ENGLISH LEGAL SYSTEM

# ENGLISH LEGAL SYSTEM IN CONTEXT

*Fifth Edition*

**FIONA COWNIE**

*Professor of Law, Keele University*

**ANTHONY BRADNEY**

*Professor of Law, Keele University*

**MANDY BURTON**

*Professor of Socio-Legal Studies, University of Leicester*

OXFORD
UNIVERSITY PRESS

# OXFORD
UNIVERSITY PRESS

Great Clarendon Street, Oxford OX2 6DP

Oxford University Press is a department of the University of Oxford.
It furthers the University's objective of excellence in research, scholarship,
and education by publishing worldwide in

Oxford New York

Auckland  Cape Town  Dar es Salaam  Hong Kong  Karachi
Kuala Lumpur  Madrid  Melbourne  Mexico City  Nairobi
New Delhi  Shanghai  Taipei  Toronto

With offices in

Argentina  Austria  Brazil  Chile  Czech Republic  France  Greece
Guatemala  Hungary  Italy  Japan  Poland  Portugal  Singapore
South Korea  Switzerland  Thailand  Turkey  Ukraine  Vietnam

Oxford is a registered trade mark of Oxford University Press
in the UK and in certain other countries

Published in the United States
by Oxford University Press Inc., New York

British Library Cataloguing in Publication Data
Data available

Library of Congress Cataloging in Publication Data
Data available

Typeset by Newgen Imaging Systems (P) Ltd, Chennai, India
Printed in Great Britain
on acid-free paper by
Ashford Colour Press Ltd, Gosport, Hampshire

ISBN  978-0-19-956740-9
1 3 5 7 9 10 8 6 4 2

*For Christine and Duncan Cownie*

# Guide to the book

## Overview

This text provides a critical overview of the English legal system. It does not simply describe the law; it is concerned with analysing and evaluating the complexities of the legal system, and encouraging you to debate and look critically at the framework within which the law operates.

This approach is summed up in the Preface to the first edition, which states that 'the law is an argument not a statement... [it is] something to be debated and discussed...'

## Approach

The authors look at the wide variety of dispute resolution mechanisms currently operating in England and Wales. The main areas covered in this text are: criminal justice procedure; the civil justice system; alternative dispute resolution; and private policing.

### Criminal justice procedure

The text examines the police and their powers, as well as the Crown Prosecution Service, magistrates, and other important personnel and procedures involved in what is often the most familiar aspect of the legal system.

> **Arrest in context**
>
> This is an area where it is important to balance the operational needs of the police against the protection of civil liberties. It would be unrealistic to impose too strict a test as to when the police can make an arrest, given that officers frequently have to make speedy decisions under pressure, but if the courts interpret the standard too loosely, the concept of 'fundamental balance' which was intended by the Philips Commission to run throughout PACE, is undermined.
>
> Clearly, arrest involves depriving a person of their liberty, so that it is a serious step, which should not be undertaken lightly. Mindful of this fact, the Philips Commission was clear, in making proposals relating to powers of arrest without warrant, that it wished:
>
> to restrict the circumstances in which the police can exercise the power to deprive a person of his liberty to those in which it is genuinely necessary to enable them to execute their duty

### Private policing

The issue of private policing also falls within the realms of criminal justice, and it is an area often overlooked in books on the English legal system. Here, the authors examine the role of non-police agencies in uncovering and prosecuting crime, and discuss how their work fits into the system as a whole.

> **Private security**
>
> An increasingly important form of social control which has hitherto been largely ignored by those writing about the English legal system, is the world of private security. Private security personnel are those persons engaged in the protection of information, persons or property. They are privately employed, have different legal powers to the public police, and are accountable for the exercise of those powers to a private individual or institution, rather than to the public.
>
> The term 'private security' is used, rather than 'private policing', partly to avoid confusion with the public police, but also because that term conveys more accurately the wide range of activities carried out by private security personnel in contemporary society, activities which go far beyond the policing activities carried out by the public police.[5] The range of activities undertaken by the private secur-

### Civil justice system

The roles of judges, barristers, solicitors, and other legal professionals are examined, as well as the position of law students, some of whom will be the legal professionals of the future.

> **INTRODUCTION**
>
> It has been traditional to divide analysis of the work of the civil courts into two parts: smaller claims in the county court and larger claims in the High Court. Historically, it has been thought that this has reflected not only the formal difference in procedures between these two courts but also the very real difference in attitudes on the part of judges and others who staff the courts. As we saw in **Chapter 3**, county courts were set up to provide a cheaper way of settling civil disputes. They were not intended to be a local mirror of the High Court but, rather, to be a different type of venue. The creation of a small claims division in 1972, with its emphasis on informality and accessibility for the unrepresented lay person, further highlighted these distinctions.
>
> There are two dangers in analysing the work of the civil courts in this traditional way. First, the effect of reforms consequent on the Civil Justice Review has been to reduce the

## Alternative dispute resolution

Alternative dispute resolution (ADR) has been an area of significant growth as a mechanism for resolving disputes out of court since the latter part of the twentieth century, and this has been reflected in its increasing prominence on undergraduate courses: it is now considered to be an important element in understanding how the legal system operates in practice, without which no study of the legal system would be complete.

In a dedicated chapter, the authors discuss why and how ADR has expanded and how it relates to, and impacts on, the more traditional areas of dispute resolution.

**ADR in different settings**

Some ADR schemes are court based, and involve referrals of disputes by courts to an ADR scheme. In these schemes, cases will usually start off in the formal legal system, but be encouraged to use ADR by the court; they may resolve all or part of their dispute using an ADR process, and the interaction between the ADR process and the formal legal system may be quite considerable. Other schemes operate independently of the courts; their direct interaction with the formal legal system may be minimal, unless negotiations break down and the parties decide to take their dispute to court.

**Court-based ADR schemes**

We have already looked at the Central London County Court mediation scheme, and

# Features in the text

## Extracts from academic texts

Many different aspects of the legal system are considered both in detail and within the wider framework within which the law operates; assumptions are challenged, and practices investigated and opened up to debate. To support this approach, extracts from a range of academic texts are critically evaluated and discussed by the authors to illustrate the contentious issues at stake.

This example from Chapter 6 is a discussion of the complexities involved in the interpretation of statutes, and the authors investigate how some degree of uniformity and predictability in reading statutes came about.

**Interpretative communities**

Analysis of both the general principles of statutory interpretation and the rules of particular application show that they are by no means a closed system. They do not offer, and are not intended to offer, a complete answer to the difficulties of statutory interpretation even where they can be applied. Nor do judges always seek to use these principles. Judges have been willing to interpret statutes not only in the context of principle or logic but on the basis of 'a matter of common sense'.[111] Finally:

[t]he fact that a substantial proportion of the problems of statutory interpretation which confront them [the courts] cannot be answered on principle is something to be borne in mind when the manner in which the courts perform their interpretative function is under discussion.[112]

## Bibliography

No single text can cover every aspect of the English legal system in detail, and nor does this book attempt to. However, the extensive Bibliography is a particular feature of this book, and it provides accurate references for materials, opinions, and works cited and considered in the book.

The wide range of academic texts, journals, and other textbooks provides an excellent starting point for those wishing to embark on further research in specific areas of the legal system.

**Bibliography**

*A Time for Change: Report of the Committee on the Future of the Legal Profession* (the Marre Committee) (1988) General Council of the Bar and the Council of the Law Society, London

ABEL, M., 'The Internal Control of a Bureaucratic Judiciary: The Case of Japan' (1995) 23 International Journal of the Sociology of Law 303

ABEL, R., 'The Comparative Study of Dispute Institutions in Society' (1973) 8 Law and Society Review 217

ABEL, R., 'Western Courts in Non-Western Settings' in S. Burman and B. Harrell-Bond, *The Imposition of Law* (1979) Academic Press, New York

# Preface

As in previous editions, we have endeavoured to include material which reflects our adoption of a pluralistic perspective on the English legal system. As time goes on, an increasing number of different dispute resolution mechanisms are emerging, which we think play an important role in the overall picture of the system in which we are interested. The formal state system is also making increasing use of alternative forms of dispute resolution, which further underlines the importance of including these phenomena in our analysis.

We have also taken account of the new developments introduced in the formal state system, including the establishment of the Supreme Court, the changes in the structure of tribunals following the implementation of the Tribunals, Courts and Enforcement Act 2007, and current debates about the calculation of legal costs. We have also paid attention to the effects of the Coroners' and Justice Act 2009, particularly as it affects coroners' courts, although this Act has not yet been fully implemented. In the criminal justice area, the role of the police in uncovering and investigating crime in a proactive way is considered. At the same time, we acknowledge the importance of non-police actors, such as fraud investigators. The Crown Prosecution Service has continued to evolve and developments in the prosecutor's role have been noted. We have also included recent research evaluating the criminal courts, particularly jury trial.

As we said in the Preface to the first edition of this book, a textbook is only a beginning, but we hope that the references and analysis we have included will prove to be a useful and stimulating starting point for an exploration of the English legal system in its widest, pluralistic form.

Fiona Cownie
Anthony Bradney
Mandy Burton
*April 2010*

# Preface to the first edition

Law is an argument not a statement. It is not a fact to be learnt as we all once learnt our multiplication tables. Rather it is something to be debated and discussed. Our debate in this book starts with that which has gone before, previous books and articles, and we hope that this book adds something to that which has gone before. Your debate as a reader starts with, amongst other things, this book and we hope the book will help you to take your debate further. A textbook is only ever a beginning. We have selected that material and discussed those issues which seem to us to be most relevant in trying to understand dispute resolution in England and Wales. In reading and disagreeing with our arguments you will think of other questions and other material which will seem more important to you. Thus the debate goes on. Thus the debate expands.

Many people have helped us, sometimes unconsciously, whilst we were writing this book. In particular we would like to thank Andrew Choo, Paul Torremans and Robin White of the Faculty of Law at Leicester University and Sally Wheeler of the Faculty of Law at Leeds University. We would also like to thank Sue Collins and Trevor Aldridge QC for their assistance with material relating to the Special Educational Needs Tribunal.

Fiona Cownie
Anthony Bradney
*August 1996*

# Contents

# Table of statutes

Page numbers in **bold** type indicate where the Act is set out in part or in full

# Table of cases

# 1

# What is 'the English legal system'?

## INTRODUCTION

This book is about the English legal system. It is about how law functions in England and Wales. We intend to describe and analyse legal processes in England and Wales.[1] Before we can do this we need to be clear about what is understood by the phrase, 'the English legal system'. If we cannot define what our subject-matter is, we cannot hope to describe and analyse it properly. We need to know what law is. We need to know what we mean by 'legal processes'. How are they distinguished from 'non-legal processes'? What is the difference between 'the English legal system' and other things?

Such understanding should be easy to achieve. This is not the first book about 'the English legal system'. There are currently more than a dozen different books in print in the United Kingdom which have the phrase 'the English legal system' as part of their title. To these works can be added those books which take 'the English legal system' as their subject-matter although their title is *The Machinery of Justice in England* or some such similar phrase.[2] Moreover, books with 'the English legal system' as their subject are not new. Many of the titles currently in print are in their second or subsequent edition. One, *Jackson's Machinery of Justice in England*, is in its eighth edition, having been originally published in 1940[3] and another, *Walker and Walker's English Legal System*, is now in its tenth edition, having first been published in 1965.[4] From this weight of texts, it should be possible to distil a clear description of the essence of the topic of these books, 'the English legal system'. However, what 'the English legal system' actually is, has, in fact, become less and less clear as more and more books have been published.

---

[1] The United Kingdom contains a number of different legal systems. Apart from the legal system which applies to England and Wales, there are also separate legal systems in Scotland and Northern Ireland. Much of what we will say about England and Wales would broadly be true in these other legal systems. However, as between the various systems, there are important differences in detail and, in some instances, broad substance.

[2] J. R. Spencer, *Jackson's Machinery of Justice in England* (8th edn, 1989) Cambridge University Press, Cambridge.

[3] R. Jackson, *The Machinery of Justice in England* (1st edn, 1940) Cambridge University Press, Cambridge.

[4] R. Walker and M. Walker, *The English Legal System* (1965) Sweet & Maxwell, London; R. Ward and A. Akhtar, *Walker and Walker's English Legal System* (10th edn, 2008) Oxford University Press, Oxford.

## 'English legal system' textbooks

One point is relatively plain. Previous books about the English legal system have not been concerned with describing the substance of the legal rules of the state. A book about 'the English legal system' does not tell you about what you should and should not do. It is not an encyclopaedia of English law, telling you everything there is to know about English legal rules. Description of legal rules is to be found in books about the various subject areas which are customarily used to divide up English law: thus, there are books on criminal law, books on contract law, books on land law, and so forth. What, then, is the subject-matter of a book with 'English legal system' as part of its title? What should the reader expect to know when they have finished reading the book?

Jackson, in the first edition to his book, *The Machinery of Justice in England*, divided his text into seven chapters. The first was a historical introduction, the next two described the court structure, the fourth looked at what he called 'the personnel of the law', the fifth looked at the financing of the operation of the courts, the sixth at tribunals, and the final chapter at law reform.[5] The content and division in Jackson's book has been fairly faithfully replicated in most subsequent books.[6] Walker and Walker's first edition of their text, *The English Legal System*, written 25 years later, is rather longer than that of Jackson[7] and has more chapters.[8] Nevertheless, much of the content is substantially the same, although the coverage is more detailed. The one obvious difference in the content is that Walker and Walker devote five chapters to the law of evidence; a subject which is not mentioned at all in either the contents page or index of Jackson. This difference is probably explained by the fact that Walker and Walker was originally written with the needs of the syllabus of the then Law Society Part I Qualifying Examination in mind, whilst Jackson was conceived to meet the less specific aim of explaining, 'the system of law courts and allied matters relating to the administration of justice'.[9] Nevertheless, a significant percentage of the book deals with the courts, the personnel of this system, and the procedures therein.[10]

Jackson and Walker and Walker established a pattern whereby books about 'the English system' were books which concerned themselves with the way in which legal disputes were resolved. Such books described the rules which governed this process. They told the reader which courts could do what and who could take part in the work of the courts.

---

[5] Jackson (1940) pp. v–vi.

[6] There have been exceptions to this general pattern. For example, Radcliffe and Cross's text, *The English Legal System*, devotes over 12 of its 22 chapters to history (see G. Radcliffe and G. Cross, *The English Legal System* (3rd edn, 1954) Butterworths, London).     [7] There are 520 pages as compared with 342 pages.

[8] There are 37 chapters as compared with 7.

[9] Walker and Walker (1965) p. v; Jackson (1940) p. vii.

[10] Nineteen chapters are devoted to these topics.

In the 1980s, some new textbooks signalled a desire to move away from the pattern established by Jackson and Walker and Walker. Thus, for example, White, in the first edition to his work, *The Administration of Justice*, wrote that, 'the old institutional, historical and rule-oriented approaches to [the English legal system] ... have given way in many courses to an approach which stresses processes'.[11] The suggestion here is that the statement of rules which formed a large part of the traditional text needed to be complemented by a description of how the system worked in practice. Statements of rules tell you what should happen. Even in courts, there may be a gap between what should be done and what actually happens. White's preface to his book suggests that if one is to understand completely 'the English legal system' one needs to know both the rules and the actual practice.

However, despite the avowed difference between his book and that which had gone before, White's own text has much that mirrors previous works. Once again, there is a central concern with the state's courts, the procedures therein, and personnel who service the system. Similarly, in *The Modern English Legal System*, also first published in the 1980s, Smith and Bailey devoted three of the four parts of their book to the same topics covered in previous 'English legal system' books.[12]

Whilst there may be a common theme to the content of books about the English legal system, this is not to say that the books cited above simply repeat each another. Some are outlines of the system. Some treat it in greater depth.[13] There have been changes in the style and content of 'English legal system' books over the years. Books such as those by Jackson and Walker and Walker had tended to concentrate on a description of the legal rules that create institutions such as courts. The emphasis in newer books such as *Smith, Bailey and Gunn* was on a more equal division between description of the rules which create the institutions and discussion of how these institutions work in actual practice.[14] There is a recognition in these later books that, even for the personnel of a legal system, there is a distinction to be drawn between rules about what you should do and the behaviour which constitutes what you actually do. Some newer books have sought to look at both things. However, the degree of similarity between the first edition of Jackson and the most recent editions of White or *Smith, Bailey and Gunn* is as striking as any changes.

---

[11] R. White, *The Administration of Justice* (1st edn, 1985) Blackwells, Oxford, p. ix. This book, in a somewhat restructured form, is now in its third edition (R. White, *The English Legal System in Action: The Administration of Justice* (3rd edn, 1999) Oxford University Press, Oxford).

[12] P. F. Smith and S. H. Bailey, *The Modern English Legal System* (1984) Sweet & Maxwell, London; S. Bailey and M. Gunn, *Smith and Bailey on the Modern English Legal System* (2nd edn, 1991) Sweet & Maxwell, London. Part II, 'Solving Legal Problems', might be regarded as a departure from the pattern of previous books. This book, with a slightly different team of authors, is now in its fifth edition (S. Bailey, M. Gunn, N. Taylor, and D. Ormerod, *Smith, Bailey and Gunn on the Modern English Legal System* (5th edn, 2007) Sweet & Maxwell, London). Its structure is essentially the same as in the first edition.

[13] Compare, for example, K. Malleson's *The English Legal System* (3rd edn, 2007) Oxford University Press, Oxford, which is 260 pages long, and R. Ward and A. Akhtar's *Walker and Walker's English Legal System* (10th edn, 2008), which is 800 pages long.

[14] Current editions continue this tendency. See *Smith, Bailey and Gunn* (2007).

## The rule-centred paradigm

If we take the approach that is common to *Jackson's, Smith, Bailey and Gunn*, and other books, the core of a book on the 'the English legal system' is a focus on things like the courts, the police, barristers, solicitors, and judges who minister to those courts. To write about 'the English legal system' is to describe the rules that create and control these institutions and, sometimes, to analyse how these institutions work in practice. Moreover, it is to write about those institutions which have been created by the state and those personnel who are, in the end, accountable to government and Parliament.

That 'the English legal system' should be taken to refer to the state's courts within England and Wales and the people who appear within them, may seem to be unproblematic. Such a conclusion probably accords with the expectations of most of the readers of this book. However, with this approach comes a number of difficulties.

The main problem with this approach, where interest rests on the state's courts and those people and institutions whose work leads to the courts, is why is it, precisely, that these things, rather than other things, are being looked at? Why is it that these things, rather than other matters, constitute 'the English legal system'? What is it about these things which makes them different from other things within society in some interesting and important way?

There is a coherence to the established content of 'English legal system' texts. Such books have, hitherto, taken what Comaroff and Roberts, in another context, have termed a 'rule-centred paradigm'[15] as a basis for their subject. A 'paradigm' is a collection of ideas which are taken as axiomatic, as unquestionable, and which form the basis for a particular academic discipline.[16] What defines 'the English legal system' is seen, not in relation to function, what various institutions seek to achieve, but in provenance, where the bodies derive their authority from. Even for texts which take a more modern, broader approach to 'the English legal system', what defines their focus is the fact that the dispute-solving agencies they are concerned with are created by rules. Moreover, the paradigm implicit in 'English legal system' texts is not just a rule-centred paradigm but a state-rule-centred paradigm. For people writing books

---

[15]  J. Comaroff and S. Roberts, *Rules and Processes* (1981) University of Chicago Press, Chicago at pp. 5–11. Comaroff and Roberts use this term as a description of a particular approach to the definition of law in the work of anthropologists.

[16]  The term was first used by Thomas Kuhn to describe the way in which scientists work. He suggested that in periods of 'normal science', scientists did not, as had hitherto been thought, seek either to prove or disprove all their ideas. Rather, he argued, they accepted some ideas as axioms and then experimented within the limits of those accepted ideas. Experiments did not provide absolute proof of anything. Even where the accepted axioms, the 'paradigm', was known to contradict observed phenomena, scientists continued to accept it. Only in periods of 'revolutionary science', such as the move from Newtonian to Einsteinian physics, was the paradigm challenged and changed. Proof was only proof if you accepted the framework (T. Kuhn, *The Structure of Scientific Revolutions* (2nd edn, 1970) University of Chicago Press, Chicago). An examination of how Kuhn's ideas can be used outside the sphere of the natural sciences can be found in B. Barnes, *T.S. Kuhn and Social Science* (1982) Macmillan, London.

about 'the English legal system', the given framework is that 'the English legal system' is the system of state courts and those institutions which feed into those state courts. 'The English legal system' is seen as being 'a matter of sovereignty, rules, courts, and enforcement agencies'.[17] Judges, appointed by the state, lawyers who serve in the courts, the police who are appointed by the state – these are the stuff of 'the English legal system'. This framework, this paradigm, is simply asserted or implied. Whether we describe the rules which create these institutions (as in *Walker and Walker*) or the way in which the institutions work (as in *Smith, Bailey and Gunn*) the framework remains essentially the same. It is the bodies which either create or administer legal rules which lie at the heart of 'the English legal system'.

We would not wish to argue that the explanation for the content of 'English legal system' textbooks simply lies in this adherence to the state-rule-centred paradigm. What does fall and what does not fall within the purview of textbooks on 'the English legal system' is, in one sense, entirely arbitrary. Textbooks reflect, not natural divisions in law or legal institutions, but the needs of course divisions drawn up for teaching purposes in university law schools. When we divide land law from family law, we have to decide whether consideration of the law relating to property owned jointly by spouses falls into land law or family law or both. Any of these answers are right. Each answer is arbitrary. The same problem occurs in considering what to put in an 'English legal system' textbook. On one level, to ask why a particular thing is or is not discussed in English legal system textbooks is to ask a question which cannot receive any reasoned answer. The question is simply, is this something customarily discussed in English legal system textbooks? The answer, whether yes or no, is justified solely by relation to that custom. In turn, the custom springs from what is usually put in the syllabus of English legal system courses in university law schools. And that content is justified, in part, by the very fact that it is customary to include or exclude a particular matter. On one level, we are talking of things which are no more than matters of fashion. However, as with fashion, the individual choices made, whilst remaining arbitrary, also reflect underlying, sometimes unconscious, philosophical decisions which in turn create and reflect a more or less coherent pattern.

Since the state-rule-centred paradigm is simply an implicit assumption in previous books, the first problem with this approach is that we do not know whether or not there might be better approaches which would generate more interesting questions and more useful ideas.[18] At this stage, the problem is not that the state-rule-centred approach is an inappropriate focus. It is simply that we have not yet considered what

[17] Comaroff and Roberts (1981) p. 6.

[18] In a review of the first editions of both Smith and Bailey, *The Modern English Legal System* and White, *The Administration of Justice*, P. Robertshaw commented '[b]oth books are permeated by empiricism, and are the better for it. They also frequently pose questions regarding the efficiency, fairness and accessibility of institutions. But how can those questions be put seriously without discussion in depth of what the system's functions are in the first place, and, since the books' major focus is on social control and dispute settlement, of what the theory of dispute settlement has to offer?' (see [1985] Public Law 743 at p. 744). The first edition of this book was a belated response to that criticism.

else we might do. In previous books, there is an assumption that, because the state has created some mechanisms for solving disputes, the mechanisms are significantly different from other things. There is an assumption in previous texts, that these mechanisms should be looked at in isolation from the other dispute-solving mechanisms. Before we adopt the same approach that has been taken by previous authors, we need to look at other possible approaches.

## Dispute avoidance, dispute settlement, and 'the English legal system'

If we ignore the source of the power of the institutions which have been a central concern in textbooks on the English legal system, we see that the other thing that links these institutions is the fact that their function is related either to dispute avoidance or, more commonly, to dispute settlement. Dispute avoidance and dispute settlement are different functions. Both are equally important. Legal systems are there to determine what will happen when people have disputes. Legal rules are also there so that people can order their lives in such a way as to avoid such disputes.[19]

Because the concern in 'English legal system' textbooks is with state courts, and with rules administered by those courts, not all institutions concerned with matters of dispute resolution and dispute avoidance are examined. Thus, for example, 'English legal system' textbooks sometimes consider the role of the police and the rules of law that give them the special powers that they possess.[20] However, such textbooks do not describe the role of private police forces. People who provide security for shopping centres or who guard industrial property, fall outside the ambit of the area considered by an English legal system textbook. Yet, on one level, both the public police force and private security firms have the same role. They have a policing function. Both are concerned with the protection of people or property from the destructive or acquisitive tendencies of others. Given that 'English legal system' texts are state-focused, ignoring private policing is logical, but what important aim is served by just focusing on the state?

There are many examples of private mechanisms and institutions which mirror the state's attempts to prevent or resolve disputes. All of these mechanisms and institutions are largely ignored in texts on 'the English legal system'.

One reason why some institutions concerned with dispute resolution and avoidance are discussed in English legal system textbooks and some are not, might lie in the different sources of authority that the various institutions have. In the state court system,

---

[19] The law has other functions, both explicit and latent. For example, law can be a symbolic expression of the values of a society. However, it is these two functions which are important for the focus of English legal system textbooks.    [20] See, for example, *Smith, Bailey and Gunn* (2007) pp. 787–838.

courts operate according to rules of law laid down by Parliament and the judges. These rules of law purport to be universal in their applicability to all of those living in this country.[21] Obedience to these laws is mandatory.[22] In the nineteenth century, John Austin described a theory of jurisprudence which regarded this general applicability of the legal system and a habit of obedience to these laws by its subjects as being part of the defining characteristics of law.[23] For Austin, law, and thus the legal system, was a quite separate phenomenon from other forms of rules or social forces and was inextricably tied up with notions of the state. Despite the fact that this philosophical position is, in Austin's simple form, no longer accepted by philosophers of law, it continues to underlie the boundaries set to much writing about the content of legal rules.[24]

This may seem acceptable. 'The English legal system' is simply 'The Bill' and whatever its civil law equivalent may be. Other forms of dispute resolution are seen as private, voluntary, and simply not law. They are therefore either not the province of an 'English legal system' book or, at best, are marginal to such a book.

Separating dispute-resolution mechanisms which owe their authority to the state from voluntary mechanisms and writing only about the former, significantly reduces the amount of dispute resolution which is being discussed. Statistically, many disputes are, in fact, resolved by non-state agencies. The form that such dispute resolution takes varies. Friends mediating between quarrelling friends is a form of dispute resolution; so are arbitration procedures established by retail associations to deal with customer disputes;[25] so are dispute resolution procedures within a Quaker Meeting;[26] so are disciplinary procedures in universities; so are many other things. The essential difference between all of these non-state structures and the state courts is that, if parties to a dispute follow the findings of such a non-state agency, they usually do so of their own volition.[27] Parties choose whether or not they will use these agencies. Both parties

---

[21] Some people, of course, would deny that they are bound by these rules (anarchists, for example). Many people, perhaps most people, would deny that they are always bound by these rules (for example, when they have a conscientious objection to the content of the rule).

[22] In the sense that all laws should be obeyed though, of course, there will be some law-breakers.

[23] J. Austin, *The Province of Jurisprudence Determined* (1970) Lenox Hill Pub, Lecture VI. For an analysis of Austinian thought see W. Morison, *John Austin* (1982) Edward Arnold, London.

[24] For many years, the most influential refutation of Austin was contained in H. L. A. Hart's *The Concept of Law* (1961) Oxford University Press, Oxford. However, Hart's own concept of law retained many features of Austin's approach and continued to take a positivistic approach to law. More modern scholars have completely rejected the notion that the study of law and legal system can be limited to the pure study of state legal rules. For very different examples of new approaches to what could count as law see M. Kelman, *A Guide to Critical Legal Studies* (1987) Harvard University Press, Cambridge, MA; S. Engle Merry, *Getting Justice and Getting Even* (1990) University of Chicago Press, Chicago; and S. Engle Merry and N. Milner (eds), *The Possibility of Popular Justice* (1993) University of Michigan Press, Ann Arbor, MI.

[25] As, for example, in the case of the Association of British Travel Agents (ABTA) Tour Operators' Code of Conduct. This can be found at <http://www.abta.com/articlesandcode.shtml>.

[26] See A. Bradney and F. Cownie, *Living without Law* (2000a) Ashgate, Aldershot.

[27] This distinction between non-state and state dispute resolution in the end collapses. In some cases, non-state institutions also claim mandatory obedience to their rules even where these rules are in conflict with state laws. Thus, for example, according to some authorities, a Muslim is bound by Muslim law wherever she or he is living even when Muslim law is in conflict with the law of the state (see the text of the fatwa

must accept their jurisdiction. In the case of state courts, the state itself can compel the presence of one of the parties to an action. Parties are obliged to take part in proceedings, whether they want to or not.

Non-state dispute resolution agencies must operate within the shadow of the law.[28] They may use state law, for example, by making their decisions the subject of a binding contract. Thus, for example, in the United Kingdom, the Jewish Beth Din, a court established under Jewish religious law (though open to both Jews and non-Jews), requires those who wish to use it to accept the provisions of the Arbitration Act 1996.[29]

The more peripheral a dispute resolving agency is to the state system, the less likely it is to be discussed in an 'English legal system' textbook.

## Problems with the state-rule-centred paradigm

English legal system textbooks concentrate on dispute avoidance and resolution mechanisms which emanate from that state. It is not the only factor which decides whether a matter is to be included in the book but it is the most important factor. Is there any loss involved in this approach to deciding what we are going to analyse? Does it in any way detract from our understanding of the way in which individual legal systems or legal systems as a whole work?

There are two possible problems with the state-rule-centred approach. The first is that this approach asserts, rather than proves, that there is an important difference between what is happening in state agencies concerned with dispute resolution and non-state agencies. The provenance of the authority of the agency, the fact that it comes from the state, is deemed to be significant. This significance has not been obvious to everyone.

De Sousa Santos, a Portuguese legal anthropologist, studied the activities of an institution, the Residents' Association, in a favela or shanty town, Pasargada, in Rio de Janeiro. The land upon which Pasargada was built belonged to the state. The residents were, so far as the Brazilian legal system was concerned, no more than squatters. They had no legal title to the land upon which they had built their houses. Brazilian state

---

issued by the Ayatollah Khomeini, *The Guardian*, 15 February 1989). (For an examination of the application of some aspects of Muslim law in Great Britain, see D. Pearl and W. Menski, *Muslim Family Law* (3rd edn, 1998) Butterworths, London.) Equally, even with voluntary dispute resolution mechanisms, there may be considerable pressure to accept the dispute resolution mechanisms ruling. A person who refuses to accept the jurisdiction of their family to mediate in a family quarrel may find that they lose contact with that family. A person refusing to accept the jurisdiction of their school may be expelled. Conversely, a person may choose to reject the jurisdiction of the state by going into exile.

[28] They cannot do that which is illegal without running the usual risks of civil or criminal action.

[29] *The Lawyer*, 7 January 1992. (At the date of this article the relevant legislation was the Arbitration Act 1979.)

law did not afford them any mechanism to buy and sell their houses.[30] However, the Residents' Association was willing to register such sales.[31] Written agreements were drawn up by the Association. Standard phrases were used in these agreements. Copies were exchanged, one being kept by the Residents' Association, others by the parties to the sale.[32] Residents of the favela were thus able to pass property amongst each other in a way similar to that which they would have been able to do had they been title-holders under Brazilian state law. When there were disputes about matters relating to housing, the Residents' Association was willing to determine which party was in the right. The Residents' Association had no power to do this under Brazilian state law. Its power came from the fact that those who lived in Pasargada regarded it as having a judicial function. De Sousa Santos concluded that the activities of the Residents' Association could be described as 'Pasargada law' which was 'an example of an informal and unofficial legal system'.[33] According to de Sousa Santos, Pasargada was an example of legal pluralism; a situation where two legal systems, Brazilian state law and Pasargada law, coexisted alongside each other. In deciding which was law there was, for de Sousa Santos, no special significance in the fact that the rules of one legal system, Brazilian state law, emanated from the state.[34] Using the approach which typifies 'English legal system' texts, a description of the work of the Residents' Association would form no part of a book on the Brazilian legal system. Yet, for de Sousa Santos, that institution was central to the way in which the inhabitants of the favela brought law into their lives.

We might want to argue that that which is true of Brazil is not necessarily true of England and Wales; that a more developed country with a different history will not allow such non-state legal systems to grow. It is certainly correct to say that we need to be cautious in applying the lessons of one country and one legal culture to another. A change of conditions which appears to be minor can result in great variations in practice.[35] However, British examples of legal pluralism are available. Pearl and Menski have described the position of some British Muslims who choose to live according to the rules of Muslim law and two of the authors of this book have described a Quaker Meeting in Great Britain whose guiding principles and rules

---

[30] B. de Sousa Santos, 'The Law of the Oppressed: The Construction and Reproduction of Legality in Pasargda' (1977) 12 Law and Society Review 5 at p. 52. For a re-assessment of his original study, see B. de Sousa Santos, *Towards a New Common Sense: Law, Science and Politics in the Paradigmatic Transition* (1995) Routledge, London, pp. 124–249.　　　　　　　　　　　　　　[31] De Sousa Santos (1977) p. 44.

[32] De Sousa Santos (1977) p. 50.　　　[33] De Sousa Santos (1977) p. 89.

[34] De Sousa Santos defined law as a 'body of regularized procedures and normative standards, considered justiciable in a given group, which contributes to the creation and prevention of disputes and to their settlement through an argumentative discourse, whether or not coupled with force' (De Sousa Santos (1977) p. 10).

[35] The difference between the jury system in England and Wales on the one hand and the USA on the other is one of the more obvious examples of this phenomenon. (Thus, for example, see the description of jury selection in England and Wales at **pp. 358–61** below and compare that with the process of voir dire in the USA as described in S. Kassim and L. Wrightsman, *The American Jury on Trial* (1988) Hemisphere, New York, ch. 3.) For this reason, in this text, we have tried to keep comparative references to a minimum.

for both decision-taking and dispute resolution are to be found in the Quaker *Book of Christian Discipline*.[36] Neither study is precisely analogous to de Sousa Santos's examination of Pasargada, but both describe groups within contemporary Great Britain who do not regard UK state law as having primary authority over the control of their lives.

From a very different theoretical perspective, Durkheim also reached conclusions which challenge the assumption that the fact that state law emanates from the state is of any special significance in itself, identifying law as something uniquely privileged and interesting.

For Durkheim, state law was one amongst a number of examples of 'social facts'. Durkheim defined social facts as being:

ways of acting, thinking, and feeling which possess the remarkable property of existing outside the consciousness of the individual.

...they are endued with a compelling and coercive power by virtue of which, whether he wishes it or not, they impose themselves upon him.[37]

Law for Durkheim was a coercive, regulatory force. But morality and religion, for example, were also social facts.[38] They were also coercive, regulatory forces. The only feature that was peculiar to state law, according to Durkheim, was its particular visibility.[39] It was easier to identify and classify legal rules objectively than it was to do so in the case of other social facts. State law could thus be more easily used to exemplify and measure the way in which social cohesion was created and changed in different types of society. Different types of legal rules reflected different forms of social cohesion.[40] Except in this, law was no different in any essential feature from other examples of social facts.[41]

For de Sousa Santos, law is not defined by its relationship to the state. For Durkheim, though he would accept that law is defined by its relationship to the state,[42] law's

---

[36] Pearl and Menski (1998); Bradney and Cownie (2000a). On Muslim law in Great Britain, see also Z. Badawi, 'Muslim Justice in a Secular State' in M. King (ed.), *God's Law versus State Law* (1995) Grey Seal, London; Y. Ihsan, 'The Challenge of Post-modern Legality and Muslim Legal Pluralism in England' (2002) 28 Journal of Ethnic and Minority Studies 343; and Y. Ihsan, *Muslim Laws, Politics and Society in Modern Nation States* (2005) Ashgate, Aldershot. The Archbishop of Canterbury has suggested that it might be necessary to consider whether or not a wider recognition of sharia law might be desirable (The Archbishop of Canterbury, *Civil and Religious Law in England: A Religious Perspective* (February, 2008) at <http://www.archbishopofcanterbury.org/1575>). For a comment on this, see S. Bano, 'In Pursuit of Religious and Legal Diversity: A Response to the Archbishop of Canterbury and the "Sharia Debate" in Britain' (2008) 10 Ecclesiastical Law Journal 282. For similar arguments from a senior judge see Lord Phillips, *Equality before the Law* (July, 2008) at <http://www.judiciary.gov.uk/publications_media/speeches/index.htm>.

[37] E. Durkheim, *The Rules of Sociological Method* (1982) Macmillan, London, p. 51.

[38] Durkheim (1982) ch. 1.

[39] E. Durkheim, *The Division of Labour in Society* (1933) Macmillan, London, p. 64.

[40] Durkheim (1933) chs 2 and 3.

[41] For an introduction to Durkheim's sociology of law, see S. Lukes and A. Scull, 'Introduction' in *Durkheim and the Law* (1983) Martin Robertson, Oxford, p. 1.

[42] Durkheim equates the term 'juridical rules' and law (Durkheim (1933) p. 68). He also rejects the notion of pluralistic concepts of law by seeing law as the direct manifestation of the *conscience collective* within a society.

provenance did not result in any particular variation in the way it functioned as a mechanism of social control. Numerous other examples of such writers could be given. Thus we can see that in implicitly asserting that the state courts and those things associated with them are 'the' English legal system and in further implicitly asserting that there is something specially interesting about this legal system, 'English legal system' textbook writers are guilty of a form of question begging; asserting the truth of something which others have found problematic. The question then remains: what is different and special about the institutions on which 'English legal system' texts have traditionally focused? Why has there been this focus?

## Textbooks for lawyers

In the first edition to their text, Walker and Walker gave a pragmatic reason for their selection of topics. They wrote '[t]he present work is designed to embrace comprehensively the syllabus for the Law Society Qualifying Examinations'.[43] Whilst other writers might not have been so forthright nor so uncomplicated in the description of the raison d'être for the contents of their books Walker and Walker's statement seems to capture the essence of the original reason for the selection of the state-rule-centred paradigm. Courses which are intended to qualify students as professional lawyers centre on the state's legal system. For such lawyers, if for no others, that particular system is uniquely interesting. More modern writers have been more equivocal in indicating who constituted the market for their texts. Thus, for example, Bailey and Gunn merely write about their work as relating to 'law students' without saying whether it was written for law students on professional law courses or academic law courses or both.[44] It is certainly the case that university law schools are no longer simply breeding grounds for future professional lawyers.[45] Thus, a book intended for such students can no longer concentrate on topics which are solely of professional interest. Once this instrumental justification for selecting topics because they are studied on a particular examination course is abandoned, then the intellectual need to justify the particular topics selected becomes more pressing.

[43]  Walker and Walker (1965) p. v.

[44]  S. Bailey and M. Gunn, *Smith and Bailey on the Modern English Legal System* (3rd edn, 1996) Sweet & Maxwell, London, p. 3.

[45]  A. Bradney, 'Ivory Towers or Satanic Mills: Choices for University Law Schools' (1992) 17 Studies in Higher Education 5 at pp. 14–15. Most legal academics in England and Wales claim to provide a liberal education; such an approach forbids treating a student as simply a future worker (see further A. Bradney, *Conversations, Choices and Chances: The Liberal Law School in the Twenty-First Century* (2003a) Hart Publishing, Oxford; and F. Cownie, *Legal Academics: Culture and Identities* (2003) Hart Publishing, Oxford). However, we should note that a small minority of writers believe that university law schools should behave as though they were simply a breeding ground for future lawyers (see, for example, H. Brayne, 'A Case for Getting Law Students Engaged in the Real Thing – The Challenge of the Sabre-Tooth Curriculum' (2000) 34 The Law Teacher 17).

## 'The English legal system' and law reform

A second difficulty with using a state-rule-centred paradigm as a focus for describing 'the English legal system' is that, even if there is something special about the state system, this does not necessarily lead to the conclusion that the state system can happily be studied in isolation from its context. One aspect of this problem can be seen when the question of reforming aspects of the state court structure is considered. If 'the English legal system' is considered in isolation, the scope of potential reforms tends to be reduced. One area of the state system can be compared with another, one state system can be compared with another state system, but the methods and processes that are unique to state systems are taken as given, thus tending to limit the range of potential reforms considered. Looking at 'the English legal system' in the context of other dispute avoidance and dispute resolution mechanisms encourages a wider perspective, suggesting more fundamental changes than are likely to be the case if the analysis is solely of the status quo. When Lord Mackay, then the Lord Chancellor, gave a series of lectures entitled 'The Administration of Justice' he looked, not only at things such as the courts and the judiciary, but also at alternative forms of dispute resolution outside the usual court structure because he thought such dispute resolution 'raises issues…and challenges some traditional assumptions about the way in which justice must be administered'.[46]

## Alternative legal theories

If the rule-centred paradigm which has been central to 'English legal system' text-books raises difficulties, what can be put in its place? In the rest of this chapter, we will describe a number of ideas about law which provide a background for a different way of viewing the 'English legal system'. Many of these ideas overlap with one another. Cumulatively, we would argue, they provide us with a richer idea of 'the English legal system' and how it works.

In order to avoid the kind of problems of the rule-centred paradigm we would argue that we need to embrace an integrated theory of law, which is broad enough to capture not only the legal system which emanates from the state, but also the numerous other kinds of legal system which are generated quite independently of the state. We need to be aware of both the differences between, and the similarities amongst, these different kinds of legal systems. In this we would differ from those who have written previous books because they have seen a strong divide between 'the English legal system' and other forms of dispute resolution in England and Wales. We also need an integrated theory which is able to look at legal worlds, not only in terms of 'positivism', which focuses on the purity of legal rules and which would look to the state system, but also

---

[46]  Lord Mackay, *The Administration of Justice* (1994) Sweet & Maxwell, London, p. 69.

in encompassing ideas based on 'structuralism', which emphasizes the importance of large socio-economic structures. Finally, it is important not to neglect the contribution of 'interactionism', that is, research which concentrates on the behaviour of individuals within a particular system. In this sense, we agree with the approach which is found in books such as White or *Smith, Bailey and Gunn*. We would, however, seek to take their approach further. We need to move away from 'common-sense' ideas of what constitutes law, legal system, and legal process and to begin by exploring a variety of approaches to legal theory which might give us a deeper idea of what constitutes 'the English legal system' and how it relates to other systems of dispute resolution within England and Wales.[47]

## The process paradigm

Comaroff and Roberts offer as an alternative to the rule-centred paradigm the 'processual paradigm'. This they define by quoting from the work of the legal anthropologist, Malinowski:

In such primitive communities I personally believe that law ought to be defined by function and not by form, that is we ought to see what are the arrangements, the sociological realities, the cultural mechanisms which act for the enforcement of law.[48]

Such a view is applicable, not only to simple or preliterate societies, but also to more complex communities.[49]

Such an approach, whilst uncommon in 'English legal system' texts, is not without precedent in other areas of legal writing. An integrated theory of law, which de-emphasizes the importance of state rules and state institutions, can draw on ideas from a number of works. Thus, for example, historically, the work of nineteenth-century thinkers like Gierke enabled people to regard law in a new way. Gierke looked in particular at the idea of a corporation, rejecting previous legal theories which had seen the corporation as a fictitious person, capable of having legal rights but unable to know or will anything. Gierke revived the old German idea of *Die Gesammte Hand* or the reality of the group. His theory, *Die Genossenschaftstheorie*,[50] viewed the corporate body as a real group person, as opposed to a fiction. He rejected the Roman Law idea that only that which the state recognizes is valid, since he argued that a corporation is a social fact, and the state cannot create social facts; its function is limited to declaring which social facts conform to the requirements of law.

Gierke characterised all organised groups as the subject of their own autonomous order of law...He proclaimed law's independence of the State...[51]

---

47  Some of which, in de Sousa Santos's terms, may constitute legal systems in their own right.
48  Comaroff and Roberts (1981) p. 11. The passage quoted is taken from Malinowski's introduction to H. Hogbin's *Law and Order in Polynesia* (1934) Harcourt Brace, New York, p. lxiii.
49  For further discussion of these issues see below.
50  G. Gurvitch, *The Sociology of Law* (1947) Routledge & Kegan Paul, London, pp. 72–4.
51  Gurvitch (1947) p. 72.

From our point of view, the importance of Gierke's work was that he saw that instead of there being only one kind of law, that generated by the state, there are many other kinds of law emanating from bodies (such as corporations) quite independent of the state. This way of looking at law provided some of the foundations of a theory of law known as 'legal pluralism'.[52]

Gierke, in focusing on social reality, made a useful contribution to juristic thought, but he still gave the state a dominant role in relation to law, since he saw the state as having pre-eminence over other groups. In order to find thinkers who are moving away from giving the state a dominant role in the production of law, it is necessary to consider the work of jurists like Gurvitch. For Gurvitch, each form of social reality 'can give birth to its own peculiar kind of law'.[53] The state, as one social form, is one source of law, but other social forms can also be sources of law.[54]

## 'Law in action' and Legal Realism

We need to do more than to consider whether law can come from other sources than the state. As previous writers such as White have argued, in order to get a true picture of the legal processes which operate within England, it is not enough to look at 'law in the books', the formal rules of procedure and substance; it is also important to look at 'the law in action', at what actually happens.[55] Looking at legal rules alone is inadequate; it assumes that people actually *do* behave in the way in which the rules say that they *should*. Many studies have shown that this is not the case.[56]

Awareness of the importance of looking at the actual operation of legal systems owes much to studies by a number of American jurists, now known as American Legal Realists, working mainly at Harvard University in the early decades of the twentieth century. In terms of the legal system, the Realists were concerned, not primarily with legal rules, that is, cases and statutes, but with what actually happened when the legal system was at work. A classic statement of the concerns of Legal Realism is that made in a book review by one of the leading Realists, Karl Llewellyn. He wrote:

[52] For more detailed discussion of legal pluralism see **pp. 20–1** below.    [53] Gurvitch (1947) p. 158.

[54] For Gurvitch, the pre-eminence of the state as a source of law was under threat in modern society (Gurvitch (1947) p. 223).    [55] See n. 11 above.

[56] Malinowski's anthropology was based on an attempt to collect data about both what people say they should do and what they actually do (B. Malinowski, *Crime and Custom in Savage Society* (1926) Routledge, London). In his view, this attempt to collect data about the full diversity of practice as well as the details of norms within a system resulted in a richer conception of law. (For examples of attempts to study the law in action in England and Wales, see J. Eekelaar and E. Clive with others, *Custody after Divorce* (1977) Oxford Centre for Socio-Legal Studies, Oxford; P. Carlen, *Magistrates' Justice* (1976) Martin Robertson, Oxford; A. E. Bottoms and J. D. McClean, *Defendants in the Criminal Process* (1976) Routledge & Kegan Paul, London; A. Leonard, *Judging Inequality: The Effectiveness of the Tribunal System in Sex Discrimination and Equal Pay Cases* (1987) Cobden Trust, London.) We are not aware of any study, in this country or abroad, which has shown a perfect fit between the 'law in books' and the 'law in action'. These studies are of state law but, in principle, there is no reason why there should be a perfect fit between the stated rules and the actual practice in any system of law.

The reviewer holds that the time has passed when the study of law could be profitably centred on legal doctrine. At the present juncture, the only serviceable focus of law study is law in action; law in action not only in the sense of... what the courts and all quasi-judicial bodies actually do; but also [in the sense of] the actual ordering of men's actions.[57]

American Legal Realism firmly shifted its focus of inquiry away from traditional study of legal rules. This thesis can be illustrated by examining some of the work of Jerome Frank, regarded as one of the more extreme practitioners of Legal Realism.

Frank was heavily critical of the work of Christopher Columbus Langdell, the American legal academic who is best known for introducing the 'case method' of teaching law into American law schools. Langdell viewed law as a science, which could be practised very simply by applying legal rules mechanically to specific cases recorded in the law reports. Langdell's method rested heavily on the positivistic notion that law resided solely in the reports of decided cases or in statutes.[58] Jerome Frank criticized this, arguing that Langdellian legal science had very little to do with law, because it overlooked such things as the lawyer-client relationship and the role of the jury.[59] He argued that Langdell's attitude towards law was typical of what he termed 'the basic legal myth'; lawyers promote the myth that legal rules can be applied in a mechanical way because they, like all human beings, are constantly looking for certainty.[60] The purpose of Realism, on the other hand, was to expose this myth. This concern with what Frank saw as law in action, rather than with the 'legal myth' of the law in the books, was typical of the concerns expressed by members of the Legal Realist movement. Given the nature of Frank's work, it is not surprising that Legal Realism 'has sometimes been seen as part of a general movement in American social thought called "the revolt against formalism"'.[61] However, it has been argued that many of the leading Legal Realists had a much more ambivalent attitude towards formalism.[62] When Jerome Frank went on to discuss the jury, he appeared to turn away from such ideas, and to embrace the very formalism which he had so wholeheartedly rejected before.[63] He argued that it would be better to abolish the jury, who, as laypeople, lacked the training to fully understand the complex legal issues before them. It would, he argued, be preferable to rely on the expertise of the judge. By placing such faith in the judge,

---

[57] K. Llewellyn, 'Review of M. Campbell's *Cases on Mortgages of Real Property*' (1926) 40 Harvard Law Review 142 at p. 144.

[58] Langdell's ideas are not only of historical interest. The notion that law lies in legal rules continues to underlie much academic research work in British university law schools, albeit in a rather more sophisticated form than that put forward by Langdell. It also underlies much teaching. See, for example, Smith's comment that '[f]or a thorough understanding of the subject [of contract law], there is no substitute for the study of the cases' (J. C. Smith, *The Law of Contract* (1989) Sweet & Maxwell, London, p. v).

[59] N. Duxbury, 'The Reinvention of Ideas: American Jurisprudence in the Twentieth Century', University of Nottingham Research Papers No. 3, June 1992, p. 11.

[60] In a similar fashion, Comaroff and Roberts argue that the rule-centred paradigm is 'founded on the notion of the irreducibility of law, [and] offers comforting boundaries' (Comaroff and Roberts (1981) p. 15). In their view, such comfort is falsely grounded.

[61] W. Twining, *Karl Llewellyn and the Realist Movement* (1973) Weidenfeld & Nicolson, London, p. 8.

[62] Duxbury (1992).     [63] Duxbury (1992) p. 12.

Frank could be seen as embracing legal formalism – the very tradition he had formerly been at such pains to undermine.

The contradiction which can be found in the work, not only of Jerome Frank, but also of other American Legal Realists,[64] is a serious flaw. However, American Legal Realism, with its emphasis on 'law in action' rather than 'law in the books', had a positive contribution to make to the development of jurisprudence.

The late 1960s saw an ever-increasing interest in how legal systems worked in practice in British university law schools. This was reflected in both the development of new areas of study, such as socio-legal studies (an attempt to use the techniques and methods of the social sciences to gain new insights into law and legal systems),[65] and in changes in old areas, with a growth in the awareness of the importance of factors other than pure legal rules.[66] The change in attitude can also be seen outside the work of university law schools, for example in the area of law reform.[67]

## Legal anthropology

Another strand of thinking which can contribute to how we view 'the English legal system' is legal anthropology. The precise scope of legal anthropology is a matter of some debate. Traditionally, legal anthropologists have been concerned with the study of law in simple or preliterate societies. More recently, legal anthropologists have begun to concern themselves with law in complex societies.[68] As noted above, Comaroff and Roberts have divided anthropologists concerned with dispute resolution and avoidance into those who follow a rule-centred and those who follow a processual paradigm.[69]

Those working within a rule-centred paradigm, for example Radcliffe-Brown,[70] tend to derive their definition of law from positivistic Western legal theory. If they cannot identify legal rules and institutions similar to those one would expect to find in Western society, they tend to assume that the society which they are studying has no law.[71] The rule-centred approach tends, not merely to state that a particular social

---

[64] Duxbury (1992) pp. 11–16.

[65] See C. Campbell and P. Wiles, 'The Study of Law and Society in Britain' (1975–76) 10 Law and Society Review 547.

[66] See, for example, P. Atiyah, *Accidents, Compensation and the Law* (1970) Weidenfeld & Nicholson, London, pp. xi–xix.

[67] Royal Commission on Criminal Justice, *Report* (1993) Cm. 2263, HMSO, London.

[68] See S. Roberts, *Order and Dispute: An Introduction to Legal Anthropology* (1979) Penguin Books, Harmondsworth, passim.

[69] As Roberts has noted, some have distinguished between legal and political anthropology with only those who follow the rule-centred paradigm being termed legal anthropologists. See Roberts (1979) pp. 198–206.

[70] A. R. Radcliffe-Brown, *Structure and Function in Primitive Society* (1952) Cohen & West, London.

[71] R. Abel, 'The Comparative Study of Dispute Institutions in Society' (1973) 8 Law and Society Review 217 at pp. 222–3.

mechanism, law, is not to be found in a society, but also to infer, or to state, that that society is less highly developed by virtue of the fact that it lacks that social mechanism. This approach has been widely criticized for its ethnocentricity.[72] If there is a separate natural phenomenon to be called law, why should we begin by assuming that it is to be characterized by those institutions which are to be found in Western societies? There may be no directly equivalent category to a particular Western 'legal' institution in a non-Western society. Why should that mean there is no dispute settlement process which should be termed 'legal'? Equally, if there is an apparently 'legal' institution, such as a third party adjudicating a dispute, why should this be termed legal when it may in fact perform a very different function in another society?[73] It may be inaccurate to assume that the conceptual categories of Western law can be used to analyse accurately the dispute-processing mechanisms found in other societies. For those interested in an integrated theory of law as an alternative to traditional conceptions of 'the English legal system', the work of rule-centred legal anthropologists is not the primary source of interest.

The strand of legal anthropology which might contribute most to the development of an integrated theory of law is research emanating from scholars working within the processual paradigm. This approach is generally acknowledged to have originated in the work of Bronislaw Malinowski, and, in particular, in the book published in 1926 as *Crime and Custom in Savage Society*.[74] In this book, Malinowski examined the 'legal conditions'[75] which he found in one society in the Trobriand Islands, in north-west Melanesia. Malinowski was interested in the legal phenomena which might be used by the Trobriand Islanders. In looking for these phenomena, he adopted a very broad definition of law:

We shall approach our facts with a very wide and elastic conception of the problem before us. In looking for 'law' and legal forces, we shall try merely to discover and analyse all the rules conceived and acted upon as binding obligations, to find out the nature of the binding forces, and to classify the rules according to the manner in which they are made.[76]

Malinowski did not look for direct equivalents of Western legal institutions within the society of the Trobriand Islanders. He noticed that in Western society, legal institutions were used to maintain order and manage conflict. He argued that those functions were performed in some way in all societies, and that it was the way in which those functions were performed which should form the subject of investigation for the legal anthropologist:

---

[72] See, for example, Roberts (1979) chs 2 and 11.

[73] See, for example, Bohannan's criticism of the work of Gluckman (P. Bohannan, *Justice and Judgement among the Tiv* (1967) Oxford University Press for International African Institute, Oxford, pp. 212–13.)

[74] Malinowski (1926).      [75] Malinowski (1926) p. 15.      [76] Malinowski (1926) p. 15.

There must be in all societies a class of rules too practical to be backed up by religious sanctions, too burdensome to be left to mere goodwill, too personally vital to individuals to be enforced by any abstract agency. This is the domain of legal rules...[77]

Malinowski's definition of law was so broad that it was very difficult to separate out law from other areas of social control. While this can be seen as a weakness, for those interested in the development of an integrated theory of law, it is this very ability to look at law in a broader context which is of interest.

Recently, there have been attempts to move legal anthropology beyond the rules/ process dichotomy. Comaroff and Roberts have argued that any dispute resolution procedure can only be understood in the context of 'the *total* fabric of the sociocultural system' that contains it.[78] To do this, they argue what is required is 'the elaboration of an approach that can account for both the *total* logic of dispute processes and for their systematic contextualisation'.[79]

## Semi-autonomous legal fields

Sally Falk Moore, another legal anthropologist, has also been concerned to arrive at a total picture of law in society. For her, it is not enough merely to study law as a formal method of social control. In particular, a narrow focus on 'rule-bound law' would be inadequate because legal institutions only partly effect control of society. If that is true, then 'any analysis which focuses entirely on the rule-bound is limited indeed, and does not place the normative in the whole context of action'.[80] She argues that it is equally important to identify those social processes 'which cause people to use rules, or abandon them, bend them, reinterpret them, sidestep them or replace them'.[81] In order to achieve a more accurate picture of law in society, Moore proposes the concept of the 'semi-autonomous legal field'. Any small field observable to an anthropologist should be studied in terms of its semi-autonomy. This involves recognizing that, while any such field can generate its own rules and customs internally, it is at the same time vulnerable to rules and decisions and other forces emanating from the larger world by which it is surrounded:

The semi-autonomous social field has rule-making capacities, and the means to induce or coerce compliance; but it is set in a larger social matrix which can, and does, affect and invade it, sometimes at the invitation of persons inside it, sometimes at its own instance.[82]

Moore's ideas have been developed by Peter Fitzpatrick,[83] who has emphasized that an important feature of law is the interaction between legal orders; it is not a case of semi-autonomous legal fields possessing their own discrete legal orders which are

---

[77]  Malinowski (1926) pp. 67–8.        [78]  Comaroff and Roberts (1981) p. 216, emphasis in original.
[79]  Comaroff and Roberts (1981) p. 246, emphasis in original.
[80]  S. Falk Moore, *Law as Process* (1978) Routledge & Kegan Paul, London, p. 3.
[81]  Falk Moore (1978) p. 4.        [82]  Falk Moore (1978) p. 55.
[83]  P. Fitzpatrick, 'Law, Plurality and Underdevelopment' in D. Sugarman (ed.), *Legality, Ideology and the State* (1983) Academic Press, London, pp. 159–80.

ultimately subordinate to the state legal order. Rather, it is a two-way process, with an interaction of legal orders. As an illustration, Fitzpatrick has attempted to show, in a Third World context, how the family and its legal order (one semi-autonomous legal field) is profoundly affected by the state (another semi-autonomous legal field) and also how the state, in its turn, is profoundly affected by the legal order of the family.[84] The emphasis on the interaction between legal orders means that '[l]aw, thence, takes on a greater diversity and richness than is usually afforded it academically'.[85]

## Informal legal systems

Since the 1980s, attention has begun to turn to the importance of informal legal systems,[86] which include a wide variety of methods of dispute resolution, for example conciliation, mediation, arbitration, and community courts. In trying to achieve a complete picture of legal worlds, informal systems are of considerable significance. However, much of the work on informalism has not focused on the way in which informal systems form a part of the whole legal world; instead, researchers have been concerned to argue, either that informal systems should be seen as complementary to the formal legal system,[87] or that the formal legal system is a failure, and that it should be replaced with the radical alternative which informal legal systems offer.[88] However, we would argue that both of these strands of thinking miss the point and that 'the informal is an integral part of the totality of law and not an alternative to it'.[89]

Some writers have, however, been concerned to explore the relationship between the formal and the informal from a broader perspective. One of these is Richard Abel,[90] who is concerned to point to a deep ambiguity in the growth of informalism; it is both a contraction and an expansion of the state system. Abel notes that, recently, reforms have taken place in an effort to decrease the complexity of the law. These reforms have been implemented in a number of different ways: sometimes, laws which are thought unnecessary are repealed; procedural reforms have attempted to make legal institutions more accessible; finally, there has been a rapid growth of informal alternatives to the formal legal process – negotiation, arbitration, community service, etc. Superficially, it might have been expected that these changes would lead to a decrease in the power of the state. However, Abel argues to the contrary. Informal institutions

---

[84] Fitzpatrick (1983) p. 159. In a somewhat similar fashion, de Sousa Santos shows how Pasargada law takes on and uses to its own ends the terminology of Brazilian state law (see de Sousa Santos, 1977, passim).

[85] Fitzpatrick (1983) p. 160.

[86] See, for example, R. Matthews (ed.), *The Politics of Informal Justice* (1988) Sage, London.

[87] R. Danzig, 'Towards the Creation of a Complementary, Decentralised System of Criminal Justice' (1973) 26 Stanford Law Review 1.

[88] E. Fisher, 'Community Courts: An Alternative to Conventional Criminal Adjudication' (1975) 24 American University Law Review 1253.

[89] S. Henry, *Private Justice* (1983) Routledge & Kegan Paul, London, p. 46.

[90] R. Abel, 'The Contradictions of Informal Justice' in R. Abel (ed.), *The Politics of Informal Justice* (1982) Academic Press, London.

tend to be less coercive; clients are 'referred' to them, staff go to great lengths to make participants feel comfortable with the process. Since coercion is much less visible than it is within the formal legal system, the result is that the state can seek to control more behaviour; for instance, behaviour which was too trivial to be dealt with by the formal system, can be dealt with by informal procedures.

Informal justice purports to devolve state authority on non-state institutions, to delegate social control to businesses, neighbourhoods, and other private entities. But, in fact, informalism expands the grasp of the state at the expense of other sources of authority that appear to be potential competitors.[91]

The dynamic relationship between formal and informal legal worlds has also been explored by de Sousa Santos.[92] In his examination of the nature of state power, he comments '[the state] is expanding through a process which on the surface appears to be a process of retraction. What appears as delegalization is indeed relegalization.'[93]

## Legal pluralism

In the analyses that have been examined so far, there has been an emphasis on a multiplicity of sources of law. Law has been seen to emanate from the state but not only from the state. Many of the ideas that have been discussed would fall broadly under the heading of 'legal pluralism'. These ideas acknowledge that the legal universe with which we are dealing does not just consist of the formal municipal legal system and its rules found in cases and statutes:[94]

[N]on-state legal orders range from the interstices within, or areas beyond the reach of, state legal systems where custom-based norms and institutions continue to exert social control, to the rule-making and enforcing power of institutions like corporations and universities, to the normative order that exists within small social groups, from unions, to sports leagues, community associations, business associations, clubs and even the family.[95]

To get an accurate picture of English legal processes, it will be necessary to look, not only at those formal rules and to acknowledge that in some legal interaction, they have a very important role; but it will also be important to look at how those rules operate in practice. To see how, even for the officials of an individual legal system, there is a gap between what people say they should do and what they actually do. However, it will also be necessary to look at a number of legal worlds which operate to some extent independently of the formal system, but which also interact with it in crucially

---

[91]  Abel (1982) p. 275.

[92]  B. de Sousa Santos, 'Law and Community: The Changing Nature of State Power in Late Capitalism' (1980) 8 International Journal of the Sociology of Law 379.          [93]  De Sousa Santos (1980) p. 391.

[94]  For an analysis of the contrast between traditional accounts of law and notions of legal pluralism, see M. Davies, 'The Ethos of Pluralism' (2005) 27 Sydney Law Review 87.

[95]  B. Tamanaha, *A General Jurisprudence of Law and Society* (2001) Oxford University Press, Oxford, p. 116. For a critique of Tamanaha's approach to legal pluralism, see W. Twining, 'A Post-Westphalian Conception of Law' (2003) 37 Law and Society Review 199.

important ways. In order to explain this approach satisfactorily, we need to adopt an integrated theory of law. It is necessary, not only to acknowledge the importance of a variety of legal systems, as legal pluralism does, but also to 'explore the processes of interpenetration of the micro-structures with the macro and vice versa'.[96]

What this means is that it is necessary to find a theory which encompasses, not only thinking about social structures (the macro), but also the effects of individual social action (the micro). Encompassing the macro involves encompassing the approach taken by structuralists like Doreen McBarnet, who emphasize the importance of looking at socio-economic structures and legal-bureaucratic rules. She argues that:

Law-enforcement, in short, is not exclusively an area for interactionist study at the micro level; it is also an issue in the politics of law at the macro level. This means a change of focus, shifting attention from the routine activities of petty officials of the state to the top of the judicial and political hierarchies where rules are made and sanctions operated...shifting the focus to the political and judicial elite also shifts the focus to the very core of the operation of the state.[97]

## An integrated theory of law

An integrated theory must encompass broad social structures and the effects of policy on our legal worlds, but it must also be able to look at the consequences of the behaviour of the actors within the legal worlds, as interactionist researchers would suggest. Interactionism, in contrast to structuralism, focuses on the behaviour of individuals; as Robert Reiner has commented, in the context of studies on the police:

In the interactionist tradition, it has largely been assumed that formal rules are primarily presentational. They are the terms in which conduct has to be justified, but do not really affect practice. It is the police sub-culture which is the key to understanding police action.[98]

Interactionism, then, looks at 'the personal and social variables which intervene between how institutions should work and how they do'.[99]

Recognition of the need to integrate macro and micro approaches has come from a number of different sources.[100] In relation to law, this is the approach which Stuart Henry has adopted in his book *Private Justice*.[101] Henry argues that:

By recognising the dialectical relationship between structure and social action and how these are interdependent and mutually implying, we begin to see the possibility of transcending the view that law is either the product of structure or the outcome of interaction.[102]

---

[96] Henry (1983) p. 62.      [97] D. McBarnet, *Conviction* (1981) Macmillan, London, pp. 7–8.
[98] R. Reiner, *The Politics of the Police* (1985) Wheatsheaf Books, Brighton, pp. 174–5.
[99] McBarnet (1981) p. 4.
[100] For example, A. Giddens, *Central Problems in Social Theory* (1979) Macmillan, London, ch. 2; K. Knorr-Cetina and A. V. Cicourel (eds), *Advances in Social Theory and Methodology* (1981) Routledge & Kegan Paul, London.      [101] Henry (1983).
[102] Henry (1983) p. 61.

It is not merely that an integrated approach simply acknowledges the importance of both macro and micro perspectives. As Henry points out:

> What is new about the recent integrative approach of [these] commentators...is that they explicitly seek to unite macro and micro perspectives in a single theoretical framework which above all recognises that action and structure presuppose one another and cannot be addressed separately.[103]

## CONCLUSION

The conclusion that we derive from the above is that we must both be more modest and more ambitious than previous authors. There is no single unique English legal system that structures British society. The rules, the courts, the lawyers which owe their authority to the state are a legal system in England and Wales. They are, as we will see, a very important legal system that is hugely influential in most people's lives. However, this is not the only legal system. Other forms of dispute resolution also have an impact on people's lives. What previous authors have described as being 'the English legal system' is merely one part of the English legal universe. In some ways, as we shall argue in the next chapter, what has traditionally been thought of as 'the English legal system' may be the most important part of the English legal universe. Nevertheless, it is merely one world among many.

This is not a novel observation. The idea is implicit in the fact that previous writers of 'English legal system' textbooks have felt obliged to discuss arbitration procedures, private courts, conciliation schemes, and other mechanisms far removed from the state apparatus. However, their discussion of such material has been peripheral to the main body of their text and we would argue it should be brought more into the centre. We see this as impoverishing both their account of 'the English legal system' and their account of legal processes in England and Wales.

## FURTHER READING

The Archbishop of Canterbury, 'Civil and Religious Law in England: A Religious Perspective' at <http://www.archbishopof canterbury.org/1575>

Lord Mackay, *The Administration of Justice* (1994) Sweet & Maxwell, London

---

[103]  Henry (1983) p. 64.

# 2

# The significance of courts

## INTRODUCTION

When we look at the legal system, the courts seem to be the most obvious place to start. *Smith, Bailey and Gunn* states that 'the courts of law are perhaps the most visible feature of the English legal system'.[1]

## The definition of courts

Courts as an institution are not unique to 'the English legal system'. They exist in the legal systems of every modern state. They also exist in other non-state legal systems. Thus, Jewish law has the Beth Din, Muslim law the United Kingdom Islamic Shari'a Council, and Scientology its Chaplain's Court.[2] Yet, despite the pervasive nature of courts in legal systems, it is easier to describe the work of individual courts within each legal system than to define the concept of a court. Indeed, 'courts' may not be a single discrete concept since '[a]cross societies, what are called courts do not necessarily handle the same matters'.[3]

Straightforwardly, courts might be defined as places concerned with settling legal disputes. However, this definition is deficient in several ways. First, courts are sometimes distinguished from other bodies which are also concerned with settling legal disputes. One such distinction you can make is between courts and tribunals. Parliament has sometimes said that disputes under a particular Act are to be determined not by

---

[1]  S. H. Bailey, J.P. L. Ching, and N. W. Taylor, *Smith, Bailey and Gunn on the Modern English Legal System* (5th edn, 2007) Sweet & Maxwell, London, p. 48.

[2]  J. Phillips, 'An Alternative Method of Settling Disputes' (1992) The Lawyer, 7 January. (This is not just a British phenomenon. See 'Rabbinical Courts: Modern Day Solomons' (1970) 6 Columbia Journal of Law and Social Problems 49.) On the Shari'a Council in particular, see D. Pearl and W. Menski, *Muslim Family Law* (3rd edn, 1998) Butterworths, London, p. 78. On Muslim law in Great Britain, see also Z. Badawi, 'Muslim Justice in a Secular State' in M. King (ed.), *God's Law versus State Law* (1995) Grey Seal, London; Y. Ihsan, 'The Challenge of Post-modern Legality and Muslim Legal Pluralism in England' (2002) 28 Journal of Ethnic and Minority Studies 343; and Y. Ihsan, *Muslim Laws, Politics and Society in Modern Nation States* (2005) Ashgate, Aldershot. For a reference to discussion of the internal structures of Scientology in terms of laws and courts, see *Hubbard* v *Vosper* [1972] 2 QB 84 at p. 99C–D.

[3]  R. Cranston, 'What do Courts do?' (1986) 5 Civil Justice Quarterly 123 at p. 124.

courts but by particular tribunals set up for the purpose. Tribunals are less formal dispute resolution bodies: typically, three people hear the case; usually one of them is legally qualified and two are experts in the subject-matter with which the tribunal is dealing. Sometimes, it is possible to appeal from the tribunals to the courts. Sometimes, the tribunals have exclusive jurisdiction and no appeal to the courts is possible.[4] So, courts are not the only bodies that resolve disputes, since tribunals also do that.

There is something more to being a court than its function as a dispute determiner. The clue to what this is might lie in *Smith, Bailey and Gunn*'s description of it as being the most visible symbol of the legal system. There are, after all, other things that might be given this title. The police, at least those parts of police forces which wear uniforms, are a very visible symbol of a legal system. Why not select them as the most visible symbol? We would suggest the reason for this is something to do with the standing of courts.[5] To call something a court is not simply to describe what it does. It is also an ascription of status.[6] Courts are seen as having a centrality to a legal system that is not true for other institutions.

## The importance of courts

For those brought up in any complex society, such as the United Kingdom, courts tend to seem central to the very idea of a legal system. The words 'court' and 'legal system' become synonyms. Lawyers, professionals in a legal system, are assumed to be people who use the law and legal system as a regular part of their professional lives, who go to courts and are thus familiar with court procedures. In 1976, Campbell published a study which suggested that half the people in Scotland thought that lawyers spent the majority of their time in court. However, according to his research, the reality was somewhat different. When he asked Scottish solicitors to estimate how much purely legal work took up their time, the estimate they arrived at was that they spent less than one hour per week in work which involved technical legal knowledge.[7] Their own perception of

---

[4] But even where a tribunal has exclusive jurisdiction, the courts can see whether or not the tribunal had the power to make a decision or not. Thus, if a tribunal with exclusive jurisdiction, and having powers to make orders increasing student grants, purports to make orders abolishing student grants the courts could still declare such orders invalid notwithstanding the lack of a right of appeal. *Anisminic v Foreign Compensation Commission* [1969] 2 AC 147. (See further W. Wade and C. Forsyth, *Administrative Law* (10th edn, 2009) Oxford University Press, Oxford, ch. 8.) The distinction is further blurred by the fact that under s. 3(5) of the Tribunals, Courts and Enforcement Act 2007, the recently created Upper Tribunal is designated as a 'superior court of record' and is therefore not susceptible to judicial review (see further Wade and Forsyth (2009) pp. 780–1).    [5] And of police forces.

[6] 'Judges are authoritative figures…' (S. Roberts, 'Three Models of Family Mediation' in R. Dingwall and J. Eekelaar (eds), *Divorce Mediation and the Legal Process* (1988) Clarendon Press, Oxford, p. 148) and, we would argue, other people settling disputes are not authoritative in the same way.

[7] C. Campbell, 'Lawyers and their Public' in D. N. MacCormick (ed.), *Lawyers in their Social Setting* (1996) W. Green, Edinburgh, p. 209.

their work was that they spent most of their time in work which either involved only 'routinised legal knowledge' or skills which were wholly non-legal.[8] These early findings about the work of lawyers have been confirmed by more recent inquiries into the work of lawyers in England and Wales.[9] Many lawyers spend very little of their time either in court or in doing work which directly leads to anything happening in court.

*Smith, Bailey and Gunn* is plainly right in saying that courts are a very visible feature of a legal system. But does the fact that they are very visible mean they are very important? What exactly does a court do? What is the relationship between courts and lawyers? What is the court's role in a legal system?

## The function of courts

Courts, we might suppose, exist to settle disputes about the application of legal rules. They might not be the only bodies that do that, but that is at least part of their function. Within the rules of the system itself, the courts of that system are the only body which can authoritatively settle disputes. Others, such as academics and journalists, may comment on court decisions, questioning their internal logic or social efficacy, but that questioning does not affect the finality of the court's decision.[10] In this sense, courts exist to determine disputes. However, we should not take from that proposition the idea that *all* legal disputes end up in court.

In 1978, the Royal Commission on Civil Liability and Compensation for Personal Injury noted that of the 250,000 tort claims in respect of personal injury, 86 per cent were disposed of without issue of a writ, 11 per cent after issue of a writ but before setting down for a hearing, 2 per cent after setting down for trial but before trial, and only 1 per cent were settled in court.[11] Ten years later, the Civil Justice Review noted that of 340,000 personal injury claims based on allegations of either negligence or breach of statutory duty 300,000 (88 per cent) were settled without issue of a writ and, once again, only 1 per cent were disposed of by trial.[12] Statistically, court action is simply not an important part of the way in which the legal system settles disputes about personal injuries. This is not just true of personal injury actions. Genn's major study of the

---

[8]  Campbell (1996) p. 209.

[9]  Thus, for example, Chambers and Harwood found that only 61 per cent of their respondent solicitors were currently engaged in advocacy work and only 25 per cent of those engaged in advocacy appeared as often as three times per week (G. Chambers and S. Harwood, *Solicitors in England and Wales: Practice, Organisation and Perceptions* (1990) The Law Society, London, p. 40).

[10]  See further H. Hart, *The Concept of Law* (1961) Oxford University Press, Oxford, pp. 138 *et seq.*

[11]  Royal Commission on Civil Liability and Compensation for Personal Injury, *Report* (the Pearson Report, vol. 2) (1978) Cmnd 7054–II, p. 20. Torts are actions in respect of civil wrongs; claims where the litigant contends that they suffered an injury contrary to law at the hands of another. Actions are commenced by issue of a writ. After the issue of the writ, indicating that court action is being contemplated, the matter is set down for trial at a later date (see **Chapter 10**).

[12]  Civil Justice Review, *Report of the Review Body on Civil Justice* (1988) Cm. 394, para. 391.

public's response to justiciable problems (i.e., those disputes that could be dealt with by the courts) concluded that:

the court and other legal proceedings play a very minor role in the resolution of justiciable problems afflicting ordinary members of the public as private individuals.[13]

Courts, then, are not as central to this part of the legal system as we might at first have thought. People can, and usually do, choose to make a final settlement of their dispute without going to court.

In some other areas of law, however, the courts must be used if legal action is to be taken. In divorce cases, for example, a divorce can only be granted after a court hearing.[14] A couple may agree to live apart without getting a divorce. However, legally they are still married. If they marry other parties, that marriage would, legally, be bigamous and therefore a criminal offence.[15] Only a court can legally separate them, allowing them to marry again.[16] Such areas, where the use of the court is mandatory, are, however, rare.[17]

Where people have a choice whether to use a court or not, there is a considerable body of evidence which attests to the reluctance of people to use courts as a means of settling their legal disputes. In an early study, published in 1975, Beale and Dugdale showed that people in business displayed a marked reluctance to use the courts to redress the wrongs done to them, even where they were aware of the possibility of legal action.[18] Since then, other studies have also suggested that courts are often something to be used in the last resort, even where those in dispute perceive that their

---

[13]  H. Genn, *Paths to Justice* (1999b) Hart Publishing, Oxford, p. 150.

[14]  Matrimonial Causes Act 1973, s. 1. Even in divorce cases, the actual degree of court involvement can be overestimated. In 1973, a 'special procedure' was introduced. Under this 'special procedure' petitions for divorce, together with accompanying affidavits and responses, are not considered in court but are, rather, referred to a Registrar. Petitioner and respondent are not present when the Registrar considers the papers. If the Registrar is satisfied that the petitioner has proven their case, the Registrar will issue a certificate to that effect. The case is then referred to court where the petition is granted without further discussion or the need for the presence of the parties. Although technically there is still a court hearing in substance, under the 'special procedure', divorce has become an administrative process (J. Masson, R. Bailey-Harris, and R. Probert, *Cretney's Principles of Family Law* (8th edn, 2008) Sweet & Maxwell, London, p. 288. The 'special procedure' is now available for all undefended divorce petitions and there are now no officially available figures for defended divorces suggesting that they are either unknown or almost so.

[15]  Offences Against the Person Act 1861, s. 57.

[16]  Not all legal systems insist on courts determining divorce. Under Islamic law, divorce may be a purely personal act involving the husband announcing that the couple are divorced (see Pearl and Menski (1998) ch. 9).

[17]  Another example would be the issue of licences for things like the sale of alcohol (see, for example, Licensing Act 2003).

[18]  H. Beale and T. Dugdale, 'Contracts between Businessmen: Planning and the Use of Contractual Remedies' (1975) 2 British Journal of Law and Society 45. The study was based upon a survey of a very small number of people in business and was described by its authors as being 'preliminary research'. One must therefore be cautious about generalizing from its findings. We should also note that people's attitudes towards law can change. Vincent-Jones has suggested that there has been a rise in the willingness of business people to take legal action when faced with a dispute (P. Vincent-Jones, 'Contract Litigation in England and Wales 1975–1991' (1993) 12 Civil Justice Quarterly 370). Conversely, Kagan has argued that in the United States, debt collection – tradition-

problem should, in part or whole, be settled by reference to the rules of the legal system.[19] Thus, for example, in her 1987 study of insurance claims in cases of personal injury, although Genn concludes that '[t]he context within which ... negotiation and settlement of claims takes place is provided by the principles of negligence which determine the legal liability of those who cause accidents, and by English civil litigation procedure',[20] she goes on to observe that 'the vast majority of claims initiated are likely to be concluded by means of a compromise rather than court adjudication',[21] citing as one major reason for this the desire of plaintiff's solicitors to be seen as being cooperative rather than confrontational when dealing with the representatives of insurance companies.[22] Similarly, in a much larger and more general survey of the way in which people deal with potentially justiciable problems, Genn found that the most common strategy for dealing with such problems was to attempt to solve the matter without resort to professional legal advice, let alone by resort to the courts.[23]

Whatever function courts do have, it is not to deal with the day-to-day activity of a legal system. Being in court does not take up most of the time of most lawyers. Courts do not resolve most legal disputes. In these senses, the courts seem rather peripheral to a legal system. Is there, then, any sense in which the courts are in reality central to a legal system?

## The centrality of courts

When courts are involved in an individual dispute, they usually impose a final legal determination of the issue on the parties involved. The parties' presence in court may be voluntary but, usually, either party can insist on going to court simply by refusing

ally a focus for court work – has now become comparatively unlitigated (R. Kagan, 'The Routinization of Debt Collection: An Essay on Social Change and Conflict in the Courts' (1984) 18 Law and Society Review 323).

[19] People may fail to see their problem as a legal problem even when it is, in principle, capable of legal redress. Thus, for example, a tenant with a lease which puts the lessor of the property under an obligation to repair it may be unaware of their rights under that lease. When a repair needs to be done, they may elect to do it themselves rather than ask the lessor to do it or they may ask the lessor to do it and when the lessor refuses then elect to do it themselves. In such situations, there is no necessary fear of, or refusal to use, courts, rather, there is a more fundamental failure to categorize the problem as being a legal problem at all. This failure is not necessarily to be seen as being problematic in terms of the end result, the non-use of the legal system. Both from society's point of view and from the individual's point of view, legal action may not be the most efficient means of selecting a problem. (See further P. Morris et al., *Social Needs and Legal Action* (1973) Martin Robertson, Oxford.) There is, however, a difference between a failure to use the legal system because it is seen as not being beneficial in the individual instance and a lack of awareness of the possibility of legal action.

[20] H. Genn, *Hard Bargaining: Out of Court Settlement in Personal Injury Claims* (1987) Oxford University Press, Oxford, p. 163. For a re-examination of Genn's work, see R. Dingwall, T. Durkin, P. Pleasance, W. Felstiner, and R. Bowles, 'Firm Handling: The Litigation Strategies of Defence Lawyers in Personal Injury Cases' (2000) 20 Legal Studies 1.

[21] Genn (1987) pp. 168–9. Genn's findings are, of course, in keeping with the statistical analyses in the Pearson Report and the Civil Justice Review discussed above.

[22] Genn (1987) pp. 164–5. Genn's research is discussed further in **Chapter 10**.

[23] Genn (1999b) p. 230.

to settle the dispute in any other way. As soon as one of the parties insists on a court settling the dispute, however, the nature of the dispute changes. The court at this point becomes central to the legal system. It is its focus. It controls what happens within the legal system. In this sense of centrality, each court which makes a final determination for any individual litigant is as important as any other. So far as the defendant is concerned, the magistrates' court's decision that decided that they are guilty is precisely as important as if the case had been taken on appeal to the Supreme Court and the Supreme Court had held that they were guilty. The finding of both courts will equally lead to their punishment.

If we say that courts provide a final legal *determination* of a dispute this is not to say that the courts provide a final *settlement* of the issue. Legal systems tend to be hierarchical. One court's decision may be overturned by another higher court. A determination may thus only be final until an appeal. Moreover, even when the highest court has ruled, even when there is no prospect of further appeal, the court does not necessarily settle an issue. Courts are of more limited importance than this. The parties, or one party, to a dispute may carry on arguing about the matter, regardless of what the courts have decided. However, this continuance must be outside the legal arena. Thus, for example, losing a court case may lead to an attempt to reform the law. In some cases this attempt to reform the law may include an attempt to alter the decision that led to the reform. In the press, we sometimes see people convicted of some crime, or their supporters, seeking to carry on a dispute in this manner.[24]

It is the fact that a court can impose a decision on the parties that normally distinguishes a court from some, but not all, other kinds of bodies involved in disputes about the law. Thus, for example, a mediator may seek to get the parties to a dispute to come to an agreement about their differences. The mediator is still concerned with settling a legal dispute. In their task of mediating, they may take account of the legal rules which affect the parties.[25] However, because they are mediators, they cannot impose a decision on the parties. Mediators seek consent and assent.[26] Courts usually simply expect obedience. It has been said that '[c]ourts obtain their power to coerce individuals at the cost of their capacity to persuade'.[27] However, this is not always the

---

[24] See, for example, the case of Sara Thornton (*The Guardian*, 23 November 1994). More generally, women who have killed their partners in a situation of domestic violence, find that their individual cases are determined by the courts according to standard criminal law rules of self-defence and provocation. However, these cases then become the basis for academic reflection on the necessity for reform. (See, for example, K. O'Donovan, 'Defences for Battered Women who Kill' (1991) 18 Journal of Law and Society 219; and C. Wells, 'Battered Woman Syndrome and Defences to Homicide: Where Now?' (1994) 14 Legal Studies 266.)

[25] G. Davis, 'The Halls of Justice and Justice in Halls' in Dingwall and Eekelaar, *Divorce Mediation and the Legal Process* (1988b).

[26] Mediation can take a number of different forms but the eventual desire to produce a resolution which is acceptable to all parties is common to all types of mediation properly so called. (See Roberts (1988).)

[27] R. Abel, 'Western Courts in Non-Western Settings' in S. Burman and B. Harrell-Bond, *The Imposition of Law* (1979) Academic Press, New York, p. 173.

case. Sometimes, judges can be seen as mediators.[28] Courts sometimes make orders because both parties want them to do so. These are known as 'consent orders'.[29] Courts may also be faced with disputes where one party refuses to take part in the case. In one survey, Cain concluded that 'the court settles disputes between two actively participating parties in only one quarter of the non-familial cases with which it deals'.[30] Nor do courts have to see themselves as being there simply to impose decisions. Whether or not they do this is partly a matter of the style the court chooses to adopt rather than anything which is necessary to the function of the court.

In Gluckman's study of the Lozi tribe, he describes the way in which the Kuta gives judgment. In his description, he emphasizes the Kuta's attempt to get the parties to admit to their errors. Thus, in one case he describes, 'the case of the biased father', three men sued their village headman for gardens. During the hearing of the case, those settling the dispute got both the headman and the men to agree that they had acted incorrectly. He describes the way in which the members of the Kuta lecture parties on their duties, rarely finding fault simply on one side. Again, in 'the case of the biased father', all parties are said to be at fault and all parties accept that they want a resolution of the dispute. We should not make the mistake of thinking that because they do this the Kuta is simply mediating between the parties. They can, if they choose, impose a decision. They are in this sense a court. However, they see their role as being partly persuasive.[31]

Gluckman argues that the Kuta adopts this style because the Lozi tribe are a comparatively small community. Each member depends on other members for mutual support. In England and Wales, it has been said that we have a legal duty of care towards our neighbours.[32] By neighbours, English tort law means fellow members of the community. If this duty is breached we may sue in the courts and the courts will impose their verdict. However, one could argue that one may sue one's neighbour precisely because one's neighbour is only one's neighbour. The more connections someone has with me the less likely I am to sue them. Indeed, I am less likely to sue someone who in fact lives next door to me; still less likely to sue them if they are also my friend, my business partner, and so forth.[33] Because we normally sue strangers, it is easier for courts to impose settlements which involve one person winning and one person losing. Such settlements may cause a break in social relationships, but it is a

[28] M. Galanter, '"...Settlement Judge not a Trial Judge": Judicial Mediation in the United States' (1985) 12 Journal of Law and Society 1; N. Kwai, 'The Judge as Mediator: The Japanese Experience' (1991) 10 Civil Justice Quarterly 108; C. McEwen and R. Maiman, 'Mediation in Small Claims Court: Achieving Compliance through Consent' (1984) 18 Law and Society Review 11; K. Rohl, 'The Judge as Mediator' (1985) 4 Civil Justice Quarterly 235.
[29] See, for example, Civil Procedure Rules 1998, r. 40.6. (These rules are available via the Ministry of Justice website at: <http://www.justice.gov.uk/civil/procrules_fin/index.htm>.)
[30] M. Cain, 'Where are the Disputes? A Study of a First Instance Civil Court in the UK' in M. Cain and K. Kulscar, *Disputes and the Law* (1983) Akademia Kiado, Budapest, p. 121.
[31] M. Gluckman, *The Judicial Process amongst the Barotse* (2nd edn, 1976) Manchester University Press, Manchester, pp. 37–45.          [32] Per Lord Atkin in *Donaghue* v *Stevenson* [1932] All ER 1 at p. 11.
[33] Beale and Dugdale (1975).

break only at one level. If the Kuta imposes a settlement, without getting the parties to accept their error and without trying to reconcile the parties, there is a risk of the community losing one of its members.

In modern complex societies, there are also courts which are under a duty to try to bring parties together. Cloutier describes the Quebec court's role in family law.[34] Under s. 528 of the Quebec Civil Code, '[i]t comes within the role of the court to counsel and foster the conciliation of the parties'. Cloutier concludes that '[a] family court is not a court of law anymore but a court of equity, more concerned with fact-conclusion than fact-finding, with regulation of the future conduct of family members rather than enforcement of individual rights'.[35]

In the last chapter, we noted that there was some interest in introducing different forms of dispute adjudication into 'the English legal system'.[36] In his report on the civil justice system, Lord Woolf argued that there was a need to introduce changes which would make 'the landscape of civil litigation fundamentally different'.[37] As a consequence of his report, the Civil Procedure Rules 1998 were passed which were intended to change the culture of the civil courts. The focus of the new Rules is on avoiding litigation, with the court having a duty to manage cases actively, and encourage and facilitate the settlement of disputes.[38]

## Courts as rule-makers

Courts are also important to 'the English legal system' because of the contribution they make to the development of the jurisprudence of the legal system. In making individual decisions, courts are not necessarily just deciding the law for the individual parties to the case. They may also be deciding the law for those litigants that come after the particular case before them. Rules of law in the English legal system come from two main sources. One source of legal rules is the statutes passed by Parliament. These are intended to create rules of law which are binding prospectively and, occasionally, retrospectively.[39] Another source of law is the decisions of the courts where no statutory provisions are to be found; the common law.

---

[34]  A. Cloutier, 'The Conciliatory Function of the Superior Court' (1985) 4 Civil Justice Quarterly 342.

[35]  Cloutier (1985) p. 357.        [36]  See **Chapter 1**.

[37]  Lord Woolf, *Access to Justice: Final Report to the Lord Chancellor on the Civil Justice System in England and Wales* (the Woolf Report) (1996) Lord Chancellor's Department, London, p. 4. For a critical account of the Woolf Report, see M. Zander, 'The Final Woolf Report: Forwards or Backwards for the New Lord Chancellor?' (1997) 16 Civil Justice Quarterly 208; and A. Zuckerman, 'Lord Woolf's Access to Justice: Plus ça change...' (1996) 59 Modern Law Review 773.

[38]  CPR 1.4. The changes are discussed at greater length in **Chapter 10**.

[39]  For an example of retrospective legislation, see the War Damages Act 1961. In *Burmah Oil Company* v *Lord Advocate* [1965] AC 75, the courts had held that the Government was obliged to compensate the Burmah Oil Company for the loss of installations which had been destroyed to prevent their falling into the hands of the Japanese during the Second World War. The War Damages Act 1961 retrospectively gave the

Courts make law when they interpret statutes, when they give a legally authoritative explanation of what the Act means. Ordinary individuals, trying to decide what a statute means, are faced with the problem that '[i]n all forms of experience, not only that of rules, there is a limit, inherent in the nature of language, to the guidance which general language can provide'.[40] Words are not precise things. With their many possible definitions and usages they do not simply tell us what to do or not to do but point in a myriad of different directions. In ordinary life, this often does not matter. However, in law where we have to decide to do or not to do a particular act this will create great difficulties. The open texture of language means that even if a literal meaning of the words in the statute is sought this meaning will always be 'an interpretative meaning'.[41] In deciding what the statute says there will always be a degree to which the reader chooses the meaning. Each reader of the statute may choose in a different way.[42] But the law can only work if each person selects the same meaning; if we thus know what following the law is or is not. In this situation of flux and uncertainty, the decisions of the courts affix (an apparently) settled reading.[43] Courts are thus creating law.

In selecting a meaning, the English courts have consistently held that they are not free to read into statutes meanings that they might like to see there but are, rather, bound to interpret the statute in the light of the intention of Parliament.[44] In doing so, they are, at least ostensibly, accepting their subordination to Parliament.[45] However, without resiling from this public acceptance of their inferior hierarchical relationship to Parliament, the courts have come to accept that when '[w]e often say that we are looking for the intention of Parliament...that is not quite accurate. We are seeking the meaning of the words which Parliament used. We are seeking not what Parliament meant but the true meaning of what they said.'[46] But, in doing this, given the inherent flexibility of language, the courts are not identifying a previously determined reading, 'the true meaning of Parliament's words', since there is no true

---

Crown authority to act in this way without being obliged to pay compensation. The Act is thus an example of a litigant, in this case the Government, successfully carrying on a dispute in another arena, despite a ruling from the courts.

[40] H. L. A. Hart, *The Concept of Law* (2nd edn, 1994) Clarendon Press, Oxford, p. 126.

[41] P. Goodrich, *Reading the Law* (1986) Blackwell, Oxford, p. 109.

[42] '[I]t is trite learning that the interpreter has nearly as much to say as the speaker so far as the meaning of words is concerned' R. Cross, *Precedent in English Law* (3rd edn, 1977) Clarendon Press, Oxford, p. 42.

[43] We will argue in **Chapter 6** that the clarity of the meaning of a statute found in a court decision is often more superficial than it seems.

[44] *Pepper* v *Hart* [1993] 1 All ER 42. See particularly Lord Browne-Wilkinson's speech at p. 74E–F.

[45] 'This formula [searching for the intention of Parliament] reminds all who deal with statute that they are operating in a field of law in which they are not free to define public policy simply according to their own judgment' J. Hurst quoted in J. Bell and Sir George Engle, *Cross: Statutory Interpretation* (2nd edn, 1987) Oxford University Press, Oxford, p. 29. However, in the recent case of *Jackson* v *Attorney-General* [2006] 1 AC 262, several judges questioned whether the notion of parliamentary sovereignty was still an appropriate doctrine for the courts to uphold. See further **Chapter 6**.

[46] Per Lord Reid in *Black-Clawson Ltd* v *Papierwierke AG* [1975] AC 591 at p. 613.

meaning, but selecting what *they decide* 'the true meaning of Parliament's words' will be. In this even stronger sense, the courts are making law when they interpret statutes.[47]

If the interpretation of statutes involves the courts in making law this is still more the case when they deal with common law. Common law is the other main source of legal rules in England and Wales. The phrase describes that area of law where the final authority for the legal rule lies not in any statute but in previous decisions of the courts. Common law is an inferior source of legal rules to statute since, where any statute has been passed, the courts will take this to be the source of the legal rule.[48] Common law is thus an area of declining importance since statutory intervention encompasses an ever greater part of social and commercial life. Nevertheless, the common law remains of some significance, particularly in areas such as the law of contract and the law of tort.

The judicial power to make law in interpreting rules is something that is inherent in the nature of judging. It exists even in those legal systems that claim that judges are simply applying law. Thus, for example, Islamic law rests on a source, the Koran, which is thought to be divine and unchallengeable.[49] Nevertheless, even here, in applying rules there is a degree of creativity.[50] However, not all legal systems allow their judges the pure power to make rules which is found in the common law system. The civil law systems of the rest of Europe are based upon judges interpreting codes.[51]

## The court as legislature

To say that judicial decisions are themselves a final source of law is a statement of greater constitutional significance than saying that in interpreting statutes judges make law. It is often argued that the theory of the separation of the powers is fundamental to any Western, liberal democracy of which the British constitutional system

[47]  This is not to say that the courts are free to make any decision about what these words will mean; merely to argue that there is in their decision an element of discretion. For this see further **pp. 133–5**.

[48]  However, 'plain words are necessary to establish an intention to interfere with common law...rights' (per Somervell LJ in *Deeble* v *Robinson* [1954] 1 QB 77 at p. 81).

[49]  R. David and J. Brierley, *Major Legal Systems in the World Today* (3rd edn, 1985) Stevens, London, pp. 457–65; M. H. Kamali, *Principles of Islamic Jurisprudence* (1989) Pelanduk Publications (M) Sdn Bhd, Petaling Jaya, ch. 11.

[50]  See Kamali (1989) for a chapter (ch. 19) on personal reasoning in Islamic law.

[51]  A. Chloros, 'Common Law, Civil Law and Socialist Law: Three Leading Systems of the World, Three Kinds of Legal Reasoning' in Csaba Varga (ed.), *Comparative Legal Cultures* (1992) Dartmouth, Aldershot, pp. 87–91.

is taken to be an example.[52] This theory, in its simplest form, holds that an abuse of governmental power is prevented, or at least made less likely, if the power of the state is shared amongst the executive, the legislature, and the judiciary. Thus, following this theory, one of the functions of a court is to be one side in a balance between the various organs of state. If, however, judicial decisions are themselves a final source of law:

A judge when dealing with a case…is applying the law to a particular instance, is 'judging' or determining the nature of the rule to be applied, and is at the same time creating a precedent to be followed by other courts. He, therefore, *of necessity*, exercises all three functions, and cannot be prevented from doing so if he is to perform the tasks which he is set.[53]

Indeed, if we accept that judges are a final source of law then, in a democratic society, by what right do these unelected officials take on this legislative role?[54]

One way to avoid such constitutional problems is to deny that judges, in any straightforward sense of the phrase, make law. Such a denial is made easier by the fact that although the statement that judges make law appears to be a simple theory 'the more closely the theory is examined the less simple does it appear'.[55] British judges plainly do not regard themselves as having the same freedom to make law as do other legislatures. If they do make law, they do so only cautiously. They often attempt to explain that their law-making is either not law-making at all or, insofar as it is law-making, it is inevitable and fits closely with the established system. This is so, even when their new rules seem to be relatively uncontroversial. In 1991, the courts overturned the centuries-old rule that a wife on marriage gave consent to sexual intercourse and could not withdraw that consent. Although the court accepted that '[i]n modern times any reasonable person must regard that conception as quite unacceptable', it took seven pages of judgment, and the examination of many authorities, for it to come to the conclusion that the old law could be overturned.[56]

The implementation of the Human Rights Act 1998 is likely to bring arguments about the legitimacy of the judicial role in making law even more to the fore. Under s. 4(1) of the Act, judges have the duty to determine 'whether a provision of primary legislation is compatible with a [European] Convention [on Human Rights] right', whilst under s. 3 they are required to interpret legislation so that 'so far as it is possible' it is compatible with the Convention rights.[57]

---

[52] See, for example, A. W. Bradley and K. D. Ewing, *Constitutional and Administrative Law* (14th edn, 2007) Longman, London, p. 81.

[53] M. Vile, *Constitutionalism and the Separation of Powers* (1967) Clarendon Press, Oxford, p. 318.

[54] See further J. A. G. Griffith, *The Politics of the Judiciary* (5th edn, 1997) Fontana, London.

[55] Sir William Holdsworth, 'Case Law' (1934) 50 Law Quarterly Review 180 at p. 180.

[56] *R v R* [1991] 4 All ER 481 at p. 484.      [57] See further **Chapter 6**.

## Limits to the judicial legislature

Historically, it was said that 'cases do not make law, but are only the best evidence of what the law is'.[58] Under this declaratory theory of law, the judges were said merely to enunciate what was part of the custom of England and Wales. They did not make law, merely describing what had in fact already existed, even though it had not been referred to by previous judges. However, in the nineteenth century, the work of legal theorists such as Austin 'killed this childish but highly convenient fiction'.[59] Austin, drawing on a phrase first used by Bentham, wrote approvingly of 'judge-made law'. 'That part of the law of every country which was made by the judges has been far better made than that part which consists of statutes enacted by the legislature.'[60] Austin argued that judges did make law but that this law was tacitly approved by the sovereign.[61] Thus, again, the inconvenient notion that judges independently make law was avoided.

In the twentieth century, Austin's concept of the relationship between 'judge-made law' and other law-making has been regarded in much the same light that Austin regarded the previous declaratory theory. 'To say that judge-made law is the tacit command of the sovereign is... a "mere artifice of speech", "a straining of language", "a forced expression."'[62] More recently, Dworkin has put forward the thesis that when judges are faced with new problems judges neither 'find nor invent law; we understand legal reasoning... only by seeing the sense in which they do both and neither'.[63] In Dworkin's account, the work of the judiciary should be seen as akin to writing a chain novel with each successive author adding new material which must make sense in the light of that which has gone previously.[64] New legal rules and concepts can only be created in the context of old ones. This account avoids the constitutional problems inherent in the notion of autonomous judicial creativity whilst not relying on the fictions of declaration of tacit consent. As a theory, it appeals to judges.[65]

---

[58] Holdsworth (1934) at p. 184. Thus, in *Bole* v *Horton*, it was said that 'if a court give judgement judicially, another court is not bound to give like judgement, unless it thinks that judgement first given was according to law' (*Bole* v *Horton* (1673) Vaughan 360 at p. 383).

[59] A. Goodhart, 'Case Law – A Short Replication' (1934) 50 Law Quarterly Review 196 at p. 197.

[60] Though he disapproved of the term itself, which he described as 'disrespectful' and 'injudicious' (J. Austin, *Lectures on Jurisprudence* (1885) John Murray, London, p. 218). Bentham had already, prior to Austin's work, baldly stated that judges made law but had argued that statute was a better form of law (J. Bentham, 'Truth *versus* Ashhurst' in *The Works of Jeremy Bentham* (1962)) Russell and Russell, New York, vol. 5, p. 233 at pp. 235–6.

[61] J. Austin, *The Province of Jurisprudence Determined* (2nd edn, 1861) Burt Franklin, New York, p. 169.

[62] W. Rumble, *The Thought of John Austin* (1985) Athlone Press, London, p. 112 quoting Maine and Gray, respectively.        [63] R. Dworkin, *Law's Empire* (1986) Fontana, London, p. 225.

[64] See Dworkin (1986) particularly ch. 7.

[65] See Lord Hoffmann's remarks in his review of Lee's *Judging Judges* ((1989) 105 Law Quarterly Review 140 at p. 144). For further analysis of judicial creativity, see **Chapters 5** and **6**.

No matter which account of the relationship between judges, the executive, and the legislature is accurate, one thing remains true. For those outside the court, the judges appear to be in a position to make law. In 1959, a publisher took legal advice as to whether or not it was a criminal offence to publish a book listing the names and addresses of prostitutes. He also sought the advice of Scotland Yard and sent a copy to the Director of Public Prosecutions. In 1961, the same publisher, having published the book under the title, *The Ladies' Directory*, was convicted of the hitherto unknown offence of conspiracy to corrupt public morals.[66] In this sense, judges make law and in this sense, courts are central to the functioning of 'the English legal system'.

## CONCLUSION

From the above, we can see that courts are in some ways central to an account of most legal systems.[67] However, it is important to underline the phrase, 'in some ways'. The courts are not simply central to either every legal system or any particular legal system. They are central when we ask some questions; inconsequential when we ask others; 'most visible' when we look for some things; impossible to see when we look for others. We must begin this book in some way and we opt to begin it with courts. In the next few chapters, we will concentrate on the courts of 'the English legal system'. We could equally legitimately have begun the book by looking at the people who are parties to disputes. We could have begun by looking at the reasons why people enter into legal disputes, what leads them to end legal disputes, and what makes them satisfied with the way in which legal disputes are conducted. We could have asked what distinctions people make between the different kinds of disputes they take part in. Legal systems are institutions but they are also people. We could have begun with these people for they are too, in one sense, central to a legal system. We could also have begun with looking at the officials of a legal system. We could have examined the sociology and psychology of people like court clerks, police-officers, judges, lawyers, and others associated with a legal system. Again, in one sense, these people are central to a legal system. That which is most visible, like the tip of the iceberg, is not always that which is most important. That which comes first is not always that which is of greatest concern.

---

[66] *Shaw* v *DPP* [1962] AC 220.

[67] There are some legal systems which do not have courts at all. Malinowski's description of the legal regime in the Trobriand Islands is a description of a legal system with no court at all where disputes are resolved against the background of an implicit notion of reciprocity (see B. Malinowski, *Crime and Custom in Savage Society* (1926) Routledge & Kegan Paul, London). In Evans-Pritchard's description of the Nuer, he begins by saying '[i]n a strict sense the Nuer have no law' (E. Evans-Pritchard, *The Nuer* (1940) Oxford University Press, Oxford, p. 162). He then goes on to describe an elaborate system of compensatory payments for wrongs done. The 'strict sense' in which there is no law is largely the fact that there is no 'legislative, judicial and executive functions' vested in any particular individual (Evans-Pritchard (1940) p. 162).

## FURTHER READING

BAILEY, S. H., CHING, J. P. L., and TAYLOR, N. W., *Smith, Bailey and Gunn on the Modern English Legal System* (5th edn, 2007) Sweet & Maxwell, London, ch. 2.

WARD, R. and AKHTAR, A., *Walker and Walker's English Legal System* (10th edn, 2008) Oxford University Press, Oxford.

# 3

# Courts in 'the English legal system'

## INTRODUCTION

In the last chapter, we looked at the nature of courts. In this chapter, we will change our focus and look at the particular courts found in 'the English legal system'. The chapter is divided into three sections. In the first section, we will look at different categories of courts. In the second section, we will look at the form of individual courts. We are not just looking for a description of the various courts. We are looking to see how the courts work and to see what links the various courts together. In the final section, we will see what general conclusions can be drawn about the nature of courts within 'the English legal system'.

## Categories of courts

Within 'the English legal system' there are a large number of courts. They vary from small courts which have a limited jurisdiction over a particular geographical area or a particular type of dispute, to courts which can hear any case about virtually any aspect of law no matter where the dispute took place.[1] They can be grouped together in a number of different ways.

### Civil and criminal courts

Many people talk about the difference between civil courts and criminal courts. This is a useful idea when you are starting to learn about the legal system, but it is not really a very accurate distinction, because many courts exercise jurisdiction in both civil and criminal matters. However, there are a few differences about which it is helpful to be aware.

Some courts deal primarily with civil matters (the county court, the High Court, the Court of Appeal (Civil Division)); the Supreme Court (formerly the House of Lords) also deals with appeals about civil matters. Civil matters often concern relationships

---

[1] For example, county courts have a limited geographical jurisdiction, whilst the Court of Appeal has an appellate jurisdiction over almost all areas of law wheresoever a dispute within England and Wales arises.

between individual people (contracts, family law, torts); these are often referred to as 'private law'. Other civil matters concern the relationships between individuals and the state (disputes about tax, or the actions of a local authority or other public body); this type of issue is often referred to as 'public law'. But whether it is private law or public law, it involves the civil law, as opposed to the criminal law.

In civil proceedings, a claimant (who used to be called a plaintiff) sues a defendant or makes an application for an order of the court. When civil cases are reported, the cases are referred to by the names of the parties involved in the dispute: *Patel* v *Jones*, for instance. The 'v' is pronounced 'and', to signify that it is a civil case. The standard of proof in a civil case is generally that things have to be proved 'on a balance of probabilities'.

Courts which deal primarily with criminal law matters are the magistrates' courts, the Crown Court, and the Court of Appeal (Criminal Division). The Supreme Court also deals with criminal appeals. Criminal matters involve a potential breach of the criminal law; someone is accused of having committed a crime (e.g., murder, theft, burglary) and the state prosecutes them.

The parties in a criminal case will be the accused person, and a prosecutor, a representative of the state, who will generally be a member of the Crown Prosecution Service (CPS), or someone acting on behalf of the CPS. Prosecutions are carried out on behalf of the Crown, so when criminal cases are reported, they are reported as *R* v... The 'R' stands for Regina, which means 'the Queen'. When criminal cases are reported (*R* v *McFadden*), the 'v' is pronounced 'against', to signify that it is a criminal case. The standard of proof in a criminal case is generally that things have to be proved 'beyond reasonable doubt'.

## Courts of record

Historically, a court of record was a court whose records were kept in the Public Records Office.[2] However, the modern usage is to describe a court as being a court of record if it has the inherent power to punish people who are in contempt of court.[3] This usage is somewhat loose because '[w]hether *all* courts of record are vested with an inherent contempt jurisdiction still has to be directly tested'.[4] Equally, Parliament has, at times, statutorily designated some courts, and even some tribunals, as being courts of record.[5] Nevertheless, this usage is of some importance.

---

[2] '[T]he technical conception of a court of record...was of slow growth...' (W. Holdsworth, *A History of English Law*, vol. V (1924) Methuen, London, p. 157). For the historical reasons for the development of this idea see Holdsworth (1924) pp. 157–60.

[3] R. Ward and A. Akhtar, *Walker and Walker's English Legal System* (10th edn, 2008) Oxford University Press, Oxford, p. 237. The High Court has a common law power to punish people in contempt of court where a court does not itself have such a power. *R* v *Davies* [1924] 1 KB 32.

[4] N. Lowe and G. Borrie, *Borrie and Lowe's Law of Contempt* (2nd edn, 1983) Butterworths, London, p. 315, emphasis in original.

[5] See, for example, the designation of the new Upper Tribunal as a superior court of record under s. 3(5) of the Tribunals Courts and Enforcement Act 2007.

In the last chapter, we argued that calling something a court ascribes a special status to that body. Although the courts have been keen to argue that 'the object of the discipline enforced by the Court in case of contempt of Court is not to vindicate the dignity of the Court or the person of the judge but to prevent undue interference with the administration of justice', in fact, the very idea of contempt of court helps to create a special status for the courts.[6] The law relating to contempt of court creates special rules which limit the degree and nature of debate about what goes on in court.[7] In some circumstances, one may not say things to judges that one could say to other people. One may not criticize judges in ways that one could criticize other people. Thus, these rules give courts a special sanctity.[8]

Although the notion of a court of record emphasizes one of the key aspects of the idea of a court, the historical division between courts of record and courts not of record now serves little practical or academic purpose.

## Superior courts and inferior courts

There is no precise principle which distinguishes superior courts from inferior courts. 'The most that can be said is that it is necessary to look at all the relevant features of the tribunal in question including its constitution, jurisdiction and powers and its relationship to the High Court.'[9] It is generally accepted that the superior courts are the Judicial Committee of the Privy Council, the Supreme Court (and therefore formerly the House of Lords), Court of Appeal, High Court, Crown Court, Employment Appeal Tribunal, the new Upper Tribunal, and the Court of Protection.[10] However,

---

[6] The quotation is taken from Bowen LJ's judgment in *Helmore* v *Smith* (1886) 35 Ch D 449 at p. 455. Lowe and Borrie describe the purpose of the law of contempt of court as being 'to protect the fairness of trials and to maintain the authority of the court' (Lowe and Borrie (1983) p. 4).

[7] These rules are either found in the inherent jurisdiction of the court, the Contempt of Court Act 1981, specific legislation (see, for example, County Courts Act 1984, s. 118) or a combination thereof.

[8] 'The law may be an ass but the ass can bite. Its teeth are its powers to punish contempt of court' (A. Nicol and H. Rogers, *Changing Contempt of Court* (1981) National Council for Civil Liberties, Campaign for Press Freedom, London, p. 5).

[9] Per Goff LJ in *R* v *Cripps* [1984] 1 QB 68 at p. 87. See also Lord Edmund-Davies's comment that '[a]t the end of the day it has unfortunately to be said that there emerges no sure guide, no unmistakable hallmark by which "courts" or "inferior court" may unerringly be identified. It is largely a matter of impression' (*Attorney-General* v *BBC* [1981] AC 303 at p. 351).

[10] See, for example, Ward and Akhtar (2008) p. 237. Section 19 of the Contempt of Court Act 1981 defines 'superior courts' as specifically including, with the exception of the Judicial Committee of the Privy Council, these courts 'and any other court exercising in relation to its proceedings powers equivalent to those of the High Court'. (The Restrictive Practices Court, mentioned in s. 19, was a superior court but was abolished by the Competition Act 1998, s. 1.) The Court of Appeal, High Court and Crown Court are defined as 'superior courts of record' by ss. 15(1), 19(1) and 45(1) of the Senior Courts Act 1981. Section 20(3) of the Employment Tribunals Act 1996 defines the Employment Appeal Tribunal as a 'superior court of record', s. 3(5) of the Tribunals, Courts and Enforcement Act 2007 defines the Upper Tribunal as 'a superior court of record' and the Mental Capacity Act 2005 s. 45 defines the Court of protection as 'a superior court of record'. In addition, the Courts-Martial (Appeals) Act 1968, s. 1(2) defines the Courts-Martial Appeals Court as a 'superior court of record'.

this list is not entirely complete. Sometimes, other courts are treated as superior courts for some purposes.[11]

The distinction between superior and inferior courts is important for two reasons. First, inferior courts have more limited powers when imposing sanctions for contempt of court.[12] Second, the work of inferior courts is subject to judicial review under the supervisory jurisdiction of the High Court.[13] This means that, not only can one appeal against a decision of an inferior court, using such rights of appeal as are available, but a litigant can also ask the High Court to use its inherent jurisdiction to issue one of its prerogative writs.[14] Successfully getting the High Court to exercise its supervisory jurisdiction does not mean, as it would if one was appealing, that one has now won a case that was previously lost. The High Court's role is literally supervisory. It can tell a court not to exercise in excess of its jurisdiction by an order of prohibition. It can order an inferior court to exercise its jurisdiction by an order of mandamus or it can quash a particular decision by an order of certiorari. Thus, the High Court can dictate decisions that the inferior courts cannot make. However, the High Court can neither make a decision for the parties of its own volition nor can it tell the inferior court which decision it can make.[15]

The traditional distinction between inferior and superior courts highlights the fact that the very notion of 'courts' within 'the English legal system' is one which is, in itself, contentious. It used to be common for writers to distinguish 'courts' within 'the English legal system' from 'tribunals'.[16] However, just as it is difficult to define what an inferior court is, so it is difficult to define a court, as opposed to a tribunal, for the purpose of 'the English legal system'.[17] We will discuss tribunals within 'the English legal system' in the next chapter. At this point, we should note that the Employment Appeal *Tribunal* is also a superior court, as is the new Upper Tribunal. Tribunals and courts merge into one another, just as 'the English legal system' merges into dispute resolution and avoidance generally.

---

[11] In *R* v *Cripps* [1984] QBD 68 at p. 86, Goff LJ gives the example of the county court exercising jurisdiction under the Bankruptcy Acts 1883 and 1890 where s. 100 of the 1883 Act gives the county court 'all the powers and jurisdiction of the High Court'.

[12] Contempt of Court Act 1981, s. 14(1) limits the penalty for contempt under the Act to two years for superior courts and one month for inferior courts. However, under s. 14(4A) a county court is treated as a superior court for the purposes of this section.

[13] Although the Crown Court is for most purposes a superior court, under s. 29(3) of the Senior Courts Act 1981, the High Court can issue orders of prohibition, mandamus, and certiorari in relation to all of the jurisdiction of the Crown Court 'other than its jurisdiction in matters relating to trial on indictment'.

[14] Sir W. Wade and C. Forsyth, *Administrative Law* (10th edn, 2009) Oxford University Press, Oxford.

[15] For discussion of the constitutional principles lying behind the High Court's position see Wade and Forsyth (2009) ch. 2.

[16] See, for example, R. White, *The English Legal System in Action: The Administration of Justice* (3rd edn, 1999) Oxford University Press, Oxford, p. 321.       [17] *Attorney-General* v *BBC* [1981] AC 303.

## Reported courts

A third distinction that we could draw is between courts whose decisions are regularly reported and those courts whose decisions are rarely reported. This distinction is important in thinking about the function of a court. It is only those courts whose decisions are reported which can contribute directly to the development of the law.

We will discuss the way in which courts make law in **Chapters 5** and **6**. At this point, it is sufficient to note that the law-making is based upon a system of precedents wherein courts look back to previous decisions in deciding how to make new decisions. Any decision which has been reported by a barrister or a solicitor with a right of audience in relation to all proceedings in the Supreme Court or any other person with such a right may be used as a precedent.[18] Such reports are then published in one of a number of series of law reports.

Law reports take one of three forms. First, there are *general reports*. These are series which report a broad range of courts dealing with all of English law. The Incorporated Council of Law Reporting produces two such series: the Weekly Law Reports and the Law Reports. Both series contain verbatim accounts of judgments. The Law Reports are judgments which were first found in volumes 2 and 3 of the Weekly Law Reports. When reported in the Law Reports, the reports include not only the full judgment found in the Weekly Law Reports but also a summary of the argument used by counsel in the case. Lawyers are required to cite a report from the Law Reports where one is available when arguing in court.[19] There is also a third general series of the law reports, the All England Law Reports. The second type of law reports is the ever-increasing number of *commercial law reports* devoted to particular areas of law.[20] Finally, there are those reports which are found recorded on *electronic databases*. Of these, the largest are LEXIS and Westlaw. Both databases contain a wide range of cases taken from many areas of law and from many different courts.[21] Some of these cases are reported in other law reports. Sometimes, the only publicly accessible report of a case is that to be found on an electronic database. Whilst cases published in one of the two traditional forms of reports may always be cited in court, the courts have sought to limit the use of electronic databases. In *Roberts Petroleum Ltd* v *Bernard Kenny Ltd*, Lord Diplock held that transcripts of unreported judgments by the Civil Division of the Court of Appeal should only be used in argument before the (then) House of Lords with the leave of the court. Furthermore, he held that leave should only be given if those cases disclosed some new principle of law not to be found in cases reported in traditional

---

[18]  *Birtwistle* v *Tweedale* [1954] 1 WLR 190; Courts and Legal Services Act 1990, s. 115.

[19]  *Practice Note* [1991] 1 All ER 352.

[20]  Examples include the Family Law Reports, Immigration Appeal Reports, and Housing Law Reports.

[21]  The Supreme Court publishes its judgments on the Web. They can be found on the 'Decided Cases' section if its website at <http://www.supremecourt.gov.uk/decided-cases/index.html>.

form.[22] The very large number of reports and transcripts now available to lawyers in both electronic and printed form means that the courts could be overwhelmed by the number of authorities cited. They have therefore sought to limit the number of authorities to which they are referred. In 2001, a Practice Direction was issued on *Citation of Authorities in Civil Courts*. This aimed to limit the citation of authority to cases which are 'relevant and useful to the court', requiring advocates to explain, in respect of each authority they want to cite, the proposition of law it supports, and the parts of the judgment that support that proposition.[23]

Notwithstanding the large number of law reports, cases in some courts are rarely published. These courts are also those which have the largest volume of business. Cases in the magistrates' court and the county court constitute the greatest volume of business in the criminal and civil jurisdictions respectively. The Crown Court is the next most important court in terms of volume of business. Cases in all these three courts are rarely reported.[24] Cases in the High Court and above are more regularly reported. Westlaw and LEXIS now report all decisions of the Court of Appeal or the Supreme Court. There is thus an inverse ratio between the importance of the court in terms of its volume of business and the importance of the court in terms of its ability to make law.

Splitting courts into those whose decisions are regularly reported and those whose decisions are only rarely reported allows the inclusion in the former category of the European Court of Justice and the European Court of First Instance. These courts, which have jurisdiction over European Community law, are neither inferior or superior courts nor are they courts of record or courts not of record since they lie outside the United Kingdom. However, their decisions are binding in English law.[25]

Whilst the division between those courts which are regularly reported and those courts which are not is an important one, like the more traditional categories it has its limitations. Foremost amongst these limitations is the fact that some tribunals regularly have their decisions reported.[26] This limitation once again draws attention to the fact there is no clear distinction between courts and tribunals within 'the English legal system'.

---

[22]  *Roberts Petroleum Ltd* v *Bernard Kenny Ltd* [1983] 1 All ER 564 at pp. 567–8.

[23]  *Practice Direction (Citation of Authorities)* [2001] 1 WLR 1001. Lord Judge LCJ (as he then was) reiterated the point in relation to criminal proceedings in *R* v *Erskine, R* v *Williams* [2009] 2 Cr App 29.

[24]  For an example of a report of a magistrates' court case, see *Bruskin* v *London County Council* (1951/52) 2 Planning and Compensation Reports 264. For a report of a county court case, see *B* v *M* [1994] 1 FLR 342. For a report of a Crown Court case, see *Lenten* v *MAFF* [1991] 2 Ll Rep 305.

[25]  These two courts are discussed later in this chapter. See also A. Arnull, *The European Union and its Court of Justice* (2nd edn, 2006) Oxford University Press, Oxford.

[26]  For example, the Employment Appeal Tribunal, the Employment Tribunal, and the Asylum and Immigration Appeal Tribunal.

# Individual courts

## The European Court of Justice

Since the passage of the European Communities Act in 1972, the United Kingdom has, by virtue of that statute, been subject to European Community law.[27] Individuals arguing in courts within 'the English legal system' can base their case on rights found in the international treaties that created the European Community.[28] However, there are also two courts that belong not to the national legal systems of the Member States of the European Union but to the Union itself. These are the European Court of Justice and the European Court of First Instance.

The European Court of Justice was created by Articles 3 and 4 of the Convention on Certain Institutions common to the European Communities which was signed at the same time as the two treaties of Rome which set up the original European Economic Community.[29] The court has two main types of jurisdiction.[30] First, it can consider direct actions. These include infringement proceedings under Article 226, annulment actions under Article 230, actions for failure to act under Article 232, and actions for damages under Article 235. The other principal category of action is where a judge of a national court within the European Union has referred a case to the Court of Justice for a ruling on a point of interpretation regarding European Union law. The court also has minor jurisdictions dealing with matters such as disputes between the Community and its staff and disputes under arbitration clauses in contracts entered into by the Community. Finally, the court may be called upon to give its opinion about the compatibility with European law of proposed treaties the Community intends to enter into with non-member states.

Under Article 222 of the EC Treaty, the court consists of 25 judges. Under Article 223, judges must be 'chosen from persons whose independence is beyond doubt and who possess the qualifications required for appointment to the highest judicial offices in their respective countries or who are juriconsults of recognised competence'. Judges are selected by the Member States by 'common accord' and are appointed for a period of six years.[31] Rasmussen, in his study of the court, has noted that 'most of the members of the Court have pursued quite varied professional and political activities' and that '[p]ractically all [judges] ... were in close contact and co-operation with the political branches of their home governments'.[32] Several judges of the court have previously

---

[27]  Prior to the passage of the Maastricht Treaty, which was intended to mark a new stage in European integration, the European Community was referred to as the European Economic Community.

[28]  *Van Gend en Loos* v *Nederlandse Administratie der Belastingen*, Case 26/62 [1963] ECR 1 at p. 13.

[29]  J. Usher, *European Court Practice* (1983) Sweet & Maxwell, London, p. 3.

[30]  For a detailed discussion of the jurisdiction of the court, see Arnull (2006).

[31]  Article 223 of the EC Treaty.

[32]  H. Rasmussen, *On Law and Policy in the European Court of Justice* (1986) Martinus Nijhoff, Dordrecht, p. 216. The Community has always adopted the policy of having an odd number of judges. When, during its

held ministerial office within their home countries.[33] Thus, their background is different from that which is normal for judges in courts within 'the English legal system' where direct contact by judges with political parties is not usual.[34] There is no requirement under the Treaty as to nationality of the judges. 'Practice is different. Indeed, an unwritten but steadily followed tradition gives each member State "its" judge.'[35] The judges themselves elect a President of the Court from amongst their number.[36] The President serves a three-year term of office which can be renewed.[37] The President directs both the judicial and the administrative business of the court.[38] The judges also appoint Presidents of Chambers who serve in office for a period of one year. This period is renewable.[39] Presidents of Chambers exercise the power of the President when a case is heard in Chambers and substitute for the President when the President is not available. Each case has a judge appointed as Judge Rapporteur.[40] The Judge Rapporteur's job is to manage the progress of the case and draft the final decision of the court.[41] Judges are assisted in their work by legal secretaries who conduct research on cases and provide preliminary drafts of documents. Each judge has three such assistants.[42]

Judges can either sit in a Grand Chamber of 11 judges or in Chambers.[43] When sitting in Chambers, the court consists of three or five judges. Exceptionally, the court can sit in a plenary session. The court can sit in Chambers when looking at preparatory inquiries or when considering particular categories of case. The number of such categories that can be decided by the court sitting in Chambers has gradually been increased. Writing in 1983, Usher noted that approximately half of the cases before the court were heard in Chambers.[44] However, with the creation of a Court of First Instance, commentators have noted that Chambers have become underused.

Judges are not the only important members of the court. The court also has eight Advocates General.[45] The court appoints a First Advocate General for a term of one year.[46] The First Advocate General is responsible for assigning cases to individual

expansion, the Community came to consist of an even number of states, an extra judge was created. Before the last increase in Community membership, the thirteenth judge was appointed by the five largest Member States in rotation.

[33] For example, Neville Brown and T. Kennedy identified seven such judges (L. Neville Brown and T. Kennedy, *Brown & Jacobs: The Court of Justice of the European Communities* (5th edn, 2000) Sweet & Maxwell, London, pp. 58–9.).

[34] For a detailed discussion of the background of judges, see Neville Brown and Kennedy (2000) pp. 58–63.    [35] Rasmussen (1986) p. 214.

[36] Rules of Procedure of the Court of Justice of the European Communities (2009) OJ C 65, Article 7(1).

[37] Rules of Procedure of the Court of Justice of the European Communities (2009), Article 7(1).

[38] Rules of Procedure of the Court of Justice of the European Communities (2009), Article 8.

[39] Rules of Procedure of the Court of Justice of the European Communities (2009), Article 10(1).

[40] Rules of Procedure of the Court of Justice of the European Communities (2009), Article 9(2).

[41] A. Dashwood, 'The Advocate General in the Court of Justice of the European Communities' (1983) 2 Legal Studies 202 at p. 204.    [42] See further Neville Brown and Kennedy (2000) pp. 23–4.

[43] EC Treaty, Article 221.    [44] Usher (1983) p. 176.    [45] EC Treaty, Article 222.

[46] Rules of Procedure of the Court of Justice of the European Communities (2009), Article 10(1).

Advocates General.[47] Advocates General do not determine cases. However, they have a very powerful role in each decision. In order to be an Advocate General, a person must have the same qualifications as a putative judge of the court.[48] They have the same independence that a judge has.[49] The Advocate General assigned to a particular case sits alongside the judges in the court and listens to submissions from counsel. The Advocate General has the same power as the judges in the court to question counsel. Having listened to argument, the Advocate General then produces an opinion which sets out the facts and legal provisions relevant to the case and provides the court with the Advocate General's 'impartial and independent view of the case'.[50] Armed with this opinion, the judges consider their decision in private. Some commentators have described the Advocate General's opinion as having a similar status to that of a first instance decision with the court's ruling representing an appellate decision which either concurs with, or overturns, the Advocate General's decision.[51]

Another person having an important role in the functioning of the Court of Justice is the Registrar. The Registrar is appointed by the court.[52] The Registrar's functions, unlike those of the judges and the Advocates General, are wholly administrative. The Registrar is responsible for maintenance of the records of the court and the management of the day-to-day activities of the court.[53]

## The Court of First Instance

Between 1978 and 1987, the time taken to deal with direct actions before the European Court of Justice rose from 9 months to 22 months. Similarly, the time taken to deal with requests for preliminary rulings from the court on points of community law rose from 6 months to 18 months.[54] One response to this was the creation of the European Court of First Instance.[55] The jurisdiction of the court has widened over the years and

---

[47] Dashwood (1983) p. 208.

[48] For discussion of the background of Advocates General, see Neville Brown and Kennedy (2000) ch. 4.

[49] K. Borgsmidt, 'The Advocate General at the European Court of Justice: A Comparative Study' (1988) 13 European Law Review 106 at p. 107.

[50] Dashwood (1983) p. 207. The Advocate General will usually begin preparation of the opinion before the oral hearing of the parties and may take a further two weeks before writing the opinion (Neville Brown and Kennedy (2000) p. 68.

[51] Borgsmidt (1988) p. 107. Borgsmidt describes the Advocate General as a 'collaborator in the process of divining the law' (Borgsmidt (1988) p. 108). Like judges, Advocates General have three legal secretaries to assist them in research and in preparing drafts of documents (Neville Brown and Kennedy (2000) p. 23.

[52] EC Treaty, Article 12.

[53] For a fuller discussion of the office of Registrar see Neville Brown and Kennedy (2000) pp. 24–6.

[54] T. Kennedy, 'The Essential Minimum: The Establishment of the Court of First Instance' (1989) 14 European Law Review 7 at p. 8.

[55] This was set up by the Council of Ministers following the passage of the signing of the Maastricht Treaty. The decision that set up the court is reported at OJ 1989 C215/1. In that cases have been heard by the Court of First Instance rather than by the European Court of Justice this has been a success. However, cases still experience considerable delay before being heard. Direct actions before the European Court of Justice in 1991 took 20.8 months to be heard. Direction actions before the Court of First Instance in the same year

now includes disputes between the Community and its civil servants, actions for judicial review under Article 230, and some references from national courts under Article 234.

The qualifications for appointment to the Court of First Instance are somewhat different to those for appointment to the Court of Justice. Article 225(3) requires only that a person be independent and that they have the 'ability required for appointment to judicial office' rather than to the 'highest judicial office'. This difference reflects the status of the court. There are 25 members of the court, with one being elected the President by the judges themselves.[56] The court has no Advocates General but a judge may be asked to act as an Advocate General in a particular case. The court can sit either as a Grand Chamber of 13 judges, in Chambers (of three or five judges) or in plenary session.[57]

Decisions made by the Court of First Instance are subject to a right of appeal to the Court of Justice.[58]

## The Supreme Court

The Supreme Court came into existence in 2009 as a result of the implementation of the Constitutional Reform Act 2005. It exercises the former appellate jurisdiction of the House of Lords and the former devolution jurisdiction (i.e., matters relating to devolution within the United Kingdom) of the Privy Council.[59] It is the final court of appeal within 'the English legal system'. It is a court of record, a superior court and a court whose cases are regularly reported.[60] The establishment of the Supreme Court means that there will be a more complete 'separation of powers' between the judiciary and the legislature, because judges in the Supreme Court will not have a right to sit in the House of Lords when it acts as a legislature. The principle of the separation of powers, which is often argued to be basic to the organization of political life in a liberal democracy, contends that power is less likely to be abused if the legislative, executive, and judicial bodies balance each other.[61] Whereas, formerly, the judges of the highest court of appeal were members of the Appellate Committee of the House of Lords (and were also entitled to sit in the House), the Supreme Court is an entirely separate institution.

Another anomaly that has been removed as a result of the establishment of the new court is the ability that the Lord Chancellor had to sit as a judge in the House of Lords. Historically, a Lord Chancellor was both a judge, a member of the House of Lords and

---

took 23 months to be heard (L. Neville Brown, 'The Court of First Five Years of the Court of First Instance and Appeals to the Court of Justice: Assessment and Statistics' (1995) 32 Common Market Law Review 743 at p. 749).

[56] Article 2 [1989] OJ C215/1. The number of judges in the court was increased following the accession of Austria, Finland, and Sweden (OJ 1994 C241).                   [57] Article 2 [1989] OJ C215/1.

[58] EC Treaty, Article 225.          [59] Constitutional Reform Act 2005, s. 40.

[60] Constitutional Reform Act 2005, s. 40(1).

[61] A. W. Bradley and K. D. Ewing, *Constitutional and Administrative Law* (14th edn, 2007) Longman, London, p. 84.

thus a member of the legislature, and, as a Cabinet Minister, a member of the Executive, accepting collective responsibility and speaking on behalf of the Government.[62] The three branches of power were thus combined in one person, which clearly went against the principle of the separation of powers. This practice was subjected to sustained criticism, on the basis that it threatened the independence of the judiciary.[63] For example, Hartley and Griffiths argued that '[the Lord Chancellor's] judicial functions...are clearly contrary to the concept of judicial independence: when sitting as a judge he cannot be independent of the Government since he is part of it'.[64] The removal of the Lord Chancellor from the pool of those who are eligible to sit as judges in the Supreme Court answers this criticism and is at the same time another way of reinforcing the principle of separation of powers. The decision by the Government to abolish the role of Lord Chancellor, taken in June 2003, and the decision by Lord Falconer (appointed as Lord Chancellor with the task of implementing the abolition of the office) not to sit as a judge whilst the abolition took effect, in part reflected a realization by the Government of the merits of the argument against a government minister sitting as a judge.

The Supreme Court consists of 12 judges, known as 'Justices of the Supreme Court'.[65] The first members of the court were those judges who had been Lords of Appeal in Ordinary immediately before the establishment of the Supreme Court.[66] Future appointments to the Supreme Court will be governed by the Constitutional Reform Act 2005, which created a new selection process to choose future Justices of the Supreme Court. In order to be eligible for appointment, candidates must either have over 15 years' qualifying legal practice, or have previously held high judicial office for at least two years.[67]

When a vacancy occurs, an ad hoc Supreme Court Selection Commission will be appointed, which will include the President and Deputy President of the court, together with one member of each of the Judicial Appointments Commissions for England and Wales, Scotland, and Northern Ireland (at least one of whom must be a non-lawyer).[68] The Selection Commission will decide upon its own selection process, but it must consult the Lord Chancellor and senior judges, as well as senior ministers in Scotland, Wales, and Northern Ireland.[69] Selection will be made on merit, though the Selection Commission will be required to take into account any guidance issued by the Lord

---

[62] For a discussion of collective ministerial responsibility, see G. Marshall *Constitutional Conventions* (1986) Clarendon Press, Oxford, ch. 4.

[63] For further analysis of this, see A. Bradney, 'The Judicial Role of the Lord Chancellor 1946–1987: A Pellet' (1989) 16 Journal of Law and Society 360; and A. Bradney, 'The Judicial Role of the Lord Chancellor' in P. Carmichael and B. Dickson (eds), *The House of Lords* (1999) Hart Publishing, Oxford. For an analysis of the work of different Lord Chancellors see R. Heuston, *Lives of the Lord Chancellors, Volume 1: 1885–1940* (1964) Clarendon Press, Oxford; and R. Heuston, *Lives of the Lord Chancellors, Volume 2:1940–1970* (1987) Clarendon Press, Oxford.

[64] T. C. Hartley and J. A. G. Griffith *Government and Law* (1975) Weidenfeld & Nicolson, London, p. 180.

[65] Constitutional Reform Act 2005, s. 23(6).         [66] Constitutional Reform Act 2005, s. 24.

[67] Constitutional Reform Act 2005, s. 25.

[68] Constitutional Reform Act 2005, Sch. 8 paras 1(1) and 6(3).

[69] Constitutional Reform Act 2005, s. 27(2).

Chancellor as to matters to be taken into account when making a selection.[70] In addition, s. 27(8) of the Constitutional Reform Act 2005 provides that the Commission must, when making selections for the appointment of judges, also take into account the need for the court to have among its judges those with knowledge and experience of practice in the law in every part of the United Kingdom. This is intended to maintain the convention that previously applied to the House of Lords that there should generally be at least two Scottish judges and usually one from Northern Ireland.

Once the selection has been made, there is a complex procedure which is designed to deter political considerations from playing a part in the selection process. After making its selection, the Selection Commission will be required to report to the Lord Chancellor, who must then consult senior judges, as well as the senior ministers in Scotland, Wales, and Northern Ireland.[71] After having done that, the Lord Chancellor has a number of options: to notify the selection to the Prime Minister, to reject the selection, or to require the Commission to reconsider its selection.[72] The effect of this is that, unlike the previous system, the Lord Chancellor no longer selects the candidates for presentation to the Prime Minister, but he or she will retain a veto on who may be appointed. However, a candidate may only be rejected on the grounds that, in the Lord Chancellor's opinion:

(a) there is not enough evidence that the person is suitable for the office concerned,
(b) there is evidence that the person is not the best candidate on merit, or
(c) there is not enough evidence that if the person were appointed the judges of the Court would between them have knowledge of, and experience of practice in, the law of each part of the United Kingdom.[73]

Once a candidate has been finally selected, the appointment will be made by the Queen on the advice of the Prime Minister.[74] The controversy which can surround an appointment to the Supreme Court was reflected in the media reports of the first appointment exercise to the court. Despite a change in the eligibility criteria introduced by s. 25 of the Constitutional Reform Act 2005, permitting lawyers with 15 years' experience to apply for appointment to the Supreme Court, it was suggested that senior judges had lobbied to ensure that such a person, without previous judicial experience, was not appointed.[75] The changes to the method of appointing judges to the Supreme Court are discussed in more detail in **Chapter 9.**

Under s. 42 of the Constitutional Reform Act 2005, the Supreme Court is duly constituted if it consists of an uneven number of judges, of whom there must be at least three, and more than half of them must be permanent judges (as opposed to being 'acting judges' under s. 38 of the Act). In the House of Lords, it was the norm for five judges to hear each case, although sometimes in cases which were likely to be important for

---

[70] Constitutional Reform Act 2005, s. 27(5) and (9).        [71] Constitutional Reform Act 2005, s. 28(5).
[72] Constitutional Reform Act 2005, s. 29(2).        [73] Constitutional Reform Act 2005, s. 30(2).
[74] Constitutional Reform Act 2005, ss. 23(2) and 26(2).
[75] See 'Supreme ambition, jealousy and outrage' *The Times,* 4 February 2010, p. 52.

the development of the law more than five judges heard the case.[76] It appears likely that these practices will continue in the Supreme Court. Having an uneven number of judges hearing the case means that there will always be a clear decision as to who wins and who loses.

It was noticeable that, despite its pre-eminent position in the hierarchy of the courts, the atmosphere in the House of Lords was relatively informal. This is likely to continue to be the case in the Supreme Court. The justices of the Supreme Court are not robed as they are in most other courts. The hearing is a re-examination of all the documents in a case, together with transcripts of the previous court hearings in the lower courts. Counsel (the barristers or solicitors representing the parties) are expected to present argument to the court and to answer questions put by the judges. The precise nature of the hearing depends on the individual judges. Some judges ask many questions; some ask few.[77] The court is pre-eminently a lawyer's court. It is not a court where witnesses are examined.[78] In this it differs from the very lowest courts. There the arguments are mainly about questions of fact. In the Supreme Court, the arguments are quasi-scholarly examinations of the rules of law.

It is likely that other aspects of the practice of the court will also continue to be similar to that of the House of Lords. For example, after a case has been heard it is likely that the judges will meet to share their views of the case, just as they used to in the House of Lords. Paterson's study of the House of Lords showed that the judges were likely to have already had informal conversations during the case. However, after the case, they are able to see if they have a unanimous view. Although five judges usually hear a case, this does not mean that five judges always give judgment. In some cases, one judge may decide to adopt the views of another judge. In others, the judges may decide that, given their unanimity, there is no point in having more than one judge write an opinion which the other four can then all adopt. The decision whether or not to write an opinion reflects more than the individual choices of the judges.[79] In his work, Paterson notes opinions were more likely to be written if the judges were clearly divided.[80] However, such matters clearly change from time to time. Analysis of House of Lords' cases between 1974 and 1983 shows a marked rise in the number of single judgments from 1979 onwards, and there is no reason to think that this trend will change in the Supreme Court.[81]

---

[76] See, for example, *Pepper* v *Hart* [1993] AC 593 where seven judges heard the case.

[77] Paterson's study of the House of Lords, based upon interviews with law lords and counsel, describes the effect that different law lords have had on the court atmosphere over the years (see A. Paterson, *The Law Lords* (1982) Macmillan, London, chs 3 and 4; see also L. Blom-Cooper and G. Drewery, *Final Appeal* (1972) Clarendon Press, Oxford, ch. 8).

[78] Although litigants may elect to represent themselves rather than be represented by counsel (see Blom-Cooper and Drewery (1972) p. 101).

[79] Notwithstanding the fact that several judges interviewed by Paterson claimed that this was the sole reason (see Paterson (1982) pp. 96–7). [80] Paterson (1982) p. 97.

[81] See further A. Bradney, 'The Changing Face of the House of Lords' (1985b) Juridical Review 178. For an analysis of a similar phenomenon in the Court of Appeal see R. Munday, 'All for One and One for All: The

## The Judicial Committee of the Privy Council

In many ways, the Judicial Committee of the Privy Council is similar to the Supreme Court in its composition and its work. Most cases are heard by judges drawn from the Supreme Court. Its work is largely appellate.[82] It is a multi-judge court. Technically, it delivers not judgments but opinions which are then acted upon through Orders in Council.[83] Like the Supreme Court, the Privy Council has an appellate jurisdiction over certain, albeit in the main minor, areas of British law. When the High Court sits as a prize court in matters of admiralty law, appeal lies to the Privy Council.[84] Appeals from ecclesiastical courts are heard by the Privy Council.[85] Those who have had their names struck off the registers of a number of professional bodies, thus preventing them from practising, have in the past been able to appeal to the Privy Council. However, with the exception of veterinary surgeons, these appeals are now made to the High Court.[86] The minor nature of this jurisdiction is illustrated by the fact that, in 2005, in the exercise of its ecclesiastical jurisdiction the Privy Council heard no cases and, in the same year, only two appeals from veterinary surgeons were listed.[87]

Membership of the Judicial Committee of the Privy Council is not limited to English or even British judges. Orders in Council have extended the membership to include persons holding high judicial office in Commonwealth countries. This is because the jurisdiction of the Privy Council is not merely specific to the United Kingdom. The court acts as a court of final appeal for a number of Commonwealth countries.[88] In deciding cases that come from these countries, the court is deciding cases that do not strictly fall under the ambit of British law. Although Commonwealth countries have a similar legal history to that of the United Kingdom and will, at some time in their past, have fallen under direct British rule, the laws they now operate are different, subtly or greatly, to those that pertain within the state system in the United Kingdom. Decisions of the Privy Council, therefore, do not bind the other courts discussed in this chapter in the way that decisions of the Supreme Court do. However, because the judges in the Privy Council are virtually

Rise to Prominence of the Composite Judgment within the Civil Division of the Court of Appeal' (2002) 61 Cambridge Law Journal 321.

[82] Judicial Committee Act 1833, s. 4 gives the Privy Council a jurisdiction to advise on matters of law as well as to hear individual cases.

[83] Such an order must then be obeyed by every other court (*Pitts v La Fontaine* (1880) 6 App Cas 482).    [84] Senior Courts Act 1981, s. 16(2).

[85] Ecclesiastical Jurisdiction Measure 1963, s. 8 and Pastoral Measure 1983, s. 9.

[86] See, for example, Dentists Act 1984, s. 29; Medical Act 1983, s. 40; Opticians Act 1989, s. 23G; and Veterinary Surgeons Act 1966, s. 17.    [87] *Judicial Statistics 2005: Revised* (2006) Cm. 6903, p. 9.

[88] This number, however, is diminishing. By 1975, 19 countries had either abolished the right of appeal to the Privy Council or had stated that such a right did not exist (see *Halsbury's Laws of England*, Volume 10 (4th edn, 1975) Butterworths, London, para. 770). This decline has continued since then. Thus, for example, in 1994, Singapore abolished the right of appeal to the Privy Council (*Judicial Statistics 1994* (2005) Cm. 2891, p. 6). In 2008, the Privy Council heard cases from 17 overseas jurisdictions (Ministry of Justice, *Judicial and Court Statistics 2008* (2009b) Cm. 7697, HMSO, London, Table 1.1).

the same people as the judges in the Supreme Court, judgments of the Privy Council are of great persuasive authority when they are considered by other courts.

## The Court of Appeal

The Supreme Court is a relatively small court with a restricted number of people who can act as judges.[89] It hears a relatively small number of cases. In 2008, the House of Lords (as it then was) disposed of 96 cases.[90] By contrast, the Court of Appeal is a much larger court with a much wider group of people who can act as judges. In 2008, 1,215 civil cases were filed and disposed of in the Court of Appeal whilst the Criminal Division heard 2,532 cases.[91] Membership of the court comprises any former Lord Chancellor who held office before 12 June 2003, judges of the Supreme Court who were, at the time of their appointment to that court, sitting in the Court of Appeal or were qualified to do so, the Lord Chief Justice, the Master of the Rolls, the President of the Queen's Bench Division, the President of the Family Division, the Chancellor of the High Court, and not more than 38 Lord Justices of Appeal.[92] Like the Supreme Court, the Court of Appeal is largely an appellate court.[93] Like the Supreme Court, the Court of Appeal is a court of record, a superior court and a court whose cases are mainly reported. These similarities between the two courts raise the immediate question why, in effect, have two courts of appeal?

Several judges in the Court of Appeal have said that the Court of Appeal occupies a position that is very similar to, or the same as, the Supreme Court. Thus, Sir Donald Nicholls has argued that 'it should be recognised that for most cases the Court of Appeal is the ultimate court'.[94] Clearly, there are many comparisons between the work of the Court of Appeal and the Supreme Court. Both are appellate courts. Both have jurisdictions which range across English law rather than focusing on some particular

[89]  The Supreme Court will consist of 12 judges: Constitutional Reform Act 2005, s. 23(2).

[90]  *Judicial and Court Statistics 2008* (2009b) Cm. 7697, Table 1.4. This figure does not include applications for leave to appeal.

[91]  *Judicial and Court Statistics 2008* (2009b) Cm. 7697, Tables 1.7, 1.8. This figure does not include applications for leave to appeal or interlocutory appeals.

[92]  Senior Courts Act 1981, s. 2(1), (2). The Lord Justices of Appeal are called ordinary judges; the others are termed ex-officio judges.

[93]  The court's inherent jurisdiction includes the power to make an order for the protection of property (*Hyde* v *Warden* (19876) 1 Ex D 309), to grant an injunction either pending an appeal to the Court of Appeal (*Wilson* v *Church* (1879) 11 Ch D 576) or from the Court of Appeal (*Polini* v *Gray* (1979) 12 Ch D 438), to make an order requiring fulfilment of an undertaking given to the court (*Jonesco* v *Evening Standard Ltd* [1932] 2 KB 340) and the inherent jurisdiction to strike out an appeal when it is incompetent (*Aviagents Ltd* v *Balstavest Investments Ltd* [1966] 1 All ER 450). Its appellate jurisdiction includes hearing cases referred to it by the Criminal Review Commission which can refer cases to the Court of Appeal where a person has been convicted on indictment and the Commission believes there is a 'real possibility' that their sentence or conviction will not be upheld (see Criminal Appeals Act 1995, ss. 9(1), 13(1)).

[94]  Sir Donald Nicholls, 'Keeping the Civil Law Up to Date: Flexibility and Certainty in the 1990s' (1991) Current Legal Problems 1. See also the remarks of Lord Denning in *Davis* v *Johnson* [1978] 1 All ER 841 at pp. 852–3.

area of law.[95] Indeed, in some rare circumstances, the Court of Appeal may be precisely in the same position as the Supreme Court for, on occasion, no appeal lies beyond the Court of Appeal to the Supreme Court.[96] If the Court of Appeal is, for all practical purposes, on the same level as the Supreme Court, it is then possible to argue that it should be treated in the same manner as the Supreme Court.

One important way in which the two courts are not treated in the same manner is in their freedom to make new law. The Supreme Court, like the House of Lords before it, is not bound by its own previous decisions.[97] In deciding a particular case, it is not forced to come to the same decision that it did in another case with similar facts, even if that similar case was decided only a very short time previously.[98] The Court of Appeal is bound by its own decisions.[99] It is thus more restricted in its law-making. In a series of cases in the 1970s, culminating in *Davies* v *Johnson*, Lord Denning argued that because the House of Lords was able to decide not to follow its past decisions and because the Court of Appeal was in a similar position to that of the House of Lords, the Court of Appeal should be able to vary its own rules and depart from its own previous decisions.[100] Lord Denning's argument was rebutted in the House of Lords by Lord Diplock. He stated that:

In an appellate court of last resort a balance must be struck between the need on the one side for legal certainty resulting from the binding effect of previous decisions and on the other side the avoidance of undue restriction on the proper development of law. In the case of an intermediate appellate court, however, the second desideratum can be taken care of by appeal to a superior appellate court, if reasonable means of access to it are available; while the risk to the first desideratum, legal certainty, if the court is not bound by its own previous decisions grows ever greater with increasing membership and the number of three-judge divisions in which it sits ... So the balance does not lie in the same place as the court of last resort.[101]

However, subsequent to these remarks Sir Donald Nicholls has argued that 'certainty in the law can be obtained at too high a price'.[102] He has gone on to suggest that '[t]here are signs that the Court of Appeal, very cautiously indeed, may be moving in the direction of an extra degree of freedom'.[103]

---

[95] 'It is almost impossible to state exhaustively the appeals which may come to the Court of Appeal' (R. White, annotation to Supreme Court Act 1981, s. 15 in Supreme Court Act 1981, *Current Law Annotated Statutes* (1981) Sweet & Maxwell, London).

[96] For example, it was held that refusal to grant leave to appeal to the Court of Appeal by the Court of Appeal, since no order or judgment had been made within the meaning of Appellate Jurisdiction Act 1876, s. 3, was not something for which there was a right of appeal to the House of Lords (*Whitehouse* v *Board of Control* [1960] 1 WLR 1088).

[97] *Practice Statement* [1966] 3 All ER 77. This point is discussed at greater length in **Chapter 5**.

[98] See, for example, *R* v *Shivpuri* [1986] 2 All ER 334, where the House of Lords reversed a rule of law that they had laid down only 12 months previously in *Anderton* v *Ryan* [1985] 1 AC 560.

[99] *Young* v *Bristol Aeroplane Co Ltd* [1944] KB 718. This rule is subject to an increasing number of exceptions. Again, this point is discussed at greater length in **Chapter 5**.

[100] *Davis* v *Johnson* [1978] 1 All ER 841 at pp. 852–7.

[101] *Davis* v *Johnson* [1978] 1 All ER 1132 at pp. 1137–8.    [102] Nicholls (1991) p. 1.

[103] Nicholls (1991) p. 5.

Whilst there may be some merit in the argument that the Court of Appeal and the Supreme Court occupy similar positions, caution has to be exercised in accepting the argument too quickly. Writing in 1951, Lord Justice Cohen stated that 'the majority of appeals which come from the county courts and many of those which come from the High Court do not involve a lengthy hearing'.[104] The number of cases disposed of by the Court of Appeal noted above does not suggest that there have been significant changes since 1951. Much of the work in the Court of Appeal falls on the 38 Lord Justices of Appeal, although it is the usual practice for criminal law cases to be heard by a Lord Justice of Appeal and one or more judges from the High Court.[105] The large number of cases disposed of and the relatively small number of judges to hear them indicate a more rapid turnover of cases than in the Supreme Court. This in turn suggests that the quasi-legislative role of the Supreme Court in considering the development of the law is not the usual kind of work in the Court of Appeal.

The Court of Appeal is divided into two divisions, the *civil division* and the *criminal division*.[106] The criminal division inherited the jurisdiction of the now defunct Court of Criminal Appeal.[107] Both divisions are usually multi-judge courts with three judges being the norm to hear each case. However, there are occasions when the court may sit with just two judges and, far more rarely, with just one judge.[108]

## The High Court

Like the Supreme Court, Privy Council, and Court of Appeal, the High Court is a superior court of record whose decisions are frequently reported.[109] Unlike the two previous courts, the High Court is a court which has both a substantial appellate and a substantial original jurisdiction.[110] It now consists of three divisions. These are the Chancery Division, the Family Division, and the Queen's Bench Division. In law, each of these divisions is part of the same court.[111] However, in practice, the different divisions act as though they were separate courts. The distribution of business in the different divisions is set out in the Senior Courts Act 1981.[112] Thus, for example,

---

[104] Lord Justice Cohen, 'Jurisdiction, Practice and Procedure of the Court of Appeal' (1951) 11 Cambridge Law Journal 3 at p. 13.

[105] Such judges sit by virtue of the Senior Courts Act 1981, s. 9(1). Examination of any volume of the Criminal Appeal Reports will demonstrate this practice. Judges from the House of Lords also sat in the Court of Appeal. (See, for example, *Mallett* v *Restormel Borough Council* [1978] 2 All ER 1057.) It is likely that this practice will continue, with Justices of the Supreme Court sitting in the Court of Appeal.

[106] Senior Courts Act 1981, s. 3(1).

[107] Criminal Appeal Act 1966, s. 1(1). The right of criminal appeal is now mainly to be found in Criminal Appeal Act 1968, s. 1. As has been noted above, there are a multiplicity of sources for the right of appeal to the civil division.          [108] See Senior Courts Act 1981, s. 55(4) and Criminal Appeal Act 1968, s. 31.

[109] Though, unlike the previous three courts, only a selection of its decisions are reported. Even LEXIS and Westlaw do not contain a complete set of reports.          [110] Senior Courts Act 1981, ss. 19–28, 61–65.

[111] *Practice Direction (High Court; Divisions)* [1973] 2 All ER 233.

[112] Senior Courts Act 1981, s. 61.

cases about foreclosure of a mortgage will always be heard in the Chancery Division.[113] Judges are assigned to one of the divisions.[114]

The Supreme Court and the Court of Appeal are multi-judge courts. The High Court is normally a single judge court.[115] The court consists of the Lord Chief Justice, the President of the Queen's Bench Division, the President of the Family Division, the Chancellor of the High Court, the Senior Presiding Judge, the Vice-President of the Queen's Bench Division, and not more than 108 puisne judges.[116]

Much of the work of the court is done by the heads of the divisions, the Chancellor of the High Court, the President, the Lord Chief Justice or by the puisne judges of the High Court.[117] However, not all judges hearing cases in the High Court are High Court judges. The Civil Justice Review noted that 30 per cent of High Court sittings were conducted by people who were not High Court judges. These hearings are conducted by either circuit judges or recorders who sit as deputy High Court judges.[118] An important question of principle arises here. If Parliament has laid down rules indicating that cases should be heard by the High Court, is it right that such a large percentage of cases should be heard by judges who do not have the experience to be full-time High Court judges? The justification for use of circuit judges or deputy High Court judges has been variously given as the need to give experience to potential recruits to the bench, temporary upsurges in work or temporary shortages in the number of judges. However, respondents to the Civil Justice Review did not feel that these reasons justified the number of cases heard by such judges.[119]

Divisional courts of each of the three divisions exercise most of the High Court's appellate jurisdiction. When the divisions proceed in this manner, two judges sit together.[120]

The Supreme Court, Privy Council, and the Court of Appeal all sit in London. However, the Court of Appeal (Civil Division) has developed a programme of regional sittings, and has sat in locations outside London, such as Birmingham, Cardiff, Manchester, and Exeter.[121] Whilst the High Court also sits in London, it has the power to sit elsewhere as well. Under s. 71 of the Senior Courts Act 1981, cases can be heard anywhere in England or Wales. In practice, the High Court only sits outside London at the 27 first-tier centres for the Crown Court.

---

[113] Senior Courts Act 1981, Sch. 1, para. 1(b). (See also the Civil Procedure Rules created under the Civil Procedure Act 1997.) There are a few instances when cases can be heard in more than one Division. Thus, for example, cases under the Inheritance (Provision for Family and Dependants) Act 1975 can be heard in either the Chancery Division or the Family Division (CPR 57.15).          [114] Senior Courts Act 1981, s. 5(2).

[115] Senior Courts Act 1981, s. 19(3).

[116] Senior Courts Act 1981, s. 4(1). The Courts and Legal Services Act 1990, s. 72(6), added the Senior Presiding Judge to those entitled to sit in the High Court. The Senior Presiding Judge is appointed from amongst the Lord Justices of Appeal (Courts and Legal Services Act 1990, s. 72(2)).

[117] Any judge in the High Court, other than the Chancellor, the President, and the Lord Chief Justice, is styled a puisne judge denoting their junior status.

[118] Civil Justice Review, *Report of the Review Body on Civil Justice* (1988) Cm. 394, HMSO, London, para. 192.

[119] Civil Justice Review (1988) Cm. 394.       [120] Senior Courts Act 1981, s. 66(3).

[121] S. H. Bailey, J. P. L. Ching, and N. W. Taylor, *Smith, Bailey and Gunn on the Modern English Legal System* (5th edn, 2007) Sweet & Maxwell, London, p. 117.

Where a case is heard in the High Court, having first been heard in the magistrates' court or the Crown Court, any subsequent appeal will be heard by the Supreme Court. In other cases, appeals are normally heard by the Civil Division of the Court of Appeal.[122]

## Chancery Division

The formal head of the Chancery Division is the Chancellor of the High Court.[123] There are also presently 18 puisne judges.[124] The jurisdiction of the Chancery Division is set out in Sch. 1 of the Senior Courts Act 1981. The jurisdiction in the main concerns:

(a)  the sale, exchange or partition of land, or the raising of charges on land;

(b)  the redemption or foreclosure of mortgages;

(c)  the execution of trusts;

(d)  the administration of estates of deceased persons;

(e)  bankruptcy;

(f)  the dissolution of partnerships or the taking of partnership or other accounts;

(g)  the rectification setting aside or cancellation of deeds or other instruments in writing;

(h)  probate business, other non-contentious or common form business;

(i)  patents, trade marks, registered designs, copyright or design right;

(j)  the appointment of a guardian of a minor's estate;

and all causes and matters involving the exercise of the High Court's jurisdiction under the enactments relating to companies and any matter relating to legislation about companies.

The Chancery Division also supplies judges for the Patents Court. Despite its name, this is not a separate court and merely consists of nominated judges within the Chancery Division. It was first established by the Patents Act 1977.[125] These judges hear patent actions at first instance and appeals from the Comptroller of Patent, Designs and Trade Marks.[126] Similarly, judges from the Chancery Division act as the judges in the Companies Court, again not a separate court, dealing with compulsory liquidation and other matters under the Insolvency Act 1986 and the Companies Acts.[127]

---

[122]  Senior Courts Act 1981, s. 16(1). Exceptions to this rule include appeals in the case of prize courts noted above.                    [123]  Senior Courts Act 1981, s. 5(1)(a).

[124]  *Judicial and Court Statistics 2008* (2009b) Cm. 7697, p. 32. The membership of theSupreme Court, Court of Appeal, and the various divisions of the High Court is listed at the front of each volume of the All England Law Reports.

[125]  See now Senior Courts Act 1981, s. 6(1)(a).

[126]  For a brief description of the working of this court, see B. Reid, *A Practical Guide to Patent Law* (3rd edn, 1999) Sweet & Maxwell, London.

[127]  For a description of the work of the Companies Court see S. Mayson, D. French, and C. Ryan, *Company Law* (26th edn, 2009) Oxford University Press, Oxford, ch. 1.

The appellate jurisdiction of the Chancery Division is limited. Single judges hear a small range of appeals.[128] The divisional court of the Chancery Division hears appeals in certain bankruptcy and land registration cases.

## Family Division

The head of the Family Division is the President. There are 19 puisne judges in the Family Division at present.[129] However, cases can also be heard by district judges of the principal registry of the Family Division. The jurisdiction of the division, set out in Sch. 1 of the Senior Courts Act 1981, is:

(a)  all matrimonial causes and matters (whether at first instance or on appeal);

(b)  all causes and matters (whether at first instance or on appeal) relating to

  (i)   legitimacy;
  (ii)  the exercise of the inherent jurisdiction of the High Court with respect to minors, the maintenance of minors and any proceedings under the Children Act 1989, except for proceedings solely for the appointment of a guardian of a minor's estate;
  (iii) adoption;
  (iv)  non-contentious or common form probate business;

(c)  applications for consent to the marriage of a minor or for a declaration under s. 27B(5) of the Marriage Act 1949;

(d)  proceedings on appeal under s. 13 of the Administration of Justice Act 1960 from an order or decision made under s. 63(3) of the Magistrates' Courts Act 1980 to enforce an order of a magistrates' court made in matrimonial proceedings or proceedings under Part IV of the Family Law Act 1996 or with respect to the guardianship of a minor;

(e)  applications under Part III of the Family Law Act 1986;

(f)  proceedings under the Children Act 1989;

(g)  all proceedings under –

  (i)   Part IV or 4A of the Family Law Act 1996;
  (ii)  the Child Abduction and Custody Act 1985;
  (iii) the Family Law Act 1986;
  (iv)  s. 30 of the Human Fertilisation and Embryology Act 1990;
  (v)   Council regulation (EC) No 2201/2003 of 27th November 2003 concerning jurisdiction and the recognition and enforcement of judgments in matrimonial matters and matters of parental responsibility, so far as the Regulation relates to jurisdiction, recognition and enforcement in parental responsibility matters; and

---

[128]  For example, under Taxes Management Act 1970, s. 56.    [129]  See [2009] 4 All ER at front.

(fa) all proceedings relating to a debit or credit under s. 29(1) or 49(1) of the Welfare Reform and Pensions Act 1999;

(g) all proceedings for the purpose of enforcing an order made in any proceedings of a type described in this paragraph;

(h) all proceedings under the Child Support Act 1991;

(i) all proceedings under ss 6 and 8 of the Gender Recognition Act 2004;

(j) all civil partnership causes and matters (whether first instance or on appeal);

(k) applications for consent to the formation of a civil partnership by a minor or for a declaration under para. 7 of Sch. 1 to the Civil Partnership Act 2004;

(l) applications under s. 58 of that Act (declarations relating to civil partnerships).

The distinction between the Chancery Division and the Family Division is not merely a bureaucratic matter. It reflects a belief that family law is inherently different from other kinds of law.[130] Family law cases are inevitably about disputes that arise in what has often been regarded as the most personal and private part of people's lives. In 1970, Parliament considered a suggestion that there need only be two divisions to the High Court: the Chancery Division and the Queen's Bench Division. This was rejected, with MPs arguing that the welfare issues raised in family law cases needed a different kind of judge from those in the other divisions.[131]

## Queen's Bench Division

The Queen's Bench Division is the largest of the three divisions both in terms of the number of cases it deals with each year and in terms of the number of judges assigned to the division. The head of the division is the Lord Chief Justice. There are currently 68 puisne judges who assist the Lord Chief Justice. As in the other divisions, deputy judges can also sit.[132] Finally, the division has a number of Masters who can perform many of the administrative and judicial functions of a judge.[133] As long ago as 1960, Diamond noted the importance of Masters in allowing a court staffed by a comparatively small number of judges to deal with a relatively large number of cases.[134] Masters are not

---

[130] Thus, for example, in his interim report on the civil justice system, Lord Woolf distinguishes between the civil justice system, the criminal justice system, and the family justice system (Lord Woolf, *Access to Justice: Final Report to the Lord Chancellor on the Civil Justice System in England and Wales* (the Woolf Report) (1996) Lord Chancellor's Department, London, p. 58).

[131] See, for example, the comments of the then Lord Chancellor, Lord Gardiner (Hansard, House of Lords, vol. 306, cols 197–8).

[132] *Judicial and Court Statistics 2008* (2009b) Cm. 7697, p. 42; for deputy judges, see Senior Courts Act 1981, s. 9(4).

[133] For the duties of a Master see CPR 2.4 and the *Practice Direction* in Brooke LJ (ed.), *Civil Proceedings: Volume 1* (2006) Sweet & Maxwell, London, pp. 60–4.

[134] A. Diamond, 'The Queen's Bench Master' (1960) 76 Law Quarterly Review 504, which includes discussion of the actual work of Masters.

merely minor figures but are, on the contrary, significant in the day-to-day work of the jurisdiction.[135]

The Queen's Bench Division has a much wider jurisdiction than either of the two other jurisdictions of the High Court. Under Sch. 1 of the Senior Courts Act 1981, the jurisdiction of the division covers:

(a)   applications for writs of habeus corpus, except applications made by parent or guardian of a minor for such writ concerning the custody of the minor;

(b)   application for judicial review;

(ba)  all control order proceedings (within the meaning of the Prevention of Terrorism Act 2005);

(bb)  all financial restrictions proceedings within the meaning of Chapter 2 of Part 6 of the Counter-Terrorism Act 2008 (see s. 65 of that Act);

(c)   all causes and matters involving the exercise of the High Court's Admiralty jurisdiction or its jurisdiction as a prize court; and

(d)   all causes and matters in the commercial list.

However, to this is added all the jurisdiction of the three superior common law courts of first instance that existed immediately before the major reorganization of the courts which was begun with the Supreme Court of Judicature Act 1873.[136] These jurisdictions, now a major part of the Queen's Bench Division, cover large areas of both civil and criminal law.[137]

In the same way that judges from the Chancery Division provide judges for the Patent Court, so judges are taken from the Queen's Bench Division to sit in cases in the Commercial Court.[138] This is not a separate court but the procedures followed in commercial law cases are different to those normally followed in the Queen's Bench Division.[139] Similarly, the Queen's Bench Division also provides judges for the Admiralty Court and the Technology and Construction Court.[140]

---

[135] Diamond (1960).

[136] These courts were the Court of Common Pleas, the Court of Exchequer, and the Court of Queen's Bench. See further Sir W. Holdsworth, *A History of English Law*, Volume 1 (3rd edn, 1922) Methuen, London, pp. 638–42.

[137] The precise details of each jurisdiction are to be found in the individual statutes that create the causes of action.                                    [138] Civil Procedure Rules Part 58.1.

[139] The function of the Commercial Court is to provide 'speed, simplicity, service' (R. Goode, *Commercial Law* (2004) Penguin, Harmondsworth, p. 1,126). The jurisdiction is diverse, covering both cases that may take six months to hear and those that concern only one legal issue (Sir J. Jacob (ed.), *Supreme Court Practice 1995* (1994) Sweet & Maxwell, London, p. 1,249). Part 58 of the Civil Procedure Rules lays down the procedure in the Commercial Court. A report on the work of the Commercial Court, including a study of its actual practice by Coopers and Lybrand, is to be found in the Civil Justice Review (1988) Cm. 394, ch. 11 (see also R. Bradgate, *Commercial Law* (3rd edn, 2000) Butterworths, London, pp. 869–71).

[140] The work of the Admiralty Court is governed by Part 61 of the Civil Procedure Rules and the work of the Technology and Construction Court by Part 60 of the Civil Procedure Rules. Information about these courts can be found on Her Majesty's Court Service website at: <http://www.hmcourts-service.gov.uk>.

The Queen's Bench Division has a relatively small civil appellate jurisdiction. For example, appeal from the decision of the Solicitor's Disciplinary Tribunal is, amongst others, to the Queen's Bench Division.[141] However, its criminal appellate jurisdiction is more extensive. The Queen's Bench Division hears criminal appeals from both the magistrates' court and from the Crown Court.[142] Nevertheless, even here, the appellate jurisdiction of the court is relatively limited in quantitative terms. Appeal from either the magistrates' court or the Crown Court to the High Court is by way of 'case stated'. This is not intended to be a regular means of appeal (for which other mechanisms exist) but, rather, is to be used in exceptional cases where a sentence is 'truly astonishing'.[143] The 'case stated' mechanism cannot be used when the appeal is on a basis of a challenge to issues of fact.[144]

The final aspect of the Queen's Bench Division's jurisdiction is its supervisory jurisdiction over other inferior courts and tribunals and other bodies exercised through the Administrative Court.

## The Crown Court

Unlike the English courts previously discussed in this chapter, the Crown Court is of relatively recent origin. It owes its origins to the Courts Act 1971 which implemented the recommendations of the Beeching Commission which had reported in 1969.[145] The Beeching Commission surveyed the system of courts extant at the time of its work and assessed according to a number of different criteria. These were grouped together under the headings of convenience, quality, and economy.[146] The Commission recommended the abolition of a number of existing courts and their replacement by a single new court, the Crown Court.[147]

The jurisdiction for the Crown Court is now to be found in the Senior Courts Act 1981. Unlike the Supreme Court, Court of Appeal, and High Court, the Crown Court largely specializes in trying criminal cases. The 1981 Act gives the Crown Court exclusive jurisdiction over all trials brought on indictment.[148] In addition,

[141]  Solicitor's Act 1974, s. 49(1).

[142]  Magistrates Court Act 1980, s. 111(1); Senior Courts Act 1981, s. 28(1).

[143]  Per Goff LJ in *Universal Salvage* v *Boothby* (1983) 5 Cr App R(S) 428 at p. 423.

[144]  Per Pill J in *Tucker* v *DPP* [1992] 4 All ER 901 at p. 902.

[145]  Royal Commission on Assizes and Quarter Sessions (the Beeching Commission), *Report* (1969) Cmnd 4153.

[146]  Beeching Commission, para. 112. The Commission expanded on these criteria, listing more detailed standards as being ease of access, early date of hearing, reasonable notice of hearing, suitable accommodation, judicial expertise, adequate and dependable legal representation, efficient use of manpower, and optimum use of buildings. 'Judicial integrity' was said to be taken for granted (Beeching Commission).

[147]  The courts that were recommended for abolition were the Courts of Assize, the Central Criminal Court, the Lancashire Crown Courts, and the Courts of Quarter Sessions (Beeching Commission, para. 124).

[148]  Senior Courts Act 1981, s. 46. Indictable offences are, in the main, more serious criminal offences than those that are not indictable. For the procedure for trial on indictment, see Administration of Justice (Miscellaneous Provisions) Act 1933, s. 2(1).

the court also took over the appellate jurisdiction of the previous Court of Quarter Sessions, hearing appeals from criminal cases in the magistrates' courts.[149] It also hears cases remitted to it from the magistrates' court for sentencing.[150] Finally, in the area of criminal law, the Crown Court hears cases referred to it by the Criminal Cases Review Commission where a person has been convicted summarily and the Commission believes there is a 'real possibility' that their conviction or sentence will not be upheld.[151] However, the court is not exclusively a court with a criminal jurisdiction. It can also hear appeals from magistrates' courts in a variety of civil cases.[152]

Any judge of the High Court can sit to hear cases in the Crown Court.[153] In addition, cases may be heard by either circuit judges or recorders.[154] Finally, there is provision for not more than four magistrates to sit in addition to one of the above.[155] Magistrates must sit with one of the above if the case is either an appeal or a committal for sentence.[156]

The Crown Court is a single court and as such is part of the Supreme Court of England and Wales.[157] However, the court sits at a number of different venues throughout England and Wales. There are currently 77 such venues.[158] Crown Court cases are classified into three separate classes, according to their seriousness. Class 1 includes offences such as murder, treason, and genocide. These may normally only be tried by a High Court judge. Class 2 includes offences such as manslaughter, rape, and incest. Cases in this class are also normally heard by a High Court judge but there is wider provision for such cases to be heard exceptionally by a circuit judge. Class 3 offences cover all other offences. Such cases cannot be listed for hearing by a High Court judge except with the consent of the presiding judge.[159]

An appeal from a trial on indictment in the Crown Court will be heard by the Criminal Division of the Court of Appeal.[160] An appeal from a case involving the Crown Court's appellate jurisdiction will be heard by the High Court.[161]

Up to now, this chapter's discussion of the jurisdiction and composition of courts has largely been based on the statutes which created these courts. This has been inevitable because of the paucity of other material available. However, there have been a number of detailed studies of various aspects of the Crown Court which give the

---

[149] This was implemented by the Courts Act 1971, s. 8 and Sch. 1. This jurisdiction is now to be found in the Senior Courts Act 1981, s. 45(2).        [150] Powers of Criminal Courts (Sentencing) Act 2000, s. 3(2).

[151] Criminal Appeal Act 1995, ss. 11(1), 13(1).        [152] Senior Courts Act 1981, s. 45(2).

[153] Senior Courts Act 1981, s. 8(1)(a).        [154] Senior Courts Act 1981, s. 8(1)(b).

[155] Senior Courts Act 1981, s. 8(1)(c).        [156] Senior Courts Act 1981, s. 74(1).

[157] Senior Courts Act 1981, s. 1(1).

[158] *Judicial and Court Statistics 2008* (2009b) Cm. 7697, p. 104.

[159] For full details of this division of workload, see *Practice Direction (Crown Court: Classification and Allocation of Business)* [2005] 1 WLR 2215.        [160] Criminal Appeal Act 1968, s. 1(1).

[161] Senior Courts Act 1981, s. 28(1).

possibility of a deeper understanding of the nature of the court than would otherwise be possible. Some of these studies will be discussed later in the chapters on criminal procedure. One, however, is relevant at this point.

Paul Rock's book, *The Social World of an English Crown Court*, is an ethnographic account of one Crown Court, the Crown Court at Wood Green.[162] The book is based upon a year's period of study spent watching the work of Wood Green Crown Court.[163] It provides important information which supports the need for an integrative theory of law if we are to understand legal processes.

One observation Rock makes is about the nature of those involved in the work of the court. The court, he points out, is more than just the judiciary. Although '[w]hen judges spoke of the Court they meant themselves' there are a wide range of other staff involved in the work of the court.[164] We have already seen in this chapter that other courts have officers such as Masters or Registrars who occupy a near-judicial office. But Rock points to the importance of others in the work of the court from listing staff, who are responsible for planning the timetable of the court, to security staff and court ushers.[165]

The flowchart below, taken from Rock's book, gives some idea of the actual complexity of the personnel who constitute the court.

These staff are not all equally important. However, the Crown Court would no more be the institution that it is without each of these staff than it would be the same institution without judges. In some cases, the degree to which it would be different would be slight. Nevertheless, in other cases, the importance of court officials who are not judges is easy to underestimate. '"Some people describe me as the most powerful person in the Court. I might dispute that," said the listing officer.'[166] The emphasis here is surely on the 'might'. Listing staff, with their power to determine the day-to-day workload of the court, play a vital part in determining the balance that is to be drawn between the optimum use of the building and staff on the one hand and the need to give each case due time for consideration on the other. Similarly, the Chief Clerk is described by Rock as having a 'baronial power complete with a fief and subordinates, a power surrounded by other baronies with *their* territories and personnel'.[167] In analysing the social world of the Crown Court, Rock describes a series of circles in which not only judges but also these other officials interact.[168]

---

[162] P. Rock, *The Social World of an English Crown Court* (1993) Clarendon Press, Oxford. The primary purpose of ethnographic accounts is to attempt to describe the culture of a particular community from the perspective of the members of that community. Rock's work is thus, in one sense, an attempt to follow in the tradition of legal anthropologists such as Malinowski and Gluckman, whose works were discussed in earlier chapters.

[163] In an ethnographic inquiry, the researcher attempts, in so far as is possible, to become part of the community being studied.                                      [164] Rock (1993) p. 151.

[165] Rock (1993) ch. 4.        [166] Rock (1993) p. 137.        [167] Rock (1993) p. 135, emphasis in original.

[168] Rock (1993) ch. 5.

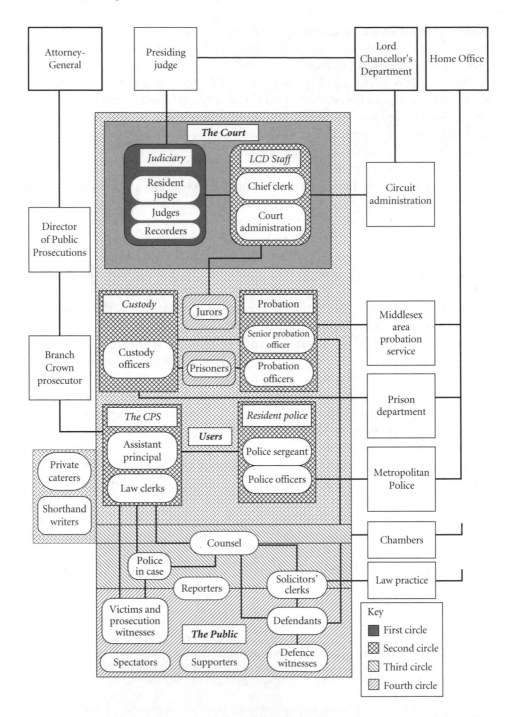

**Fig. 3.1** The administrative organization of the Crown Court Centre at Wood Green*

*P. Rock, *The Social World of an English Crown Court* (1993) Clarendon Press, Oxford, p. 133 Reproduced by permission of Oxford University Press.

The importance of Rock's work lies not just in the context of the Crown Court. From it, we see that the Crown Court is not just about the work of the judges. But if this is true of the Crown Court, why should it not also be true of the other courts we have already discussed in this chapter?[169]

## The county court

Like the Crown Court, the county court is a specialized court. However, whilst the Crown Court is predominantly a criminal court, the county court is a civil court. County courts were first set up under the County Courts Act 1846. In many ways, their original jurisdiction duplicated the jurisdiction of the High Court. Their purpose was not to offer a jurisdiction that had not hitherto been found in the courts but, rather, to offer a local and therefore more effective way of taking legal action. The High Court was seen then, as now, as being an expensive and time-consuming way of taking legal action. Cost meant that it was effectively open only to a relatively small part of the population. Equally, cost meant that it was of use only when some comparatively large sum of money was involved.[170] The 1846 Act attempted to set a court jurisdiction that could efficiently deal with minor civil claims.

The setting up of the county court points to a tension in the court system. Courts exist not simply to hear cases but to deal efficiently with dispute settlement. But determining what counts as efficiency is difficult. Something can be efficient because it is quick, because it is accurate or because it is cheap. The three things may not be compatible. Lord Woolf, in his report on the civil justice system, said the system should:

(a) be *just* in the results it delivers;
(b) be *fair* in the way it treats litigants;
(c) offer appropriate procedures at a reasonable cost;
(d) deal with cases with reasonable *speed*;
(e) be *understandable* to those who use it;
(f) be *responsive* to the needs of those who use it;
(g) provide as much *certainty* as the nature of the particular cases allows;
(h) be *effective*, adequately resourced and organized.[171]

The litigant wants a case to be heard expeditiously by suitably qualified judges. Litigants also want due time to be given over to the assessment of the facts and law which relate to their case. But, if all cases are to be heard quickly, large numbers of courts and large numbers of staff are needed. Similarly, more time given to individual cases means that more courts are needed. Highly qualified staff are also expensive staff. The financial costs of such a system must be met either by the state or by

---

[169] On this, see below.

[170] Holdsworth (1922) pp. 187–93. See also B. Abel-Smith and R. Stevens, *Lawyers and the Courts* (1967) Heinemann, London, pp. 32–7.

[171] Lord Woolf (1996) p. 2. This passage has become, with minor stylistic amendments, 'The Overriding Objective' in the Civil Procedure Rules (see r. 1.1(2) CPR 1998), emphasis in original.

individual litigants through fees levied when they bring their case. For litigants, court fees are a discouragement to bringing a case. They may be unable to afford the fees or the fees may outweigh the financial value of that which is in dispute. Yet, in creating a legal system which has legal rights, it might be argued that the state implicitly gives citizens a promise that there will be an effective way of enforcing those rights.[172] The state creates an expectation that law will be enforced, not that law will be enforced if one has sufficient wealth to do so. A system where only the rich can enforce their rights is no more obviously attractive than one where only the physically strong can enforce their rights.[173]

Balancing the imperatives of the need to operate a just legal system and the need to operate within scarce financial resources is something that is done not just through the courts system. Legal aid to individual litigants also plays its part.[174] However, different court jurisdictions are also a way of trying to balance the need for appropriate courts to hear cases which are different, not in a legal sense, but in an economic sense.

The jurisdiction of the county court largely corresponds with the civil jurisdiction of the High Court. It is, however, local in nature. County courts are separate courts, unlike the Supreme Court, Court of Appeal, High Court, and Crown Court.[175] These are all single courts, though some of them may sit at various centres throughout the country.[176]

Historically, the jurisdiction of the High Court and that of the county court has been separated largely by the value of the matter in dispute. Thus, immediately before 1991, contract actions or tort actions could be taken in either the High Court or the county court. If, however, the value of the matter in dispute was no more than £5,000 the case would have been heard in the county court.[177] This separation reflected a perception that smaller claims merited a separate court system. Since 1991, the High Court and county court jurisdictions have been brought much more closely together following the proposals of the Civil Justice Review.[178] Following Lord Woolf's report on the civil justice system, this process of closer integration has been carried much further with the creation of a single set of court rules, the Civil Procedure Rules 1998, and a division of business between the High Court and the county courts which, whilst both courts will usually have jurisdiction over a dispute, envisages most cases being taken in a county court.[179]

[172] For a discussion of the economics of using the legal system, see R. Cooter and T. Ulen, *Law and Economics* (1988) Harper Collins, New York, ch. 10; and R. Bowles, *Law and the Economy* (1982) Martin Robertson, Oxford, ch. 11.

[173] The classic liberal argument for the creation of the state is that it enables avoidance of a state of nature wherein life is, in Hobbes's words, 'solitary, poor, nasty, brutish, and short' (T. Hobbes, *Leviathan* (n.d.) Basil Blackwell, Oxford, p. 82).    [174] See **Chapters 10** and **16**.

[175] County Courts Act 1984, s. 1. In 2005, there were 218 county courts throughout the country (*Judicial Statistics 2005: Revised*, p. 43).    [176] See the discussion of the Court of Appeal, above.

[177] County Court Act 1984, s. 15(1).    [178] Civil Justice Review (1988) Cm. 394.

[179] The rules were created under the authority of Civil Procedure Act 1997, s. 1(1). For an analysis of the new rules, see N. Andrews, 'A New Civil Procedural Code for England: Party-Control "Going, Going, Gone"' (2000) 19 Civil Justice Quarterly 19.

The new arrangements have been described as being 'the most radical reform of civil litigation since 1875'.[180] Under them, not only are the vast majority of cases to be heard in the county court rather than the High Court, either as small-claims cases having a value of not more than £5,000 or as fast-track cases with a value of not more than £25,000, but the court will also have an overriding duty to manage cases.[181] The new notion of case management means that judges become involved in a case, not just at trial stage, but from the moment that a claim is made. Judges are responsible for seeing that a case is allocated to the correct court and seeing that the case comes to court expeditiously, with the maximum of cooperation between the parties, under 'the overriding objective' of the Civil Procedure Rules.[182]

County courts are grouped together into districts, with a single circuit judge being assigned to each district.[183] The administrative work of the circuit is the responsibility of a district judge.[184]

Appeals from the county court are to the Court of Appeal, except in cases where bankruptcy is the subject of the trial. In these cases, an appeal is heard by a single judge in the High Court.[185]

## Magistrates' courts

Magistrates' courts are inferior courts. They are not courts of record. Their decisions are rarely reported. In many senses, they are at the bottom of the hierarchy of courts within 'the English legal system'. They are its least important court. Yet, in other ways, they have great significance. They have a heavy workload; much heavier than that of the other courts mentioned above. They are also the most local of courts. Their location is distributed through the country in such a way as to make them as physically accessible as possible. The average member of the population is far more likely to come into contact with the magistrates' court than with the High Court or even the Crown Court.

A key feature of the courts discussed in this chapter so far is the fact that those doing the judging are professional judges. Judges are barristers or solicitors, trained lawyers, who have become judges.[186] Magistrates' courts and magistrates are atypical in that those performing the judicial role are usually not trained lawyers. They are unpaid and part-time.[187] Normally, they sit in benches of three.[188] In 2008, there were

---

[180]  C. Plant (ed.), *Blackstone's Guide to the Civil Procedure Rules* (1999) Blackstone Press, London, p. 1.

[181]  CPR, r. 26.6; CPR, r. 1.4. These rules are available on the Web at: <http://www.justice.gov.uk/civil/procrules_fin/>.

[182]  Part 26 CPR 1998. For early assessment of the effects of the Woolf reforms, see 'Further Findings: A Continuing Evaluation of the Civil Justice Reforms' (2002) <http://www.dca.gov.uk/civil/reform/ffreform.htm>.                                  [183]  County Courts Act 1984, s. 5(1).

[184]  County Courts Act 1984, ss. 6, 12(1). District judges were created following the Courts and Legal Services Act 1990, s. 74.                                  [185]  Insolvency Act 1986, s. 375.

[186]  This generalization is subject to exceptions. There is the limited exception of the role of magistrates in the Crown Court noted above.

[187]  But they are permitted to claim allowances for travelling expenses, subsistence, and financial loss (Courts Act 2003, s. 15).

[188]  Magistrates' Court Act 1980, s. 121 (SI 2002/193); Courts Act 2003, s. 18.

approximately 30,000 lay magistrates.[189] Skyrme's justification for using lay magistrates rather than professional judges is typical of that of many commentators:

The collective views of a cross-section of the population, representing different shades of
opinion, can be more effective in dispensing justice acceptable to the public than the decision of a single individual necessarily drawn from a fairly narrow social class and whose
experience of local problems may be limited.[190]

However, there is also provision for the appointment of district judges (magistrates'
court) who are paid, full-time lawyers.[191] In 2008, there were 140 full-time district
judges (magistrates' court).[192]

Lay magistrates are assisted in their work by a legally qualified justices' clerk.[193] The
task of these officials is wider than the administrative role of many officials in other
courts. They are responsible for advising magistrates on the law pertaining to cases
heard by the magistrates.[194] However, they have no power to decide cases.

Magistrates have a national jurisdiction but are assigned to particular local justice
areas and so, in practice sit locally.[195]

Magistrates' courts are primarily *criminal courts*. The cases they hear are relatively
trivial. Either the offence is in itself a minor matter, for example a parking offence,
or the particular incident is of little consequence, for example theft of an item of little value. Magistrates' courts cannot try the more serious criminal cases which are
tried on indictment.[196] The powers of the court are limited. They can both fine and
imprison those convicted, as well as making a range of other orders, but their power
to punish is less than that of the Crown Court.[197] The less serious nature of cases in
the magistrates' court is illustrated by the fact that since 1957 there has been a procedure enabling people to plead guilty to some cases by post.[198]

The criminal jurisdiction of the magistrates' court is not limited to trying the less
serious cases. The court also acts as a first-stage filter in more serious criminal cases.
Before a case can be heard on indictment in the Crown Court, there must usually be a
preliminary hearing in a magistrates' court to determine whether or not there is prima
facie case to answer.[199]

Although the magistrates' court is primarily a criminal court, it also has a range
of other jurisdictions. The closest of these to its criminal jurisdiction is its *youth
jurisdiction*. The Criminal Justice Act of 1991 retitled the old juvenile courts 'youth

---

[189] *Judicial and Court Statistics 2008* (2009b) Cm. 7697, p. 137.
[190] Sir T. Skryme, *The Changing Image of the Magistracy* (2nd edn, 1983) Macmillan, London, p. 8. See
also M. King and C. May, *Black Magistrates* (1985) Cobden Trust, London, p. 38.
[191] Courts Act 2003, s. 22(1).      [192] *Judicial and Court Statistics 2008* (2009b) Cm. 7697, p. 137.
[193] Courts Act 2003, s. 27.      [194] Courts Act 2003, ss. 28(4) and 28(5).
[195] Courts Act 2003, ss. 8 and 10.
[196] Magistrates' Court Act 1980, s. 1. In some instances, a case may either be tried in a magistrates' court
or in the Crown Court (Magistrates' Court Act 1980, s. 17 and Sch. 1).
[197] See, for example, Powers of Criminal Courts (Sentencing) Act 2000, s. 78(1).
[198] This procedure is now found in the Magistrates' Court Act 1980, s. 12.
[199] Magistrates' Court Act 1980, s. 6(1).

courts'.[200] The youth court jurisdiction attempts to separate the juvenile offender from the atmosphere of the criminal court.[201] Unlike other criminal cases in the magistrates' court or Crown Court, youth courts hear cases in private.[202] Magistrates hearing the cases are drawn from a special panel. At least one of the three magistrates hearing the case must be a woman.[203] The press cannot report details of a case in such a way as to identify the defendant, even if they are found guilty, unless the court so orders.[204]

Whilst the youth court jurisdiction is in part a criminal jurisdiction, it is also a jurisdiction which is intended to assist the offender. The court's role is in part paternal. This welfare role for the magistrates' court becomes even more pronounced when the court sits as a family proceedings court.[205] Magistrates sitting in the family proceedings court are once again drawn from a special panel.[206] Under the Domestic Proceedings and Magistrates' Court Act 1978, the court has the jurisdiction to hear cases where a party to a marriage has failed to provide reasonable maintenance for the other party or for a child of the family.[207] Appeals from the family proceedings court lie to the Family Division of the High Court.[208]

The final jurisdiction of the magistrates' court is its extensive *civil jurisdiction* which covers a wide range of quasi-administrative matters, ranging from the recovery of debts for things such as income tax, council tax, or water charges, to the granting of licences for businesses.[209]

## Courts of special jurisdiction

The courts described above are commonly discussed in textbooks on 'the English legal system'. However, they are not the only state courts to be found within Great Britain. There are also a number of courts which have limited jurisdictions but which are of great significance in the areas they cover. They are, in the main, inferior courts which are not of record and whose cases are not usually reported.[210]

### Coroners' courts

The coroners' court is an inferior court which is not of record. Its decisions are not reported. The legal rules relating to coroners' courts will be changed by the Coroners and Justice Act 2009 when it is fully in force. The changes introduced by this statute are intended to address concerns about the system of coroners' courts raised in the

---

[200] Criminal Justice Act 1991, s. 70.

[201] The jurisdiction covers those under the age of 18 (Children and Young Persons Act 1933, s. 107).

[202] Children and Young Persons Act 1933, s. 47(2).

[203] Benches may be as big as seven (Children and Young Persons Act 1933, s. 45; Youth Court (Constitution) Rules 1954).                                                      [204] Children and Young Persons Act 1933, s. 39.

[205] Children Act 1989, s. 92.        [206] Magistrates' Court Act 1980, s. 67.

[207] Domestic Proceedings and Magistrates' Court Act 1978, s. 1.

[208] Domestic Proceedings and Magistrates' Court Act 1978, s. 29(1).

[209] See, for example, the Licensing Act 2003.

[210] The exceptions to this general rule are noted below.

Luce Report, which concluded that the system of investigation of deaths by coroners had been seriously neglected for several decades and there was a widespread recognition of the need for reform.[211] In particular, it was recognized that there was a need to give better support to bereaved families.[212]

Under the 2009 Act, all coroners must be legally qualified (previously, it was also possible for a registered medical practitioner to be appointed as a coroner).[213] The Act also introduces the office of Chief Coroner, who must be a circuit or High Court judge.[214] Coroners must investigate deaths where the deceased 'died a violent or unnatural death', when 'the cause of death is unknown' or the deceased 'died while in custody or otherwise in state detention'.[215] Generally, a coroner must hold an inquest as part of the investigation.[216] There is a general rule that an inquest will be held without a jury, but s. 7 of the Act sets out the exceptions to this rule. A jury must be summoned where the death took place in custody or otherwise in state detention and the death was violent or unnatural or of unknown cause; also, where the death was as a result of an act or omission of a police officer or a member of a service police force, or where the death was caused by an accident, poisoning, or disease which must be notified to a government department or inspector.[217] Although a jury is not compulsory in any other case, the coroner is able to summon a jury in any other case where he or she believes there is sufficient reason for doing so.[218] If a coroner's jury is summoned, it must consist of no fewer than 7 and no more than 11 people.[219]

At the end of the inquest, the coroner (or the jury, if there is one) must make a 'determination' as to who the deceased was, and how, when, and where the deceased came by his or her death.[220] The coroner or jury is also usually required to make a 'finding' about the cause of death.[221] The finding will normally be a short summary of the cause of death, such as accident or misadventure, suicide, natural causes, or, where no clear cause of death has been established, the finding will be known as 'open'.

Under the previous law, there was no appeal against a coroner's decision. However, s. 40 of the 2009 Act provides for a right of appeal to the Chief Coroner. The right of appeal includes an ability to appeal against a number of matters, including the coroner's decision whether to summon a jury or not, and the determination as to who the deceased was, and how, when, and where the deceased came by his or her death.[222] A decision of the Chief Coroner can be appealed on a point of law only to the Court of Appeal.[223] The court of appeal may affirm the decision, substitute any decision that the Chief Coroner could have made, or quash the decision and remit the matter to the

---

[211] *Death Certification and Investigation in England and Wales: The Report of a Fundamental Review* (Luce Report) (2003) Cm. 5831, p. 3.          [212] Luce Report (2003) Cm. 5831, pp. 16–17.
[213] Coroners and Justice Act 2009, s. 23 and Sch. 3.          [214] Coroners and Justice Act 2009, Sch. 8.
[215] Coroners and Justice Act 2009, s. 1.          [216] Coroners and Justice Act 2009, s. 6.
[217] Coroners and Justice Act 2009, s. 7.          [218] Coroners and Justice Act 2009, s. 7(3).
[219] Coroners and Justice Act 2009, s. 8.          [220] Coroners and Justice Act 2009, s. 10(1)a.
[221] Coroners and Justice Act 2009, s. 10(1)b.          [222] Coroners and Justice Act 2009, s. 40(2).
[223] Coroners and Justice Act 2009, s. 40(9).

Chief Coroner for a fresh decision.[224] The lack of a right of appeal against coroners' decisions was one of the aspects of the previous law which came in for much criticism, and the introduction of this right was one of the recommendations made in the Luce Report.[225]

## Courts of Chivalry

Courts of Chivalry have an ancient jurisdiction over disputes about coats of arms. However, the Court of Chivalry only sat once in the last century.[226] The judge in the court is the Earl Marshal, an official in the College of Arms.

## Courts-martial

Members of the United Kingdom armed forces are subject to a separate system of military law as well as being subject to the normal laws of the land. Under these laws, people may be tried summarily by senior officers or before a court-martial in the case of more serious offences. However, in the case of the most extreme offences, such as murder or rape, the matter must be tried in the ordinary criminal courts.[227]

Courts-martial are similar in many ways to criminal courts.[228] Trial before a district court-martial is before two officers who are assisted by a judge advocate from the Judge Advocates Department.[229] The judge advocate is a lawyer who advises the court on matter of law.[230] The judge advocate thus fulfils a similar role to that of the justice's clerk in the magistrates' court. Lawyers may be present to represent either the prosecution or the defence. However, officers from the armed forces may also fulfil these roles. The court-martial decision is by majority verdict.[231]

## Courts-Martial Appeals Court

Unlike courts-martial, the Courts-Martial Appeals Court falls more squarely within the usual civilian court system described in this chapter. Judges in the court are normally taken from members of the Court of Appeal or the High Court.[232] Procedure before the court is similar to that in the criminal division of the Court of Appeal. Three judges sit with only one judgment being delivered. Appeal is to the House of Lords on similar terms as in normal criminal cases.[233]

---

[224] Coroners and Justice Act 2009, s. 40(10).      [225] See, Luce Report (2003) Cm. 5831, p. 232.

[226] *Manchester Corporation* v *Manchester Palace of Varieties Ltd* [1955] 1 All ER 387. No other case is found on the LEXIS database. A description of the history of this court and its jurisdiction is to be found on pp. 392–4 of the report. See also P. Goodrich, *Languages of Law* (1990) Weidenfeld & Nicolson, London, p. 133.                                          [227] See, for example, Army Act 1955, s. 70(4).

[228] Procedure for the courts is laid down in delegated legislation. See, for example, Courts-Martial (Army) Rules 2007 (SI 2007/3442). In all cases below similar provisions exist in the cases of the Royal Air Force and the Royal Navy.

[229] Army Act 1955, s. 84D. Judge advocates can be appointed by the officer convening the court.

[230] Courts-Martial (Appeals) Act 1951, s. 31; Army Act 1955, s. 84B.

[231] See, for example, Army Act 1955, s. 96(1).

[232] Courts-Martial (Appeals) Act 1968, s. 2(1). Although the Lord Chancellor does have the discretion to appoint 'other persons of legal experience' (Courts-Martial (Appeals) Act 1968, s. 2(2)).

[233] Courts-Martial (Appeals) Act 1968, s. 39.

## Ecclesiastical courts

Just as members of the armed forces are subject to a separate system of military law as well as to normal civil law, so members of the Church of England are subject to a separate system of ecclesiastical law. This law is more limited since, in the main, it pertains only to matters relating to the functioning of the Church of England. However, it has a history which is as long as the history of English common law.[234]

Ecclesiastical law has its own system of ecclesiastical courts.[235] Each diocese has its own consistory court.[236] A judge in a consistory court must be a lawyer but must also either be in Holy Orders or a communicant member of the Church of England.[237] Judges are called chancellors.[238] The jurisdiction of these courts mainly covers the conduct of those in Holy Orders.[239] Appeal lies either to the Arches Court of Canterbury or to the Chancery Court of York.[240] There are five judges in each of these courts.[241] One judge, who sits in both courts, must be a lawyer.[242] The other judges are taken from those in holy orders and the laity.[243] Appeal from these courts lies to the Privy Council.[244]

Ecclesiastical law also has its own courts when dealing with matters of doctrine or ritual.[245] Jurisdiction in these matters is exercised by the Court of Ecclesiastical Causes Reserved which consists of five judges, two of whom must have held high judicial office

---

[234] Separate ecclesiastical courts have existed 'since the time of William the Conqueror, who provided that they should "have care of pleas affecting episcopal jurisdiction" and "any cause concerning the government of souls"' (A. Manchester, *Modern Legal History* (1980) Butterworths, London, p. 143). In *Re St Mary of Charity, Faversham* [1986] 1 All ER 1 at p. 8, the separation of ecclesiastical and temporal courts was said to date from 1072. This joint jurisdiction has not always been to the benefit of litigants since they have sometimes had to choose which courts to bring their case in (see Sir W. Holdsworth, *A History of English Law*, Volume 12 (3rd edn, 1922) Methuen, London, pp. 695–702; and Manchester (1980) p. 125).

[235] For a full description of these courts, see G. Moore, *English Canon Law* (1963) Clarendon Press, Oxford, ch. 14. On canon law, see N. Doe, *Canon Law in the Anglican Communion* (1998) Oxford University Press, Oxford; N. Doe, *The Legal Framework of the Church of England* (1996) Oxford University Press, Oxford; and M. Hill, *Ecclesiastical Law* (3rd edn, 2007) Oxford University Press, Oxford.

[236] Ecclesiastical Jurisdiction Measure 1963, s. 1(1). Judgments of these courts are regularly but not frequently reported in the law reports. See, for example, *Re St James Malden* [1994] 1 All ER 85, a report of a case in the Southwark Consistory Court. Westlaw lists 196 such cases.

[237] Ecclesiastical Jurisdiction Measure 1963, s. 2(2).

[238] Chancellors may be chancellors of more than one diocese at a time. Moore notes that in 1963, there were 42 dioceses but only 18 chancellors (Moore (1963) p. 131). Under the Diocesan Chancellorship Regulations 1993, a person may not hold more than two chancellorships at one time, though persons holding more than two at the time of the regulations may continue to do so (Diocesan Chancellorship Regulations 1993, SI 1993/1841, regs 2, 3).    [239] Ecclesiastical Jurisdiction Measure 1963, s. 6(1).

[240] Ecclesiastical Jurisdiction Measure 1963, s. 7(1).

[241] Ecclesiastical Jurisdiction Measure 1963, s. 3(1).

[242] Ecclesiastical Jurisdiction Measure 1963, ss. 3(2)(a), 3(3).

[243] Ecclesiastical Jurisdiction Measure 1963, s. 3(2)(a)(c).

[244] Ecclesiastical Jurisdiction Measure 1963, s. 8(2).

[245] Ecclesiastical Jurisdiction Measure 1963, s. 10(1).

and three of whom must be diocesan bishops.[246] Appeal lies to a Commission of Review which consists of three Lords of Appeal in Ordinary and two Lords Spiritual.[247]

## Election courts

Separate election courts exist to deal with disputes about the conduct of European parliamentary, parliamentary, and local government elections.[248] The court which deals with European parliamentary and parliamentary elections is a court of record.[249] It has the authority, powers, and jurisdiction of a judge of the High Court.[250] Two judges sit to hear cases. Judges on the rota for hearing these cases also appoint lawyers to hear disputes about local government elections.[251]

## CONCLUSION

The purpose of this chapter is to see what looking at the courts within the state legal system in England and Wales will tell us about the nature of 'the English legal system'. Information can mislead. From the above, it might appear that we have a detailed picture of the courts that constitute one facet of 'the English legal system'. This is not, in fact, the case. Comparing the above with our first chapter, which discussed what we needed to know in order to understand a legal process, it is plain that we know very little about the courts. It is true that we know quite a lot about the rules which describe the jurisdictions of the courts, something of the rules of the procedures of those courts, and something of the pathways for appeal and review. However, what we do not know, even after all this description, is much more significant.

The information we have tells us a great deal about the formal powers of judges in the courts. It tells us very little about what those judges actually do. We have already seen that anthropologists would tell us that, in order to understand a culture, we need to know both what people say they should do (in this case, the rules of the court) and what people actually do. Moreover, we know very little about what people other than judges do in the courts. Indeed, we hardly know that they exist; for us, they are shadows. In this respect, comparing the picture of the Crown Court that emerges from the work of Rock with our picture of each of the other courts is highly instructive. For Rock, the Crown Court is a complex network of personal interrelationships. It seems implausible to suggest such relationships do not exist in other courts but we have very limited data on what they might be.[252]

---

[246] Ecclesiastical Jurisdiction Measure 1963, s. 5.

[247] Ecclesiastical Jurisdiction Measure 1963, s. 11(4). For a detailed treatment of canon law see Doe (1998).          [248] Representation of the People Act 1983, ss. 123(1), 130(1).

[249] Representation of the People Act 1983, s. 123(2).

[250] Representation of the People Act 1983, s. 123(2).

[251] Representation of the People Act 1983, s. 130 (3).

[252] Equally, of course, Rock's picture of the Crown Court might be accurate only for the particular Crown Court that he studied.

What we do know about the courts above, however, is useful if we come to ask the question, in what sense is this group of courts a 'system'? From what we have seen they are plainly a very diverse set of institutions. What separates them is as apparent as that which unites them.

No single factor can be seen which runs through the courts above and which does not run through other institutions in England and Wales concerned with dispute resolution. Their personnel differ from court to court. Not all courts, for example, have lawyers as their judges.[253] The way in which they reach their conclusions differs. Not all courts, for example, use the same system of legal reasoning.[254] The function of the courts varies widely. Thus, for example, the European Court of Justice, the Supreme Court, and the Privy Council might, in some senses, be said to be constitutional courts charged with a general duty to protect the administration of the law. They make decisions at a high level which apply broadly. Their work frequently has immediate political impact. This is clearly not true of some other courts above whose duties are more local and more particular. Some are courts of first instance. Their work is largely concerned with ascertaining the facts of a particular case and then applying largely unargued law. This is not to say that their work is less important than the constitutional courts, but it is different. Still other courts are appellate and decisions in them regularly revolve around the minutiae of legal reasoning.

The courts above are interconnected. They are either subject to appeal to other courts, review by other courts or they hear appeals from or review the decisions of other courts. But this, as we will see, does not distinguish them from other institutions of dispute settlement for Great Britain. These, too, interact with the courts. What, then, makes the courts different from these other bodies? What, if anything, unites them apart from the simple assertion that they are part of the English legal system?

## FURTHER READING

BAILEY, S. H., CHING, J. P. L., and TAYLOR, N. W., *Smith, Bailey and Gunn on the Modern English Legal System* (5th edn, 2007) Sweet & Maxwell, London, ch. 2.

WARD R. and AKHTAR, A., *Walker and Walker's English Legal System* (10th edn, 2008) Oxford University Press, Oxford, ch. 8.

---

[253] Figures as different as lay magistrates, medical practitioners, and, until the resignation of Lord Irvine, the Lord Chancellor hold judicial office.

[254] The reasoning in the European Court of Justice owes very little to English legal reasoning as practised in the Court of Appeal. Reasoning in the coroners' court can hardly be called legal reasoning at all since the process is one of factual inquiry.

# 4

# Tribunals

## INTRODUCTION

It might seem appropriate to begin this section with a definition of what a tribunal is. However, as we have already seen, distinguishing tribunals from courts within 'the English legal system' is very difficult. Typically, a tribunal is a decision-making body established by the state to resolve disputes arising between individual citizens and the state.[1] A typical tribunal is composed of a legally qualified chairperson, and two 'wing people' who generally have knowledge and experience of the subject-matter over which the tribunal has jurisdiction. The decisions which tribunals make are legally binding, and generally there is a limited right of appeal to a court.

Tribunals cover a wide range of subjects. In 2001, the Leggatt Review of Tribunals found 70 different tribunals dealing with matters covering the whole range of social and political life, including social security benefits, health, education, tax, agriculture, immigration and asylum, rents, and parking.[2] One of the defining features of a tribunal, as opposed to a court, is that ordinary people should be able to take their dispute to a tribunal and have it resolved without the need to be represented by a lawyer. The Leggatt Review commented:

First, the widest common theme in current tribunals is the aim that users should be able to prepare and present their own cases effectively, if helped by good-quality, imaginatively presented information, and by expert procedural help from tribunal staff and substantive assistance from advice services.[3]

Within 'the English legal system', courts and tribunals are both generally established by the state and both are concerned with settling disputes. As we will see in **Chapter 9**, appointment to chair a tribunal is, like appointment to be a judge in a court, appointment to a judicial office, and as a result of the Tribunals, Courts and Enforcement Act 2007, chairs of tribunals (who were formerly called 'chairs') are now called judges.[4] Equally, the judicial independence

---

[1] There are also some bodies that are called tribunals which operate outside the English legal system. Thus, for example, the bodies that make decisions about nullity cases under Roman Catholic canon law are called Tribunals (see further G. Read, 'The Catholic Tribunal System in the British Isles' (1991) 9 Ecclesiastical Law Journal 213.

[2] Sir A. Leggatt, *Tribunals for Users: One System, One Service*, Report of the Review of Tribunals by Sir Andrew Leggatt (Leggatt Review) (2001) The Stationery Office, London, paras 1.9 and 1.16.

[3] Leggatt Review (2001) para. 1.11.

[4] Tribunals, Courts and Enforcement Act 2007, s. 4.

of tribunal judges and members is guaranteed in a similar way to other judges.[5] However, just as there are courts which operate outside 'the English legal system', so, too, are there tribunals which operate outside 'the English legal system'.[6] Nevertheless, the majority of tribunals are set up by the state, and, although they are different from courts, as we shall discuss below, they are part of the state system and not, strictly speaking, a form of 'alternative dispute resolution' or Alternative Dispute Resolution (ADR).

In some cases, whether something is said to be a tribunal or a court may be of little importance. The current collection of tribunals has grown up in an almost entirely haphazard way to deal with disputes in a range of disparate areas, as government departments have developed new statutory schemes:[7]

Often the allocation of a jurisdiction to either a tribunal or to a court, in preference to its retention within the [government] department, is purely a matter of historical accident or political whim or convenience. There are fads and fashions which come and go in this area as elsewhere and there are also developments which defy any rational analysis.[8]

Notwithstanding this observation, to say that there is no distinction between tribunals and courts is as inaccurate as saying that you can easily distinguish all tribunals from all courts. The fact is that there is no simple dividing line between the two types of institution; what we will find is differences of emphasis and direction.[9]

## The Franks Report

Commentators frequently begin any analysis of tribunals with the Franks Report into tribunals and inquiries of 1957.[10] The Franks Report said of tribunals, '[t]ribunals are not ordinary courts' thus implying that, in some sense, tribunals were courts even if they were courts of an extra-ordinary character.[11] This impression is confirmed by the fact that the Franks Report saw proceedings in tribunals as ones which should be characterized by 'openness, fairness and impartiality'.[12] The analogy with cases heard in court is obvious. Indeed, the Franks Report noted evidence

---

[5] See Tribunals, Courts and Enforcement Act 2007, s. 1 and Constitutional Reform Act 2005, s. 3.

[6] See above n. 1.        [7] Leggatt Review (2001) para. 1.3.

[8] J. Farmer, *Tribunals and Government* (1974) Weidenfeld & Nicholson, London, p. 4. See also B. Abel-Smith and R. Stevens, *In Search of Justice* (1968) Allen Lane, London, p. 219.

[9] Individual examples of courts and tribunals merge into each other in borderline cases. Tribunals hold some things in common with courts. To say, however, that the differences are not 'fundamental' (Abel-Smith and Stevens (1968) pp. 224, 228) is to miss the point. In the important sense that all dispute-solving institutions, state or non-state, merge into each other in their function, tribunals and courts are part of the same thing. However, there are fundamental differences in their raison d'être even if those differences vary from example to example.

[10] Franks Committee, *Report of the Committee on Administrative Tribunals and Enquiries* (the Franks Report) (1957) Cmnd 218, HMSO, London.        [11] Franks Report (1957) p. 9.

[12] Franks Report (1957) p. 5.

criticizing the then existing rent tribunals as being 'insufficiently judicial in their methods of handling cases' because they did not have legally qualified chairpersons and proposed that such chairs should be appointed.[13] However, the similarity between courts and tribunals found in Franks can be overstated. The Report has to be read in the light of the evidence that was given to it and the view commonly taken of tribunals at the time. 'Much of the official evidence...appeared to reflect the view that tribunals should properly be regarded as part of the machinery of administration.'[14] Tribunals were seen by some as merely being a part of, or at least ancillary to, the Government departments to which their work related. In reacting to this evidence, the Franks Report emphasized the formal independence of the tribunals, and their discreteness. In this sense, tribunals could be said to be similar to courts. However, it does not follow that they are similar to courts in all other respects. The Franks Report itself accepted that there were 'certain characteristics which give them [tribunals] advantages over the courts'.[15] In the following section, we will consider some of the similarities and differences between tribunals and courts.

## The differences between courts and tribunals

Most tribunals within 'the English legal system' are of much more recent origin than the courts within the same system. Writing about tribunals in 1928, Robson said:

the social legislation of the past seventy years has introduced an entirely new element into the British constitution, or, to state it more accurately, has reintroduced an old element in a new form.[16]

However, even if the idea of the tribunal can be traced back to the nineteenth or earlier centuries, none of the tribunals which are commonly discussed can show the ancient lineage that many courts within 'the English legal system' can.

Most courts have a general, or at least a wide, jurisdiction. Tribunals, however, tend to have relatively restricted jurisdictions. Moreover, 'most typical tribunals are appellate and concern appeals by a member of the public against some organ of the

13 Franks Report (1957) pp. 37–8. The Franks Report (p. 35) also criticized the then existing County Agricultural Executive Committees on grounds of their partiality.        14 Franks Report (1957) p. 9.
15 Franks Report (1957) p. 9.
16 W. Robson, *Justice and Administrative Law* (3rd edn, 1951) Stevens, London, p. 89. Holdsworth notes that '[f]rom the medieval period onwards the Legislature have given to specialized tribunals...jurisdiction over certain matters which ordinary courts were unable to deal satisfactorily...' (W. Holdsworth, *A History of English Law*, Volume 14 (1964) Methuen, London, p. 182).

State'.[17] Each has been created in relation to a specific need and as specific needs have changed, so new tribunals have been created and old ones have been abolished.[18] As government action has impinged more and more on society, so the number of tribunals has grown.[19] Nevertheless, the jurisdictional distinction between courts and tribunals can be over-emphasized. The Restrictive Practices Court, for example, was of recent origin and its jurisdiction was less extensive than that of the industrial tribunal.[20] However, there is a general truth that each tribunal tends to have a much more limited function, and a different kind of function, than do the courts.

Tribunals can also be distinguished from courts by looking at who takes the decisions in a tribunal. In a court, one finds judges and judges are legally trained.[21] In the case of tribunals, decisions are often made by a panel of three individuals, one of whom is legally trained (and who generally takes the chair) with the others, commonly called wing people, who are not legally trained, but are present because of their expertise in the area of dispute to which the tribunal relates. Thus, in the case of the Employment Tribunal, wing people are drawn from the two sides of industry, employers, and trade unionists.[22]

The distinction between the kind of people who take decisions in a tribunal and the kind of people who take decisions in a court points to a further distinction between courts and tribunals. Decisions in courts are essentially about questions of law. The assessment of facts is important but at the root of the matter it is supposed that some legal point must be at issue. Legal qualification for the person making the decision is therefore vital. In the case of a tribunal, the balance between complexity and importance of fact and law is much more equal. Therefore, specialist expertise in a particular area is as much a qualification for passing judgment as legal expertise. Again, exceptions to this general truth exist. Lay magistrates and jurors, who are involved in decision-making in courts, are not legally qualified.[23]

---

[17] M. Sayers and A. Webb, 'Franks Revisited: A Model of the Ideal Tribunal' (1990) 9 Civil Justice Quarterly 36.

[18] For a discussion of historical tribunals see Holdsworth (1964) pp. 183–8 and P. Cane, *Administrative Tribunals and Adjudication* (2009) Hart Publishing, Oxford, ch. 2.

[19] Wade has described the 'phenomenal growth' rate of tribunals in the two to three decades preceding the 1960s (W. Wade, *Towards Administrative Justice* (1963) University of Michigan Press, Ann Arbor, MI, p. 14).

[20] Restrictive Trade Practices Act 1956, s. 2. The court was abolished by s. 1 of the Competition Act 1998. Equally, some tribunals do have a claim to a fairly long history. The General Commissioners of Income Tax, for example, were set up in 1799. The General Commissioners have been variously described as 'amateurs' (P. de Voil, *Tax Appeals* (1969) Butterworths, London, p. 35) and 'busy men acting under a sense of public duty' (per Lord Reid in *Re Vandervell's Trust* (1971) 46 Tax Cases 341 at p. 361). For a discussion of their work see de Voil (1969) pp. 33–7.

[21] There are, of course, exceptions, most notably that of the magistrates' court, which we have discussed in the previous chapter.

[22] Employment Tribunals (Constitution and Rules of Procedure) Regulations 2004 (SI 2004/1861) para. 8(3)(a) and (b).

[23] The situation is not exactly analogous. The function of lay magistrates and jurors is, amongst other things, to represent the community as a whole. Members of tribunals who are not legally qualified usually

Some further distinctions between courts and tribunals can be identified if we look at what Sayers and Webb put forward as the most important aims of a tribunal:

(1)  to reach the right decisions under law;

(2)  to give the parties what they will recognize as an impartial, fair and sufficient hearing (even though one of them will probably not win his case); and

(3)  to use the advantages of a tribunal, like informality, speed, independence, expertise, accessibility, and efficiency and cheapness both for the parties and for society as a whole.[24]

The first two aims continue the Frank tradition of linking tribunals with the courts. The third aim brings in the wider question of the purpose of tribunals which points to some differences with courts, and links with the reasons why tribunals were set up and why people are appointed to tribunals. Tribunals are frequently cheaper than courts, frequently quicker than courts, and frequently able to deal with a wider range of more policy-oriented and less legalistic questions when looking at individual disputes. These are aspects of tribunals which tend to differentiate them from courts.

The Leggatt Report on Tribunals (2001) continued the approach adopted by Sayers and Webb by suggesting that there were three tests which could be used to identify whether a court or a tribunal was an appropriate body for determining a dispute. Tribunals, the Report argued, were more efficacious than courts where there was a desire to let people put their disputes directly without the use of lawyers, where there was a need for special expertise on the part of the body determining the dispute, or where a dispute concerned that 'mixture of fact and law often required to consider decisions taken by administrative and regulatory authorities'.[25]

However, whatever their merits, these tests do not provide a clear distinction between the work of courts and the work of tribunals. As we have seen in **Chapter 3**, there are courts which share a number of features with tribunals, such as courts where litigants often appear without lawyers, courts which are specialized in their nature, and there are courts which deal with disputes involving administrative agencies. Although differences do exist between courts and tribunals, it is not possible to draw a clear-cut distinction. There are some differences between courts and tribunals, but they also share certain features.

## Tribunals and administrative agencies

So, although tribunals can be distinguished from courts in some ways, there are also similarities between tribunals and courts. It has been argued that to accept these similarities is to misunderstand the nature of tribunals or, at least, to misunderstand the

sit by virtue of their actual knowledge and, in some cases, by virtue of their professional, albeit non-legal, expertise.

[24] Sayers and Webb (1990) pp. 38–9.      [25] Leggatt Review (2001).

nature of some tribunals. Some writers include within their definition of tribunals various Commissioners, inquiries, and other bodies set up to deal with decisions made about the exercise of statutory powers. In this context, Abel-Smith and Stevens distinguish court-substitute tribunals from policy-oriented tribunals.[26] Examples given of policy-oriented tribunals include licensing bodies and inquiries, for example planning inquiries, empowered to make recommendations which government ministers may then choose to follow if they wish.[27]

Such bodies are clearly different from those tribunals which make mandatory decisions about discrete disputes between individual parties. However, it would be wrong to dismiss them as a wholly separate form of state power. To separate these agencies off as being so clearly distinct from court-substitute tribunals that they fall within a separate category would be to ignore the similarities they have with these bodies. What they do, orders people's lives, allocates resources, and results in the imposition of decisions sanctioned by the state. Rather, the existence of policy-oriented tribunals strengthens the argument for the fluidity of institutions in the state and society, where one kind of institution merges into another; a fluidity which belies the fixed notion of 'the English legal system', where everything falls either clearly within it or plainly outside. There are a variety of tribunals, some clearly within the state legal system, others operating on the margins of the system or outside it. Some of these tribunals share many features of courts, while others can be clearly differentiated from courts. This fluidity reflects the nature of the integrated legal system to which this book draws attention.

## Reforming tribunals

Tribunals have recently been the subject of major reforms, following the passing of the Tribunals, Courts and Enforcement Act 2007. This piece of legislation was the culmination of a major review of tribunals undertaken by the Government, which started in the year 2000 with the Leggatt Review, when Sir Andrew Leggatt, a retired Lord Justice of Appeal, was asked to head a review to look at 'the delivery of justice through tribunals'.[28] When the Review reported in 2001, it identified a number of criticisms of tribunals. One concern was that some tribunals were not truly independent from their sponsoring government departments, so that citizens using tribunals did not feel their dispute was being adjudicated by a truly independent body.[29] Another major problem was that each tribunal tended to operate completely separately, using its own practices and standards.[30] This caused considerable confusion for those dealing with tribunals, not only users, but also solicitors and other advisers, who often failed to appreciate the peculiarities of particular tribunals' practices. It was also inefficient in its use of

---

[26] Abel-Smith and Stevens (1968) pp. 220–1. See also Farmer (1974) p. 183.

[27] See, for example, Farmer (1974) p. 184.

[28] Leggatt Review (2001); see: <http://www.tribunals-review.org.uk/leggatthtm/leg-fw.htm>.

[29] Leggatt Review (2001) para. 2.23.     [30] Leggatt Review (2001) para. 3.2.

administrative and other resources.[31] Leggatt also found that some tribunals were not sufficiently user-friendly, so they did not fulfil their basic function of allowing people to use them without the need for legal representation.[32]

In the light of these concerns, the Leggatt Review made a number of recommendations for the reform of tribunals. The most fundamental recommendation was that tribunals needed to be rationalized into a coherent system, with administrative support provided by the Lord Chancellor's Department (LCD) (now the Ministry of Justice), which is the government department primarily responsible for the administration of justice.[33] This would address concerns about lack of consistency, and also ensure independence:

The important place which tribunals now play in the modern system of administrative law would best be recognised by forming them into a coherent system to sit alongside the ordinary courts, with administrative support provided by the LCD.[34]

To achieve this objective, Leggatt proposed that a new Tribunals Service should be established which would be responsible for the administration of all tribunals.[35] This would sit alongside the Court Service, which is responsible for the administration of the courts in England and Wales, and, like the Court Service, be the responsibility of the Lord Chancellor. The establishment of a separate Tribunal Service would also serve the purpose of ensuring that tribunals were not regarded as inferior to courts, which Leggatt regarded as a possibility if tribunals were to become the responsibility of the Court Service:[36]

we want an organisation committed to producing a distinctive tribunal service and tribunal approach and directed at providing tribunal 'services of the highest quality, matching the best anywhere in the world…responsive to the user and…seamless'.[37]

In addition, Leggatt suggested that a separate Service would have the potential to be sufficiently focused to develop and communicate to users the sense of coherence in line with the Review's major recommendations.[38] Leggatt also saw the Tribunal Service as answering concerns about the complexity of the existing system, arguing that it would simplify matters for users:

Any citizen who wished to appeal to a tribunal would only have to submit the appeal, confident in the knowledge that one system handled all such disputes, and could be relied upon to allocate it to the right tribunal.[39]

The other significant recommendation made by the Review was that major changes should be made to the organization of tribunals. It recommended the establishment

31  Leggatt Review (2001) para. 3.4.
32  Leggatt Review (2001) ch. 4.
33  Leggatt Review (2001) para. 3.8.
34  Leggatt Review (2001) para. 2.25.
35  Leggatt Review (2001) ch. 5.
36  Leggatt Review (2001) para. 5.3.
37  Leggatt Review (2001) para. 5.3.
38  Leggatt Review (2001) para. 5.4.
39  Leggatt Review (2001) para. 3.8.

of a new Tribunals System, with a coherent structure which would enable the effective management of the workload and encourage consistency, furthering a common approach to decision-making and case management, as well as to appeals.[40]

Finally, Leggatt recommended that a greater effort should be made to ensure that tribunals adopted an 'enabling approach' to users, so that people could bring their disputes to tribunals confident that, with advice from the Tribunal Service and information produced to assist them, they could present their cases without the need for legal representation.[41] The Review noted that tribunals had developed different ways of assisting unrepresented parties, especially where the dispute was with the state, and the state was represented by an official or advocate who was familiar with the relevant law, the tribunal and its procedures:

In these circumstances, tribunal chairmen may find it necessary to intervene in the proceedings more than might be thought proper in the courts in order to hold the balance between the parties, and enable citizens to present their cases. All the members of a tribunal must do all they can to understand the point of view, as well as the case, of the citizen. They must be alert for factual or legal aspects of the case which appellants may not bring out, adequately or at all, but which have a bearing on the possible outcomes. It may also be necessary on occasion to intervene to protect a witness or party, to avoid proceedings becoming too confrontational. The balance is a delicate one, and must not go so far on any side that the tribunal's impartiality appears to be endangered.[42]

Despite the need to assist unrepresented parties to present their case effectively, tribunals must always retain their impartiality and ensure that both parties to a dispute are treated fairly. In order to achieve this, Leggatt recommended that the approach must be an 'enabling' one, supporting both parties in ways which give them confidence in their own ability to participate in the proceedings and also in the tribunal's capacity to compensate for any lack of skills or knowledge on the part of either of the parties, yet maintaining a balanced approach.[43] The approach adopted in tribunals is particularly important, because one of their purposes is to enable people to have their cases heard without the need for legal representation. If tribunals fail to adopt a sufficiently enabling approach, users will feel excluded from the tribunal which is adjudicating their dispute, thus undermining one of the basic features of the tribunal. This type of perception was reflected in the opinion of one of the respondents to a research study carried out for the Leggatt Review, who said: 'I really don't think any tribunal is suitable for a layman like me...My solicitor did all the talking for me. I didn't speak at all because it was way over my head.'[44] Delivering the enabling approach which would help to overcome this feeling of alienation from the tribunal process requires great skill on the part of tribunal chairs and members, and Leggatt recognized that more training of chairs and members would be needed to ensure the enabling approach is adopted consistently and effectively.[45]

---

[40]  Leggatt Review (2001) para. 6.2.          [41]  Leggatt Review (2001) ch. 7.
[42]  Leggatt Review (2001) para. 7.4.          [43]  Leggatt Review (2001) para. 7.5.
[44]  Leggatt Review (2001) para. 7.5.          [45]  Leggatt Review (2001) paras 7.13–7.35.

The Leggatt Review was the first comprehensive review of tribunals to take place since the Franks Committee reported in 1957.[46] Overall, the Review succeeded in addressing many of the major concerns which had been raised about tribunals by researchers and commentators in the intervening years, such as the inconsistencies in approach, the difficulties for unrepresented users to present their cases effectively, and the legalistic nature of some tribunals.[47]

In 2004, the Government issued a White Paper, *Transforming Public Services: Complaints, Redress and Tribunals*.[48] This adopted many of the recommendations of the Leggatt Review, and in some ways went further. Not only were tribunals to resolve disputes in 'the best way possible', but they were also to 'stimulate improved decision-making so that disputes do not happen as a result of poor decision-making'.[49] The White Paper also indicated that the former Council on Tribunals would be replaced by a new Administrative Justice Council, which would not only have a supervisory role in relation to all types of tribunals, but would also become an advisory body for the whole administrative justice system:

What is needed for the future is a Council which can focus on improvements for the user across the whole administrative justice field, so that the new organisation, and tribunals outside the new organisation, develop and operate under the strategic oversight of an independent and authoritative body with a very wide perspective.[50]

The Government indicated in the White Paper that it had ambitious aims for the administration of justice, and that reform of the tribunal system was a key part of this:

we see this new body as much more than a federation of existing tribunals. This is a new organisation and a new type of organisation. It will have two central pillars: administrative justice appeals, and employment cases. Its task, together with a transformed Council on Tribunals, will not be just to process cases according to law. Its mission will be to help to prevent and resolve disputes, using any appropriate method and working with its partners in and out of government, and to help to improve administrative justice and justice in the workplace, so that the need for disputes is reduced.[51]

It remains to be seen to what extent these ambitions will be fulfilled, but the aim was clearly to do more than merely replicate the old system of tribunals in a new form.

---

[46]  Franks Report (1957).

[47]  See, for example, concerns raised in H. Genn and Y. Genn, *The Effectiveness of Representation at Tribunals* (1989) Lord Chancellor's Department, London. In relation to employment tribunals in particular, see E. Blankenburg and R. Rogowski, 'German Labour Courts and the British Industrial System' (1986) 13 Journal of Law and Society 67; and R. Munday, 'Tribunal Lore: Legalism and the Industrial Tribunals' (1981) 10 Industrial Law Review 146.

[48]  Department for Constitutional Affairs, *Transforming Public Services: Complaints, Redress and Tribunals* (2004b) Cm. 6243, HMSO, London.

[49]  Department for Constitutional Affairs (2004b) Cm. 6243, para. 6.4.

[50]  Department for Constitutional Affairs (2004b) Cm. 6243, para. 11.11.

[51]  Department for Constitutional Affairs (2004b) Cm. 6243, para. 1.14.

## The new tribunals system

When the Tribunals, Courts and Enforcement Act 2007 came into force, it implemented the reforms which had been proposed in the White Paper (many of which had also been recommended by the Leggatt Review). The Act created two new tribunals, the First-tier Tribunal and the Upper Tribunal, into which existing tribunals have been merged.[52] Each of these tribunals consists of a number of Chambers (a similar concept to that of the divisions in the High Court).[53] An office of Senior President of Tribunals was created, and Lord Justice Robert Carnwath, a Lord Justice of Appeal, was appointed as the first Senior President.[54] In his first Annual Report, Carnwath LJ noted that:

The statutory functions of the Senior President are modelled in many respects on those of the Lord Chief Justice under the CRA. They confer wide-ranging responsibility for judicial leadership, including training, welfare and guidance of the tribunal judiciary, and for representing their views to Parliament and to ministers.[55]

The statutory responsibilities of the Senior President, set out in s. 2 of the Tribunals, Courts and Enforcement Act, give a good indication of some of the distinctive features of tribunals which the Government intended should be reflected in the new system. Section 2(3) provides that the Senior President must have regard to:

(a) the need for tribunals to be accessible,

(b) the need for proceedings before tribunals—

   (i) to be fair, and
   (ii) to be handled quickly and efficiently,

(c) the need for members of tribunals to be experts in the subject-matter of, or the law to be applied in, cases in which they decide matters, and

(d) the need to develop innovative methods of resolving disputes that are of a type that may be brought before tribunals.

Fairness, speed of disposal, expertise and innovative methods of dispute resolution are intended to be the key features of the new system. It may be questioned to what extent speed of disposal is compatible with the need to be fair, but the system will, in the future, have to reconcile these two potentially conflicting aims as best it can.

## The First-tier Tribunal

The First-tier Tribunal comprises seven Chambers: War Pensions and Armed Forces Compensation; Social Entitlement; Health, Education and Social Care; General

---

[52] Tribunals, Courts and Enforcement Act 2007, s. 3.
[53] Tribunals, Courts and Enforcement Act 2007, s. 7.
[54] See: <http://www.tribunals.gov.uk/Tribunals/About/president.htm>.
[55] Carnwath LJ, *Senior President of Tribunals' Annual Report: Tribunals Transformed* (2010) Ministry of Justice, London, para. 23.

Regulatory; Tax; Immigration and Asylum; and Land, Property and Housing. The Employment Tribunals in England, Scotland, and Wales also come under the judicial leadership of the Senior President, but are not part of the system other than that.[56]

The tribunals which lie within each of the Chambers are as follows:[57]

- War Pensions & Armed Forces Compensation:

   Pensions Appeals Tribunal

- Social Entitlement Chamber:

   Social Security & Child Support Appeals
   Asylum Support Tribunal
   Criminal Injuries Compensation Appeal Panel

- Health, Education and Social Care Chamber:

   Mental Health Review Tribunal
   Special Educational Needs & Disability Tribunal
   Care Standards Tribunal
   Family Health Services Appeal Authority

- General Regulatory Chamber:

   Charity Tribunal
   Consumer Credit Appeals Tribunal
   Estate Agents Appeals Tribunal
   Transport Tribunal
   Driving Standards Agency Appeals
   Information Tribunal
   Claims Management Services Tribunal
   Immigration Services Tribunal
   Adjudication Panel for England

- Tax Chamber:

   General Commissioners
   Special Commissioners
   VAT & Duties Tribunal
   Section 70 Tribunal

- Immigration & Asylum Chamber:

   Asylum and Immigration Tribunal

- Land, Property and Housing Chamber:

   (The content of this Chamber and the timetable
   for its establishment are yet to be decided.)

---

[56] See diagram giving the structure of the tribunal system in Carnwath LJ (2010) p. 10.
[57] Carnwath LJ (2010) p. 10.

The former Presidents of each of the tribunals which have been transferred in to the First-tier Tribunal have become 'Principal Judges' of the equivalent jurisdiction within the new structure, and they are also judges in the Upper Tribunal.[58]

## The Upper Tribunal

The Upper Tribunal comprises four Chambers: the Administrative Appeals Chamber, the Immigration and Asylum Chamber, the Tax and Chancery Chamber, and the Lands Chamber.[59] The Administrative Appeals Chamber hears appeals from the Social Entitlement Chamber, the Health, Education and Social Care Chamber, the War Pensions and Armed Forces Compensation Chamber and some appeals from the General Regulatory Chamber.[60] The Immigration and Asylum Chamber hears appeals from the First-tier Immigration and Asylum Chamber, while the Tax and Chancery Chamber hears appeals from the Tax Chamber and some appeals from the General Regulatory Chamber.[61] The Lands Chamber presently consists of the Lands Tribunal; it will hear appeals from the Land, Property and Housing Chamber, but this is not yet fully functioning.[62] In addition, the Senior President is responsible for providing overall leadership for the Employment Appeal Tribunal, which hears appeals from employment tribunals in England, Scotland, and Wales.[63]

Each of the four Chambers of the Upper Tribunal has a Chamber President (a High Court judge in each case, except for the small Lands Tribunal) and a body of specialist judges.[64] The creation of the Upper Tribunal means that there is now one clear appeal system for all the tribunals transferred into the new system. This is in stark contrast to the situation which previously existed, whereby routes of appeal varied greatly between different specialist tribunals.[65] Since the Upper Tribunal is a superior court of record, its establishment will enable a body of specialist jurisprudence to be developed at a higher level than previously, by a group of specialist judges. The Senior President commented in his first Annual Review:

Over time, the Upper Tribunal should come to play a central, innovative and defining role in the new system, enjoying a position in the judicial hierarchy at least equivalent to that of the Administrative Court.[66]

The Upper Tribunal does not just hear appeals from the First-tier Tribunal. It also has some original jurisdiction. For example, the Administrative Appeals Chamber hears first instance appeals from those barred from working with children and others under the safeguarding Vulnerable Groups Act 2006. It also hears references in forfeiture cases (for instance, where an individual convicted of the homicide of their partner

---

[58] Carnwath LJ (2010) para. 39.    [59] Carnwath LJ (2010) paras 31–5.
[60] See diagram giving the structure of the tribunal system in Carnwath LJ (2010) p. 10.
[61] Carnwath LJ (2010) p. 10.    [62] Carnwath LJ (2010) p. 10.    [63] Carnwath LJ (2010) p. 10.
[64] Carnwath LJ (2010) para. 30.    [65] Carnwath LJ (2010) para. 26.
[66] Carnwath LJ (2010) para. 27.

later claims bereavement benefit).[67] It also has a statutory judicial review function. As Judge Wikeley explained in an early article about the Upper Tribunal:

Some judicial reviews [JR] can be started in the Administrative Appeals Chamber (indeed, the only way to challenge a First-tier Tribunal decision on criminal injuries compensation is by JR), whilst others can be transferred in, on either a mandatory or discretionary basis, from the High Court. Similarly, the Tax and Chancery Chamber can hear tax JRs, while the new Immigration and Asylum Chamber of the Upper Tribunal has a limited JR function as a result of amendments made by the Borders, Citizenship and Immigration Act 2009, designed in large part to reduce the workload of the Administrative Court.[68]

The question whether decisions of the Upper Tribunal can themselves be judicially reviewed has proved controversial. In an early ruling on this point by the Divisional Court, it was held that judicial review will only lie against the Upper Tribunal in exceptional circumstances.[69] Laws LJ, giving the judgment of the court, held that as the Upper Tribunal was 'an authoritative, impartial and independent judicial source for the interpretation and application of the relevant statutory texts', it was in effect an 'alter ego' of the High Court.[70] It was a court possessing for itself the final power to interpret for itself the law that it had to apply and the High Court could only correct it if it embarked on a decision that was clearly beyond the extent of its statutory remit or where there had been a wholly exceptional collapse of fair procedure.[71]

## Tribunal personnel

The establishment of the two new tribunals involved bringing together very large numbers of legal and non-legal tribunal personnel. Within the tribunals transferred into the new structure there were over 7,000 tribunal appointments, the majority of which (4,400) were fee-paid or non-paid part-time non-legal appointments. There were also over 2,500 fee-paid (part-time) judge appointments, as well as 447 salaried (full-time) judges and 4 salaried (full-time) non-legal members.[72]

The Tribunals, Courts and Enforcement Act 2007 introduced a number of changes affecting those working in tribunals. Section 1 of the Act enshrined in statute the guarantee of judicial independence which was conferred on the judiciary in general by s. 3 of the Constitutional Reform Act 2005. In addition, s. 4 of the 2007

---

[67] Tribunals, Courts and Enforcement Act 2007, ss. 15 and 18.

[68] N. Wikeley, 'So what Exactly *is* the Upper Tribunal?' (2010) The Reporter, Society of Legal Scholars.

[69] *The Queen (on the application of Rex, C, U, XC) v The Upper Tribunal, Special Immigration Appeals Commission* [2009] EWHC 3052. At the time of writing, this decision had been referred to the Court of Appeal.

[70] *The Queen (on the application of Rex, C, U, XC) v The Upper Tribunal, Special Immigration Appeals Commission* [2009] EWHC 3052, para. 97.

[71] *The Queen (on the application of Rex, C, U, XC) v The Upper Tribunal, Special Immigration Appeals Commission* [2009] EWHC 3052, para. 99.

[72] Carnwath LJ (2010) para. 54.

Act conferred the title of judge on the legally qualified members of the tribunals, whereas previously they had been known as the 'Chair' of the tribunal. Judges and members of the new tribunals were also required to take the oath of judicial allegiance.[73] All of these innovations could be seen as moves which might have the result of making tribunals more legalistic, and more like courts, rather than reinforcing their distinctive identity. The Senior President himself commented that 'Extending salary protection, the title of judge and the provision for taking the judicial oaths place tribunals very firmly in the judicial family.'[74] On the other hand, he has also indicated that 'As expected the title of judge has not changed the way in which tribunal judges behave or the way hearings are conducted.'[75] The extent to which the distinctive nature of tribunals will, in fact, be preserved under the new structure, remains to be seen.

## Evaluating the new structure

While it is too soon for any research to have been carried out to evaluate the effectiveness of the new tribunal structure introduced by the Tribunals, Courts and Enforcement Act 2007, there are a number of matters upon which it is possible to comment. The new structure has greatly reinforced the independence of tribunals, completely taking them away from the government departments from which their appeals arise and giving statutory protection to the independence of legal and non-legal members.[76] The routes of appeal have been greatly simplified, as opposed to the great variety of routes of appeal which existed before.[77] Another significant change, though often overlooked, has been the introduction of new sets of procedural rules for all the Chambers, with consistent overriding objectives.[78] Prior to the establishment of the new structure, many jurisdictions had out-of-date and much-amended procedural rules, which were difficult for users and their representatives to follow.[79] The introduction of the new rules has made the administration of the tribunals system more efficient, as well as clarifying procedures for users and their representatives, thus improving access to justice.

However, there are some matters which are yet to be satisfactorily resolved.[80] The new structures do not fit neatly with arrangements in the devolved jurisdictions: some Chambers are confined to England; others to England and Wales; others to Great Britain; and some to the United Kingdom.[81] There is also the continuing question of the extent to which tribunals will be able to preserve their distinctive ways of working and their specialist expertise. The implementation of the Tribunals, Courts and Enforcement Act 2007, has involved uniting a large number of people, used to working within separate tribunals, into a coherent and unified structure.

---

[73] Tribunals, Courts and Enforcement Act 2007, Sch. 2, para. 9.    [74] Carnwath LJ (2010) para. 61.
[75] Carnwath LJ (2010) para. 58.    [76] Tribunals, Courts and Enforcement Act 2007, Part 1 and s. 1.
[77] Tribunals, Courts and Enforcement Act, s. 11.    [78] Carnwath LJ (2010) para. 46.
[79] Carnwath LJ (2010) para. 53.    [80] See comments in Wikeley (2010).    [81] Wikeley (2010).

The fundamental issue underlying this task was the extent to which the new system would accommodate the special features of the former tribunals, and the specialist expertise built up by members and judges. The Senior President was clearly aware of concerns in some quarters that the new system would sweep away the individual identities and working methods of the specialist tribunals, forcing them into a homogenous whole, involving a loss of the expertise which had been built up over the lifetime of the relevant tribunal. In his first Implementation Review, the Senior President acknowledged the importance of ensuring that users, their representatives, the higher courts, and public authorities were reassured that the introduction of the new structure would bring with it 'no diminution in specialist expertise'.[82] He also said that he regarded it as important 'to seek where possible to maintain continuity of leadership within the various specialist jurisdictional groups' as this would 'help to reassure the tribunal members and users that the specialist skills and collegiate traditions of the different groups are not being sacrificed'.[83] However, concerns were raised by the Administrative Justice and Tribunals Council (which replaced the former Council on Tribunals) that under the new structure, there was a danger that some of the tribunals which adopted a particularly informal (and arguably user-friendly) approach, were becoming more legalistic. The Council commented:

We had occasion to raise early concerns with senior Tribunals Service officials about our perception of increasing formality of hearings in some jurisdictions as a consequence of hearings taking place in rooms set out as formal courtrooms...hearings in some tribunal jurisdictions, such as social security, war pensions and special educational needs, particularly lend themselves to less formal surroundings. We intend in the coming year to monitor this matter closely, not just in respect of hearing venues but also the tribunal proceedings themselves.[84]

While research has shown that it should not be assumed that informality will produce better outcomes for users, since some forms of representation generally increase applicants' chances of success, the question of the extent to which the new structure is able to preserve best practice from the previous regime, together with the unique approaches of the individual jurisdictions, remains an important one.[85]

---

[82] Carnwath LJ, *Senior President of Tribunals First Implementation Review* (2008) para. 32, available at: <http://www.tribunals.gov.uk/Tribunals/Documents/News/%5B30june%5DSPImplementationClean 7b.pdf>.

[83] Ibid. para. 26.

[84] Administrative Justice and Tribunals Council, *AJTC Annual Report 2008/9* (2009) The Stationery Office, London, ch. 3, para. 19.

[85] See Genn and Genn (1989) p. 94, which suggested that representation by lawyers significantly improved an applicant's chance of success. Leonard's 1987 survey of sex discrimination cases suggests that what is needed is representation by lawyers who are knowledgeable about the area of law (A. Leonard, *Judging Inequality: The Effectiveness of the Tribunal System in Sex Discrimination and Equal Pay Cases* (1987) Cobden Trust, London, p. 89.) See also comments in Wikeley (2010).

## CONCLUSION

In the future, it is likely that the integration of the different specialist tribunals within the new structure will increase, especially with the increased use of 'cross-ticketing' (a practice whereby judges can be flexibly deployed both within and across chambers, whatever their original expertise). The Senior President indicated in his first Implementation Review that he wished in due course to encourage interaction between the specialist groups within the new system, commenting that, 'It will be important in due course to encourage interaction between groups, and breaking down of artificial barriers, and to exploit the opportunities presented by cross-ticketing and assignment...but I see this as an evolving process.'[86] It is unclear whether such moves will enable different Chambers (or parts of Chambers) to retain their distinctive working practices. Given the great variety of tribunals involved, some of which (such as social security, war pensions, and special educational needs) are very informal in approach, it will be interesting to see whether that informality can be retained.

## FURTHER READING

CARNWATH LJ, *Senior President of Tribunals' Annual Report: Tribunals Transformed* (2010) London, Ministry of Justice.

GENN, H. and GENN, Y., *The Effectiveness of Representation in Tribunals* (1989) Lord Chancellor's Department, London.

LEGGATT, SIR A., *Tribunals for Users: One System, One Service*, Report of the Review of Tribunals by Sir Andrew Leggatt (Leggatt Review) (2001) The Stationery Office, London.

---

[86]  Carnwath LJ, *Senior President of Tribunals First Implementation Review* (2008) para. 26.

# 5

# English legal reasoning: the use of case law

## INTRODUCTION

In previous chapters we have begun to get some understanding of what 'the English legal system' might be by looking at some of its institutions. We have noted that we have relatively little information about many facets of these institutions and that this inhibits our ability to understand how they work. However, even if we were satisfied with the quality of information that we had obtained about the institutions, it is clear from our first chapter that this would be insufficient to obtain a complete understanding of 'the English legal system'. The integrated theory we outlined in the first chapter points to the need to understand the full complexity of legal processes. One thing we do not yet know is how disputes are settled within these institutions. We have some knowledge of the jurisdiction of the institutions. We know a little about the personnel who staff. As yet we know nothing about how disputes are processed. How does a dispute become a legal event? How does a dispute become a case? How does a dispute become a judgment?[1]

Analysing the processing of disputes can be done in two ways. First, we can look at the way in which conflict between two or more individuals is gradually translated into a court case and, from there, into the judgment of a court. Looking at this involves both looking at the legal rules which help effect this and also looking at the impact of the different inputs from individuals, both from within and outside the legal system. It involves asking both what is happening and in what way is that which is happening different from other ways of solving disputes? This we will do in **Chapters 10** to **17**. A second way of looking at the process by which disputes become decisions is to concentrate on what actually happens in court and, in that, to focus on what is specifically legal; that is, the process of legal argument. In looking at this, we can hope both to understand how legal decisions are generated and also what makes 'the English legal system' unique.

---

[1] In saying this, we should remain aware of the possibility that disputes that become legal events are no different, in any important way, from disputes that are settled by other means.

# The legal system as legal reasoning

It has been said that:

> a legal system is a 'closed logical system' in which correct legal decisions can be deduced
> by logical means from predetermined legal rules without reference to social aims, policies,
> moral standards...[2]

If this is true, the essence of a legal system can be said to lie in its form of reasoning. What is being said is that when judges give judgment in English courts, and when lawyers argue before these courts, they do so in a distinctive, manner. The form of speech they adopt, the ideas they find persuasive, and the manner in which they construct their arguments are all particular to the English legal system and are also general throughout that system. English legal reasoning takes the same form whether the area of law is contract law, family law, or the law of taxation. English legal reasoning remains the same whatever the change to the content of the rules. Thus, English legal reasoning can be said to be one of the ways in which English legal rules acquire their systematic character in application.

To say English legal reasoning is particular to the legal system is not to say that it has no connection with other forms of legal reasoning. There are many similarities between the approach taken by English lawyers and that taken by other lawyers within the common law legal world (broadly those countries which were once part of the British Empire). However, each jurisdiction has its own unique features. Equally, there may be similarities between common law legal reasoning and civil law or other legal forms of reasoning.[3] Nor does the above quotation argue that legal reasoning is unconnected with other forms of reasoning.[4] The point is simply that each system has its own internal coherence and that that coherence gives it a particular identity.

In this chapter and in the next one, we will look at analyses which have sought to identify the important features of English legal reasoning. At the same time, we will look at critiques of these accounts. These critiques both suggest deficiencies in traditional accounts and also suggest that English legal reasoning may neither be unique nor even specifically legal. These critiques may either be used to supplement traditional theories or to offer a radical challenge. Thus, for example, Kelman has argued that traditional accounts of common-law reasoning function as ways of protecting

---

[2] H. L. A. Hart, 'Positivism and the Separation of Law and Morals' (1958) 71 Harvard Law Review 593 at p. 602.

[3] Indeed, it would be strange to find that there were no connections between different forms of legal reasoning. Legal reasoning, whether it be common law or, for example, Islamic, is still an attempt to apply general propositions about behaviour to particular sets of facts. See further G. Samuel, *The Foundations of Legal Reasoning* (1994) Maklu, Antwerp.

[4] Again, it would be strange if it were. Legal reasoning must be understood, at least to some extent, by those who are untrained in it. On the relationship between legal reasoning and other forms of reasoning, see further G. Samuel, 'Can Legal Reasoning be Demystified?' (2009) 29 Legal Studies 181.

a hierarchical relationship between academics and students or well-established and fledgling lawyers. 'Only by creating a technical fog to obscure the true concerns [of law], concerns about which they have nothing much to say that would make them stand out, have the masters been able to make the initiates bow, scrape, and believe themselves to be deeply unfit and inferior.'[5]

## The idea of precedent

Traditionally, it has been said that the key to English legal reasoning lies in its use of precedent:

Our common law system consists in the applying to new combinations of circumstances those rules of law which we derive from legal principles and judicial precedents; ... and we are not at liberty to reject them, and to abandon all analogy to them.[6]

In looking at a new set of facts, a new dispute, English legal reasoning always demands that one first ask how previous judges would have decided the legal problem that one is now facing. One looks back to old judgments, and the legal rules, concepts, and principles found therein, and decides how they would have been applied in these new circumstances. Judges do not decide de novo. Equally, judges do not simply approach a new case on the basis of broad principles. They do not begin each case and decide what they think the law is or should be. Rather they take the law as being something that is given in what has gone before. Of course the old law was about a different situation. No two sets of facts ever recur precisely. There is always some element of change even if that element involves some relatively slight matter. In looking backwards, therefore, one looks not for past circumstances where the present case is repeated but, rather, past circumstances where one might draw a comparison between them and the present and one might say, that is what was decided in the past about that set of circumstances, therefore, in this very similar set of facts, the same thing would have been decided. One draws an analogy between the past and the present.

## The advantages and disadvantages of precedent

Law is not just a mechanism for settling disputes. It is also, more importantly, a way of avoiding disputes; of telling people how they might order their lives so that disputes can be avoided. If people are to do this, they must know what the law is; they must

---

[5]  M. Kelman, 'Trashing' (1984) 36 Stanford Law Review 293 at p. 325. Kelman's comments are couched in the context of American universities but could be equally applied in the English context.

[6]  Per Mr Justice Peake in *Mirehouse v Rennel* [1833] 1 Cl and Fin 527 at p. 546.

know how judges will settle a dispute should a matter come to court. Law must be predictable. Lawyers must be able to tell their clients how to run their affairs. Judges must be able to announce what the law will be to the world at large. One must be able to know what the law is before going to court, for this would be expensive both financially and socially. Moreover, the law must be removed from the judges. Judges must be there, not to decide cases on their own initiative, but to apply a known set of rules to the facts before them. The job of the judge must be stripped of any subjective or personal element. Law must be a system of rules not of men.[7] It has been argued that a system of precedent can be of assistance in allowing all these things to be done.

A past Lord Chancellor, Lord MacKay, has described the advantages of precedent in this way:

a scheme of precedent is clearly capable of providing important benefits. It assists litigants to assess the nature and scope of legal obligations and, to the extent that it enables them to predict the likely outcome of disputes, it restricts the scope of litigation. By allowing the vast bulk of disputes to be settled in the shadow of the law, a system of precedent prevents the legal apparatus from becoming clogged by a myriad of single instances. It reflects a basic principle of the administration of justice that like cases should be treated alike and therefore generates a range of expectations from different participants in the legal process. Rules of law based on a system of precedent are therefore likely to exhibit characteristics of certainty, consistency and uniformity.[8]

Precedent, on this argument, provides certainty, consistency, and thus a measure of clarity. People know not only what the law is but also what it will be. In principle, the ordinary person, the ordinary lawyer, the humblest judge, is in just as good a position as the judge in the highest court to look back and see what the law was and, thus, see what the law will be. However, in providing this consistency, precedent also carries with a disadvantage.

Precedent carries with it the unlikely message that those that came before us knew as much as we do now; that those in the past are good judges of what we should do in the present. One past Lord Chancellor, in a book on political philosophy, caricatured the lawyer's idea of precedent thus:

Failing all else, their last resort will be: 'This was good enough for our ancestors, and who are we to question their wisdom?' Then they'll settle back in their chairs, with an air of having

---

[7] It has long been argued that an important feature of 'the English legal system' is the fact 'no man is punished or can be lawfully made to suffer in body or goods except for a distinct breach of law established in the ordinary legal manner before the ordinary Courts of the land' (A. V. Dicey, *Introduction to the Law of the Constitution* (5th edn, 1897) Macmillan, London, p. 179). Not everyone accepts that liberal states have, in fact, reached this position. Thus, Kairys has asserted that '[o]urs is a government by people, not law. These robed people sitting behind ornate oversized desks are not controlled or bound by law; regardless of their honest self-appraisals and their pretensions, they are in the business of politics' (D. Kairys (ed.), *The Politics of Law* (rev. edn, 1990) Pantheon, New York, p. 8).

[8] Lord Mackay, 'Who Makes the Law', *The Times* (1987) 3 December. Lord Mackay was a Lord Chancellor and therefore at that time, both a member of the highest court and a minister with responsibility for appointing judges. See also Jacob LJ in *Actavis UK Ltd* v *Merk Co* [2009] 1 WLR 1186 at p 1209.

said the last word on the subject – as if it would be a major disaster for anyone to be caught being wiser than his ancestors![9]

Precedent is conservative. It favours the status quo. Precedent slows down the pace of change within a legal system.[10] In a world where things are constantly in flux, where things are always changing, and where the pace of change seems ever to increase, the very advantages of precedent can thus be a disadvantage. By making the law predictable, precedent also makes it predictable that law will be suitable for old social conditions but not for those that presently obtain. Law is certain but also certainly out-dated. Law is consistent but also consistently wrong.

For traditional theorists the solution to these problems is clear. The legislature exists to change legal rules. Parliament has the political legitimacy to amend the rules of the game. The judiciary, being unelected professionals who merely have a particular technical competence, are simply there to apply those rules which the legislature have made, or by implication, approved.

There are several problems with this account of the judge's role. One difficulty is its political naiveté. The parliamentary timetable is a crowded matter. There is not the time to debate all the legislation that a government would like to put forward in order to fulfil its own programme. There is still less time for measures which may be of great moment or importance within a narrow area of law but which is of no pressing weight for the population taken as a whole. There is almost no time at all for ideas for legislation which are not favoured by the government.[11] A second problem for this traditional account of precedent is that most people, including most judges, now accept that judges do indeed make law.[12] It is perhaps for this reason that the then Lord Chief Justice, Lord Woolf, cautioned against an over-reliance on a rigid view of precedent:

---

[9] T. More, *Utopia* (1965) Penguin, Harmondsworth, pp. 42–3. See similarly J. Swift in *Gulliver's Travels*:

  [i]t is a maxim among these lawyers, that whatever hath been done before, may legally be done again, and therefore they take special care to record all their decisions formerly made against common justice, and the general reason of mankind. These under the name of precedent, they produce as authorities to justify the most iniquitous opinions; and the judges never fail to direct accordingly. (J. Swift, *Gulliver's Travels* (1975) JM Dent, London, p. 266.)

[10] Which is not to say that it stops it altogether. In an essay published in 1939, Lord Wright wrote of the 'elasticity in the authorities' that allowed the law to advance (Lord Wright, 'The Common Law in its Old Home' in Lord Wright, *Legal Essays and Addresses* (1939) Cambridge University Press, Cambridge, pp. 341–2). See further R. Buxton, 'How the Common Law Gets Made: *Hedley Byrne* and other Cautionary Tales' (2009) 125 Law Quarterly Review 60.

[11] For an account of the pressures on the parliamentary timetable and the different time given over to government and non-government measures, see P. Norton, *The Commons in Perspective* (1981) Martin Robertson, Oxford, ch. 5. The suggestion that Parliament does not have the time to deal with precedents that have lost their value is not a new one. See, for example, Maitland's assertion that '[w]e cannot, I fear, affirm that Parliament adequately performs this scavenger's task' (F. Maitland, 'The Making of the German Civil Code' in F. Maitland, *Collected Papers* (1911) Cambridge University Press, Cambridge, vol. III, p. 487).

[12] See, for example, Sir Louis Blom-Cooper in *R v London Borough of Brent, ex parte Awua* (1993) 25 HLR 626 at p. 636: 'Judges do make laws regularly.' In this judgment, Sir Louis Blom-Cooper then goes on to cite Lord Reid's statement: 'There was a time when it was thought almost indecent to suggest that judges

The rules of precedent reflect the practice of the courts and have to be applied bearing in mind that their objective is to assist the administration of justice. They are of considerable importance because of their role in achieving the appropriate degree of certainty as to the law. This is an important requirement of any system of justice. The principles should not, however, be regarded as so rigid that they cannot develop in order to meet contemporary needs.[13]

## The problem of the concept of precedent

Contained within the bald account of the basic concept of precedent, in the quotation from *Mirehouse* v *Rennel* above, are its major problems as a theory of legal reasoning.

First, in this quotation we are told that precedent is a matter of looking back to both 'judicial precedents' (by which is meant judgments) and 'legal principles'. These are very different kinds of things. Judgments are relatively objective things. We can at least identify what a judgment is. We can agree about which physical reported case we are taking about, although, as we shall see, we may disagree about what it decided or what it means. If two people are told to look to past judgments, there is a reasonable expectation that, if they are diligent, they will both find the same material. Legal principles are less clear.[14]

A legal principle is not simply what was decided or found in a particular case. It is an idea which runs through a whole series of cases and, perhaps, across many different areas of law. It is a general statement about behaviour. Dworkin argues that the distinction between legal rules and legal principles is a logical one which goes to their very essence.[15] Legal rules are applicable in an all-or-nothing manner whilst principles have weight. If a legal rule says you should not murder that is an end to the matter.[16] With a principle it is not simply a question of whether or not a principle applies but, rather, a question of how important it is in a particular situation. An example of a legal principle is the statement that 'no person can benefit from their own wrong'. From this general principle English law deduces the particular rule that a person who

make law – they only declare it.... But we do not believe in fairy tales any more... for better or worse judges do make law' (at p. 637). For Lord Reid's reflections on the limits to legitimate judicial law-making, see Lord Reid, 'The Judge as Law Maker' (1972) 12 Journal of the Society of Public Teachers of Law 22.

[13]  *R* v *Simpson* [2003] 3 All ER 531 at p. 538.

[14]  Some writers have asserted that the distinction between a legal rule and a legal principle is 'too vague to be of much significance' (A. Simpson, 'The *Ratio Decidendi* of a Case' (1957) 20 Modern Law Review 413 at p. 414).

[15]  For a statement of these arguments, see R. Dworkin, *Taking Rights Seriously* (1977) Duckworth, London, pp. 22–8.

[16]  Although, of course, there will be much argument as to what act of killing constitutes 'murder'.

is a beneficiary under a will cannot inherit if they murder the testator.[17] Yet we cannot say that in every situation the English courts prevent a person benefiting, directly or indirectly, from their wrong. Were we to argue this, we would be arguing that English courts are courts of morals simply deciding who has acted unfairly and rectifying that unfairness.[18]

Legal principles are, by their very nature, less clear than rules. We cannot be certain of the content of a legal principle. We cannot be certain where we will find it. We cannot be certain how it will be applied. And yet legal principles, themselves uncertain, are one of the two sources of precedent: something which we are told will bring the law certainty.

A second difficulty in the very idea of precedent which we find in the quotation from *Mirehouse* v *Rinnel* above is that we are told, in applying precedent, to take that which has gone before and apply it by a process of analogy. Analogy means comparing two or more things and seeing they are the same in important respects though they be very different in other less important matters. But deciding what is important is something which seems inherently subjective. What is important to me may not be important to you:

The whole point of argument by analogy in law is that a rule can contribute to a decision on facts to which it is not directly applicable; cases of 'competing analogies' involve rules pulling in different directions over debatable land between.[19]

Precedent is not a way for us to decide what the law should be. It is a way for us to decide what the law is, or, alternatively, for us to decide what judges will say that the law is. If analogy involves arguments that are 'debatable', how are we to decide what will be important for a judge? How does analogy provide consistency in deciding what is important? How does a theory of precedent tell us which cases in the past we should use?

This problem is answered in very different ways by traditional theorists of precedent and by more modern writers who have been heavily influenced by accounts of linguistics and the philosophy of language. For traditional theorists, the point about precedent was that it gave you a series of rules which, at least in the vast majority of cases, would lead to everyone knowing which part of which cases should be applied in the future.[20] For more modern writers, the problem is more complicated.

One analyst has begun by suggesting '[i]n order to understand what one has read [and one might add apply what one has read], one must be able to recognise what

---

[17] *Cleaver* v *Mutual Reserve Fund Life Association* [1892] 1 QB 147.

[18] For some reflections on the possible limitations to this principle, see J. Chadwick, 'A Testator's Bounty to his Slayer' (1914) 30 Law Quarterly Review 211. Goodhart raises the query whether this principle covers a beneficiary whose negligent driving kills the testator (A. Goodhart, *Essays in Jurisprudence and Common Law* (1931) Cambridge University Press, Cambridge, p. 7).

[19] N. MacCormick, *Legal Rules and Legal Reasoning* (1978) Clarendon Press, Oxford, p. 155.

[20] Hart's 'logical system' noted above.

is significant in the text, and what is trivial'.[21] However, he has gone on to observe, notions of what is trivial and what is important are determined not just by some kind of inherent value in the thing that one has read or by an understanding of technical 'legal' words but, rather, by one's subjective reactions which, in turn, result, in large part, from the group from which one comes. In looking at a car-crash, artists and lawyers see different things as being important and trivial. Artists are concerned with the scene's graphic possibilities; lawyers with questions of blame. To the extent that one's subjective reaction results from the group from which one comes, those reactions are predictable. They will be the same, or similar, to other members of the group. Thus, if you are part of a group of lawyers, what you will see as important and what you will see as trivial in past judgments will be the same or similar to the choices made by other lawyers.[22]

Two points need to be made about these modern accounts. First, these arguments supplement traditional theories. They do not replace them. The new approaches considerably change the significance of old accounts. Traditional accounts had purported to be the whole, or almost the whole, explanation of the nature of English legal reasoning.[23] More modern accounts stress the need to place discussion of the rules and principles of precedent in the social context wherein that reasoning takes place. Second, descriptions of legal reasoning, which suggest that we need to take account of the nature of the group of people doing the reasoning, are similar to arguments in other academic and professional areas, which suggest that the kind of reasoning used is partially constructed by the dynamics of the group of people who do the reasoning. Thus, for example, the American poet and critic, J. V. Cunningham, writing for a friend who is being examined for a doctorate in English, asks:

> After these years of lectures heard,
> Of papers read, of hopes deferred,
> Of days spent in the dark stacks

---

[21]  M. Davies, 'Reading Cases' (1987) 50 Modern Law Review 409 at p. 409.

[22]  Thus, Kennedy argues that a student's experience of being in a law school is both an experience of learning a new language and a process of being socialized into a particular way of seeing the world (D. Kennedy, 'Legal Education as Training for Hierarchy' in D. Kairys (ed.), *The Politics of Law* (1990) Pantheon, New York).

[23]  Some writers have argued that traditional accounts of legal reasoning have never pretended to be complete accounts. Thus, for example, Farrar and Dugdale comment that such accounts have never 'purported to provide a scientific route to the truth' (J. Farrar and A. Dugdale, *Introduction to Legal Method* (3rd edn, 1990) Sweet & Maxwell, London, p. 82). It is true that some traditional theorists have been aware of the shortcomings of their own theories, though they have not been able to remedy these failings. However, it is less clear that they have realized the full implications of these problems. Thus, for example, Cross stated that he could not provide a formula for determining the ratio decidendi of a case (R. Cross, *Precedent in English Law* (3rd edn, 1977) Clarendon Press, Oxford, p. 76). However, despite this and other acknowledged limitations to his analysis he continued to maintain that '[t]he peculiar feature of the English doctrine of precedent is its strongly coercive nature' (Cross (1977) p. 4). Moreover, other writers do appear to believe that a scientific form of precedent exists enabling us to deduce the law from a simple reading of cases (see, for example, J. C. Smith, *The Law of Contract* (1989) Sweet & Maxwell, London, p. v).

> In learning the impervious facts
> So well you can dispense with them,
> Now that the final day has come
> When you shall name the date
> Where fool and scholar judge your fate
> What have you gained?

and answers:

> ... you have learned, not what to say,
> But how the saying must be said.[24]

The point he makes is that that which is learnt is not a set of facts but a method of articulating arguments that will be convincing to a particular group. Thus it is with English legal reasoning. That which is learnt in learning English legal reasoning is not simply a set of rules and principles but also a set of social responses suitable for a certain body of people.

In his lectures to first-year law students, Karl Llewellyn argued that only total immersion would enable students to understand the language of law. The published version of his lectures begins with the fairy story of the man who throws himself into a bramble bush losing his sight and then throws himself in again and so regains his sight. 'The life of the words is in the using of them', argues Llewllyn.[25] In becoming lost in using them when they are new to us so, he argued, we begin to understand them.

In learning these responses, one learns not just what particular words mean:

the legal significance of the text does not depend solely on the presence or absence of recognisably 'legal' words. It is not an understanding of the words 'appellant' and 'respondent' that separates the legal reader's understanding...from those of his or her non-legal colleagues. Rather it seems to be the ability to recognise certain combinations of words, whether 'ordinary' or 'legal' as having some significance other than that which is immediately apparent as their surface meaning.[26]

In learning, in the hackneyed phrase, to 'think like a lawyer' (or perhaps more pertinently speak and write like a lawyer) one has to become a 'native speaker'; not merely conversant with the language but able to sound as though it is one's first language. One learns to listen to the way in which things are said:

> I listen to you speak, hear only tone;
> I feel the weight of words, not what they mean.[27]

---

[24] J. V. Cunningham, 'To a Friend, on her Examination for the Doctorate in English' in J. V. Cunningham, *The Poems of J.V. Cunningham*, edited and with an introduction by Timothy Steele (1997) Swallow Press Ohio University Press Athens, Press, Athens.

[25] K. Llewellyn, *The Bramble Bush* (1960) Oceana Publications, New York, p. 41.

[26] Davies (1987) p. 415.

[27] Neil Powell, 'Soliloquy' in *A Season of Calm Weather* (1982) Carcanet New Press, Manchester.

## The present system of precedent

Precedent is a concept; the form of legal reasoning to be found in 'the English legal system' at present is one system of precedent. All systems of precedents have the general feature of incorporating the necessity of taking into account previous legal opinions. However, each system has its own individual characteristics. Traditional accounts of precedent regard the present English system as being comparatively rigid.[28] By this, theorists mean that the present system provides for a comparatively high degree of control over the courts; that judges have relatively little discretion in their decision-making.

Precedent works as a way of controlling judges' behaviour. Precedent dictates or at least influences decisions. It says to a judge, this case must be decided or should be decided in this way. By doing that, it enables a lawyer to predict the movement of the law. However, the current system of precedent does not simply involve looking back to every previous analogous case.

## Ratio and obiter

At the Common Law not every opinion expressed by a judge forms a Judicial Precedent. In order that an option may have the weight of a precedent, two things must concur: it must be, in the first place, an opinion given by a judge, and, in the second place, it must be an opinion the formation of which is necessary for the decision of the particular case, in other words, it must not be obiter dictum.[29]

Traditional accounts of precedent distinguish between that which is ratio decidendi, an opinion which is necessary for the decision in the case, and that which is obiter dictum, remarks in a judgment which are made merely in passing. It is the ratio that binds the future court.[30] Ratio is that which another court is obligated to follow. Those parts of a previous judgment which are obiter dictum are not binding on any court though they will be of persuasive value.[31]

It is, in part, the notion of ratio which gives the current English system of precedent its relatively strict character. Being required to look to previous cases for your ideas of how to deal with a new case is in itself something which reduces the range

---

[28] Cross (1977) p. 4.    [29] Professor John Chipman Gray quoted in Goodhart (1931) p. 1.

[30] Not every case has a ratio. For example, a case which is heard in a multi-judge court like the Court of Appeal or Supreme Court may have a number of judgments which reach the same conclusion as to who wins and who loses by different routes. Jacob LJ has recently observed that, although judges try to articulate a ratio when they write their judgments, they do not always succeed (*Actavis UK Ltd* v *Merk & Co* [2009] 1 WLR 1186 at p. 1209).

[31] N. MacCormick, 'Why Cases have Rationes and what these are' in L. Goldstein (ed.), *Precedent in Law* (1987) Clarendon Press, Oxford, p. 157.

of options which is open to a judge. However, this restriction is something which is in itself limited. As cases grow so the range of decisions grow. If judges can pick and choose amongst different previous decisions, and amongst different parts of different decisions, then a skilful and knowledgeable judge (or lawyer) will find it easier and easier to find previous judgments which justify any decision they wish to arrive at. It becomes just a matter of finding a useful quotation which will seem to rationalize the argument that the judge wishes to make.

The use of ratio calls for a much more precise use of previous cases. Ratio requires lawyers to analyse past cases, not for arguments which we may find useful, but, rather, for them to look at past cases for lines of reasoning which are binding. At the same time, ratio tells us that parts of past cases, perhaps large parts of past cases, are merely obiter and therefore not binding in precedent at all.

Yet, traditional accounts complicate the system of precedent for, at the same time as emphasizing the importance of ratio, traditional accounts of ratio also note that:

[i]t is a truism…that dicta [obiter] are of varying degrees of persuasiveness…Dicta of the highest degree of persuasiveness may often, for all practical purposes, be indistinguishable from pronouncements which must be treated as ratio.[32]

To say that obiter remarks still have some importance, even though they are not binding, would not be incompatible with arguing for the overriding significance of ratio. Where no ratio exists, where upon a particular point there is no existing line of binding legal reasoning, one might expect the courts to turn to obiter statements. One might say 'obiter [is]…something of less force than a rule but…might be worth following'.[33] The courts are then continuing to use precedent but in the looser sense of simply looking back at past decisions for ideas about how the new case might be decided. A degree of consistency in decision-making is still preserved even though the new court may not choose to follow every previous obiter decision. However, to say that obiter remarks can be so persuasive as to be indistinguishable from ratio is much more troubling.

There is in the traditional theory of precedent an inherent conceptual difference between the importance of ratio and the significance of obiter. Ratio is important because of its obligatory character. Courts must follow a ratio whether they agree with it or not. For courts rationes are like the law of theft. One may not agree with the law of theft, one may feel like Proudhon that it is property that is theft, but legally one is obliged not to steal. The law of theft does not require agreement, merely acquiescence. Obiter statements, however, are worthy of consideration first because they have been made by judges within the same system. If consistency is a virtue for a legal system it is worthwhile seeing whether there is good reason for departing from arguments which have previously been used. Second, obiter statements are in themselves reflections on the law. A new decision is improved the more judges have the benefit of previous

---

[32] Cross (1977) p. 81.    [33] Farrar and Dugdale (1990) p. 96.

argument before determining which side to find for in the case before them. Obiter statements are in this sense commentaries on the law. Like the work of academic lawyers, they may convince others by their logic or their rhetoric that they offer the most plausible account of the law. Obiter judgments are, amongst other things, capable of being persuasive in the same manner that anyone's arguments can be persuasive. But if this is the sense of persuasive, how can one ever say an obiter remark can be likened to a ratio?

There are two possible ways of explaining the powerful effects of obiter which are consistent with the traditional divide between ratio and obiter. One is to say that obiter remarks from higher courts reflect the way in which that court is reasoning. Thus, for a lower court, these remarks must be treated as though they were ratio because, should the case before them be taken on appeal, that is the way in which the case will be decided by the higher court. On this account, treating some obiter statements as ratio is merely a way of reducing the quantity of litigation within a legal system by forestalling the possibility of appeal. Second, one might argue that the higher the court in the legal system the more experienced and the more able the judge. It may be sensible to treat the arguments of judges of great learning as though they were ratio because, in fact, they are always likely to be very persuasive.[34] Both these arguments have some merit in them. Both, however, are only partial accounts of the problem, both are only limited explanations. First, to treat obiter remarks as binding because they represent the view of an appellate court is to forget that, if the remarks are obiter, they concern things that have not been central to the decision made by the court. They, thus, refer to matters upon which the court has not heard complete argument. In an adversarial system courts may make different decisions when they have heard longer arguments. Obiter remarks may be a clue to how higher courts will decide cases in the future but they are neither unambiguous or determinant in their meaning. Second, to argue that judges in higher courts are more learned and therefore their words are likely to be more persuasive may accord with their own view of themselves. However, this view raises a number of problems. Plainly judges in higher courts cannot all be uniformly able. Nor can they all be equally able about all areas of law. Some courts see some types of law but rarely and their pronouncements on such areas when they do see them may be of a low standard.[35] Even able judges writing in areas that they are familiar with

34  In *WB Anderson & Sons v Rhodes* [1967] 2 All ER 850 at p. 857, Cairns J stated that '[w]hen all five members of the House of Lords have all said, after close examination of the authorities, that a certain type of tort exists, I think that judge of first instance should proceed on the basis that it does exist...'. This statement could be taken to reflect either or both of these two arguments.

35  Thus, for example, in an article on *Anderton v Ryan* [1985] 1 AC 560, a criminal law case decided in the House of Lords, Professor Glanville Williams wrote:

the tale I have to tell is unflattering of the higher judiciary. It is an account of how judges invented a rule based upon a conceptual misunderstanding; of their determination to use the English language so strangely that they spoke what by normal criteria would be termed untruths; of their invincible ignorance of the mess they had made of the law; and of their immobility on the subject, carried to the extent of subverting an Act of Parliament designed to put them straight. (G. Williams, 'The Lords

may make mistakes. Expertise in a writer can alert a reader to the probability that the writer is expressing a view that is accurate. It can never tell the reader the view is correct. Only the internal reasoning of the writer's argument can do that.

Whilst neither argument above provides a compelling reason for treating obiter as though it were ratio the traditional injunction to do so in some cases reflects an important point in the actual application of the theory of precedent. Whilst traditional theories of precedent hinge on the importance of ratio, in practice judges and lawyers make a very heavy use of obiter remarks in their arguments.[36] One question which will recur in the following pages is whether this heavy use of obiter is wholly consistent with traditional accounts of English legal reasoning.

## Finding the ratio

There have been many different explanations which have sought to show how rationes are to be distinguished from other parts of a judgment. This proliferation of competing explanations is, in itself, a strange feature of traditional accounts of English legal reasoning. If precedent is about the search for certainty and consistency, and if the use of rationes is the way in which the present system of precedent provides a comparative degree of strictness, then it seems troubling that neither academics nor judges can provide any clear account of how rationes are to be found. If you were one of a group of students and, in trying to ascertain the circumference of a circle, you were not told the correct formula to use but, rather, were told that there was no agreement about the correct formula, you would not expect your group to agree about the size of the circumference. Yet, it has been said by one of the foremost theorists of precedent that '[i]t is almost impossible to devise a formula for determining the *ratio decidendi* of a case...'.[37] Indeed, the matter goes further. What we mean precisely by the term 'ratio decidendi' remains a matter of dispute. Goodhart described the

and Impossible Attempts, or Quis Custodiet Ipsos Custodes?' (1986) 45 Cambridge Law Journal 33 at p. 33.)

In a survey of cases decided in the House of Lords in 1979, Murphy and Rawlings noted that 5 of the 58 cases were criminal law cases (W. Murphy and R. Rawlings, 'After the Ancien Regime: The Writing of Judgments in the House of Lords 1979/80' (1981) 44 Modern Law Review 617 at p. 617). In a subsequent judgment of the House of Lords, *R. v Shivpuri* [1986] 2 All ER 334, which reversed *Anderton* v *Ryan*, Lord Bridge said of Williams' article '[t]he language is not conspicuous for its moderation, but it would be foolish...not to recognise the force of the criticism' (*R. v Shivpuri* [1986] 2 All ER 334 at p. 345).

[36] Thus, for example, for many years the English law of negligence hinged upon an obiter doctrine, Lord Atkin's neighbour principle, annunciated in a Scottish case (*Donoghue* v *Stevenson* [1932] AC 562 at p. 580). Markesenis and Deakin wrote of this principle '[i]ts status is at best that of a guide-line of general principle; in no sense is it a formula which can be mechanically applied' (B. Markesinis and S. Deakin, *Tort Law* (3rd edn, 1994) Clarendon Press, Oxford, p. 67). Some judges have argued that there is too heavy a use of obiter remarks in legal argument (see, for example, Wright (1939) p. 345).    [37] Cross (1977) p. 76.

term as 'the most misleading expression in English law'.[38] Writing in 1957, Montrose distinguished between 'classical' and other uses of the term ratio.[39] More recently, Andrews has suggested that there are four possible definitions of the term ratio.[40] Others have even suggested that 'it is a mistake to seek...a prescriptive definition of the concept of *ratio decidendi*'.[41]

Each account of how to find a ratio offers its own problems. By looking at one account we can see the general kind of difficulties that are raised. Goodhart's description of the ratio and how to find it is especially worth looking at for two reasons. First, Goodhart's account is not only developed by the author and defended by him at length.[42] It is also analysed by Cross in his leading monograph on precedent.[43] Second, in his book on judges in the House of Lords, Paterson notes that Cross and Goodhart are two of the very few academics whose work was said to interest the judiciary.[44] Neither of these two facts mean that Goodhart's account of how to find a ratio is in fact correct. They do, however, suggest that his work might be instructive.[45]

Goodhart begins by distinguishing the search for a ratio in a case from the attempt to find the logic in a judgment. 'The logic of the argument, the analysis of prior cases, the statement of the historical background may all be demonstrably incorrect in a judgment, but the case remains a precedent nonetheless.'[46] Each reported case, no matter how wrong, is a precedent. For Goodhart, '[t]o determine the principle [the ratio] of a case the first and most essential step is...to determine what were the material facts on which the judge based his conclusion'.[47] Upon its face, this may seem a strange starting point. Ratios are, after all, essentially reasons even though they may be bad or illogical reasons. The distinction between a reason and a fact is one which seems clear. However, common law legal reasoning is always reasoning about something; it is never reasoning about an abstract concept. Ratios are statements of reasons about the law in relation to a particular set of facts. It is therefore with these facts that Goodhart begins. Since rationes concern the law as the judge sees it '[w]e are bound by the judge's statement of facts even though it is patent that he has misstated them'.[48] The facts we

---

[38] '[W]ith the possible exception of malice...' (Goodhart (1931) p. 2).

[39] J. Montrose, 'Ratio Decidendi and the House of Lords' (1957a) 20 Modern Law Review 124 at p. 124.

[40] N. Andrews, 'Reporting Case Law: Unreported Cases, the Definition of a Ratio and the Criteria for Reporting Decisions' (1985) 5 Legal Studies 205 at pp. 209–14.    [41] Farrar and Dugdale (1990) p. 94.

[42] Goodhart (1931) ch. 1; A. Goodhart, 'The Ratio Decidendi of a Case' (1959) 22 Modern Law Review 117.

[43] Cross (1977) pp. 66–76. This passage is retained in the most recent edition of this work edited by Cross and Harris (R. Cross and J. Harris, *Precedent in English Law* (1991) Clarendon Press, Oxford, pp. 63–72).

[44] A. Paterson, *The Law Lords* (1982) Macmillan, London, p. 19.

[45] Goodhart's analysis is not accepted by everyone. Montrose and Simpson, in an interchange of opposing views on the nature of the ratio, are agreed in finding Goodhart's analysis unsatisfactory (see Montrose (1957a); Simpson (1957); J. Montrose, 'The *Ratio Decidendi* of a Case' (1957b) 20 Modern Law Review 587; and A. Simpson, 'The *Ratio Decidendi* of a Case' (1958) 21 Modern Law Review 155). Similarly, Stone has argued that the assumptions underlying Goodhart's theory are unacceptable (J. Stone, 'The *Ratio* of the *Ratio Decidendi*' (1959) 22 Modern Law Review 597 at pp. 603–10). Andrews also finds fault in Goodhart's thesis (Andrews (1985) particularly at pp. 210–11). However, were we to write only about an approach that had universal, or even large-scale, acceptance we would have to be silent.    [46] Goodhart (1931) p. 2.

[47] Goodhart (1931) p. 10.    [48] Goodhart (1931) p. 12.

are searching for are the facts in the case not the facts in the real world. The judge might have decided the case differently had he or she known that the facts stated were incorrect but the search for a ratio is about looking for the law as it was stated in a case not as it might have been stated.

Goodhart's phrase 'material facts' is an important part of his theory of how to identify a ratio. Not all facts in a case are 'material facts'. 'Too often the cautious judge will include in his opinion facts which are not essential to his judgement, leaving it for future generations to determine whether or not these facts constitute a part of the ratio decidendi.'[49] The reader must identify those facts in a case which are material and discount those which are immaterial. Facts are material when they are vital to the legal decision, immaterial when they are irrelevant. If the alteration of a factual detail would make a difference to the conclusion in the case, then that fact is material. However, the reader is bound by the opinion of the judge if that opinion is stated. '[A]ll the facts which the court specifically states are material must be considered material.'[50]

Goodhart suggests some basic principles for deciding whether or not facts are material:

[T]he facts of person, time, place, kind and amount are presumably immaterial ... [A]ll the facts which the court impliedly treats as immaterial must be considered immaterial ... If the opinion does not distinguish between material and immaterial facts, then all the facts set forth in the opinion must be considered material with the exception of those that on their face are immaterial. There is a presumption against wide principles of law, and the smaller the number of material facts in a case the wider the principle will be ... [If there are multiple judgments in a case] the principle is limited to the sum of all the facts held material by the various judges.[51]

Once the material and immaterial facts in a case, as seen by the court, have been established, the ratio of the case is the conclusion to the case based on the material facts.[52] Having found the ratio we are then in a position to apply it:

[T]he final step is to determine whether or not it is a binding precedent for some succeeding case in which the facts are prima facie similar. This involves a double analysis. We must first state the material facts in the precedent case and then attempt to find the material ones in the second one. If these are identical, then the first case is a binding precedent for the second, and the court must reach the same conclusion as it did in the first one.[53]

What is surprising about Goodhart's method of finding a ratio is not what it says but what it remains silent about. Many of the steps suggested by Goodhart raise the question of whether the theory can be said to be a complete explanation of legal reasoning given the number of questions unanswered. Thus, for example, in assessing the utility of the suggestions for how to determine what are the material facts in the case it is

---

[49]  Goodhart (1931) p. 15.    [50]  Goodhart (1931) p. 20.    [51]  Goodhart (1931) pp. 16–17.
[52]  Goodhart (1931) p. 22.    [53]  Goodhart (1931) pp. 23–4.

necessary to remind ourselves of the function and advantages of precedent. Precedent is there to guide and control judicial decision-making. It is a way of providing certainty in the law by making sure everyone will make the same decisions about new cases. It is a way of providing predictability in the law by allowing others to anticipate what a judge's decision will be before they have arrived at it. In this context, several of Goodhart's suggestions are problematic. In criticizing Goodhart's theory, Stone has argued that one of the central theses of the theory is the notion of the material fact but 'there will often be the gravest doubt as to what facts the precedent court "explicitly or implicitly" "determined" to be material'.[54] If we cannot know, with certainty, what a material fact is, how, when this lies at the centre of Goodhart's thesis, are we to use the method? Similarly, there is a presumption that something like the identity of the party to the case is not a material fact. But presumptions are rebuttable. When is this presumption not to be followed? On this, Goodhart is silent. Facts set forth in the judge's opinion are material with the exception of those 'that on their face are immaterial'. How does one recognize a fact that is on its face immaterial? How does one know that others will make the same judgment? How does one know that judges will make the same decision? Again, on this matter Goodhart is silent. As a predicative tool, Goodhart's theory seems deficient.[55] It exemplifies Cross's statement that there is no formula for finding a ratio and showing what problems that brings.[56]

In seeking to provide a cure for the deficiencies in Goodhart's approach to finding a ratio, two broad approaches might be suggested. The first would be to provide a more precise theory which would tell the reader when, for example, a fact presumed immaterial was in fact material or what exactly was meant by a fact 'immaterial on its face'. This approach would be to say that the broad picture painted by Goodhart was essentially correct but that what was needed was more detailed brush-work, using the same style, to fill in the minutiae. A completely different approach would be to say that the problems seen in Goodhart's suggestions, when viewed in the context of the general difficulties in the general concept of precedent noted above, suggests that this approach to legal reasoning, at least if taken as a complete explanation, is fundamentally flawed.[57]

---

[54] Stone (1959) p. 605.    [55] Which is not to say that it has no merit or no advantage.

[56] There are other criticisms to be made of the theory which if accurate point not to its limitations but, rather, to the fact that it might be wholly misdirected. A particular problem is arguably the strong emphasis that Goodhart gives to the importance of facts in finding a ratio. This emphasis has the advantage of making the process potentially more objective but it runs the risk of being inaccurate as a description of what courts do and what courts say they do. It devalues, perhaps to too great an extent, the importance of reasoning in the process of reaching a conclusion in a judgment (see Cross (1977) pp. 70–6).

[57] A third approach would be to select some other theory of the ratio constructed in terms of traditional theories of precedent.

# The hierarchy of courts

Precedent is not just about identifying a ratio. It also involves consideration of the status of the court. Precedent is a broadly hierarchical system, with courts being bound by the courts above them. Thus, the Supreme Court, formerly the House of Lords, is the highest court. Its rulings are binding on all courts below it, including the Court of Appeal.[58] However, the Supreme Court is not bound to follow its own previous rulings. In 1966, the House of Lords, as it then was, issued a practice statement saying that it would depart from its own previous decisions in cases where it 'appeared right to do so'.[59] This power to depart from its own previous decisions was not used lightly by the House of Lords. The practice statement notes the importance of precedent in providing certainty. The statement also emphasizes the need for the House to consider the retrospective nature of any failure to stand by its own previous decisions. Those who have based their actions on the law as annunciated in House of Lords and Supreme Court decisions, are likely to be aggrieved if a subsequent decision sets aside past law. In his analysis of the House of Lords, Paterson argues that the House made very sparing use of their new power in the period between 1966 and 1980.[60] This continues to be the case, with there being no suggestion that the Supreme Court will behave differently. However, there can be striking exceptions. The decision to depart from the judgment in *Anderton* v *Ryan* came only 11 months after the decision had been made.[61]

The Court of Appeal's position in the hierarchy of the courts is somewhat equivocal. In *Young* v *Bristol Aeroplane Co. Ltd*, the Court of Appeal laid down the general rule that it was bound by its own previous decisions.[62] This rule was subject to a limited number of exceptions. Where the court was faced with conflicting previous decisions, it would have to choose between them. If a decision was made per incuriam, it need not be followed. Finally, where a subsequent decision of the House of Lords could not stand with a previous decision of the Court of Appeal, even though the House of Lords had not explicitly overruled it, a new Court of Appeal need not follow it.[63]

---

[58] Per Lord Diplock in *Davies* v *Johnson* [1979] AC 264 at p. 328. See also Lord Hailsham in *Broome* v *Cassell* [1972] AC 1027 at p. 1054 and Lord Denning in *Gallie* v *Lee* [1969] 2 Ch 17 at p. 37. It is decisions of the Supreme Court that are binding, not, technically, decisions of the Privy Council. Thus, in the High Court Diplock J was free not to follow the Privy Council decision of *Lord Strathcona Steamship Co. Ltd* v *Dominion Coal Co. Ltd* [1926] AC 108 (*Port Line Ltd* v *Ben Steamers Ltd* [1958] 2 QB 146). Diplock J did, however, say that the composition of the court in the *Strathcona* case was 'entitled to respect which in a common lawyer borders upon awe' (p. 165).                                                    [59] [1966] 3 All ER 77.

[60] Paterson (1982) pp. 162–6.

[61] *Anderton* v *Ryan* [1985] 1 AC 560; *R* v *Shivpuri* [1986] 2 All ER 334. On the way in which the House of Lords' power to overrule itself ought to be used see B. Harris, 'Final Appellate Courts Overruling their Own "Wrong" Precedents: The Ongoing Search for Principle' (2002) 118 Law Quarterly Review 408.

[62] [1944] KB 718.

[63] In *Limb* v *Union Jack Removals Ltd*, the Court of Appeal re-emphasized the importance of it not departing from it own previous decisions ([1998] 1 WLR 1354 at p. 1364). See, however, Lord Woolf's comments in *R* v *Simpson* [2003] 3 All ER 531 at p. 538.

Read literally, the potential scope of the exceptions to the rule in *Young* v *Bristol Aeroplane Co. Ltd* was such as to cast the very rule in doubt. The per incuriam exception in itself could be read as putting the foundations of the doctrine of precedent at risk. The rule, briefly stated, holds that where a decision is made without taking account of some statutory or other authority binding on the court the decision can be discounted. The problem that this raises is that virtually any decision can be discounted if all that is required is evidence of some failure to cite some authority. The wealth of previous case law means that only a small percentage is ever cited in court. For this reason, the per incuriam rule has usually been strictly interpreted.[64] Courts have consistently limited the doctrine to cases where citing a relevant authority would, not might, have resulted in a different conclusion to the case.[65] However, at the same time, other exceptions to the rule have been found. In *Boys* v *Chaplin*, it was held that a decision made in an interlocutory hearing would not be binding upon a subsequent Court of Appeal.[66] In *Rickards* v *Rickards*, it was held that a decision involving a 'manifest error' need not be followed.[67] This process of adding exceptions to the general rule continues to the present day. In *Acatvis UK Ltd* v *Merk & Co*, the Court of Appeal ruled that it was not bound by its own previous decisions where they were incompatible with what had become the 'settled view' of the European Patent Office Boards of Appeal on a matter relating to European patent law.[68] By 1979, Lord Denning felt that exceptions were 'in the process of eating up the rule itself' and he suggested that the court no longer regard itself as being bound by its own previous decisions.[69]

We have already discussed the merits of the view that the Court of Appeal should feel free to depart from its own previous decisions.[70] What is more important here is the question of the status of precedent that is raised in this case. Lord Denning had argued that rules about precedent were not rules of law but rules of practice laid down by a court for its own use. As evidence for this, he cited the fact that the House of Lords had prior to the 1966 practice statement been bound by its own previous decisions.[71] If the House of Lords had the power to change its own practice, if it was not bound by a rule of law decided in 1898, it must logically follow that the Court of Appeal, and indeed any other court, could change its practice. This view had implicit support in the House of Lords. Lord Salmon pointed out that the significant difference between the 1966 practice statement and Lord Denning's arguments in *Davies* v *Johnson* was the fact that the practice statement had the agreement of all the Law

---

[64] According to Evershed MR, per incuriam cases must be 'of the rarest occurrence' (*Morelle Ltd* v *Wakeling* [1955] 2 QB 379 at p. 406).          [65] *Morelle Ltd* v *Wakeling* [1955] 2 QB 379 at p. 406.

[66] [1968] 2 QB 1.

[67] [1989] 3 All ER 193. The Criminal Division of the Court of Appeal had already made a similar pronouncement in *R* v *Gould* [1968] 2 QB 65.

[68] [2009] 1 WLR 1186 at p. 1215. In *National Westminster Bank plc* v *Spectrum Plus Ltd and other* [2004] EWCA Civ 570, Lord Phillips suggested, at para. 58, that it was not open to the Court of Appeal to expand the list of exceptions to the rule created in *Young* v *Bristol Aeroplane Company*.

[69] Per Lord Denning in *Davies* v *Johnson* [1979] AC 264 at p. 283. He had made a similar suggestion ten years before in *Gallie* v *Lee* [1969] 2 Ch 17 at p. 37.          [70] See pp. 51–3.

[71] *London Street Tramways Co. Ltd* v *London County Council* [1898] AC 375.

Lords, whereas Lord Denning's view was a minority one, at the time, even within the Court of Appeal.[72] However, the majority of the House of Lords rejected the argument, instead insisting on the legitimate authority of the House of Lords in applying its view of precedent to the Court of Appeal.[73] Subsequent academic opinion has not followed the House of Lords, with the majority uneasy about the inherent logic of the view being espoused by the House of Lords.[74] However, if precedent is merely a matter of practice it does make it potentially more unstable than would be the case if it was a rule of law. Changes in culture in courts have the potential to change precedent itself.

The position of the High Court is clearer than that of the Court of Appeal. Judges in the High Court are not bound to follow decisions of other judges in the same court though they will tend to do so 'as a matter of judicial comity'.[75] Thus, though judges in the High Court recognize the importance of the coherence and certainty which is achieved if they follow each other's decisions, there may be clear conflict with opposing decisions being made by different judges. Judges in the High Court are, however, bound by decisions of a Divisional Court.[76]

## Using precedents

We have now described the broad technical features of the present English system of precedent. The next step is to see how these features are used in practice. How do they contribute to the process of legal reasoning that results in judgments in individual cases?

The use of ratios, and the use of precedent generally, is just as puzzling as is identifying a ratio. One much-cited passage about the use of precedent was written by Lord Halsbury: 'A case is only authority for what it actually decides. I entirely deny that it

---

[72] *Davies* v *Johnson* [1979] AC 264 at p. 344. The fact that there are now 43 judges who sit in the Court of Appeal makes universal agreement on any major change of practice unlikely.

[73] Other judgments in the House of Lords have also supported this view. Perhaps the clearest is Lord Simon of Glaisdale's statement that 'it is clear law that the Court of Appeal is bound … by a previous decision of the Court of Appeal itself' (*Miliangos* v *Frank (Textiles) Ltd* [1976] AC 443 at p. 470). However, in a later case, *Attorney-General* v *Reynolds*, Lord Salmon stated that House of Lords decisions about precedent in the Court of Appeal were only of persuasive authority ([1980] AC 637 at p. 659). In *National Westminster Bank plc* v *Spectrum Plus Ltd and other* [2004] EWCA Civ 570, Lord Phillips, citing the House of Lords judgments in *Davies* v *Johnson*, restated the view that the Court of Appeal was bound by the rule laid down in *Young* v *Bristol Aeroplane Company*.

[74] See Paterson (1982) at p. 152, where he lists other academic authorities who do not accept this view. See also Sir Donald Nicholls, 'Keeping the Civil Law Up to Date: Flexibility and Certainty in the 1990s' [1991] Current Legal Problems 1, for an example of continued judicial unease about the restrictions on the Court of Appeal.

[75] Per Lord Goddard CJ in *Police Authority for Huddersfield* v *Watson* [1947] KB 842 at p. 848.

[76] Per Lord Goddard CJ in *Police Authority for Huddersfield* v *Watson* [1947] KB 842 at p. 848.

can be quoted for a proposition that may seem to flow logically from it.'[77] This is a strict and restricted view of the use of precedent. It is in keeping with the idea that precedent is a binding system of rules which governs the court's behaviour. It limits the number of cases referred to in any new judgment to those whose ratio is clearly to the point. Yet, Lord Halsbury's statement seems at odds with how judges actually write about previous cases. Their language is frequently more discursive. In *Dorset Yacht Co.* v *Home Office*, Lord Pearson stated that:

> It is true that the *Donaghue* v *Stevenson* principle [Lord Atkin's neighbour principle] as stated in the passage which has been cited is a basic and general but not universal principle and does not in law apply to all the situations which are covered by the side words of the passage. To some extent the decision in this case must be a matter of impression and instinctive judgement as to what is fair and just.[78]

Judges can be vague about the exact status of the precedent they are citing. In giving judgment on behalf of the court in *Hynds* v *Spillers-French Baking Ltd*, Lord Thompson said '[w]e agree broadly with the views expressed ... in *Newell* v *Gillingham Corporation*'.[79] Is the case cited a binding ratio or an obiter remark? We have noted above difficulties in ascertaining precisely what a ratio is and how it is to be identified. Yet, judges rarely refer to difficulties in locating the ratio of a case. Judgments are cited but their technical status remains unstated.[80] Both these examples illustrate a broader use of past cases than just referral to that which is binding. We have already noted the heavy use of obiter remarks in constructing judgments. Nothing in the above discussion of ratio, obiter, and the hierarchy of the courts accounts for the way in which precedent is actually used. Traditional accounts of precedent emphasize the orderliness of legal reasoning. We have already noted Hart's description of a 'closed logical system'. Yet, judges have frequently rejected the view that the common law is either logical or, at least, 'strictly logical'.[81] Finally, we need to take account of the fact that patterns of legal linguistic usage are also affected by matters other than the doctrine of precedent. In their study, 'After the Ancien Regime', Murphy and Rawlings offer an analysis of the way in which judgments in the House of Lords were constructed in 1979.[82] Their concern is with the way judgments in cases are 'glued' together; with 'the sequence and progression of the arguments deployed' and with other linguistic elements in the judgment which are not, in the strict sense, argument at all.[83] They show how particular phrases (for example, 'ordinary natural meaning', 'common sense' and 'the ordinary man') can be used to construct arguments which have a lawyerly feel even though the techniques have nothing to do with the traditional doctrine of precedent nor with

---

[77] *Quin* v *Leathem* [1901] AC 459 at p. 506. For an example of the use of this passage see Cross (1977) p. 59 and P. Atiyah, *Pragmatism and Theory in English Law* (1987) Stevens, London, pp. 8–9.

[78] *Dorset Yacht Co.* v *Home Office* [1970] AC 1004 at p. 1054.

[79] *Hynds* v *Spillers-French Baking Ltd* [1974] IRLR 281 at p. 283.

[80] Indeed, use of the WestLaw database suggests that the words ratio and obiter rarely pass judicial lips.

[81] Atiyah (1987) p. 12.      [82] Murphy and Rawlings (1981); and (1982) 45 Modern Law Review 34.

[83] Murphy and Rawlings (1981) p. 617.

formal logical reasoning. Similarly, two of the authors of this book have shown how the Chancery Division of the High Court and the Family Division, which both have jurisdiction over the Inheritance (Provision for Family and Dependants) Act 1975, use very different metaphors and analogies when constructing their judgments.[84] To explain all these phenomena we need, therefore, to turn elsewhere to either supplement or replace traditional accounts of precedent.

## The use of language

Much of the common law tradition is essentially a written tradition.[85] Although judgments are given orally, they are then written down. Argument is mainly oral but it is those written judgments that are reviewed when judges, lawyers, and others want to know how the law will develop. It is those written judgments that are referred to when lawyers are seeking to construct their arguments. Theories of precedent are attempts to explain how there is order in the way that lawyers read this collection of written texts, how they select those that are important and those that are not important and how they read them in the same way. However, in looking for rules to describe this process lawyers may be looking in the wrong direction or, at least, they may not be considering something which is just as important as whatever rules of precedent there may be.

We can see an alternative to the traditional approach to precedent if we return to one of the essential features of any theory of precedent: the desire to treat similar cases in the same fashion and thus bring both certainty and consistency to the law. Here, the basic question is how do we decide that two cases are or are not alike? Traditional theories approach this question on the basis that it is simply a matter of close reasoning to see what are and what are not the significant and trivial aspects of the two cases in issue. However, we have seen that, in law, as in other disciplines, what makes something trivial or significant does not depend solely on linguistic features. Nothing is essentially significant or essentially trivial. Meaning is socially defined by the small community of English lawyers. Thinking like a lawyer means not arguing more rigorously than others but, literally, thinking in the way that a lawyer would.

[T]he legal significance of the text does not depend solely on the presence or absence of recognisably 'legal' words. It is not an understanding of the words 'appellant' and 'respondent'

---

[84]  F. Cownie and A. Bradney, 'Divided Justice, Different Voices: Inheritance and Family Provision' (2003) 23 Legal Studies 566.

[85]  Goodrich has written that 'the primary source of law [common law] within the English legal system is unwritten law' (P. Goodrich, *Reading the Law* (1986) Blackwell, Oxford, p. 40). This is correct. Whether common law can now be said to be unwritten in any helpful sense is less clear. Historically, records of cases were badly kept and were little more than a brief précis of judgments. As late as the mid-seventeenth century, reports commonly took less than one page, even though they included the argument of counsel as well as the judgment of the court. However, in the modern era, where full reports are commonly available and assiduously read, the matter seems somewhat different.

that separates the legal reader's understanding…from those of his or her non-legal colleagues. Rather it seems to be the ability to recognise certain combinations of words, whether 'ordinary' or 'legal' as having some significance other than that which is immediately apparent as their surface meaning.[86]

Prediction is achieved not just because the same rules are followed but because of an ability to empathize with those whose thought processes are being considered. One seeks to use words and judgments in the way other English lawyers would use them.[87]

Several writers have argued that, in considering how this social effect of language occurs, we need to consider the influence of what they have called the legal canon in legal reasoning:

[T]he decided cases within any particular body of substantive law represent the equivalent of a literary canon or…a specific speech-community within which possible choices of the court are strictly defined and limited by reference to legal criteria, by reference to rules, principles and values established in previous case law.[88]

A canon is an accepted body of literature which it is said one should know if one is to be knowledgeable about a particular area. But a canon is more than simply a certain set of books (or in the case of a legal system, judgments). The works that constitute the canon are chosen for their alleged value; this value is, amongst other things, a matter of moral or political judgement. Works in the canon say something about the spirit of the system.[89] However, since the canon reflects values in the system, the selection of what is and what is not in the canon is in itself a value-laden act. The canon reflects and reinforces the politics of those who constitute the community for whom it operates.[90] In the context of law, this means that the influence of the canon on legal argument is itself not a value-free act. Arguments which are not reflective of the values of the canon will find it harder to find a purchase within the system.[91]

The notion of the canon provides a framework within which the more traditional accounts of ratio and obiter can work. It allows us to understand how legal arguments can be acceptable even if they are not logical.[92] The idea of a canon helps to explain

[86] Davies (1987) p. 415.

[87] This emphasis on the use of language within a community corresponds to Wittgenstein's rejection of the view that language had essential meaning and his search for a description of the way in which languages were used. See particularly L. Wittgenstein, *Philosophical Investigations* (1963) Basil Blackwell, Oxford.

[88] Goodrich (1986) p. 75.

[89] Thus, within English literature, Leavis argued for novels representing 'the great tradition' of English literature (F. Leavis, 'The Great Tradition: George Eliot, Henry James, Joseph Conrad' (new edn, 1960) Chatto and Windus, London).

[90] See, for example, B. Doyle, 'The Hidden History of English Studies' and C. Belsey, 'Re-reading the Great Tradition' in P. Widdowson (ed.), *Re-Reading English* (1982) Methuen, London.

[91] See, for example, P. McAuslan, 'Administrative Law, Collective Consumption and Judicial Policy' (1983) 46 Modern Law Review 1.

[92] J. Bell, 'The Acceptability of Legal Arguments' in N. MacCormick and P. Birks (eds), *The Legal Mind* (1986) Clarendon Press, Oxford, pp. 46–64.

how, on the one hand, there can be the irresolvable problems in traditional accounts of precedent and yet, on the other hand, there still be a reasonable degree of consistency and certainty in English legal reasoning. Social pressures supplement the principles of English legal reasoning to produce comparatively predictable outcomes to legal arguments. This explanation, though, has consequences for our understanding of the nature of legal reasoning. If reasoning is in part social, in part about values, who does the reasoning matters. The social background of judges and lawyers will affect how they respond to, and help construct, the atmosphere that in turn creates the canon.

## CONCLUSION

In previous chapters looking at the institutions that might be said to constitute 'the English legal system', we have emphasized their essential incoherence; the fact that, far from being a uniform set of bodies, they are divided in both form and function. The above account of legal reasoning might suggest that here we have found something that could account for the idea of 'the English legal system'. Legal reasoning, for all its difficulties and ambiguities, might be thought to be sufficiently coherent to constitute the unifying feature for 'the English legal system'.

In our view, there is much merit in the suggestion that the essence of 'the English legal system' lies not in its institutions but rather in the way it approaches its arguments. Many writers would argue that the combination of rules, principles, and social constraints inherent in legal reasoning is such as to produce a closed system, impervious to arguments from outside.[93] However, in our view, there are several problems with suggesting that this coherence in reasoning is sufficient to justify the idea of a clear and distinct 'English legal system'.

First, the legal reasoning described above is most typically that kind of reasoning which goes on in court or in the writing of judgments. We have already emphasized the amount of legal activity that takes place outside the arena of the court. Law is not just the courts and it is not just judges. Of course, any other kind of legal activity takes place in the light of the knowledge that the court may be the final place to resolve a dispute. This possibility of court action does not justify us ignoring the other forms of reasoning used when interviewing clients, negotiating settlements, taking part in alternative dispute resolution, or any of the other myriad activities associated with 'the English legal system'. Equally, it does not justify us in treating as reasoning of 'the English legal system' only that reasoning which is paradigmatically judicial. Second, even within the court not all those giving judgments are involved in the kind of reasoning described above. Two of the courts we described in **Chapter 3**, the European Court of Justice and the European Court of First Instance, have their own separate

---

[93]  See, in particular, G. Teubner, *Law as an Autopoetic System* (1993) Basil Blackwell, Oxford.

system of legal reasoning.[94] Other courts within 'the English legal system', and still more tribunals in that system, have people making decisions who are not trained in legal reasoning.[95] Since they cannot involve themselves in such reasoning, how can legal reasoning be the signature of 'the English legal system'? Some courts and, once again, still more, some tribunals, emphasize the fact that arguments need not be couched in legal terms.[96] Again, this would seem to indicate that legal reasoning is not a necessary feature of activity within the legal system. Finally, the legal reasoning described above is what lawyers say they ought to do. Studies of courts suggest it is not always what judges actually do. In Lord Woolf's interim report on the civil justice system, he noted that research that he had commissioned showed that some judges:

saw it as their unequivocal duty to apply the principles of English law, while those at the other end of the spectrum spoke of a wider responsibility to 'do justice' even if that meant disregarding the strict requirements of law and adopting a more common sense approach in some cases.[97]

This finding replicates many previous studies.[98] The empirical evidence suggests that we cannot simply assume that lawyers or, indeed, judges do, in fact, always pay heed to the apparent constraints on the way in which they reach decisions. In all these circumstances, it would be an exaggeration to suggest that English legal reasoning unites all the things that might be said to constitute 'the English legal system'.


## FURTHER READING

CROSS, R. and J. HARRIS, *Precedent in English Law* (1991) Clarendon Press, Oxford

KELMAN, N., 'Trashing' (1984) 36 Stanford Law Review 293

---

[94] On this, see J. Benoetvea, *The Legal Reasoning of the European Court of Justice: Towards a European Jurisprudence* (1993) Clarendon Press, Oxford.

[95] The most obvious examples are lay magistrates and tribunal wing-people.

[96] Within the court system, the most obvious example is the small claims track under Part 27 of the Civil Procedure Rules 1998.

[97] Lord Woolf, *Access to Justice: Interim Report to the Lord Chancellor on the Civil Justice System in England and Wales* (1995) Lord Chancellor's Department, London, p. 109.

[98] See, for example, W. Barrington Baker, J. Eekelaar, C. Gibson, and S. Raikes, *The Matrimonial Jurisdiction of Registrars* (1977) Centre for Socio-Legal Studies, Oxford.

# 6

# English legal reasoning: reading statutes

## INTRODUCTION

Judgments in cases are, in the first instance, pragmatic solutions to the particular dispute before the court. Only secondly can they be attempts to formulate some general principle of law. Statutes, by contrast, start by 'laying down general rules for application to particular facts'.[1] Their primary purpose is to enable people to order their affairs and understand what their legal position will be in the future. Judgments have this only as a secondary task.

Within 'the English legal system' statutes are generally said to be more important than cases in making law. Historically, most academic commentators and most judges have accepted that the judicial capacity to make law is limited by Parliament's ability to pass statutes.[2] Parliament can pass statutes which order or forbid any behaviour whatsoever and the judiciary, as much as anyone else, are bound by those statutes.[3] Judges cannot make law, cannot determine cases, in a way which contradicts the provisions of a statute.[4] This doctrine of parliamentary sovereignty thus asserts a hierarchical relationship between the judiciary and Parliament in which the judiciary are the inferior body.

The doctrine of parliamentary sovereignty dominates much traditional writing about the judicial approach to the interpretation of statutes.[5] Judges obey Parliament. They are therefore there to interpret and apply a statute in the way intended by Parliament. They must

---

[1]  F. Bennion, *Bennion on Statute Law* (3rd edn, 1990) Longman, London, p. 9.

[2]  However, this has never been a universal view. For an example of apparent judicial doubts about the principle of parliamentary sovereignty, see Lord Denning, *Misuse of Power* (1980) BBC, London. For early academic commentary doubting the conceptual coherence of the principle of parliamentary sovereignty, see A. Bradney, 'Parliamentary Sovereignty – A Question of Status' (1985a) 36 Northern Ireland Legal Quarterly 2.

[3]  See, for example, Lord Simon of Glaisdale's statement that 'a fundamental principle of our Constitution is the sovereignty of Parliament' (*Dockers' Labour Club* v *Race Relations Board* [1974] 3 All ER 592 at p. 600), and Sir Robert Megarry's view that 'once an instrument is recognized as being an Act of Parliament, no English court can refuse to obey it or question its validity' (*Manuel* v *A-G* [1982] 3 All ER 786 at p. 793).

[4]  Though, following the implementation of the Human Rights Act 1998, in October 2000, the higher courts can, under s. 4 of the Act, make a declaration of incompatibility between a statute and Convention rights (as defined by s. 1 of the 1998 Act).

[5]  For an example of this traditional approach, see J. Bell and Sir George Engle, *Cross: Statutory Interpretation* (3rd edn, 1995) Oxford University Press, Oxford, p. 29.

therefore search for the original meaning of the statute.[6] To find that meaning, all the courts need to do is to construe the actual language of the statute. Thus, we find the nineteenth-century comment:

The only rule for the construction of Acts of Parliament, is that they should be construed according to the intent of the Parliament which passed the Act. If the words of the statute are in themselves precise and unambiguous, then no more can be necessary than to expound those words in that natural and ordinary sense. The words themselves alone do, in such a case, best declare the intention of the lawgiver.[7]

If language were a simple matter the process could perhaps be left there. The judiciary's job would simply be to explain the statute to the population at large. However, in the previous chapter we saw that language is not a simple matter. Even those who follow traditional theories would agree that:

even at a relatively elementary stage, the existence of borderline cases [in the meaning of words] is forced upon our attention, and this shows that the assumption that several instances of the general term must have the same characteristics may be dogmatic. Very often the ordinary, or even the technical, usage of the term is quite 'open' in that it does not *forbid* the extension of the term to some cases where only some of the normally concomitant characteristics are present.[8]

Far from being clear or plain, language is inherently open-textured allowing, at least in some instances, a variety of meanings. 'Words,' said Mr Justice Holmes, 'are not crystals.'[9] 'Language,' writes Lord Steyn, 'is a labyrinth.'[10] Equally, the purpose of a statute does not always allow even the most precise use of the imprecise tool of language. 'They [statutes] seek to regulate a future which is certain only of constant surprise.'[11] Language in statutes cannot always address the exact problem because the exact problem cannot be foreseen. Statutory

---

[6] This traditional approach is not just limited to 'the English legal system'. For example, in the USA, '[t]heories of statutory interpretation in the United States have in this century emphasized the original meaning of statutes, and debates have focused on identifying the best evidence of that original meaning' (W. Eskridge Jr, *Dynamic Statutory Interpretation* (1994) Harvard University Press, Cambridge, MA, p. 13).

[7] Per Tindal CJ in *Sussex Peerage Case* (1844) 11 Cl & Fin 85 at p. 143.

[8] H. L. A. Hart, *The Concept of Law* (1961) Clarendon Press, Oxford, p. 15.

[9] Quoted in M. Radin, 'Statutory Interpretation' (1929–30) 43 Harvard Law Review 863 at p. 866.

[10] J. Steyn, '*Pepper v Hart*: A Re-examination' (2001) 21 Oxford Journal of Legal Studies 59 at p. 60. Commentators differ on how frequently the open-textured nature of language creates problems. Thus, for example, Farrar and Dugdale assert that '[i]n spite of the difficulties arising from the English style of drafting, many cases are clear cases. They fall squarely within a legislative category and rule' (J. Farrar and A. Dugdale, *Introduction to Legal Method* (3rd edn, 1990) Sweet & Maxwell, London, p. 143). On the other hand, Hutchinson and Monahan argue that '[l]egal doctrine not only does not, but also cannot, generate determinant results in concrete cases. Law is not so much a rational enterprise as a vast exercise in rationalization' (A. Hutchinson and P. Monahan, 'Law, Politics and the Critical Legal Scholars: The Unfolding Drama of American Legal Thought' (1984) 36 Stanford Law Review 199 at p. 206).

[11] F. Bennion, *Statutory Interpretation* (2nd edn, 1992) Butterworths, London, p. 2.

language must generalize.[12] Even the early nineteenth-century statement of the judiciary's approach to statutory interpretation noted above goes on to add:

[b]ut if any doubt arises from the term employed by the legislature, it has always been held a safe mean of collecting the intention to call in aid the ground and cause of making the statute.[13]

Even then, where the judiciary are forced to look beyond the bald words of the statute itself, the core of their task, according to traditional theories, remains their submission to the will of Parliament.

In this chapter, we will look at how the courts approach the difficult task of making sense of statutes. Theories of statutory interpretation need to do two things. They must describe how judges (and perhaps others) actually approach the process of statutory interpretation. Second, they must justify the manner of that process, explaining why it is legitimate for the interpretation to be done in that way. In this chapter, we will examine traditional accounts of statutory interpretation and see how these explain how judges cope with the limitations of language on the one hand and the political imperatives of the doctrine of parliamentary sovereignty on the other hand. At the same time, we will see how more recent accounts of statutory interpretation have sought to supplement or supplant these traditional accounts.

## The statute as a text

Traditional accounts of statutory interpretation presume the existence of a text that has a meaning independent of whoever is reading that text. When judges refer to 'the intention of Parliament' in their judgments, as they frequently do, the picture of legislative interpretation given is of a writer who writes a book that conveys a meaning which must be discerned by the reader.[14] Parliament is the writer; a judge the reader. The reader is not free to make up the meaning of the text. This picture might well accord with ordinary common sense notions of what the act of reading requires. However, the picture conceals as much as it reveals.

The first problem with the notion of the statute as a text is the question of who wrote the text. What do we mean when we talk about 'the intention of Parliament'? 'The intention of Parliament' cannot be exactly the same kind of thing as the intention of an individual.[15] Parliament, as a legislative body, is made up of the two Chambers,

---

[12] For a discussion of the draftsman's functions in writing a bill, see D. Miers and A. Page, *Legislation* (2nd edn, 1990) Sweet & Maxwell, London, pp. 51–7.

[13] Per Tindal CJ in *Sussex Peerage Case* (1844) 11 Cl & Fin 85 at p. 143.

[14] Use of this phrase by judges is very frequent. WestLaw lists 99 cases where the phrase was used in 2009 alone.

[15] For discussion of this issue, see Bell and Engle (1995) pp. 22–30 and R. Dworkin, *Law's Empire* (1986) Fontana Press, London, pp. 318–37. The proposition that legislative intention is a problematic notion is not

the House of Lords and the House of Commons, and the monarch. All three must give their consent before a bill can become a statute. Each of the two Chambers contains many members who are entitled to vote on each bill although they may or may not be present when any individual part of any bill is considered. Equally, since each Chamber is a democratic body, a bill or a part thereof may be passed by that Chamber even though an individual in the Chamber objects to its contents. A member of one of the Chambers may vote for a bill or a clause in a bill because they have construed its meaning quite differently from another member of the Chamber.[16] In these circumstances, the phrase 'the intention of Parliament' must have a somewhat different meaning to the phrase 'the intention of the individual'. Thus, Lord Steyn has noted that:

[i]t is sometimes meaningful and appropriate for a judge to refer to the intention of Parliament in recognition of its supreme law-making power … it is quite a different matter to ascribe to a composite and artificial body such as a legislature a state of mind deduced from exchanges in debates.[17]

## Enacting coalitions

One way of dealing with the problems created by the notion of 'the intention of Parliament' might be to suggest that such intention referred only to those members of Parliament who actually voted for a particular measure.[18] This method appears to have an obvious advantage in that it limits intention to those who have positively taken part in enacting the legislation. If this is so, the courts need only concern themselves with the intention of these people. However, this seeming advantage disappears under closer analysis. First, it is logically no more likely that those legislators who are in favour of a particular piece of legislation are at one as to its meaning than that the whole legislature will understand the legislation in the same way. Second, the American commentator Eskridge's comment on Congress and legislation is equally accurate in a British context: 'Legislators routinely vote for legislation simply because their president, their party leaders or relevant interest groups favor it.'[19] Such legislators have no intention

---

a new one. In 1929, Radin described the idea as 'a queerly amorphous bag of slag' and asked '[a]re we really reduced to such shifts that we must fashion monsters and endow them with imagination in order to understand statutes?' (Radin (1929–30) p. 872). His answer was in the negative.

[16] A frequently cited example of this is the agreement of Winston Churchill and Sir Thomas Inskip that the Statute of Westminster's application to the Irish Free State was perfectly clear and their disagreement as to that clear meaning (see Bell and Engle (1995) p. 23 and G. Marshall, *Constitutional Theory* (1971) Clarendon Press, Oxford, p. 76. The original interchange can be found at 259 HC Deb col. 1194 and col. 1250). All these problems are well known to the judiciary who are required to interpret statutes (see, for example, Lord Simon of Glaisdale in *Ealing LBC* v *Race Relations Board* [1972] AC 342 at pp. 360–1).

[17] Steyn (2001) p. 64.

[18] See, for example, G. MacCullum, 'Legislative Intent' (1966) 75 Yale Law Journal 754 at pp. 777–80.

[19] Eskridge (1994) p. 16.

regarding the meaning of the legislation; their intention is simply to vote for it. Finally, different legislators will come together at different points during the passage of a piece of legislation in order to vote for it.

Attempts to replace 'the intention of Parliament' with 'the intention of those who enact the legislation' founder on the fact that 'no robust theory of enacting coalitions' has yet been articulated which could say how such persons combined together to provide a single meaning.[20]

## 'The words which Parliament used'

If the judiciary cannot ascertain meaning directly by looking into the mind of Parliament or some part of Parliament, they must look elsewhere for meaning. What they have before them as the direct evidence of Parliament's intention is the statute itself. It can therefore be argued that it is appropriate to start by simply interpreting the words of the statute:

We often say that we are looking for the intention of Parliament, but that is not quite accurate. We are seeking the meaning of the words which Parliament used. We are seeking not what Parliament meant but the true meaning of what they said...[21]

Parliament used those words so, following constitutional principle, it is legitimate to presume that Parliament meant those words.

Even if we accept this formulation, at its surface value it creates difficulties for the doctrine of parliamentary sovereignty. Parliament, as much as an individual, may presumably misspeak itself. We can fail to explain properly our will to others. So, then, may Parliament. If others follow our orders but do not do what we want because we are unclear in our commands, we could not say they are following our will.[22] So it is with the judiciary. Following the words of the statute may be all that they can do but there is a significant gap between that and following the will of Parliament.

Equally important, is the fact that this formulation seems to contradict what we have already seen is now largely accepted about the nature of language. If each judge approaches a statute simply on the basis that their job is to derive meaning from the words of the statute itself, and if language is a complex matter, how can we be sure either what judges will decide in the future or that each judge will derive the

---

[20]  Eskridge (1994) p. 32. However, the decision by the House of Lords to permit the use of Hansard to ascertain what the person proposing a bill had said about its intention might be taken to be tacit support for this concept of the enacting coalition (see *Pepper* v *Hart* [1993] 1 All ER 42 at p. 64; see **pp. 126–7** for discussion of this case).

[21]  Per Lord Reid in *Black-Clawson* v *Papierweike* [1975] 1 All ER 810 at p. 814.

[22]  Though we may blame ourselves, not them, for their failure.

same meaning as their fellow judges? How will meaning be both predictable and uniform?

# Principles of statutory interpretation

Scholars have identified a number of different principles of statutory interpretation. In traditional accounts of statutory interpretation, these help to explain the coherence of the judiciary's approach to statutory interpretation. These principles, if they exist at all, are, in the Dworkinian sense we examined in the last chapter, principles and not rules.[23] These principles, however, are often referred to as rules.[24] Nobody argues that these principles are capable of concrete application in each case so as to give a clear determinate result. Rather, they are matters to be taken into account and weighed by the judge when they reach their decision about the interpretation of a particular piece of legislation.[25] This fact in itself limits the efficacy of traditional accounts of statutory interpretation since adherence to principle must create less predictability and uniformity in results than adherence to mechanical rules.

## The literal rule

The first principle of statutory interpretation is that which springs most closely from the judiciary's general support for the doctrine of parliamentary sovereignty:[26]

If the words of an Act are so inflexible that they are incapable in any context of having but one meaning, then the court must apply that meaning, no matter how unreasonable the result – it cannot insert other words. But such cases are rare because the English language is a flexible tool.[27]

It has been argued that this principle of statutory interpretation is first not only in the sense that it springs most naturally from constitutional theory, but also in the sense

---

[23]  Bell and Engle (1995) pp. 33–43. See **pp. 94–5** above for discussion of the concept of Dworkinian principles.                                    [24]  See, for example, Bell and Engle (1995) p. 49.
[25]  Bennion argues that '[t]he basic rule of statutory interpretation is that it is taken to be the legislator's intention that the enactment shall be construed in accordance with the guides laid down by the law; and that where in a particular case these do not yield a plain answer but point in different directions the problem shall be resolved by a balancing exercise, that is by weighing and balancing the factors they produce' (Bennion (1990) p. 104). This, he argues, is a rule in the strict sense of the word.
[26]  Bennion has argued that the practice of reducing the judicial approach to statutory interpretation to a small number of principles is fatally flawed, since it misses the full complexity of a process where no single rule is ever selected by the courts (see Bennion (1990) pp. 104–5). Bennion's arguments may be seen to gain some support from Lord Wilberforce's remark that the interpretation of legislation is 'a multi-faceted thing, calling for many talents; not a subject which can be confined to rules' ((1981) 418 HL Deb col. 73). Whilst there may be some truth in this argument, the practice of treating the rules as Dworkinian principles could be taken to rebut the central thrust of Bennion's approach.
[27]  Per Lord Reid in *Kammins Ballrooms Co. Ltd* v *Zenith Investments (Torquay) Ltd* [1971] AC 850 at p. 859.

that it is a primary rule with all other rules having secondary status.[28] In the past, there may have been good arguments for this position. In the nineteenth century and before, when judges were prepared to believe that their role in making decisions was purely 'expounding, declaring and publishing what the law of this kingdom is' – the so-called 'declaratory theory of law' – they might also have believed that their role in interpreting statutes was just mechanically to expound the words of the text.[29] However, such a rule of primacy is difficult to equate with the modern tendency to regard the rules of statutory interpretation as principles having weight.[30] At most one might argue that the literal rule could be said to have greater weight than other rules:[31]

Cross's formulation of the literal rule brings out some of its limitations:

The judge must give effect to the grammatical and ordinary or, where appropriate, the technical meaning of words in the general context of the statute; he must also determine the extent of general words with reference to that context.[32]

This description of the rule directs our attention to two facts. The first is that courts rarely, if ever, interpret words in a statute if, by that, we mean interpret single, isolated words. Instead they have to give meaning to phrases, sentences, and sections of statutes. Isolated words may have a comparatively clear meaning, ascertainable from a dictionary.[33] However, when we seek to put words into the context of each other, and into the context of a matter in dispute, we have to call on principles of grammar to assist us in gaining meaning.[34] Calling on these aids will rarely, if ever, tell us how we must interpret a particular word or phrase. Rather they will give us a range of alternative interpretations. The second issue raised in Cross's description is the fact that even the purest formulations of the literal rule insist on the distinction between ordinary and technical words in a statute. This involves the exercise of discretion by the judge. When is a word 'technical' rather than ordinary? Technical words are not always obviously technical upon their face. In *Fisher v Bell*, the defendant placed a flick knife in his shop window. Section 1(1) of the Restriction of Offensive Weapons Act 1959 made it a criminal offence 'to offer for sale' a flick knife. 'Offer for sale' may appear to be plain language. However, the defendant was found not guilty because the court said the phrase 'offer for sale' had

---

[28]  P. Langan, *Maxwell on the Interpretation of Statutes* (12th edn, 1969) Sweet & Maxwell, London, p. 28.

[29]  The quotation is taken from the 1820 work, Hale's *History of the Common Law* cited in G. Williams (ed.), *Salmond on Jurisprudence* (11th edn, 1957) Sweet & Maxwell, London, p. 163.

[30]  One may doubt the soundness of the proposition even if it is taken to be a historical truth. Authority for another rule of statutory interpretation, the mischief rule, is to be found in the sixteenth-century case *Heydon's Case* (1584) 3 Co Rep 7a. Other examples could be given.

[31]  Even this argument might be difficult to sustain given the difficulty in applying the literal rule.

[32]  Bell and Engle (1995) p. 49.

[33]  Though, in this instance, there will be boundary cases and instances of multiple meaning.

[34]  Bennion has argued that to say judges ever seek a literal meaning is incorrect. He argues that judges must look for a *legal* meaning which should take into account the legal considerations of the case (Bennion (1990) pp. 87–8). For others, this approach may be seen simply as pointing to the limitation in the number of instances that the literal rule can be used.

to be construed in its technical sense under the English law of contract. Under this, placing goods in a shop window was an invitation to treat and not an offer to sell, which would come at a later stage in the transaction when the shopkeeper named a price to a prospective purchaser.[35]

These problems with the literal rule show its inherent contradiction:

A literal meaning is, at the end of the day, always an interpretative meaning. A selection or choice has to be made – consciously or unconsciously – to prefer one of several possible literal meanings in the context of the phrase or statutory rule to be interpreted.[36]

This is not to say that the literal rule is a sham. The principles of statutory interpretation are mechanisms for improving the predictability and uniformity of judicial interpretations of statutes. Even if the literal rule involves choosing from a number of literal meanings, it still restricts the degree of choice that can legitimately be made by a judge. However, it does not, as its more crude formulations might suggest, dictate that choice.

It is sometimes said that whilst the judiciary should follow the literal rule even if it will produce a result that was not intended by Parliament, they should not follow the literal rule if its application will produce 'either an improbable result or a manifest absurdity'.[37] This formulation further dilutes the apparent clarity of the literal rule.[38] It requires the judiciary to make a judgement, and thus exercise discretion, about the acceptability of a particular meaning. It also does so without giving judges any criteria against which they can judge whether or not something is 'a manifest absurdity'. Thus, once again, the chances of the application of this principle bringing predictability and uniformity to judicial interpretation are thus much reduced.

The main advantage of the literal rule is that it fits easily with constitutional principle. Its main difficulty is that, in its purest form, it will very rarely be capable of application. It is difficult to think of many words that will always have a single literal application.[39] However, once one moves away from its pure form and uses a formulation of the literal rule that gives it operative effect in a wider number of cases, the task that it asks the judiciary to perform, an act of interpretation, appears to be at odds with its supposed focus.

---

[35] [1961] 1 QB 394. The ambiguities of the phrase 'technical meaning' are discussed in Bell and Engle (1995) pp. 72–5.        [36] P. Goodrich, *Reading the Law* (1986) Basil Blackwell, Oxford, p. 109.

[37] See, for example, R. Ward and A. Akhtar, *Walker and Walker's English Legal System* (10th edn, 2008) Oxford University Press, Oxford, p. 48.

[38] This formulation is of comparatively recent origin. Historically, it has been said that where there is a single literal interpretation, '[i]f the words of an Act are clear, you must follow them, even if they lead to a manifest absurdity' (per Lord Esher MR in *R v Judge of City of London Court* [1892] 1 QB 273 at p. 290).

[39] One example is indications of speed in laws concerning speed limits. What 70 mph is, will always be clear. The only difficulty in applying the statute will be the factual difficulty inherent in determining whether or not somebody exceeded 70 mph.

## The golden rule and the purposive approach

Given its inherent limitations, it is debatable that the courts were ever able to follow even the most attenuated form of the literal rule in many cases. However, historically, there has been considerable evidence for their apparent acquiescence to it. This acquiescence has not been without criticism. The Law Commission's view is typical:

To place undue emphasis on the literal meaning of the words of a provision is to assume an unattainable perfection; it presumes that the draftsmen can always choose words which will leave no room for a difference of opinion as to their meaning. Such an approach ignores the limitations of language ... [40]

This kind of criticism has created a pressure for the judiciary to consider principles of statutory interpretation other than the literal rule when passing judgment. Perhaps more importantly, a more professional and thus more reflective judiciary, as compared with that of previous centuries, may feel less comfortable with the obvious contradictions which use of the literal rule involves.[41] Finally, an increase in the quantity of statute law has persuaded some judges this must 'inevitably result in ambiguities in statutory language which are not perceived at the time the legislation is enacted'.[42] Thus, other principles of statutory interpretation take on greater significance. As Lord Griffiths has put it: '[t]he days have long passed when the courts adopted a strict constructionist view of interpretation which required them to adopt the literal meaning of the language'.[43]

Lord Blackburn attributed the second rule of statutory interpretation, the golden rule, to Lord Wensleydale and stated it thus:

[W]e are to take the whole statute together, and construe it all together, giving the words their ordinary signification, unless when so applied they produce an inconsistency, or an absurdity or inconvenience so great as to convince the Court that the intention could not have been to use them in their ordinary signification, and to justify the Court in putting them in some other signification, which, though less proper, is one which the Court thinks the words will bear.[44]

---

[40] The Law Commission, *The Interpretation of Statutes* (Law Com. No. 21) (1969) HMSO, London, para. 30.

[41] For evidence of this improvement in the professionalism in the case of the House of Lords, see R. Stevens, *Law and Politics* (1979) Weidenfeld & Nicholson, London.

[42] Per Lord Griffiths in *Pepper* v *Hart* [1993] 1 All ER 42 at p. 50.

[43] *Pepper* v *Hart* [1993] 1 All ER 42 at p. 50.

[44] *River Wear Commissioners* v *Adamson* (1977) 2 App Cas 743 at pp. 764–5. The courts do sometimes use the term 'the golden rule' when interpreting statutes (see, for example, Rix LJ in *Yarl's Wood Immigration Limited and others* v *Bedfordshire Police Authority* [2009] EWCA Civ 1110 at para. 68). However, the phrase 'purposive approach' is now more common (see, for example, Lord Walker in *Office of Fair Trading* v *Abbey National* [2009] 3 WLR 1215 at p. 1228).

The golden rule has clear connections with the literal rule.[45] Both require the court to begin by looking at ordinary meaning. However, in the golden rule, there is greater stress on the court's duty to make assessments about the desirability of using particular meanings in their judgments.

It is possible to reconcile the use of the literal rule and the golden rule by saying that the golden rule can be used only where there are two or more literal meanings or where use of the literal rule would lead to a manifest absurdity.[46] However, to argue this is to miss the reality of the application of the literal rule. In most cases, even where the literal rule is used, the court will be applying what it deems to be a literal meaning even though other meanings exist.

Careful analysis of the golden rule as stated above suggests two different cases where the literal interpretation of a statute might be avoided: one where 'inconsistency' would result if a particular interpretation was followed; and another if 'absurdity or inconvenience so great' as to justify the court in not applying a particular interpretation is to be found. These, it might be argued, are not parallel cases. 'Absurdity' is stronger and requires more than 'inconvenience'. However, such an approach would be too narrow and too pedantic. It might be better to say what the rule requires is that, under the golden rule, the courts require a very strong reason before they can refuse to follow a particular interpretation of a statute.

Some of the difficulties noted above that are inherent in the application of the literal rule apply even more strongly in the case of the golden rule. How is a court to know what is appropriate inconvenience, absurdity, or inconsistency? Not every inconvenience, absurdity, or inconsistency will do. The rule asks the judge to consider how 'great' is the fault. The rule suggests a subjective approach by the courts and can be criticized on this account. Yet, despite this, this approach, or a milder version sometimes described as the purposive approach, has been recommended in recent judgments.

The thrust of the golden rule is to consider an interpretation of a statute in the light of its effect. The purposive approach extends this by asking the judiciary to interpret a statute in the light of its purpose. Thus, in *Bank of Scotland* v *Grimes*, Sir John Arnold felt unable to arrive at any understanding of the actual language of one part of s. 8(1) of the Administration of Justice Act 1973. However, because he felt able to understand the general intention of the statute when applied to the particular dispute, he was able to give meaning to the section. He interpreted, not the words of the section, but

---

[45]  Indeed, it is difficult to distinguish some formulations of the literal rule from that of the golden rule. For example, in *Becke* v *Smith*, Baron Parke held '[i]t is a very useful rule in the construction of a statute to adhere to the ordinary meaning of the words used, and to the grammatical construction, unless that is at variance with the intention of the legislature to be collected from that statute itself, or leads to any manifest absurdity or repugnance, in which case the language may be varied or modified so as to avoid such inconvenience, but no further' (*Becke* v *Smith* (1836) 2 M & W 191 at p. 195). It is difficult to distinguish this from the modern formulation of the literal rule which requires the court to avoid absurdity noted above. However, it has been described as 'the best known statement' of the golden rule (R. Ward, *Walker and Walker's English Legal System* (8th edn, 1998) Butterworths, London, p. 40). Bell and Engle, however, treat it as an example of the literal rule (Bell and Engle (1995) p. 16).

[46]  Ward and Akhtar (2008) p. 48; Bell and Engle (1995) p. 17.

the intention of the Act.[47] According to the WestLaw database, the phrase 'purposive approach' was first used in 1971 in *Kamins Ballrooms Co. Ltd* v *Zenith Investments (Torquay) Ltd*.[48] The fact that the phrase was only used in ten cases in the ten years after *Kamins Ballrooms Co. Ltd* v *Zenith Investments (Torquay) Ltd* but was used in 31 cases in 2009, is indicative of the greater use that the judiciary are now making of this notion.[49] Recently, one senior judge has commented, 'purposive construction is like mother's milk and apple pie: who can argue against it?'[50]

## The mischief rule

Although the literal rule may arise most closely from constitutional principle, it is not the only rule which has an ancient parentage. In the sixteenth-century case, *Heydon's Case*, the Barons of the Court of Exchequer laid down:

that for the sure and true interpretation of all statutes in general (be they penal or beneficial, restrictive or enlarging of the Common Law), four things are to be discerned and considered:

1st   What was the common law before the making of the Act.

2nd   What was the mischief and defect for which the common law did not provide.

3rd   What remedy the Parliament hath resolved and appointed to cure the disease of the commonwealth.

And,

4th   The true reason of the remedy; and then the office of all the Judges is always to make such construction as shall suppress the mischief, and advance the remedy, and to suppress subtle inventions and evasions for continuance of the mischief, and *pro privato commodo*, and to add force and life to the cure and remedy, according to the true intent of the makers of the Act, *pro bono publico*.[51]

This mischief rule goes much further than either the golden rule or the purposive approach. It allows for a much fuller investigation into the position of the statute in relation to the law taken as a whole and gives the courts more latitude in their construction of the statute. The court's attention is focused more firmly on the purpose of the statute and the intention of the legislature than on the words before them. This can be illustrated by considering the use made of the mischief rule in a modern case, *Davies* v *Johnson*.[52]

In *Davies* v *Johnson*, the House of Lords was faced with a dispute where a woman had left the flat she had shared with her boyfriend because of his violence and threats of violence. The Domestic Violence and Matrimonial Proceedings Act 1976, the relevant

---

[47]   *Bank of Scotland* v *Grimes* [1985] 2 All ER 254 at p. 258. This is an extreme use of the approach. It is rare for a judge to say they can find no meaning for a particular phrase in a statute.          [48]   [1971] AC 850.

[49]   This is not to say that the use of the purposive approach is limited to these cases. Judges may have used this approach without discussing their use of it in their judgments.          [50]   Steyn (2001) p. 70.

[51]   (1584) 3 Co Rep 7a at p. 7b.          [52]   [1979] AC 264.

legislation, was intended to deal with domestic violence. Under it, those living together as husband and wife were to be treated as though they were married.[53] However, although the 1976 Act gave the courts jurisdiction to grant an injunction excluding a violent party from the matrimonial home in the circumstances of the case, previous courts had argued that, since the Act did not explicitly grant property rights to those who were unmarried cohabitees nor give power to suspend or restrict the property right in favour of a cohabitee, they should not grant exclusion orders in these circumstances to cohabitees. To grant an exclusion order would, it was argued, be the equivalent of giving a property right and this was not authorized by the Act.[54] In *Davies* v *Johnson*, Lord Scarman said, 'the question which I consider to be crucial to a correct understanding of the scope of the section … [is] what is the mischief which Parliament has provided the remedies specified [for] … '.[55] He described the mischief thus:

[c]onduct by a family partner which puts at risk the security, or sense of security, of the other partner in the home. Physical violence, or the threat of it, is clearly within the mischief. But there is more to it than that. Homelessness can be as great a threat as physical violence to the security of a woman (or man) and her children. Eviction – actual, attempted or threatened – is, therefore, within the mischief: likewise, conduct which makes it impossible or intolerable, as in the present case, for the other partner, or the children, to remain at home.[56]

Unmarried cohabitees applying to the court under the 1976 Act were statistically more likely to be women rather than men.[57] As women, they were more likely not to have any exclusive legal property rights in the home they had shared with their partner.[58] If the Act was construed so as not to allow the suspension of property rights in favour of those who had been abused or threatened, this would be to say that in relationship to cohabitees 'Parliament decreed a trifling and illusory remedy for a known disgraceful mischief, and to hold it in the interest of the conceptual purity of the law'.[59] In order to avoid this, the House of Lords held that, despite the absence of explicit words in the 1976 Act, the statute did, indeed, allow for the temporary suspension of property rights in favour of the victim of domestic violence.

The greater scope given to the courts by the application of the mischief rule is clear from the above. It did far more than allow them to choose between two different meanings of the statutory language or infer into the statute a small number of words.[60] It

---

[53]  Domestic Violence and Matrimonial Proceedings Act 1976, s. 1(2).

[54]  See, for example, *B* v *B* [1978] Fam 26.     [55]  *Davies* v *Johnson* [1979] AC 264 at pp. 347–8.

[56]  *Davies* v *Johnson* [1979] AC 264 at p. 348.

[57]  J. Dewar with S. Parker, *Law and the Family* (2nd edn, 1992) Butterworths, London, p. 224.

[58]  Women are less likely than men to have access to full-time paid work. When they do have access to full-time paid work, they will, on average, earn less than men. They are therefore in a poorer position to acquire property. See A. Coote and B. Campbell, *Sweet Freedom* (1987) Basil Blackwell, Oxford, ch. 2.

[59]  Per Lord Kilbrandon in *Davies* v *Johnson* [1979] AC 264 at p. 339.

[60]  Although, in fact, the latter was also necessary in this case. The 1976 Act applied to cohabitees 'living together as husband and wife'. Because of the threats of violence, Ms Davies had fled to the Chiswick refuge for battered wives. She was thus not at the time of her action living with Mr Johnson. Nevertheless, the court construed the statute so as to include Ms Davies and those others in her situation.

allowed them to discern the creation by Parliament of the equivalent of a new species of legal property right even though this was not apparent from the language of the statute.

The social advantages of the House of Lords' ruling in *Davies* v *Johnson* are clear. However, equally manifest are the difficulties that the application of the mischief rule creates for notions of uniformity and predictability in statutory interpretation. If it is possible to criticize the golden rule or the purposive approach because of their supposedly subjective nature, this must still more be the case with the mischief rule. This can be illustrated once again by looking at the court's approach to the Domestic Violence and Matrimonial Proceedings Act 1976.

The House of Lords in *Davies* v *Johnson* were not the first court to consider the intention of Parliament in passing the 1976 Act. In *B* v *B*, the Court of Appeal had considered what Parliament's intention must have been when they passed the 1976 Act. Bridge LJ noted that Parliament had created an 'elaborate code regulating the rights inter se of spouses in relation to the occupation of the matrimonial home' when it passed the Matrimonial Homes Act 1967. It had not chosen to do so in relation to unmarried couples. The 1976 Act applied only to county courts. It gave no jurisdiction to the High Court although there was an extensive family jurisdiction in that court similar to that of the county court. To give jurisdiction to the county court to suspend property rights under the 1976 Act would mean that there was a different system of law operating in the county courts on the one hand and the High Court on the other hand.[61] In the light of these arguments, and in the context of the fact that two decades ago even more than now it was possible to argue marriage should create more legal rights and thus more legal protection than merely cohabiting, it did not seem implausible to argue that Parliament did intend cohabitees to have much inferior protection as compared with those who were married under the 1976 Act. The point is not that the argument in *B* v *B* is better than *Davies* v *Johnson*, or vice versa, but that both arguments are tenable. In such a case, how can uniformity and predictability be achieved? How will we predict what mischiefs the court will think were being remedied and what way was being chosen by Parliament to remedy them? This may be why the mischief rule has been used only sparingly by the courts. The WestLaw database lists only 42 cases where the term has been used in judgment.

When *Davies* v *Johnson* was decided, one factor that arguably added to the air of uncertainty in statutory interpretation was the fact that the courts were unwilling to look at Hansard in seeking to determine what the mischief was that Parliament was trying to remedy. Indeed, this rule was reaffirmed in *Davies* v *Johnson* itself.[62] This rule may appear rather strange in the context of any principle of statutory interpretation which seeks to look to the intent of Parliament as opposed simply to the plain language of the statute. 'It is self-evident that in order to understand a statute a court

---

[61] *B* v *B* [1978] Fam 26 at pp. 36–7.
[62] See, for example, Lord Scarman in *Davies* v *Johnson* [1979] AC 264 at pp. 349–50 and Viscount Dilhorne at p. 337.

has to take into account many matters which are not to be found within the statute itself.[63] It had long been accepted that some materials other than the records of parliamentary debates could be used when interpreting a statute. In 1898, for example, the House of Lords had turned to a report of commissioners appointed to enquire into the duties of the Patent Office when seeking to interpret s. 64 of the Patents, Designs and Trade Marks Act 1883.[64] Thus, the actual debates of Parliament regarding the Act might be regarded as relevant. It might be thought that consulting them would at least restrict the number of meanings which might plausibly be regarded as lying within Parliament's intent. However, it had long been argued that, because of the expense involved in consulting them, it was impracticable to expect lawyers to refer to debates of Hansard and that, in any event, being a record of adversarial debate, it gave no clear indication of the will of Parliament.[65]

In 1993, using the power given to it by the 1966 Practice Statement, the House of Lords decided to depart from its previous practice and permit the use of Hansard in the case of legislation:

which is ambiguous or obscure or the literal meaning of which leads to absurdity. Even in such cases references...should only be permitted where such material clearly discloses the mischief aimed at or the legislative intention lying behind the ambiguous or obscure words. In the case of statements made in Parliament, as at present advised I cannot foresee that any statement other than the statement of the minister or other promoter of the Bill is likely to meet these criteria.[66]

Lord Griffiths stated that one of the reasons for the change in practice was the fact that courts were now adopting a purposive approach to statutory interpretation.[67] At the same time, Lord Oliver said the courts had to be 'very cautious in opening the door' to the use of Hansard.[68]

The relaxation of the rule regarding the citing of Hansard is as much of symbolic or illustrative importance as of practical significance. The fact that the House of Lords are willing to countenance argument which does not go directly to the plain language of the statute, suggests just how pervasive the purposive approach and the mischief rule are in the operation of the court. It has been said that the use of Hansard since *Pepper* v *Hart* already exceeds the boundaries set in that case.[69] The WestLaw database lists 548 decisions where *Pepper* v *Hart* had been cited.[70] Although not all of these cases were ones where the use of Hansard was finally accepted, the sheer number of

---

[63] Law Commission (1969) para. 46.

[64] *Eastman Photographic Materials Co.* v *Comptroller-General of Patents, Designs and Trade-Marks* [1989] AC 571 at p. 575.

[65] See, for example, Lord Scarman in *Davies* v *Johnson* [1979] AC 264 at p. 350.

[66] Per Lord Browne-Wilkinson in *Pepper* v *Hart* [1993] 1 All ER 42 at p. 64.

[67] *Pepper* v *Hart* [1993] 1 All ER 42 at p. 50.          [68] *Pepper* v *Hart* [1993] 1 All ER 42 at p. 52.

[69] Bell and Engle (1995) pp. 159–60.

[70] This figure includes a small number of cases where the term is used in a case analysis provided by WestLaw rather than in the decisions made by the judges.

citations in such a short space of time does suggest that this argument is correct.[71] One conclusion to draw is that in deciding the ambit of statutes, the courts are increasingly willing to draw on arguments other than plain language.

## Fundamental rights

In *R v Secretary of State for the Home Department, ex parte Simms*, Lord Hoffmann noted that:

Parliamentary sovereignty means that Parliament can, if it chooses, legislate contrary to fundamental principles of human rights...But the principle of legality means that Parliament must squarely confront what it is doing and accept the political cost. Fundamental rights cannot be overridden by general or ambiguous words...In the absence of express language or necessary implication to the contrary, the courts therefore presume that even the most general words were intended to be subject to the basic rights of the individual.[72]

Although one senior judge has said that the proposition that '[g]eneral words in a statute should not be allowed to abrogate fundamental rights' is one that was until recently 'dormant', it seems to be more accurate to say that it is a new approach to statutory interpretation.[73] One question raised by this approach, which is quite separate from the new duties of the courts under the Human Rights Act 1998, is what rights are the courts going to regard as being fundamental so as to require clear words in a statute to limit or extinguish them? Another question raised by the new principle of statutory interpretation is more deep-seated. In commenting on a series of articles by one judicial proponent of the new approach, Sir John Laws, Griffith observes that:

[t]he proposals advanced by Sir John Laws openly advocate a massive shift of power from the executive and Parliament to the judiciary. The political question is whether or not this is to be supported, whether it is likely to result in a society more just, more free, more equal.[74]

[71] However, one senior judge has noted that '[I]t remains my view the *Pepper v Hart* has substantially increased the costs of litigation to very little advantage. Many appellate judges share this view' (Steyn (2001) p. 59). See also the House of Lords' decision in *Wilson v First County Trust Ltd (No. 2)* [2003] 3 WLR 568. For academic criticism of *Pepper v Hart*, see A. Kavanagh, '*Pepper v Hart* and Matters of Constitutional Principle' (2005) 121 Law Quarterly Review 98.                    [72] [2001] 2 AC 115 at p. 131.
[73] Lord Steyn, 'Democracy Through Law' (2002) 6 European Human Rights Law Review 723 at p. 729.
[74] J. A. G. Griffith, 'The Brave New World of Sir John Laws' (2000) 63 Modern Law Review 159 at p. 173. For Sir John Laws' arguments, see, for example, Sir John Laws, 'Is the High Court the Guardian of Fundamental Constitutional Rights?' [1993] Public Law 59; Sir John Laws, 'Law and Democracy' [1995] Public Law 72; Sir John Laws, 'Public Law and Employment Law' [1997] Public Law 455; and Sir John Laws, 'The Limitations of Human Rights' [1998] Public Law 254. For Griffith's views on another judicial proponent of fundamental rights, Sedley LJ, see J. A. G. Griffith, 'The Common Law and the Political Constitution' (2001) 117 Law Quarterly Review 42. For Sedley LJ's response see S. Sedley, 'The Common Law and the Political Constitution: A Reply' (2001) 117 Law Quarterly Review 68.

Citing traditional arguments about the non-accountability and the unrepresentative nature of the judiciary, Griffith's own view is in the negative.[75]

Lord Hoffman has recently argued that the notion of fundamental rights is 'largely superseded, in its application to human rights, by section 3 of the 1998 [Human Rights] Act'.[76] However, other judges seem to take a different view, with the idea still being cited in judgment.[77]

## A changing paradigm

Whilst there is no doubt that the notion of parliamentary sovereignty has dominated statutory interpretation in the past, whether it will continue to do so, at least in its classical form, is now a matter of some doubt. Indications of judicial unease with the concept first became apparent in the 1990s. Thus, for example, in 'Droit Public – English Style', the then Master of the Rolls, Lord Woolf, argued that parliamentary sovereignty is subservient to the doctrine of the rule of law.[78] In a similar spirit, Sedley LJ, as he now is, argued that there was 'a bi-polar sovereignty of the Crown in Parliament and the Crown in its courts'.[79] Subsequently, after some criticism of early comments by judges on the doctrine of parliamentary sovereignty, Lord Woolf observed that 'the courts accept the sovereignty of Parliament' but went on to argue that '[t]he sovereignty of Parliament is but an important aspect of the rule of law'.[80] Such statements were extra-judicial, being made in various academic journals and, thus, in strict terms, did not have the status of legal authority. However, in *Jackson v Attorney-General*, several judges voiced doubts about the doctrine of parliamentary sovereignty in their judgments.[81] Lord Steyn observed that the 'classic account... pure and absolute as it was, can now be seen to be out of place in the modern United Kingdom', whilst Lord Hope held that 'parliamentary sovereignty is no longer, if it ever was, absolute', and Lady Hale said that '[t]he courts will treat with particular suspicion (and might even reject) any attempt to subvert the rule of law by removing governmental action affecting the rights of the individual from all judicial scrutiny'.[82] In a subsequent article, written after his retirement as a Law Lord, Lord Steyn has argued that:

the dicta in *Jackson* are likely to prevail if the government tried to tamper with fundamental principles of our constitutional democracy, such as five-year parliaments, the role of the

---

[75] See also R. Ekins, 'Judicial Supremacy and the Rule of Law' (2003) 119 Law Quarterly Review 127.

[76] *RB (Algeria) FC v Secretary of State for the Home Department; OO (Jordan) v Secretary of State for the Home Department* [2009] 2 WLR 512 at p. 566.

[77] See, for example, LJ Pill in *JT (Cameroon) v Secretary of State for the Home Department* [2009] 1 WLR 1411 at p. 1417.          [78] [1995b] Public Law 57 at pp. 67–9.

[79] J. Sedley, 'Human Rights: A Twenty-First Century Agenda' [1995] Public Law 386 at p. 389.

[80] Lord Woolf, 'Judicial Review – The Tensions between the Executive and the Judiciary' (1998) 114 Law Quarterly Review 579.          [81] [2005] UKHL 56; [2006] 1 AC 262.

[82] *Jackson v Attorney-General* [2006] 1 AC 262 at pp. 302, 303, and 318.

ordinary courts, the rule of law, and other such fundamentals. In such exceptional cases the rule of law may trump parliamentary sovereignty.[83]

It is now clear that there is a division in both academic and judicial opinion about the concept of parliamentary sovereignty. *Jackson* is part of a much wider reassessment by the British judiciary of their proper role in political governance.[84] For some academics, the dicta in *Jackson* 'are a signal that the judiciary no longer wishes to play a part in maintaining fairytales'.[85] Just as Lord Reid once decried the previously established notion that judges never make law, so some judges are now rejecting the notion that they are simply subservient to Parliament, no matter what Parliament does.[86] If this is correct, there is a need for a fundamental reconsideration of the principle of parliamentary sovereignty.[87] However, not everyone takes the same approach. For some, the circumstances in which the courts might ignore the doctrine of parliamentary sovereignty are so extreme as to be unlikely ever to occur.[88] Others take the view that the traditional concept of parliamentary sovereignty should not be changed by unilateral action on the part of the judiciary. In a recent book, Lord Bingham, once the Senior Law Lord, has argued that:

We live in a society dedicated to the rule of law; in which Parliament has power, subject to limited, self-imposed restraints, to legislate as it wishes; in which Parliament may therefore legislate in a way which infringes the rule of law; and in which the judges, consistently with their constitutional duty to administer justice according to the laws and useages of the realm, cannot fail to give effect to such legislation if it is clearly and unambiguously expressed.[89]

However, when considering the principles of statutory interpretation that are used by the courts, what is important is not the conclusions that might eventually be arrived at as these matters are debated. Instead, the fact of the debate itself is of central sig-

---

[83] Lord Steyn, 'Democracy, the Rule of Law and the Role of Judges' (2006) 3 European Human Rights Law Review 243 at p. 253.

[84] J. Jowell, 'Parliamentary Sovereignty under the New Constitutional Hypothesis' [2006] Public Law 562.

[85] A. Kavanagh, *Constitutional Review under the Human Rights Act* (2009) Cambridge University Press, Cambridge, p. 415.

[86] Lord Reid, 'The Judge as Law Maker' (1972) 12 Journal of the Society of Public Teachers of Law 22

[87] See, for example, S. Larkin, 'Debunking the Idea of Parliamentary Sovereignty: The Controlling Factor of Legality in the British Constitution' (2008) Oxford Journal of Legal Studies 709 and M. Gordon, 'The Conceptual Foundations of Parliamentary Sovereignty: Reconsidering Jennings and Wade' [2009] Public Law 519.

[88] A. W. Bradley and K. D. Ewing, *Constitutional and Administrative Law* (14th edn, 2006) Longman, Harlow, p. 61.

[89] T Bingham, *The Rule of Law* (2010) Allen Lane, London p. 168. In his book, Lord Bingham accepts the existences of constitutional problems resulting from the fact that the House of Commons, dominated by the government, now has virtually untrammelled power when it comes to the passage of legislation. He refers to Lord Hailsham's notion of 'the elective dictatorship' (Bingham (2010) p. 169). Lord Steyn had referred to Lord Hailsham's work in his judgment in *Jackson v Attorney-General* ([2006] 1 AC 262 at p 294). However, for Lord Bingham, the solution lies in a codified constitution, setting limits on the legislature's power to make law (Bingham (2010) p. 170).

nificance. It could once be said that the starting point for construing principles of statutory construction was the principle of parliamentary sovereignty. Some judges no longer accept this principle, at least in its traditional form, and their starting point for interpreting statutes must, at least on occasion, be different to that which we have traditionally conceived.

## Rules of particular application

The three rules discussed thus far are rules of general operation. There are also a large number of rules of particular application.[90] Once again, these are better regarded as Dworkinian principles than rules. There is no rule of priority in their operation; no rule to say which rule of particular application should be applied in preference to another, nor even when it should or should not be applied. To some degree, these rules must operate to produce greater consistency and predictability by restricting the range of meanings a court can legitimately give to a statute. How far they do this is, however, another matter.

An example will illustrate how these rules operate. The ejusdem generis rule is said to be:

The rule that where particular words are followed by general words, the general words are limited to the same kind as the particular words. Thus, the Sunday Observance Act, 1677, s 1, provides that 'no tradesman, artificer, workman, labourer or other person whatsoever shall do or exercise any worldly labour, business, or work of their ordinary callings upon the Lord's Day (works of necessity and charity only excepted)'. The words 'or other person whatsoever' are to be construed *ejusdem generis* with those that precede them so that an estate agent is not within the section. (*Gregory* v *Fearn* [1953] 1 WLR 974.)[91]

The meaning of the rule is thus clear. Its effect when applied is plain.[92] When it is to be used is not, however, self-evident. Its use is not automatic. Bennion notes that '[a] n intention to exclude the *ejusdem generis* principle may be shown expressly or by implication'.[93] Explicit exclusion of the rule is a relatively easy phenomenon to deal with when predicting the behaviour of the judiciary. However, the conclusion that the rule has implicitly been excluded requires the exercise of discretion by the judge and is an inherently subjective process.[94] Thus, how far this rule or other rules of particular

---

[90]  For examples of these rules, see Bennion (1990) ch. 12 and Bennion (1992) Parts 27 and 28.

[91]  P. Osborn, *A Concise Law Dictionary* (5th edn, 1964) Sweet & Maxwell, London, p. 119.

[92]  The rule continues to be used by the courts. See, for example, Blair J's judgment in *Bank of New York Mellon* v *GV Films Limited* [2009] EWHC 3315 (Comm) at para. 28.

[93]  Bennion (1990) pp. 198–9.

[94]  The example of implicit exclusion given by Bennion is *Young* v *Grattidge* (1968) LR 4 QB 166 (Bennion (1990) p. 199). In this case, Lush J asserts rather than argues for the exclusion of the ejusdem generis rule. This illustrates the subjective nature of its application.

application operate to produce uniformity and predictability in statutory interpretation is questionable.

## The Human Rights Act 1998

The Human Rights Act 1998 altered judicial practice with regard to interpretation in three ways. First, under s. 3 of the Act, the courts are required to interpret legislation so that 'so far as it is possible' it is compatible with the Convention rights defined under the Act.[95] Second, under s. 2 of the Act, the courts must 'take into account' the jurisprudence of the European Court of Human Rights, together with opinions and decisions of the European Commission of Human Rights and the decisions of the Committee of Ministers with regard to these rights, when deciding any question about Convention rights.[96] Finally, under s. 4 of the Act, in appropriate cases, where in interpreting a statute the courts find that the contents of that statute contravene Convention rights the High Court, Courts-Martial Appeal Court, Court of Appeal, Supreme Court, or Privy Council can make a declaration of incompatibility.[97]

How these new powers will alter the behaviour of courts is a matter for debate. During the passage of the Act through Parliament, one Law Lord commented that 'they [the provisions of the Human Rights Act] will not turn our world upside down'[98] with other Law Lords and retired Law Lords taking a similar, relaxed stance. Lord Scarman, for example, suggested that '[t]he Bill is modest'.[99] On the other hand, the then Government's intention in introducing the new legislation seemed to have been more radical. In the House of Lords, Lord Irvine, then Lord Chancellor, assented to Lord Lester's proposition that:

the court's obligation will be to strive wherever possible, to read existing legislation in accordance with the convention, using whatever interpretative tools they think fit.[100]

In the House of Commons Jack Straw, the then Home Secretary, said that:

we want the courts to strive to find an interpretation of legislation that is compatible with convention rights, so far as the plain words of the legislation allow, and only in the last resort to conclude that the legislation is incompatible with them.[101]

---

[95] These being broadly the rights and freedoms that are to be found in the European Convention on Human Rights (see further Human Rights Act 1998, s. 1 and Sch. 1).

[96] For an examination of this jurisprudence, see C. Ovey and R. White, *Jacobs and White, The European Convention on Human Rights* (4th edn, 2006) Oxford University Press, Oxford.

[97] See F. Klug, 'The Human Rights Act 1998, *Pepper* v *Hart*, and All That' [1999] Public Law 246, for a general examination of how the Act should be interpreted.

[98] Lord Bingham, Hansard, vol. 582, col. 1246.      [99] Hansard, vol. 582, col. 1256.

[100] Hansard, House of Lords, vol. 583, col. 523.

[101] Hansard, House of Commons, vol. 313, cols 421–2. It is noteworthy that in both the House of Lords and the House of Commons, the Government rejected amendments to s. 3 that would have limited courts to giving only 'reasonable' interpretations of legislation (Klug (1999) p. 253).

In the light of this Butler's comment seems accurate:

Through section 3(1) of the HRA Parliament intends the courts to adopt a new approach to the interface between statutes and human rights norms and has signalled a commitment to human rights principles.[102]

However, as Sedley LJ has observed, 'one major imponderable [in assessing what the impact of the 1998 Act will be] is the measure of the courts' receptivity to human rights issues'.[103] Early indications seemed to suggest that the courts would make liberal use of s. 3(1). In *R v A (No. 2)*, Lord Steyn said that 'the interpretative obligation under s. 3 of the 1998 Act is a strong one' and then went on to say that:

[i]n accordance with the will of Parliament as reflected in section 3 it will sometimes be necessary to adopt an interpretation which linguistically may appear strained. A declaration of incompatibility is a measure of last resort. It must be avoided unless it is plainly impossible to do so.[104]

Other judgments, however, have been more restrained. In *R v Lambert*, Lord Hope argued that legislation's:

primary characteristic ... is its ability to achieve certainty by the use of precise and clear language. It provides a set of rules by which, according to the ordinary meaning of the words used, the conduct of affairs may be regulated. So far as possible judges should seek to achieve the same attention to detail in their use of language to express the effect of section 3(1) as parliamentary draftsmen would have done if he had been amending the statute.[105]

In looking at how the courts can now draw the boundary between interpreting legislation and making legislation, given their power under s. 3(1), Lord Nicholls has observed:

[n]owadays courts are more 'liberal' in the interpretation of all manner of documents. The greater the latitude with which courts construe documents, the less readily defined is the boundary. What one person regards as sensible, if robust, interpretation, another regards as impermissibly creative. For present purposes it is sufficient to say that a meaning which departs substantially from a fundamental feature of an Act of Parliament is likely to have crossed the boundary between interpretation and amendment.[106]

---

[102]   A. Butler, 'Declaration of Incompatibility or Interpretation Consistent with Human Rights in New Zealand' [2001] Public Law 28 at p. 34. See also Lord Cooke, 'The British Enactment of Human Rights' (1998) 3 European Human Rights Law Review 243 at p. 256; Lord Lester, 'The Art of the Possible – Interpreting Statutes under the Human Rights Act' (1998) 6 European Human Rights Law Review 665 at p. 669; and Lord Steyn, 'Incorporation and Devolution – A Few Reflections on the Changing Scene' (1998) 2 European Human Rights Law Review 153 at p. 155 for similar comments.

[103]   Sedley LJ, *Freedom, Law and Justice* (1999) Sweet & Maxwell, London, p. 20.

[104]   [2002] 1 AC 45 at p. 68.      [105]   [2001] 3 WLR 206 at p. 234.

[106]   *Re S* [2002] 2 AC 291 at p. 313.

On the basis of judgments such as these, Klug and O'Brien concluded, two years after the 1998 Act came into force in England and Wales, that:

the emerging view is the 'plain meaning' of statutory language cannot be 'ignored or simply changed in the cause of securing compatibility [with convention rights].[107]

However, in *Ghaidan* v *Godin-Mendoza*, the House of Lords took a more robust view. Lord Nicholls, for example, stated that:

the interpretative obligation decreed by section 3 is of an unusual and far-reaching character. Section 3 may require a court to depart from the unambiguous meaning the legislation would otherwise bear [in order to ensure its compatibility with Convention rights].[108]

In a later case in the House of Lords, Lord Bingham cited *Ghaidan* v *Godin-Mendoza* in support of four propositions about the current state of the law:

first, the interpretative obligation under section 3 is a very strong and far reaching one, and may require the court to depart from the legislative intention of Parliament. Secondly, a Convention-compliant interpretation under section 3 is the primary remedial measure and a declaration of incompatibility under section 4 an exceptional course. Thirdly, it is to be noted that during the passage of the Bill through Parliament the promoters of the Bill told both Houses that it was envisaged that the need for a declaration of incompatibility would rarely arise. Fourthly, there is a limit beyond which a Convention-compliant interpretation is not possible, such limit being illustrated by *R (Anderson)* v *Secretary of State for the Home Department* [2003] 1 AC 837 and *Bellinger* v *Bellinger* (Lord Chancellor intervening) [2003] 2 AC 467.[109]

*Ghaidan* v *Godin-Mendoza* appears to have heralded a rather more liberal use of the powers given to the courts by s. 3.[110]

## Interpretative communities

Analysis of both the general principles of statutory interpretation and the rules of particular application show that they are by no means a closed system. They do not offer, and are not intended to offer, a complete answer to the difficulties of statutory

---

[107] F. Klug and C. O'Brien, 'The First Two Years of the Human Rights Act' [2002] Public Law 649 at p. 654. See also K. Starmer, 'Two Years of the Human Rights Act' (2003) 1 European Human Rights Law Review 14 at p. 16 for a similar view. [108] [2004] 2 AC 557 at p. 571

[109] *Sheldrake* v *DPP* [2005] 1 AC 264 at p. 303.

[110] For an analysis of *Ghaidan* v *Godin-Mendoza*, see J. van Zyl Smit, 'The New Purposive Interpretation of Statutes: HRA Section 3 after *Ghaidan* v *Godin-Moendoza*' (2007) 70 Modern Law Review 294. For a general assessment of the use made by the House of Lords of the Human Rights Act see B. Dickson, 'Britain's Law Lords and Human Rights' (2006) 26 Legal Studies 329. Even if *Ghaidan* v *Godin-Mendoza* does indicate a change in attitude by the courts it is still arguable that they could, and on occasions should, make even more use of their s. 3 powers. Thus, for example, despite Lord Bingham's approval in *Sheldrake* of the refusal of the House of Lords to use its s. 3 powers in *Bellinger* v *Bellinger* and instead issue a declaration of incompatibility, it is possible to argue that the use of s. 3 would have been more appropriate ([2003] 2 AC 467; on this, see A. Bradney, 'Developing Human Rights? The Lords and Transsexual Marriages' (2003b) 33 Family Law 583).

interpretation even where they can be applied. Nor do judges always seek to use these principles. Judges have been willing to interpret statutes not only in the context of principle or logic but on the basis of 'a matter of common sense'.[111] Finally:

[t]he fact that a substantial proportion of the problems of statutory interpretation which confront them [the courts] cannot be answered on principle is something to be borne in mind when the manner in which the courts perform their interpretative function is under discussion.[112]

Yet, notwithstanding all of this, it is clear that the interpretation of statutes by the judiciary is to some extent uniform and to some extent predictable. 'The English legal system' is not wholly anarchic. Lawyers feel able to advise clients. Thus, we must ask how this uniformity and predictability comes about if not solely through the mechanism of the principles and rules discussed above.

One way of explaining this phenomenon is to argue that:

all the phrases concerning the supremacy of Parliament in the matter of certain sets of words having been promulgated under a given set of rules, and all the other rules of statutory interpretation with which lawyers are familiar and to which judges constantly resort, constitute the interpretative strategies of these [legal] communities, which in turn constitute what will count as a statutory text. Interpreters, no less than texts which their strategies constitute, are themselves constituted by conventional ways of thinking.[113]

The important phrase here is 'conventional ways of thinking'. Important in the principles and rules of statutory interpretation is what they signal about the way the legal community (and in particular judges) think about the construction of statutes. The prescriptive force that the rules and principles have in dictating how statutes must be interpreted is less significant than the values they suggest. There are large logical lacunae in the rules and principles of statutory interpretation and these do indeed breed a degree of uncertainty in saying how a statute will be interpreted. But, just as the notion of the canon supplements the traditional theories of precedent and helps to explain the predictability of legal reasoning based upon case law, so the idea of the interpretative community assists principles of statutory interpretation in explaining the coherence of the lawyer's approach to statutes. It is the social pressure of the legal community as much as the normative force of a rule which generates given interpretations.[114] This necessity of understanding both the importance of the formal principles of statutory

---

[111] Per Lord Parker in *Smart* v *Allan* [1963] 1 QB 291 at p. 298. Although it should also be borne in mind that judges have held that it is 'statutory interpretation rather than common sense which must at the end of the day prevail if the two do not coincide' (per Lord Jauncey in *Bruce* v *Legal Aid Board* [1992] 3 All ER 321 at p. 326).                                                    [112]  Bell and Engle (1995) p. 76.

[113] D. Miers, 'Legal Theory and the Interpretation of Statutes' in W. Twining (ed.), *Legal Theory and Common Law* (1986) Basil Blackwell, Oxford, p. 122.

[114] Therefore, as with case law legal reasoning, the questions of who constitutes that community and where they derive their values from and how those values relate to the wider society become of central import.

interpretation and the influence of social construction underscores the importance on an integrated theory in understanding 'the English legal system'.

## CONCLUSION

Unsurprisingly, in considering how far the above can contribute to an integrated theory of 'the English legal system', there are many connections to be made between the conclusions that we can draw in this chapter and those that we already drew in the previous chapter on legal reasoning in cases.

Traditional analyses of rules and principles of statutory interpretation are important. They are part of the explanation for how statutes are interpreted by lawyers and particularly by judges. Within the areas wherein they operate, they reflect a particularly distinct notion of community and thus system. They connect with the rules of case law reasoning and help build a stronger whole, distinguishing those who use them from those who do not. As in the instance of case law reasoning, these rules have to be supplemented by notions of social construction. Community, like canon, is as important as Dworkinian principles.

As with case law reasoning, there are many, who are ostensibly within 'the English legal system', who do not form part of this unity. Once again, those in the European courts as well as the legally untrained members of English courts and tribunals and those who should but do not follow the rules fall wholly or partially outside this system. However, when we consider statutory interpretation there is a further limitation to the extent that the principles of statutory interpretation can truly be said to apply to 'the English legal system' taken as a whole.

Judgments, in the main, are considered only by those to whom they directly apply or by lawyers seeking assistance in deciding what their clients can do. Reasoning about cases is thus mainly limited to lawyers. However, we started off this chapter by pointing out that statutes are intended to be of general application. They apply to the world at large. This means that many people are involved in considering what statutes mean. Yet 'the vast majority of statutes never come before the courts for interpretation'.[115] Statutes apply to the world and are interpreted by the world. The interpretative community for statutes extends well beyond the judiciary. 'Most interpretation is done in the lawyer's office, on the police officer's beat, and at the bureaucrat's desk.'[116] There is not so much an interpretative community for statutes as interpretative communities and the rules and principles discussed above apply strongly only to some of those communities. Indeed, most interpretation of statutes is not done by any official of a legal system but is done, rather, by the ordinary individuals to whom the statutes apply.

---

[115] Bell and Engle (1995) p. 1.      [116] Eskridge (1994) pp. 71–2.

For many people, their understanding of statutes comes indirectly through secondary commentaries on statutes.[117] These may be contradictory or, from the point of view of the rules and principles stated above, inaccurate.[118] Nevertheless, if we ask, from the perspective of an integrated theory, how are statutes understood in 'the English legal system' as a whole, this understanding should constitute part of the picture. Unfortunately, it is a part of the picture that is unexplored by the academic community.

## FURTHER READING

CROSS, R., J. BELL, and G. ENGLE, *Cross: Statutory Interpretation* (1995) Oxford University Press, Oxford

GOODRICH, P., *Reading the Law* (1985) Basil Blackwell, Oxford

[117] Bennion writes: '[t]he subject who is bound by legislation must be classed as an interpreter of it. Nevertheless, unless an expert the subject is unwise to trust to his or her unaided understanding. Professional advice is needed' (Bennion (1992) p. 21). If by this, recourse to lawyers is being suggested, this seems, at the very least, expensive and impracticable given the all-pervasive nature of statutory regulation.

[118] For an example of this in relation to advice to nurses about the operation of the conscience clause (Abortion Act 1967, s. 4(1)), see A. Bradney, 'Making Cowards' [1990] Juridical Review 129 at p. 146.

# 7

# The university law school and law students

## INTRODUCTION

To start a section of this book devoted to looking at the personnel of 'the English legal system' with a discussion of the university law school might seem an eccentric enterprise. This is the first textbook to have taken this approach.[1] Whatever other function they have, university law schools are not institutions which help society in providing either dispute resolution or dispute avoidance.[2] They might therefore seem to be irrelevant to 'the English legal system'. However, in previous chapters, we have emphasized the importance of the idea of community in understanding how some personnel in 'the English legal system' work. We have argued that understanding English legal reasoning involves understanding the very small communities within which this reasoning takes place. We now wish to argue that part of the background to those communities, part of their source of values, is to be found in the university law school. University law schools are therefore intimately tied up with 'the English legal system'.[3] An understanding of the latter is possible only with an understanding of the former.[4]

---

[1] Stychin and Mulcahy's *Legal Method*, the first edition of which was published after the first edition of this book, also looks at university law schools (C. Stychin and L. Mulcahy, *Legal Method* (3rd edn, 2003)) Sweet & Maxwell, London, pp. 371–3.

[2] Universities are, however, sites of dispute resolution and avoidance. Members of universities are bound by codes of behaviour which are both formal and informal. Students, for example, find themselves constrained by regulations. Universities have their own police force which they normally call security officers. They have their own courts and judges who sit individually or in panels to hear accusations that students have been in breach of these regulations. Students may represent themselves at these hearings. Frequently, however, they may choose to be represented by others who we might regard as analogous to lawyers. Legal anthropologists might regard a university as a separate community with its own semi-autonomous legal system.

[3] Although an examination of university law schools is new to 'English legal system textbooks', it is far from new to analyses of the function of law in society. Thus, for example, Bankowski and Mungham's 1976 monograph *Images of Law* included a section 'Liberation and the law teacher' (Z. Bankowski and G. Mungham, *Images of Law* (1976) Routledge & Kegan Paul, London, pp. 106–9).

[4] This chapter is only concerned with the university law school, insofar as it directly affects law students. For a discussion of the wider issues relating to university law schools, see W. Twining, *Blackstone's Tower* (1994) Sweet & Maxwell, London; A. Bradney, *Conversations, Choices and Chances: The Liberal Law School in the Twenty-First Century* (2003a) Hart Publishing, Oxford; and F. Cownie, *Legal Academics: Culture and Identities* (2003) Hart Publishing, Oxford.

The importance of the university law school in contributing to the formation of the values of the legal communities has to be seen in context. No legal community in England and Wales requires its members to have been to a university law school. One legal community, that comprising solicitors, does not even require its members to be university graduates.[5] Thus, whatever effect universities have on the values of their students will not necessarily affect all lawyers. However, the statutory rules which govern membership of legal communities do not necessarily reflect the actual reality of those coming into the community. Of the 8,491 solicitors admitted in 2008–9 (excluding the 1,895 who were admitted by virtue of being a foreign lawyer), only 147 came via a route that permitted entry for non-graduates;[6] 316 were formerly barristers, where entry into the profession now demands a degree before the taking of the professional qualification; 3,843 had a law degree; whilst 1,446 were graduates from a discipline other than law.[7] Thus, at least 45.3 per cent of those admitted as solicitors were originally educated in a university law school.[8] Lawyers tend to be educated to tertiary level and to be educated at a university law school. The law school therefore has an important influence on the values of legal communities. An understanding of those communities is predicated on an understanding of the law school.

## Law students

Before analysing the work of the university law school, we need to look at the nature of university law students. Law students are not a typical cross-section of the population of England and Wales.[9] First, their gender balance does not reflect national norms. They are somewhat more likely to be female than male – in 2008, 63.7 per cent of all those accepted onto law degree programmes were women.[10] In the same year, 32.1 per cent of those accepted onto law degree programmes were from ethnic minorities.[11] Halpern's 1994 longitudinal survey of law students showed that students are largely

---

[5] The other major legal community, that comprising barristers, does now normally require its members to be graduates. For a description of the training route for a solicitor, see the Law Society's website at: <http://www.lawsociety.org.uk/becomingasolicitor.law>. For a description of the training route for a barrister, see the Bar Council's website at: <http://www.barcouncil.org.uk/CareersHome/TrainingtoBecomeaBarrister/>.

[6] *Annual Statistical Report 2009* (2009) The Law Society, London, p. 46.

[7] *Annual Statistical Report 2009* (2009) p. 46.

[8] The figure will, in fact, be greater than this because many barristers and some overseas lawyers are educated in British university law schools. Indeed, the non-degree routes into the solicitors' profession do not preclude candidates having a law degree.

[9] Equally, the concept of a law student is a broad one. Thus, for example, Francis and McDonald point out that not all law students are full-time and go on to argue that part-time students are not simply a subset of law students taken as a whole but instead, as a body, have distinctive characteristics of their own (A. Francis and I. McDonald, 'Part-time Law Students: The Forgotten Cohort' (2005) 39 The Law Teacher 277).

[10] *Annual Statistical Report 2009* (2009) p. 30.

[11] *Annual Statistical Report 2009* (2009) p. 30.

drawn from a middle-class background. Only 18 per cent came from a working-class background.[12] Moreover, students are likely to come from a relatively highly edu-cated background. Halpern's study showed that 26 per cent of students had a father with a degree (2.4 times the national average), whilst 16 per cent had a mother with a degree (4 times the national average).[13] Of the students in university law schools, 18 per cent had a close relative in one of the legal professions.[14] In Halpern's survey, 31 per cent came from independent schools as compared with the 6 per cent of the population who are in independent schools at the age of 14.[15] Law students are highly successful at A levels, having, in Halpern's study, an average score of 11.2 points.[16] In other words, in social terms, typically law students come from a relatively privileged, relatively high-achieving background.[17]

The study of law at university is often seen as being 'vocational, but with a strong academic content'.[18] This view is reflected in the reasons why students decide to study law. Although not all university law students will become lawyers, and not all students enter university law schools with the intention of becoming lawyers, there is a strong 'practical bias' amongst law students.[19] Purcell and Pitcher's 1996 sur-vey showed that 72.2 per cent of all law students surveyed chose their degree for 'pragmatic' (broadly career-oriented) reasons, whilst only 23.7 per cent chose it for 'hedonistic' (broadly interest in the subject) reasons.[20] This practical bias, in turn, both reflects and reinforces values held by students before they enter the university law school.

The values of university law students, and the kind of community they will wish to become part of, is to some extent set by their background before they reach the university law school. Nevertheless, the university law school makes its own contri-bution to the development of these values.

---

[12] D. Halpern, *Entry into the Legal Profession: The Law Student Cohort Study Years 1 and 2* (1994) The Law Society, London, p. 21. This figure is supported by earlier studies that showed the predominant middle-class nature of university law students. See, for example, P. McDonald, '"The Class of 81" – A Glance at the Social Class Composition of Recruits to the Legal Profession' (1982) 9 Journal of Law and Society 267 at pp. 268–70; and A. Sherr and J. Webb, 'Law Students, the External Market and Socialization: Do We Make Them Turn to the City?' (1989) 16 Journal of Law and Society 225 at p. 231.

[13] Halpern (1994) p. 23. A figure almost precisely replicated by Sherr and Webb (1989) p. 230.

[14] Halpern (1994) p. 24.        [15] Halpern (1994) pp. 26–7.

[16] Halpern (1994) p. 27. This figure is based on grading students' A levels as A = 5, B = 4, C = 3, D = 2 and E = 1.

[17] This 'typical' picture conceals great variations both in terms of individual background and, more significantly, institution. Thus, for example, there is a variation in all these figures if one considers new universities and old universities separately. However, even in the case of new universities, law students still come from a comparatively privileged and successful background as compared with the average in the population.

[18] Baroness Warnock, *Universities: Knowing our Minds* (1989) Chatto and Windus, London, p. 12.

[19] Sherr and Webb (1989) p. 246.

[20] K. Purcell and J. Pitcher, *Great Expectations* (1996) Institute of Employment Research, University of Warwick, p. 11. By contrast, the figure for humanities students were respectively 8.3 per cent and 85.1 per cent (Purcell and Pitcher (1996)).

# The nature of university law schools

University law schools are not simply one of the bureaucratic divisions of a university. Law schools, like departments of other disciplines in universities, are examples of specific cultures which are separated both from the outside world and from other cultures within the university:

The tribes of academe...define their own identities and defend their own patches of intellectual ground by employing a variety of devices geared to the exclusion of illegal immigrants. Some...are manifest in physical form ('the building occupied by the English department', in Clark's words); others emerge in the particularities of membership and constitution (Waugh's 'complex of tribes, each with its own chief and elders and witch-doctors and braves'). Alongside these structural features of disciplinary communities, exercising an even more powerful integrating force, are their more explicitly cultural elements: their traditions, customs and practices, transmitted knowledge, beliefs, morals and rules of conduct, as well as their symbolic forms of communication and the meanings they share.[21]

It is this culture which helps define the values of university law schools. Identifying the culture of the university law school is difficult. 'Our law schools, despite sharing a common culture, are probably too diverse to lend themselves to reliable generalisation.'[22] Individual variations in practice can appear to be more important than common themes. University law schools are found in old and new universities. They may be faculties on their own or departments within a faculty of social sciences. The largest schools number in excess of 1,000 students, whilst the smallest may be no more than several hundred. Staff sizes vary in similar proportions. However, despite all these important variations there are, nevertheless, some dominant ideas which prevail in most law schools and which constitute the culture of the university law school.

# The black-letter tradition

Traditionally, law schools have assumed that 'although law may appear to be irrational, chaotic and particularistic, if one digs deep enough and knows what one is looking for, then it will become evident that law is an internally coherent and unified body of rules'.[23] One of the earliest professors of law in Britain, A. V. Dicey, began his academic

---

[21] T. Becher and P. Trowler, *Academic Tribes and Territories* (2001) SRHE and the Open University Press, Buckingham, p. 47.

[22] Twining (1994) p. 66. For an analysis of the changing nature of university law schools, see A. Bradney and F. Cownie, 'British University Law Schools in the Twenty-first Century' in D. Hayton (ed.), *Law's Future(s)* (2000b) Hart Publishing, Oxford.

[23] D. Sugarman, 'Legal Theory, the Common Law Mind and the Making of the Textbook Tradition' in W. Twining (ed.), *Legal Theory and Common Law* (1986) Basil Blackwell, Oxford, p. 26.

career by arguing that '[i]t is for law professors to set forth the law as a coherent whole – to analyse and define legal conceptions – to reduce the mass of legal rules to an orderly series of principles'.[24] This became translated into a more modern proposition that, for example, 'the English law of real property rests on the logical development of clear principles, and it is these principles that throughout we have sought to emphasise [in writing our textbook]'.[25]

Following this idea, the university law school's function is to identify legal principles.[26] These are to be found in law reports and statutes and are written up in textbooks and legal periodicals.[27] Students are present in law schools to inculcate both these principles and that which is the method of understanding these principles, English legal reasoning. This approach is not necessarily something which is unwelcome and imposed on law students. There is some evidence to suggest that it is in accord with their expectations and desires. Sherr and Webb's study of students in Warwick University law school, an avowedly non-traditional law school, found that '[t]he students thought that most emphasis is and should be placed on thinking like a lawyer and on substantive legal doctrine and rules'.[28] Increasingly, British university law schools are moving away from this traditional approach. Cownie's study of contemporary British law schools showed that only a minority of university academics work simply within the black-letter law tradition.[29] Nevertheless, the analysis of legal rules, albeit often an analysis that draws on a range of concepts and techniques from disciplines outside law, remains at the centre of the law school.

## Training for a hierarchy

To say that English university law schools are dominated by an attempt to analyse legal rules does not seem to say anything about the values that law students will imbibe or the kinds of communities they will form or wish to enter because of the nature of this

---

[24]  A. V. Dicey, *Can English Law be Taught at the Universities?* (1883) Macmillan, London, p. 18.

[25]  R. Megarry and W. Wade, *The Law of Real Property* (1966) Stevens, London, p. vii. See also J. C. Smith's, *The Law of Contract*, which the author states is an attempt 'to elucidate the fundamental principles of the subjects from the authorities' (J. C. Smith, *The Law of Contract* (1989) Sweet & Maxwell, London, p. v) and Williams' influential skills textbook, *Learning the Law*, which states that '[i]t is through applying oneself to cases that one gets to understand how legal problems present themselves and how legal argument is conducted' (G. Williams, *Learning the Law* (11th edn, 1982) Stevens, London, p. 48).

[26]  This view is not just to be found in academic writing. It is also a view held by some within the judiciary. See Lord Goff, 'The Search for Principle' (1983) 69 Proceedings of the British Academy 169 and 'Judge, Jurist and Legislator' (1987) Denning Law Journal 79.

[27]  Twining (1994, p. 94) quotes the 1974 guide to the Bodleian Law Library 'Legal literature is vast but almost universally consists of four main classes: (1) Legislation, (2) Law Reports, (3) Legal Periodicals, (4) Textbooks.'                                               [28]  Sherr and Webb (1989) p. 246.

[29]  Significant numbers describe themselves as being black-letter lawyers but then go on to describe their work in terms that would be unfamiliar to, for example, Dicey (Cownie, 2003, pp. 54–8).

education. It might appear to be merely descriptive. One might want to argue that a diet of material limited to cases, statutes, and textbooks is too restricted; that law should involve a wider study which includes materials taken from the social sciences.[30] This, however, is a separate point.

During the last 30 years, many academics have argued that to concentrate on the form of the material used in black-letter law teaching is to miss its social effect and political impact. 'Law school can be an intense, powerful experience.'[31] For most students, it involves largely unfamiliar materials in a wholly unfamiliar atmosphere. 'We cope with law school by reducing the chaos to manageable terms.'[32] But, it is argued, this ordering of chaos is more than simply an intellectual process of taking on new knowledge.[33]

In an early, very influential article Kennedy argued that '[l]aw schools are intensely political places despite the fact that the modern law school seems intellectually unpretentious, barren of theoretical ambition or practical vision of what social life might be'.[34]

Kennedy's argument pointed to a number of features which he thought were important in the ideological impact of the university law school. First, the law school was hierarchical, with the nature of the relationship between lecturer and student being determined by the lecturer. Secondly the study of law involved the study of a new language. Thirdly, law was put forward as a matter of rules. Fourthly, in applying these rules one's emotions or sympathies were deemed to be irrelevant. Finally, the law school provided no overt theory in its teaching which could act as a source for critique:

Teachers convince students that legal reasoning exists, and is different from policy analysis, by bullying them into accepting as valid in particular cases arguments about legal correctness that are circular, question-begging, incoherent, or so vague as to be meaningless. Sometimes these are just arguments from authority, with the validity of the authoritative premise put outside discussion by professorial fiat. Sometimes they are policy arguments (eg security of transaction, business certainty) that are treated in a particular situation as

---

[30] See, for example, P. Atiyah, *Accidents, Compensation and the Law* (1st edn, 1970) Weidenfeld & Nicolson, London, pp. xv–xvi; and Bradney (2003a) pp. 98–101.

[31] J. Elkins, 'Coping Strategies in Legal Education' (1982) 16 The Law Teacher 195 at p. 195.

[32] Elkins (1982) p. 197.

[33] In itself, this argument is not wholly new. See, for example, J. Taylor, 'Law School Stress and the Deformation Professionelle' (1975–6) 27 Journal of Legal Education 251. What are new are the radical conclusions that are drawn about the effects of this process.

[34] Reprinted as D. Kennedy, 'Legal Education as Training for Hierarchy' in D. Kairys (ed.), *The Politics of Law* (1990) Pantheon Books, New York, p. 38. The original version of this article was published as D. Kennedy, 'Legal Education and the Reproduction of Hierarchy' (1982) 32 Journal of Legal Education 591. Some parts of Kennedy's argument rest on the particular pedagogic practices of American university law schools and are not directly applicable in the British context. Kennedy was not the first person to argue for the political effect of the university law school. For example, the 1982 volume of the Journal of Legal Education also saw the publication of Halpern's article 'On the Politics and Pathology of Legal Education'. Halpern, formerly a professor of politics, based his article on his experience of law school as a student and argued that much of legal education was subliminal political indoctrination (S. Halpern, 'On the Politics and Pathology of Legal Education' (1982) 32 Journal of Legal Education 383).

though they were rules that everyone accepts but that will be ignored in the next case when they would suggest that the decision was wrong. Sometimes they are exercises in formal logic that wouldn't stand up for a minute in a discussion between equals (eg the small print in a form contract represents the 'will of the parties').[35]

Using these methods, black-letter law presents itself, through the cases, statutes and textbooks, as a form of objective knowledge; there is a legally correct outcome to a particular dispute which, with proper training, the student will discern. A failure to see the objectively right answer by the student is characterized by the lecturer (and frequently the student) as a failure to learn the language of law or a failure in knowing the correct rules or an inability to disentangle one's emotional or political sympathies from one's intellectual understanding of the law.[36] However, in Kennedy's view, in fact all there is in law is a distinctive argumentative technique. This technique does not determine any particular outcome; does not produce a closure which will require a predestined answer. Legal technique is simply a form of argument that literally will sound right to another lawyer.

One of the results of the black-letter approach to law teaching is that there appears to be a strict separation of the question of what law is and what law should be. In learning the former, questions about the latter do not need to be raised. Outcomes of cases do not need justifying from either an ethical or a political standpoint.[37] They simply are the law. Thus, in the British context, Fitzpatrick has argued that '[t]he deep complicities between professional and academic conceptions of law produced an English jurisprudence that...protected law from significant engagement with political and social issues'.[38] Indeed, it has been argued that raising questions about the social impact of particular legal rules is not appropriate within a law school.[39] 'The desired result, at the end of legal training, is a competent lawyer who can analyse and apply legal doctrine in an intelligent and disinterested fashion.'[40] Law is seen as a value-free tool.

Kennedy's argument directly opposes this traditional approach. In his view, the outcomes to cases are determined, not by the content of the rules themselves or by the nature of legal argument, but by the policy biases, conscious and unconscious, of those who deal with them. '[E]verything taught [in the university law school], except

[35]  Kennedy (1990) pp. 43–4.

[36]  See also Foster's comment that '[l]aw school is a lonely place for idealists. Its obsession is the real world, not the world as it ought to be' (J. Foster, 'The "Cooling out" of Law Students: Facilitating Market Co-operation of Future Lawyers' in R. Gambitta, M. May, and J. Foster (eds), *Governing through Courts* (1981) Sage Publications, Beverley Hills, p. 179) and that '[t]his sense that lawyering has something to do with justice is largely beside the point in law school. Justice is the concern of philosophers – lawyers represent clients' (p. 180).

[37]  '[T]he truth claims of legal knowledge are not only treated as unproblematic but are rarely raised in education at all' (A. Thompson, 'Critical Legal Education in Britain' in P. Fitzpatrick and A. Hunt (eds), *Critical Legal Studies* (1987) Basil Blackwell, London, p. 184).

[38]  P. Fitzpatrick, 'The Abstracts and Brief Chronicles of the Time: Supplementing Jurisprudence' in P. Fitzpatrick (ed.), *Dangerous Supplements* (1991) Pluto Press, London, p. 28.

[39]  See B. Barrett, 'A Plea for Conservation' (1981) 15 The Law Teacher 146 at p. 156.

[40]  N. Naffine, *Law and the Sexes* (1990) Allen & Unwin, London, p. 32.

the formal rules themselves and the argumentative techniques for manipulating them, is policy and nothing more.[41] The constant repetition of particular policy outcomes in individual cases reinforces a message that such outcomes are natural, inevitable, and right. Students are learning an '[i]ndividualism [that] provides a justification for the fundamental legal institutions of criminal law, property, tort and contract'.[42] The fact that these policy outcomes are not explicitly examined or set into any kind of social context further reinforces this message about their naturalness.[43] On this view, by 'learning the law' students are also learning a set of political and ethical values that are oriented towards the status quo:[44]

[Legal] method is meant to be applied to a body of law presented, to a limited but significant degree, as a repository of intelligible purposes, policies, and principles rather than as merely a collection of shaky settlements in a constant war for the favors of government. Yet the real message of the curriculum is the denial of all this...It teaches that a mixture of low-level skills and high-level sophistic techniques of argumentative manipulation is all there is – all there is and all there can be – to legal analysis and, by implication, to the many methods by which professional expertise influences the exercise of state power.[45]

The ideological impact of the university law school lies not just in the way in which things are taught; it is also concerned with what it is that is taught. Kennedy notes that not all courses have equal status within the curriculum.[46] What the law school makes compulsory, what it teaches first, what it regards as basic to further more advanced work is also that to which it grants greater status. Other subjects are marginalized. Thus, for example, it has been said that '[j]urisprudence does have a reputation [as the] final retreat of the incompetent or exhausted black-letter lawyer'.[47]

Stanley has applied Kennedy's argument to the British context. Most law in the curriculum, he argues, is private law rather than public law; contract law or the law of tort rather than social security law or planning law. 'This dominance of rule based,

---

[41] Kennedy (1990) p. 45.

[42] D. Kennedy, 'Form and Substance in Private Law Adjudication' (1976) 89 Harvard Law Review 1685 at p. 1,715. Kennedy maintains that there is a contradiction in the rhetoric that lawyers use:

> One formal mode favors the use of clearly defined, highly administrable, general rules: the other supports the use of equitable standards producing ad hoc decisions with relatively little precedential value...altruist views on substantive private law issues lead to willingness to resort to standards in administration, while individualism seems to harmonize with an insistence on rigid rules rigidly applied. (Kennedy (1976) p. 1,685)

[43] Thompson argues that central to this critique of the traditional approach to legal education is 'the concept of ideological domination, the idea that we are dominated by not seeing how we see ... [It is] a crucial critical concept, and ideology critique, which seeks to thematise the invisible structures of thought, becomes a dominant methodology' (Thompson (1987) p. 190).

[44] In 1948, the President of the Society of Public Teachers of Law, W. Stalleybrass, said in his Presidential Address: 'you cannot be a good lawyer unless you have a respect of property, life and order' (W. Stalleybrass, 'Law in the Universities' [1948] Journal of the Society of Public Teachers of Law 157 at p. 164).

[45] R. Unger, *The Critical Legal Studies Movement* (1986) Harvard University Press, Cambridge, MA, pp. 112–13.                                                        [46] Kennedy (1990) p. 44.

[47] C. Stanley, 'Legal Fictions: Discourse and Archaeology. Notes on the Construction of a Jurisprudence Course' (1991) 25 The Law Teacher 241 at p. 241.

procedural subjects which are of relevance only to certain sections of society ensures the continued individualist, free-market ethos.[48] The subjects which command the curriculum are of relevance only to the lives of a small section of the population. The disputes they concern are largely disputes about property which are settled on an individual basis. Large sections of the population have relatively little property. What is of greatest importance to them is not individual dispute resolution but, rather, collective decisions about general resource allocation. Quite simply, on this argument, the lives of the majority of the population are written out of the law school curriculum in favour of the needs of the economic system. This teaches the student that the important areas of law are the areas which involve large amounts of money, major companies, or significant economic actors. Law for other purposes is of little account.

If the arguments above are accepted, university law schools teach not just particular facts but also particular values. They inculcate into students the ideas that law is fixed and that law is neutral. Moreover, they do this not by proving either of these two points but by assuming that they are so and then by repeating that assertion until the majority of the audience, students, believe them. Equally important, is what university law schools do not teach. By not giving the same prominence to theoretical courses as they do to black-letter courses, university law schools fail to give law students any method by which they might criticize the material that they are being presented with.

University law schools are not, of course, fixed entities, wholly unable to escape their past. A number of writers have argued that the research paradigm in university law schools is changing and that theoretical work or socio-legal studies rather than doctrinal law now represents the dominant mode.[49] Teaching tends to lag behind research. In the main, only that which is known can be taught and, in the main, that which is known is only that which has been published. Nevertheless, some writers have argued that a different approach to purely doctrinal study is now required from law students and we have noted above the results of Cownie's survey which shows that adherence to the purest forms of doctrinal teaching no longer dominate the law school in the way that they once did. Students now need a general mastery of, amongst other things, the social sciences.[50] This being so, a changing approach to teaching in law will change the process of acculturation that occurs in the law schools, perhaps making the law school less simply a place for the replication of hierarchies.

---

[48] C. Stanley, 'Training for the Hierarchy? Reflections on the British Experience of Legal Education' (1988) 22 The Law Teacher 78 at p. 83. Kennedy argues that the law in those courses which dominate the curriculum 'are the ground rules of late nineteenth-century laissez-faire capitalism' (Kennedy (1990) p. 44).

[49] For an example of this argument put in the specific context of company law, see B. Cheffins, 'Using Theory to Study Law: A Company Law Perspective' (1999) 58 Cambridge Law Journal 19. For this argument in a more general context, see A. Bradney, 'Law as a Parasitic Discipline' (1998) 25 Journal of Law and Society 71.

[50] See, for example, B. Hepple, 'The Renewal of the Liberal Law Degree' (1996) 55 Cambridge Law Journal 470. In a similar vein, Brownsword has argued that the purpose of the law degree is not to make students better lawyers but to make them better citizens (R. Brownsword, 'Teaching Contract: A Liberal Agenda' in P. Birks (ed.), *Examining the Law Syllabus: The Core* (1992) Oxford University Press, Oxford, p. 48). See also Bradney (1998) passim and Bradney (2003a) passim.

## University law schools and gender

University law schools are now overtly neutral about matters of gender. Historically, women were debarred from entering law schools.[51] This period of legal exclusion is now, however, long since over and, as we have noted above, women are now found in larger numbers than men in the student body in university law schools.[52] Nevertheless, some would argue that this does not necessarily indicate that university law schools treat women equally and that, on the contrary, patterns of discrimination found in legal communities are begun in law schools.[53]

Although women are represented more than equally with men in the student body in most university law schools this pattern is not followed if one looks at numbers of academic staff who are male and female. Clare McGlynn's 1999 survey suggested that, while women formed 40 per cent of all legal academics (and 49 per cent of lecturers), they accounted for only 14 per cent of professors and 22 per cent of readers.[54]

We saw above that it is possible to argue that the traditional black-letter approach to law implies that the interests of some sections of society are more important than others. If the law school curriculum gives greater priority to subjects that are concerned with property and the protection of property, it is implicitly saying that the interests of those people who own property are more important than the interests of those people who, for example, live on state benefits. For the latter group, the law relating to social security may be of more obvious concern than that relating to property. Similarly, the law school's curriculum can be argued to reflect male rather than female interests.[55]

The very priority that the law school curriculum gives to property might in itself be said to reflect a male bias. If the majority of the property owners are male, and if men on average earn more than women, property is more obviously a male rather than a female concern. This is not to say that the law school curriculum is overtly biased towards either gender. Women are not explicitly excluded from the curriculum.

---

[51] A. Sachs and J. Hoff Wilson, *Sexism and the Law* (1978) Martin Robertson, Oxford, pp. 27–8, 31–3, and 170–4.

[52] This does not necessarily indicate an absence of discriminatory practices on the part of university law schools. If more well-qualified women than men applied to law schools for places and an equal number received places, the result would be discriminatory. If the criteria used to allocate places were discriminatory then, even if an equal number of women found places in law schools, the process would be discriminatory.

[53] 'There is probably a strong correlation between the existence of gender bias in American courts and gender bias in law school classrooms' (T. Lovell Banks, 'Gender Bias in the Classroom' (1988) 38 Journal of Legal Education 135 at p. 138). See also A. Jacobs, 'Women in Law Schools: Structural Constraint and Personal Choice in the Formation of Professional Identity' (1972) 24 Journal of Legal Education 462.

[54] C. McGlynn, 'Women, Representation and the Legal Academy' (1999) 19(1) Legal Studies 68 at p. 75.

[55] For a general discussion of gender bias in law teaching, see R. Graycar and J. Morgan, *The Hidden Gender of Law* (1990) The Federation Press, Leichhardt, pp. 25–9. For a discussion of the possibilities for a feminist legal curriculum, see R. Auchmuty, 'Agenda for a Feminist Legal Curriculum' (2003) 23 Legal Studies 377.

But neither is any single course clearly dealing with matters which are solely, or even mainly, of concern to women.[56] Instead, issues which are of direct concern are split up in the curriculum, making possible connections between them difficult to spot and marginalizing their importance within individual courses. An illustrative example of this phenomenon can be seen in traditional accounts of rape, offences of sexual violence, and domestic violence. These are split between criminal law courses and family law courses. Moreover, in traditional legal analysis, the discussion of rape can itself be reduced to a discussion of the technical issues which are drained of any sense of the significance of the crime being discussed. One leading textbook, for example, took three pages to discuss one reported case concerning what constitutes the legal concept of mistake. The nature of the 'mistake' in the case, the inaccurate belief in a woman's consent to sexual intercourse with multiple partners, that belief allegedly being held despite the fact that she had expressed her lack of consent, becomes evident only at the very end of the discussion.[57]

Gilligan has argued that there are separate 'voices' for women and men. The female voice is one that sees itself in relation to others. In looking at moral problems, it seeks answers that work for everyone involved in the problem. The male voice is individualized. In looking at moral problems, it seeks answers in terms of the rights that each individual has in the particular situation.[58] Many writers have seen lessons for university law schools in these differentiated voices.[59] It has been said that women, 'like racial minorities, often feel alienated in the classroom. As a result they become silent in the class.'[60] One reason for this alienation might be:

a rigid focus on the rights of disconnected individuals...an uncaring law whose sole concern is getting right abstract principles without reference to the particular human beings involved. In it, competing claims between individuals are settled bloodlessly, according to standards of supposed fairness and impartiality. People must be treated alike whatever the individual need, whatever the social context and whatever the unfortunate consequences for nearest and dearest.[61]

The female voice is alienated from the individualized, rights-based approach in law.

Another reason for alienation might be the very manner of law school teaching acts differently upon the female and male voice:

The politics of masculinity involves recognising that historically specific institutional practices – for example, how we behave as legal academics, how we interact with

---

[56] With the exception of the relatively new innovation of courses concerned with either feminism and law or women and law.

[57] See the discussion of *R v Morgan* [1976] AC 182 in Sir John Smith, *Smith and Hogan's Criminal Law* (10th edn, 2002) Butterworths, London, pp. 237–9. Following criticism of the decision in *Morgan* the law was amended by statute. The present law is discussed in D. Ormerod, *Smith and Hogan: Criminal Law* (12th edn, 2008) Oxford University Press, Oxford, pp. 694–703.

[58] C. Gilligan, *In a Different Voice* (1982) Harvard University Press, Cambridge, MA.

[59] For a discussion of the argument that there are both conservative and progressive readings of Gilligan's work see, M. Frug, *Postmodern Legal Feminism* (1992) Routledge, London, ch. 3.

[60] Lovell Banks (1988) p. 139.     [61] Naffine (1990) p. 11.

colleagues and students, how the 'working' lives relate to 'home' lives, draw and transform a gender order in which at present hegemonic masculinism constitutes the dominant ideology.[62]

Thus, individual questions (and answers) in tutorials, a hierarchical ordering of marks for students, the assertion that the individual must present her ideas and the demarcation of status between lecturer and student might all, amongst other things, be argued to be features of the law school which will affect the male voice and the female voice very differently.[63]

The gender distinctions noted above might teach one of two things. First, they might teach a woman that she was partially or wholly excluded from the law and thus partially or wholly excluded from the legal profession. Second, they might teach her that in order to succeed within the law it is necessary to take on Gilligan's male voice. In either case, the gender distinctions involve the inculcation of value preferences.[64]

However, here again, we need to be careful about drawing too static a picture of the law school. Whilst the general picture outlined might still be accurate, we also need to be aware of the possible direction of change.[65] Of the heads of school listed in the Society of Legal Scholars Directory for 2008/9, 50 were men but 27 were women.[66] The Society is both the oldest and largest association for legal academics, having been founded in 1909. It elected its first women president in 1997/98; a president holding office for one year. However, since then, there have been a further four women presidents.[67] Other examples of women holding senior positions in the legal academy can be given.[68] Nevertheless, law schools continue to be gendered with this having an inevitable effect on students.[69]

---

[62]  R. Collier, 'Masculism, Law and Law Teaching' (1991) 19 International Journal of the Sociology of Law 427 at p. 433.

[63]  Indeed, a textbook such as this can be argued to be the product of, and the affirmation of value in, the male voice given its implicit assertion of the authority of the text. For a different approach to academic writing, see 'Define and Empower: Women Students Consider Feminist Learning' (1990) 1 Law and Critique 47.

[64]  Equally, of course, men might be taught that their values are inherently superior, or at least more acceptable within the legal world.

[65]  For a more detailed analysis of this point, see F. Cownie, 'Women in the Law School: Shoals of Fish, Starfish or Fish out of Water?' in P. Thomas (ed.), Discriminating Lawyers (2000) Cavendish, London.

[66]  The Directory entries are not exhaustive. However, there are sufficient to provide a broadly accurate picture.

[67]  For a history of the Society, see F. Cownie and R. Cocks, 'A Great and Noble Occupation': The History of the Society of Legal Scholars (2009) Hart Publishing, Oxford.

[68]  Thus, for example, the chair of the last Law Sub-Panel that assessed the quality of research in university law schools was female (see: <http://www.rae.ac.uk/panels/members/>).

[69]  For a recent examination of the gendered nature of law schools, see R. Collier, 'The Restructured University: Rethinking the Gendered Law School' in R. Collier, Men, Law and Gender: Essays on the 'Man' in Law (2010b) Routledge, London.

## CONCLUSION

The arguments above are strongly put by their proponents; perhaps too strongly. As we have already noted, university law schools are not all identical; nor are all courses identical; nor are all lecturers identical; law schools are constantly in a process of change. Each law student, no matter which law school they are in, will meet a number of different examples of approaches to the study of law during the time they are studying. Some law schools are much more diverse than others in the methods and material that they use in their teaching. Moreover, they can see still more examples of different approaches to the study of law in the books and articles available to them in their university library. This variety serves to dilute the ideological effect of the law school on the student.[70]

It is probably pertinent to observe that the criticisms of the ideological effect of university law schools on law students noted above are offered by writers who are all themselves working in just such an environment. Universities are sites of resistance as well as places where established power will reproduce itself. Russell has argued that one of the most important functions of a university is inculcating intellectual independence into a student. This independence, he argues, gives the student the strength of purpose to resist illegitimate occupational pressures when they enter into employment after graduation. The examples he gives are of civil servants who have to tell a minister that what the minister wants doing cannot be done or an engineer asked to design a bridge in an unsafe manner. In Russell's view, a university education provides graduates with a respect for truth which will enable them to resist such demands.[71] His argument could easily be applied to the university law school and its effects on law students. Even within the black-letter tradition, it could be said that what the law school seeks to teach is a requirement for evidence for an argument. If the evidence is not there, then the argument, no matter who puts it forward, is invalid.[72] It is easy to argue that the ideological effect of university law schools is not all negative.

The history of British legal education over the last four decades is replete with those who have rejected the black-letter tradition. There is nothing new in the suggestion that the

---

[70] Although the proponents of the arguments above would argue that alternative approaches to teaching are marginalized within the law school and that this marginalization affects the way in which students accept these approaches (see, for example, R. Abel, 'Evaluating Evaluations: How Should Law Schools Judge Teaching?' (1990) 40 Journal of Legal Education 407 at pp. 408–10). For a notorious example of such marginalization, see Carrington's assessment of those who favour the Critical Legal Studies movement:

> In an honest effort to proclaim a need for revolution, nihilist teachers are more likely to train crooks than radicals. If this risk is correctly appraised, the nihilist who must profess that legal principle does not matter has an ethical duty to depart the law school, perhaps to seek a place elsewhere in the academy. (P. Carrington, 'Of Law and the River' (1984) 34 Journal of Legal Education 222 at p. 227.)

[71] C. Russell, *Academic Freedom* (1993) Routledge, London, p. 27.

[72] But the proponents of the views above would immediately wish to add that what counts as evidence and what the evidence shows are rarely simple matters and whether the evidence is being distorted in university law schools is precisely what is being debated.

study of legal doctrine is insufficient on its own.[73] Philosophical approaches to law, the law in context movement, socio-legal studies, economic analyses, as well as the Critical Legal Studies movement and feminism which lie behind the criticism above, all find the place in the law school and have done so for some time.[74] Indeed, the writing of this book would have been impossible without the articles and books which are themselves evidence of a wider approach to legal scholarship than is suggested by the black-letter tradition. Yet, the writing of this book also demonstrates the strength of the criticisms above. In writing this book, we have been forced on many occasions to observe that we have no evidence about how a particular legal process works in practice or that the evidence is very limited. In many areas, non-doctrinal legal scholarship is thinly spread. Perhaps the criticisms put above are put too strongly. Nevertheless, they contain strong elements of truth. The black-letter tradition is not all-pervasive, and it is much weaker than it once was, but it is still there and it still exerts a powerful influence on the psyche of the graduate who becomes a lawyer.

## FURTHER READING

BRADNEY, A., *Conversations, Choices and Chances: The Liberal Law School in the Twenty-first Century* (2003) Hart Publishing, Oxford

COWNIE, F., *Legal Academics: Culture and Identities* (2003) Hart Publishing, Oxford

TWINING, W., *Blackstone's Tower* (1994) Sweet & Maxwell, London

---

[73] See, for example, Twining's call for the reassessment of the view that 'legal doctrine is *the* subject-matter of legal studies' (W. Twining, 'Pericles and the Plumber' (1967) 83 Law Quarterly Review 396 at p. 420).

[74] For a discussion of the widening nature of legal scholarship see Twining (1994) pp. 141–6 and Cownie (2003) ch. 3.

# 8

# Solicitors and barristers

## INTRODUCTION

Lawyers are a ubiquitous feature of modern life. This is true not just for England and Wales but for developed societies generally. In a study of legal evolution, Schwartz and Miller noted that '[i]t is a striking feature of the data that damages and mediation are characteristic of the simplest (as well as the most complex) societies, while legal counsel are found only in the most complex'.[1] Social complexity and lawyers seem to go together.[2] Yet, at the same time, it has been noted that '[t]he effective handling of legal problems does not necessarily require the use of lawyers'.[3] Many legal problems are dealt with by people who cannot strictly be called lawyers.[4] Lawyers are important. If we are to understand how disputes are resolved in 'the English legal system', we need to understand the work of lawyers. But we need to do more than this. We need to begin by seeing how lawyers relate to, and are different from, other people offering advice about legal problems. For the purposes of this chapter, we will use Schwartz and Miller's term 'counsel' to describe both lawyers and others who offer advice about legal problems. In their study, Schwartz and Miller defined the use of counsel as being the 'regular use of specialized non-kin advocates in the settlement of disputes'.[5] Using this definition, solicitors and barristers are counsel. However, there are many other examples of 'specialized non-kin advocates [involved] in the settlement of disputes' within present-day Great Britain.

Even if we limit the notion of counsel to those professionals who are entitled to represent clients in courts and tribunals within 'the English legal system' we would have to include people other than solicitors and barristers. Patent agents or patent attorneys, for example,

---

[1] R. Schwartz and J. Miller, 'Legal Evolution and Social Control' (1964–5) 70 American Journal of Sociology 159 at p. 167.

[2] 'A complex society is almost necessarily legalized' (L. Friedman, 'Lawyers in Cross-Cultural Perspective' in R. Abel and P. Lewis, *Lawyers in Society: Volume Three* (1989) University of California Press, Berkeley, p. 13). For a discussion of the changing role of lawyers in modern society, see I. Ramsay, 'What Do Lawyers Do? Reflections on the Model for Lawyers' (1993) 21 International Journal of the Sociology of Law 355.

[3] M. Zander, *Legal Services for the Community* (1978) Temple Smith, London, p. 298.

[4] 'Most services which are "legal", in the sense that a lawyer often performs them in the ordinary course of his practice, may also be performed by non-lawyers' (Lord Chancellor's Department, *The Work and Organisation of the Legal Profession* (1989) Cm. 570, para. 2.1).

[5] Schwartz and Miller (1964–5) p. 161.

are entitled to represent clients in the Patents County Court.[6] However, it would be difficult to justify limiting the term counsel in this way. We will show below that the work of solicitors and barristers involves a lot more than appearing in court for clients. If this is so, we must look more widely than court work in deciding who might count as counsel.

There are a number of different directions in which we might look for counsel other than solicitors and barristers. We might start by considering the role of those who work in advice centres of various kinds. Thus, when Abel-Smith, Zander and Brooke surveyed the provision of legal services in three London boroughs, they looked, not just at the work of solicitors, but also at the work of organizations such as Citizens Advice Bureaux, Legal Advice Centres, and the Probation Services. They also considered the work of local authority departments which gave legal advice to the general public.[7] Whilst many of these organizations employed some solicitors, it was equally true that many of the people giving advice were not professionally qualified in this way. We would argue that such advisers can still be counted as counsel since they fit the definition used by Schwartz and Miller. Similarly, in Morton's account of a law centre, Liverpool 8, he discusses the work of the Welfare Rights Advice Worker as well as that of a solicitor employed by the centre.[8] Both are involved in acting as advocates in settling disputes so both might legitimately be called counsel.

A second direction in which we might look for lawyers other than solicitors and barristers is by looking at the organization of firms of solicitors. Not everybody employed in a firm of solicitors is a trained solicitor. Firms employ support staff to assist the work of solicitors. They also employ people who provide legal advice to clients even though they are not solicitors. Many firms now employ legal executives. Their work is varied. Much of it will be relatively routine. In theory, they will usually work under the supervision of a solicitor, though in practice they will be comparatively autonomous.[9] In a number of areas, legal executives can act independently for clients.[10] Employed by lawyers, many would not regard them as strictly being lawyers, but they are certainly counsel in Schwartz and Miller's terms.[11]

---

[6] Copyright, Designs and Patents Act 1988, s. 292. There is some discussion of the work of patent agents in court in J. Adams, 'Choice of Forum in Patent Disputes' (1995) 10 European Intellectual Property Review 497 at pp. 409–551. These are not the only such examples of counsel. For example, official receivers and deputy official receivers have rights of audience in insolvency proceedings in both the county court or the High Court (SI 1986/1925, para. 1).

[7] B. Abel-Smith, M. Zander, and R. Brooke, *Legal Problems and the Citizen* (1973) Heinemann, London.

[8] J. Morton, 'Liverpool 8 – Anatomy of a Law Centre' (1988) 138 New Law Journal 141.

[9] For a description of the work of legal executives, see Zander (1978) p. 299 and the Report of the Royal Commission on Legal Services (the Benson Report) (1979) Cmnd 7648, ch. 31.

[10] Thus, for example, the Institute of Legal Executives is a prescribed body for the purposes of the Legal Services Act 2007 (see Sch. 4 para. 1). For a full description of the rights of audience of legal executives, see the Institute of Legal Executives website at: <http://www.ilex.org.uk/professional_issues/advocates.asp>.

[11] The Institute of Legal Executives contends that 'ILEX is recognised as the third branch of the legal profession, alongside solicitors and barristers. Legal Executives are professional lawyers' (<http://www.ilex.org.uk/press_office/article.asp?theId=341&themode=1>) but gives no evidence for this assertion. See further A. Francis, 'Legal Executives and the Phantom of Legal Professionalism: The Rise and Rise of the Third Branch of the Legal Profession?' (2002) 9(1) International Journal of the Legal Profession 5.

Finally, in looking for lawyers other than solicitors and barristers, we might look for other occupational groups such as licensed conveyancers.[12] These are groups, with greater or lesser degrees of organization, who specialize in legal advice in particular areas. They do not, as a group, hold themselves out as having the general knowledge about law that barristers as a group or solicitors as a group would purport to have. However, within their own specialist areas, they may claim to have a greater degree of specialized knowledge than lawyers or to offer a more efficient service. Accountants and patent agents would both fall into this category.[13]

We will say relatively little about the work of these other people who are engaged in giving legal advice in this chapter because relatively little is known about how they work. This lack of knowledge is not accidental. Where research is done in part reflects perceptions of the importance of the area researched. We know too little about the work of lawyers but, since legal advice given by non-lawyers is seen as being of less consequence, we know even less about their work.[14] This lack of knowledge serves, in turn, to focus attention and discussion on what we do know something about, lawyers, and thus reinforces traditional preoccupations with the personnel and institutions of 'the English legal system'. This is unfortunate because what we do know about these other sources of legal advice suggests that they may have a significant impact on both the work of lawyers and on the general map of the settling of disputes.[15]

The significance of non-lawyers giving legal advice can be illustrated in two different ways. First, they can be seen to be important in quantitative terms. For example, a study of legal staff who were employed in organizations other than firms of solicitors found that over a period of ten years the percentage of such staff who were paralegals varied from 26 per cent to 43 per cent.[16] Second, remembering the existence of counsel who are not lawyers can be important in a qualitative sense. In previous chapters, we have argued that one of the ways in

[12]  The Legal Services Act 2007 describes licensed conveyancers, commissioners for oaths, Trade Mark attorneys, Patent attorneys, immigration advisers, and immigration service providers and claims management services as 'other lawyers' (see Legal Services Act 2007, ss. 182–7).

[13]  It has been argued that accountants are now taking over 'the more generalised role of professional adviser, previously enjoyed by solicitors' (G. Lee, 'An Introduction' in G. Lee, *The Changing Professions: Accountancy and Law* (1991) Aston Business School, Birmingham, p. 3).

[14]  Even our knowledge of lawyers is limited and partial. Abel, in his book, *The Legal Profession in England and Wales*, argued that there was insufficient research to enable him to write a sociology of lawyers' work as opposed to a sociology of the profession (R. Abel, *The Legal Profession in England and Wales* (1988a) Basil Blackwell, Oxford, p. 3).

[15]  This is not to suggest that the role of those engaged in giving legal advice who are not solicitors or barristers is entirely unrecognized. The 1989 Green Paper on the organization of the legal profession included one appendix, Annex B, which was entitled, 'The Providers of Legal Services'. Four of its six pages were given over to a description of ten institutions or occupations other than barristers and solicitors who provided legal services (Lord Chancellor's Department (1989)).

[16]  R. Woolfson, J. Plotkinoff, and D. Wilson, *Solicitors in the Employed Sector* (1994) The Law Society, London, p. 15. The Benson Report estimated that the number of legal executives grew by 16 per cent between 1966 and 1976 (Benson Report (1979) p. 408). However, Abel has argued that legal executives are less important than they once were (Abel (1988a) pp. 207–10). Nevertheless, Chambers and Harwood's survey showed that the mean staff size for a firm of solicitors was 5.8 solicitors with 3.5 paralegal staff, whilst the very largest firms had an average of 70.9 solicitors and 36.6 paralegals (G. Chambers and S. Harwood, *Solicitors*

which a view of the law is constructed, is not merely through the logical analysis of legal rules, but through the expression of community values which influence a lawyer in the approach they take to the law. In turn, this view of what the law is will naturally affect the advice given to clients. However, it is important not to over-emphazise the dominance of these community values. The communities we have referred to are, in the first instance, communities of lawyers; communities of solicitors, barristers and judges who are in part separate communities and in part one inter-related community.[17] If there are other groups of people giving legal advice the effect of the values of these communities on the public to whom advice is supplied is to some extent dissipated.[18] Equally, organizations like Citizens Advice Bureaux and local government departments work in ways which are not typical for lawyers. They are usually publicly funded.[19] Their advice is usually free. They are mainly concerned with those who are relatively poor.[20] The areas of law that they are most concerned with are therefore areas like social security law or housing law which are of direct interest to their clients.[21] Finally, the strategies that they adopt may not involve dealing with the individual problems of individual clients in the fashion which is typical of traditional lawyers. Instead, they may choose to address a particular area of difficulty by campaigning for legal reforms, by suing group actions or by engaging in community education in order to heighten people's awareness of their legal position.[22]

# The legal profession(s)

The term 'profession' indicates more than the fact that something is an occupation. A shop assistant has an occupation. A doctor is part of a profession. However, exactly what the term 'profession' indicates is somewhat elusive. Various writers have defined the term in different ways and there is not even agreement as to how these different definitions should be grouped together.[23] Thus, for example, Abel has argued that '[t]here are three principal theoretical traditions in the study of professions: Weberian,

*in England and Wales: Practice, Organisation and Perceptions - First Report: The Work of the Solicitors in Private Practice* (1990) The Law Society, London, p. 19).

[17] The values of these communities are not, of course, unrelated to the values of the wider community of which they are part. On the other hand, neither are they simply reflective of that wider community.

[18] Although the communities of lawyers retain dominance in important areas because of their greater influence in the courts and tribunals of 'the English legal system'.

[19] Abel has noted that there is a historical dominance of private practitioners in the common law world (R. Abel, 'Lawyers in the Civil Law World' in R. Abel and P. Lewis (eds), *Lawyers in Society: Volume Two* (1988b) University of California Press, Berkeley, p. 5). Because of this numerical dominance, the term 'lawyer' has become almost synonymous with 'private practitioner'.

[20] By contrast, '[t]he work of lawyers consists mostly of representing the powerful and wealthy against others of the same class or group' (Friedman (1989) p. 12).

[21] For a discussion of the role of the Citizens Advice Bureaux, see Benson Report (1979) pp. 71–6.

[22] See further J. Cooper, *Public Legal Services* (1983) Sweet & Maxwell, London, pp. 10–11.

[23] For examples of different approaches to the nature of the professions, see A. Abbott, *The System of Professionals* (1988) University of Chicago Press, Chicago; M. Larson, *The Rise of Professionalism* (1977)

Marxist and a structural functional approach with roots in Durkheim', whilst Johnson has divided different approaches to the definition of profession into 'trait' and 'functionalist' models.[24]

On the basis of his survey of the academic literature on the subject, Millerson, adopting the trait approach, has suggested that there are six essential features to the notion of a profession:

(a) A profession involves a skill based on theoretical knowledge.

(b) The skill requires training and education.

(c) The professional must demonstrate competence by passing a test.

(d) Integrity is maintained by adherence to a code of conduct.

(e) The service is for the public good.

(f) The profession is organized.[25]

Whilst we would accept that there are problems with this trait approach to the definition of profession, Millerson's key features do serve to point to some of the important differences between the idea of an occupation and that of a profession.[26] The Royal Commission on Legal Services' description of a profession as implying the presence of a central organization, the giving of advice by the members of the profession, the control of entry based on adequate education, self-regulation, and the acceptance of the notion of duty to the client mirrors Millerson's approach.[27] At the same time, however, Millerson's key features may serve to conceal the essence of the nature of a profession.

Central to Millerson's approach, is the idea of the profession's duty to those other than themselves. This idea of professional duty is often to be seen in lawyers' descriptions of themselves.[28] However, it can be argued that the control that the profession exerts is as much or more for the benefit of the profession than it is for the benefit of the public at large.[29] By controlling admission to the profession and by creating standards according to which work must be done, professions control the market for their services. Entry standards can be used to limit the number of members of a particular profession. Standards according to which work has to be

University of California Press, Berkley; and H. Perkin, *The Rise of Professional Society* (1989) Routledge, London.

[24] Abel (1988a) p. 4; T. Johnson, *Professions and Power* (1972) Macmillan, London, p. 23.

[25] G. Millerson, *The Qualifying Associations* (1964) Routledge & Kegan Paul, London, p. 4.

[26] For a discussion of the limitations of the trait approach, see Johnson (1972) pp. 23–32. For a discussion of the functional approach to the concept of the legal profession, see Friedman (1989) pp. 2–5. For a discussion of Weberian, Marxist and structural functionalist approaches see Abel (1988b) ch. 1.

[27] Benson Report (1979) pp. 28–30.

[28] See, for example, R. du Cann, *The Art of the Advocate* (rev. edn, 1993) Penguin, Harmondsworth, ch. 2; and D. Pannick, *Advocates* (1992) Oxford University Press, Oxford, ch. 4.

[29] 'In the common law world, professions dominated by private practitioners and exposed to market forces sought to control production *by* producers once they had attained sufficient control over the production *of* producers' (Abel (1988b) p. 22).

done can be used to reduce the amount of competition between members of the profession. Both these things will tend to increase the price for the services of the profession.[30]

One point that is clear is the fact that professions are organized. For this reason, it seems better to talk about legal professions in England and Wales rather than the legal profession because there are two very different regulatory bodies for solicitors and barristers.[31]

# Solicitors

## The training of solicitors

Entry into the solicitor's profession involves two types of training: participation in a course of vocational education and a period of apprenticeship as a trainee solicitor. The course of vocational education is divided into two parts. The first part is waived for those candidates who have a qualifying law degree. The second part can be completed either in a course taught at one of the old or new universities or at one of the institutions owned by the College of Law.

As we noted in **Chapter 7**, the most frequently used form of entry into the solicitor's profession is now via the completion of a law degree. The vast majority of entrants are graduates.[32] The dominance of this route has consequences for the social composition of the profession. Although universities have moved somewhat from the position of providing an education only for the elite to more of a mass-market provision, the extent of that change can be over-emphasized.[33] In 2008, there were 13,803 students who graduated in law, with 19,020 being accepted for entry into law school.[34] Previous studies have indicated that social class continues to advantage application to university.[35] McDonald's small-scale survey found that 70 per cent of law students had fathers who came from a professional or managerial background, whilst the Royal Commission on Legal Services had found that 54 per cent of people studying law had

---

[30] For a discussion of these arguments in relation to solicitors and barristers, see Abel (1988a) chs 2, 5, 10, and 12.

[31] It is, however, very common to write about 'the' legal profession in England and Wales. See, for example, Abel (1988a) and the Lord Chancellor's Department (1989).    [32] See **p. 138** above.

[33] See, for example, O. Fulton, 'Elite Survivals? Entry "Standards" and Procedures for Higher Education Admissions' (1988) 13 Studies in Higher Education 15. For an analysis of the extent to which university law schools have moved away from the elite entry model, see A. Bradney, 'English University Legal Education: Elite Education or Mass Education? Some Preliminary Thoughts' in P. Torremans (ed.), *Legal Convergence in the Europe of the New Millennium* (2000) Kluwers, The Hague.

[34] *Annual Statistical Report 2009* (2009) The Law Society, London, pp. 29 and 31.

[35] See C. Connolly, 'Shades of Discrimination: University Entry Data 1990–92' in S. Haselgrove (ed.), *The Student Experience* (1994) Open University Press, Milton Keynes, p. 29.

fathers in a professional or managerial job.[36] Notwithstanding the large number of ethnic minority students in university law schools, the general literature shows that ethnic minorities are disadvantaged in applications to university.[37] The most popular entry route into the profession thus helps to distort the social composition of the profession.[38]

After completing a law degree, the prospective solicitor must enter the vocational training course, the Legal Practice Course. Entry onto this course is not automatic. Although an increasing number of institutions offer the Legal Practice Course, students still report difficulties in securing a place.[39] Halpern's longitudinal study of law students suggested that students' A level performance had a significant effect on their chances of gaining a place on a Legal Practice Course. Because A level results are not evenly distributed throughout the population, this, in turn, meant that there was a correlation between age, sex, and ethnicity and the chance of gaining a place on a Legal Practice Course.[40] As with the fact that a law degree is the most popular method of starting off the qualifying process to become a solicitor, this difficulty in gaining places on Legal Practice Courses also increases the degree to which the social background of solicitors is not representative of the population as a whole.

The number of people sitting the final vocational examination has risen greatly over the past decades. In 1985, 3,236 students sat this examination. By 2009, the figure had risen to 7,759.[41] With this rise in the number of students sitting the final examination has come a change in the gender breakdown. In 1985, more men than women sat the examinations. Since 1987, there has been a consistent pattern of more women than men sitting the examinations and in 2008/9, 60.1 per cent of those admitted to the Roll (that is, those who had passed both their Legal Practice Course examinations and had done the two-year period of training) were women.[42]

The final stage of training to become a solicitor is the period of employment as a trainee solicitor.[43] Training should not simply be seen as technical training.

---

[36] P. McDonald, '"The Class of 81" – A Glance at the Social Class Composition of Recruits to the Legal Profession' (1982) 9 Journal of Law and Society 267 at p. 269; Benson Report (1979) vol. 2, p. 59. By comparison, the Royal Commission on Legal Services found that 21 per cent of all children aged 16–19 had fathers who had a professional or managerial job (Benson Report (1979), vol. 2, p. 59). More recently, Punt and Cole found that 17 per cent of solicitors had a parent or close relative who was a solicitor (T. Punt and B. Cole, *Routes into the Solicitors' Profession and the Utilisation of Professional Time* (1999) The Law Society, London, p. 9).                                    [37] Connolly (1994) passim.

[38] For an examination of the backgrounds of law students, see D. Halpern, *Entry into the Legal Professions: The Law Student Cohort Study: Years 1 and 2* (1994) The Law Society, London, ch. 5. Punt and Cole's 1999 survey suggested that 69 per cent of solicitors had a law degree, with 18 per cent having a degree in some other subject (Punt and Cole (1999) p. 7).                                    [39] Halpern (1994) p. 69.

[40] Halpern (1994) pp. 70–2.        [41] *Annual Statistical Report 2009* (2009) p. 35.

[42] *Annual Statistical Report 2009* (2009) p. 44.

[43] For a study of recruitment practices, see H. Rolfe and T. Anderson, 'A Firm Choice: Law Firms' Preferences in the Recruitment of Trainee Solicitors' (2003) 10 International Journal of the Legal Profession

One recent study of the ways in which large law firms portray training concludes that:

I have charted a narrative of developing a career as a successful lawyer… [that] is marked by a number of recurring features and focal concerns: ideas about consumption, identity and youth; of space, place and practice; of appearance, class and respectability. On closer examination, I have argued, a workplace which appears ostensibly equitable and just, open and inclusive, is in fact a site *already* constituted at the point of entry by reference to the making of certain assumptions which, I have suggested, are mediated in complex ways by ideas about class, gender, race and ethnicity.[44]

Just like entry onto the Legal Practice Course, securing a position as a trainee solicitor is not an automatic matter.[45] The number of trainee positions available tends to be related quite closely to small changes in the health of the economy. Thus, in the year, 1 August 1992 to 31 July 1993, there were 3,689 new articles registered with the Law Society. This was a decrease of 6.8 per cent on the previous year.[46] In 2009, the number of traineeships had risen to 5,809, with 20.3 per cent being awarded to students from ethnic minorities.[47] Notwithstanding this rise, it is likely that law students still experience difficulties in finding a position as a trainee.[48] In Halpern's study, the average number of applications made was 30.2 per student.[49]

Students have very varying experiences when applying for a position as a trainee. For example, Halpern's study shows that students from Oxford and Cambridge make far fewer applications for trainee positions than do those from other institutions.[50] A level grades, class mark, the type of institution the student studied in, having a relative who was in the legal profession, and ethnicity all played a part in influencing a student's chance of getting a position as a trainee.[51] Shiner's Year 5 report on the

---

315, and M. Carroll, M. Marchington, J. Earnshaw, and S. Taylor, 'Recruitment in Small Firms' (1999) 21 Employee Relations 230.

[44] R. Collier, '"Be Smart, be Successful, be yourself…"'? Representations of the Training Contract and Trainee Solicitor in Advertising by Large Law Firms' (2005) 12 International Journal of the Legal Profession 51 at p. 75.

[45] By way of contrast, the transition from trainee to qualified solicitor does seem, in practice, if not in form, to be automatic. Of the participants in the sixth Law Society cohort survey, only 3 per cent of those people who completed their training contract failed to secure positions as a salaried solicitor (E. Duff, M. Shiner, A. Boon, with A. Whyte, *Entry into the Legal Professions: The Law Student Cohort Study: Year 6: Research Study No. 39* (2000) The Law Society, London, p. 14).

[46] *Annual Statistical Report: 1993* (1993) The Law Society, London, p. 68.

[47] *Annual Statistical Report 2009* (2009) p. 38. The percentage for the number of trainee contracts awarded to students from ethnic minorities relates to the 91.6 per cent of students whose ethnicity has been reliably recorded.

[48] There were fewer traineeships available in 2009 than there had been in 2008 (*Annual Statistical Report: 2009* (2009) p. 37).

[49] Halpern (1994) p. 73. This shows a considerable rise in the number of applications made by students in the past. For discussion of this, see Abel (1988a) pp. 152–4.        [50] Halpern (1994) p. 73.

[51] Halpern (1994) pp. 78–9.

cohort previously studied by Halpern shows that ethnicity and being a woman still disadvantage a person who is applying for a training contract.[52]

As important as this information about the background to obtaining a position as a trainee solicitor is, it is less important than what happens during the process of training itself. It is at this stage that we would expect the most intense period of acculturation to take place as the law student becomes absorbed into the community of solicitors. However, it is precisely at this point that we know the least. Whilst Shiner's Year 5 report on the cohort study found high levels of satisfaction amongst those who had taken training contracts this, in itself, tells us little about how the training process works to induct trainees into the solicitors' profession.[53] His study does suggest that the discriminatory behaviour which is to be found in the process of securing a training contract can continue during the training itself, with 18 per cent of respondents saying that they had received discriminatory treatment or had been harassed during their contract.[54]

## Ethnicity and entry into the solicitors' profession

In 1987, King, Israel, and Goulbourne carried out a study of English and Welsh students who were intending to practise as lawyers.[55] Their study showed that being a member of an ethnic minority had an effect on the way in which a person was treated when they tried to become a solicitor. However, they were less clear about precisely how this effect occurred. Students interviewed by King, Israel, and Goulbourne certainly reported instances of offensive behaviour and hearing racially insensitive jokes in interview.[56] But racially insensitive jokes do not, of themselves, necessarily indicate that a candidate is being treated worse in terms of getting a job. Candidates were interviewed about matters pertaining to their background but whether this showed interest on the part of the interviewer, poor interviewing technique, or racism was unclear.[57] King, Israel, and Goulbourne were able to show that solicitors seemed to favour candidates from the then polytechnics which became universities after 1992 less than those from universities and those with a middle-class background.[58] This, indirectly, made it less likely that candidates from ethnic minorities would get a job.

---

[52] M. Shiner, *Entry into the Legal Professions: The Law Student Cohort Study: Year 5* (1999) The Law Society, London, p. 13.

[53] Shiner (1999) p. 31. See further A. Boon, 'From Public Service to Service Industry: The Impact of Socialization and Work on the Motivation and Values of Lawyers' (2005) 12 International Journal of the Legal Profession 229 at pp. 240–3.          [54] Shiner (1999) p. 36.

[55] M. King, M. Israel, and S. Goulbourne, *Ethnic Minorities and Recruitment to the Solicitors' Profession* (1990) Law Society on Behalf of the Commission for Racial Equality, London.

[56] See, for example, King et al. (1990) p. 72. They do, in themselves, indicate that a candidate is less likely to be happy working in a firm where such jokes are thought appropriate.

[57] King et al. (1990) pp. 76–80.          [58] King et al. (1990) pp. 78, 84–7.

Individual candidates were clear that they 'experienced a lot of racial prejudice' and that their 'racial background was a major factor' in their rejection.[59] Equally, however, a smaller number of candidates felt that their ethnic background was an advantage in obtaining a job.[60] It is plainly very difficult to prove that the largely subjective matter of awarding one candidate rather than another is due to discrimination, whether direct or indirect, unless such discrimination is explicitly acknowledged by the person choosing the employee.

In 1993, the Law Society Council agreed a policy that made racism unacceptable professional conduct, both within the profession and amongst the profession.[61] The Law Society also began to keep detailed statistics on the position of ethnic minorities and there was a clear awareness of a potential problem. The number of solicitors from ethnic minorities holding practising certificates has shown a rise over the last few years. In 1990, the figure was 1.3 per cent. By 2009, it had grown to 10.6 per cent.[62] However, this percentage should be compared with the fact that 32.1 per cent of students of students starting a law degree course in 2008 were from an ethnic minority.[63] Plainly, the solicitor's profession has gone a long way in securing equal representation of those in the ethnic minorities and, even more importantly, in securing equal representation of those from the ethnic minorities who aspire to the profession. However, one must be cautious in assuming that this shows ethnic minorities face no discrimination within the solicitors' profession. Law Society figures show that whilst 38.4 per cent of white European solicitors in private practice are partners, the comparable percentage for ethnic minority solicitors is 25.9 per cent. Although this may be explained, at least in part, by the fact that many ethnic minority solicitors are comparatively new to the profession, the same figures also show that 8.1 per cent of ethnic minority solicitors are sole practitioners, compared with 4.4 per cent of white European solicitors and 50.2 per cent of ethnic minority solicitors in private practice work in firms with four partners or less, whilst the percentage for white European solicitors is 28.1 per cent.[64] As we noted above, Shiner's Year 5 report on the cohort study indicated that ethnicity was still a barrier to securing a training contract.[65] A recent report from the Law Society noted that, whilst the median earnings for white solicitors in private practice in 2007/8 was £55,000, median earnings for black and ethnic minority solicitors was £45,000. However, the report concluded that ethnicity on its own was not responsible

---

[59]  King et al. (1990) p. 90. See also S. Vignaendra, *Social Class and Entry into the Solicitors' Profession: Research Study 41* (2001) The Law Society, London, ch. 6.        [60]  King et al. (1990) pp. 90–1.

[61]  J. Ames, 'Council Endorses Anti-bias Policy' (1993) 90 Law Society Gazette, 13 October.

[62]  *Annual Statistical Report: 1993* (1993) p. 15; *Annual Statistical Report 2009* (2009) p. 17.

[63]  *Annual Statistical Report 2009* (2009) p. 30. Comparison between the percentage of students enrolling in law at university or enrolling in the Law Society with the total percentage of the ethnic minorities in the population taken as a whole suggests that, at least amongst some groups, there is a greater desire to become a lawyer than there is amongst the white population. This possibility is supported by previous research which suggests that some ethnic minority groups have greater aspirations than average to professional status. (See, for example, R. Penn and H. Scattergood, 'Ethnicity and Career Aspirations' (1992) 19 New Community 75 at p. 78.)        [64]  *Annual Statistical Report 2009* (2009) p. 20.

[65]  Shiner (1999) p. 13.

for this disparity. instead, it reflects differences such as the area of law that the two groups were likely to work in or the size of the firm that employed them.[66] The report did not investigate what led to these differences.

## Gender and the solicitor's profession

In 1914, the Court of Appeal held that a woman was not a 'person' for the purposes of the Solicitors Act 1843 and therefore could not become a solicitor.[67] However, the Sex Disqualification Removal Act of 1919 overturned that judgment, and a number of other similar decisions, and women have been legally capable of being solicitors for many decades.[68]

Women and men do not seem to have an equal place in the solicitors' profession.[69] In 1993, 60 per cent of male solicitors were partners in their firms. Only 27 per cent of women held the same position.[70] This discrepancy might be explained by the fact that women have begun to enter the solicitor's profession in large numbers only comparatively recently.[71] The percentage of women being admitted to the profession only first rose to above 10 per cent of the total annual admissions in 1972.[72] Women first exceeded 50 per cent of the total number of admissions in 1992/3.[73] Promotion to partnership depends on a combination of seniority, ability, and luck. However, an examination of the partnership progression of solicitors according to their years of admission showed that in every category, 0–9 years, 10–19 years, 20–29 years, and 30 plus years, a much larger percentage of men had become partners.[74] In 2009, some 16 years after women had first exceeded 50 per cent of admissions, they continued to be statistically less likely than men to have a partnership, with 49.1 per cent of men but only 21.5 per cent of women being partners.[75] As in previous years, the Law Society's annual statistical report for 2009 noted that, in what has now become a routine observation, in 'all experience bands a lower proportion of women than men are partners'.[76]

---

[66] Law Society, *Ethnicity and Earnings in Private Practice* (2009b) The Law Society, London p. 7, pp.10 and 11.

[67] *Bebb v Law Society* [1914] 1 Ch 286. The decision is briefly discussed in A. Sachs and J. Hoff Wilson, *Sexism and the Law* (1978) Martin Robertson, Oxford, pp. 31–3.

[68] For an examination of the historical exclusion of women from the solicitors' profession, see H. Sommerlad and P. Sanderson, *Gender, Choice and Commitment: Women Solicitors in England and Wales and the Struggle for Equal Status* (1998) Ashgate, Aldershot, ch. 3.

[69] P. Sanderson and H. Sommerlad, 'Professionalism, Discrimination, Difference and Choice in Women's Experience in Law Jobs' in P. Thomas (ed.), *Discriminating Lawyers* (2000) Cavendish, London. Differential gender experience of participation in the professions is not unique to law. See, for example, Law Society, *Women in the Professions: A Report Compiled by the United Kingdom Inter-Professional Group Working Party on Women's Issues* (1990) The Law Society, London, passim.

[70] *Annual Statistical Report 1993* (1993) p. 13.

[71] As we noted above, this is the explanation given for the low percentage of ethnic minority solicitors who have partnerships.          [72] Abel (1988a) p. 415. Abel's table gives figures for the 1920s to 1985.

[73] *Annual Statistical Report 1993* (1993) p. 58.          [74] *Annual Statistical Report 1993* (1993) p. 13.

[75] *Annual Statistical Report 2009* (2009) p. 15.          [76] *Annual Statistical Report 2009* (2009) p. 16.

Women's unequal place in the profession is not only to be seen in their rate of promotion. The ruling body of the Law Society is its Council. According to the Law Society's website, the vast majority of its members are men.[77]

As we will see below, not all solicitors pursue the same kind of work. And not all work is equally valued. In their survey of lawyers, Podmore and Spencer found that:

men solicitors had higher scores in terms of importance in their workload for company and commercial, European and personal injury, criminal and other litigation work, and women had higher scores for matrimonial, wills and probate, estate duty, and property and conveyancing work.[78]

This evidence that women participate unequally in the solicitor's profession has long been known.[79] It continues to be the case that there are fewer women than men in some areas of activity. Thus, a 2004 study showed that 58 per cent of male solicitors were regularly doing business or commercial work, but only 33 per cent female solicitors were similarly engaged.[80] It is important to realize that the evidence above suggests that the profession is 'both male dominated and male-orientated'.[81] It is not just that there are more men than women in the profession, but, rather, that expectations and attitudes make the profession (or parts of it) more comfortable for men.

In a study by Spencer and Podmore based upon interviews with lawyers, they identified a number of assumptions about the legal profession made by members of the profession themselves.[82] The practice of law was seen as being aggressive and objective. Women were seen as lacking these qualities. Prejudice was seen as a fact of life and to come just as much from clients as from the legal profession itself. Women were expected to leave practice to start a family. They were therefore of short-term value to a practice. They were seen as different, emotional, and weak. There was for women a 'basic incongruity between their personal identity as "feminine" and their membership of a profession which is strongly "masculine"'.[83]

---

[77] <http://www.lawsociety.org.uk/>.

[78] D. Podmore and A. Spencer, 'Gender in the Labour Process: The Case of Women and Men Lawyers' in D. Knights and H. Wilmott (eds), *Gender in the Labour Process* (1986) Gower, Aldershot, pp. 38–9. For further analysis of the divided experience of women and men solicitors, see Chambers and Harwood, *First Report* (1990) pp. 18–20.

[79] See, for example, the Benson Report (1979) vol. 2, s. 15. Equally, it would be possible to go on adding many other examples of women's differential participation in the profession. For example, Nott's survey found that only 15 per cent of women worked in firms of less than three partners (S. Nott, 'Women in Law – 2' (1989) 139 New Law Journal 785). In 1993, 35.7 per cent of the profession taken as a whole worked in firms with four principals or less (Law Society, *Trends in the Solicitors' Profession: Annual Statistical Report 1994* (1994) The Law Society, London, p. 28).

[80] Law Society, *Women Solicitors 2004: Research Findings* (2004) The Law Society, London, p. 15.

[81] A. Spencer and D. Podmore, 'Women Lawyers – Marginal Members of a Male-dominated Profession' in A. Spencer and D. Podmore (eds), *In a Man's World* (1987) Tavistock Publications, London, p. 113.

[82] Spencer and Podmore (1987) p. 113. This study was of 'the legal profession' looking both at solicitors and barristers as one group.

[83] Spencer and Podmore (1987) p. 129, see also H. Sommerlad, 'Women in a Changing Profession: The Myth of Feminisation' in J. Shapland and R. Le Grys (eds), *The Changing Shape of the Legal Profession* (1994a) Institute for the Study of the Legal Profession, University of Sheffield, Sheffield, pp. 40–4. See also

These attitudes cannot be dismissed as simply sexist and prejudiced.[84] Rather, the attitude towards the nature of the legal profession reflects further feelings about the nature of 'the English legal system'. 'The English legal system' is implicitly seen as being confrontational and adversarial. Those areas where it best shows those features are seen as being typical and also as exemplars. In this book, we seek to argue that this view of 'the English legal system' is partial and, further, that it is a view of 'the English legal system', something which is an ideological construct, rather than a view of dispute processes within England and Wales. Thus, as a view of lawyering, this attitude is inaccurate. Lawyering is also about settlement negotiation and mediation:

The assumption that a care orientation cannot accompany the ability to be a good lawyer falls into the trap of dichotomous thinking prevalent in the legal system. assuming a sharp division between reason and emotion, linear and associative thought, cold rationality and warm empathy reinforces the exclusion of traditional feminine traits from the practice of law – Just as culture in the past has taught that these traits are mutually exclusive and gender specific, in the future the message should be one of integration and compatibility.[85]

However, the word 'also' in the last sentence before the quotation is crucial. The view that the practice of law is confrontational and adversarial may be partial but that is different from saying that it is wholly inaccurate.[86] Those qualities are part of at least some solicitors' everyday lives. The attitudes towards women solicitors can be compared with the work of Gilligan seen in the previous chapter. Her idea of a feminine voice can be seen to support, in non-pejorative terms, for example, the notion that women are not aggressive and are not subjective.[87] If it is true 'that many women experience society in significantly different ways from men and that there are certain real *or* potential experiences that can be described as constituting the basis for feminist development of a "gendered" life', it might be argued that it is not surprising that women experience the profession of solicitor in a different way from men.[88] Discrimination within the profession against women on the grounds that they were women would be wrong.[89] Failing to select particular women for entry into, or promotion within, the profession because they lacked the necessary attributes would be a different matter. On this argument, this latter practice would be acceptable.

---

H. Sommerlad, 'The Myth of Feminisation: Women and Cultural Change in the Legal Profession' (1994b) 1 International Journal of the Legal Profession 31.

[84]  Although it may be both.

[85]  D. Jack and R. Jack, 'Women Lawyers: Archetype and Alternatives' in C. Gilligan (ed.), *Mapping the Moral Domain* (1988) Harvard University Press, Cambridge, MA, p. 287.

[86]  Although whether it is necessary or desirable for it to be aggressive is another question.

[87]  See pp. 147–8 above.

[88]  For arguments about the feminist development of a theory of gendered life, see M. Fineman, 'Feminist Legal Scholarship and Women's Gendered Lives' in M. Cain and C. Harrington (eds), *Lawyers in a Postmodern World* (1994) Open University Press, Buckingham, p. 239, emphasis in original.

[89]  And would be contrary to the profession's non-discrimination policy.

Nott's survey of women solicitors showed that 9 per cent of her sample had turned down the offer of a partnership.[90] Whilst there is clear evidence of discrimination against women in the solicitor's profession, there is also plain evidence that some women choose not to take advantage of those opportunities that they have. This raises the question of how far the profession should change its attitudes and working practices to suit the new gender division within the profession. Thus, for example, in Nott's survey, only 1 per cent had experience of a job share whilst 15 per cent had taken time out of the profession. The profession makes relatively little allowance for those women who want to start a family.[91] This can result in careers divided by a period of child-raising. Studies of women solicitors which have involved interviewing women about their working lives have been consistent in suggesting that, not only is there discrimination against women, but there is also a particular form of discrimination against women with children.[92] Yet, in professional jobs generally:

in those circumstances where women were able to take advantage of the availability of flexible employment, some kind of labour force participation had been almost continuous (even when children were quite young) and no serious conflict was perceived between work and family life.[93]

Chamber and Harwood's survey of the profession showed that, whilst 97.3 per cent of male solicitors between the age of 25 and 29 surveyed expected to be in the profession in five years' time, the percentage for women was only 88.4 per cent.[94] Equal participation by women and men in the solicitors' profession demands a change in values and attitudes on the part of the profession generally.[95] As Webley and Duff observe, 'the retention and advancement of women in the [solicitors'] profession remains slow.[96]

[90]  Nott (1989) p. 785.

[91]  But there is some evidence to suggest that this may be changing. A survey of the 100 largest solicitors' firms show that 43 per cent of respondents allowed partners to work part-time and 79 per cent allowed assistant solicitors to do so (C. McGlynn, 'Soliciting Equality – The Way Forward' (1995) 145 New Law Journal 1065 at p. 1066). Although the difference in the results of these two surveys might be explained by an improvement of the position of women over time, it might also be explained by a difference in the type of firms surveyed. Larger firms may be able to offer their employees better facilities.

[92]  C. McGlynn, *The Woman Lawyer* (1998) Butterworths, London, pp. 100–3; Sommerlad and Sanderson (1998) ch. 7.

[93]  R. Crompton and K. Sanderson, 'Professional Women's Careers' in S. McRae, *Keeping Women In* (1990) Policy Studies Institute, London, p. 12.

[94]  Chambers and Harwood (1990) pp. 62–3. The reason why women intended to leave was not investigated nor were they asked whether or not they intended to return. Not all women leave the profession because of problems associated with child-rearing. In one study, 40 per cent of women who were not practising had left for reasons unrelated to childcare and 27 per cent had reasons for not returning which were not related to childcare (Sommerlad (1994b) p. 38).

[95]  The Law Society's Solicitors' Anti-Discrimination Rule came into effect on 18 July 1995. This gives each firm the right to institute an anti-discrimination policy. If it does not do so, the Law Society's Model Policy applies in lieu. However, for a recent study suggesting that there has been no general change in the culture of law firms, see H. Sommerlad, 'Women Solicitors in a Fractured Profession: Intersections of Gender and Professionalism in England and Wales' (2002) 29 International Journal of the Legal Profession 213.

[96]  L. Webley and L. Duff, 'Women Solicitors as a Barometer for Problems within the Legal Profession – Time to Put Values before Profits?' (2007) 34 Journal of Law and Society 374 at p. 375.

## The work of the solicitor

Writing about the solicitors' profession implies a homogeneous and uniform group of workers. This is misleading.[97] Solicitors lead diverse working lives, with differences between individuals, age-groups, firms, gender groups, and geographical areas. Moreover, '[t]he claim that the legal profession has been experiencing a period of extensive change is a long established one.[98] Within these differences it is, however, possible to trace some patterns.

In their survey of the profession, Chambers and Harwood divided solicitors into general practitioners, moderate specialists, and extreme specialists. Most solicitors, whether male or female, described themselves as specialists although only 28.7 per cent of men, as compared with 42 per cent of women, described themselves as extreme specialists.[99] Thus, the very type of work that solicitors do divided them up into separate sub-groups.[100] Chambers and Harwood then divided the work of solicitors up into 15 different categories. When solicitors were asked how many of those different categories they had dealt with, 51 per cent said that they had dealt with 11 to 15 different types of work and 25 per cent said that they had dealt with 7 to 10 types of work;[101] 76 per cent had thus dealt with half or more of the categories of work. However, 41 per cent of those surveyed were dealing with no more than three types of work at the time when they were surveyed.[102] Solicitors thus appear to be specialists at any immediate point in time but generalists over the period of their careers or in terms of their willingness to take on isolated pieces of unfamiliar work. In either instance, this gives them a greater degree of common purpose than their self-defined specialist interests would seem to admit.[103]

The range of work that a solicitor might do is vast. Chambers and Harwood's 15 categories range from commercial property to childcare and wardship or personal

---

[97] This has consequences for the governance of the solicitors' profession. See further A. Francis, 'Out of Touch and Out of Time: Lawyers, their Leaders and Collective Mobility within the Legal Profession' (2004) 24 Legal Studies 322

[98] D. Muzio and S. Ackroyd, 'Change in the Legal Profession: Professional Agency and the Legal Labour Process' in D. Muzio, S. Ackroyd, and J. Chanlat, *Redirections in the Study of Exopert Labour: Established Professions and New Occupations* (2008) Palgrave Macmillan, London p. 31

[99] Chambers and Harwood (1990) p. 57. See also A. Boon, L. Duff, and M. Shiner, 'Career Paths and Choices in a Highly Differentiated Profession: The Position of Newly Qualified Solicitors' (2001) 64 Modern Law Review 563.

[100] For an illustration of the consequences of this in terms of work life, see R. Moorhead, 'Legal Aid and the Decline of Private Practice: Blue Murder or Toxic Job?' (2004) 11 International Journal of the Legal Profession 159 particularly at pp. 173–6.

[101] Chambers and Harwood (1990) p. 14.

[102] Chambers and Harwood (1990) p. 16.

[103] Seniority made a difference to the range of work a solicitor was engaged in, with the most senior equity partners being engaged in a wider range than assistant solicitors. As Chambers and Harwood suggest, this could indicate that those with ultimate responsibility for a firm may engage in a wider range of activities, they may be able to make more choices about what they do or the profession may becoming more specialized so that those who are younger do a smaller range (Chambers and Harwood (1990) p. 17).

financial management and advice.[104] They are themselves further subdivided.[105] Equally, this list is intended to apply only to the work of solicitors in private practice. Solicitors are also employed by organizations other than firms of solicitors. The range of work, and the concentration in different types of work, varies for employed solicitors as compared with those in private practice. Thus, for example, Woolfson, Plotkinoff, and Wilson's study of the employed sector showed 5 per cent of the legal work performed by local authorities was in the area of environmental protection and 3 per cent was in the area of waste collection.[106] Neither type of work fits clearly into any of Chambers and Harwood's categories. Equally, whilst one might find some private practitioners engaged in a small amount of general local government work, it is not surprising to find that this is the largest single area of legal work done by local authorities.[107] Finally, we should note that the specifically legal elements to these areas of work may be very routine or even very limited. Scottish solicitors interviewed by Campbell estimated they spent an average of one hour per week on technical issues of law.[108]

## Form of organization

Solicitors can work on their own as sole practitioners, as part of a firm of solicitors (wherein they may be assistant solicitors, salaried partners or equity partners) or as solicitors employed by other organizations. Once again, within these individual variations, patterns, and concentrations emerge.

Most solicitors' firms are small. However, most solicitors work for larger firms. Thus, for example, firms with 81 or more partners account for only 0.6 per cent of all firms but employ 25.1 per cent of all solicitors.[109] In contrast, in 2009, there were 4,163 solicitors who were sole practitioners.[110]

The 1980s and 1990s saw a huge growth in the size of a small number of firms of solicitors. Until 1967, the number of partners in a firm of solicitors was limited by statute to 20 and this effectively restricted the total size of a firm. The 1967 Companies Act saw the removal of this limitation.[111] The economic changes of the 1980s brought with them changes in commercial organization, particularly changes in the City, and the

---

[104] Chambers and Harwood (1990) pp. 12–13. Podmore has suggested that of Johnstone and Hopson's 19 different work tasks for American lawyers many are applicable to solicitors (D. Podmore, *Solicitors and the Wider Community* (1980) Heinemann, London, p. 34).

[105] The non-inclusive list for commercial property is of four items.

[106] Woolfson et al. (1994) p. 26.        [107] Woolfson et al. (1994) p. 26.

[108] C. Campbell, 'Lawyers and their Public' in D. N. MacCormick (ed.), *Lawyers in their Social Setting* (1976) W. Green, Edinburgh, p. 209.

[109] *Annual Statistical Report 2009* (2009) p. 25. The differences between a small firm and a large one do not simply relate to size. For example, small firms have more difficulty in recruiting staff than do large firms (T. Williams and T. Goriely, *Recruitment and Retention of Solicitors in Small Firms: Research Study 44* (2003) The Law Society, London).        [110] *Annual Statistical Report 2009*, p. 15.

[111] Companies Act 1967, s. 120(1)(a). Now Companies Act 1985, s. 716(2)(a).

result was the development of a small number of very large firms of solicitors.[112] This growth was partly achieved by increased business and increased recruitment of staff but also by the merging of firms. Chambers and Harwood-Richardson's study of firms in 1989 showed that the larger the firm, the greater the chance that it had experienced a merger within the previous five years.[113] These practices are very different from most other firms of solicitors. Most City firms work only in the corporate and commercial, property, litigation, and tax areas.[114] The fees billed are much greater, the clients almost solely corporate, and the range of work limited. In 1999/2000, the top quartile of 81 plus partner firms of solicitors in England and Wales earned £160,387,000 or more in fees.[115] At the opposite end of the scale, in 1999/2000, 25 per cent of sole practitioners earned gross fees of less than £57,000.[116] The *Annual Statistical Report* from the Law Society no longer gives information about firms' earnings. However, in 2008/9, Clifford Chance, a large law firm, had a revenue of £1,262 million;[117] it had offices in 29 countries;[118] and profits per equity partner in 2009 were £736,000.[119] Lee, in his study of large City practices, observes that:

[t]he largest firms in the City of London are distinctive institutions…not only in terms of their size and financial base, but also in terms of their works and their increasingly international presence.[120]

# Barristers

## The training of barristers

Training for barristers in many ways replicates that for solicitors. It consists of a first degree, followed by a vocational course, followed by a process of apprenticeship. However, within this similar pattern, there are a number of differences which

[112] Lee (1999) pp. 33–4.

[113] G. Chambers and S. Harwood-Richardson, *Solicitors in England and Wales: Practice, Organisation and Perceptions – Second Report: The Private Practice Firm* (1991) The Law Society, London, p. 89.

[114] J. Flood, 'Megalaw in the UK: Professionalism or Corporatism? A Preliminary Report' (1989) 64 Indiana Law Journal 569 at p. 581. On the work of large firms, see Lee (1999) and J. Lewis with J. Keegan, *Defining Legal Business: Understanding the Work of the Largest Law Firms* (1997) The Law Society, London.

[115] *Annual Statistical Report 2001* (2002) p. 44.

[116] *Annual Statistical Report 2001* (2002) p. 44.

[117] *Annual Review 2009* <http://www.cliffordchance.com/reports09/pdf/CliffordChance_AR09.pdf>.

[118] <http://gradsuk.cliffordchance.com/a-global-view.html>.

[119] <http://www.cliffordchance.com/reports09/ar/other/financial-information.html#income>. Firms with 81 or more partners, which constitute 0.6 per cent of the total number of firms in the profession, employ 25.1 per cent of all solicitors (*Annual Statistical Report 2009* (2009) p. 25.

[120] R. Lee, *Firm Views: Work of and Work in the Largest Law Firms* (1999) The Law Society, London, p. 66. The very notion that these large law firms are in any simple sense just part of the English legal system is open to question. See further J. Faulconbridge, J. Beaverstock, D. Muzio, and P. Taylor, 'Global Law Firms: Globalization and Organizational Spaces of Cross-border Legal Worlds' (2008) 28 Northwestern Journal of International Law and Business 455.

are important. Unlike the solicitors' profession, the Bar only accepts graduates. It also only accepts those who have become members of one of the four Inns of Court. Being accepted by an Inn of Court involves attending dinners in London.[121] Finally, whilst trainee solicitors may be paid from the moment they commence their period of apprenticeship, pupil barristers may only accept fees in the second six months of their apprenticeship or period of pupillage.[122] Even then, they will only receive fees if a solicitor chooses to instruct them. Awards for pupillages do exist but demand outstrips supply.[123] Like all barristers, they cannot advertise their services. Even when fully qualified, before a barrister can practise, they must join a set of chambers. As a member of a set, they are a sole practitioner. They are not paid by the set and must rely on attracting clients, though, once again, they cannot advertise.[124] However, they become immediately liable for their share of chambers' expenses.[125]

Whatever its reasons and intentions, the training path for a barrister is more exclusionary than that for a solicitor.[126] The potential barrister must pay more than the potential solicitor for a longer time and there is no clear career path. The barrister as a barrister will always be a sole practitioner, relying solely on their own efforts. Thus, the path advantages the financially more secure or the risk taker. In doing so, in turn, it advantages some social classes rather than others.

## The Bar and discrimination

Many of the things said above about the solicitors' profession could also be said about the barristers' profession. Details differ but the pattern remains much the same.

Discrimination in the Bar is historical and continuing. As long ago as 1979, the Benson Committee noted that barristers from the ethnic minorities tended to be confined to 'ghetto' sets of chambers.[127] In May 1995, it was reported that a survey of 822 Bar students showed that 40 per cent of female students experienced sexual harassment during pupillage or in practice and that in 10 per cent of these cases

---

[121] Dining is a social rather than an intellectual process, designed to promote contact between students and practitioners (Benson Report (1979) para. 39.50).

[122] The national minimum starting salary for a trainee solicitor in 2009 normally permitted by the Law Society was £19,160 in Central London and £17,160 outside of London (*Annual Statistical Report 2009* (2009) p. 41). Actual average salaries ranged from £34,158 in Central London to £17,790 in Wales (*Annual Statistical Report 2009* (2009) p. 42). The Court of Appeal has ruled that pupils do not have a contract of employment with their master so as to qualify for the minimum wage (*Edmonds* v *Lawson* [2000] 2 WLR 1091).

[123] TMS Consultants, *Without Prejudice? Sex Equality at the Bar and in the Judiciary* (1992) TMS Management Consultants, Bournemouth, p. 14.

[124] Shapland and Sorsby's survey of the junior Bar notes 'large variations [in the amount of work done] ... with some barristers working every day, including weekends, while one barrister reported no work and another reported working only a couple of days' (J. Shapland and A. Scorsby, *Starting Practice: Work and Training at the Junior Bar* (1995) Institute for the Study of the Legal Profession, Faculty of Law, University of Sheffield, Sheffield, pp. 40–1).

[125] For a somewhat dated discussion of entry into the profession of barrister, see Abel (1988a) pp. 37–46.

[126] This, of course, in the comparison with a profession whose entry procedures are, as we have seen above, already highly exclusionary.    [127] Benson Report (1979) para. 35.33.

were of a serious nature. A separate internal, unpublished report from the Bar in the same year 'denounced certain graphic and disturbing accounts of harassment as "disgraceful"'.[128] Like the solicitors' profession, the Bar continues to be dominated by white males. As with the solicitors' profession, this is so despite the rapid rise in the number of women being called to the Bar and despite the number of women practising at the Bar. In 1970, 77 women were called to the Bar, representing 8.2 per cent of those called that year. In 2008, 910 women were called to the Bar, 52.2 per cent of those called that year.[129] In 2008, there were 3,772 female barristers in the self-employed Bar and 8,364 male barristers in the self-employed Bar.[130]

A survey of sex discrimination in the Bar published in 1992 showed strong evidence of direct discrimination in recruitment to the Bar. Fifty-four per cent of women reported that they had been asked questions about marriage, children, and plans to stay at the Bar during pupillage interviews. Only 27 per cent of men were asked similar questions. In tenancy interviews, 39 per cent of women were asked such questions, whilst only 14.6 per cent of men were asked such questions.[131] As with solicitors, there was a consistent pattern of women working in family law and certain areas of criminal law, with men working in commercial law.[132] Career progression is a little more difficult to check than is the case with solicitors, given that most barristers are self-employed. One route for promotion is appointment as Queen's Counsel. In October 1999, women represented only 8.2 per cent of all Queen's Counsel.[133] In 2008, there were 1,146 male barristers who were Queen's Counsel and 127 female barristers who had that rank.[134] Malleson and Banda, in their report on the system for appointing both judges and Queen's Counsel, noted that women barristers they had questioned were particularly critical of the way in which people were appointed to be a Queen's Counsel, '[a] recurring theme...was the need for networking and being "known" in order to be appointed'.[135]

---

128  Both reports are referred to in B. Hewson, 'A Recent Problem?' (1995) 145 New Law Journal 626.

129  *Bar Council Annual Statistics – 2008* at: <http://www.barcouncil.org.uk/assets/documents/Annual%20Statistics%20Dec%2008.pdf>.

130  *Bar Council Annual Statistics – 2008* at: <http://www.barcouncil.org.uk/assets/documents/Annual%20Statistics%20Dec%2008.pdf>. In addition to this, there are 1,635 male barristers in the Employed Bar working for organizations like the Crown Prosecution Services and 1,411 female barristers in the Employed Bar.

131  TMS Consultants (1992) p. 8.

132  TMS Consultants (1992) p. 9. In a 2005 survey, the Commercial Bar Association (COMBAR) noted that 1,203 members of the Commercial Bar were male whilst 288 were female. Of those members under 7 years of call, 234 were male whilst 91 were female (COMBAR (Commercial Bar Association), *Pupillage, Maternity Leave and Pro Bono Work* (2005) Annex A).          133  TMS Consultants (1992) p. 19.

134  *Bar Council Annual Statistics – 2008* at: <http://www.barcouncil.org.uk/assets/documents/Annual%20Statistics%20Dec%2008.pdf>. In 2008, 94 per cent of all Queen's Counsel were classified as 'White British', see:   <http://www.barcouncil.org.uk/assets/documents/Self%20Employed%20Bar%20QC%27s%20by%20Ethnicity%20and%20Gender%20Apr%2009.pdf>.

135  K. Malleson and F. Banda, *Factors Affecting the Decision to Apply for Silk or Judicial Office* (2000) Lord Chancellor's Department, London, p. 24. It is important to note that some male respondents were also critical of this aspect of the system (see Malleson and Banda (2000) ch. 5).

Detailed analysis of the position of barristers from the ethnic minorities is less readily available than data about the position of women. However, 'ghettoization' continues. It still appears to be the case that '[b]lack barristers are working disproportionately in chambers with a criminal legal aid practice and [are] servicing an increasingly black clientele'.[136]

## The barrister and the barristers' clerk

One difference between the person who acts as a solicitor and the person who acts as a barrister is the fact that the barrister is always a self-employed person. A barrister must work as an individual out of a set of chambers. A barrister may be employed by an organization but they cannot then normally act as a barrister unless they are also part of a set of chambers.

Sets of chambers employ various administrative staff who do clerical work for the barristers in the set. Not all these administrative staff are of equal importance. Historically, a set of chambers has normally appointed a senior barrister's clerk to oversee the administration of the set.[137] Legally, the status of the barristers' clerk is relatively clear. He or she is an employee. They have no managerial control over the barristers in the set of chambers for which they are responsible, no matter how junior a barrister may be. In practice, many have argued that the position is rather more complicated.

The job of the barristers' clerk is to act as a broker. Under Bar rules, barristers may not advertise their services. This is a particular problem for young barristers. In theory, the barrister must gain clients because of the reputation secured by representing people in court. But until they have clients, how can they acquire a reputation? Even for the older barrister, this remains a problem. The reputation the barrister has will be for the work they have done. But what is a barrister to do when they wish to change the type or quality of work they are doing? Part of the role of the barristers' clerk lies here. The clerk can negotiate directly with solicitors, indicating the qualities of the barristers in the set of chambers for which they work. If a barrister is new or wishes to change the nature of their work, this can be particularly useful. Equally, the barrister can negotiate with court listings officers seeking to juggle schedules of cases in order to ensure, both that there are barristers for all cases, and that barristers make the most efficient use of their time.

Flood has argued that barristers' clerks seek to create a healthy set of chambers. They want a range of barristers who can provide advocacy at various different levels for potential clients and they want firms of solicitors who regard their set as the first

---

[136] N. Kibble, 'Access to Legal Education and the Legal Professions in England' in R. Dhavan, N. Kibble, and W. Twining, *Access to Legal Education and the Legal Professions* (1989) Butterworths, London, p. 154. See also Abel (1988a) pp. 76–9. The Bar Council approved an Equality Code in September 1995.

[137] There is an Institute of Barristers' Clerks. Its website is to be found at: <http://www.barristersclerks.com/>.

place to turn to when they need such advocacy. To this end, the clerks are engaged, not just in managing the careers of individual barristers, but also in ensuring that the balance of the chambers is maintained as a whole. Although they have no direct say in whom the set accepts as a member, they will not infrequently have considerable indirect influence.[138]

Some commentators have seen the power of barristers' clerks as being detrimental to the Bar. Thus, Zander has argued that the barristers' clerk 'exercises an influence over the distribution of work amongst his supposed principals which is out of all proportion to his qualifications or other attainments'.[139] Flood instances examples of discriminatory behaviour by barristers' clerks, quoting one clerk as saying '[w]omen aren't physically or emotionally suited to the Bar…It's something to do with their glands.'[140] Clerks can promote or ruin careers, depending on their perhaps prejudiced view of a barrister. But, as Flood observes, the work that the clerk does is not necessarily to the overall detriment of the barristers. Since barristers do not advertise, since they do not negotiate directly about fees or the collection of fees, and since they take little part in administering the chambers out of which they work, the barristers' clerk steps forward to fill gaps left.[141]

This traditional picture is now complicated by the fact that some sets of chambers are now appointing a more complex array of support staff. Examination of any one of a number of weekly newspapers directed towards lawyers will show that terminology is changing and becoming more varied and complex. Terms like 'senior clerk' and 'practice manager' are becoming more common and denote a new way of working, but, as yet, these new forms have not been the subject of adequate research.

## Barristers and rights of audience

The formal divide between the role of the solicitor's profession and the barrister's profession has always been expressed in terms of monopolies enjoyed by the two professions. Solicitors, for example, hold a virtual monopoly on instructing barristers.[142]

---

[138] J. Flood, *Barristers' Clerks* (1983) Manchester University Press, Manchester, passim.

[139] M. Zander, *Lawyers and the Public Interest* (1968) Weidenfeld & Nicholson, London, p. 85. See also pp. 83–95 generally.

[140] Flood (1983) p. 50. Flood also instances examples of discriminatory behaviour on grounds of race (Flood (1983) pp. 50–1).

[141] Flood (1983) ch. 8. See also J. Morison and P. Leith, 'The Barrister's World and the Nature of Law' (1992) Open University Press, Buckingham, pp. 29–34.

[142] In limited circumstances, a number of other people can instruct barristers. Amongst these groups are 'parliamentary agents, patent agents, trade mark agents, London notaries, licensed conveyancers, the Government legal service, the legal departments of local or public authorities and employed barristers' (Lord Chancellor's Department (1989) para. 8.4). The Bar now operates a scheme, BarDIRECT, 'whereby organisations or individuals who are suitable to instruct barristers because they have expertise in particular areas of the law can apply to the Bar Council to be licensed to instruct barristers directly in those areas'. A description of the scheme and a list of those individuals and organizations licensed to approach barristers directly can be found on the Bar Council's website at: <http://www.barcouncil.org.uk/>.

Barristers usually may not be approached directly by a member of the public.[143] On the other hand, barristers have had rights of audience in courts not enjoyed by solicitors. The less formal divide has been the idea that barristers enjoy an expertise not found in solicitors.[144] The reality of the divide between the two professions has always been more complex, less rigid, and more changeable than these two dichotomies suggest. In the last decade, it has come under increasing pressure.

At the beginning of the 1980s, solicitors held a monopoly on conveyancing. This was an important source of revenue for them. The Benson Committee had concluded that it was in the public interest that this monopoly be retained by solicitors.[145] However, during the 1980s, it was argued that the monopoly merely increased the price of conveyancing to the public at large. Although the Law Society argued that the monopoly protected the public from conveyancing by the unqualified, the introduction of Austin Mitchell's Private Members' Bill, which would have ended the monopoly, persuaded the Government to introduce its own legislation, Part II of the Administration of Justice Act 1985, which permitted licensed conveyancers to undertake conveyancing in competition with solicitors.

The withdrawal of the conveyancing monopoly increased the pressure on solicitors to look for new sources of income. The barristers' monopoly over rights of audience was one potential source of new income. Solicitors had long had rights of audience in some courts. These courts, however, tended to be the lower courts where work involved cases with relatively little legal complexity and relatively small fees.[146]

Tensions between the Bar and the Law Society resulted in the setting up of a joint committee, the Marre Committee, to consider the future of the profession. However, the resulting report did little to resolve the problem of the relationship between the two professions, not least because of the strong Note of Dissent from the barrister members of the committee, together with some independent members, about the question of rights of audience.[147]

The Marre Committee had concluded that '[a]ny changes which weaken the ability of the Law Society and the General Council of the Bar to regulate the conduct and competence of their members are unlikely to be in the public interest'.[148] This espousal of the traditional idea that professions should regulate themselves was challenged in 1989 by the Government's Green Paper on 'The Work and Organisation of the Legal Profession'. This set the debate about the relationship between the two legal professions

---

[143] Solicitors have not always been the only profession generally able to instruct barristers. The now abolished attorneys once also held that position (R. Cocks, *Foundations of the Modern Bar* (1983) Sweet & Maxwell, London, p. 1).                    [144] Morison and Leith (1992) p. 50.

[145] Benson Report (1979) ch. 21.

[146] Thus, for example, solicitors had rights of audience in the county court under the County Court Act 1959, s. 89(c) and rights of audience in the magistrates' court under the Magistrates' Court Act 1980, s. 122(1).

[147] *A Time for Change: Report of the Committee on the Future of the Legal Profession* (the Marre Committee) (1988) General Council of the Bar and the Council of the Law Society, London.

[148] Marre Committee (1988) para. 4.23.

in general, and the question of rights of audience in particular, in an entirely new context. In its introduction, the Green Paper set out new parameters for the professions:

The Government's overall objective in publishing this Green Paper is to see that the public has the best possible access to legal services and that those services are of the right quality for the needs of the particular client. The Government believes that this is best achieved by ensuring that:—

(a) a market providing legal services operates freely and efficiently so as to give clients the widest possible choice of cost effective legal services; and

(b) the public can be certain that those services are being supplied by people who have the necessary expertise...

The Government believes that free competition between the providers of legal services will, through the discipline of the market, ensure that the public is provided with the most efficient and effective network of legal services at the most economical price, although the Government believes that the public must also be assured of the competence of the providers of those services.[149]

The Bar did not welcome the idea that the traditional monopolies of the profession be justified according to the discipline of the marketplace. In an early comment, the then Chairman of the Bar Council wrote that '[j]ustice cannot be measured in terms of competition and consumerism; justice is not a consumer durable; it is the hallmark of a civilised and democratic society'.[150] Nor did the judiciary welcome the Green Paper's proposal that the Lord Chancellor, rather than the professions themselves, should be responsible for setting the principles according to which professional conduct was judged.[151] Responding to this suggestion in the particular context of rights of audience, the judiciary argued the proposal that 'the Lord Chancellor should make the final decision on standards of education and training for advocates...*represent[s] a grave breach of the doctrine of separation of powers*'.[152]

The debate which the Green Paper began finally resulted in the Courts and Legal Services Act 1990.[153] This Act did not implement all of the original Green Paper's proposals. The idea that the Lord Chancellor should have final control over the professional standards of the two professions was abandoned but the Act did set out a statutory objective for the provision of legal services, 'making provision for new and better ways of providing such services and a wider choice of persons providing them', and did create mechanisms to allow solicitors, amongst others, wider rights of audience and rights to conduct litigation.[154]

---

[149] Lord Chancellor's Department (1989) paras 1.1–1.2.     [150] *The Times*, 3 July 1989.

[151] Lord Chancellor's Department (1989) para. 4.11.

[152] Judges Response 'Summary' para. 3 (emphasis in original).

[153] For a discussion of this debate, see F. Cownie, 'The Reform of the Legal Profession or the End of Civilization as We Know It' in F. Patfield and R. White (eds), *The Changing Law* (1990) Leicester University Press, Leicester.

[154] The 1990 Act created a new body, the Lord Chancellor's Advisory Committee on Legal Education and Conduct, which has, amongst its duties, consideration of issues relating to training in advocacy and the

The change that the 1990 Act has brought to the relationship between the profession of solicitor and that of barrister can be over-emphasized. Only barristers have rights of audience in all courts by virtue of their profession. Even where solicitors have been granted increased rights of audience there are limitations on those solicitors who can take advantage of this extension.[155] Increasing rights of audience for solicitors, and others, have been negotiated but presently it remains the case that 'the Bar is the profession for specialist advocates'.[156] In March 2002, there were 1,401 solicitor advocates.[157] How much this number will increase in the future remains unclear.[158]

## CONCLUSION

The chapters in this book on legal reasoning emphasized the notion of the legal community as a way of explaining the predictability of the development of legal thought. Yet, much of what we have seen above suggests that lawyers are a divided group. Solicitors and barristers pursue different vocations. Both are separated off from the wide range of other counsel who offer legal advice. Within themselves, the professional groups are further split. The title

conduct of litigation. It has the power to make recommendations to professional bodies. Its role is, however, purely advisory (Courts and Legal Services Act 1990, s. 19 and Sch. 2). The statutory objective is set out in the Courts and Legal Services Act 1990, s. 17(1). Sections 27 and 28 set out provisions which allow for rights of audience and litigation to be widened.

[155] Three qualifications are now available for solicitors which give them wider rights of audience. The higher courts (criminal proceedings) qualification gives solicitors rights of audience in the Crown Court. The higher courts (civil proceedings) qualification gives solicitors rights of audience in the High Court and in all other courts in the case of civil proceedings. The higher courts (all proceedings) qualification combines the rights of audience granted by the first two. These qualifications are not open to all solicitors. Before applying, they must normally have held a practising certificate for three years and have two years' experience of advocacy (this is defined as 20 to 25 appearances before a court or tribunal a year). They should have attended a higher court, preferably as an instructing solicitor. If they are thus qualified, they are then given examinations on various matters relating to advocacy ((1993) Law Society Gazette, 17 December).

[156] N. Addison, 'The Defeatist Talk of Frightened Men' (1995) 145 New Law Journal 860.

[157] J. Swann, 'Comment' (2002) Law Society Gazette, 30 August. There is a society for solicitor advocates, the Solicitors Association of Higher Court Advocates (see: <http://www.sahca.org.uk/>).

[158] New advocates need not come only from the solicitors' profession. In the course of a discussion of the Courts and Legal Services Act 1990, the revised edition of Richard du Cann's *The Art of the Advocate* now concludes with the observation:

> If the professional lawyers have priced themselves out of this huge field so that, save in a handful of cases, the public cannot afford to employ them as advocates, and if public money is truly not available to allow the employment of the professional advocate under the Legal Aid Act, then there is no reason now why a specialist body of advocates drawn from the Law Centres, Citizens' Advice Bureaux and Welfare Groups should not be licensed and paid to do the work of the professional advocate. (du Cann (rev. edn, 1993) p. 239.)

Du Cann's views take on a special significance in the light of the fact that he is a past chairman of the Criminal Bar Association and a past chairman of the Bar's General Council. The Institute of Legal Executives is now an 'authorised body' for the purposes of the Courts and Legal Services Act 1990, s. 27, and its members have limited rights of audience in the magistrates' court and county courts.

'solicitor', and to a lesser extent the title 'barrister', tell us less and less about what a person will actually do in the pursuit of their profession.

These perceptions of diversity are important but they have to be set in their proper context. Much still unites the legal professions, both within themselves and with each other. The common training that they have at university and in their professional courses provides a core of a common culture. Perhaps the best evidence for this lies in the comparative failure of lawyers to break out of their traditional United Kingdom markets. It has been argued that '[b]usiness and commerce are no longer captive to the time zones and politics of their home states'.[159] Yet, despite this globalization of business, 'lawyers are tied to particular conceptions of the role of law and operate within particular legal systems'.[160] Good evidence for the common bonds that still tie together lawyers within England and Wales also lies in comparing lawyers from the common law world with those from the civil law world. 'There are strong family resemblances within each and major divisions between them.'[161] Lawyers are loosely bound together, but bound they are.

## FURTHER READING

ABEL, R., *English Lawers Between Market and State* (2003) Oxford University Press, Oxford

MORISON, J. and P. LEITH, *The Barrister's World and the Nature of Law* (1992) Open University Press, Buckingham

---

[159] J. Flood, 'The Culture of Globalization' in Y. D. Dezalay and D. Sugarman (eds), *Professional Competition and Professional Power* (1995) Routledge, London, at p. 142.    [160] Flood (1995) p. 161.
[161] Abel (1988b) p. 42. These divisions, in turn, being part of what prevents the full globalization of lawyering.

# 9

# Judges and judging

## INTRODUCTION

The dominant image of the judge within England and Wales is of a male figure, wigged and gowned, sitting, raised above the rest of the court, holding forth on some point of law.[1] Judges are seen as people learned in the law; as major contributors to the development and application of the jurisprudence of 'the English legal system'. Judges are those people who will be the final determiners of what English legal reasoning says about any particular set of facts before them. They are part, and arguably the most important part, of the constellation of legal communities that make up 'the English legal system'.[2]

The popular image of judges, like all stereotypes, carries significant elements of truth. For example, most judges in courts like the Supreme Court, Court of Appeal, and High Court are male.[3] Yet, again, like all stereotypes, it is also misleading in important respects. Perhaps the paradigmatic example of the judge within the popular image is the circuit court judge spending his time hearing cases which occasionally reach the national newspapers and, more regularly, become the subject of discussion within legal circles. Nevertheless, the majority of people occupying judicial office within 'the English legal system' hold only part-time appointments. They need not necessarily have any legal training and, if they do have such training, it may be at a comparatively low level. The cases they hear are of moment only to the parties concerned. They involve no great matters of legal principle. Their determination, one way or another, will have no discernible effect on the development of English jurisprudence. They will never be the subject of comment in the national press and they will not be reported so as to be the subject of discussion by lawyers. The majority of those holding judicial office are not Justices of the Supreme Court nor are they High Court judges. They are not even circuit judges sitting in the Crown Court or judges in the county courts. Rather, they are magistrates

---

[1] For a discussion of the significance of judicial attire, see D. Pannick, *Judges* (1987) Oxford University Press, Oxford, pp. 143–7.

[2] Thus, when Lee set out to provide an impressionistic portrait of the judiciary, he provided sketches of five judges in the then House of Lords (S. Lee, *Judging Judges* (1988) Faber and Faber, London, chs 17–21).

[3] In 2010, of the 11 judges in the House of Lords, 1 was a woman, 3 out of 38 in the Lord Justices of Appeal were women, and 11 out of 106 in the High Court were women (<http://www.judiciary.gov.uk/>). In the High Court, 17 judges in the Chancery Division were men whilst one was a woman; in the Queen's Bench Division there were 62 judges who were men and 8 who were women; whilst in the Family Division there were 12 judges who were men and 7 who were women.

and judges in tribunals. Their numbers far outweigh all other people holding judicial office.[4] For organizational reasons, most of our discussion of magistrates is in **Chapter 16**, but this should not be taken to indicate that we feel that magistrates hold judicial office in any less significant sense than judges in the House of Lords.

Understanding the contribution that judges make is vital to understanding 'the English legal system'. But equally important, is understanding the way in which our image of the judge has been constructed so as to reflect and reinforce our notion of what 'the English legal system' consists of. In order to do this, we need to begin by considering what we mean by the term 'judge' and what the notion of 'judging' implies.

## The separation of powers

In the traditional liberal philosophy which has characterized the dominant political discourse in England and Wales judges have an important political function.[5] Their work balances that of the legislature and the executive. Each are seen as semi-autonomous bodies with distinctive roles contributing to the polity as a whole. Each has power over the others and power over the population at large.[6] This idea has, in turn, been seen to be of vital significance in the elaboration of an effective constitutional framework. Hayek, for example, describes the development of this idea as being one of the two 'crucial conceptions' in safeguarding individual liberty.[7] In the USA, this philosophy finds its strictest expression. Under the US constitution, the judiciary, the legislature (Congress), and the executive (the President) have clearly defined roles. None of the three are subservient to either of the other two. Rather, each has its own sphere and must work within its own area according to the rules laid down by the US constitution.[8] The power of one limits the power of each of the others and thus serves to prevent tyranny.

[4] Thus, for example, in 2008, there were 640 circuit court judges but there were 29,270 lay magistrates (Ministry of Justice, *Judicial and Court Statistics 2008* (2009b) Cm. 7697, HMSO, London, p. 185 and p. 189).

[5] Montesquieu is usually seen as the progenitor of this idea in its modern form (see C. de Montesquieu, *The Spirit of the Laws* (1989) Cambridge University Press, Cambridge). The idea is confined to liberal philosophy. Aristotle, for example, divided the different political functions in the same manner in his book *Politics* (Aristotle, *Politics* (rev. edn, 1981) Penguin Books, Harmondsworth, pp. 276–91).

[6] For an application of this argument in the British context, see Lord Steyn, 'The Weakest and Least Dangerous Department of Government' [1997] Public Law 84 and R. Stevens, *The English Judge: Their Role in the Changing Constitution* (2002) Hart Publishing, Oxford, ch. 7.

[7] F. Hayek, *The Constitution of Liberty* (1960) Routledge & Kegan Paul, London, p. 169.

[8] For a description of the development of the idea in the USA, see M. Vile, *Constitutionalism and the Separation of Powers* (1967) Clarendon Press, Oxford, chs 6 and 10. Although the idea of the separation of powers finds formal expression in the US constitution, not every commentator agrees that it works in practice. See, for example, D. McKay, *Politics and Power in the USA* (2nd edn, 1994) Penguin, Harmondsworth, passim.

This concept of the 'separation of powers' has been widely applied to modern liberal states. In *The Spirit of the Laws*, Montesquieu applied the idea to the English constitution.[9] Historically, many writers since have argued that the idea of the separation of powers is not an accurate analysis of the present reality of the British constitutional position.[10] It is certainly true that some features already discussed in this book seem contrary to the spirit of the separation of powers. The triple role of the Lord Chancellor as judge, Cabinet minister, and Speaker of the House of Lords and the spectacle of Lords of Appeal in Ordinary sitting in the House of Lords when it acts as a legislature have, historically, been but two of the more obvious contradictions. Nevertheless, the idea has always retained some potency, even in the British context. Judges have sometimes referred to it approvingly when giving judgment and some commentators have used it as a measure of the success of the constitutional framework.[11] The abolition of the judicial role of the Lord Chancellor, announced in June 2003, and the creation of a Supreme Court with its members having no place in the legislature have strengthened the notion of the separation of powers in England and Wales.[12]

## The independence of the judiciary

Inherent in the idea of the separation of powers is the linked but discrete concept of the independence of the judiciary.[13] A past Lord Chancellor, Lord Mackay, has written that the 'independence of the judiciary is rightly regarded as a key principle of the constitution'.[14] Even some of those commentators who have disavowed the application of the separation of powers to the British constitutional situation have supported the notion of the independence of the judiciary.[15] Equally, commentators who do not discuss the notion of the separation of powers in relation to the British constitution may still discuss the idea of the independence of the judiciary. Thus, for example,

[9] Montesquieu (1989) pp. 156–66.

[10] For a full discussion of the attitude of British constitutional lawyers to the separation of powers in Great Britain, see C. Munroe, *Studies in Constitutional Law* (1987) Butterworths, London, pp. 193–6.

[11] See, for example, *R v Secretary of State for the Home Department, ex parte Fire Brigade Union* [1995] 2 All ER 244 at pp. 267–8; and *R v Secretary of State for the Home Department, ex parte Hickey (No. 2)* [1995] 1 All ER 490 at pp. 495–6. See also the *Report of the Committee on Ministers' Powers* where it was stated that '[i]n the English Constitution there is no such thing as the absolute separation of powers…in practice it is inevitable that there should be overlap…[but] [t]he distinction is nonetheless real, and for our purposes important' (*Report of the Committee on Ministers' Powers* (1932) Cmd 4060, HMSO, London, p. 4, see also pp. 8–10, 73–5, and 81–2).

[12] 18 June 2003 HC Debs, cols 357–8. See further the Constitutional Reform Act 2005.

[13] R. Stevens, *The Independence of the Judiciary* (1993) Oxford University Press, Oxford. The best recent account of these issues is to be found in K. Malleson, *The New Judiciary* (1999) Ashgate, Aldershot.

[14] Lord Mackay, *The Administration of Justice* (1994) Sweet & Maxwell, London, p. 12.

[15] See, for example, Lord Hailsham, 'The Office of Lord Chancellor and the Separation of Powers' (1989) 8 Civil Justice Quarterly 308.

Harden and Lewis, in their analysis of the British constitution, describe the notion of the independence of the judiciary as being one of two central aspects of the orthodox version of the rule of law.[16] Under s. 3(1) of the Constitutional Reform Act 2005, 'The Lord Chancellor, other Ministers of the Crown and all with responsibility for matters relating to the judiciary or otherwise to the administration of justice must uphold the continued independence of the judiciary.'

What the independence of the judiciary involves is a matter of some dispute. Complete independence for the judiciary is, of course, impossible. They are a part of the society in which they live and are influenced by the things around them. As one judge has put it, 'the habits you are trained in, the people with whom you mix, lead to your having a certain class of ideas of such a nature that, when you deal with other ideas, you do not give as sound and accurate judgements as you would wish'.[17] Independence implies, not isolation, but a willingness to resist external pressures when passing judgment. Central to the concept is the idea that judges will not be influenced in their decisions by anybody or anything outside the court. From this proposition, one can deduce a variety of different things; that judges should be comparatively well-paid so they will not be financially tempted, that judges should not take part in party politics, that judges should not be part of the government, that judges should not have any direct pecuniary or other interest in a case which would cause them to be (or appear to be) biased in their judgment, that judges should not make controversial statements in public which might lead to a feeling that they were biased about any particular issue, and that judges should be immune to being sued about their decisions so that they can make them without fear.[18]

Some of these points are either more controversial or more difficult to apply than others. For example, when Lord Mackay became Lord Chancellor judges were required to apply to the Lord Chancellor before contributing to public discussion. The so-called 'Kilmuir rules' which laid out this procedure were first enunciated by Lord Kilmuir when he was Lord Chancellor.[19] Lord Mackay took the view that this requirement was incompatible with judicial independence and abolished it.[20] However, it might be argued that judicial independence will be compromised by increased incursion into the arena of public debate. Lord Kilmuir had asserted, when laying down the Kilmuir rules, that judicial independence required judges to be insulated from criticism and that '[s]o long as a Judge keeps silent his reputation for wisdom and impartiality

---

[16] The other they variously describe as being the supremacy of Parliament and the idea of the common law. See I. Harden and N. Lewis, *The Noble Lie* (1988) Hutchinson, London, pp. 37 and 190.

[17] T. Scrutton, 'The Work of the Commercial Courts' (1921) 1 Cambridge Law Journal 6 at p. 8.

[18] For a discussion of points similar to these, see S. H. Bailey, J. P. L. Ching, and N. W. Taylor, *Smith, Bailey and Gunn on the Modern English Legal System* (5th edn, 2007) Sweet & Maxwell, London, pp. 264–7. See also D. Casson and I. Scott, 'Great Britain' in S. Shetreet and J. Deschenes (eds), *Judicial Independence: The Contemporary Debate* (1985) Martinus Nijhoff, Dordrecht; and Stevens (2002) ch. 6.

[19] The text of his letter setting out this rule is to be found in A. Bradley, 'Judges and the Media – The Kilmuir Rules' [1983] Public Law 383 at pp. 384–6.     [20] Mackay (1994) pp. 25–6.

remains unassailable'.[21] In the contemporary era, not only do judges make speeches, but they are also advertised on the judiciary's website.[22] One consequence of this has been judges not sitting in cases which raise issues on which they have already made extra-judicial pronouncements.[23]

Judicial independence has traditionally been thought of in terms of independence of individual judgment: a particular judge in a particular case should not have their decision affected by any outside influence. However, in the past decade judges have begun to argue that threats to the independence of the judiciary as a collective body are as important as threats to the independence of individual judges. The central threat has been seen to come from the executive via mechanisms of financial control:

> Judges are sitting in an environment wholly determined by executive decision in the Lord Chancellor's Department, which is in turn operating under financial constraints and pressures imposed by the Treasury. The yardstick for decision-making is financial value for money, not the interests of justice.[24]

At one extreme, all commentators would agree that financial control can compromise the independence of the judiciary. An executive which did not provide any financial support for the courts or for judicial salaries could not be said to be supporting the principle of the independence of the judiciary. However, it might equally be argued that, even under the doctrine of the separation of powers, the decision as to the precise percentage of the nation's wealth that can be spent on the legal system in general, and the courts in particular, properly falls within the powers of the executive or the legislature.[25] Several previous Lord Chancellors have urged caution in taking arguments for judicial independence too far, arguing that financial constraints have, to date, never impinged upon the integrity of the judiciary.[26]

Other commentators have raised questions about how far the judiciary are independent when making their individual judgments. No serious writer has suggested that judges make decisions which are the result of direct pressure. Rather, queries have been raised about the degree to which judgments are the result of indirect pressures that arise out of the particular social position of the judiciary. One persistent critic of the judiciary has argued that they are subject to subtle political influences in their decision-making although this influence does not mean that it necessarily results in

---

[21]  Bradley (1983) p. 383.          [22]  <http://www.judiciary.gov.uk/publications>.

[23]  See, for example, Lord Steyn's comments in '2000–2005: Laying the Foundations of Human Rights Law in the United Kingdom' (2005) 4 European Human Rights Law Review 349 at p. 350 n. 4.

[24]  Sir N. Browne-Wilkinson, 'The Independence of the Judiciary in the 1980s' [1988] Public Law 4 at p. 50. See also Lord Lane, 'Judicial Independence and the Increasing Executive Role in Judicial Administration' in Shetreet and Deschenes (1985).

[25]  For one comment on the relationship between the judiciary and the executive see Lord Woolf, 'Judicial Review – The Tensions between the Executive and the Judiciary' (1998) 114 Law Quarterly Review 579. Under s. 3(6)(b) of the Constitutional Reform Act 2005, the Lord Chancellor must have regard to 'the need for the judiciary to have the support necessary to enable them to exercise their functions'.

[26]  See Hailsham (1989) passim and Mackay (1994) pp. 17–18.

subservience to the dominant political party in Parliament. Writing about judges at the time of the last Conservative administration Griffith comments:

many of the judges did seem to regard ministers as mildly disreputable and not very intelligent.

Judges today mostly reflect moderate Conservative opinion of the middle 'consensus' years of [the twentieth century].[27]

## Independence, separation, and judicial office

These arguments about the judiciary are carried on in the context of particular judges. They are not extended to those holding judicial office as a whole. The official handbook for new magistrates in Scotland states that:

In order to understand accused persons and witnesses, to weigh their evidence, to understand their problems and to make appropriate decisions and sentences, the justices need to be part of the local community, to be aware of its diversity and to know how its members live, work and play.[28]

Such a view stresses, not the separateness of the judicial role, but the degree to which the judiciary are part of society taken as a whole. This argument is not limited to magistrates. The Justice Report on Industrial Tribunals (now termed Employment Tribunals) said of the wing members, those people who were not legally qualified, '[t]he aim is to have a good spread of members on the panel in terms of age, sex, industry, occupation, public sector, private sector, size of firm etc' and criticized the tribunals for failing to achieve that aim.[29] Writing about Social Security Appeal Tribunals, Baldwin and his colleagues said:

The shift from lay to legal chairmen inevitably means that at least one-third of any tribunal panel comes from a professional background, often with no direct experience of the kind of problems faced by appellants. This makes it all the more important, given the aim of achieving some kind of social balance on a panel, that the people recruited as lay members on the tribunal be drawn from a range of backgrounds.[30]

This is not to say that either lay magistrates or wing members of tribunals are expected to be mere delegates of their communities, determining cases in a manner that they think would be approved of by the groups from which they come. Magistrates, as much as judges in the Court of Appeal, are expected to assess cases on their merits

[27] J. A. G. Griffith, *The Politics of the Judiciary* (5th edn, 1997) Fontana, London, p. 328.

[28] Quoted in Z. Bankowski, N. R. Hutton, and J. J. McManus, *Lay Justice?* (1987) T. & T. Clark, Edinburgh, p. 56. See also J. Raine, *Local Justice: Ideals and Realities* (1989) T. & T. Clark, Edinburgh, pp. 30–1.

[29] Justice (Society), *Industrial Tribunals* (1987) Justice, London, p. 49.

[30] J. Baldwin, N. Wikeley, and R. Young, *Judging Social Security* (1992) Clarendon Press, Oxford, pp. 132–3.

and according to law. They, too, must have 'the capacity or potential to act judicially and thereby to make fair and proper decisions'.[31]

Arguments about the independence of the judiciary and the separation of powers do not seem to be so easily applied to magistrates or members of tribunals and the main debates about these notions have not been carried on in the context of these offices. This shows us how distorted our common-sense idea of a judge is, for the essential role of these offices is the same as that for a judge in the better-known courts. Just as we view the idea of a court from a picture of one particular type of court, so we view the idea of a judge from one particular, and not necessarily very representative, idea of a judge. If the judiciary should be separate and independent then all the judiciary should be separate and independent. If it is only some who should be separate we need an argument, which has not been put, for the identification of different kinds of judiciary.

## The selection of the judiciary

In many countries, there are career judiciary. The judiciary in such countries can either be seen as being part of the legal profession or as being a profession alongside other legal professions. The decision to become a judge is made at the same time and in the same way that decisions to become other types of lawyers are made. You can choose to train as a judge just as you choose to train as a lawyer.[32] Within 'the English legal system', a different approach is found. Judicial appointment is something to which one can aspire only after a period spent in another occupation. In most cases, this separate occupation is prior experience as a solicitor or barrister but in the case of lay magistrates more general experience is required.

### Barristers and judges

Historically, appointment to judicial office has been linked to previous practice as a barrister. Thus, for example, when it was first passed, s. 10(1)(b) of the Supreme Court Act 1981 limited appointment as a Lord Justice of Appeal to those who had 'at least fifteen years' standing' as a barrister and to puisne judges. Section 10(1)(c) limited appointment as a puisne judge of the High Court to barristers 'of at least ten years' standing'. This excluded, not just non-lawyers, but also solicitors. In 1981, opposing

---

[31] Lord Chancellor's Department, 'The Qualities Looked for in a Justice of the Peace', quoted in Raine (1989) p. 54.

[32] This approach is common through much of the world. Thus, for example, in the case of France, see B. Dickson, *Introduction to French Law* (1994) Pitman Publishing, London, p. 31; in the case of Germany, see N. Foster, *German Law and German Legal System* (1993) Blackstone Press, London, p. 73; and in the case of Japan, see H. Oda, *Japanese Law* (1992) Butterworths, London, p. 95 and M. Abe, 'The Internal Control of a Bureaucratic Judiciary: The Case of Japan' (1995) 23 International Journal of the Sociology of Law 303.

an attempt to widen appointments to include solicitors, Lord Hailsham, the then Lord Chancellor, asserted that appointment to such an office required the previous experience of appearing in the court.[33]

Limiting judicial office to those who are barristers is neither without advantage nor without effect. In previous chapters, we have noted the ways in which law arises not from the mechanical operation of pure legal rules but, in part, from the socially conceived results of the operations of communities of lawyers. We have seen how the very notion of 'the English legal system' can arise from arbitrary distinctions between things in and things not in the legal system made by groups whose social relations with each other and collectively with others gives them the power to legitimize the validity of these distinctions. Drawing judges from barristers meant that a very small legal community, judges, could be distilled from what was already an enclosed group, barristers. The advantage of this is that a common professional background can lead to a coherence of views and thus a predictability of behaviour.[34] The community will speak with one voice. The disadvantage is that the distortions and faults of the barrister's community are at best repeated and at worst amplified in the judicial community.

## Changes to methods of judicial selection

The observation that judges are not a statistical cross-section of the society in which they live, does not automatically lead to the conclusion that the only way in which they can either judge fairly or be seen to judge fairly is for there to be changes so that they can be that cross-section. First, it is clearly possible for people to understand and empathize with those who are not from the same background as themselves. Lord Mackay has argued that:

[o]bviously every judge comes to a case with previous experience and opinions formed in the light of that experience. But the criterion for a good judge is, to my mind, the extent to which he is able to apply his judgement afresh to issues put before him and to relegate any such pre-formed views.[35]

Equally, it is possible for them to persuade others that they can do this. Training can help. Thus, for example, the Ethnic Minorities Advisory Committee of the Judicial Studies Board began organizing a seminar on issues related to ethnic awareness for judges, magistrates, and tribunal chairs in 1992.[36] There is some evidence to suggest that this type of training has produced a cultural change in the judiciary. One survey concluded that:

[t]he ethnic awareness training that had been carried out...appears to have had an effect not just on the formal ways in which judges deal with ethnic minorities, but on their

---

[33] Hansard, House of Lords, vol. 417, col. 1237.    [34] See, for example, Pannick (1987) p. 50.
[35] Mackay (1994) p. 9.
[36] *Judicial Studies Board Report 1991–1995* (1995) Judicial Studies Board, London, pp. 28–33.

recognition that they need to examine their prejudices and degree of ignorance about the lifestyles, culture, religion and languages of members of minority ethnic groups if they are to treat them fairly.[37]

Yet, this having been said, the same survey found that small numbers of defendants continued to believe that they were treated unfairly in courts because they were from minority ethnic groups and also noted that racist remarks continued to be made by a small number of magistrates.[38]

The passage of the Courts and Legal Services Act 1990, saw the beginning of a process of reform which gave people other than barristers increasing rights of audience in the courts and, as a consequence, enlarged the number of people who were eligible for judicial office. Solicitors became eligible to act as advocates in the higher courts, providing they had obtained appropriate advocacy qualifications in addition to their qualification as a solicitor.[39] This, in turn, meant that such solicitors became qualified to be appointed as judges in the higher courts. One Justice in the current Supreme Court, Lord Collins, is a solicitor.[40] Subsequent developments have widened even further the range of people who are qualified to hold judicial office. In 2003, a government report, *Constitutional Reform: A New Way of Appointing Judges*, called for even further diversity in the appointment of judges. This is reflected in the provisions of the Tribunals, Courts and Enforcement Act 2007. The 2007 Act both gives the power to recognize a wider range of qualifications as being relevant to the appointment of judiciary and recognizes a wider range of experience as being relevant.[41]

Changes to the judicial appointments process have not just involved widening the pool of potential applicants. Under the Constitutional Reform Act 2005, with effect from 3 April 2006, the process of recruiting and selecting judges was put in the hands of the independent Judicial Appointments Commission.[42] The Commission has 15 members, 5 of whom are lay people with the rest being drawn from the legal professions and the judiciary. Whilst s. 63(2) of the 2005 Act says that selection of the judiciary 'must solely be on merit', s. 64(1) says that '[t]he Commission...must have regard to the need to encourage diversity in the range of persons available for selection'.[43] The process of the selection of the judiciary has thus been fundamentally altered. Whether outcomes will similarly be affected remains to be seen.

[37] R. Hood, S. Shute, and F. Seemungal, *Ethnic Minorities in the Criminal Courts: Perceptions of Fairness and Equality of Treatment* (2003) Research Series Report No. 2/03, Lord Chancellor's Department, London, p. 133.                                              [38] Hood et al. (2003) pp. 47 and 110.

[39] These qualifications are currently to be found in The Higher Courts Qualification Regulations 2000 which are due to be replaced by The Solicitors Higher Rights of Audience Regulations 2009.

[40] See the Supreme Court website at: <http://www.supremecourt.gov.uk/about/biographies.html>.

[41] Thus, for example, the statute treats acting as a mediator and teaching or research into law as being 'law-related activities' for the purpose of appointment as a judge (see s. 52(4)(f) and (h) Tribunals, Courts and Enforcement Act 2007). Being a Fellow of the Institute of Legal Executives is a qualification for some judicial appointments (see Judicial Appointments Order 2008/2975).

[42] For information on the Commission and how it operates, see <http://www.judicialappointments.gov.uk/>.

[43] In a recent statement, the then Lord Chancellor, Lord Falconer, said that '[i]ncreasing the diversity of the judiciary...remains one of my key priorities' <http://www.dca.gov.uk/pubs/statements/2006/>.

Solicitors have been able to be appointed as recorders for over three decades.[44] Despite this fact, in 1998, only 53 of the 403 assistant recorders were solicitors.[45] In a speech in October 1999, the then Law Society President, Robert Sayer, called solicitor judges 'the rare exception'.[46] Solicitors have consistently argued that the process of selecting judges makes it difficult for them to be appointed, even if they are formally qualified.[47] Even in the current era, solicitors continue to argue that, in practice, they are largely excluded from the full range of judicial appointments.[48] If this is true for solicitors it may be that it is unlikely that the reality of judicial appointments will change very greatly. Most judges may still come from the bar with all that entails for judicial diversity.

## Discrimination and the judiciary

The distortions that drawing judges from barristers can produce is best exemplified by considering the gender balance amongst the judiciary. As we have already noted, there are considerably more senior male judges than female judges. A recent report found that 26 per cent of the judiciary were women.[49] In their 1992 survey, *Without Prejudice? Sex Equality at the Bar and in the Judiciary*, Holland and Spencer note that the appointments procedure to the judiciary 'attracted the largest number of comments in the survey'.[50] Of the respondents, 112 suggested that the system need more openness. This was twice as many comments as on any other issue.[51] According to the Lord Chancellor's Department, the process of judicial appointment involves a process of 'continuous consultation with judges and senior members of the profession' about the abilities of those who might be suitable for office.[52] Individual applications are assessed in the light of the 'views of the judicial and professional community'.[53] Holland and Spencer noted that many respondents to their survey commented adversely on

[44] Courts Act 1971, s. 21(2). The office of recorder was originally only open to those who were barristers (see A. Kiralfy, *The English Legal System* (1954) Sweet & Maxwell, London, pp. 205–6).

[45] A. Clarke et al., 'Solicitors in the Judiciary' (1999) Law Society Gazette, 13 October. The same source notes that only 74 of the 559 circuit judges were solicitors, although 95 per cent of all district judges were solicitors.

[46] 'Law Society President Calls for One Unified Legal Profession', 30 October 1999 <http://www.lawsociety.org.uk/>.

[47] See, for example, the views of Harvey Crush, a solicitor circuit court judge, Paul Hampton, a solicitor assistant recorder, and Rivers Hickman, a solicitor recorder, in R. Verkailc, 'Be the Judge' (1996) Law Society Gazette, 31 January.

[48] A. Rice, 'Solicitor Judges Face Exclusion from Senior Judicial Posts' (2007) Law Society Gazette, 16 August.

[49] *Judicial Diversity: Findings of a Consultation with Barristers, Solicitors and Judges: Final Report* (2006) Opinion Leader Research, p. 7. Figures vary, depending on which part of the judiciary is being considered. For detailed figures, see Department of Constitutional Affairs, *Increasing Diversity in the Judiciary: Consultation Paper: CP25/04* (2004a) DCA, London, Annex G.

[50] L. Holland and L. Spencer, *Without Prejudice? Sex Equality at the Bar and in the Judiciary* (1992) TMS Consultants, London, p. 22.           [51] Holland and Spencer (1992).

[52] Lord Chancellor's Department, *Judicial Appointment* (1986) Lord Chancellor's Department, London, p. 3.                    [53] Lord Chancellor's Department (1986) p. 3.

both the secrecy of this procedure and on the fact that it involved a largely male refer-ence group.[54] The Bar's acceptance of 'stereotypical and discriminatory remarks', the lack of opportunity to appear in high-profile cases, and the perception of QC status, something not equally enjoyed by men and women, as a criterion for appointment to the judiciary were all also mentioned as reasons why women failed to be appointed to the judiciary.[55] In other words, the barristers' community, which was seen as sex-typed, naturally produced a judicial community which was itself sex-typed.[56] Even in Malleson and Banda's study, which was based upon a survey of lawyers, 'the most notable feature of responses taken overall... [was] the high level of criticism of the appointments process'.[57]

The uneven balance of men and women in the judiciary raises questions of fairness and equality. Positions of power and advantage are, it is argued, being illegitimately denied to women. More than this, it is arguable that the nature of judicial work at the highest level has changed, resulting – in the view of Lady Hale, the sole woman judge in the Supreme Court – in a 'greater constitutional and "small p" political significance... [in] the work of the higher judiciary'.[58] The lack of diversity in the judiciary thus raises constitutional issues if aspects of governance are largely matters of male governance. However, the inequality of representation also raises other questions.[59] If the judiciary are largely male, if it is a sex-typed profession, can judges properly deal with women and issues which have a particular concern for women in their courts? This general argument has been raised in many particular instances. O'Donovan and Szyszczak, for example, in their study of sex discrimination, quote a judicial statement that 'a woman's hair is her crowning glory' and another telling a woman that 'when she had dried her tears, she would have had to look for new employment and count herself lucky to find it'.[60] Such remarks trivialize and belittle women. O'Donovan and Szyszczak argue that they also bespeak of an underlying lack of sympathy for the legislation relating to sex discrimination. In a similar vein, judicial comments when sentencing in rape trials

[54] Holland and Spencer (1992) p. 24. The 1999 Peach Report on the judicial appointments process noted that this remained, for some, 'the most controversial element of the selection process' (Sir Leonard Peach, 'Independent Scrutiny of the Appointment Processes of Judges and Queen's Counsel' (1999) Lord Chancellor's Department, London).                    [55] Holland and Spencer (1992) p. 24.

[56] D. Podmore and A. Spencer, 'The Law as a Sex-typed Profession' (1982) 9(1) Journal of Law and Society 21.

[57] K. Malleson and F. Banda, *Factors Affecting the Decision to Apply for Silk and Judicial Office* (2000) Lord Chancellor's Department, London, p. 39.

[58] Lady Hale, 'Making a Difference? Why We Need a More Diverse Judiciary' (2005) 56 Northern Ireland Legal Quarterly 281 at p. 283.

[59] On gender inequality within the judiciary, see generally E. Rackley, 'Representations of the (Woman) Judge: Hercules, the Little Mermaid, and the Vain and Naked Emperor' (2002) 22 Legal Studies 602; K. Malleson, 'Justifying Gender Inequality on the Bench: Why Difference Won't Do' (2003) 11 Feminist Legal Studies 1; and E. Rackley, 'Difference in the House of Lords' (2006) 15 Social and Legal Studies 163.

[60] K. O'Donovan and E. Szyszczak, *Equality and Sex Discrimination Law* (1988) Basil Blackwell, Oxford, p. 84. The statements quoted are by Lord Denning in *Ministry of Defence* v *Jeremiah* [1980] ICR 13 at p. 22 and Shaw LJ in *Skyrail Oceanic Ltd* v *Coleman* [1981] ICR 864 at p. 873. Similar such comments are legion.

have sometimes caused concern.[61] Judicial interventions during trials have also resulted in adverse comment.[62] Such judicial comments are reported in the media. The media are not, of course, scientific or representative in their selection of which judicial comments to report. Moreover, some of these press reports are of some age. Those reported may thus wholly misrepresent the attitude of the current judiciary taken as a whole.[63] Two separate but interrelated arguments are raised by the points above. First, are women and women's particular interests treated properly by the judiciary? Second, can women reasonably be expected to feel that they and their interests are being treated properly by a group which is so much dominated by men? Even if the first question can be answered in the affirmative, the second might be answered in the negative. Even if, after lengthy research, it were possible to show that women and women's interests were treated sensitively by the judiciary taken as a whole it could be argued that a legitimate suspicion of mistreatment is raised by the gender imbalance in the judiciary: that the judiciary should not just treat people equally but should appear to have the ability to do so.

It is important to remember that any legal system is constantly in a state of change. As McGlynn has noted, '[r]eforms are being implemented, and more women and lawyers from ethnic minorities are being appointed'.[64] However, the base from which reform starts is very low and reform is very slow. Between the first and present editions of this book, the number of women judges in the Court of Appeal increased fourfold, but an increase from one to four is not an impressive achievement in a highly developed country at the beginning of the twenty-first century.[65]

## Judges and the legitimacy of the legal system

Problems about the way in which judges are selected and their relationship to the population as a whole can be related to issues other than those of gender discrimination. Judges are largely white.[66] Griffith has noted instances of racist remarks made by judges as has Crawford.[67] In a broader vein, Griffith has argued that judges are drawn

---

[61] See, for example, J. Temkin, *Rape and the Legal Process* (1987) Sweet & Maxwell, London, pp. 18–19 and Pannick (1987) pp. 33–4.

[62] See, for example, Z. Adler, 'Rape – The Intention of Parliament and the Practice of the Courts' (1982) 45 Modern Law Review 664 at pp. 673–4.

[63] K. Soothill, S. Walby, and P. Baigguley, 'Judges, the Media and Rape' (1990) 17 Journal of Law and Society 211. [64] C. McGlynn, *The Woman Lawyer* (1998) Butterworths, London, p. 187.

[65] For arguments for the importance of women being appointed as judges, see Dame Brenda Hale, 'Equality and the Judiciary: Why Should We Want More Women Judges?' [2001] Public Law 489; and Rackley (2002).

[66] In 1994, the highest rank of the judiciary which contained judges from the ethnic minorities was that of circuit judge. Only three such judges were drawn from the ethnic minorities (D. Harvie, 'Equal Opportunities at the Bar' (1994) 144 New Law Journal 503 at p. 503).

[67] J. A. G. Griffith, *The Politics of the Judiciary* (5th edn, 1997) Fontana, London, pp. 12–13, 38; L. Crawford, 'Race Awareness Training and the Judges' (January/February 1994) Counsel 11 at p. 12.

from a comparatively narrow social background.[68] Pannick has asserted that judges 'lack expertise and knowledge of many of the matters which are central to the lives of those people who come into court as litigants or witnesses'.[69] Once again, these criticisms raise questions of fairness and knowledge but equally questions of legitimacy. Will the population as a whole think the judges understand the people they are judging if they are so far removed from them? Will they regard the system as legitimate?[70] A 1985 survey showed that 45 per cent of people thought that judges were influenced by government and 50 per cent thought that judges favoured the rich.[71]

## Judicial style

In this and previous chapters, we have argued that 'the English legal system' in part is to be explained by the existence of various legal communities which draw people together and cause them to act in similar ways. Judges and magistrates are two such communities. At the same time, we should remember the limitations of this argument. Judges are not clones, sharing precisely the same education and training or precisely the same beliefs. Each judge or magistrate differs from every other judge or magistrate. There are differences in style, as between individual judges and as between different periods of judges. These differences need to be taken into account when analysing the work of the judiciary.

Studies of judicial behaviour invariably show some variations in individual judicial behaviour which can be accounted for only by reference to differences in individual judicial activities. Thus, for example, a study by Baldwin of district judges showed four different ways of conducting court hearings:

(a) 'going for the jugular' (identifying the central issues at an early stage and sticking to them)

(b) 'hearing the parties' (allowing the parties greater latitude to develop their arguments in their own way)

(c) 'passive' (talking to each of the parties like a solicitor interviewing clients) and

(d) 'mediatory' (encouraging parties to agree their own solutions).[72]

---

68  Griffith (1997) pp. 18–22. For more recent work on the background of the judiciary, see P. Darbyshire, 'Where Do English and Welsh Judges Come From?' (2007) 66 Cambridge Law Journal 365.

69  Pannick (1987) p. 55.

70  Lord Mackay has noted that judges are appointed 'to serve the general public, not just the [legal] profession, and that accordingly the type of impression an applicant makes on a lay person may well give a useful insight into his or her potential performance as a judge' (Mackay (1994) p. 7).

71  Quoted in D. Oliver, 'Politicians and the Courts' (1988) Parliamentary Affairs 13 at pp. 13–14.

72  J. Baldwin, 'Small Claims Hearings: The "Interventionist" Role Played by District Judges' (1998) 17 Civil Justice Quarterly 20 at pp. 25–7.

Variations in judicial behaviour are not just important in a descriptive sense. They will sometimes alter the outcome of a case. Nor are such variations necessarily minor. One study of judicial behaviour in relation to determining the result of applications by step-parents to adopt their step-child described some variations in outcome as 'enormous'.[73]

In theory, one might expect judicial behaviour to be constrained by the rules under which they operate. Whatever the judge's own predisposition, she or he is bound to apply the law as it is. However, as we have seen, the law is a debatable rather than a fixed concept. Judges are thus relatively unconstrained. Moreover, there is some evidence to suggest that judges will, on occasion, ignore even that which is relatively clear law.[74]

Whilst some have argued that judicial decision-making reflects the social background of the judiciary, it is clear that some judges' decisions are based much more on their own personal views.[75] Thus, for example, Geary has argued of Lord Denning:

his style of law-making is such that there is no coherent pattern of legal thought behind it…he expresses his own ideas, his own morality, his own ideology…[76]

However, there are not many clear examples of judicial decision-making based upon personal morality or ideology making a significant difference to the outcome of a case. Even where an individual variation in decision-making can be seen, the difference is usually modest in nature.[77]

Judicial style varies over time. A current judge, Sedley LJ (then Sedley J), writing about what were then recent decisions in the High Court, Court of Appeal, and House of Lords, argued that there is now 'a culture of judicial assertiveness to compensate for, and in places repair, dysfunctions in the democratic process'.[78] Stevens, in his analysis of the House of Lords, has shown how an increasing professionalization of the judiciary in the House of Lords changed the way in which it worked.[79] Paterson has compared the work of the House of Lords during the time when Lord Reid was the

---

[73] J. Masson, D. Norbury, and S. Chatterton, *Mine, Yours or Ours?* (1983) HMSO, London, p. 84.

[74] Thus, for example, a study of registrars showed that 32 per cent of them took minor instances of bad conduct into account when determining maintenance applications, even though the Court of Appeal had said that such conduct should be taken into account only if it was 'gross and obvious' (W. Barrington Baker, J. Eekelaar, C. Gibson, and S. Raikes, *The Matrimonial Jurisdiction of Registrars* (1977) Centre for Socio-Legal Studies, Oxford, p. 90).

[75] Direct party political bias is now difficult to show. However, it does seem to have existed in the past and to have affected the outcome of cases which are law today. See, for example, A. Bradney, 'Facade: The Poplar Case' (1983) Northern Ireland Legal Quarterly 1.

[76] R. Geary, 'Lord Denning and Morality' in P. Robson and P. Watchman (eds), *Justice, Lord Denning and the Constitution* (1981) Gower, Aldershot, p. 74. Of course, these views in part may be based upon Lord Denning's social background.

[77] See, for example, B. Dickson, 'The Contribution of Lord Diplock to the General Law of Contract' (1989) 9 Oxford Journal of Legal Studies 441.

[78] Sedley J, 'Human Rights: A Twenty-First Century Agenda' [1995] Public Law 386 at p. 388. For articles which illustrate this assertiveness, see Lord Woolf, 'Droit Public – English Style' [1995b] Public Law 57; and Laws J, 'Law and Democracy' [1995] Public Law 72.

[79] R. Stevens, *Law and Politics* (1979) Weidenfeld & Nicholson, London.

senior judge and after.[80] Such changes are reflective, both of major issues such as variations in social conditions and changes in social mores, and more minor matters such as, for example, variations in court workload affecting the time the judiciary have to consider each case.[81]

Despite the above, we know relatively little about the nature of judicial behaviour. We know that such behaviour varies and we know that that variation is important but in many areas of law how it works is, as yet, unclear. Part of the reason for this ignorance lies in the fact that for many years legal academics regarded such behaviour as unimportant. However, part of the reason is the judiciary's unwillingness to cooperate in research. A pilot project on sentencing in the Crown Court showed that there was considerable diversity in the approaches that experienced judges took to sentencing. The researchers engaged in this project proposed further research in order to ascertain more clearly how judges approached sentencing decisions and thus reached very different decisions about what were apparently similar cases. The then Lord Chief Justice, Lord Lane, refused permission for such research on the ground that he 'could not think of any aspects of judicial sentencing upon which research might prove helpful'.[82] Such uncooperative attitudes make it difficult to assess exactly what role judges and magistrates play in 'the English legal system'.

## CONCLUSION

How is a person occupying judicial office different from someone else? What makes being a judge different? It might be said that those occupying judicial office make authoritative statements about disputes about rules. But, then, so do football referees. In previous chapters, we have seen that 'the English legal system' is not a discrete entity which is sharply differentiated from that which surrounds it but, rather, that it merges into the society in which it is found. So it is with those holding judicial office. Being a Justice of the Supreme Court is in most ways very different from being a magistrate.[83] That which unites the two offices, the fact that the holders are called to give judgment, does not distinguish them from many other jobs that we would not describe as judicial. Making judgments is, after all, something we must all do all the time. Existentialists argue that that constant necessity of making judgments is central to the nature of human existence.[84] On a more trivial level, anybody who occupies any position of authority within a hierarchy, is required to make decisions, to pass judgments, about

---

[80]  A. Paterson, *The Law Lords* (1982) Macmillan, London.

[81]  A. Bradney, 'The Changing Face of the House of Lords' [1985b] Juridical Review 178 at p. 187.

[82]  A. Ashworth, E. Genders, G. Mansfield, J. Peay, and E. Player, *Sentencing in the Crown Court* (1984) Centre for Criminological Research, Oxford, p. 64.

[83]  For a study of the work of district judges, see P. Darbyshire 'Cameos from the World of District Judges' (2006) 50 Journal of Criminal Law 443.

[84]  'Man is nothing else but which he makes of himself' (J. Sartre, *Existentialism and Humanism* (1973) Eyre Methuen, London, p. 28).

other people. This applies equally to the more obvious cases such as managing directors and the less obvious ones such as section leaders. Anybody who is 'a line manager' is thereby a judge.

What distinguishes judicial office from others who are involved in judging is just the status that we attribute to it. Judges can be described but not defined. That status, in turn, arises in part because of the nature of the job being done and in part because of the social position of judges. It is not distributed equally. A judge in a tribunal is not treated in the same way as a Court of Appeal judge.[85] Whilst there are powerful elements which bind judges together, the community of judges is also fractured and divided. If it is one thing which helps pull together 'the English legal system', it is also one thing which exemplifies the amorphous nature of that system.

## FURTHER READING

MALLESON, K., *The New Judiciary: The Effects of Expansion and Activism* (1989) Dartmouth, Aldershot

STEVENS, R., *The English Judges: Their Role in the Changing Constitution* (2002) Hart Publishing, Oxford

---

[85] By the legal system as well as by others. Judges in tribunals are not appointed in the same way as judges in the Court of Appeal and they do not have the same protection from dismissal.

# 10

# The civil court in action

## INTRODUCTION

It has been traditional to divide analysis of the work of the civil courts into two parts: smaller claims in the county court and larger claims in the High Court. Historically, it has been thought that this has reflected not only the formal difference in procedures between these two courts but also the very real difference in attitudes on the part of judges and others who staff the courts. As we saw in **Chapter 3**, county courts were set up to provide a cheaper way of settling civil disputes. They were not intended to be a local mirror of the High Court but, rather, to be a different type of venue. The creation of a small claims division in 1972, with its emphasis on informality and accessibility for the unrepresented lay person, further highlighted these distinctions.

There are two dangers in analysing the work of the civil courts in this traditional way. First, the effect of reforms consequent on the Civil Justice Review has been to reduce the distinction between the High Court and the county courts. Following the publication of Lord Woolf's report on the civil justice system, *Access to Justice*,[1] the introduction of the Civil Procedure Act 1997 and the Civil Procedure Rules 1998 were intended to further hasten the integration of the two courts. Whilst there is no suggestion that the distinction between the High Court and the county courts will be entirely lost within the foreseeable future their relationship seems to be destined to be a much closer one than has been the case in the past. An analysis which divides consideration of the two may, therefore, be less appropriate. Second, an analysis which concentrates on and contrasts the work of the High Court and county court tends to concentrate on certain sorts of civil actions. There is a tendency to look at actions in contract and tort and treat these as paradigmatic of the work of the civil courts.[2] Again, this approach has several advantages. Actions based directly or indirectly on contract and tort form an important part of the work of the civil courts. In 2008, the three

---

[1] Lord Woolf, *Access to Justice: Final Report to the Lord Chancellor on the Civil Justice System in England and Wales* (1996) Lord Chancellor's Department, London.

[2] Thus, in *Smith, Bailey and Gunn on the Modern English Legal System*, the treatment of the civil process uses contract actions as an example (S. H. Bailey, J. P. L. Ching, and N. W. Taylor, *Smith, Bailey and Gunn on the Modern English Legal System* (5th edn, 2007) Sweet & Maxwell, London, pp. 706–27).

largest types of claim brought in the Queen's Bench Division of the High Court in the Royal Courts of Justice were:

Claims for debt – 1,065
Personal Injuries – 1,205
Breach of contract – 710.[3]

Discussion of these areas therefore conveys an important sense of how people's actual disputes are dealt with in the courts. It reflects not just the remote reaches of the courts, where points of law are argued at a high level of abstraction, but the day-to-day activity of the law in context. However, important as these areas are, the work of the civil courts encompasses a far wider range of actions than is to be seen in those based on contract and tort.

In previous chapters, we have argued that the idea of 'the English legal system' can be misleading because of the way it both ignores divisions within 'the system' and things that actors and institutions within 'the system' have in common with actors and institutions that are deemed to be not part of 'the system'. Treating the work of the civil courts as being largely the operation of contract and tort can give civil courts the appearance of a false unity and coherence. This is true, not just in the sense that there are actions in the civil courts based on areas of law other than contract or tort. More important, is the fact that the civil court's approach to many civil disputes can be very different to the approach which is taken to the kind of contract and tort actions noted above. In some instances, these other kinds of civil disputes are just as important in terms of the workload of the court, and perhaps more central to the lives of the majority of the population, as actions in contract and tort. For example, 2008 saw 128,000 divorce petitions filed in court.[4] The average individual is far more likely to be involved with the courts because of a divorce case than because of a contract case in the High Court. As we will see, the court's role in a divorce action is very different from its role in other areas of law. Similar points can be made about a number of other areas of the work of the civil courts.

It is arguable that the civil courts are becoming much more diverse in their activities than has been the case in the past. Jurisdictions which were once trifling and obscure have now become large and central. Thus, in 1980, there were a mere 525 public law applications to the courts. In 1991, this figure had risen to 2,089 and the next five years saw a further 50 per cent rise in the number of applications.[5] In 2008, the Administrative Court received 7,169 applications by way of judicial review and 5,052 appeals and applications other than by way of judicial review.[6] The important point here, is not just that

---

[3]  Ministry of Justice, *Judicial and Court Statistics 2008* (2009b) Cm. 7697, HMSO, London, Table 3.2.
[4]  Ministry of Justice (2009b) Cm. 7697, p. 87.
[5]  Lord Woolf, 'Droit Public – English Style' [1995b] Public Law 57 at p. 60. By 2007, Shah and Poole noted that 40 per cent of cases in the House of Lords were rights-related (i.e., public law cases): S. Shah and T. Poole, 'The Impact of the Human Rights Act on the House of Lords' [2009] Public Law 361.
[6]  Ministry of Justice (2009b) Cm. 7697 p. 16.

there are now a relatively large number of public law applications (though this is the case). Public law represents a very different form of civil law from tort or contract. The differences are to be seen not just in its rules of procedure and substantive law but in the nature of its subject-matter. Public law directly concerns the fundamental relationship between the state and the individual.[7] The rise in the number of public law applications represents, in part, a reappraisal by the judiciary of their attitude to this relationship. As one judge has put it '[t]he courts...are by now engaged on a broad highway of constitutional adjudication along which issues of fundamental rights relentlessly present themselves'.[8] A public law case has the potential to include many interests; not just the interests of individuals in the case, but also those of the state, society as a whole and groups within society. How those interests are represented and recognized, how they are balanced and how they are determined is a very different problem for the courts than the issues in most contract cases.

It is no longer possible to describe the approach of the courts to all civil disputes in a single textbook. To attempt to do so would be to write an encyclopaedia of law. It is not even possible to describe the typical action in the civil courts. It seems doubtful that any such creature exists. Instead, in this chapter, we will look at some of the varied ways in which civil disputes are played out in the courts, illustrating some of the various dynamics and problems that occur. The picture will be partial and incomplete but sufficient to show the diversity of the courts.

## Personal injury claims

One main type of personal injury action is a claim for injury done to an individual where that injury was due to an accident caused by the *negligence* of another. It is thus a claim in tort. For example, the driver injured in a road accident by another's negligent driving may make a personal injury claim. The other main source of personal injury claims is an action where the injury done was due to another's *breach of statutory duty*. Somebody who injures their leg due to an improperly maintained public footpath may, for example, sue the relevant local authority.

The purpose of personal injury claims is to allow one person, the injured, to force another person who was at fault to compensate them for the injury that was done to them. Personal injury claims are, thus, a mechanism for allowing the redress of the balance of loss due to accident. Such a mechanism deters people from causing injury to others in the first place when they can do so without costing themselves more than the payment of compensation.[9]

---

[7] All law emanating from the state might be said to be concerned with this but often the relevance of the state/individual relationship is tangential.

[8] Sedley J, 'Human Rights: A Twenty-first Century Agenda' [1995] Public Law 386 at p. 395.

[9] R. Bowles, *Law and the Economy* (1982) Martin Robertson, Oxford, pp. 106–7.

Not all accidents result in personal injury claims. As long ago as 1986, a consultation paper prepared for the Civil Justice estimated that there were about 3 million accidents involving personal injuries each year. Of these, 215,000 were estimated to occur on the roads, 350,000 at work, and the rest mostly in the home.[10] Of all these, it estimated that only 10 per cent became the subject of legal action.[11] This finding is similar to that of the earlier Pearson Committee which estimated that only 11 per cent of people involved in accidents took steps to seek legal redress.[12] In a large-scale survey in the late 1990s, Genn found that only 8 per cent of those people in her survey having injuries or work-related ill-health started a court case.[13] This is not just something that relates to personal injury claims. A more recent survey by the Legal Services Commission found that in 19 per cent of instances where justiciable problems were reported no action had been taken.[14]

The fact that not every person who is injured makes a claim in the courts does not, of itself, indicate that there is any fault in the legal system, even if those people were legally entitled to make a claim. In cases of trivial damage, where there is an absence of intention or recklessness on the part of the person doing the injuring, there is little benefit to anybody in a legal action occurring even if there has been legal fault.[15] However, the likelihood of not taking action is not spread evenly throughout the population. The Legal Services Commission survey of justiciable problems showed that, for example, men were more likely than women not to take action and people from ethnic minority groups were less likely than white people to take action.[16] Equally, the likelihood of experiencing justiciable problems is not spread equally through the population. The same survey showed that those who are most vulnerable in society, such as the unemployed or lone parents, are those who are most likely to experience such problems.[17] Thus, the question of why people do not take action, even when they have a legal case, is an important one.

[10] *Civil Justice Review: Personal Injuries Litigation* (1986) Lord Chancellor's Department, London, p. 7.

[11] *Civil Justice Review* (1986) p. 7. The fact that there has been an accident does not necessarily mean that a tort claim can be made. Somebody other than the victim must be legally liable. (On the differential likelihood of legal liability depending on the type of accident, see P. Cane (ed.), *Atiyah's Accidents, Compensation and the Law* (5th edn, 1993) Butterworths, London, pp. 171–2.)

[12] Royal Commission on Civil Liability and Compensation for Accidental Injury, *Report* (the Pearson Report) (1978) Cmnd 7054-II, p. 119.

[13] H. Genn, *Paths to Justice* (1999b) Hart Publishing, Oxford, p. 52.

[14] P. Pleasence with A. Buck, N. Balmer, A. O'Grady, H. Genn, and M. Smith, *Causes of Action: Civil Law and Social Justice* (2004) Legal Services Commission, London, p. 50.

[15] Cases of trivial damage might still arguably merit trial where, for example, a person deliberately decided that to avoid harming others would be economically inefficient because there would be cost involved and nobody would think it worthwhile suing if they were injured. The harm done here would then be, not merely the actual physical injury to others, but the studied disregard of others' legal rights. This latter harm might be seen as a challenge, on a small scale, to the legal and hence social fabric of society.                                        [16] Pleasence et al. (2004) p. 55.

[17] Pleasence et al. (2004) p. 106. Moreover, having one justiciable problem makes it more likely that you will experience another (Pleasence et al. (2004) p. 31).

In 1978, the Pearson Committee sought to analyse the reasons for the discrepancy between the number of accidents and the number of personal injury claims. The Pearson Committee produced evidence that the following reasons were involved in people deciding not to claim:

| Reasons for not Claiming | Percentage of Respondents |
| --- | --- |
| Not seriously injured | 22 |
| Did not know how to claim/that they could claim | 19 |
| It was just an accident | 11 |
| Too much trouble/did not want to make a fuss/too upset | 11 |
| It would have meant claiming against a member of the family/friend | 10 |
| Felt that it was partly own fault | 9 |
| Did not lose any/much money/not off work | 8 |
| Did not know who was responsible/identity of wrongdoer | 8 |
| Could not prove anyone at fault/no witnesses/no evidence | 6 |
| Did not think about it/glad to be alive/more concerned about injuries | 5 |
| Thought it would cost too much/might lose money | 4 |
| Others | 13[18] |

Subsequent surveys have broadly supported these findings.[19] The Legal Services Commission survey notes that '[a]s few people are familiar with the complexities of the framework of civil law that bears on everyday life, the existence of unidentified solutions is no doubt commonplace'.[20] It also goes on to observe that:

even if people believe that something can be done to resolve a problem, action may yet not be taken because of concerns about the physical, psychological, economic or social consequences of doing so...[21]

This survey found that personal injury cases were one of the problem areas where people were least likely to think that taking action would not be successful. However, in some problem areas such as discrimination, more than half of the respondents who reported a problem felt that there was no point in taking action.[22]

Findings such as the above are evidence of serious structural shortcomings in the way in which the civil system deals with cases. They show that it is not that people do not want to use the courts to settle their disputes: rather, some people feel they cannot

---

[18] Pearson Report (1978) p. 121. This table is also reproduced in *Civil Justice Review* (1986) p. 8.

[19] See, for example, H. Genn, 'Who Claims Compensation: Factors Associated with Claiming and Obtaining Damages' in D. Harris et al. (eds), *Compensation and Support for Illness and Injury* (1984) Clarendon Press, Oxford; and more recently, Genn (1999b) and Pleasence et al. (2004) ch. 3.

[20] Pleasence et al. (2004) p. 50.      [21] Pleasence et al. (2004) p. 50.

[22] Pleasence et al. (2004) p. 51.

use the courts. The Pearson Committee, for example, found evidence of fear of the courts on the part of some people. Respondents were quoted as saying:

The ordinary working man doesn't know half of the law and some lawyers aren't too keen on telling you.

And:

People are frightened by the law, I know I am.[23]

The Civil Justice Review found that cost was a significant factor in the making of claims. In 71 per cent of all county court cases, for example, the plaintiff's costs were in excess of 75 per cent of the compensation recovered.[24] The same study found that High Court cases 'take 4, 5, 6 or more years from accident to conclusion' and county court cases took 3 years or more from accident to conclusion, even where the amount involved was less than £3,000.[25] Perhaps as important as these complaints is the fact that different surveys conducted decades apart have continued to produce similar results. In her 1999 survey, Genn concluded that:

[t]he responses to questioning in this study suggest that although the public regard the courts as important, there is some lack of confidence in the fairness of hearings, a belief that the courts serve the interests of the wealthy, and that the judiciary are remote and out of touch. There is also a strong view that lawyers' charges are unreasonably high.[26]

For people to make a calculated decision, on the basis of full knowledge and in a calm atmosphere, not to use the civil courts as a way of obtaining compensation may be acceptable. The civil courts are a facility. Litigation is not necessarily a good thing. However, the decision to make or not to make a claim is influenced by factors extraneous to the merits or seriousness of the case. Genn has identified four main explanations for why people make claims in an unequal manner. These are:

(1) That there is an unequal distribution of economic resources making it financially easier for some people to claim.

(2) That there is an unequal distribution of knowledge, access to social networks and general competence so that some people are socially better equipped to claim.

(3) That legal services are organized in such a way that the concerns of the wealthy are more likely to be handled by lawyers.

(4) That some people have higher rates of participation in economic and social life and so are more likely to be exposed to legal risks.[27]

---

[23] Pearson Report (1978) p. 126.    [24] *Civil Justice Review* (1986) p. 29.
[25] *Civil Justice Review* (1986) p. 34.    [26] Genn (1999b) p. 246.
[27] Genn (1984) p. 48. More recently, she has concluded that:

[The remoteness of the legal system from justiciable problems] derives from the real and imagined cost and discomfort of becoming involved in the procedures that currently exist for the resolution of

The first three reasons, and arguably the fourth, give rise to concern because they would suggest that the civil courts serve citizens unevenly; that what matters is not the legal nature of your difficulty but who you are.

Even where the system for making claims for personal injuries has been successful, that success has been of disproportionate advantage to different sectors of the community. Genn, for example, in her analysis, noted that the most important factor in making a successful personal injury claim was the type of accident involved. Claims which resulted from injuries on the road or at work were far more likely to succeed than any other type of claim.[28] Given the nature of these potentially successful claims, it is not surprising that Genn's analysis of her sample of personal injury claims found that although housewives constituted 14 per cent of the victims of personal injury they only constituted 5 per cent of the successful claimants.[29] Part of the explanation for some types of accidents leading to a greater proportion of successful claims lies in factors such as compulsory insurance. However, factors which are in themselves neutral lead to distortions in the way the system serves society; in this instance resulting in a gender bias.

## Claims consciousness

The first stage in making a claim, whether in relation to personal injury or anything else, is having the awareness that a claim is a legal possibility. Claims consciousness is not automatic. As we saw above, 19 per cent of respondents in the Pearson Commission's 1978 analysis gave as a reason for not making a claim either the fact that they did not know how to make a claim or that they did not know they could make a claim. Almost 30 years later, the Legal Services Commission survey reported that the biggest reason for people not taking action with respect to a problem was because they 'did not think anything could be done'.[30] Legal knowledge is unequally distributed throughout society as is the ability to seek advice:

Most people seek legal advice and assistance at some stage in their lives. But most approach lawyers rarely and only after much thought and discussion.[31]

For most people a lawyer is not the first person they consult in the event of trouble. First, they may not see their problem as being a legal problem.[32] Second, even if they are aware of the legal aspects of their problem, they may see lawyers as being expensive,

civil disputes and claims. There is a widespread perception that legal proceedings involve uncertainty, expense and potential long-term disturbance and that only the most serious matters could justify enduring these conditions. (Genn (1999b) p. 254.)

[28] Even here, only one in three and one in five of all claims were successful (Genn (1984) p. 50).

[29] Genn (1984) p. 56.    [30] Pleasence et al. (2004) p. 50.

[31] National Consumer Council, *Ordinary Justice* (1989) HMSO, London, p. 44.

[32] Most people's knowledge of the civil law is quite restricted. For example, a study by the Consumer Council showed that 78 per cent of respondents did not know about their rights if they were sold faulty goods (A. Diamond, 'Codification of the Law of Contract' (1968) 31 Modern Law Review 361 at pp. 372–3).

forbidding or intimidating. It might be thought that claims consciousness and a willingness to litigate is linked to class position; that the middle classes are more likely to go to court than those of a lower class. Class, however, is of little significance, at least in the case of personal injury litigation.[33] Age and sex can have a more significant effect on the likelihood of a person consulting a lawyer:

[W]omen, children, and the elderly are in general less likely to obtain damages, [but] this failure stems primarily from a low propensity to *think* about compensation or to seek legal advice...[34]

Claims consciousness is also cultural. To make a claim in the case of personal injuries claims, is to blame someone else for the accident. There is strong evidence to indicate that some cultures are more likely than others to apportion blame to others.[35] However, Genn has argued that there is an 'error in thinking about what certain kinds of "people" do, rather than focusing on what people do *in relation to particular problems*'.[36] Some kinds of claims are more likely to be regarded as being justiciable than others even though, in law, there is no difference in their actual justiciability.[37]

Equally significant in explaining why claims are made, is the fact that for most people the idea of seeking legal advice comes not from themselves but from other people.[38] The range of people giving initial advice is very wide. Surveys have suggested the importance of trade union officials, hospital personnel, doctors, the police and advice bureaux.[39] Other authors have suggested the use of local councillors, MPs, social workers, and community groups.[40] The important point to note about these various bodies and individuals is that the sources of advice available are unstructured. Some are intended to be sources of advice. Some do it as an ancillary or voluntary adjunct to their main tasks. The sources are in no sense coordinated with one another. It is thus not surprising that people make differentiated use of the sources of advice. Whether people are aware of these sources, and whether they feel comfortable using them, will depend upon variable social factors such as class, race, sex and age.[41]

---

[33] Cane (1993) p. 176.    [34] Genn (1984) p. 61.

[35] H. Kritzer, 'Propensity to Sue in England and the United States of America: Blaming and Claiming in Tort Cases' (1991) 18 Journal of Law and Society 400.    [36] Genn (1999b) p. 253, emphasis in original.

[37] Pleasence et al. (2004) p. 52.    [38] Genn (1984) p. 65.

[39] See, for example, Genn (1984) p. 66. See also Pleasence et al. (2004) pp. 66–72.

[40] National Consumer Council (1989) p. 44. Other people are not only a source for prompting the idea of seeking legal advice. They can themselves be a mechanism for solving the problem and obtaining compensation (see M. Zander, *Legal Services for the Community* (1978) Temple Smith, London, ch. 10).

[41] The use of different sources of advice can also vary over time. For example, the National Consumer Council has noted the rise in the number of advice centres and thus, presumably, the rise in the number of people using them as a source of advice (National Consumer Council (1989) p. 46). Conversely, the importance of trade unions as a source of advice has been noted in the past (see Genn (1984) pp. 67–70). The decline in the number of trade union members must, in turn, affect their importance as a source of advice.

## The cost of litigation

One feature that will affect people's willingness to use lawyers in a personal injuries case or in any other case, is the cost of the service. Legal costs are high. A study of personal injury cases for the Civil Justice Review showed that in 85 per cent of successful cases in the county court and nearly 50 per cent of cases in the High Court, the plaintiffs' costs for the case amounted to 50 per cent or more of the compensation recovered.[42] Lord Woolf, in his report on the civil justice system, noted that:

Costs are a significant problem because:

(a) litigation is so expensive that the majority of the public cannot afford it unless they receive financial assistance;
(b) the costs incurred in the course of litigation are out of proportion to the issues involved; and
(c) the costs are uncertain in amount so that the parties have difficulty in predicting what their ultimate liability might be if the action is lost.[43]

The cost of litigation is a major factor when people are contemplating whether or not to pursue a dispute in the courts. The costs of litigation are assessed by the court. The judge must decide who should pay the costs and on what basis. It is the general rule in litigation that 'costs follow the event'. In other words, the losing party pays the legal costs of the winning party.[44] However, the court has a great deal of discretion in deciding whether or not to award costs, and on what basis. The rules relating to costs are set out in the Civil Procedure Rules.[45] They direct the court, when assessing costs, to have regard to all the circumstances, including:

- the conduct of the parties;[46]

- the manner in which a party has pursued or defended his case or a particular allegation or issue;[47]

- whether a claimant who has succeeded in his claim, in whole or in part, exaggerated his claim.[48]

It is important to understand that the costs regime operated by the courts means that, while the successful party will often receive some payment from the losing party towards his or her legal costs, this will not necessarily cover all the costs actually incurred. This is because costs are often awarded by the court on a standard basis, which generally covers 60 to 70 per cent of the actual costs incurred.[49]

---

[42] Civil Justice Review, *Report of the Review Body on Civil Justice* (1988) Cm. 394, HMSO, London, p. 79.
[43] Woolf (1996) p. 78.
[44] CPR r. 44.3(2) 'If the court decides to make an order about costs – (a) the general rule is that the unsuccessful party will be order to pay the costs of the successful party, but (b) the court may make a different order.'      [45] CPR Parts 43–8.
[46] CPR r. 44.4      [47] CPR r. 44.5.      [48] CPR r. 44.5.
[49] See Bailey, Ching, and Taylor, *Smith, Bailey and Gunn* (2007) p. 650.

The costs of civil litigation have recently been subjected to a thorough review on behalf of the Government by Sir Rupert Jackson.[50] The basic purpose of the review was to make recommendations in order to promote access to civil justice at proportionate cost.[51] Sir Rupert found that conditional fee agreements have been the major contributor to disproportionate costs in civil litigation.[52] This is because of the inclusion of the lawyer's 'success fee' and the 'after-the-event' insurance premium that is usually taken out to cover the claimant against the risk of having to pay the defendant's costs. Both the success fee and the insurance premium are recoverable from the defendant if the claimant wins.[53] Sir Rupert recommended that these items should no longer be recoverable as costs. If a success fee is charged, it should be borne by the claimant.[54] In order to overcome the problems caused by after-the-event insurance, in particular, Sir Rupert recommended the introduction of 'qualified one-way cost shifting'.[55] This would mean that the claimant would not be required to pay the defendant's costs if unsuccessful, but the defendant, if successful, would be required to pay the claimant's costs. This idea was accompanied by the recommendation that any unreasonable behaviour by either party should, however, lead to a different costs order.[56] Sir Rupert envisaged that only certain categories of litigation should be subject to one-way costs shifting, and recommended that the precise details of such a regime should be further explored.[57]

Another major recommendation made in the Review, was that there should be fixed costs in fast-track litigation.[58] Cases in the fast track are those up to a value of £25,000, where the trial can be concluded within one day, and a substantial proportion of litigation is conducted in the fast track.[59] Sir Rupert recommended that the costs recoverable for fast-track litigation should be fixed for personal injury cases, and that for other types of cases in the fast track there should either be fixed costs or a financial limit on the costs recoverable.[60] The intention of this recommendation is to provide certainty about the extent of costs, avoid disputes over the amount of recoverable cots, and to ensure that costs are proportionate to the litigation being undertaken.[61]

Sir Rupert also made a number of specific recommendations relating to the conduct of personal injury cases, and a number of general recommendations designed to control the costs of litigation, including an increased use of ADR, an enhanced role for the courts in case management, to ensure that realistic timetables are observed and costs are kept proportionate, and an enhanced incentive

---

[50] Sir R. Jackson, *Review of Civil Litigation Costs: Final Report* (2010) The Stationery Office, London.
[51] Jackson (2010) para. 1.1.
[52] Jackson (2010) ch. 10 and para. 2.1. Conditional fee agreements are discussed later in this chapter.
[53] Jackson (2010) ch. 10, para. 2.1.        [54] Jackson (2010) ch 10 and para. 2.2.
[55] Jackson (2010) ch. 9.        [56] Jackson (2010) ch. 9, para. 2.6.        [57] Jackson (2010) ch. 9, para. 2.7.
[58] Jackson (2010) ch. 15. The fast track is discussed later in this chapter.
[59] Jackson (2010) ch. 15, para. 2.9.        [60] Jackson (2010) para. 2.9.
[61] Jackson (2010) para. 2.10.

to parties to make settlements under Part 36 of the Civil Procedure Rules.[62] In terms of the future funding of civil litigation, Sir Rupert made another important recommendation, which was that the 'indemnity principle' should be abolished. The principle prevents a party recovering more by way of costs from an opponent than it is obliged to pay to its own lawyers.[63] Sir Rupert noted that supporters of the indemnity principle maintained that it was a vital tool in the battle to control excessive costs, while critics saw it as the cause of much 'satellite litigation' and wastage of costs.[64] On balance, he decided that the principle should be abolished, but that the existing costs rules should be amended to reinforce the position that the courts will generally only allow 'reasonable amounts in respect of work actually and reasonably done'.[65] This recommendation has been welcomed by some commentators, who see it as opening up the possibility of a whole new range of options for funding civil litigation.[66]

It remains to be seen to what extent Sir Rupert's recommendations are implemented, but there is no doubt that, at 557 pages, his report was thorough and far-reaching.

## Legal aid

It has been said that '[i]t is one of the marks of a civilised society that it provides support for its citizens in gaining access to their rights within the rule of law'.[67] At the same time, the cost to the state of providing legal aid is a significant matter. In 1992/93, the cost of civil and family legal aid was £463 million; in 1998/99 the cost was £659 million. However, although there had been a 42 per cent increase in the state's spending on civil and family legal aid, the number of people helped had fallen by 30 per cent.[68] The increasing costs of legal aid and perceptions about the efficiency of the system led to the reforms which were included in the Access to Justice Act 1999.[69]

The 1999 Act created a new regime for civil legal aid.[70] Under the Act, the Legal Services Commission became responsible for establishing and maintaining the

---

[62] Jackson (2010): on the increased use of ADR, see ch. 36; on case management, see ch. 39, and on settlements, see ch. 41.                                                         [63] Jackson (2010) ch. 5.1(1).

[64] Jackson (2010) ch. 5.3(1).        [65] Jackson (2010) ch. 5.3(6).

[66] See, for example, S. Sime 'What Price Justice' (2010) Counsel, March, p. 12.

[67] Lord Chancellor's Department, *Legal Aid, Targeting Need: The Future of Publicly Funded Help in Solving Legal Problems and Disputes in England and Wales: A Consultation Paper* (1995) Cm. 2854, HMSO, London, p. 3.

[68] Explanatory Notes to Access to Justice Act 1999, para. 36. In 2008, the cost was just over £2 billion (Legal Services Commission, *Legal Services Commission Annual Report and Accounts 2008-9* HC731 (2009) The Stationery Office, London, p. 3).

[69] P. Mirfield, *Silence, Confessions and Improperly Obtained Evidence: Modernising Justice: The Government's Plans for Reforming Legal Services and the Courts* (1997) Cm. 4155, The Stationery Office, London, ch. 3.

[70] R. Moorhead, 'Third Way Regulation? Community Legal Service Partnerships' (2001) 64 Modern Law Review 543.

Community Legal Service[71] and was required to set priorities in accordance with any directions given by the Lord Chancellor.[72] The Community Legal Service is responsible for, amongst other things, 'the provision of general information about the law and legal system and the availability of legal services' and the provision of help in giving advice to prevent, resolve or settle disputes or legal proceedings.[73]

The range and manner of the work carried out by the Community Legal Service is rather different from that of the previous Legal Aid Board. Thus, for example, the Community Legal Service has established a website to give legal advice as a 'first port of call for legal help and information' and a telephone advice service.[74] In 2008–9, its specialist telephone advisors handled 100,851 cases, an increase of 19 per cent on the previous year.[75]

The Legal Service Commission is also required to establish a Community Legal Service Fund, which replaces legal aid, and monies from this can be used for individual assistance.[76] However, Schedule 2 to the Act lays down types of work that cannot be funded. These are quite extensive. Thus, for example, personal injury claims are excluded under para. 1(a) of Schedule 2.[77] Moreover, work must be done with approved contractors who must meet systems of quality control set up by the Commission (the 'quality mark').[78] The Community Legal Service Fund is spent in accordance with the Funding Code. The Code sets out the criteria and procedures to be used when deciding whether a particular case should be funded. The chances of success must be at least 50 per cent and the potential recovery must generally bear a specified minimum ratio to the anticipated costs of the case. The merits of the case are also taken into account.[79]

In some ways, these provisions widened the state's role in ensuring that citizens have access to information and assistance in relation to their legal problems. The website and telephone advice service, for example, are available to all, irrespective of their means.[80] Equally, the scheme covered the provision of advice by non-lawyers, such as advisors employed by non-profit organizations.[81]

However, these provisions raise questions, both about the independence of the legal assistance that is being provided and its quality. In the main, the Act ensures that the state determines which lawyers will be used (even though the state may itself be a party to the litigation in question), because parties obtaining legal assistance can only use lawyers holding a contract from the Legal Services Commission. For specialist areas

---

[71] Access to Justice Act 1999, ss. 1 and 4.      [72] Access to Justice Act 1999, s. 6(1)(a).

[73] Access to Justice Act 1999, s. 4(2).      [74] See: <http://www.communitylegaladvice.org.uk/>.

[75] *Legal Services Commission Annual Report and Accounts 2008–9* HC731, p. 19.

[76] Access to Justice Act 1999, s. 5(1).

[77] Although Lord Irvine has noted that a 'few' cases may still require public subsidy (Hansard, House of Lords, 12 May 1999).      [78] Access to Justice Act 1999, ss. 4(8) and 12(4).

[79] Legal Services Commission, *Funding Code* (n.d.) Legal Services Commission, London, available at: <http://www.legalservices.gov.uk/civil/guidance/funding_code.asp#updates>.

[80] Providing, of course, they have access to the internet and/or telephone.

[81] I. Magee, *Review of Legal Aid Delivery and Governance* (2008) Ministry of Justice, London, paras 7 and 43.

of law, such as family law, immigration, mental health, and clinical negligence, only specialist firms are funded to do the work. Parties are not free to decide exactly which lawyers they want to use. Moreover, it is clear that the changes are driven, at the very least in part, by concerns about costs and leave open the question whether, in a drive to provide a cheaper service, the Act also operates so as to provide a worse service.[82] One commentator has noted that there is an increasing concentration of legal aid in specialist legal aid practices, with smaller, mixed practices withdrawing from such work, and that the existence of practices with legal aid contracts is geographically spread in an uneven fashion throughout the country.[83]

Continuing concern about the size of the legal aid budget has stimulated a series of reviews and policy initiatives relating to legal aid, including the Government's long-term strategy for legal aid, *A Fairer Deal for Legal Aid*, which was published in 2005.[84] Around the same time, Lord Carter was asked to carry out a review of legal aid procurement, with the objective of ensuring that the system delivered maximum value for money, whilst ensuring quality and the fairness of the system. He concluded that the best way forward was 'a system of best value competition, based on quality, capacity and price'.[85] The Government largely accepted Lord Carter's recommendations, and set out its strategy for legal aid in a document entitled, *Legal Aid Reform: The Way Ahead*.[86] It stated that the following principles would in future structure its approach to buying legal aid:

- A focus on service to the client, rather than simply hours worked
- Best value competition based on quality, price and capacity
- Fixed and graduated fees ... to prime the market and stabilize spending ...
- Measures to ensure sustainability ... [87]

*The Way Ahead* initiated a major programme of legal aid reform, which the Legal Services Commission has been working on, changing the way it pays for and procures services.[88]

Reforms of the legal aid system appear likely to continue, with a review of the Legal Services Commission carried out by Sir Ian Magee, who published his report in 2010.[89] Sir Ian notes that the Legal Services Commission has focused on implementing the reforms set out in *The Way Ahead*, trying to maximize the number of people who

---

[82] See, for example, H. Sommerlad, '"I've Lost the Plot": An Everyday Story of the "Political" Legal Aid Lawyer' (2001) 28 Journal of Law and Society 335.

[83] R. Moorhead, 'Legal Aid and the Decline of the Private Practice: Blue Murder or Toxic Job?' (2004) 11 International Journal of the Legal Profession 157.

[84] Department for Constitutional Affairs, *A Fairer Deal for Legal Aid* (2005) Cm. 6591, HMSO, London.

[85] Lord Carter of Coles, *Legal Aid: A Market-based Approach to Reform* (2006) Department for Constitutional Affairs, London, p. 3, para. 9.

[86] Department for Constitutional Affairs, *Legal Aid Reform: The Way Ahead* (2006) Cm. 6993, HMSO, London.                    [87] Department for Constitutional Affairs, *Legal Aid Reform* (2006) p. 9.

[88] *Legal Services Commission Annual Report and Accounts 2008–9* HC731, p. 12.

[89] Magee (2010).

can be helped within a limited legal aid budget.[90] The reform programme it has put in place has succeeded in halting a year-on-year 8 to 10 per cent growth in expenditure on legal aid.[91] However, while recognizing that the Legal Services Commission and its sponsoring Department, the Ministry of Justice, have delivered a significant amount of legal aid policy reform, Sir Ian also points out that legal aid policy-making could be significantly improved.[92] He also raises concerns about the Legal Services Commission's systems and processes, and emphasizes the urgent need to clarify the relationship between the policy and delivery functions of the legal aid system.[93] In response to these concerns, it would appear likely that the Legal Services Commission will become a government agency, focused on delivery, while responsibility for policy remains within the Ministry of Justice.[94]

Despite the large numbers of reforms to the system, it is likely that legal aid will remain a contested subject. Concerns are raised by users and providers about the operation of the system, with commentators drawing attention to the entire exclusion of the middle classes from the scheme, despite the rising costs of legal services, including those arising out of the increasing amount of quality assurance and audit requirements of the legal aid authorities.[95] Lawyers are concerned that fixed fees will prevent them from offering legal aid services, because it will be economically unviable. A recent example of such protests is the outcry from family lawyers, following the proposal to pay fixed advocacy fees in family legal aid cases from 2010.[96] Overall, legal aid is likely to remain a controversial subject for the foreseeable future.

## Trade unions, legal expenses insurance, and conditional fees

In the past, writers have noted the importance of trade unions as a source of funding for legal actions. One survey showed that 33 per cent of all personal injury claims were funded by trade unions.[97] Having such a source of funding considerably changes the nature of the personal injury claim. The plaintiff is no longer burdened by any fear of legal costs and is thus freer to pursue the claim on the basis of its intrinsic legal merits.[98] However, the drop in the number of trade unionists is likely to have resulted in a drop in the number of personal injury claims being funded by trade unions.[99]

Legal expenses insurance gives a personal injury litigant the same kind of advantages and security as being funded by a trade union. The number of people buying

---

[90] Magee (2010) para. 50.     [91] Magee (2010) para. 50.     [92] Magee (2010) paras 65–9.

[93] Magee (2010) pp. 3–4.

[94] See Press Release, 'Review of Legal Aid Delivery and Governance Published' (2010) 3 March, at: <http://www.legalservices.gov.uk/aboutus/press_releases_11173.asp>.

[95] See, for example, the discussion in R. Cranston, *How Law Works: The Machinery and Impact of Civil Justice* (2006) Oxford University Press, Oxford, p. 51.

[96] See: <http://www.lawgazette.co.uk/news/family-barristers-attack-legal-aid-fixed-fee-scheme>.

[97] H. Genn, *Hard Bargaining: Out of Court Settlement in Personal Injury Claims* (1987) Oxford University Press, Oxford, p. 110.     [98] Genn (1987) p. 113. See further 'Settlement' at **pp. 209–10** below.

[99] A recent survey showed that in relation to justiciable claims as a whole, only 7 per cent of claimants had consulted a trade union or professional association about the claim (Pleasence et al. (2004) p. 67).

legal expenses insurance has increased considerably over the past two decades.[100] Those who have it have many of the advantages of the trade union funded or the litigant who is supported by the Legal Services Commission. However, in the case of the person supported by legal expenses insurance, their degree of protection is limited by the terms of the insurance policy. This may not give full coverage.[101]

An even newer method of paying for legal action is to fund a lawyer who is willing to work on a conditional fee basis. Conditional fee agreements (often colloquially referred to as 'no win, no fee' agreements), involve a lawyer agreeing to be paid only if they are successful in pursuing a claim. In return, they may expect remuneration at a higher rate than normal if they are successful. This usually involves a 'success fee', which can be recovered from the losing party, if the lawyer's client wins the case. The success fee is a percentage uplift on the lawyer's standard fee, and is supposed to compensate them for the risk they have taken.[102] The Courts and Legal Services Act 1990 legalized conditional fees in England and Wales from 1995 for the first time.[103] Since then, the regime has been extended to all areas of civil litigation, except certain family matters.[104] Whilst conditional fee arrangements have the advantage that they enable a person to employ lawyers even if they do have any significant financial resources, they also have several disadvantages. First, since damages are intended to be compensation for the injury suffered, paying for the litigation out of those damages means that the victim is not fully and properly recompensed. Second, unscrupulous lawyers might seek to take very high fees, vastly out of proportion to the value of their work or the degree of financial risk they are incurring by taking on the work, because of the vulnerable position of the victim. For this reason, the government regulates the manner and content of contingency fee arrangements.[105] Having surveyed the use of such arrangements, White and Atkinson concluded that in 'straightforward personal injury cases where prospects of success are high and where the investigations costs are low conditional fee agreements and after-the-event insurance are an effective form of funding the claim'.[106] They expressed more doubts, however, about the suitability of

---

[100] However, this is from a low base. In 1984, White suggested that the total legal expenses insurance market was worth only £10 million (R. White, 'Legal Expenses Insurance' (1984) 3 Civil Justice Quarterly 245 at p. 252). By 1991, it was still estimated that only 2 to 3 per cent of the population had legal expenses insurance. By comparison, in West Germany at the same time, 50 per cent of the population had such insurance and the market was worth £1 billion (J. Harris, 'Legal Expenses Insurance' (1991) 135 Solicitors Journal 668 at p. 669).

[101] White noted that most policies were limited to traditional civil litigation work (White (1984) p. 253). The same thing can be said about the person supported by a trade union or a person who is using legal aid. However, in these two instances, the systems seem to be more generous in terms of the type of claims covered.                                                                 [102] Cranston (2006) p. 65.

[103] Courts and Legal Services Act 1990, s. 58.

[104] Conditional Fee Agreements Order 2000, SI 2000/823.

[105] Conditional Fee Agreements Order 2000 (SI 2000/823) and the Conditional Fee Agreements Regulations 2000 (SI 2000/692).

[106] R. White and R. Atkinson, 'Personal Injury Litigation, Conditional Fees and After-the-event Insurance' (2000) 19 Civil Justice Quarterly 118 at p. 133.

such mechanisms for complex cases.[107] Fenn and his colleagues, on the basis of their survey of personal injury cases where a conditional fee agreement had been used, concluded that the agreements were taking the place of legal aid but that they increased costs for both defendants and claimants.[108] This conclusion is borne out by the findings of Sir Rupert Jackson in his review of civil litigation costs, discussed above. It is for this reason that he recommended major changes to the costs regime in relation to conditional fee agreements.[109]

## Issuing proceedings

The Civil Justice Review concluded that, in personal injury cases, High Court cases frequently took between four and six years from the original accident to the final conclusion of the case.[110] Even county court cases which involved sums of less than £3,000 could take three years or more.[111] This finding reflected a general situation where delay and cost were the hallmarks of much of the civil justice system. The Civil Procedure Act 1997 and the Civil Procedure Rules 1998 passed consequent to Lord Woolf's report on the civil justice system are designed to end that situation, changing, as they do, both the terminology and the procedures of the system.

The Act and the Rules establish a system of three paths by which a case may be brought in court: the small claims track, the fast-track, and the multi-track routes. The small claims track is the normal route for most civil claims of not more than £5,000 and in the case of personal injury claims for claims of not more than £1,000.[112] The fast track covers most defended cases involving claims between £5,000 and £25,000.[113] The multi-track is the route for all cases which are not on any other track.[114] Thus, in principle, a personal injury claim might be found on any one of these tracks. The key feature of each of these tracks is that the formality and speed with which the case is treated is intended to reflect the actual complexity of the particular case in question rather than reflect some general view of the complexity of cases of this type. Allocation of cases and management of the speed by which the case passes through the legal system (both before and when it reaches court) has become the province of the judiciary who are charged with a general overriding objective to manage cases so as to ensure that parties cooperate and deal with the cases expeditiously.[115] In relation to personal injury claims, as in the case of a number of other areas of litigation, a pre-action protocol has been created under the Civil Procedure Rules which sets out a timetable for

---

[107]  White and Atkinson (2000) p. 133.

[108]  P. Fenn, A. Gray, N. Rickman, and H. Carrier, *The Impact of Conditional Fees on the Selection, Handling and Outcomes of Personal Injury Cases* (2002) Lord Chancellor's Department, London. For further doubts about the efficacy of conditional fee agreements, see D. Ryan, 'Conditional Fee Agreements: Strutting their Stuff around a Circle that Cannot be Squared?' (2006) 25 Civil Justice Quarterly 20.

[109]  Jackson (2010) ch. 10.          [110]  *Civil Justice Review* (1986) p. 80.

[111]  *Civil Justice Review* (1986) p. 80.          [112]  Civil Procedure Rules 1998, r. 26.6(6).

[113]  Civil Procedure Rules 1998, r. 26.6(4).          [114]  Civil Procedure Rules 1998, r. 26.6(6).

[115]  CPR r. 1.1.

litigation indicating what letters should be sent when, what their content should be, when they should be replied to and so forth.[116]

The principle of allocating cases to different courts on the basis of the quantum of the claim has always been problematic and remains so even in the present system. Ever since the small claims system was introduced, concern has been expressed about the compatibility of procedures designed to reduce expense and improve accessibility on the one hand and the dictates of justice and the proper application of law on the other.[117] Small claims, by definition, involve small sums of money. That does not necessarily mean they involve people with limited means or even that they involve individual litigants. Research done for the Civil Justice Review indicated that 5 per cent of cases involved large organizations as both plaintiff and defendant, whilst large organizations were either plaintiff or defendant in a further 27 per cent of cases.[118] At the same time, it should be noted that the same survey showed that 75 per cent of all plaintiffs were either small businesses, local professional firms or private citizens, whilst 88 per cent of all defendants fell into one of the same categories.[119]

A 1995 study by Baldwin of the small claims system showed evidence of considerable satisfaction amongst those who used the system. This satisfaction included both business users and private individuals.[120] Indeed, Baldwin has described his sample as 'to an astonishing extent an uncomplaining group'.[121] Observations of actual cases suggested that most district judges have become 'adept...at putting people at their ease'.[122] However, whether this provides evidence for the success of the small claims system is debatable. As Baldwin notes, his sample was not a cross-section of society. 'Most were well-heeled and articulate individuals.'[123] The absence of significant sections of the population, in both economic and educational terms, from his sample supports earlier research which suggests that large sections of the population simply do not see the small claims system as a way of solving their problems. Excluding lawyers from the jurisdiction is not necessarily of advantage to all sections of society, since some people may feel they lack the skills or confidence to present their case.[124] The Woolf reforms were intended to minimize this disadvantage by decreasing the complexity of court proceedings. Baldwin, in a study published in 2002, noted that 'what has been striking about recent developments is...how little difference they have made' and that the courts continue to be 'regarded as institutions that are to be avoided at all costs'.[125] However, Peysner and Seneviratne, on the basis of their study of eight county

---

[116] See: <http://www.justice.gov.uk/civil/procrules_fin/contents/protocols/prot_pic.htm>.

[117] See, for example, K. Economides, 'Small Claims and Procedural Justice' (1980) 7 British Journal of Law and Society 111.                                         [118] Civil Justice Review (1986) p. 89.

[119] Civil Justice Review (1986) p. 89.

[120] J. Baldwin, The Small Claims Procedure and the Consumer (1995) Office of Fair Trading, London, p. 5. Notwithstanding their satisfaction, most litigants found their case a 'nerve-wracking experience' (Baldwin (1995) p. 8).                                         [121] Baldwin (1995) p. 6.

[122] Baldwin (1995) p. 8.        [123] Baldwin (1995) p. 8.

[124] Although, equally, some people may lack the confidence necessary to consult lawyers.

[125] J. Baldwin, Lay and Judicial Perspectives on the Expansion of the Small Claims Regime (2002) Lord Chancellor's Department, London.

courts, have argued that the new procedures have been successful in reducing delays in the courts.[126]

## Settlement

Most personal injury cases are settled before the dispute comes to court. However, for a significant minority of cases, the process of bringing a case to court forms part of the background to, and part of the reason for, settlement.[127]

Many, but not all, personal injury cases involve unequal parties. Where the personal injury results from an accident in a situation where compulsory insurance is required the victim, an individual citizen, will be dealing with in effect not the party who did the damage but their insurer.[128] The victim will be, in Galanter's terminology, a 'one-shotter', someone who is for the first time and perhaps the only time in their lives involved in litigation.[129] On the other hand, the insurance company will be a repeat player, an organization for whom litigation is a continuing part of their business.[130] If the victim employs a lawyer, they are unlikely to pick them because of their expertise in personal injury litigation.[131] The insurance company will employ staff simply to deal with claims and possible litigation and will only use solicitors who are expert in this area.[132] Victims will usually be ignorant of the legal technicalities that surround their position; they will not know what compensation they are entitled to or what are the legal strengths and weaknesses of their case. They will be expert only in the question of their own financial needs.[133] The insurance company, on the other hand, will not only employ experts – its employees will themselves be expert on the legal niceties of claims, gathering their own information so as to aid them in instructing their solicitors and assessing the advice of those solicitors.[134] Insurers will begin the case with knowledge of what evidence is necessary.[135] Victims will begin the case in pain and in ignorance, perhaps for these reasons failing to keep vital evidence about the circumstances of the accident.[136] Victims must somehow finance their claim. And all this, in the context of the possibly protracted nature of court proceedings described above:

Uncertainty about liability, uncertainty about quantum, uncertainty about what might happen during court proceedings, together with the effects of delay and cost considerations,

---

[126] J. Peysner and M. Seneviratne, 'The Management of Civil Cases: A Snapshot' (2006) 25 Civil Justice Quarterly 312 at p. 325.

[127] Research done for the *Civil Justice Review* suggested that 85 per cent of personal injury cases were settled before the issue of proceedings (*Civil Justice Review* (1986) p. 19). However, in at least a proportion of these cases, the possibility of legal action would form part of the context of settlement.

[128] The most obvious kind of case will be one involving a road accident.

[129] They may be particularly vulnerable because of the economic or medical consequences of their accident.        [130] M. Galanter, 'Why the "Haves" Come Out Ahead' (1974) 9 Law and Society Review 75.

[131] Although there is an association of personal injury litigators and some firms of solicitors may advertise this as a specialty.                                        [132] Genn (1987) pp. 35–6.

[133] Harris (1991) pp. 125–6.        [134] Genn (1987) p. 36.        [135] Genn (1987) pp. 62–6.

[136] Genn (1987) pp. 66–7.

represent the main pressures on the parties to achieve a negotiated compromise rather than to hold out and take their chances on a formal adjudication of the claim in court.[137]

Even if proceedings are issued at each stage described above, whether in the High Court or the county court, some litigants will settle. Even when the case reaches court and the trial has begun, parties may settle rather than take the risk of waiting for the judge's decision.[138]

The importance of settlement is not that the procedures described in previous sections are irrelevant to most cases. Rather, these procedures, and particularly the delay inherent in these procedures, form part of the negotiating tools used in reaching a settlement. Settlement may not be to the advantage of all or even most victims. It may not even be to the advantage of society at large.[139] Victims receive less damages than they are entitled to by law and thus behaviour which might cause accidents is discouraged to a lesser degree than might otherwise be the case. Nevertheless, settlement is the defining feature of the system.

## Obtaining damages

For the victim who does not settle, the court case does not represent the end of their dispute. In a personal injury case, the victim who is successful in court will be awarded damages.[140] However, in civil disputes, being awarded damages and receiving damages are separate things.[141] Where an insurance company is concerned, they will both have the funds and the willingness to pay the damages. However, if the defendant is an individual citizen, they may have neither. The plaintiff must then go back to the court to seek enforcement of the judgment. Once again, the plaintiff is faced with the legal complexities of civil actions. Depending on where the original action was taken, and the type of enforcement order sought, the judgment may be enforced in either the High Court or the county court. The difficulties of enforcing a judgment are one further reason for settlement.

## Divorce

The picture of a civil court action presented in a divorce case is very different from that presented in personal injury litigation. Participation in personal injury litigation is a voluntary matter. People can choose not to claim compensation for an injury. If

---

[137] Genn (1987) p. 99.    [138] *Civil Justice Review* (1986).

[139] O. Fiss, 'Against Settlement' (1984) Yale Law Journal 1073.

[140] Both plaintiffs and defendants have rights of appeal. These are discussed above in **Chapter 3**.

[141] 'When the judgement is delivered the layman is apt to assume that the case is effectively finished; in fact, nothing could be further from the truth, for the judgement does nothing more than declare the respective rights of the parties and says nothing about how the order of the court is to be enforced' (D. Barnard and M. Houghton, *The New Civil Court in Action* (1993) Butterworths, London, p. 347).

they do decide to claim compensation, they can settle their claim without ever going to court. The existence of the court may affect what they do but it does not determine it. In the case of divorce the reverse is the case. If an individual wants a divorce which will be recognized by the state, they must go to court.[142] However, when most people go to court, the court's part in their divorce is largely bureaucratic in nature. The fact of the divorce is registered but there is little by way of contest. Personal injury cases are usually a matter of two parties trying to assert their respective rights against each other. This is so, whether the dispute is carried on inside or outside the court. Divorce does not involve this contest.[143]

In order for a person to obtain a divorce, they must establish a legal ground for divorce.[144] In 1973, a procedure was established whereby the person wishing to obtain the divorce, the petitioner, and witnesses do not need to attend court. Instead, the court considers only written pleadings and evidence to see whether the parties to the case fall within the legal grounds for divorce. This 'special procedure' has been extended so that it now covers all cases where the petition for divorce is not opposed by the other party to the marriage.[145]

Under the 'special procedure', there is no prescribed form for the divorce petition. Appendix 2 of the Family Proceedings Rules 1991 sets out the information that the petition must contain.[146] These include particulars of the factual incidents which lead the petitioner to think that they are entitled to a divorce, an actual request for a divorce, and any request as to ancillary matters about maintenance. Service of the petition on the other party to the marriage may be made by the petitioner or their solicitors but, more usually, the court serves notice of the proceedings by post.[147] The service of notice of proceedings includes a form to be used for acknowledgement. This has to be returned to the court within eight days and, if the other party wishes to defend the petition, they have to file an answer to the petition with the court within 29 days.[148] If the other party does not wish to defend the petition the petitioner can, after acknowledgement of service, ask the court for directions for trial. With that application, the petitioner must also file an affidavit establishing the facts necessary for the legal ground of divorce.[149] If the divorce is undefended, there is no-one to challenge the version of events set out in the affidavit. '[T]he hearing of the suit is therefore a formality at which neither the parties nor their representatives need attend.'[150] The court has little option but to accept the case put to it because there is no-one to supply an

---

[142] Individuals can also obtain religious divorces which will be recognized by their own religions but will not be recognized by the state.

[143] *Judicial Statistics 2005 (Revised)* (2006) Cm. 6903 Department of Constitutional Affairs, London, recorded no instance of a defended divorce. Actions with respect to maintenance, the division of property or children are a separate matter. Here, there may well be a contest between the parties.

[144] Matrimonial Causes Act 1973, s. 1(1).

[145] See further P. Bromley and N. Lowe, *Bromley's Family Law* (8th edn, 1992) Butterworths, London, p. 235.                                          [146] Family Proceedings Rules 1991 (SI 1991/1247) r. 2.3.

[147] Family Proceedings Rules 1991, rr. 2.9(2)(b), 2.9(4).

[148] Family Proceedings Rules 1991, r. 2.12(1).        [149] Family Proceedings Rules 1991, r. 2.24(3).

[150] D. Barnard, *The Family Court in Action* (1983) Butterworths, London, p. 33.

alternative account of the events. A district judge considers the petitioner's affidavit and, if satisfied that it does show the legal ground for divorce, certifies that fact and serves the parties notice of when a judge will pronounce a decree.[151] Cases are then considered in batches and a district judge or judge pronounces a decree of divorce.[152] A decree nisi is first pronounced. A decree may not usually be made absolute until six weeks after the pronouncement of the decree nisi. It is only when the decree is pronounced absolute that it takes effect.

In personal injury litigation, there is frequent resort to lawyers. Lawyers assist clients in saying how they can use the court system. In undefended divorces, using the special procedure legal aid is not available although advice and assistance can be obtained.[153] Most parties do, however, seek legal help. One study of undefended divorces showed that 99 per cent of petitioners and 92 per cent of respondents had consulted lawyers.[154] However, survey evidence suggests that lawyers strongly advise not using the court system to defend a divorce.[155]

The system of hearing undefended divorces is, in many ways, a model for what Lord Woolf would like the whole system of civil courts to move towards. The atmosphere is not adversarial, cases are compromised, and there is minimal use of court resources in each case. However, there is significant evidence which suggests that some people feel pressurized into not contesting divorce actions. They are advised not to do so by lawyers and there is little financial support from the state for a defended action. Even the courts will suggest that they should not defend an action.[156] In some instances, the result is litigants who feel a sense of injustice about the way in which their case has been dealt with; because the case has not been argued through in court some people feel the divorce has been obtained unfairly:[157]

The present policy may be *efficient* in terms of cutting back on the number of defended suits, but it certainly doesn't test irretrievability [the ground for divorce] and it also, in many cases, leaves respondents feeling that they have been badly done by.[158]

Whilst Baldwin's research into the operation of the small claims procedure suggests that people are willing to accept a streamlined court system, research into undefended divorces suggests that they are less happy about having their dispute excluded from the court system altogether.

---

[151] Family Proceedings Rules 1991, r. 2.36. It is possible for an affidavit to be so badly drafted that it is contradictory or discloses no legal ground for divorce. In such cases, the registrar considering the petition can transfer the case onto a list of undefended cases where a full trial is necessary (Family Proceedings Rules 1991, r. 2.36(1)(b)).                                 [152] This is done in a county court.

[153] See section on **Legal aid**, above.

[154] G. Davis, *Partisans and Mediators* (1988a) Clarendon Press, Oxford, p. 85.

[155] '[N]o solicitor *wants* a defended suit – waste of time and money, emotionally distressing for the client, and a decree is almost inevitable in any event' (G. Davis and M. Murch, *Grounds for Divorce* (1988) Clarendon Press, Oxford, pp. 125–6).                                 [156] Davis and Murch (1988) ch. 8.

[157] Davis and Murch (1988) p. 128.        [158] Davis and Murch (1988) p. 129.

The bureaucratic and uncontested nature of the undefended divorce extends only to the divorce itself. If there are children to the marriage, the court will need to consider the arrangements that have been made for the children before the divorce can be granted.[159] The court will have to certify that these arrangements are satisfactory.[160] The parties may disagree about these arrangements or the court may conclude independently that they are not suitable arrangements. Equally, the parties may disagree about financial matters relating to division of property or future payments of maintenance between the parties or for children. In both these areas, the court makes decisions about substantive points of law and disputed fact.[161] However, the divorce action itself remains merely a formalized ritual. A personal injury claim enables a party to claim compensation. A divorce action signifies little in itself.[162] Rather, it allows a party to move on to the next stage, whether that be a legal dispute about children or money or the possibility of a new legal marriage.[163]

## CONCLUSION

In many ways, it is hard to see the civil court as a single thing, either in terms of its procedures or in terms of the ways in which that which the court does relates to society as a whole. Personal injury cases and undefended divorce cases represent opposite poles in the civil court's work but other contrasts could have been chosen.[164] In this context, to talk of the work of the civil courts, is to contribute to a myth of the solidity of 'the English legal system' that is belied by reality.

## FURTHER READING

JACKSON, SIR R., *Review of Civil Litigation Costs: Final Report* (2010) The Stationery Office, London.

WOOLF, LORD, *Access to Justice: Final Report to the Lord Chancellor on the Civil Justice System in England and Wales* (1996) Lord Chancellor's Department, London.

---

[159] Matrimonial Causes Act 1973, s. 41.     [160] Family Proceedings Rules 1991, r. 2.36(1).

[161] Even here, there is evidence to suggest that lawyers tend to act in a conciliatory rather than adversarial manner. R. Ingleby, 'The Solicitor as Intermediary' in R. Dingwall and J. Eekelaar (eds), *Divorce Mediation and the Legal Process* (1988) Clarendon Press, Oxford.

[162] For some people, it can have the same symbolic purpose as marriage. Where the latter is a public testimony to unity, a divorce testifies to separation.

[163] Proposals in the Family Law Act 1996 to substantially amend the process of divorce have not, at the time of writing, been implemented.     [164] Public law cases, for example, or tax cases.

# 11

# Alternative dispute resolution

## INTRODUCTION

We have noted throughout this book that for many people, the 'English legal system' is composed solely of state legal rules, state courts, and the personnel, such as judges, police, barristers, and solicitors, who work with those rules and in those courts. However, since the latter part of the twentieth century, there has been a noticeable growth in different mechanisms for resolving disputes, outside the courts. These different types of dispute resolution are referred to as 'alterative dispute resolution', commonly called ADR.

There are many types of dispute resolution which fall under the heading ADR. Some of them, like arbitration, are relatively formal, and very similar to courts. Arbitration involves a decision being made by an independent third party, the arbitrator (who may be an expert in the field of the dispute, or may be a lawyer), with the arbitrator's decision being legally binding on both sides. Other forms of ADR, such as mediation, are much more informal than traditional courts; they involve assisted dispute settlement, rather than adjudication by a third party. In mediation, the parties agree to use the services of a mediator to help them reach an agreement which is acceptable to both sides. No settlement can be imposed on the parties, and they are not automatically legally bound by the agreement which is reached (though the parties may agree to have their agreement set out in a legally binding contract). Thus, a very wide range of dispute resolution mechanisms, from those which are almost indistinguishable from courts, to those which are very informal, fall under the heading of ADR. However, what all these forms of dispute resolution have in common is that they are *not* actually courts, and it is in that sense that they are 'alternative'. They provide a different way of resolving a dispute than that which is offered by courts.

Interest in ADR has developed for a number of different reasons. Concern about the costs, delays, and general inaccessibility of courts led in the 1960s to calls for quicker, cheaper, and more readily available methods of resolving disputes. At the same time, other people were pointing to the advantages of the type of settlement which could be achieved by ADR over the costly and divisive nature of litigation. Others, prompted by a growing sensitivity to the nature of disputes gained from research in the social sciences (and in particular from anthropology), were looking for a genuine alternative to court-based litigation.[1] Since the early interest in ADR, many different schemes have been implemented, so that nowadays, ADR can clearly be said to form a part of the legal landscape.

In some cases, the dispute resolution offered by ADR is independent from the formal legal system – for example, the mediation services offered by private providers such as ADR Group.[2] In these cases, interaction with the formal legal system will be implicit, rather than explicit, in that the parties will often be aware, to some extent, of the relevant legal rules, but they will not form the main focus of discussions. In other cases, ADR will interact much more closely with the legal system. For instance, a court may suggest the use of ADR to resolve all or part of a dispute – the judges of the Commercial Court have been actively encouraging the use of ADR for some time – in 1994, they issued a Practice Note indicating that they wished to encourage parties to consider the use of ADR as a possible means of resolving either particular issues in their disputes, or whole disputes, and they would, in appropriate cases, invite parties to consider the use of ADR.[3] Initiatives such as this very clearly interact with the formal legal system, and indicate the relevance of adopting an integrated theory approach.

In this chapter, we will look at just two types of ADR: mediation and arbitration. They have been chosen because they represent two very different approaches to ADR. Mediation tends to be very informal and is a form of dispute resolution which is very different from that found in a court, while arbitration shares many of its characteristics with courts. Considering mediation and arbitration also illustrates the importance of adopting an integrated theory approach to the legal system, so that all the different types of dispute resolution can be taken into account when you are evaluating the system as a whole.

# Mediation

It is important to be aware of the wide range of dispute resolution practices which are referred to as 'mediation'. Roberts and Palmer remind us that mediation can range from a minimal intervention aimed merely at improving the quality of communication between the parties (passing messages, facilitating the exchange of information) to an active, direct intervention including the provision to the parties of specialist evaluation and advice. Thus, the mediator can either be thought of as simply providing the linkage through which negotiations may take place, or as actively seeking to eliminate differences.[4]

[1]  S. Roberts and M. Palmer, *Dispute Processes: ADR and the Primary Forms of Decision-making* (2005) Cambridge University Press, Cambridge, pp. 45– 6.                    [2]  See: <http://www.adrgroup.co.uk>.
[3]  *Practice Note (Commercial Court Alternative Dispute Resolution)* [1994] 1 All ER 34.
[4]  Roberts and Palmer (2005) p. 154.

Genn's report on the pilot mediation scheme operated by the Central London County Court gives a good picture of mediation in action.[5] In this mediation scheme, the role of the mediator was to facilitate the parties' negotiations and act as an expert consultant – nearer to the second type of mediation noted by Roberts and Palmer than the first.

Genn begins her account by giving us a clear description of what was involved in the mediations. She notes that it is important that the surroundings are comfortable and the sessions are conducted in an atmosphere that is 'informal, but orderly'. The mediator and the disputing parties (and their legal representatives, if any) usually sit round a table, or in a circle. The mediator will explain how the session is going to proceed, and will stress that the process is entirely voluntary, so either party is free to leave at any time if they are unhappy with the process. Genn comments that this preliminary meeting can sometimes be rather tense, but the role of the mediator is to reduce tension, and produce a calm and constructive atmosphere. In the opening session, the mediator will give each party about 15 minutes to summarize their complaint against the other side. This can be a very satisfying part of the process for the parties, and can be very helpful in reaching a compromise agreement to end the dispute. However, if relations between the parties are so bad that they do not want to be in the same room together, mediators will carry on the mediation without a preliminary meeting, and will shuttle between parties who are sitting in separate rooms.

After the opening joint session (if it takes place), each side will go into separate rooms for private meetings with the mediator and any advisers who are present. The mediator will then begin a process of 'shuttle diplomacy', exploring with each party alternately the details of their case and discussing the strengths and weaknesses of their claim. Information given to the mediator at this stage is strictly confidential, and will only be disclosed to the other side with the express permission of the party involved. During this process, the mediator tries to establish whether there is any common ground between the parties, and to discover the scope for compromise. They will also try to establish the most important points of disagreement and try to understand why the disputing parties take different views of those points.

Usually, after a period spent in private sessions, possibilities for agreement begin to emerge. Once this happens, the mediator will spend some time working out the exact terms of an agreement, ensuring that both sides are happy with them. Genn notes that this stage can often involve some intense bargaining. Once overall agreement has been reached, the mediator brings the parties together to work out the details and draft a document setting out the agreed terms. Even if the parties fail to reach agreement, the mediator will use this session to draw attention to any progress which has been made.

---

[5] H. Genn, *Mediation in Action* (1999a) Calouste Gilbenkian Foundation, London.

The Central London County Court scheme involved an offer of mediation being made to parties who were involved in litigation which would otherwise be dealt with by the court. In her evaluation of this project, Genn found that a wide variety of cases were mediated, and that the majority of them reached a settlement by the end of the mediation appointment. Overall, mediated cases had a much higher settlement rate than non-mediated cases, lending support to the argument that mediation is successful in promoting settlement.[6] She also found that settlements of mediated cases occurred more quickly than non-mediated cases.[7] Genn concludes that 'Mediation is clearly capable of promoting early settlement in a wide range of civil cases where parties have *volunteered* to attend mediation sessions.'[8]

However, Genn also expresses some concerns about the quality of the mediators, and the power they were able to exert over the parties. She notes that:

Successful mediation requires a formidable combination of natural talent, honed skills and accumulated experience on the part of the mediator. When this combination is present, mediation seems to offer opportunities for genuine dispute resolution that even the best-designed litigation procedure and best-run adjudication procedure might not be able to offer. However, when those qualities are absent, mediation has the potential for degenerating into rather squalid horse-trading, in which parties with a genuine grievance may be bullied into capitulation, and an imbalance of power is magnified in a way that might not occur in private negotiations between solicitors or in open court adjudication.[9]

Nevertheless, in general both the parties and solicitors attending mediations were very positive in their evaluations of the mediation process. The parties appreciated the opportunity to participate fully in the process and the lack of legal technicality and 'jargon'. Solicitors pointed to the benefit of an opportunity for parties to state their grievances in a non-threatening arena, to focus on commercial realities, and, on occasion, to repair damaged relationships.[10]

Despite all these positive aspects of mediation, very few litigants who were involved in litigation at the Central London County Court actually wanted to have their dispute mediated, rather than going to court: 'even within the current climate of dissatisfaction with the cost and delay of civil courts, the proportion of cases in which both parties volunteered to mediate was pitifully small'.[11]

Genn found widespread lack of knowledge about mediation, both among litigants and representatives, including solicitors. It would appear from this study, that the demand for mediation as an alternative to litigation is likely to remain low until both litigants and the legal profession become knowledgeable about what is involved and its potential benefits.[12]

---

[6] H. Genn, *The Central London County Court Pilot Mediation Scheme Evaluation Report* (1998) Lord Chancellor's Department Research Series 5/98, London, para. 3.14.1.    [7] Genn (1998) para. 4.2.6.
[8] Genn (1998) para. 7.7.1.    [9] Genn (1998) para. 7.7.5.    [10] Genn (1998) para. 5.17.2.
[11] Genn (1998) para. 7.7.4.    [12] Genn (1998) para. 7.7.7.

# Arbitration

Arbitration involves a neutral third party (chosen by the parties) listening to the evidence and arguments and then deciding a question which the parties have brought before him or her. The neutral third party has the power to issue a binding decision. Consequently, there is much less of a contrast between arbitration and traditional litigation in a court than is the case with other forms of ADR, such as mediation.

Roberts and Palmer identify a number of features of arbitration which differentiate it from litigation. First, the parties both agree to go to arbitration and agree that the arbitrator's decision will be binding upon them. Second, the usual practice is for arbitration to be carried out as a private process, and the parties have influence over the rules which will be used – often they design the process to be employed and state the substantive standards to be used by the arbitrator in making an award. Third, arbitrators do not consider themselves bound by any doctrine of precedent. Finally, in arbitration the parties themselves select the arbitrator. Usually they select a person who has expert knowledge of the subject-matter of the dispute, with personal experience of the same sort of business and a good grasp of its working norms.[13]

Arbitration has been used by disputing parties for many years, especially in the context of international commercial arbitration.[14] Arbitration is governed by the Arbitration Act 1996, which was designed to provide a statement of the relevant law and procedure in clear and comprehensible language, as well as complying with relevant international rules and principles relating to arbitration.[15] Under the Arbitration Act 1996, if parties agree to refer a dispute to arbitration in a contract, it must be in writing if the Act is to apply.[16] Section 1 of the Act sets out the general principles governing arbitration:

(a)   the object of arbitration is to obtain the fair resolution of disputes by an impartial tribunal without unnecessary delay or expense;

(b)   the parties should be free to agree how their disputes are resolved, subject only to such safeguards as are necessary in the public interest;

(c)   in matters in England and Wales governed by the Act, the court should not intervene except as the Act provides.

The Arbitration Act provides that the arbitrator must act impartially and fairly, giving each party a reasonable opportunity of putting their own case and dealing with their opponent's case, and must adopt procedures suitable to the circumstances of each case, avoiding unnecessary delay and expense, so as to provide a fair means for the

---

[13]   Roberts and Palmer (2005) pp. 265–6.

[14]   See information on the Chartered Institute of Arbitrators website: <http://www.arbitrators.org>.

[15]   See Department for Trade and Industry, *Report of the Department of Trade and Industry Departmental Advisory Committee on International Commercial Arbitration* (the Mustill Report) (1985) HMSO, London.

[16]   Arbitration Act 1996, s. 5.

resolution of the dispute.[17] This provision gives some flexibility to the arbitrator, and means they can adopt an inquisitorial approach, rather than the adversarial approach which has traditionally been adopted by courts.

Disputes are arbitrated for a number of reasons: for example, a court may refer a dispute to arbitration; sometimes contracting parties agree that, in the event of a dispute arising, they will refer it to arbitration and sometimes if a dispute occurs, parties may then decide to go to arbitration. In essence, arbitration is a private form of adjudication, which brings with it flexibility, and simplified procedures. The opportunity for speedier and cheaper resolution of disputes has made arbitration very popular within the commercial world for some time.[18]

# ADR in different settings

Some ADR schemes are court based, and involve referrals of disputes by courts to an ADR scheme. In these schemes, cases will usually start off in the formal legal system, but be encouraged to use ADR by the court; they may resolve all or part of their dispute using an ADR process, and the interaction between the ADR process and the formal legal system may be quite considerable. Other schemes operate independently of the courts; their direct interaction with the formal legal system may be minimal, unless negotiations break down and the parties decide to take their dispute to court.

## Court-based ADR schemes

We have already looked at the Central London County Court mediation scheme, and mentioned the encouragement of the use of ADR by judges of the Commercial Court, but there are many other court-based ADR schemes, including a voluntary scheme operated by the Court of Appeal. Since 1996, in a wide variety of civil cases, the Court of Appeal has sent a letter to the parties inviting them to consider the use of ADR. If both parties agree to mediate, the Court of Appeal arranges mediations and mediators provide their services without charge. Parties refusing to mediate are asked to give reasons for refusal.[19] Just over ten cases a year were mediated as a result of this scheme in its first few years. Solicitors' experiences of successful mediation were largely positive, but there were some concerns about clients' perceptions about being pushed into mediation, and a widespread view that the Court of Appeal should carefully select those cases in which it encouraged the parties to use ADR.[20] Clearly, some adjustments need to be made to this scheme, but from the point of view of the legal system

---

[17]  Arbitration Act 1996, s. 33.      [18]  Roberts and Palmer (2005) p. 265.
[19]  H. Genn, *Court-based ADR Initiatives for Non-family Civil Disputes: The Commercial Court and the Court of Appeal* (2002) DCA Research Series 1/02, Department for Constitutional Affairs, London, ch. 5.
[20]  Genn (2002) ch. 5.

the Court of Appeal scheme provides a clear example of a court-based scheme operating at a very high level of the system.

## ADR and employment cases

Since the late 1990s, in certain employment disputes, where the parties agree, instead of going to an employment tribunal, cases can be arbitrated by Acas (an organization which exists to promote resolution of employment disputes).[21] The scheme was developed as a result of the Employment Rights (Dispute Resolution) Act 1998, which inserted a new section (s. 212A) into the Trades Union and Labour Relations (Consolidation) Act 1992. The scheme was introduced in 2001. It is a voluntary scheme, and where parties both agree in writing to submit the dispute to arbitration, and Acas is sure that the employee has received independent advice, Acas will refer the dispute to an arbitrator.[22] Parties wishing to use the scheme must do so through a legally binding agreement and in agreeing to use the scheme parties accept that the arbitrator's decision will be final and binding.[23] Acas stresses that the procedure is informal and inquisitorial, with no formal pleadings or cross-examination, and instead of merely applying the law, the arbitrator will have regard to general principles of fairness and good conduct. There are only very limited possibilities for appeal, and the whole intention is that the scheme should provide a quick final outcome for the parties involved in an unfair dismissal dispute.[24] Although the intention of the scheme is clearly that disputes should be resolved informally, there is some concern that this may not turn out to be the case in practice. In South Africa, where arbitration is the usual method of resolving certain types of dismissals, the process has remained essentially adversarial.[25]

## ADR and trade associations

One of the areas in which there are considerable opportunities to use ADR to resolve disputes, is that of consumer disputes. The Office of Fair Trading (OFT) promotes codes of practice for trade associations, and many trade organizations operate schemes which involve some form of arbitration or mediation to resolve disputes between retailers of goods and services and consumers.[26]

In August 2003, the Department of Trade and Industry commissioned the National Consumer Council to research the current provision of ADR for consumer disputes in the UK and to suggest ways in which ADR might be promoted and developed in this

---

[21] For information on Acas see <http://www.acas.org.uk>.

[22] *The Acas Arbitration Scheme for the Resolution of Unfair Dismissal Disputes (England and Wales)* accessed 16 April 2010 at: <http://www.acas.org.uk> paras 19 and 20.

[23] *The Acas Arbitration Scheme for the Resolution of Unfair Dismissal Disputes (England and Wales)* para. 21.

[24] See *The Acas Arbitration Scheme for the Resolution of Unfair Dismissal Disputes (England and Wales)*.

[25] J. Clark, 'Adversarial and Investigative Approaches to the Arbitral Resolution of Dismissal Disputes: A Comparison of South Africa and the U.K.' (1999) 28(4) Industrial Law Journal 319.

[26] See: <http://www.oft.gov.uk>.

area.[27] The researchers found that the provision of ADR to resolve consumer problems is very ad hoc. Some sectors are served relatively well, in that there is an existing ADR scheme in place. Sectors covered in this way include travel agents/holidays, upholstered furniture, floor coverings, and telecommunications. However, this leaves some problematic areas such as home maintenance and repairs which are without an ADR scheme, and other areas, such as consumer credit, which have limited coverage.[28]

The research also found that there was a very low level of usage of ADR for the resolution of consumer problems, even when a scheme was in place. It appears that even when an ADR scheme exists consumers who have a problem face a 'gatekeeper' to the ADR scheme, often a trade association, which ensures that the majority of claims are handled using internal procedures. Only when these are exhausted, is the consumer allowed to proceed to ADR.[29] This may mean that a large number of disputes are settled at an early stage. However, these informal procedures are rarely independent, and they lack transparency – it is not possible to assess whether or not the consumers involved are being treated fairly.

Awareness of ADR is very low, not only among consumers, but also among advisers and the business community, which does not encourage its use.[30] Another difficulty uncovered by the research, is that cost can also be a barrier to the use of ADR. Costs to access ADR schemes ranged from no fees to fees of several hundred pounds. Since most consumer disputes are of relatively low value, the cost of trying to resolve them using some of these schemes is disproportionate to the value of the claim.[31]

From the point of view of the legal system, the existence of ADR in these different settings reinforces the importance of adopting an integrated approach which takes account of the huge variety of alternative dispute resolution processes which are used on an everyday basis. It also reminds us of the potential for interaction between the traditional legal system and other means of resolving disputes. In the following section, we will look at some of these interactions more closely.

# Courts and ADR: interaction with the formal legal system

The reform of the Civil Procedure Rules (CPR) as a result of Lord Woolf's work on the reform of civil justice in England and Wales gave ADR a much higher profile in the rules governing court procedure.[32] CPR 4 imposes a duty on courts to engage in active

---

[27] M. Doyle et al., *Seeking Resolutions: The Availability and Usage of Consumer-to-business Alternative Dispute Resolution in the United Kingdom* (2004) Department of Trade and Industry, London, p. 8.
[28] Doyle et al. (2004) ch. 5.        [29] Doyle et al. (2004) pp. 61–2.        [30] Doyle et al. (2004) p. 62.
[31] Doyle et al. (2004) p. 2.
[32] Lord Woolf, *Access to Justice: Interim Report to the Lord Chancellor on the Civil Justice System in England and Wales* (1995) Lord Chancellor's Department, London; Lord Woolf, *Access to Justice: Final*

case management, which specifically includes encouraging the parties to use an ADR procedure, if the court considers that appropriate, as well as facilitating the use of such procedures.[33] In addition, CPR 26.4 allows the court to grant a 'stay' (i.e., to suspend the proceedings) for the purposes of allowing the parties to settle their dispute using ADR or other means when one or all of the parties request this, or when the court considers this would be appropriate. If a party fails to use ADR when the court thinks this would have been appropriate, the party can be penalized through a costs order.[34]

Although the Rules are clearly designed to encourage the use of ADR, it has become clear that the courts will not *compel* a party to use ADR. In *Halsey* v *Milton Keynes General NHS Trust*,[35] the court considered whether a party who won a case, having refused to use ADR when it could have been used, was entitled to claim its legal costs. Giving the judgment of the court, Lord Justice Dyson held that:

It is one thing to encourage the parties to agree to mediation, even to encourage them in the strongest terms. It is another to order them to do so. It seems to us that to oblige truly unwilling parties to refer their disputes to mediation would be to impose an unacceptable obstruction on their right of access to the court.

If a judge takes the view that the case is suitable for ADR, then he or she is not, of course, obliged to take at face value the expressed opposition of the parties. In such a case, the judge should explore the reasons for any resistance to ADR. But if the parties (or at least one of them) remain intransigently opposed to ADR, then it would be wrong for the court to compel them to embrace it.[36]

The question whether a party has acted unreasonably in refusing ADR (which would mean that the court might decide to penalize that party by not awarding costs) must be decided having regard to all the circumstances of the particular case, including such matters as the nature of the dispute, whether the costs of the ADR would be disproportionately high and whether the ADR had a reasonable prospect of success.[37]

While *Halsey* remains good law, it appears that the courts will not go as far as *forcing* parties to use ADR rather than engaging in litigation. Nevertheless, the courts have been keen to *encourage* the use of ADR. Various schemes have been set up: in Exeter, the county court set up a scheme which involved the referral of some cases which were listed for the small claims track being referred to mediation instead; while in Manchester, the county court has a trained in-house mediator providing a free service for court users, giving parties the option of a mediation session before the court hearing. Mediations last up to one hour, and if the mediation is not successful, the case will progress to the hearing as normal.[38]

*Report to the Lord Chancellor on the Civil Justice System in England and Wales* (1996) Lord Chancellor's Department, London.

[33]  CPR 4(2)e.

[34]  CPR 44.5.      [35]  [2004] EWCA Civ 576.      [36]  [2004] EWCA Civ 576, paras 9 and 10.

[37]  [2004] EWCA Civ 576, para. 16.

[38]  S. Prince, *Court-based Mediation: A Preliminary Analysis of the Small Claims Mediation Scheme at Exeter County Court* (2004) Report prepared for the Civil Justice Council; see <http://www.adr.civiljustice-council.gov.uk>; on the Manchester scheme see: <http://www.dca.gov.uk/civil/adr/index.htm>.

Research by Genn on the use of ADR by the Commercial Court suggests that in commercial disputes, the use of ADR may be increasing.[39] As we noted above, since 1993, the Commercial Court has been identifying cases regarded as appropriate for ADR. In such cases, judges may suggest the use of ADR, or they may make an order, directing the parties to attempt ADR. If, following an ADR order, the parties fail to settle their case, they must inform the court of the steps they took towards using ADR, and why they failed. Genn found that of the cases in which ADR was attempted, 52 per cent settled following ADR, and the experiences of the litigants involved in these cases was overwhelmingly positive. The factors most valued were the skills of the mediator, the ability of ADR to get past sticking points in negotiation, the opportunity to focus on the strengths and weaknesses of cases, and client satisfaction. There was also a perception that successful mediation avoids trial costs, leading to substantial savings for clients. Genn found that in the years she examined (1996/2000) there was evidence of increasing use of ADR towards the end of the review period, suggesting a developing interest in the use of ADR among commercial litigants.[40]

However, there is considerable evidence that, other than in commercial disputes, ADR has not yet been absorbed into the culture of conventional litigation. In their research for the (then) Department for Constitutional Affairs on the 'post-Woolf landscape', Peysner and Seneviratne found that, although there has been a large increase, post-Woolf, in the number of cases settled, there has not been a corresponding increase in the use of ADR. Most judges interviewed for the study thought that there was little use made of ADR and that there was either 'real resistance' or 'little enthusiasm' for it.[41]

Peysner and Seneviratne found that judges very rarely 'stay' (i.e., suspend) a case to allow the parties the opportunity to try mediation. The most they do is to give fairly pointed hints about trying to get the matter settled.[42] However, they also found that judges could see an important role for ADR, particularly in boundary disputes and local authority housing disputes, which tend to be cases which are time-consuming and difficult to resolve legally, and where the judges felt that a compromise could be obtained through the use of ADR, rather than the 'win–lose' outcome of litigation. However, at present, the judges indicated that most unrepresented parties at fast-track trials never think in terms of mediation. Their focus is on the trial, and they do not think of other ways of resolving the dispute.[43]

Many of the practitioners interviewed by Peysner and Seneviratne were keen to see the courts intervening more in certain cases to force the parties to mediate. The general view was that this would be most useful in commercial litigation, rather than personal injury or clinical negligence or other complex areas of expert opinion, especially because these areas already have pre-action protocols, unlike the commercial area.

---

[39] Genn (2002).    [40] Genn (2002) chs 2–4.

[41] J. Peysner and M. Seneviratne, *The Management of Civil Cases: The Courts and Post-Woolf Landscape* (2005) DCA Research Series 9/05, Department for Constitutional Affairs, London, p. 43.

[42] Peysner and Seneviratne (2005) p. 45.    [43] Peysner and Seneviratne (2005) p. 44.

However, the perception of interviewees was that mediation did not really seem to play any part in the court process.[44]

It would appear that judges have a crucial role to play in the development of ADR. Genn's finding that in the Commercial Court there were signs of an increasing interest in the use of ADR seems to be closely related to the fact that the court itself was actively suggesting the use of ADR. This factor emphasizes the way in which ADR and the formal legal system interact, and shows again how important it is to adopt an integrated approach to your study of the legal system, so that you can pay proper attention to such phenomena.

## The legal profession and ADR

The attitude of the legal profession to ADR is likely to be crucial to the rate at which it develops as part of the legal landscape. We saw in Genn's evaluation of the London County Court Pilot Mediation Project that both litigants and their representatives had very little knowledge of ADR, while in the Commercial Court the judges' active role in suggesting that litigants try ADR appeared to be highly significant in encouraging lawyers and their clients to consider using ADR.[45] In her evaluation of the Department of Health's mediation pilot scheme, Mulcahy suggests that much of the responsibility for lack of take-up of ADR lies with the legal profession. She suggests that since the legal profession, particularly solicitors, act as gatekeepers to many of the new schemes, if they are uninformed about, or unsympathetic to, ADR, they are in a position to put their clients off using ADR. Mulcahy comments that when she was considering the use of mediation in her research project, she found that it was not a form of dispute resolution commonly used by High Street practitioners and not something which clients automatically associated with lawyers. This level of ignorance, coupled with a fear on the part of practitioners that cases would be diverted away from the courts, thus putting at risk their investments in handling litigation, led to reluctance to use ADR. She also found some more principled objections from those lawyers who continue to believe that the courtroom is the most appropriate backdrop to settlement negotiations. In the view of this group, diverting cases away from courts to ADR brings with it the danger that too many cases will be decided by reference to the standards of the parties, rather than the wider needs of the society in which we live.[46]

However, Mulcahy also goes on to note that other members of the legal profession have proved much more open to change. Many lawyers have trained as mediators, and the governing bodies of the professions have pledged their support for ADR.[47] From the point of view of an integrated theory of the legal system, the interaction between

---

[44]  Peysner and Seneviratne (2005) p. 45.        [45]  Genn (1998) para. 5.2.2; Genn (2002) chs 2–4.

[46]  L. Mulcahy, 'Can Leopards Change their Spots? An Evaluation of the Role of Lawyers in Medical Negligence Mediation' (2001) 8(3) International Journal of the Legal Profession 203.

[47]  The Law Society, for example, has an ADR Committee – see <http://www.lawsociety.org.uk>.

judges, lawyers, and forms of ADR provides another example of the way in which legal personnel belonging to the traditional legal system interact with forms of ADR.

## CONCLUSION

ADR has a number of advantages over formal litigation, which are reflected in the discussion above. Many ADR schemes try to work without the need for legal representation, thus reducing cost. Even if legal representatives or other advisers are used, ADR schemes tend to offer speedier resolution of disputes, which also reduces cost. In general, ADR offers a much more informal procedure than traditional litigation, allocating more power to the parties and attempting to be less intimidating and stressful than court proceedings. Sometimes, ADR schemes will offer access to assistance from persons having specialized knowledge of the relevant subject-matter, which can promote confidence, as well as helping to speed up the process.

However, we should not assume that alternative methods of dispute resolution necessarily improve the position of disadvantaged litigants. A number of concerns have been expressed about the use of ADR. One of the most significant critiques of the use of ADR to settle disputes can be found in an article written by Owen Fiss, called 'Against Settlement'.[48] Fiss worries about ADR because of the possibility that it will enhance differences in power between the parties, rather than redressing them:

> settlement is also a function of the resources available to each party to finance the litigation, and these resources are frequently distributed unequally. Many disputes do not involve a property dispute between two neighbours but rather concern a struggle between a member of a racial minority and a municipal police department over alleged brutality or a claim by a worker against a large corporation over work-related injuries. In these cases the distribution of financial resources, or the ability of one party to pass along its costs, will inevitably 'infect' the bargaining process and settlement will be at odds with a conception of justice that seeks to make the wealth of the parties irrelevant.[49]

Fiss's main concerns are: first, the litigant with less resources may be less capable than his/her opponent of gathering and analysing the information necessary to gain a reasonably accurate picture of the probable outcome of litigation so they have a baseline from which to bargain. Second, Fiss is concerned that litigants with less financial resources may be under pressure to settle because they need the money; and, finally, he worries that the poorer disputant may be forced to settle using ADR because he/she lacks the financial resources to take their dispute to court.

However, Fiss's views are not shared by all commentators. McThenia and Shaffer, in their response to the Fiss article, argue that he 'assumes that the ADR movement is one that wants peace at any price'.[50] Their own view is that:

> In many, in fact most, of the cultural traditions that argue for ADR, settlement is neither an avoidance mechanism nor a truce. Settlement is a process of reconciliation in which the anger of broken

---

[48] O. Fiss, 'Against Settlement' (1984) 93 Yale Law Journal 1073.    [49] Fiss (1984) p. 1076.

[50] A. W. McThenia and T. L. Shaffer, 'For Reconciliation' (1985) 94 Yale Law Journal 1660, at p. 1662.

relationships is to be confronted rather than avoided, and in which healing demands not a truce but confrontation.[51]

In another important critique of ADR, Richard Abel argues that, although many people might regard the growth of informal types of dispute resolution as a sign of reducing state power, in fact, the opposite is true, and the increase in ADR represents an increase in state power, because every time the state assists ADR schemes (for instance, by referring litigants to them, or by giving grants to voluntary sector schemes), it expands its influence into an area in which it previously would not have been active.[52]

Abel also points to the difficulties which arise because ADR involves relaxing the procedural rules which govern litigation in the courts, which are there to try and ensure that all parties to litigation are treated fairly and have an equal opportunity of presenting their case. There is a danger that without the procedural rules found in courts, the weaker parties are disadvantaged. There is also the danger that ADR will allow the intervening third party (such as the mediator) to impose solutions by coercing or manipulating one or both of the parties, rather than enabling the parties to come to an agreement on their own terms.[53]

While acknowledging the difficulties posed by ADR, Roberts and Palmer remind us that it has become a significant part of the legal landscape, and that it is part of an emerging transformation of the culture of dispute resolution within the English legal system. We are witnessing the emergence of new professionals in dispute resolution – mediators, arbitrators, and so on, who are quickly developing the use of ADR, and whose existence presents a challenge to the monopoly over dispute management hitherto claimed by lawyers. In responding to the emergence of these new professionals, the traditional legal profession has moved quickly to add ADR to their own repertoire. ADR is already recognized by some lawyers as 'something lawyers do', a change reflected, as Roberts and Palmer point out, in the way 'ADR units' have been established in many large commercial law firms, and in the number of City lawyers now claiming to be 'trained mediators'.[54]

As all this change takes place, it is unclear precisely how the legal universe will look in the future. However, from a theoretical point of view, it will become increasingly important for anyone studying the legal system to take a pluralistic, integrated approach, which acknowledges the many ways in which ADR and the traditional legal system interact with each other.

## FURTHER READING

ROBERTS, S. and PALMER, M. *Dispute Processes: ADR and the Primary Forms* *of Decision-making* (2005) Cambridge University Press, Cambridge

---

[51] McThenia and Shaffer (1985) p. 1665.

[52] See R. Abel, 'Introduction' in R. Abel (ed.), *The Politics of Informal Justice*, Volume 1: *The American Experience* (1982) Academic Press, New York.            [53] Abel (1982) pp. 295–8.

[54] Roberts and Palmer (2005) p. 363.

# 12

# Private security and other non-police agencies

## INTRODUCTION

Applying an integrated theory to the criminal justice system, it immediately becomes clear that it is important not to take too narrow a view as to what constitutes the criminal justice system. There has been a tendency for those carrying out research into this area to be preoccupied with the study of the public police, while relatively little study of less formal methods of policing has been carried out:[1] 'No-one questioned what "the police" meant. Thus private police forces, citizen protection groups and other government policing bodies were ignored.'[2] The narrow definition of the criminal justice system adopted by many researchers has hitherto been reflected in the majority of 'English legal system' textbooks.[3]

However, we think it is important to acknowledge that the criminal justice system does not merely consist of the activities of the public police: it is composed of a number of forms of social control, which interact to make up the complex web of relationships which makes up the entire English criminal justice system. The world of the public police forms one part of the criminal justice system, but there are many other parts. Indeed, the range of bodies engaged in policing activities is now so wide that commentators refer to the 'pluralisation' of policing.[4] Only when the relationships between *all* these different aspects of policing are examined, can one be said to have an accurate picture of 'the English criminal justice system'.

In examining some of the other forms of social control which form the criminal justice system, it is important to realize that these other activities should not be regarded as merely minor adjuncts to the formal system of policing, which can be dismissed as

---

[1] T. Jones and T. Newburn, *Private Security and Public Policing* (1998) Clarendon Press, Oxford, p. 1.

[2] M. Cain, 'Trends in the Sociology of Police Work' (1979) 7 International Journal of the Sociology of Law 143 at p. 145.

[3] See, for example, S. H. Bailey, J. P. L. Ching, and N. W. Taylor, *Smith, Bailey and Gunn on the Modern English Legal System* (5th edn, 2007) Sweet & Maxwell, London, or R. Ward and A. Akhtar, *Walker and Walker's English Legal System* (10th edn, 2008) Oxford University Press, Oxford.

[4] D. H. Bayley and C. D. Shearing, 'The Future of Policing' (1996) 30(3) Law and Society Review 585 at p. 591.

relatively unimportant, but that they have very important roles within the English legal system.

## Private security

An increasingly important form of social control which has hitherto been largely ignored by those writing about the English legal system, is the world of private security. Private security personnel are those persons engaged in the protection of information, persons, or property. They are privately employed, have different legal powers to the public police, and are accountable for the exercise of those powers to a private individual or institution, rather than to the public.

The term 'private security' is used, rather than 'private policing', partly to avoid confusion with the public police, but also because that term conveys more accurately the wide range of activities carried out by private security personnel in contemporary society, activities which go far beyond the policing activities carried out by the public police.[5] The range of activities undertaken by the private security sector is very wide.[6] It involves the provision of manned services – guarding, patrolling, transporting cash, etc., as well as providing bodyguards, private investigators, and involvement in the management of prisons and escort services. Private security entities are also involved in the provision of physical or mechanical devices, such as locks, safes, and cash bags, supplying electrical and electronic devices, such as alarms, video motion-detection devices, etc., and 'security hardware', that is, the manufacture, distribution, and servicing of a wide variety of security equipment.

It is impossible to obtain accurate figures relating to the number of persons involved in private security in Britain today. Estimates vary greatly, partly depending on the definition of private security which is used. Figures reported by the Home Affairs Select Committee in its 1995 report on the industry ranged between 126,900 and 300,000.[7] The 1999 White Paper, *The Government's Proposals for the Regulation of the Private Security Industry in England and Wales*, estimated that there were then a total

---

[5] For a more elaborate discussion of the definition of private security, see C. D. Shearing and P. C. Stenning, 'Modern Private Security: Its Growth and Implications' in M. Tonry and N. Morris (eds), *Crime and Justice*, Volume 3 (1981) University of Chicago Press, Chicago, pp. 193–245 at pp. 194ff. Also see N. South, 'Private Security, the Division of Policing Labour and the Commercial Compromise of the State' in S. Spitzer and A. T. Scull (eds), *Research in Law, Deviance and Social Control*, Volume 6 (1984) JAI Press, Greenwich, CT.

[6] For details of the activities of the private security industry in Britain, see, for example, M. Button, *Private Policing* (2002) Willan Publishing, Cullompton; T. Jones and T. Newburn, *Private Security and Public Policing* (1998) Clarendon Press, Oxford; and L. Johnston *The Rebirth of Private Policing* (1992) Routledge, London.

[7] Home Affairs Select Committee First Report, *The Private Security Industry: Volume 1* (1995) HMSO, London, paras 7–10. See also Johnston (1992) p. 73.

of 240,000 individuals employed in some 8,000 companies.[8] All commentators are unanimous, however, in agreeing that the number of persons employed in the sector is growing rapidly and many have noted that it is probable that the number of persons employed in the private security industry is larger than the number of persons working in the police service.[9] Thus, in terms of quantity alone, we are dealing with a significant factor in the criminal justice system.

## The role of private security

In terms of the criminal justice system, the activities carried out by private security with which we are most concerned are those involving the provision of manned services. These services can be supplied 'in-house' or on a contractual basis by enterprises specializing in the provision of private security services. In addition, there are services provided by private investigators, which may at times form part of the criminal justice system, if, for example, they are employed to search for stolen property, or to check an alibi in relation to criminal litigation.

Some commentators have taken the view that private security personnel perform a role which is complementary to that of the public police, in that they carry out functions which the public police cannot perform either because of lack of resources or legal restraints,[10] and that they are serving the public interest by acting as junior partners in the fight against crime. However, others argue that to assume a unity of purpose between private security and the public police is mistaken, since in fact the police and private security are motivated by different sets of objectives, which only overlap slightly.[11] Police and private security are therefore seen as seeking to further different objectives, which may sometimes be in competition with each other.

It is interesting that some private security executives have fostered the view of private security as complementary to police activity, promoting its image as a force which does not in any way threaten the established order and so deserves little attention,[12] whereas Shearing and Stenning, for example, see the role of private security in a much more threatening way:

the corporate concept of security in the private sector which emerges from interviews and discussions across a wide range of private organisations is one of a highly sophisticated and largely decentralized system of social control, which draws its authority for action from historically based and legitimated notions of property. This is quite unlike police authority

[8] Home Office, *The Government's Proposals for Regulating the Private Security Industry in England and Wales* (1999) Cm. 4254, HMSO, London, para. 5.19.

[9] Home Affairs Select Committee First Report (1995) para. 9. See also, for example, N. South, 'The Corruption of Private Justice: The Case of the Private Security Sector' in M. Clarke (ed.), *Corruption: Causes, Consequences and Control* (1983) Pinter, London, p. 39.

[10] J. S. Kakalik and S. Wildhorn, *Private Policing in the United States: Findings and Recommendations* (1971) Rand Corporation, Santa Monica, CA, p. 19.

[11] C. D. Shearing, P. C. Stenning, and S. M. Addario, 'Corporate Perceptions of Private Security' (1985) 9 Canadian Police College Journal 367 at p. 368.          [12] Shearing et al. (1985) p. 369.

which derives from state conveyed powers arising out of criminal statutes. Such corporate systems are motivated not by objectives of public interest, but by overriding concerns with the increase of profits and the prevention of losses.[13]

Of great interest from the point of view of the legal system, is that, not only do the two institutions have different objectives, but they also have different systems of justice. The public police use the public criminal justice system, whereas private security personnel do not invariably refer potential crimes to the police, but may deal with events themselves, according to a private set of rules laid down by their employer or the client for whom they are working.[14] Typically, the mandate and objectives of private security can be expressed in terms of the particular interests and objectives of those who employ them. The activities of private security are directed towards protecting the assets of its clients. Frequently, this involves 'policing for profit', in the sense that the policing carried out is directed towards the profit-making objectives of employers such as retailers or manufacturers. This is very different from the approach of the public police, who judge situations against an externally defined moral standard and who perform their duties in the public interest. It can lead to the obvious danger that pressure to cut prices will result in rule-bending or flouting of the law.[15] Even when public and private security personnel are discussing similar functions, their different orientations soon become apparent. Public police often describe one of their roles as being 'crime prevention', but private security personnel talk in terms of 'loss prevention',[16] revealing their prime concern with the protection of their clients' assets. It soon becomes clear that the world of private security is controlled to a large extent by the clients who employ private security personnel. By employing private security, they ensure that their concerns as potential victims of crime or other security problems are given priority in policing. 'Private security is essentially victim-controlled policing.'[17]

Private security's concern with loss prevention leads it to carry out a number of activities which can best be described, in general terms, as 'surveillance'. Surveillance involves a wide range of activities, from foot patrols on the alert for any potential security problems, checking locks, fences, and so on, to activities concerned with controlling access to and from the areas for which they are responsible, screening visitors, searching employees, etc.[18] The scope of the surveillance work carried out by private security has increased greatly in recent times, due to the development of privately owned public spaces, or 'mass private property',[19] that is, shopping centres, residential estates, office, industrial, and recreational complexes. Such places are privately owned, but are routinely used by large sections of the public. The public police have not had routine access to such places, so their surveillance has generally been confined to publicly owned spaces. The use of private security forces to police areas of mass private

[13]  Shearing et al. (1985) p. 369.
[14]  C. D. Shearing and P. C. Stenning, 'Private Security: Implications for Social Control' (1983) 30 Social Problems 500.                                                             [15]  South (1983) p. 40.
[16]  Shearing and Stenning (1981) p. 212.        [17]  Shearing and Stenning (1983) p. 500.
[18]  Shearing and Stenning (1981) p. 213.        [19]  Shearing and Stenning (1983) p. 496.

property means that surveillance has been extended into new areas. Considerable spaces, which are apparently public, are in reality under the ownership and control of private individuals or corporations. This has significant consequences in terms of civil liberties. Since private security operate as the agents of the owners of private property, they then have access to many of the powers and much of the authority associated with private property and its protection. Such powers are based on assumptions about the nature of property relations which are not true in relation to mass private property – for example, the assumption that places which are privately owned and controlled are normally 'private' places:[20]

Most of the elaborate protections which have been established to ensure the liberty of an individual when he is in a publicly owned place become subject to the property rights of the owner and his agents as soon as that individual steps into a privately owned public place. In the exercise of such rights the owner (or his private security agent) is free to impose almost unlimited infringements on the liberty and privacy of the individual (e.g. a requirement to submit to search of his person or property, to be photographed or temporarily to surrender his property) as conditions of access to or exit from the premises.[21]

   The legal authority originally granted to private individuals to protect their property is now used for:

massive and continuous intrusions upon the privacy of citizens (as customers and employees) by those who own and control the mass private property on which so much public life takes place. Nevertheless, the traditional association between the institution of private property and the protection of liberty has historically been such a powerful source of legitimacy that, despite these important changes in the nature of private property, the exercise of private security authority is rarely questioned or challenged.[22]

When the powers of private security guards are examined, it becomes clear that their status as the agents of property owners allows them to exercise a degree of legal authority which far exceeds the powers of the public police; for instance, they may insist that persons submit to random searches of their person or property as a condition of entrance to or exit from the premises.[23] A common example of this is the security checks carried out at museums and art galleries. Of course, it would theoretically be possible to avoid such situations, but this would be generally regarded as impractical. It is interesting that many people have perceived state power as posing the greatest threat to individual liberty, but the emergence of mass private property has given private corporations a sphere of influence which forms a serious rival to the power of the state, yet this phenomenon is often overlooked.[24] Private property owners have an interest in policing their spaces, and because that ownership is usually associated with

---

[20] Shearing and Stenning (1981) p. 238.     [21] Shearing and Stenning (1981) p. 238.
[22] Shearing and Stenning (1983) p. 498.
[23] For a discussion of the rights of property owners in this context, see R. Stone, *Entry, Search and Seizure* (4th edn, 2005) Oxford University Press, Oxford, esp. chs 1 and 2.
[24] Shearing and Stenning (1983) p. 498.

large resources, it is possible for these owners to hire a security force. It is the large public corporations who control vast industrial and commercial premises, as well as residential complexes, who are the principal users of private security.[25]

Researchers have recently turned their attention to the ways in which private security plays a key role in the policing of public order, particularly in terms of the 'night-time economy' (NTE). City centres are environments in which, particularly at night, informal methods of social control are often weak, yet they are contested spaces, and subject to a considerable amount of violence. The leisure economies which flourish in city centres at night are youth dominated, and a heavy emphasis is placed upon the sale and consumption of alcohol. The resources and policing methods of the public police are frequently inadequate to deal with the public order issues which arise.[26] Private security, in the form of bouncers, fills the void left by the police. Research has shown that bouncers, although they do not possess the same legal powers as the public police, have developed ways of working which maintain their personal authority, creating a 'moral mandate' for their actions.[27] Like other forms of private security discussed in this chapter, there is also evidence that bouncers have a preference for informal methods of dispute resolution. Apprehending criminal offenders has considerable potential to increase conflict, as well as increase the chances of personal injury to the bouncer or customer. Bouncers prefer, therefore, to resolve disputes informally.[28]

Another significant example of the importance of understanding the place of private security in the criminal justice system, lies in the extension of the industry's activities over new objects of surveillance.[29] The public police have generally directed their surveillance towards potential troublemakers. Whilst this population is also surveyed by private security operatives, it does not form their primary focus of interest. Private security is interested in preventing security breaches, so it focuses, not just on potential troublemakers, but also on those who are in a position to create opportunities for such breaches. This means that the target population is larger, and may consist largely of innocent, law-abiding citizens. This can be seen, again, as a matter of concern in terms of civil liberties.

An interesting feature of private security, as far as the legal system is concerned, is that its importance is often underestimated because its operations can seem so 'Mickey Mouse'. This amateurish appearance means that private security work does not appear as important as public police work, such as apprehending criminals. However, some commentators regard the growth of private security as being of no little significance in terms of the social control of society. It has been argued[30] that private police are an example of Foucault's 'disciplinary society',[31] that is to say, a society that is not based

---

[25] Shearing and Stenning (1981) p. 229.

[26] D. Hobbs, P. Hadfield, S. Lister, and S. Winlow, *Bouncers: Violence and Governance in the Night-time Economy* (2003) Oxford University Press, Oxford, ch. 1.    [27] Hobbs et al. (2003) ch. 5.

[28] Hobbs et al. (2003) p. 191.    [29] Shearing and Stenning (1981) p. 214.

[30] Shearing and Stenning (1981) p. 218.

[31] See M. Foucault, *Discipline and Punish: The Birth of Prison* (1977) Pantheon, New York.

on physical coercion, but on a more subtle form of coercion which draws its power from surveillance and inspection.

## Interaction with the public police

From the point of view of the English legal system, the interaction between private security and public police is significant. The existence of this relationship emphasizes how important an integrated theory is – a theory which acknowledges that the legal system encompasses many different legal worlds, which form a complex pattern of interrelationships. As far as the relationship between the police and the world of private security is concerned, it can sometimes be a negative one, in the sense that private security personnel can act as a filter which stops potential crimes ever coming to the attention of the public police. Private security personnel are often the first to encounter a problem, so they play a pivotal role in deciding what will and will not be brought to the attention of the public police.[32] Since private security focuses primarily on the interests of the client, it is not interested in things which do not threaten those interests, even if a breach of the criminal law may be involved. If a traditional offender is caught by private security, the client's interest may be best served by taking a course of action other than involving the public police, such as sacking the offending employee. This attitude can be seen in the following remark made by one Canadian security director: 'I'm not responsible for enforcing the Criminal Code. My basic responsibility is to reduce theft and minimize disruption to the orderly operation of business.'[33] Such attitudes on the part of private security operatives were also found in a UK context by Michael, who concluded on the basis of her empirical research that the private security guards she interviewed were not oriented to public policing work. They were not enthusiastic about the prospect of making an arrest, they did not want greater legal powers and they did not perceive many similarities between their work and that of a police officer.[34]

The private security industry tends to be focused on economic pragmatism, rather than on serving the public interest, and it means that many criminal disputes do not ever reach the public system. Researchers have found that private security personnel often regard the public justice system as something to turn to only as a matter of last resort.[35] This attitude is based on a number of different considerations. It might be that going to court is regarded as involving too much 'hassle', or that, especially in financial institutions, such as banks, the need to maintain a high level of public confidence in the security of the institution means that any public admission of lapse of security is undesirable. Whatever the rationale, the result of this attitude is that matters tended to be dealt with outside the public system of justice, and by behaving in this way, the employers of private security are able to retain control of the process in a

---

[32] Shearing and Stenning (1983) p. 503.     [33] Quoted in Shearing et al. (1985) p. 374.
[34] D. Michael, 'The Levels of Orientation Security Officers Have Towards a Public Policing Function' (1999) 11 Security Journal 40.     [35] Shearing et al. (1985) p. 375.

way which would not be possible if the matter was referred to the police. The attitude of many private institutions is that the courts take too little notice of the institution's perspective and interest. The main objectives of private security personnel are the restitution of the stolen property and the removal of the offender, with minimum disruption to the institution involved. This 'screening out' process, whereby many potential crimes never come to the attention of the police or the courts, emphasizes the important role which private security plays in the criminal justice system as a whole.

There are, nevertheless, some occasions on which private security personnel do turn to the public police. In the retail sector, for example, security personnel hand over to the public police about a million cases annually.[36] Some commentators have argued that this interaction is quite common, and that when private security personnel interact with the public police, they do so as 'junior partners',[37] handing over all but the most minor matters to the public police. Some private security firms have a policy which instructs their employees to call in the public police to take over any situation as soon as it becomes apparent that it is necessary to use any significant law enforcement powers.[38] However, this is not inevitably the case, and some private security personnel have been shown to deal routinely with all employee theft, even cases involving large amounts of money, and also with other serious matters, such as assault.[39]

Another important aspect of the relationship between the public police and the world of private security is the large amount of interchange among personnel. The relationship between the public police and private security has been described as 'a co-operative one', in which information and services are regularly exchanged between the two bodies.[40] Working in private security can be a stepping stone to a job in the public police. Equally, private security offers an obvious career opportunity for those leaving the public police.[41] This interchange of personnel is highly significant. Not only does it mean that personnel in both sectors are likely to share similar attitudes and social backgrounds, but it also encourages information-sharing, and other forms of cooperation. Many people have expressed concern about the existence of an 'old boy' network, which allows private security personnel access to criminal records and other information held by the public police, and researchers have frequently commented on this phenomenon.[42]

The traditional criminal justice system and the world of private security also exchange personnel at an entirely different level. Much concern has been expressed

[36] British Retail Consortium, *10th Annual Retail Crime Survey* (2002) BRC, London.

[37] Kakalik and Wildhorn (1971) p. 19.

[38] C. D. Shearing, M. F. Farnell, and P. C. Stenning, *Contract Security in Ontario* (1980) Centre of Criminology, University of Toronto, Toronto.          [39] Shearing and Stenning (1983) p. 502.

[40] Shearing and Stenning (1983) p. 503.          [41] Shearing and Stenning (1981) p. 223.

[42] H. Draper, *Private Police* (1978) Penguin Books, Harmondsworth, p. 156; South (1983) p. 49; Shearing et al. (1985) p. 145.

about the existence of criminality within the private security industry, with former criminals finding it easy to obtain jobs guarding property, or setting themselves up in the private security business.[43] Public police and private security personnel also act as consumers of each other's services in other, legitimate, ways. With the growth of the alarm industry, additional demands are made on the public police who are expected to answer alarm calls. Public police, for their part, will sometimes use the technical expertise of private security personnel, for example in cases involving highly technical equipment.[44]

Recently, the interrelationships between public police and private security have been emphasized by some commentators who have pointed to the lack of clear distinctions between public and private policing agencies. McManus argues that public police administrators are seeking to achieve inter-agency cooperation in many different ways, reflected in his study of neighbourhood private security patrols in the high degree of cooperation which he found to exist between the public police and the private security agency.[45] Livingstone's analysis of the growth of the private security industry emphasizes the interdependence between the two sectors in terms of the crises in public policing and the boom in private security activity, both of which, he argues, arise from the same causes: the rising crime rate, the emergence of new types of crime, the increasing cost of crime, both to the state and the private sector, and an increasing fear of crime.[46] The result of these factors has been to generate a greater demand for security than the public police can satisfy. This pressure on the public police has been combined with moves on the part of the Government to decrease the cost of policing. In the 1995 Home Office *Review of Police Core and Ancillary Tasks*, it was estimated that £200 million could be saved by removing some tasks from the police and giving them to private security companies.[47] The ultimate result is that relationships between public police and the private security industry are likely to become increasingly complex. Jones and Newburn's study of public policing and private security in Wandsworth revealed a vast network of people involved in policing activities, some of whom belonged to the public sector and some to the private sector.[48] They comment in particular on the high degree of functional overlap between public and non-public policing organizations which their research uncovered.[49] The existence of these interrelationships demonstrates yet again the relevance of an integrated theory of the legal system, which acknowledges the existence of the many interlocking legal worlds which go to make up the criminal justice system.

---

[43]  See, for example, Home Affairs Select Committee First Report (1995) vol. 1.

[44]  Shearing et al. (1980).

[45]  M. McManus, *From Fate to Choice: Private Bobbies, Public Beats* (1995) Avebury, Aldershot, p. 123.

[46]  K. Livingstone, *Managing the 'Policing Business'* (1996) Research Paper 6, Scarman Centre for the Study of Public Order, University of Leicester, p. 13.

[47]  Home Office, *Review of Police Core and Ancillary Tasks* (1995) HMSO, London.

[48]  Jones and Newburn (1998) chs 5 and 6.        [49]  Jones and Newburn (1998) p. 245.

## Control of private security

The growth in the private security industry, with its attendant implications for civil liberties, has given rise to much concern. Frequently, this has resulted in legislation being passed which attempts to control the behaviour of those involved in the industry. Countries in both North America and Europe have had licensing or certification schemes for some time.[50] However, until recently, this was not true in Britain, where the Government preferred to encourage self-regulation in the industry. There were repeated calls for some form of controlling legislation from a wide range of critics, who regarded self-regulation as an ineffective way of controlling the private security industry.[51]

The Private Security Industry Act was finally passed in 2001. Section 1 of the Act establishes the Security Industry Authority (SIA), which is responsible for the licensing of individuals operating in those sectors of the private security industry which are subject to regulation. It also conducts inspections, monitors the activities and effectiveness of those working in the industry and sets and approves standards of conduct, training and supervision. Everyone working within designated sectors of the industry is required to have a licence issued by the Authority. It is an offence to work in those sectors without a licence, and is also an offence to employ an unlicensed person, except where there is a valid defence. There are limited exceptions to the requirement to obtain a licence. Schedule 2 to the Act sets out the activities liable to control; these include security officers in the static guarding and 'cash-in-transit' sectors, door supervisors (bouncers), bodyguards, wheelclampers, private investigators, and security consultants. Licences are granted to those who are considered 'fit and proper persons' to engage in the relevant private security activities,[52] and the SIA has wide-ranging powers to impose conditions upon the grant of a licence, such as specifying training.[53] The legislation also sets up a voluntary system of inspection of 'providers' of security services (i.e., firms, as opposed to individuals). Under the scheme, those firms which satisfactorily meet agreed standards will be registered as approved by the SIA, and will be able to advertise themselves as such.[54]

The limitations on the extent of the regulatory system which is contained in the Act will dismay those who have argued that the *whole* of the private security industry should be subject to statutory regulation, especially in view of the fact that the different sectors of the industry are frequently interrelated, with the same companies

[50] Home Affairs Select Committee First Report (1995). Appendix 1 (Home Office Memorandum) Annex J sets out a summary of the position in each Member State of the European Union. See also B. George and M. Button, 'Private Security Industry Regulation: Lessons from Abroad for the United Kingdom?' (1997) 2(3) International Journal of Risk, Security and Crime Prevention 187.

[51] Home Affairs Select Committee First Report (1995); and see also B. George and M. Button, '"Too Little Too Late"? An Assessment of Recent Proposals for the Private Security Industry in the United Kingdom' (1998) 10 Security Journal 1.    [52] Private Security Industry Act 2001, s. 7.3(b).

[53] Private Security Industry Act 2001, s. 9.    [54] Private Security Industry Act 2001, ss. 14–18.

offering security services in different fields. However, the system which has been established is sufficiently flexible to allow it to be expanded to cover other sectors in the future.[55]

# Other non-police forms of social control

Private security firms are not the only non-police agencies which interact with the criminal justice system. A wide variety of bodies have been given various powers of enforcement in relation to a wide variety of areas. They range from local trading standards officers to representatives of the Driver and Vehicle Licensing Centre, from the Factory Inspectorate to environmental health officers, and include representatives of non-governmental agencies as well, such as the RSPCA and the NSPCC. Their powers often include the power to prosecute offenders. There are also other actors who carry out important policing roles, such as the staff employed as DJs and bar staff in high-street nightclubs, as well as members of the public.

A wide-ranging study by Lidstone et al.[56] explored the wide variety of non-police prosecutors which exist within the criminal justice system. The researchers noted not only the great variety of prosecutors, from large government departments through local authorities, retail stores and voluntary societies right down to private individuals, but also the variety of prosecutorial arrangements, with access to legal advice on prosecution varying in extent, the decision to prosecute being taken at very different levels within different organizations and with a widely varying degree of the use of lawyers to conduct prosecutions in court. Equally, the researchers found that there were a great variety of different ways of liaising with the public police. In some cases, the relationship between the non-police prosecutor and the formal criminal justice system is very close, because some agencies, such as the British Transport Police, prosecute a large proportion of the offenders with whom they deal. However, other agencies, such as the Inland Revenue, have a very low prosecution rate and here the relationship with the formal system is more distant.[57] Such differences appeared to depend on a number of different factors, including the size of the population at risk of offending, the ease with which offences could be proved and also the existence of other powers to impose penalties and dispose of offences without recourse to prosecution – the Inland Revenue, for instance, have a wide range of other powers, including confiscation of property.[58] Equally, relationships with the police differed greatly. In

---

[55]  See Private Security Industry Act 2001, Sch. 2. For examples of reservations about a limited regime, see Home Affairs Select Committee First Report (1995) para. 102 and Cm. 4254, para. 5.16.

[56]  K. Lidstone et al., *Prosecutions by Private Individuals and Non-police Agencies* (1980) Royal Commission on Criminal Procedure Research Study No. 10, HMSO, London.          [57]  Lidstone et al. (1980).

[58]  Lidstone et al. (1980) ch. 2.

some areas, the police are reluctant to become involved, although in others there is extensive cooperation. The involvement of this wide variety of personnel in criminal prosecutions, and their varying relationships with lawyers and with the public police once again illustrates the importance of an integrated theory which is able to encompass a series of interrelating phenomena which together make up the complete criminal justice system.

In his study of the 'night-time high street', Hadfield found that some venues, which he termed 'regulars' venues' are 'off the map' as far as the younger crowds of 'action seekers' are concerned. Here, social control is frequently shared between staff and the core clientele. Within such venues, there may be implicit rules designed to ensure the preservation of a convivial atmosphere, such as the avoidance of potentially divisive conversational topics such as religion or politics. If there is some sort of trouble, staff may call upon (and/or involuntarily receive) assistance from regulars, so that these venues are to a large degree self-policing.[59]

Within high street bars and clubs, Hadfield found that all staff play a part in social control. While security staff are positioned at various strategic and often highly visible surveillance points – entrances and exits, the top of the stairs or close to bars – bar and floor staff move around the venue to collect glasses or take orders and can also contribute to monitoring activities, as do DJs, who often work on raised platforms.[60] One of the main points Hadfield emphasizes is that many previous studies of the night-time economy have tended to focus on individual elements of social control, such as venue design or managerial style. He argues that it is important to understand that control is in fact exerted as a result of a complex and interconnecting orchestration of a range of factors – including design of premises, music, lighting, and the expertise of *all* the staff (DJs, bar staff, security staff, managers) who work together as a team:

In high street venues, the maximal balancing of intoxication and control is regarded as a corporate goal which enhances profitability. The manipulation of customer mood and behaviour must comprise an artful mix of various elements. Security measures are applied with fortitude, and the creation of a 'safe' and 'controlled' environment is inevitably a hard-won accomplishment, achieved only through the sustained efforts of strategic and co-operative interactional performance. Such accomplishments require emotional management, careful orchestration, loyalty, and attention to detail.[61]

This research illustrates once more the advantage of adopting an integrated theory approach to the study of the legal system. These informal modes of policing fall completely outside the traditional boundaries of the legal system.

---

[59]  P. Hadfield, *Bar Wars: Contesting the Night in Contemporary British Cities* (2006) Oxford University Press, Oxford, p. 88.                                             [60]  Hadfield (2006) p. 95.
[61]  Hadfield (2006) pp. 115–16.

# Interaction with the criminal justice system

Many studies have shown that in the enforcement of regulation, there is a tendency for enforcement agents to prefer to secure compliance with the regulations with which they are concerned, rather than to prosecute offenders.[62] In an early study, published in 1970, Carson looked at the enforcement practices of factory inspectors and found that their preferred methods of enforcement were the least threatening procedures available to them, such as warnings, and that prosecutions were rare. A major factor in this strategy was the inspectors' perception of themselves not as industrial police officers, concerned with apprehending and punishing offenders, but as persons whose main function was to secure compliance with the standards laid down, thus achieving the ultimate goal of the legislation, the improvement of safety standards.[63] Similarly, Weait, writing about the Industrial Air Pollution Inspectorate, noted that inspectors preferred to work with companies to help achieve better standards rather than to impose punitive sanctions. It was only if the offending company's attitude was in some way morally culpable that the inspectorate would move willingly to prosecution. In other cases, a policy of securing cooperation was followed, a policy which was disrupted only if a complaint was received, or an incident was so serious that people were harmed or when influential people (such as councillors) or groups (such as Friends of the Earth) took an interest.[64] As far as the formal criminal justice system is concerned, this means that many incidents which would otherwise be prosecuted and fall squarely within the formal system are being dealt with in other ways.

Hawkins argues that there are two major strategies of enforcement available to enforcement agents, which he terms 'compliance' and 'sanctioning'. A compliance strategy involves a conciliatory approach, where the attitude is to assist those in trouble, whereas a sanctioning strategy adopts a penal style, punishing breaches of the relevant code. This latter strategy involves a high degree of interaction with the formal legal system, whereas with a compliance strategy, recourse to the formal legal system is seen as a last resort.[65] These two strategies can be seen as two extremes of a continuum, and any particular agency may be operating simultaneously at several points on the continuum, so that its interaction with the legal system is highly complex.

Hawkins found in his study of the control of water pollution that prosecutions were rare. The field officers whom he observed preferred to gain the cooperation of their clients with a view to increasing compliance with the relevant regulations, regarding prosecution as a last resort. Prosecution was not seen as a helpful tool in securing

---

[62] See, for example, W. G. Carson, 'White-collar Crime and the Enforcement of Factory Legislation' (1970) 10 British Journal of Criminology 383; I. Paulus, *The Search for Pure Food: A Sociology of Legislation in Britain* (1974) Martin Robertson, London. For discussion of earlier studies see, K. Hawkins, *Environment and Enforcement* (1984) Clarendon Press, Oxford, p. 3.          [63] Carson (1970) pp. 391–2.

[64] M. Weait, 'The Letter of the Law?' (1989) 29 British Journal of Criminology 57.

[65] Hawkins (1984) p. 2.

compliance, because it destroys the relationship between officer and client, thus sacrificing any influence the officer might otherwise have had. Prosecution also involves a lot of work and disrupts the other activities of the agency, and Hawkins found that in practice prosecutions tended to occur only when the officer had exhausted all other tactical possibilities, but had still failed to secure compliance.[66] However, prosecutions did occur, so that it was clear that at least on some occasions, officers were prepared to adopt a sanctioning strategy.

The type of enforcement strategy which is adopted by any particular agency appeared to be influenced by a number of different factors. Hawkins argues that where the deviant behaviour is essentially a discrete activity and appears straightforward, a penal response is likely, whereas if the deviance is a state of affairs rather than an isolated act – unfenced machinery, a leaking pipe – then the behaviour tends to be characterized as a 'problem' and a compliance strategy is used.

Another significant factor was the attitude of the officials concerned. In Hawkins' study, the field officers tended to regard their job as educative rather than penal. Their perception of an illegal act of pollution as a 'problem' rather than a 'crime' leads to them defining a large proportion of cases as outside the proper province of the criminal law: 'To enforce the law against the blameless is to diminish the moral authority of that law.'[67] Lidstone et al. emphasized that even the agencies which had a high level of involvement in prosecution did not regard criminal law enforcement as their primary function, and that the decision to prosecute, always a matter of discretion, was further complicated by its inextricable relationship with a much wider set of policy considerations.[68]

Hawkins also argues that the type of victim is significant; if personal injury is involved, it provokes a sanctioning strategy, but a compliance strategy is often used where there is no readily identifiable victim and harm has been suffered by 'the general public'.[69] His study also revealed that the staff of the agency provided another significant factor in the decision as to which type of enforcement strategy was used. Frequently, those field officers who had joined the agency more recently were more highly educated than their predecessors and saw pollution control as a scientific matter, calling for the application of scientific principles. They also tended to see the formal legal process as the primary means by which pollution is to be controlled, leading to their use of a sanctioning strategy. For older officers, pollution control was less about the application of scientifically derived principles and more about managing relationships. They preferred a compliance strategy, negotiating wherever possible and regarding the formal legal system as the last resort.[70]

Hawkins identified several other factors which influence the enforcement strategy which will be adopted in relation to a particular incident. Public relations play an important role; regulatory agencies operate in a public arena and are sensitive to

---

[66] Hawkins (1984) ch. 10.      [67] Hawkins (1984) p. 205.      [68] Lidstone et al. (1980) ch. 3.
[69] Hawkins (1984) pp. 6–7.      [70] Hawkins (1984) ch. 3.

public opinion. In the case of water authorities, the conflicting demands of environ-
mentalists and of businesses have to be balanced when considering prosecution, and
the degree to which the agency turns to prosecution will depend to some extent on its
perception of the relative strength of these two constituencies. The law is used when
the enforcers can rely on what they perceive to be a consensus of values. The legal process has a symbolic role, in that it censures morally blameworthy conduct.[71]

The moral culpability of the offender is also a significant factor in the decision to
prosecute. Apart from major incidents, where action has to be taken regardless of
fault, it is the extent of the moral culpability of those involved which makes prosecution more or less likely. In cases of persistent failure to comply, prosecution was
highly likely, since it was necessary to preserve the credibility of the agency and its
officers. Equally, if an incident occurred which caused substantial and noticeable
damage, or involved the agency in heavy expenditure, prosecution was necessary to
show that the agency was fulfilling its public duty, and here action would be taken
regardless of blame, for such cases demand a symbolic display of authority by the
agency.[72]

Enforcement agents enforce a code of behaviour which corresponds with their perceptions of the moral sentiments of the community. This results in a highly selective use of prosecution, since pollution incidents are frequently not clear-cut in moral
terms. Officers see pollution as occurring because of limited economic resources, inefficient management, carelessness, or accident, all of which are highly ambiguous in
moral terms. In addition, the complex industrial settings in which many incidents
occur make it difficult for an officer to establish a clear chain of causation so as to
ensure that blame is fairly allocated. It is a relatively small number of wrongdoers who
satisfy the officers' moral view of just desserts so as to justify prosecution.[73]

Prosecution also serves another purpose, in that it provides visible evidence that
the agency is doing its job. Successful prosecutions illustrate the effectiveness of the
agency. However, having recourse to the legal system moves affairs into a very public
arena, so there are strong incentives only to prosecute cases which are highly likely
to result in a conviction. The agency regards losing a case as highly inefficient from a
deterrence point of view, so is keen to ensure that this does not occur.[74]

From the point of view of the criminal justice system, it is interesting to note the
extent to which the public police cooperate with and are to an extent dependent on,
other agencies in respect of the investigation and prosecution of criminal offences.
Lidstone et al. cited the example of the Drugs Inspectorate, involved in enforcing legislation relating to drug manufacture, distribution, and use. The researchers noted that
the work of the Inspectorate was largely confined to the inspection of manufacturers
and wholesale distributors and the investigation of alleged cases of over-prescribing
of controlled drugs. Cases could be conducted in conjunction with the police, who

[71] Hawkins (1984) ch. 10.    [72] Hawkins (1984) ch. 10.    [73] Hawkins (1984) ch. 10.
[74] Hawkins (1984) ch. 10.

would then handle any prosecution. Where there was no police involvement, cases were referred directly to the DPP.[75]

The Lidstone study also revealed that many of the smaller agencies routinely rely on the police to help in the investigation and where possible, prosecution of offenders. The RSPCA, for example, brings specialist knowledge to the area in which it works, but has limited resources and many other animal welfare commitments which tend to prevent it from routinely investigating and prosecuting all the offences reported to it. In relation to agencies such as the RSPB, the NSPCC, and the RSPCA, there is a certain dependence in relation to investigation and prosecution on the police or on government departments. This relationship of dependency is often regarded as highly unsatisfactory by the private agencies, because of the limited interest and frequent lack of specialist expertise in the public sector. Often, effective law enforcement in these areas may be dependent upon the quality of the informal relationships between personnel in different agencies. Consequently, private agencies regard their own ability to bring prosecutions as an important safeguard against the ignorance or inertia of public bodies.[76]

Lidstone et al. also identified more than 20 statutory or private police forces, about half of which were involved in the prosecution of offences. In the majority of these forces, more serious crimes are passed to the traditional police for investigation, but in some forces, such as the British Transport Police, almost all offences are investigated and prosecuted independently of the traditional police force. Interestingly, it was also true of these forces that their prosecution policy tended to be strongly affected by the perceived functions and obligations of the organization, so that river police, whose primary function is the conservation of rivers, tended to prosecute pollution offences routinely, though in other areas of their work they tried to educate, rather than to punish. Park police saw their function as preserving amenities for the use of the general public, and whilst they were hard on vandalism, they tended to deal with most breaches of park byelaws by warning offenders, rather than prosecuting them.[77]

## Further interaction between public police and private agencies

In the context of this discussion about the interaction between the public police and other policing agencies, it is also appropriate to draw attention to some of the ways in which the police have divested themselves of some policing activities, which have then been taken over by the private security industry. Button has pointed to the effects of 'load-shedding' and 'contracting out' by the police, both of which have resulted in private security carrying out functions which were formerly the province of the

---

[75] Lidstone et al. (1980) ch. 4.    [76] Lidstone et al. (1980) ch. 4.    [77] Lidstone et al. (1980) ch. 7.

public police.[78] 'Load-shedding' involves consciously moving services from the public to the private sector. Sometimes, the police abandon certain functions altogether; for example, they no longer escort cash-in-transit vehicles, which they once did routinely, and they have greatly limited their response to intruder alarms. In both these cases, private security firms have stepped in to undertake the policing activity. In addition to load-shedding, a wide range of police functions have been contracted out to the private sector. One of the most well-known examples of this is escorting prisoners. Following the enactment of the Criminal Justice Act 1991, this activity, formerly carried out by police and prison officers, was transferred to a number of private security firms.

## CONCLUSION

In this discussion of private security and other non-police enforcement agencies, we have tried to show the need for an integrated theory of justice. In particular, such a theory allows us to conceptualize, not only the traditional formal English criminal justice system, but also to include those other forms of social control which interact with the traditional institutions and play a hitherto unacknowledged role in the system as a whole.

## FURTHER READING

BUTTON, M., *Security Officers and Policing: Powers, Culture and Control in the Governance of Private Space* (2007) Ashgate, Aldershot.

JONES, T. and NEWBURN, T., *Private Security and Public Policing* (1998) Clarendon Press, Oxford.

---

[78]  Button (2002) ch. 3.

# 13

# The public police: uncovering crime and powers of stop and search

## INTRODUCTION

This section of the book focuses on the public police, rather than private policing. However, in accordance with the integrated theory on which the book is based, examples of the interaction of the public police and other actors within the criminal justice system will be discussed.

## Uncovering crime

### The public's role in uncovering crime

The number of offences with which the criminal justice system deals is generally acknowledged to be less than the number of offences which actually take place. That is because a large number of offences are not reported to the police, and therefore do not feature in statistics relating to recorded crime.[1]

The police play a surprisingly small role in actually uncovering crime. Research for the Royal Commission on Criminal Procedure (the Philips Commission), which reported in 1981,[2] showed that the great majority of offences were reported to the police, either by the victim or someone acting on the victim's behalf, and that when crimes reported by witnesses were also taken into account, it meant that 75 to 80 per cent of crimes are reported to the police by ordinary members of the public, rather

---

[1] A. K. Bottomley and K. Pease, *Crime and Punishment: Interpreting the Data* (1986) Open University Press, Milton Keynes, p. 25. The official crime statistics are increasingly being replaced by other sources of data about crime (see M. Maguire, 'Crime Data and Statistics' in M. Maguire, R. Morgan and R. Reiner (eds), *The Oxford Handbook of Criminology* (4th edn, 2007) Oxford University Press, Oxford).

[2] Royal Commission on Criminal Procedure, *Report* (the Philips Report) (1981a) Cmnd 8092, HMSO, London.

than the police discovering the crimes for themselves.[3] In addition, the same research study showed that a significant number of offences are discovered by the police when they are admitted by persons who are in custody or because the police find stolen property in the possession of persons who have been arrested.[4] Thus, police officers play only a very small role in the discovery of offences. This data is confirmed by other similar research studies,[5] including research carried out for the Royal Commission on Criminal Justice (the Runciman Commission), which reported in 1993, which found that the initial source of information linking the suspect to the offence came from the police themselves in only 37 per cent of cases.[6]

Not only do the police play a surprisingly small role in uncovering crime, but it has also been discovered that members of the public play an important role in carrying out some policing activities, as well as in bringing matters to the attention of the police. The importance of informal social control exercised by ordinary citizens is emphasized in the work of Shapland and Vagg, who investigated the nature of informal social control in both villages and urban centres, discovering not only that ordinary citizens carry out certain types of policing activities themselves, but that interaction between informal and formal processes of social control is of vital importance:[7]

We argue that the actions, and more particularly, the effectiveness of major public institutions such as the police depend crucially upon these processes of informal social control.[8]

The interaction between the police and members of the public is largely ignored by 'English legal system' textbooks, yet it is arguable that such relationships are fundamental to the operation of the formal legal system. An integrated theory of justice can encompass such phenomena with ease, for its basis is that the legal world is composed of many such interactions, both between parts of the formal legal system and informal processes of social control, and between different parts of the formal system and different processes of social control.

Shapland and Vagg studied two groups of villages and four city districts, all of which appeared, prima facie, to be considered as neighbourhoods or communities by the people living and working in them. The researchers observed what went on, talked to people, and finally used semi-structured interviews to build up a rich picture of concerns held by members of the communities about matters of social control, and

---

[3] D. Steer, *Uncovering Crime: The Police Role*, Royal Commission on Criminal Procedure Research Study No. 7 (1980) HMSO, London.                                          [4] Steer (1980) pp. 66–71.

[5] For example, R. Mawby, *Policing the City* (1979) Saxon House, Farnborough; M. Zander, 'The Investigation of Crime: A Study of Cases Tried at the Old Bailey' (1979) Criminal Law Review 203; M. McConville and J. Baldwin, *Courts, Prosecution and Conviction* (1981) Clarendon Press, Oxford.

[6] M. McConville, *Corroboration and Confessions: The Impact of a Rule Requiring that No Conviction can be Sustained on the Basis of Confession Evidence Alone* (1993) Royal Commission on Criminal Justice Research Study No. 13, HMSO, London, p. 12.

[7] J. Shapland and J. Vagg, *Policing by the Public* (1988) Routledge, London.

[8] Shapland and Vagg (1988) p. 6.

about the formal and informal processes of social control which existed in the areas being studied.

The researchers found that when they asked people about problems in their area, a comparatively small list of problems, very similar in all areas, accounted for the majority of all problems mentioned.[9] Damage to property, problems with parked cars (other people's cars outside one's own house, parking on pavements and grassed areas, obstruction by lorries), noise (diverse sources, including low-flying military planes, farm machinery, traffic, lorries, nightclubs), and teenagers (hanging about, looking as if they were 'up to something', sometimes acting rudely) accounted for a large part of the problems raised. In the urban areas, crime was also seen as a major problem. In each area, some of these problems were continuous, some were sporadic.

It was noted that, while there were common themes, many problems were localized in time and space, their occurrence limited to early mornings or later evenings and to specific areas, such as particular street corners, back alleys, or bus shelters.[10] The extreme localization and diversity of problems meant that any effective solution also had to be very specific, and the researchers found that many informal social processes existed which attempted to ameliorate the situation. The process of informal social control starts with someone seeing something, classifying it as problematic in some way and deciding that something must be done about it. Shapland and Vagg noted that people watched their neighbours' activities and that in both urban and rural areas this was generally regarded as a socially desirable practice. 'I love it, it's not really nosy, it's caring about what's going on', explained one respondent.[11] People who watched tended to fall into two categories: the elderly, who were more likely to be at home during the day and saw watching as a service they could perform for their neighbours; and businesspeople, working in shops, garages, pubs, as farmers or delivering goods. People who were working frequently monitored what was going on outside their place of business.[12]

When they looked at what it was that people noticed in this context, Shapland and Vagg discovered that people remembered things they regarded as 'suspicious'. Suspicious incidents or people were those which did not fall into the watchers' view of how life was generally lived in their area, so that suspicious incidents all involved conduct which was seen to be deviant or was disapproved of. Suspicious happenings usually involved somebody doing something, rather than inanimate objects in odd places. Men, particularly adult, unknown men, were often thought to be 'up to something'.[13]

Once something has been noticed, the next step is for the observer to decide what to do about it. A range of possible options extends from informal responses such as continuing to watch or discussing an event with family and friends to interaction with the formal legal system, by contacting the police. Shapland and Vagg found that the

---

[9] Shapland and Vagg (1988) p. 47.    [10] Shapland and Vagg (1988) p. 64.
[11] Shapland and Vagg (1988) p. 68.    [12] Shapland and Vagg (1988) p. 70.
[13] Shapland and Vagg (1988) p. 79.

clearest situation in which the police would definitely be called was an instance of real crime. In these situations the offence would be regarded, once reported, as becoming the responsibility of the police and they would be expected to take the decision as to how to proceed.[14] However, other interactions with the police also took place, because the police were also called to a wide range of other kinds of incident, some of which had no criminal content at all, for example if the watchers felt they could not cope with a particular kind of suspect. The assistance of the police might also be sought when informal options had been tried and failed, or where the problem seemed to be getting worse. Interestingly, from the point of view of an integrated theory of justice, the police also became involved more informally, for example if there was a known local officer an informal chat might take place. People in the community known to have a relationship with a local police officer might be 'briefed' to bring about such informal contacts.[15]

The informal social control we found operating in our areas was crucially tied in with the activities of the police and other agencies of formal social control...We found informal and formal control to be dependent on each other.[16]

Although the majority of policing remains 'reactive' rather than 'proactive', the Government has been keen to encourage proactive policing to deal with certain types of crime and anti-social behaviour.[17] This has led to new kinds of relationships between the police and local communities being fostered through neighbourhood policing teams and 'reassurance'-style policing, whereby the police are under pressure to provide a visible street presence to tackle low-level crime and disorder.[18] Sanders et al. observe: 'that the police are here engaged in a distinctive form of reactive policing. Rather than responding to reports of specific incidents or crimes, they are being asked to react to more generalised anxieties and concerns.'[19]

It is this kind of interdependency between informal and formal processes of social control which is generally ignored by textbooks dealing with 'the English legal system', but which in fact serves to emphasize once again the need for an integrative, pluralistic theory of justice, which can encompass all such relationships without ignoring a large part of what goes to make up the English legal world.

## The police's role in uncovering crime

Even if the importance of the public's role in the criminal justice system is acknowledged in the way suggested above, it is still necessary for the police to process the information which is brought to their attention, using their professional

---

[14] Shapland and Vagg (1988) p. 107.     [15] Shapland and Vagg (1988) p. 108.
[16] Shapland and Vagg (1988) p. 181.
[17] A. Sanders, R. Young, and M. Burton, *Criminal Justice* (4th edn, 2010) Oxford University Press, Oxford, pp. 62–5.
[18] A. Henry and D. Smith (eds), *Transformations of Policing* (2007) Ashgate, Aldershot.
[19] Sanders et al. (2010) p. 64.

expertise to analyse it and see whether it can be used for their purposes, for example in crime prevention or crime control. Police discretion is central even in reactive policing. It also remains the case that the state has given the police extensive powers which may assist them in uncovering crime: powers of search, arrest, and detention of persons, and seizure of property. These powers allow the police to behave in ways which would otherwise constitute torts or crimes (for example, false imprisonment, assault, or theft). They also have the effect of permitting infringements of civil liberties.[20] Since the powers given have such serious consequences, the state has also provided a legal framework for the way in which they are to be exercised, laying down conditions as to the circumstances in which they may be used.

The most important piece of legislation in this area is the Police and Criminal Evidence Act 1984 (PACE). This Act largely implemented the recommendations of the Philips Commission,[21] whose terms of reference were to review the criminal process from the start of investigation to the point of trial.[22] The Philips Commission itself arose out of concerns felt about the investigation of the rising amount of crime in society. Two opposing strands of opinion had emerged: that effective investigation of crime was being hampered by the restraints of criminal procedure; or, on the other hand, that the police were abusing the investigative powers which they had.[23]

In carrying out its work, the Philips Commission stressed the concept of a 'fundamental balance'.[24] This was the balance which it felt had to be drawn between the interests of the community in bringing offenders to justice, and the right of the individual citizen not to have their civil liberties arbitrarily infringed. Drawing this kind of balance, as the Commission rightly pointed out, raised difficult questions, for example about how community interest was defined.[25] The Commission proceeded by undertaking an analysis of existing police powers. It found that powers of stop and search were highly fragmented,[26] and recommended a single, uniform, nationally applicable power of stop and search, based on reasonable suspicion and subject to strict safeguards.[27]

It is this objective which s. 1 of PACE tried to achieve. However, the proliferation of stop and search powers since PACE was enacted has undermined the legislative objective to require reasonable suspicion of specific offences.

---

[20] On this aspect, see D. Feldman, *Civil Liberties and Human Rights in England and Wales* (2nd edn, 2002) Oxford University Press, Oxford, ch. 6.    [21] Philips Report (1981a) Cmnd 8092.

[22] Philips Report (1981a) para. 1.1.    [23] Philips Report (1981a) para. 1.2.

[24] Philips Report (1981a) paras 1.11ff.    [25] Philips Report (1981a) para. 1.11.

[26] There was no general, nationally applicable power to stop and search. In some areas of the country, the police were able to rely on statutes of local application. Although some nationally applicable powers of stop and search did exist, there was no common rationale to these powers (Philips Report (1981a) para. 1.20ff).    [27] Philips Report (1981a) para. 3.17.

## The legal powers to stop and search

Section 1 of PACE allows a constable to stop and search a person or vehicle in a place to which the public has access,[28] provided that he or she has reasonable grounds for suspecting that they will find stolen articles, prohibited articles, or an article relating to offences under s. 139 of the Criminal Justice Act 1988 (i.e., offences relating to having, in a public place, an article with a blade or sharp point, other than a folding pocketknife with a blade less than three inches long).[29] Prohibited articles include offensive weapons or articles made or adapted for use in connection with a number of listed offences, including burglary, theft, and taking a motor vehicle without authority.[30] The Criminal Justice Act 2003 added items intended for causing criminal damage to this list of offences and the Serious Organised Crime and Police Act 2005 added prohibited fireworks.[31]

It is crucial that the constable has reasonable grounds for suspecting that they will find the relevant articles. The question of what constitutes a reasonable ground of suspicion is a difficult one, which clearly gives the police officer on the street a wide discretion. It is a concept which is used in relation to a large number of statutory powers of stop and search, apart from the power in s. 1 of PACE. The difficulty of the concept was recognized when the Act was drafted, but the Royal Commission felt that it would be impracticable to give a comprehensive definition of matters which might give rise to reasonable suspicion.[32] Discussion of pre-PACE cases on police powers, where the powers were restricted by the requirement that a police officer had to have 'reasonable grounds' or 'reasonable cause' for exercising a particular power, suggests that the courts do not find such concepts easy to deal with, resulting in apparently irreconcilable decisions.[33] The post-PACE case law suggests that the courts do not find the concept of reasonable suspicion any easier to deal with.[34]

Some light is shed on the concept of reasonable suspicion by the Code of Practice for the Exercise by Police Officers of Statutory Powers of Stop and Search (Code A). Section 66 of PACE imposes a duty on the Home Secretary to issue a number of Codes of Practice of which Code A is one. A revised version of Code A came into force in January 2009.[35] The object of Code A is to assist police officers with their implementation not only of PACE, but of all the other statutory powers of stop and search to which

---

[28] PACE, s. 1(1) and (2).

[29] PACE, s. 1(3). Note the detailed interaction between different subsections. The section must be read closely.                                                                      [30] PACE, s. 1(7).

[31] Criminal Justice Act 2003, s. 1 and the Serious Organised Crime and Police Act 2005, s. 115.

[32] Royal Commission on Criminal Procedure (1981) para. 3.25.

[33] S. Bailey and D. Birch, 'Recent Developments in the Law of Police Powers' (1982) Criminal Law Review 475.                                                        [34] Sanders et al. (2010) p. 74.

[35] The Codes are published in a separate booklet: Police and Criminal Evidence Act 1984 (ss. 60(1)(a) and 66) Codes of Practice A–H. They can be downloaded from the Home Office website at: <http://www.homeoffice.gov.uk>. References here are to the revised edition in force from January 2009.

it applies. Interestingly, the Act expressly provides that persons other than police officers who are charged with investigating offences are also required to 'have regard' to
relevant provisions of such codes of practice.[36] This subsection points to yet another
instance when persons other than the police become involved in policing activities.
The personnel involved here are immigration officers or customs and excise officers
who are charged, under the relevant legislation, with investigating offences. This is
another example of the need for an integrated theory of justice which can encompass
the existence of a wide range of persons taking part in the policing activities of the
formal legal system.

A list of powers of stop and search requiring 'reasonable suspicion' to which Code
A is given as the Annex to the Code, and includes searching for firearms, controlled
drugs, poaching equipment, and evidence of wildlife offences. Annex A to the Code
also includes a list of other stop and search powers which *do not* require reasonable
suspicion at the time of the stop and search but to which Code A and other parts of
PACE apply. They include the powers to stop and search in anticipation of incidents
involving serious violence found in s. 60 of the Criminal Justice and Public Order Act
1994. Section 60(1) of the 1994 Act provides that an officer of or above the rank of
inspector may authorize police officers to stop and search people and/or vehicles for
offensive weapons or dangerous instruments provided that he or she:

reasonably believes –

   (a) that incidents involving serious violence may take place in any locality in his police
       area, and that it is expedient to give authorisation under this section to prevent their
       occurrence,[37] or
   (b) that persons are carrying dangerous instruments or offensive weapons in any locality
       in his police area without good reason.[38]

Section 87 of the Serious Crimes Act 2007 extended s. 60 to enable authorization to
be made if the authorizing officer reasonably believes that an incident involving serious violence has taken place in that officer's police area, that a weapon or dangerous
instrument used in that incident is being carried in any locality within that area, and
it is expedient to give an authorization to find that article.

Section 44 of the Terrorism Act 2000 provides a similar power to conduct searches
in a particular locality if it appears to a senior police officer that it is expedient
to have such powers in order to look for articles that could be used in connection
with the commission, preparation, or instigation of acts of terrorism. It should
be noted that there is no need for individualized reasonable suspicion where the
blanket authorization under s. 60 or s. 44 is in place. The authorization that can be
given under s. 44 of the Terrorism Act may cover an entire police area. The House of
Lords has upheld the practice of issuing successive authorizations for the whole of

---

[36]  PACE, s. 67(9).        [37]  Criminal Justice and Public Order Act 1994, s. 60(1).
[38]  PACE, s. 60(1) as amended by the Knives Act 1997.

London.[39] However, the European Court of Human Rights recently ruled that the powers interfered with the right to a private life under Article 8 as they were 'neither sufficiently circumscribed nor subject to adequate legal safeguards against abuse'.[40] The Government is likely to challenge this conclusion but if it is unsuccessful, then a change to domestic law and policy is likely to be required. However, even if this led to a reasonable suspicion requirement for all stop and searches, the impact on police practice, for example in terms of preventing discrimination in the use of powers, might be limited.

Code A tries to explain, in everyday language, various aspects of statutory stop and search powers. It includes a statement of principle that: 'Powers to stop and search must be used fairly, responsibly, with respect for people being searched and without unlawful discrimination.'[41] This addition to the Code was partly a response to research, examined below, showing the differential use of powers in relation to ethnic minority and white people. Thus, the opening statement of Code A continues with a reminder that: 'The Race Relations (Amendment) Act 2000 makes it unlawful for police officers to discriminate on the grounds of race, colour, ethnic origin, nationality or national origins when using their powers.'[42]

As far as the concept of reasonable suspicion is concerned, Code A emphasizes that there must be an objective basis for the suspicion based on facts, information, and intelligence.[43] It states that reasonable suspicion should never be based on personal factors alone without reliable supporting intelligence or information or some specific behaviour by the person concerned.[44]

This new emphasis on information and intelligence in the revised version of the Code is somewhat diluted in subsequent paragraphs, which illustrate how reasonable suspicion can sometimes exist without specific information or intelligence. However, in the 2009 version of the Code it is asserted:

For example, other than in a witness description of a suspect, a person's colour, age, appearance, or the fact that he is known to have a previous conviction, cannot be used alone or in combination with each other as the reason for searching that person. Reasonable suspicion cannot be based on generalisations or stereotypical images of certain groups or categories of people as more likely to be involved in criminal activity. A person's religion cannot be considered as reasonable grounds for suspicion and should never be considered as a reason to stop or to stop and search an individual.[45]

The reference to a person's religion was a new addition to the Code, following the London underground bombings in July 2005 which led to concern that the police were

---

[39]  R (on the application of Gillan) v Commissioner of Police of the Metropolis [2006] 2 WLR 537 (HL).
[40]  Gillan and Quinton v the United Kingdom (Application no. 4158/05) Judgment 12 January 2010.
[41]  Code A, para. 1.1.
[42]  Code A, para. 1.1. See L. Lustgarten, 'The Future of Stop and Search' [2002] Criminal Law Review 603. Lustgarten analyses the significance of the Race Relations (Amendment Act) 2002 for the legality of stop and search in the context of the evidence of 'direct' and 'indirect' discrimination in empirical research on the use of those powers.      [43]  Code A, para. 2.2.      [44]  Code A, para. 2.2.      [45]  Code A, para. 2.2.

targeting Muslims.[46] The emphasis on the objective nature of the concept of reasonable suspicion and the statement that it should normally be linked to accurate and reliable information and intelligence is related to arguments that such searches are more likely to be effective, minimizing inconvenience to law-abiding members of the public and helping to justify searches.[47]

## Stop and search in practice

Pre-PACE there was considerable controversy about the use of stop and search powers, notably the 'sus' laws which researchers found disproportionately impacted upon certain communities.[48] The resentment felt, particularly among the black community, about the use of stop and search powers, was a major contributing factor to the Brixton riots which took place in 1981.[49] Research for the Home Office in 1983 showed that black people, particularly young black males, were much more likely to be stopped and searched than white people.[50] However, the proportion of persons stopped who were subsequently prosecuted was the same for blacks as whites, thus raising the suspicion that black persons were stopped unnecessarily.[51]

The controversy about discriminatory use of stop and search powers continued well beyond repeal of the 'sus' laws and the enactment of PACE. In the post-PACE decade, there was a large number of research studies which showed that a disproportionate number of black people are stopped and searched by the police.[52] Despite the best efforts of various versions of Code A, it appeared that the racially discriminatory aspect of policing did not change significantly,[53] as the MacPherson Inquiry into the death of Stephen Lawrence seemed to confirm.[54] The Inquiry found evidence

---

[46] N. Chakraborti, 'Policing Muslim Communities' in M. Rowe (ed.) *Policing beyond Macpherson* (2007) Willan, Cullompton.    [47] Code A, paras 2.4 and 2.5.

[48] The 'sus' laws (repealed by the Criminal Attempts Act 1981) were contained in s. 4 of the Vagrancy Act 1824. They prohibited 'every suspected person or thief' from loitering in a variety of places, including the street, with intent to commit an arrestable offence. Use of 'sus' law powers by the police had had adverse effects on police relations with the public, especially with young black males. Having a record of past criminal encounters with the police also put one at substantially greater risk of being stopped, as did going out frequently at night and driving a car a great deal. W. Skogan, *The Police and Public in England and Wales – A British Crime Survey Report* (1990) Home Office Research Study No. 117, Home Office, London.

[49] Lord Scarman, *The Brixton Disorders* (1981) Cmnd 8427, HMSO, London.

[50] C. Willis, *The Use, Effectiveness and Impact of Police Stop and Search Powers* (1983) Home Office Research and Policy Planning Unit Paper No. 15, Home Office, London. See also D. Smith and J. Gray, *Police and People in London: Volume 4: The Police in Action* (1983b) Policy Studies Institute, London, p. 322.

[51] Willis (1983) p. 22.

[52] See, for example, C. Norris, N. Fielding, C. Kemp, and J. Fielding, 'Black and Blue: An Analysis of the Influence of Race on Being Stopped by the Police' (1992) 43(2) British Journal of Sociology 207; P. Southgate and D. Crisp, *Public Satisfaction with Police Services* (1993) Home Office Research and Planning Unit Paper No. 73, Home Office, London; T. Jefferson and M. Walker, 'Ethnic Minorities in the Criminal Justice System' (1992) Criminal Law Review 83.

[53] D. Brown, *PACE Ten Years On: A Review of the Research* (1997) Home Office Research Study No. 155, HMSO, London, ch. 2.

[54] Sir W. MacPherson, *The Stephen Lawrence Inquiry* (1999) Cm. 4262-I, The Stationery Office, London.

of 'institutional racism' in the disproportionate application of police stop and search powers to black people.[55] Fitzgerald noted that the finding of 'institutional racism' had a deleterious effect on morale in the Metropolitan Police.[56] It also seemed to precipitate a decline in the use of stop and search powers, which have since recovered to their pre-MacPherson levels.[57]

Fitzgerald's detailed study of stop and search in London highlighted a number of reasons why the exercise of the stop and search power is so controversial. The public nature of a stop and search (in contrast to many other encounters with the police, which take place more privately) is an important factor. Equally important is police behaviour – whether officers are polite, their skill in handling confrontation, and their ability to give an adequate explanation for their actions. Following the MacPherson Inquiry, the Home Office commissioned a programme of research on stop and search.[58] The research, like Fitzgerald's, found people are less satisfied with stop and search encounters when they are not given convincing explanations or not treated politely and fairly. Ethnic minorities were more likely to experience these problems.[59] In terms of public trust and confidence, it was the officers' attitude and the way that they dealt with people that was more important than the procedure followed.[60] Whilst the recording requirement made some officers 'think twice' about stop and searches, others saw it as an imposition.[61] In the five areas where the MacPherson recommendation for recording all stops and all searches (whether consensual or not) was piloted, the researchers found under-recording of searches.[62]

The research examining *origins of suspicion* for stop and searches found wide variation in officers' understanding of the concept of reasonable suspicion and noted that the legal requirement of reasonable suspicion is probably not fulfilled for some searches.[63] The researchers found that there are a wide range of factors which arouse police suspicion. Some of these factors might be described as 'working' rules rather than legal rules,[64] although the two are not necessarily different. Thus, a significant proportion

[55] L. Bridges, 'The Lawrence Inquiry – Incompetence, Corruption, and Institutional Racism' (1999) 26(3) Journal of Law and Society 298. The Inquiry made recommendations for the introduction of a number of further 'controls' on stop and searches (see MacPherson (1999), recommendations 61–3).

[56] M. Fitzgerald, *Searches in London* (1999b) Metropolitan Police Service, London.

[57] D. Povey and K. Smith (eds), *Police Powers and Procedures, England and Wales 2007/08* (2009) Home Office Statistical Bulletin 7/09, Home Office, London.

[58] For an overview of this research, see J. Miller, P. Quinton, and N. Bland, *Police Stops and Searches: Lessons from a Programme of Research* (2000) Police Home Office Briefing Note, Home Office, London.

[59] J. Miller, N. Bland, and P. Quinton, *The Impact of Stops and Searches on Crime and the Community* (2000) Police Research Series Paper No. 127, Home Office, London.

[60] N. Bland, J. Miller, and P. Quinton, *Upping the PACE? An Evaluation of the Recommendations of the Stephen Lawrence Inquiry on Stops and Searches* (2000) Police Research Series Paper No. 128, Home Office, London. See also V. Stone and N. Pettigrew, *The Views of the Public on Stops and Searches* (2000) Police Research Series Paper No. 129, Home Office, London.          [61] Bland et al. (2000).

[62] Bland et al. (2000).

[63] P. Quinton, N. Bland, and J. Miller, *Police Stops, Decision-making and Practice* (2000) Police Research Series Paper No. 130, Home Office, London.

[64] The concept of 'working rules' is discussed in the next chapter in relation to arrest decision-making.

of officers said that they might be prompted to stop a person it they were young. A person's clothing and appearance were also significant – for example, wearing a baseball cap or hooded top signalled to the police officer that the person might be 'up to no good'.[65] The type of vehicle, either those with defects, cars which are commonly stolen, or expensive cars (particularly if being driven by ethnic minorities) were the focus of officers' attention.[66] 'Being out of place' or 'standing out', based on officers' perceptions of what was 'normal' for the area, might result in a person being stopped to find out what they were doing.[67] Although officers in the study claimed not to carry out stops and searches because of a person's ethnicity, there was evidence that ethnicity perhaps played a part on some occasions and was certainly linked to other influential factors like clothing and being incongruent.[68] Being known to the police and suspicious activity like loitering, checking out cars, and trying to avoid being seen generated suspicion.[69] Time and place are also key factors both in terms of determining the availability of officers and making individuals more suspicious.[70] In the latter respect young people and ethnic minorities appear to suffer as a result of being out at 'unusual' times.[71]

The debate about whether the police are racially discriminatory in the exercise of their stop and search powers has been taken forward by research which aims to compare the use of stop and search powers with the 'available' population. It has been argued that when the use of powers is compared with the population available in public places to be stopped and searched, then the evidence of direct discrimination looks weaker than the bare statistics on the proportion of ethnic minorities stopped and searched might otherwise suggest. Waddington and his colleagues replicated Home Office research which found ethnic minorities were at greater risk of being stopped by the police due to their use of public space. Black males are more likely to be on the streets in city centres at times of the day when the police are carrying out most of their stop and searches.[72] They conclude: 'whatever mechanisms drive "institutional racism", they are unlikely to be as simple as police officers' targeting people for stop and search on the basis of racial stereotypes'.[73] However, the conclusions of studies such as these are open to debate due to methodological limitations, such as the difficulties that the researchers had in determining the ethnicity of the available population. The technique of comparing stop and search activity with the profile of the 'available' population does not always support the non-discrimination theory.[74] Also, Sanders et al. point out 'availability' itself is a racialized phenomenon. The police may favour particular places and times for stop and searches because of racial prejudices about those

[65] Quinton et al. (2000) p. 20.     [66] Quinton et al. (2000) pp. 21–2.
[67] Quinton et al. (2000) p. 23.     [68] Quinton et al. (2000) p. 24.
[69] Quinton et al. (2000) pp. 24–7.     [70] Quinton et al. (2000) pp. 27–31.
[71] Quinton et al. (2000) p. 30.
[72] P. Waddington, K. Stenson, and D. Don, 'In Proportion: Race, and Police Stop and Search' (2004) 44 British Journal of Criminology 889.     [73] Waddington et al. (2004) p. 910.
[74] S. Hallsworth, *Street Crime* (2005) Willan, Cullompton.

'available' there.[75] Furthermore, as the Equality and Human Rights Commission has recently pointed out, disproportion rates continue to be higher in southern England than in certain parts of the north and Wales. Why should black people in the south be more 'outdoor types' (i.e., more 'available') than people in certain northern cities or rural Wales?[76] The particularly high level of disproportionality for s. 60 searches may perhaps suggest direct discrimination at work.[77] Statistics for 2006/7 show that, although black people made up only 2.8 per cent of the population, 15.9 per cent of those searched under reasonable suspicion powers and an amazingly high 29.6 per cent of s. 60 searches were of black people.[78]

In the past, racist stereotyping has been identified as a feature of 'cop culture'. In recent years, the notion of 'cop culture' and the role that it plays in the actual decision-making of the police has become rather controversial. Some would argue that the concept is unhelpful because the police do not do what they say they do; canteen banter bears little relation to police action.[79] Whilst there may be an element of truth in this, others have asserted that the gap between talk and action cannot be so wide.[80] The legal rules in PACE do tend to be subverted by police culture, although culture is an evolving thing and can be influenced by society and the changing (more diverse) composition of the police. Commentators have therefore found it unsurprising that the concept of reasonable suspicion has not proved to be a panacea for the difficulties surrounding police powers of stop and search. Researchers have for some time criticized the concept as failing to provide an effective constraint on police behaviour. Dixon et al., in their research, pointed out that the concentration by the legislators on problems of suspicion based on stereotyping meant that they ignored another type of suspicion which is very important in police work, and deeply embedded in police culture.[81] This suspicion focuses upon people who attract suspicion not because they conform to a stereotype, but because they are incongruous in some way – they do not fit into the context in which they are observed. Police officers are encouraged, as part of their professional skills, to see the world as divisible into the normal and the abnormal, and people who do not 'fit in' will be checked.[82] Thus, the new window cleaner or the scruffy youth in a middle-class area will be regarded as suspicious. There is an overlap with stereotyping here, but the incongruity procedure is more subtle than

[75] Sanders et al. (2010) pp. 97–100

[76] Equality and Human Rights Commission, *Police and Racism: What has Been Achieved 10 Years after the Stephen Lawrence Inquiry Report?* (2009) EHRC, London.

[77] For further detail on the debate, see B. Bowling and C. Phillips, 'Disproportionate and Discriminatory: Reviewing the Evidence on Police Stop and Search' (2007) 70(6) Modern Law Review 936.

[78] Ministry of Justice, *Statistics on Race and the Criminal Justice System, 2006/7* (2008b) MOJ, London, ch. 4. See also Sanders et al. (2010) pp. 97–100.

[79] P. Waddington, 'Police (Canteen) Sub-culture: An Appreciation' (1999) 39 British Journal of Criminology 286.

[80] A. Sanders and R. Young, *Criminal Justice* (3rd edn, 2006) Oxford University Press, Oxford, p. 65.

[81] D. Dixon, A. K. Bottomley, C. Coleman, M. Gill, and D. Wall, 'Reality and Rules in the Construction and Regulation of Police Suspicion' (1989) 17 International Journal of the Sociology of Law 185.

[82] Dixon et al. (1989) p. 186.

stereotyping. This use of suspicion based on incongruity is highly valued in police cul-ture. The ability to 'know the ground' and to work on the basis of instinct or common sense, are crucial characteristics of 'the good copper'.[83] Since this type of suspicion is deeply embedded in police culture, it is highly resistant to attempts at external influ-ence and change, such as the attempt to introduce the concept of reasonable suspicion in PACE.

Another problem with PACE's concept of 'reasonable suspicion' is that PACE treats stop and search as an isolated event, rather than as part of a process.[84] The practice of policing is not so neatly segmented. Stop and search is part of a social process stretching from informal contact between police and public, to arrest. It has been suggested that in order for the concept of reasonable suspicion to have a realistic chance of being operated successfully by police officers, there is a need for effective training in order to modify police culture, and for the backing of effective sanctions for non-compliance, as well as greater public knowledge of the limits of police powers.[85]

Concern has also been expressed that, despite the large number of stops, very little seems to come from many of these encounters in terms of arrests. Only 11.4 per cent of PACE stop and searches led to an arrest in 2007/8, a reduction of 2 per cent from the rate in 2000/1, when stop and search fell from over 1 million pre-Macpherson, to a low of 714,000.[86] Although stop and search were up to over 1 million again in 2007/8, it is unclear whether the larger number of searches means that the police are being less careful or simply recording more of their searches that do not result in arrest. The arrest rate suggests that many stop and search are not 'successful', but arrest is not the only measure of a 'successful' stop. Other measures of 'success', such as social con-trol and intelligence gathering, are, however, more difficult to assess quantitatively. Sanders et al. observe that stop and search might contribute to crime control in other, not necessarily desirable, ways.[87]

## Remedies for non-compliance with the Codes of Practice and PACE

The intention of the Philips Commission was clearly that the relevant Code of Practice should play an important part in ensuring that the police complied with the Act and that suspects were protected by safeguards provided by the legislature. However, it is important to note in this context that Code A (like the other Codes issued under s. 66 of PACE) is not part of the primary legislation and the Act makes it clear that failure to comply with the provisions of a Code of Practice will not automatically render a

---

[83]  Dixon et al. (1989) p. 188.     [84]  Dixon et al. (1989) p. 189.

[85]  Dixon et al. (1989) p. 192. See also J. Chan, *Changing Police Culture* (1997) Cambridge University Press, Cambridge.                          [86]  Povey and Smith (2009) Table 2a.

[87]  Sanders et al. (2010) pp. 113–18.

police officer liable to civil or criminal proceedings.[88] The absence of a specific legal remedy for breach of a provision in any of the Codes significantly weakens their status. It means that a police officer ignoring the provisions of the Codes will only be liable if he or she does something which would otherwise amount to a crime or a civil wrong. It is not easy to pursue a civil action against the police. Even if a cause of action can be established, the cost of bringing a claim and the difficulties of proof may present insurmountable burdens.[89] Alternatively, if the criminal burden of proof is met in relation to one or more offences the Crown Prosecution Service (CPS) may pursue a prosecution. Prosecutions for criminal offences committed by the police are rare and individuals have limited means for challenging CPS decisions not to prosecute police officers for assault and other more serious offences.[90] It is possible for complaints to be made against the police, even in cases where officers have been prosecuted and acquitted.[91] However, the police complaints procedure has been much maligned. The Independent Police Complaints Commission (IPCC) was established by the Police Reform Act 2002,[92] and became operational in April 2004. However, it has been suggested that it does not represent a great improvement on the previously flawed system where the police investigated themselves.[93]

Thus, at present, the remedies for non-compliance with PACE and the Codes of Practice are limited. One further possible remedy, exclusion of evidence at trial, will be given fuller consideration in **Chapter 14**. However, exclusion of evidence is of no use to people who are unlawfully stopped and searched but not taken to trial. Given the weak link between stop and search and arrest and prosecution, it is evident that most suspects are reliant on the unsatisfactory remedies described above.

## Stop and search and 'due process'/'crime control'

Even with the existence of Code A, then, it can be seen that the implementation of s. 1 of PACE remains a matter of controversy. The difficulties engendered by the concept of 'reasonable suspicion' were acknowledged by the Philips Commission when it was considering the use of this criterion in the statute:

We acknowledge the risk that the criterion could be loosely interpreted and have considered the possibility of trying to find some agreed standard which could form the grounds of reasonable suspicion and could be set out in a statute or a code of practice. Like others before us we have concluded that the variety of circumstances that would have to be covered makes

---

[88]  PACE, s. 67(10). The Codes are admissible in evidence in any proceedings if it appears to the court or tribunal that they are relevant to a question arising (PACE, s. 67(11)).

[89]  Sanders and Young (2006) pp. 604–12.

[90]  See M. Burton, 'Reviewing Crown Prosecution Service Decisions not to Prosecute' (2001) Criminal Law Review 374.

[91]  *R v Police Complaints Board, ex parte Madden and Rhone* [1983] 2 All ER 353.

[92]  See D. Ormerod and A. Roberts, 'The Police Reform Act 2002 – Increasing Centralization, Maintaining Confidence and Contracting Out Crime Control' [2003] Criminal Law Review 141.

[93]  Sanders et al. (2010) pp. 691–700.

this impracticable. We have therefore looked for other means of ensuring that the criterion of reasonable suspicion is not devalued.[94]

The solution adopted by the Philips Commission, and embodied in PACE, was to ensure that all the statutory powers of search to which PACE applies are subjected to a number of further safeguards, like the notification and recording requirements to be discussed below. This can be seen as an attempt to provide a criminal justice system which corresponds to what is known as a 'due process' system.

The criminal justice system is often analysed in terms of two different models, called 'due process' and 'crime control'.[95] These models were developed by an American criminologist, Herbert Packer,[96] in order to provide useful ways of analysing the value systems that are present in the criminal process. Although modern theorists offer different frameworks for evaluating the criminal justice process, these models represent a starting point for examining some of the tensions that are inherent in the process.

The *due process* model emphasizes the importance of the individual citizen. Emphasis on the primacy of the individual leads to an emphasis on the need to limit the powers of officials, who may otherwise abuse their position. This model stresses that official actors in the criminal justice system, such as the police, are given very wide coercive powers which they can exercise over individuals who become suspects. It then emphasizes the need for formal safeguards to protect the position of suspects at all stages of the system.

The *crime control* model, on the other hand, sees the most important function of the criminal justice system as the repression of criminal conduct in the interests of society as a whole. It assumes that the system should operate as efficiently as possible to achieve this objective, so the important thing is that actors within the criminal justice system have the capacity to investigate, try, and convict a high proportion of the offenders known to them. The acknowledgement that the resources to carry out all this work are scarce leads to an emphasis on informality rather than compliance with strict procedural rules, and extra-judicial processes are welcomed, as being more effective in achieving the ultimate goal of crime control. This model emphasizes the expertise of the police and prosecutors to screen out the innocent, rather than relying on more thorough judicial proceedings or the rights of suspects to challenge the criminal justice process if it becomes oppressive. The idea is that offenders should be dealt with as speedily as possible; a good way of achieving this is if offenders plead guilty, so there is also emphasis on the need for the police to extract confessions from suspects. This model does allow for some safeguards for individuals, but insists that they are

---

[94] Philips Report (1981a) para. 3.25.

[95] For discussion of these models see, for example, Sanders et al. (2010) ch. 1; A. Ashworth and M. Redmayne, *The Criminal Process* (3rd edn, 2005) Oxford University Press, Oxford, ch. 2; and A. E. Bottoms and J. D. McLean, *Defendants in the Criminal Process* (1976) Routledge & Kegan Paul, London, ch. 9.

[96] H. L. Packer, *The Limits of the Criminal Sanction* (1968) Stanford University Press, Stanford, CA.

kept to a minimum. While many of the provisions in PACE would seem to reflect a due process model, if one looks at the way the system actually operates in practice, it displays many features characteristic of a crime control model.[97] In relation to stop and search, Sanders et al. argue that the police still rely on 'cop culture' rooted in crime control norms.[98]

## Notification and recording requirements

In an attempt to introduce due process safeguards into the system, ss. 2 and 3 of PACE set out the notification and recording requirements for stop and search. Sections 2(1) and 3(1) make it clear that these requirements extend to all powers relating to searching persons or vehicles without first making an arrest and not just to those found in PACE.

Section 2 of PACE requires a police officer, before commencing a search, to identify herself or himself by name to the person involved and to give a brief explanation of the reason for the search and the grounds for making it. This approach accords with research evidence which shows that when people are stopped by the police they are much less likely to be antagonistic to the police officer if the grounds for the stop are explained and seem reasonable to the person stopped.[99] Before the search takes place, the officer must inform the person to be searched (or the owner/person in charge of the vehicle to be searched) that he or she is entitled to a record of the search provided an application is made within 12 months of the search being made.[100] If the person does not appear to understand what is being said (either because of hearing or language difficulties), then 'reasonable' steps must be taken to give the information.[101]

Section 2 of PACE explicitly contemplates stops without searches. It makes clear that if a police officer detains for stop and search under s. 1, the search need not take place if it subsequently appears to the officer that it is no longer necessary.[102] The Code of Practice points out that an officer who has reasonable grounds for suspicion may wish to question the person he or she has stopped about the behaviour or circumstances giving rise to the suspicion, and they may provide a satisfactory explanation about the suspicious circumstances.[103] It goes on to emphasize that reasonable grounds for suspicion cannot be provided retrospectively by questioning, the reasonable grounds of suspicion must exist before a person is stopped.[104] However, this requirement – designed to avoid fishing expeditions by the police – may easily be overlooked. It

---

[97]  See Sanders et al. (2010) ch. 1. They highlight the limitations of Packer's models and develop their own 'freedom' model (see ch. 1). The 'freedom' model has, in turn, been critiqued by Ashworth and Redmayne ((2005) ch. 2), who offer a normative human rights framework, but Sanders et al. point out the limitations of a human rights analysis.                                                        [98]  Sanders et al. (2010) p. 126.

[99]  Willis (1983). See also Quinton et al. (2000).        [100]  Code A, para. 3.10.

[101]  Code A, para. 3.11.

[102]  PACE, s. 2(1)(a). This also applies to any other power to search a person/vehicle without making an arrest (PACE, s. 2(1)(b)).                                                      [103]  Code A, para. 2.9.

[104]  Code A, para. 2.9. See also Code A, para. 2.11.

would be difficult to show that reasonable grounds did not exist prior to questioning, if a suspect wished subsequently to challenge a search.

The Code provides detailed guidance on the extent of a search. The search can take as long as is reasonably required to enable a search of the relevant person or vehicle to be carried out, either at the place where they were first detained or nearby.[105] The Code points out that the thoroughness and extent of the search will depend on what is suspected of being carried. In the case of a small article which can be easily concealed, a more extensive search may be necessary.[106] In the case of searches of persons, the Act makes it clear that when carrying out a search police officers are not authorized to ask people to remove any of their clothing in public other than an outer coat, jacket, or gloves.[107] However, when a search is being conducted under s. 44 of the Terrorism Act 2000, the police are empowered to require a person to remove headgear or footwear in public.[108] The Code goes on to explain that if a more extensive search is considered necessary, requiring, for example, a person to take off a T-shirt, this must be done out of public view and by a police officer of the same sex as the person being searched.[109] The Code also emphasizes that every effort should be made to reduce to a minimum the embarrassment that a person being searched may experience.[110] It is made clear that the cooperation of the person to be searched should be sought, and that any use of force should be regarded as a last resort.[111] However, s. 117 of PACE gives police officers the power to use reasonable force, if necessary, to exercise statutory powers, including those relating to stop and search.

Section 3 of PACE imposes a duty on constables to make a record in writing when a search is made, unless it is not practicable to do so on the spot, in which case it should be made as soon as practicable afterwards.[112] Code A states that the officer must make a record at the time 'unless there are exceptional circumstances which would make this wholly impracticable' (e.g., in situations involving public disorder or when the officer's presence is urgently required elsewhere).[113] The record of search must include the following information:

- the object of the search;
- the grounds for making it;
- the date and time and place where it was made;
- the outcome;
- whether any, and if so what, injury to a person or damage to property, appears to the constable to have resulted from the search;

---

[105] PACE, s. 2(8).     [106] Code A, para. 3.3.     [107] PACE, s. 2(9).

[108] In addition, for searches under s. 60AA of the CJPOA 1994 (inserted by the Anti-terrorism, Crime and Security Act 2001), the police are empowered to require the removal of any item worn to conceal identity. See PACE Code A, para. 3.5.     [109] Code A, para. 3.6.

[110] PACE Code A, para. 3.1. Where there may be religious sensitivities regarding the removal of items covering the head or face, the Code provides further guidance (Code A, guidance note 4).

[111] Code A, para. 3.2.     [112] PACE, s. 3(1) and (2).     [113] Code A, para. 4.1.

- the identity of the constable making the search.[114]

Code A makes it clear that the search record must explain, briefly but informatively, the reason for suspecting the person concerned (the grounds), and in the case of searches carried out under s. 60 of the Criminal Justice and Public Order Act (CJPOA) 1994, and s. 44 of the Terrorism Act 2000, that the search record must include a statement of the authority provided to carry out a search.[115] The record of the search must also include a note of the person's self-defined ethnicity,[116] and the officer's own perception of the ethnicity of the person searched.[117] These provisions have been included to assist in the monitoring of stop and search powers for disproportionality. However, this rests on an assumption that records are an effective monitoring tool. It has been suggested that the police are more likely to make a record of a search where the suspect is an ethnic minority (to 'cover their backs'),[118] but foundation for this claim is not well established and it is arguably just as plausible that they are less likely to make a record because they want to conceal evidence of discrimination.[119]

The entitlement to a copy of the search record is laid down in s. 3(7)–(9). A copy of a record made at the time of the search must be given immediately to the person who has been searched.[120] In cases where it has been wholly impracticable to make a record at the time of the search, the person must be informed of his right to a copy of the record if an application is made within 12 months.[121]

Up until 2003, the recording requirements only applied to stop and searches; if someone was stopped and questioned but then not searched, the provisions did not come into play. In 2003, the Code introduced a requirement to record a stop where no search was subsequently made.[122] This provision has subsequently been modified so that police officers need only make a record of their identity and the self-defined ethnic background of the person called to stop and account.[123]

## Consensual stop and searches

In the past, it was common for police officers to stop and search people on the street without resorting to any of their statutory powers. They did this by obtaining the consent of the person involved. Up until 2003, the Code stated: 'Nothing in this Code affects ... the ability of an officer to search a person in the street with his consent where

---

[114] PACE, s. 3(6).    [115] PACE Code A, para. 4.3(vii).    [116] PACE Code A, para. 4.3(ii).
[117] PACE Code A, guidance note 18.    [118] Bland et al. (2000).
[119] See the discussion of racial discrimination and stop and search in B. Bowling and C. Philips, *Racism, Crime and Justice* (2002) Longman, London, pp. 138–48.    [120] Code A, para. 4.2.
[121] Code A, para. 3.10.
[122] Code A, para. 4.7. This provision, based on recommendation 61 in the MacPherson Report, was piloted in several areas prior to national implementation in April 2005. An evaluation found the requirement to record stops has been 'highly contested'. Police officers have resented the underlying agenda to monitor discrimination and reformulated the requirement to reflect their own priorities, such as intelligence gathering (see M. Shiner, *The National Implementation of the Recording of Police Stops* (2006) Home Office, London).
[123] Code A, para 4.12.

no search power exists.'[124] Such consensual stops and the searches that were carried out therefore took place outside the framework of PACE (or any other statutory power). Consequently, neither the restrictions such as that in s. 1 of PACE that an officer must have reasonable suspicion of specific offences nor the notification and reporting requirements in ss. 2 and 3 of PACE applied. From the police's point of view, given the lack of regulation, obtaining consent for a search was highly desirable.[125] McConville et al. found that police officers devoted considerable effort to 'tricking' suspects into consenting.[126] In these circumstances, 'consent' took on a new meaning. Real consent depends upon the citizen having accurate knowledge of legal rights. Many people are uncertain whether or not they are entitled to refuse to be stopped, questioned, or searched by the police, and may assume that the police have the power even though the conditions of PACE may not be satisfied in their particular circumstances.

The 2003 version of Code A introduced a major change, insofar as it prohibited consensual stop and searches. Paragraph 1.5 provided that:

An officer must not search a person, even with his or her consent, where no power to search is applicable. Even where a person is prepared to submit to a search voluntarily, the person must not be searched unless the necessary legal power exists, and the search must be in accordance with the relevant power and the provisions of this Code.

This provision is repeated in subsequent versions of the Code, including the 2009 version, and means that the police should no longer be able to circumvent the legal controls of the Code through obtaining consent. However, the Code does not prohibit consensual stops for questioning, the so-called 'stop and account'. People who are stopped and asked questions, in theory could simply walk away, but in practice they may assume that the police have the right to demand an account from them. Although there are limited recording requirements for 'stop and account',[127] the efficacy of such controls remains an issue.

## Monitoring and supervision

Section 5 of PACE requires information about searches to be included in the annual report made by chief constables. Code A requires supervising officers to monitor and supervise the use of stop and search powers, in particular to consider whether there is any evidence that stop and search powers are being exercised on the basis of stereotyped images or inappropriate generalizations.[128] Any apparent disproportionate use of the powers by a particular officer or groups of officers or in relation to specific sections of the community should be identified and investigated. The provisions were

---

[124] Code A (1997 version) Note 1D(b).
[125] D. Dixon, C. Coleman, and K. Bottomley, 'Consent and the Legal Regulation of Policing' (1990) 17 Journal of Law and Society 345 at p. 348.
[126] M. McConville, A. Sanders, and R. Leng, *The Case for the Prosecution* (1991) Routledge, London, p. 94.
[127] Code A 4.7 and 4.12 discussed above.    [128] Code A, para. 5.1.

intended to give effect to a recommendation made in the MacPherson Inquiry for better monitoring and supervision of stop and search powers by senior officers. However, there are considerable problems relying on records as a tool to monitor low visibility discretion on the street. These provisions may provide an appearance of effective supervision rather than a reality.[129]

## Community support officers

Community support officers (CSOs) are a relatively recent 'civilian' addition to the police.[130] They were introduced by the Police Reform Act 2003, with the idea that they would contribute to neighbourhood policing and be engaged with the public. Research by Cooper et al. found that CSOs spent much of their time on foot patrol, dealing with youth-related disorder, alcohol-related issues, low-level crime, and anti-social behaviour. Most forces agreed that providing high-visibility patrol and interacting with the community in dealing with low-level crime and anti-social behaviour was their core role. It was found that the presence of CSOs on the streets could help to build relationships with the community and contribute to intelligence gathering. The precise range of activities undertaken by CSOs varied according to the police force involved but most of their time is spent on the street rather than at the station.

The introduction of CSOs has resulted in a blurring of the boundaries between public and private policing. Essentially, CSOs are private police personnel with some of the powers of the public police. Under s. 38 of the Police Reform Act 2002, chief police officers are given authority to confer on CSOs a range of different powers listed in the Act and added to by subsequent legislation. The powers that can be conferred upon CSOs include issuing fixed penalty notices (for example, for low value retail thefts and criminal damage); powers to confiscate alcohol and tobacco from under-age persons; and the power to demand the name and address of a person believed to be acting in an anti-social manner. Cooper et al. found that over 90 per cent of forces designated these powers upon CSOs,[131] and the most frequently used power was to demand the name and address of a person believed to be acting in an anti-social manner.[132] The study revealed that there are mixed views amongst the police and the community about whether the powers of CSOs should be further widened.[133] A limited number of forces conferred upon their CSOs a power to detain a person pending the arrival of a police officer in specified circumstances.[134] Conferring this power may be seen as

[129] Sanders et al. (2010) pp. 105–8.

[130] C. Cooper, J. Anscombe, J. Avenell, F. McLean, and J. Morris, *A National Evaluation of Community Support Officers* (2006) Home Office Research Study No. 297, Home Office, London.

[131] Cooper et al. (2006) p. 19.        [132] Cooper et al. (2006) p. 21.

[133] Cooper et al. (2006) pp. 20–3.

[134] Cooper et al. (2006) p. 23. Six forces had conferred this power at the time of the research.

taking CSOs too far into the core of public policing when they lack the training and equipment available to the police proper. How far the role of the CSO will evolve is a matter of speculation. CSOs can perform a search under s. 44 of the Terrorism Act under the supervision of a constable. Although they are already taking on tasks which can involve activities akin to stop and search, they do not, as yet, have the full powers of stop and search available to police officers under PACE, s. 1 and other legislation discussed in this chapter.

## CONCLUSION

The main focus of this chapter has been on the powers of the public police, however, it has also been relevant to acknowledge the part played by members of the public in uncovering potentially criminal acts and the roles of Community Support Officers and non-police investigators, for example, customs and excise officers. The English legal system's ability to investigate is not restricted to the activities of the public police; a fact that brings us back to the relevance of the integrated theory of justice which underpins this book. When considering the powers of stop and search of the public police and other regulatory agencies, it is important to understand the freedom that such rules frequently allow such bodies to operate in accordance with their 'crime control' values. The legal rules and codes of practice are themselves often permissive and do not necessarily have to be breached to achieve objectives that accord with 'working' rules. These working rules may be directly discriminatory, or at the very least appear to have indirectly discriminatory effect, for example in relation to race. It is also important to appreciate the limited mechanisms for challenge on occasions when the legal rules are breached.

## FURTHER READING

Bowling, B. and C. Phillips, 'Disproportionate and Discriminatory: Reviewing the Evidence on Police Stop and Search' (2007) 70(6) Modern Law Review 936.

Miller, J., Quinton, P., and Bland, N., Police Stops and Searches: Lessons from a Programme of Research (2000) Police Home Office Briefing Note, Home Office, London.

Quinton, P., Bland, N., and Miller, J., Police Stops, Decision-making and Practice (2000) Police Research Series Paper No. 130, Home Office, London.

# 14

# Arrest and detention

## INTRODUCTION

In this chapter, the role of the police in arresting and detaining suspects for the purposes of investigating criminal offences will be examined. However, it should not be assumed that investigation is the sole purpose of arrest and detention and so consideration will be given to other objectives as highlighted by socio-legal research in this area. The relationship between the powers available to the public police and those available to ordinary citizens continues to be significant for understanding the operation of the criminal justice system. For example, the arrest powers of ordinary citizens, which are relied upon by private security personnel such as store detectives, adds to the picture of an integrated theory of justice.

## Voluntary assistance

The police may wish to arrest a suspect so that they can carry out investigations. However, it is not always necessary to arrest a person to obtain further information by questioning them, since it is possible that they may agree voluntarily to 'assist the police with their inquiries'.

The Royal Commission on Criminal Procedure (the Philips Commission) recommended that the distinction between being placed under arrest on the one hand, and assisting the police voluntarily and therefore at liberty to go on the other hand, should be clarified: 'We would begin by emphasizing that [in general] there must be no half-way house between liberty and arrest...'.[1] Section 29 of the Police and Criminal Evidence Act 1984 (PACE) addresses the issue of those who volunteer to assist the police by agreeing to go to a police station or other similar place to be interviewed. The section provides:

for the purpose of assisting with an investigation a person attends voluntarily at a police station or at any other place where a constable is present or accompanies a constable to a police station or any such other place without having been arrested –

---

[1] Royal Commission on Criminal Procedure, *Report* (the Philips Report) (1981a) Cmnd 8092, para. 3.97.

(a) he shall be entitled to leave at will unless he is placed under arrest;
(b) he shall be informed at once that he is under arrest if a decision is taken by a constable to prevent him from leaving at will.

The wording is broad enough to cover both those who are true volunteers and those who believe, mistakenly, that they are under a legal duty to attend. However, the concept of 'true volunteers' is criticized by McKenzie et al., who argue that any request by a law enforcement professional to a uniformed, unadvised layperson suspected of an offence is coercive.[2] The significant point is that, as Code C states, 'Anybody attending a police station voluntarily to assist with an investigation may leave at will unless arrested.'[3] The Notes for Guidance in Code C also make it clear that such persons, unlike those who have been arrested, 'enjoy an absolute right to obtain legal advice or communicate with anyone outside the police station'.[4] If an officer's suspicions are confirmed by initial questioning, s. 29(b) makes it clear that arrest should follow without undue delay. If a person is not arrested but is cautioned, the officer who gives the caution must at the same time inform the person that he or she is not under arrest, that he or she is not obliged to remain at the police station but if he or she remains at the police station may obtain free and independent legal advice if he or she wishes.[5]

It is a matter of concern if anyone is placed under pressure to 'assist the police with their inquiries', because apart from s. 29, which is very broadly drafted, voluntary attendance at a police station is not effectively regulated by PACE.[6] The time constraints placed on detention without charge by PACE, s. 41 do not apply until the suspect has been arrested, since s. 41(2)(c) provides that in the case of a person who attends voluntarily at a police station, time begins to run from the time of his or her arrest, rather than running, for example, from the time at which the person arrived at the police station. It is therefore clear that voluntary attendance at the police station is a concept which can be used to evade the constraints on detention which are generally imposed by PACE to protect the rights of suspects who are detained at police stations.[7] However, as Sanders et al. point out, it is rare for the police to flout s. 29 because the detention limits are usually more than adequate; they do not need to delay arrest when they can detain for 24 or 36 hours under PACE.[8]

---

[2] See I. McKenzie, R. Morgan, and R. Reiner, 'Helping the Police with their Enquiries' [1990] Criminal Law Review 22 at p. 28.          [3] PACE Code C, para. 3.21.
[4] PACE Code C, Note 1A.          [5] PACE Code C, para. 3.21.
[6] See comments in D. Clark, *Bevan and Lidstone's The Investigation of Crime* (3rd edn, 2004) Butterworths, London, pp. 290–3.          [7] Discussed below.
[8] A. Sanders, R. Young, and M. Burton, *Criminal Justice* (4th edn, 2010) Oxford University Press, Oxford, p. 208.

# Powers of arrest

If the police do not obtain voluntary assistance, or they do not think it appropriate to proceed in that way, then an arrest will be made.

It is possible to apply to a magistrate for an arrest warrant under s. 1 of the Magistrates' Court Act 1980, but, more commonly, arrests are made by police officers without a warrant being issued. This means that the decision whether or not to arrest is generally taken by a police officer without any direct supervision by a court. Section 24 of PACE provides general powers of arrest without warrant.

PACE used to distinguish between arrestable and non-arrestable offences but this distinction was removed by s. 110 of the Serious Organised Crime and Police Act 2005. Section 24 now provides a power of arrest without warrant for anyone who is about to commit an offence or who is in the act of committing an offence or who is guilty of an offence already committed. The police may also arrest anyone who they reasonably suspect is about to commit an offence, reasonably suspect to be committing an offence, or reasonably suspect to be guilty of an already committed offence. The police may only arrest if they have reasonable grounds for believing that it is necessary to arrest the person. The necessity criteria are set out in s. 24(5):

(a) to enable the name of the person in question to be ascertained (in the case where the constable does not know, and cannot readily ascertain, the person's name, or has reasonable grounds for doubting whether a name given by the person as his name is his real name);
(b) correspondingly as regards the person's address;
(c) to prevent the person in question –
   (i) causing physical injury to himself or any other person;
   (ii) suffering physical injury;
   (iii) causing loss of or damage to property;
   (iv) committing an offence against public decency (where members of the public going about their normal business cannot reasonably be expected to avoid the person in question);
   (v) causing an unlawful obstruction of the highway;
(d) to protect a child or other vulnerable person from the person in question;
(e) to allow the prompt and effective investigation of the offence or of the conduct of the person in question;
(f) to prevent any prosecution for the offence from being hindered by the disappearance of the person in question.

The necessity criteria in subsections (a) to (d) are broadly similar to the old general arrest conditions for non-arrestable offences in s. 25 of PACE, which has now been repealed. However, in addition to those conditions where it was previously thought impracticable or inappropriate to proceed by summons, the new s. 24 of PACE provides two new 'necessity' criteria in subsections (e) and (f) as noted above.

The revisions to s. 24 of PACE made by the Serious Organised Crime and Police Act considerably enlarge the powers of the police to make arrests and are 'crime control' rules. Section 24 now provides that an arrest is lawful without reasonable suspicion if in fact the person arrested turns out to have been committing an offence, about to do so or having done so. Sanders et al. observe this is:

a classic crime control norm since desirable ends are regarded as justifying undesirable means. It does not matter that the arrest was speculatively made, so long as the suspect turns out to have been engaged in a crime. The police might, for instance, see a well-known burglar walking down the street and simply arrest him on a hunch that he was responsible for a burglary committed earlier that day. If, in the police station, he confessed to that crime, his guilt would be clear and his arrest would be valid as far as PACE is concerned.[9]

The necessity criteria are an effective constraint on the use of arrest powers because the police are used to justifying decisions to detain suspects to secure evidence through questioning.[10] Section 24(5)(e) allows arrest if necessary for a 'prompt and effective investigation'.

Section 24A of PACE, inserted by s. 110 of the Serious Organised Crime and Police Act 2005, governs the powers of anyone other than a police constable to make an arrest without a warrant. It provides citizens with powers to arrest anyone who is committing, or reasonably suspected to be committing, an indictable offence. Where an indictable offence has been committed, citizens may arrest anyone who is guilty of the offence or reasonably suspected to be guilty of it. It should be noted that citizens have no power of arrest for anticipated offences; they can arrest for past and present offences only. In so far as past offences are concerned, the offence must actually have been committed; thus, if it turns out that the person arrested was doing something lawful the conditions for a citizen's arrest will not have been met. Furthermore, the powers conferred upon citizens to make an arrest are exercisable only if it appears to the person making the arrest that it is not reasonably practicable for a constable to make it instead or the person making the arrest has reasonable grounds for believing that it is necessary to arrest the person in question to prevent them causing physical injury to himself or any other person; suffering physical injury; causing loss of or damage to property; or making off before a constable can assume responsibility for him.[11]

It is clear throughout s. 24 that the powers of arrest given to police officers are wider than those given to ordinary members of the public and consequently it is wise for members of the public to exercise caution before making a 'citizen's arrest'. Citizens' arrest powers are frequently used by shop assistants and store detectives in relation to shoppers whom they believe have committed thefts. This will most likely be lawful if a theft has actually been committed, since it will normally be plausible for the store staff to argue that they reasonably believed that arrest was necessary to prevent the shopper making off. However, if a theft has not in fact been committed, then the arrest will be unlawful, even though the store staff reasonably believed that it had.

---

[9] Sanders et al. (2010) p. 156.     [10] Sanders et al. (2010) p. 144.     [11] PACE, s. 24A(3)–(4).

## Breach of the peace

In addition to the powers of arrest discussed above, there is a power of arrest available at common law, both to the police and members of the public, to arrest for breach of the peace, where such a breach is taking place or is reasonably anticipated.[12] The Serious Organised Crime and Police Act 2005 did not explicitly abolish the common law power to arrest for breach of the peace and it must be assumed that it is retained. The effect of the law relating to breach of the peace is to give the police a wide band of discretion, since it is not always clear precisely what constitutes a breach of the peace. The Court of Appeal confirmed in *Howell*[13] that it must relate to violence, in the sense that there could not be a breach of the peace unless an act was done or threatened to be done which either actually harmed a person or, in his presence, his property, or was likely to cause such harm, or which put someone in fear of such harm being done. A police officer may arrest for breach of the peace if such a breach is occurring, is imminent, or is likely to recur.[14]

However, many of these concepts leave a lot of room for the exercise of judgement by the police. The effect of this was clearly illustrated in the context of the miners' strike which took place in the mid 1980s, when there were a number of incidents where miners on their way to picket pits were stopped by the police some miles away from their intended destination, and after an altercation with the police, were arrested for breach of the peace. The question here was whether a breach of the peace was imminent. While some of these incidents took place very near the intended destination, so there was a stronger argument that a breach of the peace was likely to occur fairly imminently, other incidents took place over 100 miles from the place where the miners intended to picket.[15] Sanders et al. comment that the miner's strike may seem like a long time ago but the use (or misuse) of powers resurfaces periodically, particularly in the context of policing public protests, such as the May Day demonstrations in 2001. Relying on the need to prevent a breach of the peace, the police cordoned off the area for over seven hours. The practice of 'kettling' as it is known was considered by the House of Lords in the case of *Austin and Saxby*.[16] Lord Neuberger of Abbotsbury observed that if it transpired 'that the police had maintained the cordon, beyond the time necessary for crowd control, in order to punish, or "to teach a lesson" to, the demonstrators within the cordon' then 'there would have been a powerful argument for saying that the maintenance of the cordon did amount to a detention within the meaning of article 5'.[17] In general, however, the ECHR has proved to be of limited usefulness in challenging the extent of police powers and the way that they are exercised.

---

[12] For a more detailed discussion of law and policy relating to breach of the peace, see D. Feldman, *Civil Liberties and Human Rights in England and Wales* (2nd edn, 2002) Oxford University Press, Oxford, ch. 18.

[13] *Howell* [1981] 3 All ER 383.    [14] *Howell* [1981] 3 All ER 383 at p. 388.

[15] See, in particular, the case of *Moss* v *McLachlan* [1985] IRLR 76.

[16] *Austin and Another* v *Commissioner of Police for the Metropolis* [2009] UKHL 5; Sanders et al. (2010) pp. 150–2.    [17] [2009] UKHL 5 at para. 63.

## Other powers of arrest

Prior to the Serious Organised Crime and Police Act 2005, many statutory arrest powers for specific offences were preserved in addition to the powers in ss. 24 and 25 of PACE. Now that the revised s. 24 provides powers of arrest for any offence, it is no longer necessary for so many specific powers to be maintained and many were repealed by Sch. 7 to the Serious Organised Crime and Police Act 2005. However, concerns have been raised about the scope for further arrest powers to be enacted. Some additional arrest powers, such as the power to arrest a person reasonably suspected to be a terrorist,[18] are capable of very wide interpretation.[19] These powers are all much more specific than those found in PACE but may also raise similar issues about the wide discretion afforded by concepts like 'reasonable suspicion'. In recent years, enhanced powers of arrest (and detention) have been enacted to deal with the perceived terrorist threat post 9/11 and 7/7. There is not space here to consider fully the extent of these powers or whether they are fully justified but there are arguably legitimate concerns about the use of such powers.

## Arrest in context

This is an area where it is important to balance the operational needs of the police against the protection of civil liberties. It would be unrealistic to impose too strict a test as to when the police can make an arrest, given that officers frequently have to make speedy decisions under pressure, but if the courts interpret the standard too loosely, the concept of 'fundamental balance' which was intended by the Philips Commission to run throughout PACE, is undermined.

Clearly, arrest involves depriving a person of their liberty, so that it is a serious step, which should not be undertaken lightly. Mindful of this fact, the Philips Commission was clear, in making proposals relating to powers of arrest without warrant, that it wished:

to restrict the circumstances in which the police can exercise the power to deprive a person of his liberty to those in which it is genuinely necessary to enable them to execute their duty to prevent the commission of offences, to investigate crime, and to bring suspected offenders before the courts; and to simplify, clarify and rationalise the existing statutory powers of arrest...[20]

However, the Philips Commission's proposal that arrests should only take place if *necessary* was not implemented as the Commission envisaged in the original formulation of the arrest powers in PACE. The new s. 24 does include elements of the necessity

---

[18]  Terrorism Act 2000, s. 41.      [19]  Sanders et al. (2010) pp. 144–7.
[20]  Philips Report (1981a) para. 3.75.

principle in the criteria set out in s. 24(5) discussed above, but is unlikely to prevent the police making arrests where they wish to do so.

The police tend to use their powers of arrest without warrant as a matter of routine.[21] They are aware of the fact that an arrested person is at a distinct psychological disadvantage and use their powers of arrest in a coercive way. As Holdaway comments in his ethnographic account of police work:

To take someone 'down the nick' is to place them under police control; what happens next may vary, as a sergeant from another station once explained 'As a general rule it has been my experience that in a police station a person gets as good as he gives. If he is co-operative then the police are OK with him; if he is not co-operative, then he gets it.[22]

McConville et al. comment that although the Philips Commission wished to restrict the use of arrest powers to protect the legitimate interests of citizens in going about their business without fear of unnecessary or arbitrary arrest, 'the police, in the interests of increasing the vulnerability of suspects, wish to maximise the use of arrest powers'.[23] The police tend to view the making of an arrest as another tool which may assist them in the investigation of an offence.

In his study of over 1,000 arrests carried out for the Royal Commission on Criminal Justice (the Runciman Commission), McConville found that in over 75 per cent of arrests, the evidence which existed at the time the arrest was made was very weak, so that it would not have been possible to charge the suspect. However, once the suspect was arrested, other investigations took place, such as searches of property and collection of forensic evidence and the result of all this activity was that by the time the suspect was interviewed by the police, the number of weak cases was greatly reduced.[24] It was this type of approach which the Philips Commission wished to restrict:

In attempting to limit the power of arrest, we have no intention of inhibiting the police from fulfilling their functions of detecting and preventing crime. But we do seek to alter the practice whereby the inevitable sequence on the creation of reasonable suspicion is arrest, followed by being taken to the station, often to be searched, fingerprinted and photographed.[25]

Brown argues that there is now evidence which runs counter to arguments that arrest is used routinely in the way described above, with several studies (including one he carried out himself on the investigation of household burglary) suggesting that there may have been an increase in the standard of evidence on which arrests

---

[21]  See Clark (2004) p. 310.

[22]  S. Holdaway, *Inside the British Police* (1983) Basil Blackwell, Oxford, p. 27.

[23]  M. McConville, A. Sanders, and R. Leng, *The Case for the Prosecution* (1991) Routledge, London, p. 40.

[24]  M. McConville, *Corroboration and Confessions: The Impact of a Rule Requiring that No Conviction Can be Sustained on the Basis of Confession Evidence Alone* (1993) Royal Commission on Criminal Justice Research Study No. 13, HMSO, London, pp. 24–36.        [25]  Philips Report (1981a) para. 3.75.

are based.[26] This is a contested subject, although the balance of the research evidence suggests that concerns remain about the way in which powers of arrest are used.

## 'Reasonable suspicion'

As noted above, the police do not require reasonable suspicion for lawful arrest in all circumstances. However, if it turns out that the person arrested was not in fact engaged in crime then the lawfulness of the arrest depends upon the existence of reasonable suspicion. Much criticism has been made of the use of the concept of reasonable suspicion in this part of the statute, since it gives the police a very wide discretion in the matter of arrest and it has been argued that the courts accept too low a standard of suspicion and do not explore with sufficient rigour police claims that reasonable suspicion exists.[27]

McConville et al. argue that since the requirement of 'reasonable suspicion' in PACE imposes very few restraints on police discretion, the exercise of that discretion is actually structured not by legal rules but by police working rules, of which they identify six which they regard as particularly significant.

## 'Previous'

Being known to the police is more likely to make someone a suspect. McConville et al. report an incident where the arresting officer had been looking for pickpockets in a street market:

Up walks this chap who we knew was one of the suspects. He'd been seen there before, he fitted the description, he was an associate of someone who'd already been arrested. You tend to follow the ones you know. If I hadn't known to tail him, he'd have got away with it.[28]

## Disorder and police authority

The police will use their arrest powers in order to carry out other policing functions, especially to maintain public order and their own authority. This was commonly seen in the context of the miners' strike, which took place in the mid 1980s. McCabe et al. note that during the 12 months of the dispute, 9,808 arrests were made, more than in any previous industrial dispute in the last half-century. Some of the arrests were connected with serious charges, but many were for minor offences of obstruction, breach

---

[26] D. Brown, *PACE Ten Years On: A Review of the Research* (1997) Home Office Research Study No. 155, HMSO, London, p. 54. See also D. Brown, *Investigating Burglary: The Effects of PACE* (1991) Home Office Research Study No. 123, HMSO, London.

[27] See Feldman (2002) pp. 329–39 for a more detailed discussion of the concept of reasonable suspicion in this context.    [28] McConville et al. (1991) p. 24.

of the peace, or offensive words or behaviour.[29] The implication is that the police were making arrests with the primary purpose of removing people from public situations where, in the view of police officers, there was a risk of disorder and a challenge to their own authority.

Another example of arrest powers being used for public order purposes was in relation to the 'hippy convoy' to Stonehenge to celebrate the Summer Solstice. For many years, this event had given rise to little trouble. In 1985, after injunctions were obtained banning named individuals from the site, a convoy was met by a roadblock and police in riot gear. Many people were injured in the scenes of horrific violence that ensued and 500 were arrested.[30] It would appear in retrospect that the climate of opinion against the festival, made up of local farmers, landowners, residents, and MPs from the Tory constituencies had been hardening for a number of years, and that a decision had been taken by the police that the convoy would not reach Stonehenge in 1985.[31] More recent examples include the policing of political protests, notably the G20 summit in April 2009 which led to the death of Ian Tomlinson.[32]

The use of police powers of arrest in order to maintain public order and police authority can also be seen in more everyday situations. McConville et al. report an incident when the police were called to deal with a drunk: 'Even when we approached him,' the arresting officer said, 'he was offensive towards us and generally acting in a disorderly fashion.' So he was arrested.[33]

## General suspiciousness

As we noted in the previous chapter on stop and search, stereotypical clues which tend to make individuals appear more suspicious play an important part in police decision-making. McConville et al. argue that the existence of PACE imposes few constraints on the way in which the police work. The concept of 'reasonable suspicion' in PACE has made little change to the working rules adopted by the police so that many arrests are made on very thin pretexts, in the hope that more evidence will be forthcoming – if it is, a charge will be made, if not, no further action will be taken.[34] This use of arrest as a routine part of the investigative process is very far from the recommendation of the Philips Commission that arrests should only be made when necessary.

[29] S. McCabe, P. Wallington, J. Alderson, L. Gostin, and C. Mason, *Police, Public Order and Civil Liberties* (1988) Routledge, London, p. 69.

[30] See P. Vincent-Jones, 'Private Property and Public Order: The Hippy Convoy' (1986) 13 Journal of Law and Society 343.    [31] Vincent-Jones (1986) p. 360.

[32] This example is discussed by Sanders et al. (2010) p. 162.    [33] McConville et al. (1991) p. 25.

[34] McConville et al. (1991) p. 22.

## Information received

Information which the police receive may also cause them to arrest suspects. This information comes from a wide variety of sources. Sometimes it is unsolicited by the police, but at other times it is the result of police activity. Cain's study discusses the amount of effort expended by the police in information-gathering either by direct purchase or in the course of 'casual' conversation with members or fringe members of the criminal subculture.[35] The information which is received may give rise to grounds for reasonable suspicion and lead directly to arrest, or it may cause the police to carry out further investigations. The importance of information gained from various types of informant points up once again the need for an integrated theory of justice which can encompass the interaction of the police, as members of the formal justice system, with other actors who may or may not be regarded as fully within that system.

Some interesting suggestions about the different kinds of informants with whom the police interact can be found in the work of Greer, who divides informants into two main types: *outsiders*, who are not directly involved in the activities they report to the police, but merely observe them from the outside; and *insiders*, who have themselves participated, to a greater or lesser extent, in the criminal activities which they are reporting.[36] Outsiders can be subdivided into two further types: the casual observer and the snoop.[37] The casual observer is a member of the public who, on an isolated occasion and usually by chance, happens to observe a crime or any activity which she or he thinks should be brought to the attention of the police; the snoop supplies the police with information about a number of incidents which will usually follow a pattern, such as drug dealing or vice. Just as outsiders can be subdivided into different types, Greer suggests that insiders can be classified either as one-off accomplice witnesses or as informants/agents provocateurs. One-off accomplice witnesses are those witnesses who testify on a specific occasion for the prosecution against their alleged associates, whereas informants will typically be closely involved in criminal organizations or political/social organizations which the police find suspicious.[38] In another sense, all of these types are outsiders, because they are not part of the formal criminal justice system, but their interaction with it is of vital importance. An integrated theory of justice acknowledges the importance of such interactions for the legal system as a whole.

## Workload

Arrest and prosecution figures are an important measure of success for police officers. Simon Holdaway comments, 'Constables know that whatever else they may do, arrests serve as one important indicator of competence and application.'[39] The effect of this

[35] M. Cain, *Society and the Policeman's Role* (1973) Routledge & Kegan Paul, London, p. 51.
[36] S. Greer, 'Towards a Sociological Model of the Police Informant' (1995) 46 British Journal of Sociology 509.                                                                                      [37] Greer (1995) pp. 511, 512.
[38] Greer (1995) pp. 512, 513.        [39] Holdaway (1983) p. 59.

is that officers who have a particularly low total of arrests or prosecutions will seek to make a large number of arrests in order to boost their productivity. On the other hand, officers who do not need to raise their arrest total will avoid making arrests unless it is necessary to do so.[40]

## Victim

It is clear that the type of victim of an alleged offence can play a part in influencing the police decision whether or not to arrest. Some types of victim are more successful than others in persuading the police to arrest the alleged wrongdoer. In cases of drunkenness, McConville et al. suggest that police officers would frequently be content to leave the drunks alone, were it not for the complaints they received from members of the public, which meant that action had to be taken.[41] Here, the 'victims' (i.e., members of the public who did not want to tolerate the presence of drunks in public places) were successful in persuading the police to make arrests. However, some types of victim lack the ability to persuade the police to carry out an arrest.

In the past, there has been particular concern over the difficulties faced by female victims of domestic violence when reporting incidents to the police.[42] It has been argued that police attitudes towards domestic violence include assumptions about male rights and female blame which are manifested in an unsympathetic attitude towards women complainants in such incidents.[43] This means that women involved in such complaints are less likely than men to be able to persuade the police to take the complaint seriously enough to arrest the alleged perpetrator. However, more recently it has been argued that police attitudes to domestic violence are changing. The connection between canteen culture and police (in)action has also been questioned.[44] Official policy has moved towards strongly encouraging the use of arrest powers.

Nevertheless research suggests that pro-arrest policies are not being fully implemented in practice.[45] Police officers may be reluctant to make arrests because they feel that a prosecution is unlikely to succeed, particularly if, as is commonly the case, the victim withdraws her complaint. In this respect, the introduction of effective evidence gathering to reduce the reliance on the victim's testimony might be expected to have an impact on arrest rates.[46] If the police have other evidence, such as photos and statements from independent witnesses, then the anticipated reluctance of the

---

[40] McConville et al. (1991) p. 31.    [41] McConville et al. (1991) p. 32.

[42] S. Edwards, *Policing Domestic Violence* (1989) Sage, London.

[43] See E. Stanko, 'Missing the Mark? Police Battering' in J. Hanmer, J. Radford, and E. Stanko (eds), *Women, Policing and Male Violence: International Perspectives* (1989) Routledge, London, ch. 3.

[44] See C. Hoyle, *Negotiating Domestic Violence* (1998) Oxford University Press, Oxford.

[45] Her Majesty's Crown Prosecution Service Inspectorate (HMCPSI) and Her Majesty's Inspectorate of Constabulary (HMIC), *Violence at Home: The Investigation and Prosecution of Cases Involving Domestic Violence* (2004) London, CPS, available at: <http://www.hmcpsi.gov.uk>.

[46] L. Ellison, 'Responding to Victim Withdrawal in Domestic Violence Prosecutions' [2003] Criminal Law Review 760.

complainant should not deter an arrest. However, this assumes that the police are willing and able to implement effective evidence-gathering policies. Even in the context of specialist domestic violence courts, there is little evidence that effective evidence-gathering takes place.[47] However, the profile of victim has never been higher in political and policy terms. Thus, in rhetoric, if not always in practice, the victim is a key influence on police decision-making.

## Some issues relating to arrest practices

Research shows that in the majority of cases, the person arrested is likely to be a young male, a finding which some might find unsurprising, given that other surveys show that a high proportion of offenders fall into this category.[48] Concern has been expressed, however, at the differential arrest rates as between members of the population who are white and those who are not. While age can account for some differences in the arrest rate between black and white people, largely because the West Indian population is a very young population, it cannot provide a total explanation. In the same way, Stevens and Willis found that the arrest rates of persons of different racial backgrounds were all strongly associated with common measures of deprivation, but even when these were analysed in detail, the fact that black people were found to be particularly likely to be arrested for offences where there is considerable scope for selective perceptions by the police of potential or actual offenders, prompted the researchers to query whether the suspicions of the police bear disproportionately on black people.[49] The Policy Studies Institute (PSI) study of policing in London, carried out in 1983, also showed that a disproportionately high number of young males of West Indian or African origin were arrested. These researchers commented that, while many differences in arrest rates could be explained by a combination of socio-economic and demographic factors, the high incidence of contact with the police among these sectors of the population was a matter for concern, because confidence in the police is very low among these groups.[50] Black people are nearly four times more likely to be arrested than white.[51] Sanders et al. comment that this disproportionality is partially a product of proactive policing and increased targeting of certain racial groups in the aftermath of the terrorist attacks of 7/7.[52]

---

[47]  M. Burton, *Legal Responses to Domestic Violence* (2008) Routledge-Cavendish, Abingdon.

[48]  D. J. Smith, *Police and People in London*: Volume 3: *A Survey of Police Officers* (1983a) Policy Studies Institute, London, p. 88.

[49]  P. Stevens and C. F. Willis, *Race, Crime and Arrests* (1979) Home Office Research Study No. 58, Home Office, London, p. 33.

[50]  D. J. Smith and J. Gray, *Police and People in London*: Volume 4: *The Police in Action* (1983b) Policy Studies Institute, London, p. 336.

[51]  Ministry of Justice, *Statistics on Race and the Criminal Justice System, 2007/8* (2009d) MOJ, London.

[52]  Sanders et al. (2010) pp. 173–82.

It also appears that working-class people are greatly over-represented in the arrest statistics, even when socio-economic conditions are taken into account. Robert Reiner's survey of the research in both the UK and the USA on this topic leads him to conclude that the categories informing police stereotyping reflect power in society and produce a pattern of discrimination.[53] Reiner comments that these are the same groups which, in terms of 'cop culture' can be characterized as 'police property' – low-status, powerless groups whom the dominant majority see as problematic or distasteful. The majority are content to let the police deal with such groups and turn a blind eye to the manner in which this is done. As we have discussed above, the requirement of 'reasonable suspicion' before an arrest can be made does little to inhibit such differential practices in relation to arrest. Such practices fall clearly within what Choongh calls a 'social disciplinary model' of police activity. He argues that the police believe that:

an acceptable and efficient way to police society is to identify classes of people who in various ways reject prevailing norms because it is amongst these classes that the threat of crime is at its most intense. Having identified the 'criminal classes', the police are then justified in subjecting them to surveillance and subjugation, regardless of whether the individuals selected for this treatment are violating the law at any given moment.[54]

Choongh argues that it is the lower working-class, members of ethnic minorities, and those who have no stake in society, such as travellers, who are perceived by the police as posing a special and constant threat to order and thus become the focus of particular attention.[55] Members of targeted groups are deemed to be in need of corrective treatment regardless of whether they actually do anything which could reasonably be interpreted as anti-authoritarian, and the power to arrest suspects allows police officers to extract the submissiveness which they feel is their due.[56] When the police arrest for the purpose of maintaining control over and extracting deference from target groups, the presumption is that there will be no charge, although this presumption can be rebutted. Police questioning in these circumstances is not focused on extracting confessions. The opportunity is taken to ask detainees any question the police want, in the manner they want, regardless of whether it relates to the original suspicion. Respondents in Choongh's study were asked about their personal relationships, where they got their new trainers from, about their immigration status, and why they were claiming state benefits. These questions had no connection with the original reason for the arrest. The intended effect is to make it clear that members of the target groups have no privacy from the police.[57] Choongh's study showed that in a significant minority of cases, police powers are being used, not for the purposes of enforcing the criminal law, but to further the objectives of the police, who believe

---

[53]  R. Reiner, *The Politics of the Police* (3rd edn, 2000) Oxford University Press, Oxford, p. 91.

[54]  S. Choongh, 'Policing the Dross: A Social Disciplinary Model of Policing' (1998) 38(4) British Journal of Criminology 623 at p. 627.                          [55]  Choongh (1998) p. 627.

[56]  Choongh (1998) p. 630.          [57]  Choongh (1998) pp. 631–2.

that they must have control over 'problem' communities. The power of arrest is one power that is used in this way to impress upon the target groups that challenge, resistance, and a lack of respect in relation to the police will incur punishment, even if only through an informal, police-administered system.[58] This is another study which reinforces the necessity of adopting an integrated theory by which to explain the workings of the criminal justice system. Such evidence would be ignored by a rule-centred approach.

## Requirements for a valid arrest

Although PACE provides the power to arrest, it does not actually define what an arrest is. This is a matter left to common law, where the basic principle appears to be that either the suspect must submit to the arrest, or there must be a physical act of restraint, preventing the suspect from leaving.[59] So long as the arrest is lawful, the constable may use reasonable force to effect it. Section 117 of PACE provides that a constable may use reasonable force in the exercise of any power conferred by the Act, provided that the exercise of the power does not depend on the consent of any person. This general statement covers the powers of arrest in s. 24.[60] It will always be a matter of judgement, in the circumstances of each case, how much force is reasonable.

The suspect must also be told in clear terms (as soon as is practicable) that he is under arrest, even if it is obvious.[61] The suspect must also be told (as soon as is practicable) of the ground of arrest, and again, where the arrest is by a police officer, this information must be given, regardless of the fact that it is obvious.[62] The test of practicability may take into account operational reasons for delay. In terrorism cases, the courts have given considerable leeway in interpreting the practicability requirement.[63] It has been suggested that in other cases they would be unlikely to provide such room for delay,[64] but others are more sceptical.[65]

PACE, s. 30(1) provides that if a suspect is arrested by a constable somewhere other than at a police station, or is taken into custody after being arrested by a person other than a constable, the person should be taken to a police station as soon as is practicable after the arrest has taken place unless the arrested person is granted street bail. If the arrested person is taken to a police station it should be a

---

58  Choongh (1998) p. 633.      59  *Alderson* v *Booth* [1969] 2 QB 216.
60  Criminal Law Act 1967, s. 3 contains a similar provision.      61  PACE, s. 28(1), (5).
62  PACE, s. 28(3), (4).      63  *Murray* v *Ministry of Defence* [1988] 2 All ER 527.
64  Feldman (2002) p. 345.
65  Sanders et al. (2010) p. 190.

'designated' police station[66] (that is, one designated by the Chief Constable under s. 35 of PACE as a suitable place to detain arrested persons). PACE, s. 30(10) makes provision for delay in taking an arrested person to a police station if the presence of that person elsewhere is necessary in order to carry out such investigations as it is reasonable to carry out immediately. However, where there is such delay, the reason for the delay must be recorded on arrival at the police station.[67] The question of whether a person was actually taken to a police station as soon as practicable is one which will have to be answered in relation to the circumstances of each particular case.

## Street bail

Section 4 of the Criminal Justice Act 2003 amends s. 30 of PACE to enable police officers to bail suspects at any time prior to their arrival at the police station. This means that police officers can bail suspects at the scene of arrest rather than taking them to a police station. Before they grant street bail the police need to be satisfied that they have the correct name and address for the suspect, the suspect will answer bail, the suspect is not a danger to themselves or to the public, and they understand what is happening. Home Office guidance on the exercise of powers to grant street bail is broad and leaves a wide discretion.[68] The primary considerations when deciding whether street bail should be given are the nature and seriousness of the offence, the fitness, vulnerability and awareness of the detainee, the potential for further offences to be committed, and the preservation of evidence.

The benefits of street bail for the police are obvious: it will save time transporting suspects to the station and processing them once they have arrived. The benefits to the suspect are less clear, although it is also claimed that they will be spared the delay involved in a trip to the police station and waiting for their lawyer or family member to arrive. Hucklesby has noted with concern the lack of reliable information about the extent to which pre-charge bail is used. She argues that what research evidence is available on pre-charge bail suggests that it may be used in cases where the police have no intention of pursuing investigations. The introduction of street bail may increase this abuse of pre-charge bail since, like stop and search, it is low visibility discretion not readily amenable to effective regulation by recording and monitoring requirements.[69] Bail decisions are complex and ill-suited to on-the-street decision-making by police officers who will be less experienced than those who have traditionally made bail decisions at the police station. Hucklesby speculates that street bail will be used as a bargaining tool in informal interviewing on the street and will

---

[66] PACE, s. 30(2). See PACE, s. 30(3)–(5) for details of circumstances in which suspects can be taken to non-designated police stations.                                                                      [67] PACE, s. 30(11).

[68] See A. Hucklesby, 'Not Necessarily a Trip to the Police Station' [2004] Criminal Law Review 803.

[69] Hucklesby (2004) p. 809.

result in more people being arrested and bailed than would have been arrested and released or not arrested at all.

# Arrest powers of other actors in the legal system

It is clear that the police are not the only people who have the power to make arrests. We have already seen that members of the public may make 'citizens' arrests', but there are also other actors, such as customs and excise officers and store detectives, who regularly make arrests. The significance of this phenomenon, in terms of an integrated theory of justice, lies in the fact that in order to gain a comprehensive picture of the processes relating to arrest, it is necessary to consider the roles of these other actors, rather than concentrating solely on the public police.

## Officers of Revenue and Customs

In 2005, Customs and Excise merged with the Inland Revenue to form HM Revenue and Customs (HMRC). HMRC is responsible for investigating a wide range of criminal offences including tax fraud. In order to do this, officers of Revenue and Customs require investigative powers. HMRC originally inherited investigatory powers from its predecessor departments, but a consultation was launched with a view to extending PACE powers to HMRC officers.[70] The consultation envisaged that the powers would only be available to authorized officers with special training and not to tax inspectors or other officers engaged in more routine compliance work.[71] The Finance Act 2007 amended PACE so that many of its powers became available for HMRC investigations. As the HMRC explanatory document makes clear, not all the powers in PACE are made available to HMRC investigators:

For example, HMRC does not take fingerprints, charge or bail suspects. This has to be done by the police. Some of the powers in PACE are modified for HMRC. For example, a search warrant may allow HMRC to search persons found on the premises without the need for arrest. This allows HMRC to search a bookkeeper who may have evidence in a briefcase or laptop when a company's premises are searched, but who is not considered a suspect.[72]

Investigatory powers can only be used by authorized officers and there are different levels of authority which are used as equivalents to the different ranks of police officers authorized to carry out particular tasks. A higher-ranking officer is equivalent to

[70]  HM Revenue and Customs, *Modernising, Deterrents and Safeguards: Criminal Investigation Powers – A Technical Consultation Document* (2006) HMRC, London.
[71]  HM Revenue and Customs (2006) p. 14.
[72]  HM Revenue and Customs, *Criminal Investigation Powers and Safeguards* available at: <http://www.hmrc.gov.uk/prosecutions/ci-powers-safeguards.pdf>.

an inspector and a senior officer is equivalent to a superintendent. HMRC has powers to carry out intrusive surveillance under the Regulation of Investigatory Powers Act (RIPA) 2000. These powers are available to the police and are supposed to be used to deal with serious crime such as terrorism. There has been criticism of the use of RIPA powers by the public police.[73] The possible excessive use of RIPA powers by HMRC investigators has also been queried.[74] Although HMRC officers have many investigatory powers of their own, they maintain cooperative relationships with the police in carrying out joint operations. In terms of an integrated theory of justice, such inter-relationships are highly significant.

## Private security personnel

After vehicles, shops are a major target for theft in England and Wales. Security guards and store detectives who deal with such offenders use the powers of arrest which are available to all members of the public to carry out various policing functions, although they are not members of the public police force. As we noted in **Chapter 12**, the contribution of private security personnel to the English legal system is far from insignificant, although their role is rarely referred to in most textbooks on the subject.

In her work on the private security industry in the 1970s, Hilary Draper pointed out that the job of the store detective frequently involves, not only keeping an eye on customers who might engage in shoplifting, but also surveying staff – at that time it was estimated that 75 per cent of 'shrinkage' in the retail trade was caused by employee dishonesty and general inefficiency.[75] Criminal offences involving employees in the retail sector are often not reported to the police because employers prefer to deal with these offences themselves either as a disciplinary matter or by taking civil action.[76]

Whether the wrongdoer is a member of the public or an employee, if it is necessary to apprehend a suspect, the store detective involved will have to rely on the powers of arrest given to all members of the public.

It is clear that there is a great deal of interaction between store detectives and the formal legal system, in particular with the police, who are called in to deal with shoplifters initially apprehended by store detectives. In his ethnographic study of shoplifting, Daniel Murphy found that store detectives largely control shoplifting by a policy of making arrests, although they also use a variety of other methods of control which fall short of apprehension.[77]

---

[73] Sanders et al. (2010) ch. 6.3.

[74] 'Tax inspectors granted permission to spy on potential tax evaders 15 times a day', *The Telegraph*, 13 January 2010. [75] H. Draper, *Private Police* (1978) Penguin, Harmondsworth, p. 49.

[76] J. Shury, M. Speed, D. Vivian, A. Kuechel, and S. Nicholas, *Crime against Retail and Manufacturing Premises: Findings from the 2002 Commercial Victimisation Survey* (2005) Home Office Online Report 37/05, London, available at: <http://www.homeoffice.gov.uk/rds/pdfs05/rdsolr3705.pdf> p. 64.

[77] D. Murphy, *Customers and Thieves* (1986) Gower, Aldershot, p. 113.

Murphy found that informal methods of dealing with shoplifters are employed for a number of different reasons:

(a)  If store detectives have insufficient evidence to support an arrest.

(b)  If making an arrest would interfere with the domestic arrangements of the store detective. Arresting a suspect, waiting for the police to arrive, accompanying them to the police station etc. can take several hours. Some store detectives in Murphy's study were reluctant to arrest 'trivial' shoplifters near closing time (though others were happy to make an arrest at this time in order to increase their overtime pay).

(c)  If a group of suspected shoplifters is involved, because the store detective is unlikely to know which member of the gang has taken the articles, and when they leave, it is difficult to know which person(s) to stop.

(d)  If the store was very busy, store detectives would act as a visible deterrent, rather than arresting individuals. The rationale for this approach appeared to be that during busy periods, the number of shoplifters might quickly overwhelm the security staff, and while they were dealing with wrongdoers at the police station the store would be vulnerable to subsequent thieves.

(e)  Two retailers studied by Murphy had a policy of managing shoplifters informally. They preferred to employ tactics which were aimed at preventing a situation where an arrest had to take place. Security officers were instructed to arrest only those people who ignored or rejected all attempts at informal management. Once arrested, however, the suspects were referred to the police and prosecuted.[78]

Both the formal and informal methods of dealing with shoplifters are very important, in terms of an integrated system of justice. Shoplifting is a significant offence in quantitative terms. However, in terms of the formal legal system, police involvement with the offence is significantly diminished because of the presence of store detectives. The police role is largely one of processing offenders who have been detected and arrested by store detectives. As one police officer told Murphy: 'Shoplifting creates a lot of work and no job satisfaction. It's not really police work – just clerking. Shoplifters are just "handovers."'[79] The informal methods of dealing with shoplifters reveal another aspect of the importance of the relationship between store detectives and the formal legal system, in that the use of these informal methods means that some potential crimes never actually reach the formal legal system, because they are dealt with outside the system. In terms of an integrated theory of justice, it is crucial that the existence of such practices is acknowledged, because it tells us so much about the actuality of legal phenomena.

[78]  Murphy (1986) pp. 167–70.    [79]  Murphy (1986) p. 184.

The degree of interaction with the formal legal system may vary, depending on the working methods of the store detectives involved. Murphy discusses three possible methods of operating, which he describes as 'law-enforcer', 'peace-keeper', and 'moral entrepreneur'. The store detective who adopts the 'law-enforcer' role will tend to concentrate on discovering, apprehending, and interviewing suspected shoplifters and referring them to the police with a view to prosecution taking place. In this case, there will be frequent interaction with the formal legal system. If the 'peace-keeper' role is adopted, there will be a concentration on protecting the store's goods and controlling the shoplifting population without recourse to the police. This may be achieved, for example, by arresting suspects and interviewing them, by allowing them to leave without calling the police, or manipulating them into a customer role, for example by pointing out the nearest available till at which to pay. The 'moral entrepreneur' acts as a representative of society's values and as an arbiter of morality. Typically, this role involves increasing the unpleasantness of the situation for the suspect, to emphasize the wrongness of their actions. These roles are not mutually exclusive; they can be adopted at will to deal with different situations, and may be used in tandem at different stages of dealing with an incident.[80]

Alison Wakefield's study of private security in three different settings offers an interesting analysis of the different functions performed by security officers.[81] She identifies six categories of activities performed by security guards: 'housekeeping', 'customer care', 'preventing crime and anti-social behaviour', 'rule enforcement and the use of sanctions', 'responding to emergencies and offenses in progress', and 'gathering and sharing information'.[82] The security guards were reliant on good relationships with the police to perform many of their functions, not least because the sanctions available to them (mainly exclusion) are limited. However, Wakefield observes that the relationship between the public, police, and private security is mutually beneficial, an 'active partnership', particularly in the case of the 'City Mall'. Wakefield's study provides a useful reminder of the significance of a pluralist account accommodating both private and public policing and an appreciation of the relationship between them.

# Detention

## Detention in the police station

It was noted above that once a person is arrested they must be taken to a police station as soon as is practicable unless they are given street bail.[83] The intention is that a suspect should be taken to the controlled environment of a police station, where any

---

[80] Murphy (1986) pp. 172–5.     [81] A. Wakefield, *Selling Security* (2003) Willan, Cullompton.
[82] Wakefield (2008) ch. 8.     [83] PACE, s. 30(1).

ensuing interrogation must be carried out in accordance with the safeguards provided by PACE. If the police conduct interviews with suspects outside the confines of the police station, they are acting outside the system of protection for suspects and such behaviour is a cause for concern.[84]

PACE continues to use its 'fundamental balance' approach. The intention is to provide protection for the person who is under investigation, while at the same time allowing the police to continue their investigation without undue hindrance.[85] PACE created the 'custody officer',[86] a police officer who must generally be at least the rank of sergeant[87] and independent of the investigation of the offence for which the suspect has been detained.[88] The custody officer is responsible for carrying out a wide range of functions assigned by PACE and Code C (*Code of Practice for the Detention, Treatment and Questioning of Persons by Police Officers*) Revised 2008. The custody officer's first duty is usually to decide whether or not there is sufficient evidence to charge the suspect and whether or not the suspect should be detained or released (with or without bail), and then to take the appropriate action.[89] This must be done as soon as practicable.[90] PACE, s. 37 provides that the custody officer may authorize the detention of the arrested person if the officer has reasonable grounds for believing that detention without charge is *necessary* to secure or preserve evidence relating to an offence for which the person is under arrest or to obtain such evidence by questioning the person. However, the rigour with which the necessity requirement is applied is perhaps another matter. Research suggests that the authorization of detention is a routine process. This may partly be due to the limited information the custody officer receives from the arresting officers before making his or her assessment of whether detention is necessary.[91] McConville et al. also found that custody officers are reluctant to undermine the authority of arresting officers by refusing to authorize detention.[92]

## Reviews of detention

PACE makes provision for periodic reviews of detained persons by a 'review officer'.[93] If the suspect has been detained and charged, the review officer will be the custody officer, but if no charge has been made, the review officer must be an officer of at least the rank of inspector, who has not been directly involved in the investigation.[94]

PACE is very specific about the timing of reviews. The first review must take place not later than six hours after detention was first authorized, and then at intervals not longer than nine hours,[95] although a review may be postponed in limited

---

[84] See, for example, J. Hodgson, 'Adding Injury to Injustice: The Suspect at the Police Station' (1994) Journal of Law and Society 85 at p. 96.          [85] Philips Report (1981a) ch. 4.

[86] PACE, s. 36.

[87] PACE, s. 36(3). Although under s. 36(4), an officer of any rank may perform the functions of a custody officer if a custody officer is not readily available.          [88] PACE, s. 36(5).

[89] PACE, s. 37.          [90] PACE, s. 37(10).          [91] Sanders et al. (2010) p. 216.

[92] McConville et al. (1991) p. 44.          [93] PACE, s. 40(2).          [94] PACE, s. 40(1).

[95] PACE, s. 40(3).

circumstances,[96] for example if the detainee is being questioned and the review officer is satisfied that an interruption would prejudice the investigation.[97] If the suspect has not been charged by the time of the review, the review officer must again consider the matters in s. 37 considered by the custody officer when the suspect initially became his or her responsibility.[98] Before deciding to continue detention, the review officer must give the detainee (unless he or she is asleep) or the detainee's solicitor the opportunity to make representations about continued detention.[99]

One of the principal aims of PACE was to avoid unnecessary or unnecessarily long periods of detention for suspects in police stations. Research by Maguire suggests that this aim has, broadly speaking, been achieved.[100] Usually, suspects who were eventually charged spent three to six hours in police custody, while others spent two to five hours. However, there were wide variations according to the type of crime involved; the average for shoplifting was 2.5 hours, while for burglary it was 16 hours. Maguire also noted that there was some evidence that, while the PACE rules had had the general effect of reducing detention lengths in the case of people suspected on weak evidence of more serious offences, at the other end of the scale the processing time in connection with minor or readily admitted offences has not been reduced and may even have been increased in some cases.[101]

Brown discusses two unpublished research studies which both raise doubts about the way in which reviews of detainees are carried out. This research suggests that the first two reviews tend to be routine procedures, with little heed being paid to representations made by the suspect. Reviews are often conducted over the telephone, which means it is impossible for suspects to make representations directly to the reviewing officer.[102]

## Continued detention

While the general rule is that a person should not be detained in police custody without charge for more than 24 hours, it is possible for a person to be detained for longer than that in certain circumstances. Authorization for continued detention must be given by an officer of the rank of superintendent or above, who must have reasonable grounds for believing:

(a)  continued detention without charge is necessary to secure evidence relating to the offence, or to obtain such evidence by questioning the detainee;

(b)  that the offence is an indictable offence;[103] and

(c)  that the investigation is being conducted diligently and expeditiously.

---

[96]  The review must then be carried out as soon as practicable – PACE, s. 40(4).

[97]  PACE, s. 40(4)(b).      [98]  PACE, s. 40(8).      [99]  PACE, s. 40(12).

[100]  M. Maguire, 'Effects of the PACE Provisions on Detention and Questioning' (1988) 28 British Journal of Criminology 19.      [101]  Maguire (1988) p. 26.

[102]  Brown (1997) pp. 64, 65.

[103]  Serious Organised Crime and Police Act 2005, Sch. 7(3) para. 43(7).

If that is the case, the officer may authorize detention for a period up to 36 hours from when the 'detention clock' started to run.[104]

The additional detention cannot be authorized more than 24 hours after the clock started, nor before the second review is carried out.[105] When the officer has to decide whether or not to authorize continued detention, he or she must give the detainee or any solicitor representing the detainee who is available at the time, an opportunity to make representations to the officer about the decision.[106] Such representations may be made orally or in writing.[107] However, the authorizing officer may refuse to hear an oral representation from the detainee if the officer considers the detainee to be unfit to make such representations by reason of the detainee's condition or behaviour.[108]

Where an officer authorizes continued detention, the officer must inform the detainee of the grounds for the continued detention and record the grounds in the custody record.[109] If at the time, continued detention is authorized, the detainee has not exercised his or her right under s. 56 of PACE to have someone informed of his or her arrest, or his or her right under s. 58 to consult a solicitor, the deciding officer must inform the detainee of these rights. The officer must then decide whether or not to permit the exercise of these rights, using the criteria contained in both those sections which state the circumstances in which delay in the exercise of those rights is permitted.[110]

Once the authorized period of detention is over, the detainee must be released, either with or without bail unless the detainee is charged, or further continued detention is authorized.[111]

## Further detention

Detention beyond 36 hours requires a warrant from a magistrates' court[112] and the detainee is entitled to legal representation at the hearing.[113]

An application for a warrant of further detention must be supported by an information in writing which must include the nature of the offence for which the detainee was arrested, the general nature of the evidence leading to the arrest, what inquiries have been made by the police, what further inquiries they propose to make and the reasons for thinking that the continued detention of the person involved is necessary for the purpose of such inquiries.[114] The criteria which the court applies when deciding whether or not to grant the warrant are the same as those applied by a superintendent considering further detention, that is, that the suspect is under arrest for an indict-

---

104 PACE, s. 42(1).
105 PACE, s. 42(4). As usual, the detainee must be informed of the grounds of continued detention: PACE, s. 42(5).                                                                106 PACE, s. 42(6).
107 PACE, s. 42(7).        108 PACE, s. 42(8).        109 PACE, s. 42(5).        110 PACE, s. 42(9).
111 PACE, s. 42(10).        112 PACE, s. 43(1).
113 PACE, s. 43(3). Note that s. 43(3) also provides that, if necessary, the court must grant an adjournment to enable the detainee to obtain legal representation.                                114 PACE, s. 43(14).

able offence; that detention is necessary to secure or preserve evidence relating to an offence for which the detainee is under arrest or to obtain such evidence by questioning the detainee; and the investigation is being conducted diligently and expeditiously.[115] The application to the court must be made within the 36-hour period.[116] Further applications can be made to a magistrates' court for further periods of detention without charge, up to a maximum of 96 hours. The application is made in the same way as under PACE, s. 43, and the warrant will be granted if the court is satisfied that there are reasonable grounds for believing that further detention is justified.[117]

If at any point, an extension is refused, and at any rate at the expiry of 96 hours, the detainee must be charged or released, with or without bail.[118] The custody record must, of course, be maintained.[119]

## In the police station: the custody officer and the custody record

Some of the responsibilities of the custody officer have been described above, but require further elaboration. The role of the custody officers and their ability to perform the functions envisaged for them has proved controversial. The Royal Commission on Criminal Justice noted that as far as the evidence needed to substantiate a charge is concerned, the custody officer is hardly in a position to take a different view from the investigating officer, because in the nature of things he or she will not have the same direct and detailed knowledge of the case. However, despite such difficulties, the Royal Commission felt that it was important that the role of custody officer should continue to exist. It means that the police take full responsibility for the evidence gathered during interviews, and this will only happen if they remain accountable for ensuring that such evidence is reliable because everything has been done to prevent the suspect from coming under unfair pressure.[120] There are, however, ongoing concerns about the training and experience of police officers called upon to perform the custody officer's role.[121] Given many lack adequate training, it is perhaps unsurprising that they struggle with their role.

Section 39(1) of PACE imposes a duty on the custody officer to ensure that all persons in police detention at that police station are treated in accordance with the statute and Code C.[122] A copy of Code C should be readily available for consultation at all

---

[115] PACE, s. 43(4).

[116] If it is not practicable for the court to sit within that period, the application must be heard within the 6 hours following the 36-hour period (PACE, s. 43(5)). [117] PACE, s. 44(1).

[118] PACE, s. 43(15). [119] PACE, s. 43(6).

[120] Royal Commission on Criminal Justice, *Report* (1993) Cm. 2263, HMSO, London, ch. 3.25.

[121] J. Coppen, 'PACE: A View from the Custody Suite', in E. Cape and R. Young (eds), *Regulating Policing* (2008) Hart, Oxford.

[122] There are special rules relating to juveniles and vulnerable suspects that the custody officer must see are complied with (Code C, paras 3.12–3.20). Such detainees should have an 'appropriate adult', or in the case of certain vulnerable suspects, police surgeon. However, the police do not always identify vulnerabilities or ensure adequate access to the appropriate person. An appropriate adult may be a 'volunteer', in which case, they are generally quicker to respond than a professional, more likely to intervene then a parent

police stations.[123] Code C is a very important document; it has been argued that there are some matters contained within it that should really have been included in the statute itself.[124] However, it remains the case that Code C, like the other Codes under PACE, is not part of the statute, and the sanctions for breaching it are the same as those for breaching the other Codes.[125]

The custody officer must open a 'custody record' for each arrested person at the police station.[126] Both PACE and Code C require certain information to be recorded in the custody record and it is the custody officer who is responsible for its accuracy and completeness.[127] If the suspect is moved to another police station, for example, his custody record goes with him and the time of and reason for the transfer must be recorded in it.[128] All entries in the custody record must be timed and signed[129] and a solicitor must be permitted to inspect the custody record of a detained person as soon as practicable after their arrival at the police station and at any other time whilst the person is detained.[130] At the end of detention, when the person is released or taken before a court, the person or the person's lawyer can request a copy of the custody record and it should be provided as soon as practicable.[131] This is an important right, because the custody record is often a crucial document if a dispute develops about the detainee's treatment at the police station, although it is only effective if the person involved makes the relevant request. The Royal Commission on Criminal Justice noted that the shortcoming of the custody record is that it will not necessarily reveal the circumstances surrounding the written entry. Allegations that procedures were rushed, or that inducements were used to persuade people to sign the custody record can never be entirely met merely by producing the record itself.[132]

The custody officer is under a duty to tell the detainee about certain rights the detainee has whilst in custody.[133] The detainee must also be given a written notice of these rights and this notice must include the following caution:[134]

You do not have to say anything. But it may harm your defence if you do not mention when questioned something which you later rely on in court. Anything you do say may be given in evidence.[135]

---

or professional, but are still not sufficiently interventionist (see H. Pierpoint, 'Quickening the PACE? The Use of Volunteers as Appropriate Adults in England and Wales' (2008) 18(4) Policing and Society 397).

[123] Code C, para. 1.2.    [124] Clark (2004) para. 7.2.

[125] See PACE, s. 67(10) and (11) as outlined in **Chapter 13**.    [126] Code C, para. 2.1.

[127] PACE, s. 39 and Code C, para. 2.3.    [128] Code C, para. 2.3.    [129] Code C, para. 2.6.

[130] Code C, para. 2.4.    [131] Code C, para. 2.4A.

[132] The Commission therefore recommended that there should be continuous video-recording of all the activities in the custody office and in the passages and stairways leading to the cells. It was felt that this would ensure that all parties would follow procedures to the best of their ability and it would also protect the police from allegations of malpractice or error (Royal Commission on Criminal Justice (1993) ch. 3.37).

[133] Code C, para. 3.1. See below, section entitled 'Rights of persons in custody'.

[134] Code C, para. 3.2.    [135] Code C, para. 10.5.

It has been noted that this caution may be misleading in instances where a person has asked for legal advice but who is interviewed without having received it.[136] In such instances, a different caution is needed to reflect amendments to the inference from silence provisions to be discussed more fully below.

Research by Brown et al. found that there were weaknesses in the performance of the custody officer role, especially in relation to notifying suspects of their rights, where, in about 25 per cent of cases observed, custody officers gave information about rights too quickly, or incompletely, or in a way which was incomprehensible to the suspect.[137] The Royal Commission on Criminal Justice observed that the police are not entirely comfortable with the role of custody officer.[138] The job is not a popular one and is probably often performed in poor working conditions. Maguire has noted the pressure that custody officers may come under when working in busy charge rooms.[139] This can only add to the tension already inherent in the role. The Commission recommended exploration of the possibility of some of the clerical and administrative duties of the custody officer being delegated to civilians.[140] This has been taken much further than was envisaged by Pt 4 of the Police Reform Act 2002. The Act introduces 'designated persons', civilian support staff who could perform a wide range of functions including, in relation to detainees, activities like conducting searches and taking fingerprints.[141] Although the police have been able to resist the civilianization of the custody officer role, many of the detention staff working under custody officers are now civilians.[142]

## Investigation

### Searches and the taking of fingerprints and samples

PACE, s. 54 gives the custody officer power to carry out non-intimate searches at the police station. The custody officer must ascertain articles that the arrested person has with him or her, which may, subject to the custody officer's discretion, be recorded as part of the custody record.[143] Normally, suspects will voluntarily reveal their belongings but if necessary, the person may be searched.[144] The search must be carried out by a person of the same sex as the suspect.[145] Any articles produced by the suspect

---

[136] See E. Cape, 'The Revised PACE Codes of Practice: A Further Step towards Inquisitorialism' [2003] Criminal Law Review 355.

[137] D. Brown, T. Ellis, and K. Larcombe, *Changing the Code: Police Detention under the Revised PACE Codes of Practice* (1993) Home Office Research Study No. 129, HMSO, London, ch. 2.

[138] Royal Commission on Criminal Justice (1993) para. 3.24.    [139] Maguire (1988) pp. 35–6.

[140] Royal Commission on Criminal Justice (1993) paras 3.27 and 3.28.

[141] For critical commentary of the provisions, see D. Ormerod and A. Roberts, 'The Police Reform Act 2002 – Increasing Centralization, Maintaining Confidence and Contracting out Crime Control' [2003] Criminal Law Review 141.

[142] See Sanders et al. (2010) p. 198, who observe that the legislative provisions allowing for civilianization of the custody officer role are to be repealed.

[143] PACE, s. 54(1), and (2) as amended by the Criminal Justice Act 2003, s. 8(2).

[144] PACE, s. 54(6).    [145] PACE, s. 54(8), (9) and Code C, para. 4.1.

or discovered during the search may be seized and retained by the custody officer.[146] The reasons for any seizure must be explained to the suspect and noted in the custody record.[147]

*Intimate searches* and *strip searches* may only be carried out in defined circumstances and in accordance with Code C Annex A. Strip searches can be carried out if it is considered necessary to remove an article which the detained person would not be allowed to keep, and the officer concerned reasonably considers that the person might have concealed such an article.[148] The search must be carried out by a person of the same sex as the suspect, in an area where the person being searched cannot be seen by anyone who does not need to be present.[149] Generally, at least two persons should be present other than the person being searched.[150] A strip search should be carried out with proper regard to the sensitivity and vulnerability of the person in these circumstances and every reasonable effort should be made to secure the person's cooperation and minimize embarrassment.[151] The search should be conducted as quickly as possible and the person allowed to dress as soon as it is over.[152]

An 'intimate search' is a search which consists of the physical examination of a person's body orifices other than the mouth.[153] An intimate search can only be carried out if the suspect has been arrested and is in police detention.[154] An officer of at least the rank of inspector may authorize an intimate search if the officer has reasonable grounds for believing that the arrested person may have concealed on him or her anything which the person could use to cause physical injury to himself or herself, or to others, and which the person might so use while in detention, or is concealing a Class A drug and was in possession of it with the appropriate criminal intent before the person's arrest.[155] Intimate searches must generally be made by a suitably qualified person[156] and details of the search will be recorded on the custody record.[157] Annex A makes clear that intimate searches should be avoided if possible and, if done, they should only normally be carried out by a registered medical practitioner or registered nurse. An intimate search by a police officer should only be authorized as a last resort, if the risk of injury from the article sought is sufficiently severe to justify it.[158] Intimate searches are in fact rare.[159]

---

[146] PACE, s. 54(3) – although clothes and other personal effects may only be seized in limited circumstances, e.g. if the detainee might use them to cause physical injury to himself or others (s. 54(4)).

[147] Code C, paras 4.2 and 4.5.      [148] Code C, Annex A, para. 10.

[149] Code C, Annex A, para. 11(a), (b).

[150] Code C, Annex A, para. 11(c). In the case of juveniles, normally one person should be the appropriate adult.      [151] Code C, Annex A, para. 11(d).

[152] Code C, Annex A, para. 11(g).      [153] PACE, s. 65.      [154] PACE, s. 55(1).

[155] PACE, s. 55(1). For the meaning of 'Class A drug', see Misuse of Drugs Act 1971, s. 2(1)(b).

[156] PACE, s. 55(5). For the meaning of 'suitably qualified person', see PACE, s. 55(17).

[157] PACE, s. 55(10) and Code C, Annex A, para. 7.      [158] Code C, Annex A, para. 3.

[159] There are around 100 intimate searches a year, mainly for drugs. (See D. Povey and K. Smith (eds), *Police Powers and Procedures, England and Wales 2007/08*, Home Office Statistical Bulletin 7/09 (2009) Home Office, London.)

If *fingerprints* are required, they will usually be taken with the consent of the detainee. However, fingerprints can be taken without consent if an officer of at least the rank of inspector authorizes it.[160]

*Non-intimate samples* (e.g., saliva, footprint, etc.)[161] can be taken with the suspect's written consent, or without consent subject to the conditions in s. 63 of PACE.[162] An *intimate sample* (e.g., blood, semen, urine, etc.)[163] may only be taken if the detainee consents in writing and it is authorized by an officer of the rank of inspector or above.[164] If the detainee refuses consent without good cause, a court or jury may draw such inferences as appear proper.[165]

## Rights of persons in custody

Where someone has been arrested and is being held in custody, the custody officer must inform the arrested person of his or her rights to have someone informed of the arrest; to consult privately with a solicitor; and to consult the Codes of Practice.[166]

These are continuing rights which may be exercised at any point during the period of custody.[167] However, PACE provides that in the case of persons who are in police detention for an indictable offence, the exercise of these rights can be delayed in certain circumstances.[168] Broadly speaking, any delay in the exercise of the rights discussed above must be authorized by a senior officer, who must have reasonable grounds for believing that the immediate exercise of the right would, for example, lead to interference with evidence connected with an indictable offence or the alerting of other persons suspected of having committed an indictable offence but not yet arrested.[169] If delay is authorized, it must be noted on the custody record and the detainee must be told of the reason for it.[170] Even if delay is initially authorized, the detainee must be allowed to exercise these rights within 36 hours of the 'detention clock' beginning to run.[171]

### Right to have someone informed when arrested

As far as the right to inform someone of the fact of the arrest is concerned, the detainee is entitled to have one person told about the arrest. This person can be a relative, friend, or other person who is known to the detainee or who is likely to take an interest in the detainee's welfare.[172] At the custody officer's discretion, the detainee may also receive

---

[160] Subject to the conditions in PACE, s. 61. See Feldman (2002) pp. 408–10.    [161] PACE, s. 65.
[162] See Feldman (2002) pp. 411–12.    [163] PACE, s. 65.    [164] PACE, s. 62(1).
[165] PACE, s. 62(10).
[166] Code C, para. 3.1 The detainee must be given a written notice detailing the rights along with the right to a copy of the custody record, and must be asked to sign the custody record to acknowledge receipt: Code C, para. 3.2.    [167] Code C, para. 3.1.
[168] PACE, ss. 56 and 58. See also Annex B to Code C.
[169] PACE, ss. 56(5) and 58(8). See also ss. 56(5)A and 58(8)A. See also Code C, Annex B.
[170] PACE, ss. 56(6) and 58(9).    [171] PACE, ss. 56(3) and 58(5).
[172] PACE, s. 56(1); Code C, para. 5.1 provides that if the first person cannot be contacted, the detainee may name up to two alternatives, and if they are unobtainable, further attempts at contacting may be made at the

visits.[173] Code C also provides that, unless the reasons for delay in s. 56(5) apply, the suspect may be supplied with writing materials and speak to one person for a reasonable time on the telephone.[174] The detainee must be informed that letters and calls may be monitored by the police and can be used as evidence (unless it is subject to legal professional privilege).[175] Calls may be terminated if the privilege is abused.[176] A record must be made of all letters, calls, visits, etc.[177]

Brown et al. note that there are several reasons why the take-up rate at which this right is exercised might not be very great: (a) suspects may not wish anyone to know that they have been arrested; (b) family members often know of the arrest already; and (c) suspects see no practical benefit in contacting anyone.[178]

### Right to legal advice

Until PACE came into force, detainees' access to legal advice was governed by the Judges' Rules under which suspects were entitled to ask for legal advice provided that 'no unreasonable delay or hindrance is caused to the process of investigation or the administration of justice'. In practice, the police tended to refuse access to legal advice in a large number of cases.[179] Since the Judges' Rules were not legal rules, effective enforcement of such principles was rarely possible. In addition, many suspects were completely ignorant of the possibility of seeking legal advice while in custody.[180]

PACE attempts to address both these issues, by providing a qualified right to legal advice, underpinned by the criminal defence service scheme, which attempts to ensure that legal advice will be readily available to all, regardless of means, and by ensuring that suspects are told about their rights. There are special provisions the objective of which is to safeguard the position of particularly vulnerable groups, such as juveniles, the mentally or physically disadvantaged, and those who are unable to read.[181]

Code C contains various provisions designed to ensure that a detainee is notified of the right to seek legal advice; for instance, the detainee must be reminded of his or her right before an interview starts or restarts, and informed that the interview can be delayed to allow the detainee to obtain advice (unless any of the reasons permitting the police to delay the exercise of this right apply).[182] Notifying a suspect of the right to seek legal advice includes informing the detainee that independent legal advice is available free of charge from the duty solicitor and that any communication with a

---

discretion of the person in charge. Note 5C suggests that if the detainee does not know anyone to contact, the custody officer should bear in mind any local voluntary organizations, etc. who might be able to help.

[173] Code C, para. 5.4.

[174] Code C, para. 5.6. The telephone call is in addition to any call made to tell someone about the arrest and any call made to a legal adviser – see Code C, Note 5E. These privileges can be delayed or denied in accordance with para. 5.6.    [175] Code C, para. 5.7.

[176] Code C, para. 5.7.    [177] Code C, para. 5.8.    [178] Brown et al. (1993).

[179] J. Baldwin and M. McConville, 'Police Interrogation and the Right to See a Solicitor' [1979b] Criminal Law Review 145.

[180] P. Softley, *Police Interrogation* (1980) Royal Commission on Criminal Procedure Research Study No. 4, HMSO, London, p. 68.    [181] See PACE, s. 57 and throughout Code C.

[182] Code C, para. 11.2.

solicitor may take place in private. In addition, a poster advertising the right to seek legal advice must be prominently displayed at every police station.[183]

The Code stresses that the right should be explained clearly and that no police officer should do or say anything with the intention of dissuading a person in detention from seeking legal advice.[184] The custody officer must give the detainee a written notice explaining the right and how the detainee can obtain legal advice, and the detainee has to sign the custody record to acknowledge receipt of this notice.[185]

Section 58(1) of PACE provides that 'A person arrested and held in custody in a police station or other premises shall be entitled, if he so requests, to consult a solicitor privately at any time.'[186] Requests to consult with solicitors should be recorded in the custody record, and if such a request is made, the detainee should be permitted to consult a solicitor in private as soon as is practicable, unless delay in the exercise of the right is permitted by s. 58(6). Even if delay is permitted, the detainee must be permitted to consult a solicitor within 36 hours.[187] Delay in compliance with a request to seek legal advice is only permitted in the case of a person who is in police detention for an indictable offence and if an officer of at least the rank of superintendent authorizes it. Section 58(8) sets out the circumstances in which delay is permitted:

an officer may only authorise delay where he has reasonable grounds for believing that the exercise of the right ... at the time when the person detained desires to exercise it –

(a) will lead to interference with or harm to evidence connected with a serious arrestable offence or interference with or physical injury to other persons; or
(b) will lead to the alerting of other persons suspected of having committed such an offence but not yet arrested for it; or
(c) will hinder the recovery of any property obtained as the result of such an offence.[188]

If delay is authorized, the person must be told the reason for it and it must be recorded in the custody record.[189] In the case of *R v Samuel*, the Court of Appeal interpreted s. 58 strictly, and held that the right of a person detained by the police to have access to a solicitor was a fundamental right of the citizen. A police officer attempting to justify his or her decision to delay access would have to do so by reference to the specific circumstances of the case, including evidence about the detainee or the actual solicitor to be consulted. In particular, not only did the officer have to believe that access would lead to the alerting of other suspects, but he or she had also to believe that if a solicitor was allowed access to the detained person the solicitor would thereafter commit

---

[183] Code C, para. 6.3.     [184] Code C, paras 3.1 and 6.4.     [185] Code C, para. 3.2.

[186] PACE, s. 58(1) and Code C, para. 6.1. Note that the statutory entitlement is to consult a solicitor but the Code permits representatives to be sent on the solicitor's behalf (Code C, para. 6.12).

[187] PACE, s. 58(5).

[188] There are special rules relating to drug-trafficking offences and confiscation orders under the Criminal Justice Act 1988.     [189] PACE, s. 58(9).

the criminal offence of alerting other suspects or would be hoodwinked into doing so inadvertently. Either belief could only rarely be genuinely held by a police officer.[190]

Once it has been ascertained that the detainee is in a position to exercise his or her right to seek legal advice, the general rule is that a detainee who asks for legal advice should not be interviewed until the detainee has obtained it.[191]

## Obtaining legal advice

Once legal advice has been requested, provided that there are no legitimate reasons for delay, the custody officer must ensure it is received promptly.[192] Although the right to seek legal advice is such an important right, there could clearly be practical difficulties for many people in seeking to exercise it. Arrests may take place at any time of the day or night; legal advisers may not be readily available outside office hours. Before PACE, the unavailability of solicitors to give legal advice to those detained by the police was a major problem.[193] However, the state provides a system for ensuring that all suspects are able to obtain legal advice within a reasonable time. The suspect may choose and pay for his or her own solicitor or seek legal advice through schemes regulated by the Legal Services Commission (LSC).[194] The LSC runs the Criminal Defence Service (CDS). Since April 2001, legally aided police station advice can only be provided by solicitors with a contract with the CDS. In some areas, there is also a public defence service (PDS).[195] Since 2008, all requests for publicly funded legal advice are directed to the Defence Service Call Centre which decides whether to refer the suspect to CDS direct (a telephone advice-line for minor offences) or allow the suspect to nominate his own lawyer or see a solicitor under the duty solicitor scheme. Whether these arrangements ensure that suspects receive high quality legal advice is a matter for debate.[196] There is no obligation for solicitors to participate in the duty solicitor scheme and, in some areas, it is overstretched. Furthermore, the attempts to limit public funding for defence work have made it increasingly difficult for private firms to make such work 'pay'. They are either cutting corners or not doing the work at all, restricting the 'choice' of private solicitors available.

### Putting the provision of legal advice in perspective

Most suspects do not receive legal advice at the police station. There are a number of reasons for this. Many suspects do not appreciate the significance of their right to seek legal advice and therefore do not avail themselves of the right even though they are told about it. Some suspects are dissuaded from seeking legal advice by the police. Several studies have demonstrated the importance of police influence on the suspect's decision whether or not to seek legal advice. Researchers have noted

---

[190] [1988] 2 All ER 135.      [191] Unless one of the provisos set out in Code C, para. 6.6 apply.
[192] Code C, para. 6.5.      [193] Softley (1980) p. 28.
[194] Established by the Access to Justice Act 1999.
[195] For more details on the PDS see **Chapter 16.**      [196] Sanders et al. (2010) pp. 247–9.

that the police may use various 'ploys' to discourage suspects from taking advice, including encouraging suspects to defer requests, or minimizing the significance of what is happening by saying that the person will only be at the station for a short time or emphasizing what a long time the suspect will have to wait until their legal adviser arrives.[197] For many suspects, their priority is to get out of the police station. Although there have been big increases in the proportions of suspects requesting legal advice, many will still be put off by the prospect of a long wait.[198] Skinns found that the average time between request and receipt of advice was four hours, but many suspects think (perhaps wrongly) that if they refuse advice, they will get out of the police station quicker.[199]

Even if suspects do seek advice, it cannot be assumed that the standard of custodial legal advice provided is universally good. Indeed, much of the research evidence suggests the contrary. Matters which may affect the quality of the legal advice include the willingness of the adviser to attend the station to give advice in person. Code C makes it clear that the right to legal advice includes the right to speak on the telephone.[200] Research has shown that whether or not a solicitor will attend at the police station partly depends on whether the solicitor is the detainee's own solicitor or not.[201] Sanders et al. found that many interrogations took place without solicitors being present. This was due in part to the unavailability of solicitors, but it appeared to be far more often due to the simple unwillingness of solicitors to attend.[202] Recent revisions to Code C and the introduction of CDS direct have made it more likely that suspects will receive telephone advice rather than face-to-face advice.[203] Such telephone conversations may be subject to 'eavesdropping' by the police.[204]

The standard of custodial legal advice has long been a matter of concern.[205] Solicitors' use of non-qualified representatives in a large proportion of cases was identified as a

[197] M. McConville, 'Videoing Interrogations: Police Behaviour On and Off Camera' [1992] Criminal Law Review 532; A. Sanders, L. Bridges, A. Mulvaney, and G. Crozier, *Advice and Assistance at Police Stations and the 24-Hour Duty Solicitor Scheme* (1989) Lord Chancellor's Department, London; and A. Sanders and L. Bridges, 'Access to Legal Advice and Police Malpractice' [1990] Criminal Law Review 494.

[198] L. Skinns, '"Let's Get it Over With": Early Findings on Factors Affecting Detainees' Access to Custodial Legal Advice' (2009a) 19(1) Policing and Society 58; L. Skinns, '"I'm a Detainee; Get Me Out of Here"' 49(3) (2009b) British Journal of Criminology 399; V. Kemp and N. Balmer, *Criminal Defence Services: User's Perspectives* (2008) Research Paper No. 21, Legal Services Research Centre, London.

[199] A range of factors including offence seriousness may be more determinative of the length of detention than delay incurred in waiting for a solicitor to arrive (Skinns (2009a and 2009b)).

[200] Code C, para. 6.5.

[201] Sanders et al. (1989) found that duty solicitors gave telephone advice approximately twice as often as clients' own solicitors. Phillips and Brown also found that duty solicitors were less willing to attend than the suspect's 'own' solicitor (see C. Phillips and D. Brown, *Entry into the Criminal Justice System: A Survey of Police Arrests* (1998) Home Office Research Study No. 185, HMSO, London).

[202] Sanders et al. (1989) ch. 6.    [203] Code C, para. 6B.

[204] Skinns (2009a and 2009b). However, the same applies to face-to-face consultations which take place in the custody room.

[205] Research for the Royal Commission on Criminal Justice found serious problems (M. McConville and J. Hodgson, *Custodial Legal Advice and the Right to Silence* (1993) Royal Commission on Criminal Justice Research Study No. 16, HMSO, London).

problem, particularly as there appeared to be no attempt to match the work to be done to the assumed level of competence of the person who was going to do it.[206] A scheme for the assessment and accreditation of non-legally qualified representatives was introduced and positively evaluated.[207] Sanders et al. observe that the accreditation scheme appears to have been successful in ensuring that suspects are not disadvantaged by being advised by non-solicitors.[208] They also note that the LSC requires representatives to be supervised but question how effective a quality control measure this really is. Some police interviewers 'put down' legal advisers who are not solicitors as a way of implying to suspects that their advice is incompetent.[209]

In the context of describing the circumstances when a solicitor may be required to withdraw from an interview, Code C incorporates a description of the defence solicitor's role.[210] Note 6D to the Code states that the solicitor's role is to protect and advance the legal rights of the client and that this may involve giving advice which has the effect of a client avoiding giving evidence which strengthens the prosecution case. The solicitor may also need to intervene in the interview in order to seek clarification, challenge an improper question to their client or the manner in which it is put, advise his or her client not to reply to a particular question, or to give further legal advice. The solicitor can only be excluded under the Code if his or her approach or conduct prevents or unreasonably obstructs proper questions being put to the suspect or his or her response being recorded—for example, by answering questions on a suspect's behalf.

Research by McConville et al. into the working practices, value systems, and organization of solicitors and their staff engaged in criminal defence work suggests that suspects do not always get representation that matches the role of the defence solicitor as described in the Code.[211] Their research shows that legal advisers often do not use their presence to the best advantage of their clients. Rather than protecting their clients during interview, legal advisers may facilitate the police by uncritically accepting the legitimacy of their actions:

The reason for this is that many advisers, like the police, instinctively believe, without requiring substantiation through evidence, that there is a case to answer, and that it is the client who must give the answer. This in turn springs from a working assumption that the

---

[206] Three-quarters of all police station attendances in McConville and Hodgson's study (1993) and 30 per cent of cases in Sanders et al.'s study (1989) ch. 5) involved the use of representatives.

[207] L. Bridges and S. Choongh, *Improving Police Station Legal Advice* (1998) Law Society, London.

[208] Sanders et al. (2010) p. 240.

[209] E. Shepherd, *Investigative Interviewing: The Conversation Management Approach* (2007) Oxford University Press, Oxford, at p. 311.

[210] A solicitor may only be asked to withdraw from an interview in two situations: if the client requests the solicitor to withdraw or if the solicitor's conduct prevents an investigating officer from properly putting his questions to the suspect (Code C, para. 6.9). In both situations, a record must be made (Code C, para. 6.17).

[211] M. McConville, J. Hodgson, L. Bridges, and A. Pavlovic, *Standing Accused* (1994) Clarendon Press, Oxford.

client is probably factually guilty. In line with these ideologies, advisers permit the police free rein in interrogations, and thereby legitimate dubious police methodologies.[212]

## Interviewing suspects

### General

If the suspect is arrested somewhere other than at a police station, the suspect must not usually be interviewed about the offence until he or she arrives at a police station.[213] A written record must be made of any comments made by the suspect which were made outside the context of an interview but which might be relevant to the offence; where practicable the suspect should be asked to read and sign the record.[214]

The basic assumption is that interviews should normally take place at the police station where the defendant should have the benefit of all the safeguards that PACE and the Codes of Practice provide for detainees being interviewed. It is very important to know what is and what is not an 'interview', because the provisions of PACE and the Code which provide safeguards do so for detainees being 'interviewed'.

Code C, para. 11.1A defines an 'interview' as:

the questioning of a person regarding his involvement or suspected involvement in a criminal offence or offences which, under paragraph 10.1, must be carried out under caution...

Previous attempts to define an interview have generated a body of case law. Relevant cases suggest that an objective test is applied; for example, a conversation can count as an interview even if the police officer involved genuinely believes that he or she is only having an informal chat.[215] Other cases suggest that an interview is a series of questions directed by the police to a suspect with a view to obtaining admissions on which proceedings may be founded and that the subject-matter and the likely evidential effect of the answer, or failure to answer, is the crucial factor, and not the length of the conversation.[216]

### Interview conditions

Code C, para. 12 contains detailed provisions the objective of which is to ensure that interviews in police stations are conducted in a humane manner. It is the custody officer's responsibility to decide whether the detained person is fit to be interviewed.[217] As far as practicable, interviews should take place in rooms which are adequately

---

[212] McConville et al. (1994) pp. 126, 127.

[213] PACE, s. 30 and Code C, para. 11.1. The three exceptions are set out in Code C, para. 11.1, where delay in questioning may lead to harm to evidence or persons, the alerting of other suspects or obstruction in the recovery of property. [214] Code C, para. 11.13.

[215] *R v Sparks* [1991] Criminal Law Review 128. For a more detailed discussion of relevant case law, see Clark (2004) para. 8.17, p. 505. [216] See Bingham LJ in *R v Absolam* (1989) 88 Cr App R 85.

[217] Code C, para. 12.3.

heated, lit, and ventilated,[218] with the suspect seated.[219] The Code sets out the procedure to be followed for detainees who refuse to go to an interview room.[220] In any 24-hour period, a detainee must generally be allowed a continuous period of rest of at least eight hours.[221] Breaks from interviewing should be made at recognized mealtimes and short refreshment breaks provided at approximately two-hourly intervals.[222]

### Recording the interview

An accurate record must be made of every interview which takes place.[223] The record should normally be made during the course of the interview or as soon as practicable afterwards.[224] The record can be made in writing, on audio-tape, or by visual recording; audio and visual recording must be made in accordance with the relevant Codes of Practice.[225] Unless it is impracticable, the suspect should be given the opportunity to read the interview record and sign it as correct or indicate any inaccuracies.[226]

The tape-recording of interviews in a police station of suspects alleged to have committed an indictable or triable either way offence is now routine.[227] Like all the Codes, Code E is not part of the substantive law, but the Notes for Guidance point out that any decision not to tape record may be the subject of comment in court and the authorizing officer must therefore be prepared to justify such a decision.[228] The recording should be carried out openly, to instil confidence in its reliability and impartiality,[229] and a master copy should be sealed in the presence of the suspect.[230] The Code also contains detailed provisions covering the failure of recording equipment, changing of tapes, and security of master tapes. The custody officer may authorize the interviewer not to tape record if equipment fails or a suitable interview room is not available and on reasonable grounds the interview should not be delayed[231] or if it is clear from the outset that the suspect will not be prosecuted.[232] In these cases, the interview must be recorded in writing and the custody officer must make a note of the specific reasons for not tape-recording.[233]

Although the audio recording of interviews is generally regarded with favour, research shows that despite the availability of such recordings, not much use is made of them by either the prosecution or the defence. What appears to happen instead is

---

[218] Code C, para. 12.4.    [219] Code C, para. 12.6.    [220] Code C, para. 12.5

[221] Code C, para. 12.2. The rest period may be interrupted or delayed if there are reasonable grounds for believing that it would involve a risk of harm to persons or serious damage to property, delay unnecessarily the person's release from custody or otherwise prejudice the outcome of the investigation.

[222] Code C, para. 12.8, although breaks may be delayed on the same grounds as the eight-hour rest period (see footnote above).

[223] Code C, para. 11.7(a) (whether or not the interview takes place at a police station).

[224] Code C, paras 11.7(c) and 11.8.    [225] Code E for audio-tape and Code F for visual-recording.

[226] Code C, para. 11.11.

[227] Code E, para. 3.1. Separate provisions apply to offences under the Terrorism Act 2000 (Code E, para. 3.2).    [228] Code E, Note 3B.

[229] Code E, para. 2.1.    [230] Code E, para. 2.2.    [231] Code E, para. 3.3(a).

[232] Code E, para. 3.3(b).    [233] Code E, para. 3.3.

that the parties rely on the summary, whose quality can vary greatly.[234] Baldwin and Bedward discovered a number of different deficiencies in the summaries. Some were so long that they could not be regarded as summaries at all, revealing an inability to distinguish relevant from irrelevant material. If the requirement in Code E that any admissions be written out verbatim is taken literally, the resulting transcript can be incomprehensible. At the other extreme, summaries can be so short that they omit important material. The most disturbing finding, however, was that a third of the 200 summaries examined were regarded as containing material that gave a misleading or distorted view of a case or were generally of poor quality. Research carried out by Baldwin for the Royal Commission on Criminal Justice confirmed the earlier findings; Baldwin examined interview summaries from four different police forces and concluded that in less than a third of cases could the summaries be said to form an accurate and succinct record of the interview.[235] The Royal Commission recommended that a number of different possible solutions to this problem be explored, including the preparation of transcripts, or preparation of the summaries by the CPS.[236]

One problem that can never be overcome by audio recording is that it does not provide an accurate record of non-verbal behaviour in the interview room which the suspect may find oppressive. The visual recording of interviews would perhaps address such concerns. Code F was introduced to regulate the visual recording of interviews. Any record, audio or visual, will of course remain open to concerns about exchanges that may have taken place off tape or camera.[237] Whilst digital recording may have addressed some of the problems with non-digital record, several issues may remain. For example, recordings may still focus on the demeanour of the suspect and give a less complete view of the questioner. It remains the case that prosecutors rely mainly on summaries of interview rather than viewing a digital record.[238]

## Police interviews in perspective

There is general consensus among commentators that admissions made during police questioning are one of the most useful sources for obtaining police detections.[239] Police officers, particularly detectives, perceive interrogation as the single most important stage in criminal investigation.[240] However, research suggests that the police may not be particularly skilled at interviewing suspects. In his study of police interviewing techniques based upon 600 audio- and video-tapes recorded in three police forces,

[234] J. Baldwin and J. Bedward, 'Summarising Tape Recordings of Police Interviews' [1991] Criminal Law Review 671.

[235] J. Baldwin, *Preparing the Record of Taped Interview* (1992a) Royal Commission on Criminal Justice Research Study No. 2, HMSO, London.        [236] Royal Commission on Criminal Justice (1993) ch. 3.79.

[237] McConville (1992).

[238] C. Taylor (2006) *Criminal Investigation and Pre-trial Disclosure in the United Kingdom: How Detectives Put Together a Case* (2006) Edwin Mellen Press, Lampeter.

[239] See, for example, R. Mawby, *Policing the City* (1979) Saxon House, Farnborough; A. Bottomley and C. Coleman, *Understanding Crime Rates* (1981) Saxon House, Farnborough.

[240] J. Baldwin, *The Conduct of Police Investigation* (1992b) HMSO, London.

Baldwin found that most interviews consisted of relatively straightforward inter-changes with reasonably compliant suspects. In only 4.5 per cent of the cases exam-ined did the police officer's manner seem markedly abrasive or aggressive. Nor were the interviews protracted: 89 per cent of suspects were only questioned on one occa-sion and almost 75 per cent of interviews were concluded within half an hour. Baldwin comments that most suspects in the study were thoroughly cooperative, calling into question the frequently voiced police warnings about the increasing difficulties posed by suspects in interviews.[241]

Baldwin's study confirmed the findings he had made in an earlier study, that only a minority of police officers could be said to be skilled interviewers.[242] He found that in many cases officers were ill-prepared for the interview, being unacquainted even with the basic details of the investigation; they frequently make assumptions of guilt and they are unduly repetitive or laboured in pursuing particular lines of questioning.[243]

Frequently, the early formalities (e.g., explaining the taping procedure, administer-ing the caution) were performed in a very casual manner, often garbled and clearly not in a manner designed to ensure that the suspect thoroughly understood what was going on. Police training places great emphasis on establishing rapport with suspects. Yet, most officers made no effort to do this, preferring to conduct the interview in an atmosphere of some formality rather than seek to create false bonhomie. A minor-ity were by nature good communicators, able to establish rapport with relative ease, but most attempts to put suspects at their ease were at best thoroughly artificial and at worst inappropriate. It was difficult to assess whether this process arose out of sheer ineptitude, or whether it was a deliberate attempt to unsettle or frighten sus-pects. Whatever the reason, interviews which began badly because of these techniques tended to continue that way.[244]

Baldwin identified a number of principal flaws in the way in which interviews were carried out. First, general ineptitude: the image of police interviewers as profes-sional, skilled, and forceful interrogators scarcely matched the reality which Baldwin observed. More frequently, officers emerged as ill at ease and lacking in confidence, frequently with very limited social skills. Officers were clearly preoccupied with estab-lishing relevant 'points to prove', almost regardless of the suspects' responses.[245] A second basic flaw in the interviewing technique was that crude assumptions of guilt tended to be made from the outset. Whilst this may sometimes be understandable, it is dangerous for suspects. An interview can be very unfair to a suspect where officers enter the interview room with their mind made up and treat the suspect's explanation of the circumstances, if they bother to listen to it at all, with extreme scepticism from the outset. Baldwin comments that the police are not disposed, either by training or

[241] J. Baldwin, 'Police Interview Techniques: Establishing Truth or Proof?' (1993) 33 British Journal of Criminology 325 at p. 331.

[242] J. Baldwin, *Video Taping Interviews with Police Suspects: A National Evaluation* (1992c) Home Office, London.                    [243] Baldwin (1993) p. 336.

[244] Baldwin (1993) p. 338.        [245] Baldwin (1993) pp. 338–40.

temperament, to think that they might be wrong. The questions asked merely seek to persuade suspects to accept a predetermined version of events. In several interviews examined by Baldwin, admissions were obtained only in response to a series of leading questions. Instead of allowing suspects to give their own version of events, officers merely invited them to agree with a series of propositions. Denials and alternative explanations are brushed aside. Suspects who make admissions in such interviews find, moreover, that their admissions are rarely subject to subsequent challenge.[246] Instances of coercion or belligerence when interviewing were much less frequent than feebleness and ineptitude. However, the boundaries between officers failing to listen adequately to suspects' responses and exerting undue pressures to induce a confession are very blurred. Questioning is no less coercive because officers act out of naivety, incompetence, or stupidity.

Baldwin concluded that the majority of police officers in his sample could not be described as good interviewers, however volubly they spoke (as they frequently did) about the high-level psychological concepts that they applied in interviewing. Interrogations were conducted with an eye to a subsequent trial, so that a main purpose of the interview is to seek to limit, close down, or pre-empt the future options available to the suspect, to make it more likely that a conviction will be obtained.[247]

Baldwin's findings are confirmed by the study carried out by McConville et al., which looked at how in a criminal case the prosecution constructs and presents its case.[248] The fundamental point which McConville et al. make is that during the interrogation process the police are able to construct evidence, not in terms of making it up, but in the sense that they have the ability to select, evaluate, reject, and generate facts. 'Facts, in this sense, are not objective entities which exist independently of the social actors, but are *created* by them.'[249]

In terms of rhetoric, police investigations are said to take place in circumstances which enable everyone to be fully informed as to what took place. PACE gives custody officers the responsibility of keeping records of the time taken for interviewing and for ensuring that there is full compliance with the rules relating to duration of interview. Interviewing officers must keep a record of the interview and invite suspects to verify its accuracy. However, McConville et al. found that official records of interviews constitute only a partial record of what actually happened. This is because it ignores the questioning which often precedes it. This is the 'informal interview' which takes place, quite literally, off the record. McConville et al. found that this can occur in a number of ways: the custody officer may permit the interviewing officer to visit the suspect in the cells, or questions may be asked in the police car on the way to the station. There need be nothing sinister in these exchanges. It is an important part of police culture to 'know your suspect', to learn about his or her lifestyle, hopes, fears, and problems. This is seen as essential in order to 'get under the skin' of the suspect and learn 'what

---

[246] Baldwin (1993) p. 341.     [247] Baldwin (1993) p. 350.     [248] McConville et al. (1991).
[249] McConville et al. (1991) p. 56.

makes him tick'. The system of contemporaneous recording is seen as inimical to this process. One officer told the researchers:

I'd never go cold into an interview. I always have a run over first with the person, do an informal chat without making notes. Then I do the formal interview with the note-taking being done. I'd write up some notes of the informal later...[250]

It is in these covert exchanges that the police may be able to use strategies which, if they were clearly recorded, would incur the disapproval of the courts.

The establishment of a case against a suspect requires proof of certain basic facts. It is often assumed that these facts just exist, but what this research powerfully demonstrates is that in reality these 'facts' are the outcome of a process of construction. The main forum for case construction is the interview; 'facts' are not just elicited from a suspect, they are the product of a complex interaction between suspect and officer. In practice, the weight of the evidence in a criminal trial comes not from an independent source, but from the suspect himself, and the police put most of their efforts into producing an admission by the suspect which will lead to conviction. Often, however, these 'admissions' are not volunteered by the suspect, but are created by the form of police questioning.[251] McConville et al. found that custodial police questioning is highly directive in nature, with the suspect being influenced by cues expressed in questions showing what the interrogator expects the 'correct' answer to be. This does not mean that the answers will necessarily reveal what could be regarded as objective truth.[252]

Empirical investigations of the reality of police interviewing reveal then, that while PACE does its best to balance the interests of the suspect with those of the police, there are complex social interactions taking place which may undermine the intentions of the statute. The last two decades have seen the issuing of new guidance on investigative interviewing. However, Sanders et al. observe that, despite the new guidance and training, there is little evidence of substantial improvement in practice.[253] The police still tend to focus on minor inconsistencies in accounts, despite the fact that inconsistencies are likely in truthful accounts. Police officers also wrongly assume that they are able to detect accurately lies from the physical behaviour of suspects, such as hand movements. The dominant assumption of interviewers still tends to be that the suspect is guilty. In this respect, and others, police officers and people who belong to other organizations that investigate criminal offences may behave in similar ways.

## Interviews by non-police investigators

Despite the fact that many criminal offences of a 'regulatory' nature are investigated by non-police agencies, the process of interviewing by officials working for these organizations has been relatively neglected. However, recent research has examined the

---

[250]  McConville et al. (1991) p. 59.    [251]  McConville et al. (1991) p. 67.
[252]  McConville et al. (1991) p. 68.    [253]  Sanders et al. (2010) ch. 5.

interviewing practices of investigators dealing with benefit fraud suspects.[254] Following studies such as Baldwin's in the 1980s which revealed how inept the police were at interviewing, the police received new guidance and training based on the PEACE model: planning and preparation, engage and explanation, account, closure, and evaluation. Training on this model was also offered to benefit fraud investigators. Walsh and Milne compared the interviewing performance of trained and untrained investigators and found that there was some improvement in the performance of trained investigators, for example in the use of open questions. However, many shortfalls in the interviewing technique remained even amongst those who were trained. Walsh and Milne expressed concerns about the lack of preparation, shortfalls in rapport-building, failures to explore the suspect's motive, lack of summarizing during the interview, and poor interview closure. They concluded that training had not markedly improved interview performance and that 42 per cent of investigators were demonstrating no more than adequate interviewing technique even after training. Research into the interviewing practices of benefit fraud investigators is ongoing.[255] Factors being explored include the point at which disclosure of evidence is made, and the impact of different interviewing approaches on outcomes. Whilst it has been found that the PEACE model has reduced the instances of unethical practices, and that there are few instances of oppression, investigators seem to be interviewing too early in the investigative process. This conclusion stems from the finding that, in many cases, only limited evidence is presented. Interviewers may be presuming that the suspect is guilty and adopting the approach that the suspects will admit guilt once presented with a limited amount of evidence.[256] This finding seems to echo the crime control assumptions of the police. The overall conclusion that skilled interviewing by benefit fraud investigators is rare also resonates with the finding that much police interviewing is poor.

## The right to silence

The right of a suspect to remain silent when questioned by the police or other authorities has long been a controversial subject. It is a right which is allied to two fundamental principles of criminal law: the presumption of innocence which requires that the prosecution must prove the guilt of the accused;[257] and the principle that the accused should not be put under pressure to incriminate himself or herself.[258] In the 1970s, it was suggested that the right to silence be modified to allow juries to draw adverse

---

[254] D. Walsh and R. Milne, 'Keeping the Peace? A Study of Investigative Practice in the Public Sector' (2008) Legal and Criminological Psychology 39; D. Walsh and R. Milne (2007) 'Giving P.E.A.C.E. a Chance: A Study of DWP's Investigators' Perceptions of their Interviewing Practices' (2007) 85 Public Administration 525.

[255] D. Walsh and R. Bull, 'Interviewing Suspects of Fraud' (2009) 37 Journal of Psychiatry and Law 1.

[256] Walsh and Milne (2007); Walsh and Bull (2009).

[257] Lord Sankey in *Woolmington* v *DPP* [1935] AC 462. See also the Philips Report (1981a) para. 4.35.

[258] See the Philips Report (1981a) para. 4.36.

inferences from silence during interrogation.[259] However, the Philips Commission did not favour this. Although research for the Commission showed that few suspects exercised the right to remain silent,[260] the Commission regarded the right as an essential safeguard to the weak, immature, and inadequate.[261] Despite this momentum for reforming, the right to silence gathered.[262] The matter was considered again by the Runciman Commission, which, in weighing up the views for and against modification of the right, concluded that it should be retained in an unmodified form.[263]

They took a serious view of the extra pressure on suspects to talk in the police station and the adverse inferences which could be made if they chose to remain silent and the possibility that this could result in more convictions of the innocent. This danger outweighed, for the majority, the risk that some silent but guilty persons may remain unconvicted.[264]

Despite the clear conclusion reached by the Runciman Commission, the Government decided to amend the right of silence in the Criminal Justice and Public Order Act (CJPOA) 1994, s. 34 of which provides that where, during questioning, either by the police or by other officials who have a duty to investigate offences, before or after being charged, a defendant fails to mention a fact which the defendant wishes to rely on in his or her defence and it is a fact which the defendant could reasonably have been expected to mention, then a court or jury may draw 'such inferences from the failure as appear proper'. Section 35 contains a parallel provision which relates to a decision to remain silent at trial. The accused must be told in ordinary language that if he or she refuses to be sworn, or refuses, without good cause, to answer questions, then the court or jury may draw such inferences as appear proper. Section 36 provides that where a person is arrested by the police and there is an object, substance, or mark on his or her person, clothing, or footwear which an investigating officer reasonably believes may be attributable to the participation of the suspect in an offence, and the suspect either fails to account, or refuses to account for this, then the court or jury may draw such inferences as appear proper. Similarly, in s. 37, if an accused person fails or refuses to account for his or her presence at a particular place.

The modified 'right to silence' was accompanied by a new form of caution to be administered on arrest prior to interview. The caution, as set out in para. 10.4 of Code C is:

You do not have to say anything. But it may harm your defence if you do not mention when questioned something which you later rely on in court. Anything you do say may be given in evidence.

---

[259] Criminal Law Revision Committee, *11th Report* (1972) Cmnd 4991, HMSO, London, para. 32.

[260] See J. Baldwin and M. McConville, *Confessions in Crown Court Trials* (1980) Royal Commission on Criminal Procedure Research Study No. 5, HMSO, London; and J. Vennard, *Contested Trials in Magistrates' Courts: The Case for the Prosecution* (1980) Royal Commission on Criminal Procedure Research Study No. 6, HMSO, London.                                    [261] Philips Report (1981a) para. 4.41.

[262] *Report of the Home Office Working Group on the Right of Silence* (1989) HMSO, London. The Committee concluded inferences should be possible, but the suspect should receive a modified caution before interview.                              [263] Royal Commission on Criminal Justice (1993) ch. 4.

[264] Royal Commission on Criminal Justice (1993) ch. 4, para. 22.

T. Bucke et al. found that the number of suspects exercising their right to silence in police interviews fell under the new rules.[265] Despite the amendments leading to greater significance being accorded to what suspects do or do not say during police interviews, Bucke et al. found that there was no significant rise in the number of suspects requesting and receiving legal advice.[266] However, they noted the importance of good quality legal advice. Legal advisers themselves were particularly concerned about the impact of the changes on vulnerable suspects who, because of their suggestibility, might feel pressurized into answering questions when they might best be advised to remain silent.[267]

## Silence in the police station and the European Court of Human Rights

It was speculated that the inferences from silence provisions in the CJPOA 1994 might fall foul of Article 6 of the European Convention on Human Rights.[268] Although it is now clear that the provisions will not be declared incompatible with Article 6, Strasbourg and domestic case law have restricted the operation of s. 34 of the CJPOA 1994.[269] In *Murray* v *United Kingdom*, the European Court of Human Rights has held that inferences from silence provisions do not of themselves breach the Convention, but seeking to found a conviction solely or *mainly* on such inferences would be a breach.[270] In *Condron* v *United Kingdom*, the court made a further ruling about the conditions under which an inference can be drawn.[271] The court ruled that inferences could only be drawn if the facts as established by other evidence clearly called for an explanation from the accused. Furthermore, the jury must be directed that they may draw an inference from the accused's silence in interview only if satisfied that the reason for silence was that the accused had no answer to the questions or none that he or she was prepared to have questioned or investigated.

In *Murray* v *United Kingdom* the European Court of Human Rights also ruled that the accused must be given access to legal advice before being interviewed. In response the Youth Justice and Criminal Evidence Act 1999 amended s. 34 of CJPOA 1994 so that inferences may not be drawn from a failure to mention facts if the accused has not been given an opportunity to consult a solicitor prior to being questioned.[272] A special caution applies when before being interviewed the detainee has asked for legal advice, has not been allowed to consult a solicitor (including the duty solicitor), and has not changed his or her mind about wanting legal advice.[273] In such circumstances, the

---

[265] T. Bucke, R. Street, and D. Brown, *The Right of Silence: The Impact of the Criminal Justice and Public Order Act 1994* (2000) Home Office Research Study No. 199, Home Office, London.

[266] Bucke et al. (2000) p. 21.        [267] Bucke et al. (2000) pp. 37–8.

[268] A. Ashworth, *The Criminal Process* (2nd edn, 1998) Oxford University Press, Oxford, p. 108.

[269] I. Dennis, 'Silence in the Police Station: The Marginalisation of Section 34' [2002] Criminal Law Review 25.                        [270] *Murray* v *United Kingdom* (1996) 22 EHHR 29.

[271] *Condron* v *United Kingdom* (2001) 31 EHHR 1.

[272] Youth Justice and Criminal Evidence Act 1999, s. 58.

[273] Code C, para.10.6 and Annex C, para. 1(a).

suspect must be cautioned: 'You do not have to say anything, but anything you do say may be given in evidence.'[274]

Both the domestic courts and Strasbourg have tackled the issue of drawing inferences in cases where the defendant has received legal advice and that advice was to remain silent.[275] It had appeared that if the jury decided that the defendant genuinely relied on legal advice to remain silent then no adverse inference can be drawn. However, in *Howell* the Court of Appeal said that solicitors might be encouraged to give advice to remain silent other than for good objective reasons. Following *Howell*, it would appear that, if the court thinks that the legal advice to remain silent was not based on good objective reasons, the defendant may be exposed to adverse inferences even where the defendant genuinely relied on that 'bad' advice.[276] In *Hoare and Pierce*,[277] it was held that reliance on the advice of a solicitor to remain silent was not in itself enough to prevent adverse inferences being drawn. Even where the advice to remain silent was given in good faith and the reliance upon it was genuine, an adverse inference could be drawn if the jury felt that the accused remained silent because he had either no explanation or no satisfactory explanation to give. This case confirmed that the test is an objective one of whether it was reasonable for the defendant to rely on the solicitor's advice taking into account all the circumstances of the case. In *Beckles*,[278] the defendant's conviction was overturned and a retrial ordered because the jury had not been directed to consider whether the accused had genuinely and reasonably relied on his solicitor's advice to remain silent in interview.

## Confessions

One of the points made to the Runciman Commission in favour of amending the right to silence was that it would reduce the emphasis on confession evidence. It was argued that the law as it stood put undue pressure on the police to obtain a confession because that is virtually the only way open to them of proving key elements of a criminal offence.[279] Confessions were at the heart of the concern about miscarriages of justice in cases such as the Birmingham Six and the Guildford Four, which arose out of terrorist bombings in the 1970s and which gave rise to the Runciman Commission; consequently this is a major part of the Report.[280]

The Commission acknowledged that there is a substantial body of research which suggests that people may make false confessions for a number of different reasons, ranging from a desire for publicity or notoriety, to the situation where a suspect is persuaded temporarily by interrogators that they really have done the act in

---

[274]  Code C, Annex C, para. 2. The caution is the same when a person is (exceptionally) questioned after charge (Code C, Annex C, para. 1(b)).

[275]  See *Betts and Hall* [2001] Cr App R 257; and *Beckles* v *United Kingdom* (2003) 36 EHRR 13.

[276]  See *R* v *Howell* [2003] Criminal Law Review 405 and commentary by D. Birch.

[277]  [2005] WLR 1804.        [278]  [2005] 1 WLR 2829.

[279]  Royal Commission on Criminal Justice (1993) ch. 4, para. 10.

[280]  Royal Commission on Criminal Justice (1993) ch. 4.

question.[281] Gudjonsson, for example, noted two distinct categories of confession: the 'coerced-compliant' confession, where the suspect knows the confession is false, but is prepared to confess in order to escape pressure; and 'coerced-internalized' confessions, where the suspect begins to doubt his own version of events, temporarily believing in his or her own guilt because of disorientation.[282] Given the clear research evidence on the dangers of false confessions, it is very important that the law should contain effective safeguards to try to ensure that false confessions are not believed. This has been highlighted recently by the case of Sean Hodson, who served 27 years in prison following a false confession to murder.[283]

The main safeguards against pressures to falsely confess are ss. 76 and 78 PACE which provide for the exclusion of evidence in certain circumstances. Section 76 deals specifically with confession evidence, and provides for its exclusion when it has been obtained by oppression of the person who made it, or in consequence of anything said or done which was likely, in the circumstances existing at the time, to render it unreliable. Section 78 is a more general provision, applying not only to confessions, but also to other types of evidence. Under s. 78 of PACE, the court has a discretion to exclude evidence where:

having regard to all the circumstances, including the circumstances in which the evidence was obtained, the admission of the evidence would have such an adverse effect on the fairness of the proceedings that the court ought not to admit it.

There are a large number of reported cases on ss. 76 and 78 of PACE. It has been suggested that, although the decisions do not provide a consistent pattern, the approach is broadly crime-control orientated.[284] The 'safeguard' provided by s. 78 appears inadequate.[285] In a number of cases, the admissibility of evidence has been in question because of incompetent police station advice. In at least one case, the courts ruled a confession inadmissible because of the defence lawyer's hostility towards his client. In another case, the overall deficiencies of the defence lawyer were so bad, that the court concluded that effectively he had been denied access to a lawyer.[286] Although ss. 76 and 78 may be primarily seen as 'imperfect' safeguards against police malpractice,

[281] Royal Commission on Criminal Justice (1993) ch. 4, para. 32.

[282] G. Gudjonsson, *The Psychology of Interrogations, Confessions and Testimony* (1992) Wiley, London.

[283] DNA evidence subsequently proved the murder had been committed by another man. Controversy surrounds the 'objectivity' of DNA evidence (see Sanders et al. (2010) ch. 6), but it should not be forgotten that DNA evidence has the potential to exonerate as well as to convict.

[284] Sanders et al. (2010) pp. 705–8.

[285] See, for example, A. Choo and S. Nash, 'What's the Matter with Section 78?' [1999] Criminal Law Review 929.

[286] See E. Cape, 'Incompetent Police Station Advice and the Exclusion of Evidence' [2002] Criminal Law Review 471.

they can be used to exclude confessions due to the (in)actions of the defendant's own legal adviser.[287]

A further possible safeguard against the danger of convictions based on false confessions would be a rule that the defendant could not be convicted on confession evidence alone (a *corroboration* rule). In England and Wales, as a general rule, the evidence of a single witness may be sufficient to prove any issue, no corroborating evidence is required. It was suggested to the Runciman Commission that a corroboration rule would reduce the risk of miscarriages of justice arising from false confessions.[288] McConville's research for the commission showed that in many confession cases, there was independent evidence and few cases would fail for lack of corroboration.[289] Nevertheless, the majority of the Commission decided that a corroboration rule was not justified, a conclusion that has been much criticized.[290] For example, Ashworth and Redmayne assert that: 'there are simply too many doubts about the processes which lead suspects to confess for a conviction on a confession alone ever to be justified'.[291]

## Bail or custody

Once the police have finished questioning the suspect, a decision must be made about whether the suspect is to be charged. Under the new 'statutory charging scheme', the responsibility for charging suspects has been transferred from the police to the CPS.[292] However, the police continue to play an important role in determining whether the defendant is released either with or without bail, or held in custody. First, it remains the responsibility of the police to decide if the case should be considered for charge, in this sense they are still important gatekeepers and can release the defendant without charge or bail.[293] Decisions to take no further action are not reviewed by the CPS. Custody officers also have powers to bail suspects pending further investigations or a decision about charge.[294] The police can impose conditions on this pre-charge bail. Finally, the custody officer can also, when authorized by a police inspector, remand

---

[287] This is important given, McConville et al.'s findings about the practices of defence solicitors as discussed above (McConville et al. (1994)).

[288] Royal Commission on Criminal Justice (1993) ch. 4, para. 67.

[289] McConville (1993) examined over 500 cases and found that in 86.6 per cent of cases where there was a confession, it was supported by admissible evidence from an independent source, such as a civilian or forensic witness. He estimated that only 3 per cent of confession cases would probably have become acquittals because of the lack of supporting evidence of any kind.

[290] S. Greer, 'The Right to Silence, Defence Disclosure and Confession Evidence' (1994) 21 Journal of Law and Society 102 at p. 114.

[291] A. Ashworth and M. Redmayne, *The Criminal Process* (3rd edn, 2005) Oxford University Press, Oxford.

[292] The introduction of the new 'statutory charging scheme' will be considered more fully in the next chapter.    [293] PACE, s. 37(7)(c).

[294] PACE, s. 37(7)(a)–(b).

the suspect in custody pending a future decision by a prosecutor about charge in situations where a prosecutor is not available either in person or over the phone. As discussed in **Chapter 16**, the decisions the police make about bail can be influential (affecting decisions made by the prosecution and courts) as the case continues its journey through the criminal justice system.

## CONCLUSION

In this chapter we have concentrated on the powers of the police to arrest, detain, and question suspects. We have seen that they have extensive powers to do so and the legal safeguards provided by PACE are often minimal. For example, the 'necessity' standard in relation to arrest decision-making does not prevent the police from using a range of working rules unrelated to the legal criteria for arrest. Once the suspect is arrested and detained, they have a number of rights whilst in the police station. These rights are, however, subject to limitations and exceptions. Suspects in police custody are in need of an effective representation, but, for a range of reasons, including cost and the culture of defence solicitors, may not receive it. Furthermore, they may not exercise their rights due to fear of the consequences, such as delay in getting out of the station, or in the case of the 'right' to silence, fear that adverse inferences will be drawn at trial. It would be wrong to assume that the police are effective interrogators: much of the research shows that, when it comes to questioning suspects, they are in fact fairly inept. Nevertheless, confessions can be extracted by means fair as well as foul and there is no need for any other evidence to support a conviction. The courts provide a safeguard against the admission of confessions obtained unfairly but the discretion is not always operated in a way that would encourage due process.

As in the rest of this book, we have looked at the legal system from the basis of an integrated theory of justice, one which acknowledges the significance of actors who are normally regarded as lying outside 'the English legal system'. The store detectives who carry out the vast majority of arrests for shoplifting, the officers of HMRC, are seen as part of the larger whole, in which the police also play their role. In the case of store detectives, the relationship with the police is clear and proximate, in the sense that it is not long after making an arrest that a store detective will contact the police. In the case of tax frauds, HMRC has extensive investigative powers of its own and may carry out investigation independently of the police. Although the investigative powers of non-police agencies are often neglected, in this chapter we have highlighted the interviewing practices of benefit fraud investigators. We can see that in many ways, their practices are similar to the police, for example in terms of the assumption of guilt that often seems to underlie interrogation. It is crucial that we understand these interrelationships if we are to have an accurate picture of the whole legal system.

## FURTHER READING

SKINNS, L., '"I'm a Detainee; Get Me Out of Here"'(2009) 49(3) British Journal of Criminology 399.

WALSH, D. and MILNE, R. 'Keeping the Peace? A Study of Investigative Practice in the Public Sector' (2008) 13 Legal and Criminological Psychology 39.

# 15

# Prosecutions

## INTRODUCTION

The Crown Prosecution Service (CPS) has been given an enhanced role in the criminal process in recent years. In this chapter, the role of the CPS initiating prosecutions is examined and the impact of their new powers on their relationship with the police is explored. However, in accordance with the integrated theory of justice, it must be recognized that the CPS is not the only organization with powers of prosecution. There are a number of 'regulatory bodies' that may prosecute offenders in areas of their regulatory responsibility. Furthermore, ordinary citizens retain the right of private prosecution, although this may be of limited significance in practical terms.

## The decision to prosecute

Until 1986, the decision whether or not to prosecute was the responsibility of the police. In making this decision, they were able to call on legal advice, either from their own prosecution department or from private sector solicitors. Research for the Royal Commission on Criminal Procedure showed that in 1980, 31 of the 43 police forces in England and Wales had their own prosecuting solicitors departments.[1] Prosecutions involving cases of particular difficulty or importance were taken by the Director of Public Prosecutions (DPP), and some statutes required the consent of the DPP before a prosecution could be brought, particularly if the offence involved was controversial, or there were matters of public policy involved.[2] It was felt, however, that the system whereby the police not only investigated offences, but also took the decision whether or not they should be prosecuted, was unacceptable. When the matter was examined by the Royal Commission on Criminal Procedure, it concluded that the police should retain responsibility for investigation of offences, but that after charge a prosecutor should take over the conduct of the case and decide whether or not to

---

[1] Royal Commission on Criminal Procedure, *The Investigation and Prosecution of Criminal Offences in England and Wales: The Law and Procedure* (1981b) Cmnd 8092-I, HMSO, London, Appendix 22.
[2] Royal Commission on Criminal Procedure (1981b) Appendix 12.

proceed as charged or to modify or withdraw the charge.[3] The Royal Commission's recommendations were largely accepted by the Government and the Prosecution of Offenders Act 1985 established a Crown Prosecution Service (CPS), headed by the DPP. England and Wales are divided into areas, each with a Chief Crown Prosecutor, who is responsible for supervising the operation of the CPS in that area.[4]

The Prosecution of Offenders Act 1985 set up a system whereby it is the duty of the CPS to take over proceedings instituted by the police. The fact that the police remained responsible for initiating prosecutions led some commentators to doubt whether it would be easy for them to be truly independent of the police, one reason being that once the defendant is charged some 'prosecution momentum' is established.[5] Research carried out in the early days of the CPS seemed to confirm that these concerns were well founded.

Eventually, the Government considered changing the law so that the CPS would assume the responsibility for charge.[6] CPS charging pilots were run in several areas and evaluations showed, according to the Government's White Paper, that involving the CPS in charging decisions improved the quality of the police investigation and helped to identify weak cases earlier so that they could either be dropped or further investigations be carried out to improve the evidence.[7] Consequently, the Criminal Justice Act 2003 introduced a 'statutory charging scheme' whereby the police refer cases to the CPS for them to decide whether and what to charge in all but the most minor cases.[8] The scheme can be seen as building on a range of initiatives designed to encourage a closer working relationship between the police and CPS.[9] It remains to be seen whether involving the CPS in the charging decisions will overcome or compound concerns about their independence from the police.

## The prosecution criteria

The official guidance for CPS decision-making is set out in a number of documents. The main document is the Code for Crown Prosecutors, issued by the DPP under s. 10 of the Prosecution of Offenders Act (POA) 1985.[10] The Code is currently under review, with a view to a sixth edition being published in 2010. There are unlikely to be any radical departures from the fifth edition, which was issued in 2004.[11] Under

---

[3] Royal Commission on Criminal Procedure, *Report* (the Philips Report) (1981a) Cmnd 8092, HMSO, London, para. 6.65.    [4] Prosecution of Offenders Act 1985, s. 1.

[5] A. Sanders, 'Prosecution Decisions and the Attorney-General's Guidelines' [1985b] Criminal Law Review 4.    [6] Home Office, *Justice for All* (2002) Cm. 5563, The Stationery Office, London, para. 3.31.

[7] Home Office (2002) para. 3.32.

[8] I. Brownlee, 'The Statutory Charging Scheme in England and Wales: Towards a Unified Prosecution System' [2004] Criminal Law Review 896. R. White, 'Investigators and Prosecutors or, Desperately Seeking Scotland: Reformulation of the "Philips Principle"' (2006) 69 Modern Law Review 143.

[9] J. Baldwin and A. Hunt, 'Prosecutors Advising in Police Stations' [1998] Criminal Law Review 521.

[10] POA 1985, s. 10 requires the DPP to issue a code giving guidance on the general principles to be applied by prosecutors when making decisions in relation to the prosecution of offences.

[11] See: <http://www.cps.gov.uk>.

the Code, there are two stages in the decision to prosecute: the evidential test and the public interest test.

The *evidential test* requires the prosecutor to be satisfied that there is enough evidence to provide a realistic prospect of conviction. This is an objective test, meaning that a court is more likely than not to convict the defendant. The prosecutor must look closely at all the evidence to establish whether it can be used in court, or whether it may be excluded, perhaps because of the way in which it was gathered or because of the rule against hearsay or some other evidential rule. The other aspect of evidence which the prosecutor must consider, is the reliability of the evidence. Could the credibility of the witness supplying the evidence be seriously questioned for some reason, such as a dubious motive for giving evidence? Is a confession unreliable because of the defendant's age or lack of understanding?[12]

There are a number of difficulties with the evidential test in practice, not least the fact that the objective test requires the prosecutor to ignore their opinions on the differing propensities of courts to convict. Research shows that prosecutors are well aware of the propensities of different courts to convict or acquit and sometimes find it difficult to ignore that knowledge when assessing the evidence.[13] Ashworth and Redmayne describe this tension between a 'predictive' and 'intrinsic' merits approach. The Code itself incorporates an intrinsic merits approach but in practice the predictive approach sometimes prevails.[14]

If the case does not pass the evidential test, then the Code states that the prosecution must not go ahead no matter how important or serious it may be.[15] However, there is some evidence that suggests that prosecutors have in the past applied a lower evidential test in serious cases where they feel that there is a strong public interest reason for prosecuting.[16]

There are now two evidential tests: the full Code test, described above, and a threshold test to be applied in exceptional situations. The threshold test applies where 'it is proposed to keep the suspect in custody after charge, but the evidence required to apply the Full Code Test is not yet available'.[17] The threshold test requires prosecutors 'to decide whether there is at least a reasonable suspicion that the suspect has committed an offence, and if there is, whether it is in the public interest to charge

---

[12] Code for Crown Prosecutors, para. 5.

[13] A. Hoyano, L. Hoyano, G. Davis, and S. Goldie, 'A Study of the Impact of the Revised Code for Crown Prosecutors' [1997] Criminal Law Review 556. See also Gus John Partnership, *Race for Justice* (2003) The Stationery Office/CPS, London, which found that reluctance to prosecute for racially aggravated offences was partly attributable to prosecutors' perceptions about how particular tribunals would respond to such cases.

[14] A. Ashworth and M. Redmayne, *The Criminal Process* (3rd edn, 2005) Oxford University Press, Oxford, pp. 180–2.     [15] Code for Crown Prosecutors, para. 5.1.

[16] J. Baldwin, 'Understanding Judge Ordered and Directed Acquittals in the Crown Court' [1997] Criminal Law Review 586. By contrast, prosecutors may apply a higher evidential test in cases where they are reluctant to prosecute (see O. Quick, 'Prosecuting "Gross" Medical Negligence: Manslaughter, Discretion and the CPS' (2006) 33 Journal of Law and Society 421).     [17] Code for Crown Prosecutors, para. 3.3.

that suspect'.[18] The standard of 'reasonable suspicion' is not a very rigorous test for controlling discretion, as has been seen in other contexts where the concept is used in relation to police discretion. It is doubtful whether the CPS will apply the concept of 'reasonable suspicion' more robustly than the police.[19] However, a decision to charge and not bail the defendant must be kept under review and the Code requires that: 'The Full Code Test be applied as soon as reasonably practicable.'

The *public interest test* has undergone a number of reformulations in the various versions of the Code that have been issued since 1986. All versions have incorporated the 'opportunity' principle that reminds prosecutors that there is no rule that those suspected criminal offences will automatically be the subject of prosecution.[20] However, the Code creates a presumption in favour of prosecution on public interest grounds. The Code states: 'Although there may be public interest factors against prosecution in a particular case, often the prosecution should go ahead and those factors should be put to the court for consideration when sentenced.' It envisages that: 'A prosecution will usually take place unless there are public interest factors tending against prosecution which clearly outweigh those tending in favour, or it appears more appropriate in all the circumstances of the case to divert the person from prosecution.' Under the Criminal Justice Act 2003, prosecutors acquired new powers of prosecutors to divert offenders away from prosecution to conditional cautions. The CPS has not traditionally had powers to divert from prosecution, save through no further action.[21] The CPS has not made much used of these powers as yet. Whether conditional cautions are beneficial to suspects and consistent with the right to a fair trial, is a matter of debate.[22]

Prosecutors are expected to balance the public interest factors for and against prosecution 'carefully and fairly' but may have some difficulty doing this. The Code notes some of the common factors both for and against prosecution. The list of factors in favour of prosecution begins with the statement: 'The more serious the offence, the more likely it is that a prosecution will be needed in the public interest.' Examples of common factors in favour of prosecution include the use of a weapon or threat of violence in the commission of the offence, whether the defendant was in a position of trust or the victim was vulnerable or was put in considerable

---

[18]   Code for Crown Prosecutors, para. 6.1.

[19]   Although Ashworth and Redmayne (2005) p. 183, suggested that they might.

[20]   The 'opportunity system' of prosecutions is compared by Sanders et al. to the 'legality system'. However, they observe that the systems in practice are not so diametrically opposed as the theory might suggest. In legality systems, where there is supposedly little discretion not to prosecute on public interest grounds, such discretion may in fact be exercised. By contrast, in opportunity systems, where there is supposedly complete discretion not to prosecute on public interest grounds, such discretion may be infrequently exercised in particular cases (A. Sanders, R. Young, and M. Burton, *Criminal Justice* (4th edn, 2010) Oxford University Press, Oxford, pp. 372–3).

[21]   A number of conditions must be met before such a caution can be given. See s. 23, CJA 2003 and *The Director's Guidance on Conditional Cautioning* (5th edn, 2007) CPS, London, at: <http://www.cps.gov.uk>.

[22]   I. Brownlee, 'Conditional Cautions and Fair Trial Rights in England and Wales: Form versus Substance in the Diversionary Agenda?' [2007] Criminal Law Review 129.

fear, whether the offence was motivated by discrimination, and whether there are grounds for believing that the offence is likely to be continued or repeated.[23] Public interest factors against prosecution include the fact that the offence was committed as a result of a genuine mistake or misunderstanding (though these factors must be weighed against the seriousness of the offence), the loss or harm can be described as minor and was the result of a single incident, particularly if it was caused by a misjudgment, or the fact that a prosecution is likely to have a very bad effect on the victim's physical or mental health, always bearing in mind the seriousness of the offence.[24] It is important to note that these lists are not exhaustive, which presents some difficulties in terms of accountability.[25] The lack of weighting given to specific criteria also leaves a large element of discretion to individual prosecutors. In recent years, the victim has become a powerful figure in criminal justice policy-making, at least in terms of the Government's stated objective to put the victim at the heart of the criminal justice system.[26] However, the Code makes clear that the CPS is not the victim's lawyer and prosecutors 'act on behalf of the public and not just in the interests of any particular individual'. Having said that, the Code does state that prosecutors 'should always take into account the consequences for the victim of whether or not to prosecute, and any views expressed by the victim or the victim's family'.[27] Thus, the victim's views are to be taken into account in considering the public interest, but they are not determinative. If victims are unhappy with a decision not to prosecute, then they may try to exercise the right of private prosecution, to be considered further below.

The difficulties associated with weighing up the public interest can be illustrated by a series of controversial cases on assisted suicide. In the case of Daniel James, the CPS decided not to prosecute his parents, who helped him to travel to Switzerland to die.[28] Although many assistees have not been prosecuted, Diane Purdy, a woman suffering a terminal illness, wanted clarification about whether her husband would face prosecution if he helped her when she wished to commit suicide. The House of Lords ruled that the CPS had to issue a clear policy on the criteria considered in weighing up the public interest in cases like this.[29] In 2009, the CPS issued an interim policy, pending the outcome of a public consultation. This interim policy was considered in the case of Kay Gilderdale who helped her 31-year-old daughter, who had been bedridden with ME for many years, to die. Mrs Gilderdale pleaded guilty to assisted suicide but was prosecuted for attempted murder because the CPS took the view that her actions had gone beyond providing assistance. The jury acquitted and the judge

---

[23] Code for Crown Prosecutors, para. 5.9.    [24] Code for Crown Prosecutors, para. 5.10.

[25] See A. Ashworth and J. Fionda, 'The New Code for Crown Prosecutors: Prosecution, Accountability and the Public Interest' [1994] Criminal Law Review 894.

[26] J. Jackson, 'Justice for All: Putting Victims at the Heart of Criminal Justice?' (2003) Journal of Law and Society 309.    [27] Code for Crown Prosecutors, para. 5.12.

[28] See: <http://www.cps.gov.uk/news/articles>. James sustained severe paralysing injuries in a rugby accident. His young age and lack of terminal illness made the case particularly controversial.

[29] See R (on the application of Purdy) v Director of Public Prosecutions [2009] UKHL 45.

was critical of the CPS, obviously disagreeing with their assessment of the public interest in the case.[30]

The assisted suicide policy joins a range of supplementary documents that the CPS publishes, expanding upon the way the prosecutorial discretion is guided in particular kinds of cases. One such established document is the CPS *Policy For Prosecuting Domestic Violence*, which has undergone several revisions since it was first published in 1993. The weighing of the public interest in domestic violence cases has always been problematic for prosecutors, particularly in cases where victims withdraw their support for a prosecution. Although in practice such cases are usually terminated, the policy outlines a number of factors which tend towards prosecution in the public interest and factors to be taken into account in weighing whether there is sufficient evidence to satisfy the realistic prospect of conviction test in the absence of a willing complainant.[31] Factors which point towards a prosecution include the impact upon any children of the household, the use of a weapon, and any continuing threat to the health and safety of the victim. Assessing future risk is always a difficult exercise but if the criminal justice agencies, including the CPS, fail to take appropriate steps to respond to complaints of domestic violence, then the UK could potentially be held to violate several provisions of the ECHR, including Article 3 which states individuals should be free from inhuman and degrading treatment. However, the existence of a discretionary policy which provides for prosecution without victim support in theory, if not in practice, means that the UK is probably compliant with the ECHR.[32]

In addition to the criterion governing the decision whether to prosecute, the Code also gives guidance on the selection of charges. The Code states that prosecutors should select charges which 'reflect the seriousness and extent of the offending; gives the court adequate powers to sentence and impose appropriate post-conviction orders; and enable the case to be presented in a clear and simple way'.[33] It reminds prosecutors that they should never go ahead with a greater number or more serious charges than necessary just to encourage a defendant to plead guilty to fewer or less serious charges.[34] The significance of this guidance will be explored in subsequent chapters when the research relating to plea bargaining is explored.

---

[30] 'Judge Opposed CPS Decision to Pursue Mother' (2010) *The Times*, 25 January.

[31] For a discussion of prosecution policy and practice in this area, see M. Burton, *Legal Responses to Domestic Violence* (2008) Routledge-Cavendish, Abingdon pp. 98–104. See also M. M. Dempsey, *Prosecuting Domestic Violence* (2009) Oxford University Press, Oxford.

[32] See M. Burton, 'The Human Rights of Victims of Domestic Violence: Opuz v Turkey' (2010) 22(1) Child and Family Law Quarterly 131. The ECHR has been used as a tool to argue for enhanced victims' rights but its impact on prosecution decision-making, and criminal justice decision-making more generally, has arguably been limited.

[33] Code for Crown Prosecutors, para. 7.1. See also the guidance on statutory charging discussed below.

[34] Code for Crown Prosecutors, para. 7.2.

# Prosecution in perspective: the early years of the CPS

The rhetoric of prosecution decision-making emphasizes objectivity, impartiality and individualization. The idea of establishing the CPS was to ensure that the decision to prosecute was taken away from the police and given to an independent body, which would take the decision guided by criteria of evidential sufficiency and public interest.[35] Police influence over a case was to be confined to the investigation and case preparation stage, with the ultimate decision as to whether or not to prosecute being taken by the CPS.

However, early research on the CPS showed that the reality was quite different and that the system remained dominated by the interests and values of the police, with the CPS playing an essentially subordinate and reactive role.[36] It was argued that since the police expected case review and understood the rules that informed it, they were able to anticipate and in some cases dictate later review decisions by the CPS by skilful case construction. They were able to do this because the police can choose what evidence is collected and what questions are asked of suspects and witnesses.[37] Also, police summaries of evidence and interviews may become the official account of the case.[38] The tendency of the police is to collect and present evidence of the crime, but to eschew other information which might in fact be relevant to the decision whether or not to prosecute. For instance, although the Code for Crown Prosecutors required prosecutors to consider such matters as the defendant's attitude to the offence, McConville et al. found that this information is frequently not available, because in terms of police objectives there is no reason to collect it.[39] In addition, McConville et al. found that prosecutors almost invariably deferred to the police on matters of policy and public interest, on the grounds that the involvement of the police with the community made them the best arbiters of local needs. In many cases, this deference to the police view of the public interest was expressed in uncritical acceptance of the police decision.[40] In the past, the CPS has sought to demonstrate its independence by pointing to the large number of cases that are dropped, but McConville et al. found that it was rare for the CPS to drop a case if the police

---

[35] Philips Report (1981a) ch. 7.

[36] M. McConville, A. Sanders, and R. Leng, *The Case for the Prosecution* (1991) Routledge, London, p. 126.

[37] The process of case construction through interviewing suspects has been described above. For an account of case construction through interviewing witnesses, see A. Cretney and G. Davis, *Punishing Violence* (1995) Routledge, London.

[38] Again, it was noted above how these summaries may overstate the police case (see J. Baldwin and J. Bedward, 'Summarising Tape Recordings of Police Interview' [1991] Criminal Law Review 671).

[39] McConville et al. (1991) pp. 133–6.

[40] McConville et al. (1991) p. 142; and R. Leng, M. McConville, and A. Sanders, 'Researching the Discretions to Charge and to Prosecute' in D. Downes (ed.), *Unravelling Criminal Justice* (1992) Macmillan, London, pp. 119–37 at p. 134.

wish to prosecute; in many dropped cases, the police had already signalled that there was an evidential weakness.[41]

Legislators tend to assume that the police and prosecutors are susceptible to control by legal rules and administrative guidelines. However, Leng et al. pointed out that this assumption ignores the effect of working rules, both of the police and the CPS.[42] They argued that there is no incentive for the CPS to discontinue evidentially weak cases. The CPS judges itself on its conviction rate. Hence, it pays the prosecutors to bide their time and consider dropping a case only if it appears that the defendant intends to plead not guilty.[43]

Thus, from its inception, the CPS was subjected to a considerable amount of criticism and scepticism about its ability to perform the task of independent review. In the late 1990s a review of the CPS was carried out under the chairmanship of Sir Iain Glidewell.[44] This review identified problems with the effectiveness and efficiency of the prosecution process and in the relationships between the CPS and other agencies. A major criticism was that lawyers were spending too much time on presenting less serious cases in the magistrates' court and too little time on the review and preparation of more serious cases in the Crown Court.[45] Lack of involvement in cases in the Crown Court was mooted as one possible explanation for the high level of non-jury acquittals.[46] Overall, the Glidewell Review concluded:

Our assessment of the CPS is that it has the potential to become a lively, successful and esteemed part of the criminal justice system, but that, sadly, none of these adjectives applies to the Service as a whole at present.[47]

The Glidewell review recommended the increased involvement of lay staff in the prosecution of cases in the magistrates' court to free up lawyers' time for Crown Court cases. In recent years, the CPS has considerably increased the proportion of Crown Court advocacy that is done by in-house staff.[48] The impact of this on the quality of case preparation and advocacy is mixed. A recent report found that the quality of advocacy of some CPS lawyers was poor, but they tended to be better at pre-trial hearings than the independent Bar.[49]

[41] Leng et al. (1992) p. 132.      [42] Leng et al. (1992) p. 135.      [43] Leng et al. (1992) p. 136.

[44] Sir I. Glidewell, *The Review of the Crown Prosecution Service* (1998) Cm. 3960, The Stationery Office, London.

[45] The CPS tend to instruct counsel to present cases in the Crown Court on their behalf. Initially, CPS lawyers did not have rights of audience in the higher courts, and were therefore obliged to brief counsel, but the Access to Justice Act 1999 permits prosecutors who are qualified to appear as higher-court advocates to do so.

[46] There is a range of other, probably more convincing, explanations for this alleged weakness in CPS performance (see Baldwin (1997)).      [47] Glidewell (1998) p. 6.

[48] HM Crown Prosecution Inspectorate, *Report of the Thematic Review of the Quality of Prosecution Advocacy and Case Presentation* (2009) HMCPSI, London.

[49] HM Crown Prosecution Inspectorate, *Report of the Thematic Review of the Quality of Prosecution Advocacy and Case Presentation* (2009) HMCPSI, London.

# CPS 'associate prosecutors'

The CPS has always relied on non-lawyers to help prepare cases for court. However, since 1998, some of the lay staff employed by the CPS have been able to perform certain advocacy functions: a significant development on their previous role. Whilst CPS 'associate prosecutors', as they are now known, often lack the legal training of a solicitor or barrister, they do receive specific training for their advocacy role. At first, lay presenters were used for guilty pleas in the magistrates' court, provided they were straightforward and involved no technical issues or complications of fact or law. Now, their role has been expanded so that they can be used for most types of non-trial hearing and, subject to the outcome of pilots, they may be used for some contested trial work. Is this a positive development?

One of the first thematic inspections by the CPS Inspectorate was a review of a pilot of lay review and lay presentation of cases by CPS employees.[50] The quality of review and their presentation work was found to be generally good. Representatives of other agencies were found to be generally impressed by the standard of case presentation. A more recent inspectorate report noted possible concerns about the use of 'associate prosecutors' for trials; trials do require a broader range of skills than non-contested cases.[51] Sanders et al. observe the use of less-qualified staff is indicative of the lesser importance attached to magistrates work and the 'ideology of triviality' that permeates the magistrates' court.[52] However, as will be apparent from the discussion of magistrates' courts in the next chapter, this ideology belies the reality that magistrates deal with some serious business and decisions that can have far-reaching implications for defendants.

Whilst from a bureaucratic or managerialist perspective the greater use of lay persons in the magistrates' courts makes sense, there are due process concerns about the range of decisions and tasks increasingly being taken on by lay staff with more limited training and expertise.

# Enhanced role for the CPS

It has already been noted above that the Criminal Justice Act 2003 put in place the legal framework for transferring responsibility from the police to the CPS for initiating prosecutions in all but the most minor cases.[53] This 'statutory charging scheme'

---

[50] HM Crown Prosecution Service Inspectorate, *Report on the Evaluation of Lay Review and Lay Presentation*, Thematic Report 2/99 (1999) CPSI, London.

[51] HMCPSI, *Report of the Thematic Review* (2009).

[52] Sanders et al. (2010) p. 501.

[53] Criminal Justice Act 2003, s. 29, Sch. 2.

was introduced following a recommendation by the Auld Report, which felt the CPS was failing to remedy overcharging by the police at an early stage, resulting in a number of problems, including last-minute guilty pleas.[54] The new scheme was therefore introduced with the aims of securing elimination at the earliest opportunity of hopelessly weak cases, reducing delay and reducing cracked trials (late guilty pleas).

Under the new scheme, prosecutors and police officers are co-located in police stations so that the CPS can exercise their discretion as to charge. All charging decisions should be based on an application of the full evidential and public interest test. Where there is insufficient evidence to apply the full code test then the person may, if the threshold test discussed above is met, be charged and remanded in custody. This provision was designed to give time for further evidence to be obtained to enable the application of the full code test. The DPP must issue guidance on charging decisions and a third edition of this guidance was issued in 2007.[55] The guidance specifies the nature of the report required from the police to enable the prosecutor to make a charging decision. In cases that are proceeding to the Crown Court or are expected to be contested, an evidential report must be compiled to include all the key evidence upon which the prosecution will rely and any unused material which may undermine the prosecution case or assist the defence. This report should also be accompanied by suggested charges, a record of convictions and cautions and any observations of the reporting or supervising officer. In cases where the threshold test is to be applied, an expedited report including a summary of the interview with the defence is all that is required. Summaries of evidence are also adequate in cases where suspects admit their guilt and the case is to be dealt with in the magistrates' court. It should be noted that the CPS, despite their new charging powers, remain heavily dependent on information provided by the police, and, in the past, police summaries of evidence have been found to be effective tools of 'case construction'.

The co-location of police and prosecutors may also present challenges in terms of the enhanced role envisaged for the CPS. Whilst it is hoped that it will enable weak cases to be eliminated early, this rather depends on whether prosecutors are able and willing to assert their independence in cases that the police wish to see charged. Brownlee noted the importance of recruiting lawyers sufficiently well-trained and experienced to implement the scheme. He observed that the success of the new arrangements would be dependent 'on the ability of duty prosecutors, often acting alone, in unfamiliar surroundings and in situations of some urgency and pressure, to come to the right decisions quickly'.[56]

Sanders et al. comment that prosecutors may be in a very similar situation to custody officers under the old regime, merely rubber stamping the decisions of investigating officers. Prosecution momentum may also continue to be an issue where initial decisions to prosecute have been taken speedily on low-level evidence.

---

[54]  Auld LJ, *Report by the Right Honourable Lord Justice Auld* (2001) The Stationery Office, London.

[55]  CPS, *The Director's Guidance on Charging* (3rd edn, 2007), issued by the DPP under s. 37A of the Police and Criminal Evidence Act 1984, London, available at: <http://www.cps.gov.uk/publications/directors_guidance/dpp_guidance.html>.                                                  [56]  Brownlee (2004) p. 906.

Ultimately, it is not just a change in the legal rules, but a change in culture, that will be required if the role of the CPS is to be transformed by the introduction of the statutory charging scheme. There is, as yet, very little research evidence on how the CPS and police are interacting under the new arrangements. However, a recent joint inspectorate report found that, although there have been some benefits from the new scheme, a number of problems remain. The inspectors comment:

> The implementation of the statutory charging scheme has delivered benefits to the criminal justice process. It has required close partnership working between the CPS and the police service at both senior and operational levels. It has facilitated progress within the criminal justice system in relation to linked projects improving criminal case management and reducing delay in the courts. Nevertheless some aspects of the scheme need to be substantially refined in order to be fully effective.[57]

On the positive side, the inspectors noted, amongst other factors, that the final charging decisions by prosecutors were of good quality and discontinuance happened earlier, preventing weak cases from entering the court system.[58] On the negative side, the inspectors observed that, 'police and CPS processes are inconsistent, overly complex, inefficient and lacking in pragmatism in too many instances, often leading to avoidable delays and frustration'; the practice of delivering advice in a face-to-face meeting was not providing the anticipated benefits in all cases; and that the police and CPS had conflicting targets which hindered their working together.[59]

## Private prosecution and judicial review

Prior to the establishment of the police in the nineteenth century, any prosecutions that took place were initiated by ordinary citizens, usually the victim. This right of private prosecution has survived the creation of public police and prosecution services. Technically, this right operates as a form of redress for those who are dissatisfied by decisions taken by the police and the CPS not to prosecute in 'their' case. However, it is not easy to bring a private prosecution; it is expensive and the DPP has the right to take over any prosecution and discontinue it.[60] The police and CPS may effectively bar a private prosecution by their decision-making.[61] Thus, the practical significance of the right is much diminished and even in cases where disgruntled victims have the resources (or have managed to secure financial backing) to pursue a prosecution they have not always been successful. The most high-profile example of a failed attempt to

---

[57] Her Majesty's Crown Prosecution Service Inspectorate and Her Majesty's Inspectorate of Constabulary, *Joint Thematic Review of the New Charging Arrangements* (2008) HMCPSI/HMIC, London, at para. 3.1
[58] *Joint Thematic Review* (2008) para. 3.2.      [59] *Joint Thematic Review* (2008) para. 3.3
[60] POA 1985, s. 6(2).
[61] In *Jones v Whalley* [2006] UKHL 41, a private prosecution was held to be an 'abuse of process' when a caution had been given.

bring a private prosecution is the case brought by the family of Stephen Lawrence.[62] Whilst private prosecutions may fulfil a symbolic or campaigning function, they are of limited usefulness in holding the CPS to account for failures to prosecute.[63] Judicial review is an equally problematic remedy, given that applicants must show that a decision was 'Wednesbury unreasonable' in a situation where they are not always entitled to reasons for a decision or an account of the information on which it was based. Despite some successful challenges,[64] most victims will find it difficult to show that a decision was so unreasonable that no reasonable prosecutor could have reached it, particularly if the decision was taken on the basis of public interest criteria.

## Prosecution by non-police agencies – a pluralist perspective

In **Chapter 12**, we examined the role of non-police agencies in uncovering and investigating crime. The prosecution of offences is another area of the English legal system where it is important to take a pluralistic perspective in order to gain an accurate picture of the whole of the legal system in operation. There are many people other than the CPS who are involved in the prosecution of offences. Prior to the establishment of the CPS, there were a huge range of prosecuting agencies, from the Post Office to the Department of Health and Social Security.[65] Prosecution arrangements in England and Wales have remained 'remarkably various'.[66] Prosecutions by non-police agencies form an important part of the whole picture of the prosecution of offences.

A good example of non-police criminal prosecutions are the prosecutions carried out by the Serious Fraud Office (SFO) into financial misfeasance in a commercial context.[67] The SFO was established by the Criminal Justice Act 1987, following the report of the Roskill Committee.[68] Investigations and prosecutions are conducted by multi-disciplinary teams of lawyers, police officers and accountants into allegations of complex commercial frauds. It has wide-ranging powers of investigation.[69] Prosecution policy in the SFO has recently come under critical review due to the decision not to

---

[62] For details, see the report of the inquiry into the bungled investigation of the case. Sir W. MacPherson, *The Stephen Lawrence Inquiry* (1999) Cm. 4262-I, The Stationery Office, London.

[63] Sanders at al. (2010) pp. 432–4.

[64] In *R (on application of B) v DPP* [2009] 1 WLR 2072, the victim successfully challenged the decision not to prosecute. The court decided that the evidential test had not been correctly applied.

[65] K. Lidstone et al., *Prosecutions by Private Individuals and Non-police Agencies* (1980) Royal Commission on Criminal Procedure Research Study No. 10, HMSO, London.

[66] White (2006) p. 180.

[67] See, for example, *R v Director of Serious Fraud Office, ex parte Smith* [1992] 3 WLR 66.

[68] *Report of the Roskill Committee on Fraud Trials* (1986) HMSO, London.

[69] Criminal Justice Act 1987, s. 2. See further D. Kirk and A. Woodcock, *Serious Fraud: Investigation and Trial* (2nd edn, 1997) Butterworths, London. Commentators have pointed out the possibility of extremely serious consequences arising out of these powers. See, for example, J. Jackson, 'The Right of Silence: Judicial Responses to Parliamentary Encroachment' (1994) 57 Modern Law Review 270; and P. Paulden, 'Corporate Fraud: Civil Disclosure in Criminal Proceedings' (1994) 57 Modern Law Review 280.

prosecute BAE systems for corruption in the procurement of contracts.[70] Instead, the case was 'plea bargained', as presumably will be the norm now under new arrangements for serious and complex fraud cases.[71]

In another context, prosecutions are carried out by HM Customs and Excise, for example for alcohol and tobacco smuggling, money laundering, and drugs and arms importation offences. When the Inland Revenue was merged into HM Customs and Excise, a new Revenue and Customs Prosecution Office (RCPO) was set up in 2005 to replace the prosecution arrangements of the Inland Revenue and Customs and Excise.[72] The RCPO works in partnership with the CPS to provide 'service' to the Serious Organised Crime Agency (SOCA) set up by the Serious Organised Crime and Police Act 2005.[73] Under this arrangement, the RCPO prosecutes large-scale drug-importation and money-laundering activity for SOCA. The official criteria for RCPO decision-making includes the Code for Crown Prosecutors, discussed above, and their own organization-specific guidance.[74] As with the CPS, RCPO prosecutors are formally independent of the investigator in their decision-making.[75]

As we noted before, many of the prosecution agencies operating in the 'regulatory' context have a very different approach to the police and CPS. This is particularly the case with the Environment Agency (EA) and Health and Safety Executive (HSE), who tend to see prosecution as a 'last resort' and prefer other methods of seeking compliance with the legislation with which they are concerned, such as advice or warning.[76] It has to be doubted whether advisory strategies are as effective as more coercive sanctions.[77] This is a matter of concern, given the significance of the areas in which these regulatory agencies work. The HSE, for example, has death and serious injuries in the workplace as part of its remit. Although a high proportion of personal injuries occur in the workplace, the numbers of prosecutions are low. In this respect, corporations may be escaping criminal liability in cases where they should be prosecuted.[78] The Corporate Homicide Act 2007 has created a new offence relating to workplace deaths, which may make prosecutions easier,[79] but there are no new offences relating to non-fatal workplace injuries. The compliance strategies favoured by the HSE benefit middle-class offenders who tend not be prosecuted.

---

[70] '"Outrage" as BAE Systems Probes End after £280m Deal', (2010) BBC News Online, 6 February.

[71] See **Chapter 17**.        [72]  Commissioners for Revenue and Customs Act 2005.

[73] Revenue and Customs Prosecutions Office, *Annual Report 2005–6* (2006) RCPO, London.

[74] See, for example, The Director of Revenue and Customs Prosecution Office, *Guidance on Charging* at: <http://www.rcpo.gov.uk>.                                                              [75] White (2006).

[76] K. Hawkins, *Law as a Last Resort* (2002) Oxford University Press, Oxford.

[77] R. Macrory, *Regulatory Justice: Making Sanctions Effective* (2006) Cabinet Office, London.

[78] S. Tombs and S. Whyte, *A Crisis of Enforcement: The Decriminalisation of Death and Injury at Work* (2008) Centre for Crime and Justice Studies Briefing No. 6, King's College London, London.

[79] Although not necessarily so. The legislation has been much criticized (see, for example, D. Ormerod and R. Taylor, 'The Corporate Manslaughter and Corporate Homicide Act 2007' [2008] Criminal Law Review 589.

Long ago, Sanders pointed out the differential impact of prosecution policies.[80] His observation that working-class crime is prosecuted frequently while middle-class crime is not, remains valid. This phenomenon was also clearly illustrated in Cook's study of different responses to tax and supplementary benefit fraud.[81] Cook found that welfare recipients were broadly categorized as 'takers', for whom the state lays down the conditions upon which their benefit is to be received. The state has the power to punish those who cannot, or will not, meet those criteria, so that enforcement policies, including prosecution, tend to be rigorous. By contrast, tax-payers are 'givers' to the state and the discipline to which they are subjected is less rigorous.

This finding about how the different approaches of prosecution agencies impact differently upon different social groups is important for a pluralist perspective of the legal system. Regulatory agencies tend to put their own assessments of the moral culpability of the offender above the legal rules.[82] The police also use evaluations of moral culpability in their working rules. However, whereas for regulatory offenders these moral assessment often result in cases not being prosecuted, with perhaps some notable exceptions, this is not the case with the police and CPS.[83]

## CONCLUSION

Although this chapter has necessarily concentrated on the prosecutions carried out by the police and the CPS, adopting a pluralist perspective has allowed us to acknowledge the presence of other actors who may also take part in the process of criminal prosecution. Within the CPS itself, it is not only lawyers who are responsible for prosecuting cases, but lay people ('associate prosecutors') have also begun to undertake advocacy roles. Prosecution has never been the exclusive preserve of the police and CPS, indeed it evolved from a right of private prosecution that still exists and may provide a very weak form of redress for victims of crime who are unhappy with the decisions taken by public prosecutors not to prosecute in their case. Outside the CPS, there are a range of other prosecution authorities, including the newly formed RCPO, which prosecutes revenue and customs cases. Other regulatory agencies such as the EA and HSE also have a remit for prosecuting offences within their regulatory scope, although they may focus on non-prosecution strategies in practice. Appreciating the multiplicity of arrangements for prosecuting criminal offences in England and Wales is essential to an integrated theory of law.

[80]  A. Sanders, 'Class Bias in Prosecutions' (1985a) 24 Howard Journal 176. Sanders compared police prosecution policy with that of the Factory Inspectorate. He found that the Inspectorate, which mainly dealt with middle-class people, operated an extensive system of cautioning, whereas the police (who mainly dealt with working-class persons) usually prosecuted.

[81]  D. Cook, *Rich Law, Poor Law* (1989) Open University Press, Milton Keynes.

[82]  Hawkins (2002).        [83]  See further Sanders et al. (2010).

## FURTHER READING

HER MAJESTY'S CROWN PROSECUTION SERVICE INSPECTORATE and HER MAJESTY'S INSPECTORATE OF CONSTABULARY, *Joint Thematic Review of the New Charging Arrangements* (2008) HMCPSI/HMIC, London.

TOMBS, S. and WHYTE, S., *A Crisis of Enforcement: The Decriminalisation of Death and Injury at Work* (2008) Centre for Crime and Justice Studies Briefing No. 6, King's College London, London.

WHITE, R., 'Investigators and Prosecutors or, Desperately Seeking Scotland: Reformulation of the "Philips Principle"' (2006) 69 Modern Law Review 143.

# 16

# The magistrates' court

## INTRODUCTION

The magistrates' court is the lowest court of criminal jurisdiction. It deals with a high volume of cases and its jurisdiction in more serious cases is growing due to changes to mode of trial determinations. It is therefore a matter of concern, as Darbyshire has pointed out, that much academic writing, including many textbooks, has a tendency to ignore what goes on in the magistrates' court.[1] In this chapter, some of the important decisions made by magistrates, including bail and mode of trial, are examined. The decisions of magistrates are placed in the context of their relationships with other legal actors, and in accordance with the integrated theory of this book, non-legal personnel who are increasingly to be found in the magistrates' court setting.

## Composition of the magistracy

The basic composition of the magistracy has been discussed in **Chapter 3**, where the split between lay and professional magistrates was noted. The allocation of work between lay and professional magistrates is rather ad hoc. This can affect the defendant's experience of the process but also, perhaps more importantly, the outcome. Professional magistrates are more likely to use custody at sentence and pre-trial.[2] Although the majority of magistrates are lay magistrates, the professional magistracy has been expanding.[3] Research carried out by Morgan and Russell shows that professional magistrates are more inquisitorial and efficient than lay magistrates, but that they are also less representative of the local community.[4] However, lay magistrates are far from representative of the local community themselves.[5] The selection process for magistrates, discussed in **Chapter 9**, highlights the continuing difficulties in

---

[1] P. Darbyshire, 'An Essay on the Importance and Neglect of the Magistracy' [1997a] Criminal Law Review 627 at p. 637.

[2] R. Morgan and N. Russell, *The Judiciary in the Magistrates' Courts* (2000) Home Office RDS Occasional Paper No. 66, Home Office, London.

[3] P. Seago, C. Walker, and D. Wall, 'The Development of the Professional Magistracy in England and Wales' [2000] Criminal Law Review 361.        [4] Morgan and Russell (2000).

[5] Morgan and Russell (2000).

securing a lay bench that is socio-demographically and politically representative. As lay magistrates are volunteers, it has been pointed out that, even if a satisfactory means of identifying a wider pool of potential magistrates could be identified, conscription may be the only way to recruit a more representative bench.[6] Whether a more socially representative bench is desirable is a matter of debate. It could be argued that the fairness and legitimacy of magistrates' decision-making would be enhanced if magistracy were less middle class and more in touch with the lives of the largely working-class defendants who appear before them.

It is interesting to compare the recruitment and deployment of lay magistrates in relation to 'core values' in the criminal justice system.[7] Sanders has argued that the absence of juries in the magistrates' court relates to the value of efficiency. To promote the values of fairness and participatory democracy he argues for a system where magistrates' justice can be made more judge-and-jury like.[8] At the moment, professional and lay magistrates rarely sit together as a mixed panel.[9] Sanders suggests that there should be mixed panels within the magistrates' court and cases be allocated to either a professional, lay or mixed tribunal according to the particular social fact-finding or legal skills that the hearing requires.[10] A key objection to Sanders' proposals, and one which he anticipated, was that mixed panels may be dominated by professionals. The question of whether lay wing members in a mixed panel would become 'decorative flowerpots' (having no real influence over decisions, but serving to create an appearance of legitimacy) is contested.[11] However, they appear to work reasonably well in relation to appeals from the magistrates' court to the Crown Court.[12]

## Mode of trial

All criminal offences are classified according to the way they will be tried. The Criminal Justice Act 1977, s. 14 provides that there are three kinds of offences: summary offences, tried by magistrates; offences triable on indictment in the Crown Court; and offences triable either way.

---

[6] Seago et al. (2000).

[7] An approach advocated by A. Sanders, *Community Justice: Modernising the Magistracy in England and Wales* (2001) Institute for Public Policy Research, London.  [8] Sanders (2001).

[9] Morgan and Russell (2000).  [10] Sanders (2001).

[11] The Auld Review cited the 'decorative flowerpot' theory as an objection to mixed panels in the magistrates' court, but this did not prevent Auld LJ making an (unimplemented) recommendation for a mixed tribunal himself! See Sir R. Auld, *A Review of the Criminal Courts of England and Wales: Report by the Right Honourable Lord Justice Auld* (2001) The Stationery Office, London.

[12] However, the lack of empirical research on this aspect of the criminal justice system makes it difficult to assert this reliably (Sanders (2001)).

*Trial on indictment* is reserved for the most serious offences, such as murder, robbery, rape, and blackmail. Summary offences are the less serious offences, such as minor motoring offences, common assault, and threatening behaviour in public places.

Offences which are *triable either way* include theft, burglary, arson, some assaults under the Offences Against the Person Act 1861, and certain, relatively minor sexual offences. There are special rules relating to the offence of criminal damage contrary to the Criminal Damage Act 1971, s. 1. This offence is triable either way, but where the value of the property involved is clearly less than £5,000, the offence is triable only summarily (and the magistrates have restricted sentencing powers); where the value of the property is clearly more than £5,000 the offence is triable either way and the court will proceed as it does for any other triable either way offence. If it is unclear whether the value of the damage is more or less than £5,000, the defendant can choose whether the offence is treated only summarily or as triable either way, and the court proceeds accordingly.[13]

In the case of offences triable either way, it is important that there should be a clear process for establishing their mode of trial. The procedure is laid down in the Magistrates' Court Act 1980 as amended by the Criminal Procedure and Investigations Act 1996. The latter statute introduced a new procedure, known as 'plea before venue', into the process by which the mode of trial is determined.[14] Thus, s. 17A of the Magistrates' Court Act 1980, provides that where an accused person is brought before the magistrates' court charged with an offence triable either way, the accused must be asked to indicate whether, if the offence went to trial, he would plead guilty or not guilty.[15] Before the accused answers this question, the court must explain, in ordinary language, that if the accused indicates that he or she would plead guilty, the court must proceed to deal with him or her, treating the accused as if he or she had actually pleaded guilty, and therefore proceeding to consider sentence. The accused must also be told that if the magistrates consider that their powers of sentencing are inadequate, they can commit the defendant to the Crown Court for sentencing.[16] This means that once the required explanation has been given, if the accused then indicates that he or she would plead guilty, the magistrates will proceed to consider sentence. If the accused indicates that he or she would plead not guilty, the normal procedure for determining mode of trial applies. This is contained in the Magistrates' Court Act 1980, ss 19–23.

Basically, the court must listen to representations from each side about the most suitable mode of trial and make its decision, taking into account the nature and seriousness of the offence, whether the punishment which a magistrates' court would have the power to inflict for it would be adequate and any other relevant factors.[17] If the court considers summary trial more appropriate, that should be explained to the

---

[13]  Magistrates' Court Act 1980, ss. 22 and 23.
[14]  Criminal Procedure and Investigations Act 1996, s. 49.
[15]  Magistrates' Court Act 1980, s. 17A(5).        [16]  Magistrates' Court Act 1980, s. 17A(4).
[17]  Magistrates' Court Act 1980, s. 19(3).

accused, who may still opt for jury trial if he or she wishes to do so; the accused must also be told that after a summary trial the magistrates have the power to send him or her to the Crown Court for sentencing if necessary. If the accused consents to summary trial, it can then take place; if the accused opts for trial on indictment, the case will be committed to the Crown Court. If the court considers that trial on indictment would be appropriate, it will proceed with committal and the accused has no choice in the matter.

The new 'plea before venue' procedure was expected to decrease the number of cases committed for trial at the Crown Court, with a consonant increase in the number of sentences passed by magistrates. Although magistrates could still commit to the Crown Court for sentencing if they found that their sentencing powers were inadequate, theoretically there is less need to commit a defendant who has pleaded guilty as the defendant should be entitled to a lesser sentence for his guilty plea under the 'sentence discount principle'.[18]

For many years, the government has been concerned about the proportion of triable either way cases committed to the Crown Court. Although there was a significant drop in the number of defendants electing Crown Court trial in the 1990s,[19] the Government still wanted to reduce further the number of triable either way cases going to the Crown Court.[20] A number of options, including the reclassification of more triable either way offences as summary only, were considered.[21] The preferred option was to abolish the defendant's right to elect jury trial in either way cases. This option has always been controversial. Research shows that most defendants who choose to be tried at the Crown Court do so because they believe that they will stand a better chance of acquittal and will get a fairer trial.[22] Research by Vennard suggests that for either way offences, the chances of acquittal are significantly higher in the Crown Court than in magistrates' courts.[23] However, research by Hedderman and Moxon suggests that although 50 per cent of those who elected Crown Court trial did so in the belief that if convicted they would receive a lighter sentence, this proved to be a mistaken assumption: judges were three times as likely as magistrates to impose immediate custodial sentences and sentences were on average two and a half times longer.[24] Hedderman and Moxon's research also showed that the majority of defendants who elect Crown Court trial end up pleading guilty. Thus, they never enjoy the

---

[18] Discussed more fully in **Chapter 17.**

[19] See Home Office, *Determining Mode of Trial in Either-way Cases* (July 1998) Home Office Consultation Paper, Home Office, London.

[20] See S. Cammiss and C. Stride, 'Modelling Mode of Trial' (2008) 48 British Journal of Criminology 482, for a discussion of the context of mode of trial reforms.

[21] See Home Office (1998).

[22] A. E. Bottoms and J. D. McClean, *Defendants in the Criminal Process* (1976) Routledge & Kegan Paul, London.

[23] J. Vennard, 'The Outcome of Contested Trials' in D. Moxon (ed.), *Managing Criminal Justice* (1985) HMSO, London, p. 126.

[24] C. Hedderman and D. Moxon, *Magistrates' Court or Crown Court? Mode of Trial Decisions and Sentencing* (1992) HMSO, London.

perceived benefits of a fairer trial but do expose themselves to longer sentences. In this context, the Royal Commission on Criminal Justice recommended that a defendant's right to elect a jury trial in an 'either way' offence should be completely abolished and replaced with a decision imposed by magistrates as to the mode of trial, the aim being to confine more defendants to the magistrates' court.[25] Given the research evidence discussed above, which shows that defendants have a much smaller chance of acquittal, some commentators regarded this recommendation as unacceptable.[26] It was argued that efficiency was being given priority over due process considerations. However, at the turn of the century, two bills were introduced to try to remove the defendant's right to elect jury trial.[27] Both bills were ultimately unsuccessful,[28] but had they been enacted they would have left with the magistrates the decision as to where either way offences should be heard.

For now, the policy of removing the defendant's right to elect jury trial seems to have been abandoned.[29] The implementation of other reforms aimed at reducing the committal rate, such as the provisions in the Criminal Justice Act 2003 increasing magistrates' sentencing powers and removing committal for sentence, have also been shelved or abandoned.

Scepticism had in any event been expressed about whether these reforms would lead to a greatly reduced committal rate.[30] Policy-makers have been relatively blind to the factors underlying mode of trial determinations.[31] Prosecution decision-making is possibly the most influential factor. A study of mode of trial decision-making in two courts, involving observations of 100 mode of trial hearings, found that mode of trial hearings were truncated and heavy reliance was placed on the prosecutor's presentation of the case.[32] There was found to be a shared assumption amongst participants that mode of trial was trivial, particularly in comparison to bail, and there was 'limited space for an effective challenge from the defence'.[33] As in previous research, the

[25] Royal Commission on Criminal Justice, *Report* (1993) Cm. 2263, HMSO, London, ch. 6.13.
[26] See, for example, A. Ashworth, *The Criminal Process: An Evaluative Study* (2nd edn, 1998) Oxford University Press, Oxford, pp. 225–66.
[27] The Criminal Justice (Mode of Trial) Bill 1999 and the Criminal Justice (Mode of Trial) (No. 2) Bill 2000.
[28] The bills faced strong opposition in the House of Lords, including objections that ethnic minority defendants would suffer disproportionately from having their right to elect jury trial removed.
[29] Auld recommended removal, but the Government decided not to proceed with this recommendation, or his proposal for a 'district division' comprised of a mixture of lay/professional judges. For an analysis of Auld's proposals, see R. Morgan, 'Magistrates: The Future According to Auld' (2002) 29 Journal of Law and Society 308; A. Sanders, 'Core Values, the Magistracy, and the Auld Report' (2002) 29 Journal of Law and Society 324; J. Jackson, 'Modes of Trial: Shifting the Balance towards the Professional Judge' [2002] Criminal Law Review 249.
[30] P. Herbert, 'Mode of Trial and Magistrates' Sentencing Powers: Will Increased Powers Inevitably Lead to a Reduction in the Committal Rate?' [2003] Criminal Law Review 314. See further Cammiss and Stride (2008).
[31] S. Cammiss, '"I Will in a Moment Give You the Full History": Mode of Trial, Prosecutorial Control and Partial Accounts' [2006a] Criminal Law Review 38.    [32] Cammiss (2006a).
[33] Cammiss (2006a) p. 50.

importance of local court cultures in the processing of cases was emphasized.[34] The enormous influence prosecutors wield in mode of trial hearings can, it has been suggested, result in information being manipulated to ensure summary trial in certain categories of cases. Cammiss found examples of domestic violence being minimized for this purpose.[35] That domestic violence is trivialized in this way is consistent with other research which shows that magistrates are susceptible to stereotypes which minimize the significance of violence which occurs in intimate relationships.[36] Whether the specialist domestic violence courts, which now operate in many magistrates' courts, have any impact on this will be discussed below.

## Bail decisions

For defendants facing a criminal charge, a crucial question at their first hearing, if their case is not finalized at that hearing, will be whether they will be released on bail or remanded in custody until their case is finalized. The magistrates' decision is governed by the Bail Act 1976. Under s. 4(1) there is a statutory presumption in favour of bail, since the statute provides that a defendant 'shall be granted bail except as provided in Schedule 1 to this Act'.

The Bail Act 1976, Sch. 1 makes a basic distinction between those who are charged with imprisonable or non-imprisonable offences. In the case of defendants charged with *non-imprisonable* offences, the exceptions to the 'right to bail' are limited, the main exceptions being that bail need not be granted if there has been a previous failure to answer to bail and the court believes that there would be a further failure to appear on this occasion, or if the court is satisfied that the defendant should be kept in custody for his own protection.[37] For defendants charged with *imprisonable* offences triable in the Crown Court, the grounds for refusing bail are more extensive.[38] Bail need not be granted if the court is satisfied that the defendant, if released on bail (whether subject to conditions or not) would fail to surrender to custody, would commit an offence while on bail, would interfere with witnesses, or otherwise obstruct the course of

[34] See also A. Herbert, 'Mode of Trial and the Influence of Local Justice' (2004) 43 Howard Journal of Criminal Justice 65.

[35] S. Cammiss, 'The Management of Domestic Violence Cases in the Mode of Trial Hearing: Prosecutorial Control and Marginalizing Victims' (2006b) 46 British Journal of Criminology 704. A quantitative analysis of the data in this study confirmed that domestic violence was a significant variable (see Cammiss and Stride (2008)).

[36] E. Gilchrist and J. Blissett, 'Magistrates' Attitudes to Domestic Violence and Sentencing Options' (2002) Howard Journal of Criminal Justice, 41(4), 348.              [37] Bail Act 1976, Sch. 2, Pt II.

[38] For imprisonable summary offences, the grounds for refusing bail are essentially the same as for non-imprisonable offences, but the court can also refuse bail if it has insufficient information and where it believes the defendant may commit an offence of violence or put a person in fear of violence (Bail Act 1976 as amended by s. 52 Criminal Justice and Immigration Act 2008).

justice, whether in relation to himself or any other person.[39] In taking those decisions, the court must have regard to any of the following considerations as appear to it to be relevant: the nature and seriousness of the offence and the probable method of dealing with the defendant for it; the character, antecedents, associations, and community ties of the defendant; and the defendant's record as regards the fulfilment of his or her obligations under previous grants of bail in criminal proceedings and the strength of the evidence against him or her and, in relation to defendants where there are substantial grounds for believing they would commit further offences, the risk that such offences would cause physical or mental injury to another person.[40] In addition, bail need not be granted if the court is satisfied that the defendant should be kept in custody for his or her own protection, or where the court is satisfied that it has not been practicable to obtain sufficient information for the purpose of taking the decision.

The Bail Act 1976, s. 3(6) provides that persons may be released on bail subject to such conditions as appear to the court to be necessary to secure that the defendant surrenders to the court at the appropriate time, does not commit a further offence while on bail or obstruct the course of justice, and is available for the purpose of enabling a court report to be prepared to assist in sentencing. The sort of conditions which appear to be common include reporting to the police station at stated times, residing at a specific address, or abiding by a curfew. In domestic violence cases, and other cases where there are concerns about intimidation or interference with witnesses, conditions not to contact specified persons may be imposed. Some surprise has been expressed at the wide range of conditions which courts have felt able to impose, despite the fact that there appears to be no legal authority for some of their more imaginative ideas.[41] It should be noted that the conditions imposed do not always relate to the objections to bail and can impose severe restrictions on liberty.[42] Electronic monitoring can be imposed as a condition of bail if the defendant would otherwise not be granted bail.[43]

The requirement that the court has to be satisfied that there are 'substantial' grounds for believing that one of the exceptions applies before a refusal of bail can be justified might suggest that this was intended to be a strict test, resulting, in the majority of cases, in the grant of bail. However, there was an increase in custodial remands during the 1990s, and in the twenty-first century, the number of people remanded in custody by magistrates remains high, despite a drop from 82,000 in 2002 to 67,000 in 2004, then to 52,000 in 2007.[44] It has been a matter of concern for

---

[39] Bail Act 1976, Sch. 2, Pt I, para. 2.    [40] Bail Act 1976, Sch. 2, Pt I, para. 9.

[41] See B. Block, 'Bail Conditions: Neither Logical Nor Lawful' (1990) 154 Justice of the Peace 83. The Divisional Court have held that magistrates have the power under s. 3(6) to impose a condition that the defendant should appear at his doorstep when requested by the police to do so during curfew hours (see *R (on the application of the Crown Prosecution Service)* v *Chorley Justices*, The Times, 22 October 2002). The magistrates had originally decided that they could not lawfully impose such a condition.

[42] A. Hucklesby, 'The Use and Abuse of Conditional Bail' (1994) 33 Howard Journal 258.

[43] Section 3AB Bail Act 1976 (as amended by s. 51 and Sch. 11 Criminal Justice and Immigration Act 2008).

[44] Ministry of Justice, *Criminal Statistics 2007* (2008a) MOJ, London, discussed by A. Sanders, R. Young, and M. Burton *Criminal Justice* (4th edn, 2010) Oxford University Press, Oxford, pp. 519–20.

some time that the use of custodial remands varies widely in different geographical areas of the country. It has been suggested that a possible explanation for this may be different court cultures.[45] The importance of local court cultures for understanding bail decision-making in the magistrates' courts resonates with the research on mode of trial decision-making discussed above, where court culture was also found to be significant.

One of the problems surrounding the bail decision is that the factors which magistrates are required by the Bail Act 1976 to take into account, such as whether the defendant might fail to appear, or would commit an offence while on bail, and particularly the factors indicated in Sch. 2, para. 9 (such as the defendant's character, antecedents, associations, and community ties) really require the provision of high-quality information to the court. Without such information, it is almost inevitable that para. 5 of the Schedule will apply and the court will decide that it need not grant bail because it is satisfied that it has not been practicable to obtain sufficient information for the purpose of taking the decision. Research has shown that the provision of increased amounts of information to courts about defendants results in an increase in the amount of bail granted.[46] In some areas, bail information schemes were set up to try to ensure that courts were provided with sufficient information to enable them to take a high-quality decision regarding bail. These schemes involved the probation service providing verified information to the CPS in cases where the police indicated that they had an objection to bail and research confirmed that the schemes were successful in achieving a higher rate of grants of bail.[47] Bail information schemes are supposed to operate in all prisons holding remand prisoners.[48] However, schemes in some magistrates' courts have been threatened by budgetary cuts.[49] Research has also questioned past evaluations of their success.[50]

Provision of bail hostels is another initiative which has the potential to result in more grants of bail, because such schemes ensure that the defendant has a secure environment in which to live while on bail. As McIvor and Warner point out, the issue of where a person lives is relevant to the bail decision for two reasons: to ensure that documents can be served and to ensure the defendant appears at court.[51] It is important that the court can accurately verify the existence and suitability of any address offered by the defendant. In one high profile case, the court bailed a killer

[45] A. Hucklesby, 'Court Culture: An Explanation of Variations in the Use of Bail in the Magistrates' Courts' (1997a) 36 Howard Journal 129.

[46] See, for example, C. Lloyd, *Bail Information Schemes: Practice and Effect* (1992) Home Office Research and Policy Planning Unit Paper No. 69, Home Office, London, p. 70.

[47] C. Fiddes and C. Lloyd, 'Assessing the Impact of Bail Information Schemes' (1990) 29 Home Office Research Bulletin No. 23, Home Office, London.

[48] HM Prison Service, *Instruction to Governors No. 67/1999 Bail Information Schemes* (1999) HM Prison Service, London.

[49] G. Mair and C. Lloyd, 'Policy and Progress in the Development of Bail Schemes in England and Wales' in F. Paterson (ed.), *Understanding Bail in Britain* (1996) Scottish Office, Edinburgh.

[50] K. Dhami, 'Do Bail Information Schemes Really Affect Bail Decisions' (2002) 41 Howard Journal 245.

[51] G. McIvor and S. Warner, *Bail Services in Scotland* (1996) Avebury, Aldershot, p. 11.

to an address which did not exist.[52] Bail hostels can also be useful in cases where the defendant ordinarily lives with the person against whom he or she has committed an offence, for example domestic violence. Several studies have demonstrated that the availability or otherwise of a fixed address can be an important determinant of attitudes towards the granting of bail. Melvin and Didcott found that prosecutors were opposed to the granting of bail in about 10 per cent of cases on the grounds that the defendant was 'of no fixed abode'.[53] A particular problem for defendants is the definition of a fixed address; it appears from research carried out in London that the police may have defined as being 'of no fixed abode' defendants who were living in squats or in temporary rented accommodation which, for other purposes, would be regarded as a secure address.[54] In 2007, the Government contracted with a private firm to provide 500 beds in 150 bail hostels across England and Wales. This Bail Accommodation and Support Service (BASS) has been marred by controversy,[55] but forms a key part of the Government strategy to encourage a greater use of conditional bail. One concern which has interested researchers for some time is the possibility that some defendants who are eventually found not guilty will spend considerable amounts of time remanded in custody. In 2007, 14 per cent of males and females remanded in custody were acquitted or had proceedings against them terminated.[56] However, this does not necessarily call into question the decision to refuse bail, since the criteria for refusing bail and those for conviction are different.[57]

Another question which has aroused considerable interest is whether there is any correlation between the bail decision of the police, the CPS, and the magistrates. Early studies suggested that generally magistrates seemed to act in accordance with the explicit or implicit recommendations of the police.[58] Research into CPS decision-making suggested that prosecutors are heavily reliant on police recommendations when

[52] The case of Anthony Peart. A review of the case concluded that the court was insufficiently rigorous in challenging the validity of proposed bail conditions (HM Crown Prosecution Service Inspectorate, HM Inspectorate of Constabulary, HM Inspectorate of Court Administration, and HM Inspector of Prisons, *Peart Review* (2008) HMICA, London, available at: <http://www.hmica.gov.uk/files/Peart_Review.pdf>).

[53] M. Melvin and P. J. Didcott, *Pre-trial Bail and Custody in the Scottish Courts* (1976) Scottish Office Central Research Unit, HMSO, Edinburgh.

[54] H. Lewis and G. Mair, *Bail and Probation Work II: The Use of London Probation/Bail Hostels for Bailees* (1988) Home Office Research and Policy Planning Unit Paper No. 46, HMSO, London.

[55] '150 Bail Hostels Built in Secret' *Daily Telegraph*, 30 April 2008.

[56] Ministry of Justice, *Criminal Statistics 2007* (2008a) MOJ, London. In addition, 29 per cent of those convicted were given non-custodial sentences.

[57] R. Morgan and S. Jones, 'Bail or Jail?' in E. Stockdale and S. Casale (eds), *Criminal Justice under Stress* (1981) Croom Helm, London, pp. 34–63 at pp. 38 and 39.

[58] M. King, *Bail or Custody* (1971) Cobden Trust, London, p. 45; Bottoms and McLean (1976) p. 196; F. Simon and M. Weatheritt, *The Use of Bail and Custody by London Magistrates' Courts Before and After the Criminal Justice Act 1967* (1974) Home Office Research Unit Report No. 20, HMSO, London; P. Jones, 'Remand Decisions at Magistrates' Courts' in D. Moxon (ed.), *Managing Criminal Justice* (1985) Home Office Research and Planning Unit, HMSO, London. Although Doherty and East found that there was less evidence of the police view being dominant (M. J. Doherty and R. East, 'Bail Decisions in Magistrates' Courts' (1985) 25 British Journal of Criminology 251).

considering their position regarding bail.[59] Furthermore, Morgan, and Henderson found that there is a high correlation between police and court bail decision-making.[60] Hucklesby has suggested that the police power to grant conditional bail provides the courts with clear signals about whether they think a remand in custody or conditional bail is appropriate.[61] Bail is therefore probably one of the areas where later decisions in the criminal process, both by the CPS and the courts, are heavily influenced by the police view.

The conditions in which remand prisoners are kept have been a matter of concern for some time.[62] Morgan and Jones have drawn attention to the fact that during 1990, the Council of Europe Committee for the Prevention of Torture and Inhuman and Degrading Treatment visited the UK for the first time. Among the prisons they visited were Brixton and Leeds, both of which are local prisons housing large numbers of prisoners on remand. The Committee, in a judgment unprecedented in any of their previous reports, pronounced that the conditions in which many of the prisoners were being kept were inhuman and degrading, implying that the UK was in breach of its obligations under Article 3 of the European Convention for the Protection of Human Rights and Fundamental Freedoms.[63] Morgan and Jones comment:

Crisis is an overused word. Yet, in relation to the custodial remand population, crisis is a reasonable description of the situation which has prevailed in recent years. The population has often spilled over, as has the temper of that population.

Remand prisoners frequently experience overcrowded conditions, with very restrictive daily regimes which include little opportunity for education, physical exercise, or work. In April 1990, there was a series of prison disturbances, followed by an inquiry, chaired by Lord Justice Woolf. Five of the six most serious disturbances on which the inquiry focused were in remand establishments and remand prisoners played a leading or contributory part in what happened. The Woolf Inquiry found that remand prisoners had justifiable grievances: at Glen Parva, Woolf found that remand prisoners were significantly less well-provided for than sentenced prisoners; while at Pucklechurch, a purpose-built remand centre which was 17 per cent overcrowded at the time of the riots, there was no workshop, no vocational training courses, and efforts by PE and education staff to provide activities were frequently frustrated by lack of escorts. Woolf found that remand prisoners were the object of excessive security and the control to which they were subject was inappropriate. He concluded that it must 'be part of the task of the Prison Service to enable the remand prisoner to spend his time in custody

[59] C. Phillips and D. Brown, *Entry into the Criminal Justice System: A Survey of Police Arrests and their Outcomes* (1998) Home Office Research Study No. 185, Home Office, London.

[60] P. Morgan and P. Henderson, *Remand Decisions and Offending on Bail: Evaluation of the Bail Process Project* (1998) Home Office Research Study No. 184, Home Office, London.

[61] A. Hucklesby, 'Remand Decision Makers' [1997b] Criminal Law Review 269.

[62] See, for example, R. Morgan, 'Remands in Custody: Problems and Prospects' [1989] Criminal Law Review 481.  [63] Morgan and Jones (1981) p. 35.

in as constructive a manner as possible'.[64] A decade on and a report by HM Inspector of Prisons reveals that poor conditions for remand prisoners remain a problem.[65]

The police frequently voice concerns about the incidence of defendants who offend while on bail, the so-called 'bail bandits'.[66] The Bail (Amendment) Act 1993 gave the prosecution the right, for the first time, to appeal against the grant of bail.[67] Further provisions were introduced in the Criminal Justice and Public Order Act (CJPOA) 1994, most notably s. 26 which removed the presumption of bail for defendants who have allegedly committed offences whilst on bail. Hucklesby and Marshall found that the main effect of the change was an increase in the use of conditional bail.[68] The Law Commission noted that s. 26 was probably in contravention of the European Convention on Human Rights (ECHR).[69] The Criminal Justice Act 2003 amended s. 26 to create a rebuttable presumption against bail when an offence has been committed while on bail (and when a defendant has failed to answer bail without a reasonable excuse).[70] Section 25 of the CJPOA 1994, which created an exception to bail for defendants charged with certain serious offences who had previously been convicted of such offences, was amended due to an anticipated ruling that it was in contravention of the ECHR (due to its incompatibility with the presumption of innocence until proven guilty).[71] The House of Lords in O v Crown Court at Harrow held that the amended s. 25 could be read as compatible with Article 5 of the ECHR.[72]

The Coroners and Justice Act 2009 (CJA 2009) contains provisions which reverse the presumption of bail in murder cases.[73] According to CJA 2009, ss. 114 and 115, bail may not be granted to defendants charged with murder unless a Crown Court judge is of the opinion that there is no significant risk that the defendant would commit

[64] Woolf LJ, Prison Disturbances April 1990: Report of an Inquiry by Lord Justice Woolf (Parts 1 and 2) and His Honour Judge Stephen Tumin (Part 2) Cm. 1456 (1991) HMSO, London.

[65] HM Inspector of Prisons, Unjust Deserts: A Thematic Review of the Chief Inspector of Prisons of the Treatment and Conditions for Unsentenced Prisoners in England and Wales (2000) Home Office, London.

[66] See, for example, discussion in A. Hucklesby, 'The Problem with Bail Bandits' (1992) 142 New Law Journal 558.                                    [67] The Criminal Justice Act 2003, s. 19 extended this right.

[68] A. Hucklesby and E. Marshall, 'Tackling Offending on Bail' (2000) 39 Howard Journal 150. The provision had little effect on the number of defendants who allegedly commit offences whilst on bail who were remanded in custody. Even prior to the change, defendants who had allegedly offended whilst on bail were more likely to be remanded in custody because of the assessment of the likelihood of further offences being committed.

[69] Law Commission, Bail and the Human Rights Act 1998 (1999) Law Commission Consultation Paper No. 157, para. 6.14.                                    [70] Criminal Justice Act 2003, ss. 14 and 15.

[71] Crime and Disorder Act 1998, s. 56. The European Court of Human Rights ruled that the provision was incompatible with Article 5 in Callebero v UK [2000] Criminal Law Review 587.

[72] [2006] UKHL 42. The court said s. 25 did not place a burden of proof on the defendant to make out 'exceptional circumstances' for allowing bail but could be read as simply requiring the defendant to point to material which might support the existence of such a circumstance.

[73] For background to the introduction of these provisions, see Ministry of Justice, Bail and Murder: Response to Consultation, CP (R) 11/08 (2009a) MOJ, London. The proposals followed a series of high-profile murders, including the case of Gary Weddell, a police officer who murdered his mother-in-law whilst on bail for murdering his wife (Daily Telegraph, 12 April 2008).

an offence that would cause physical or mental injury to another person. This new rebuttable presumption against bail is unlikely to be held to violate Article 5 ECHR because, by analogy with CJPOA, s. 25, it can be 'read down' to ensure compatibility with Article 5. The Government argues that it is convention compliant because it is not for the defendant to show that there is no 'significant risk', but for the prosecution to show that there is such a risk.

Section 5(1) of the Bail Act 1976 requires courts to record their reasons for refusing bail or imposing or varying conditions and supply a copy to the defendant. If remanded in custody the defendant can renew his or her application for bail at his or her next remand appearance.[74] An appeal against a refusal of bail by magistrates can be made to the Crown Court under s. 60 of the Criminal Justice Act 1982. Section 16 of the Criminal Justice Act 2003 provides the Crown Court with the power to hear appeals against conditions imposed. Although the CPS can appeal against the grant of bail it does not, as yet, have any power to appeal against a refusal to impose conditions that it requests.

In an adversarial system, it is crucial that there is an effective defence to represent defendants in bail applications and appeals. In their study of criminal defence lawyers, McConville et al. found that solicitors doing legal aid work at magistrates' courts often have very limited contact with their clients.[75] Even meetings at court immediately before a hearing are often minimal, conducted in noisy public places such as corridors or in the 'lock-up' below the court, in the hearing of the police. Solicitors who operated in more than one court had no control over their timetable and frequently had to apologize to courts and clients for their late arrival. The researchers found that solicitors tended to deal with cases, rather than clients; they worked on the basis of the file, usually produced by clerks, merely acting on the written instructions on their court list – to adjourn for instructions, or await papers, or vary bail conditions. This meant that cases could be moved through the system in a cost-effective way, but it also means that in general, solicitors in magistrates' courts have little personal contact with their clients, even at court.

When it came to making bail applications, the researchers found many examples of solicitors making clear and cogent submissions to the magistrates on the question of bail. However, there were others who were less well prepared and lacking information on which to base their application, who deployed a range of strategies, such as recharacterizing the allegations in order to reduce the apparent seriousness of the prosecution's case. The researchers concluded:

While bail hearings sometimes offer a veneer of adversariness and a forum in which solicitors can advertise their services to potential clients, they also point up the superficiality of many solicitor – client relationships, the lack of genuine commitment to the client's cause

---

[74] Any argument can be used to support that application (Criminal Justice Act 1988, s. 154), but subsequently the court need not hear arguments of law or fact it has heard previously.

[75] M. McConville, J. Hodgson, L. Bridges, and A. Pavlovic, *Standing Accused* (1994) Clarendon Press, Oxford, ch. 7.

and the importance to the solicitor of retaining credibility and status with the court even at the client's expense.[76]

The practices of defence lawyers have significant implications for the conduct of summary trial as well as the bail process.


## Summary trial

In a summary trial, the charge will be read out to the defendant and the defendant will be asked whether he or she pleads guilty or not. If the defendant pleads guilty, the court will convict without hearing the evidence, although they may go on to hold a 'Newton hearing' if a factual dispute needs to be determined for sentencing purposes.[77] If a defendant pleads not guilty, the magistrates will hear evidence from both parties and their witnesses and both parties will have the opportunity to cross-examine the other's witnesses. The magistrates will then either convict the defendant or dismiss the case.

While the defendant in the magistrates' court is theoretically free to make his or her own choice as to whether to plead guilty or not guilty, the defendant may in fact be subject to a number of pressures which will seek to influence his or her choice of plea. One of these is the practice of 'charge bargaining', whereby the defendant agrees to plead guilty to a less serious charge (regardless of whether the defendant really believes that he or she is guilty). Furthermore, the defendant may believe that he or she will benefit from a 'sentence discount'. These forms of plea bargaining will be explored more fully in relation to the Crown Court. The sentence discount principle is of less practical significance in the magistrates' court but, in theory at least, magistrates should have regard to Sentencing Guidelines on the reduction of sentence for guilty plea.

The crucial role of defence solicitors in procuring guilty pleas has been emphasized by McConville et al. They sum up the position as follows:

For the most part, solicitors do not see magistrates' courts as trial venues but as places where defendants can be processed through guilty pleas without, in general, any risk of severe sanction. The idea that the prosecution should be 'put to the proof' – required to establish a case against the defendant – is not accepted as 'valid' or 'realistic' by defence solicitors. While it would be misleading and unfair to argue that solicitors do not care about their client, so strong is their presumption of guilt and their faith in the prosecution's case that they fail to see their own role in the production of guilty pleas, and their implication in ambiguous or inconsistent pleas of guilt.[78]

---

[76] McConville et al. (1994) ch. 7.   [77] *Newton* (1982) 4 Cr App R(S) 388.
[78] McConville et al. (1994) p. 210.

Even when defendants plead not guilty, so that a full summary trial takes place, McConville et al. argue convincingly that magistrates' courts are concerned with processing guilty people. There is a very high rate of convictions in magistrates' courts.[79] McConville et al. argue that it is important to set this in the context of those factors which give the prosecution case strength or render it weak. In magistrates' courts, the prosecution tends to rely heavily upon police evidence, which is accepted as legitimate because it is depersonalized and assertive. Police evidence commends itself to magistrates because it is generally supported by notebook entries and by the testimony of other police officers. Evidence like this, of what the police allege they saw the defendant do or heard the defendant say, is much more difficult for the defence to challenge than the sort of confession evidence which may be given in Crown Court trials. The type of evidence given by the police in a magistrates' court quickly takes on the character of an impartial report, and as such appears very credible.[80]

The defence, on the other hand, frequently does not find it easy to establish a competing case with which to challenge the prosecution evidence. This is partly because of the general lack of investigation and preparation by defence solicitors and their staff. As a result, the defendant himself or herself becomes the front line of the defence, often the only witness called on the defence side. Defence solicitors in this position cannot readily challenge prosecution witnesses, in case an attack upon the integrity of the police results in the prosecution being able to explore the defendant's character.[81]

The 'structural' advantages, identified by McConville et al. as benefiting the prosecution in the magistrates' court, offer one possible explanation of the high conviction rate in contested cases. The rules on disclosure of evidence have also created some difficulties.[82] Concerns about the quality of defence work have only been increased by recent changes in the provision of public funding.

# Legal aid

The provision of publicly funded legal services has undergone a period of considerable change as the government has sought to keep some control over the rise in the cost of legal aid ('public funding'), in particular the cost of providing publicly funded criminal defence services.[83] In 2001, a public defence service (PDS) was introduced in some areas to provide competition for privately run firms doing defence work under contract with the Legal Services Commission (LSC). Recently, the Government has

---

[79] See, for example, J. Vennard, *Contested Trials in Magistrates' Courts* (1980) Royal Commission on Criminal Procedure Research Study No. 6, HMSO, London.        [80] McConville et al. (1994) p. 237.

[81] McConville et al. (1994) p. 238.

[82] J. Plotnikoff and R. Woolfson, *'A Fair Balance'? Evaluation of the Operation of Disclosure Law* (2001) RDS Occasional Paper No. 76, Home Office, London, ch. 8.

[83] Ministry of Justice, *Legal Aid: Funding Reforms*, Consultation Paper 18/09 (2009c) MOJ, London.

proposed a scheme of 'best value tendering' for private firms to bid for defence work. If implemented, this scheme may have a significant impact on the availability and quality of defence service provision in the magistrates' court. However, the likely effects are purely speculative at this stage.

There is research which has examined the effect of the introduction of the PDS on provision of defence services.[84] The service operated in six sites for a while but was found to be expensive in comparison to private sector provision and some of the more costly offices have since been closed down. The Government claimed that the aim of the scheme was never to undercut private provision but to provide a service that was as good or better than that provided by private firms. There were concerns that the PDS would lack independence but the evaluation allayed some of these fears. It found that the quality of the service provided varied across sites but that in some respects, the PDS was doing better than private practice, for example by adopting a 'more adversarial' approach in their police station work where their clients were more likely to make a 'no comment' interview.[85] In relation to magistrates' court work, it was found that there were no significant differences in bail outcomes. The PDS had more guilty pleas than private firms but they also had more discontinued cases and the levels of conviction rates and sentencing outcomes for PDS and private firms were similar

In order to qualify for publicly funded defence services, a defendant must make an application to the LSC and satisfy both means and merits testing.[86]

Representation is granted according to the 'interests of justice' test. In deciding what the interests of justice consist of in relation to any particular individual, the following factors in Sch. 3 of the Access to Justice Act 1999 must be taken into account:

(a) whether the individual would, if any matter arising in the proceedings is decided against him or her, be likely to lose his or her liberty or suffer serious damage to his or her reputation;

(b) whether the determination of any matter arising in the proceedings may involve consideration of a substantial question of law;

(c) whether the individual may be unable to understand the proceedings or state his or her own case;

(d) whether the proceedings involve the tracing, interviewing or expert cross-examination of witnesses on behalf of the individual; and

(e) whether it is in the interests of another person for the individual to be represented.

---

84  L. Bridges, E. Cape, P. Fenn, A. Mitchell, R. Moorhead, and A. Sherr, *Evaluation of the Public Defender Service in England and Wales* (2007) available from LSC website at: <http://www.legalservices.gov.uk/docs/pds/Public_Defenders_Report_PDFVersion6.pdf>.

85  Bridges et al. (2007) p. 91.

86  'Advice and assistance' covering police station work (and people appearing in the magistrates' courts who may wish to apply for bail) is not means tested. Nor is 'advocacy assistance' from a duty solicitor, although the latter is merits tested.

If the interests of justice test is satisfied, then 'full legal representation' will be available to appoint a solicitor from a private firm contracted with the LSC. Applications are determined by magistrates' court clerks under the supervision and monitoring of the LSC. Research shows that clerks tend to apply little weight to the statutory criteria, instead applying crude rules of thumb, for example regarding the seriousness of the offence. Rates of grant vary between courts, with some being more generous than others, although the level of variability and inconsistency seems to have declined over time.[87]

It has been noted that it has become increasingly difficult for solicitors working in private firms to make publicly funded criminal defence work 'pay'. It is suggested that the impact of this is that cases are increasingly dealt with in a bureaucratic fashion, with lawyers being nudged even further towards crime control goals.[88]

## Other significant actors in the magistrates' court

A pluralist perspective allows us to acknowledge the complex interactions which take place between those who have traditionally been recognized as part of the criminal justice system, such as solicitors and the police, with other actors who are not traditionally recognized as part of the criminal justice system, but who nevertheless play important roles within magistrates' courts.

The amount and importance of interaction between *solicitors* and *probation officers* should not be underestimated. Solicitors find that the probation service can be of considerable assistance. There will be at least one probation officer on duty in each remand court, whose duty includes the provision of information for bail and sentencing decisions and about bail and probation hostels. Solicitors may approach probation officers to find out about the number and type of bail hostel places available, and may find their assistance invaluable if a client has communication difficulties or has difficulty obtaining benefits (which may make them more vulnerable to committing offences while on bail).[89]

*Probation officers* and *social workers* may also have a direct influence on the criminal justice system through their preparation of pre-sentence reports. Parker et al. found that magistrates were influenced by their reports in a large percentage of cases, although not always in the ways intended.[90]

[87] R. Young and A. Wilcox, 'The Merits of Legal Aid in the Magistrates' Courts Revisited' [2007] Criminal Law Review 109.

[88] For more details on criminal legal aid representation, and a robust critique, see Sanders et al. (2010) pp. 503–14.          [89] H. Johnston, 'Court Duty Solicitors' (1992) Legal Action, May, p. 11.

[90] H. Parker, M. Sumner, and G. Jarvis, *Unmasking the Magistrates* (1989) Open University Press, Milton Keynes, ch. 8.

Another important actor in the magistrates' court is the *magistrates' clerk*. Lay magistrates rely on their clerk to ensure that they act within the law and that the rules of procedure and evidence are followed. The clerk is a central figure in the courtroom, despite the fact that their presence is largely ignored in traditional discussions of the criminal justice system, their role is of increasing significance due to enhanced powers.[91] It has been noted above that they are key figures when it comes to the determination of applications for publicly funded defence services. The two key studies of magistrates' clerks, one by Darbyshire and the other by Astor, are now quite dated but give useful insights into their role. Darbyshire's work on magistrates' clerks reveals the great variety of working practices and attitudes displayed by clerks – some are helpful and patient with unrepresented defendants, while others are unhelpful, brusque, and intimidating. Some appear to be tolerant members of Britain's multiracial society, while others appear to be motivated by racism in their dealings with defendants.[92] Given the wide variety of attitudes which Darbyshire discovered, it is not surprising that Young et al. found decisions about granting legal aid being taken very differently by different clerks.[93] Darbyshire has subsequently pointed out that the court clerks who advise lay magistrates are frequently not legally qualified, unlike their superiors, who are known as justices' clerks.[94] Furthermore, her research suggests that justices' clerks are being given responsibility for much greater numbers of courts, with the result that court clerks reported that they had often been in the position of needing to seek advice on a point of law from their (legally qualified) superior, but had been unable to obtain it at the time when it was needed because the justices' clerk was dealing with the problems of another Bench elsewhere.[95]

Astor, in her study of nine magistrates' courts, interviewed 50 magistrates' clerks.[96] She focused first on clerks' attitudes to unrepresented defendants, something about which Darybshire, in her study, had been critical. Astor found that the great majority of clerks in her study understood the difficulties of unrepresented litigants, realized that aggression and emotional outbursts were frequently a product of nerves, and that procedural complexities which made sense to them were a complete mystery to defendants. Most clerks were not only able to empathize with and understand the position of unrepresented litigants; they saw it as an aspect of the job which they positively enjoyed. Of the minority who did not enjoy it, many said that their lack of enjoyment sprang from the fact that they were always aware that they could not provide the standard of help which defendants really needed. The significance of these attitudes for a pluralist view of the legal system can be seen in an example given by Astor of the

[91] P. Darbyshire, 'A Comment on the Powers of Magistrates' Clerks' [1999] Criminal Law Review 377.

[92] P. Darbyshire, *Magistrates' Clerks* (1984) Barry Rose, Chichester.

[93] R. Young, T. Moloney, and A. Sanders, *In the Interests of Justice?* (1992) Institute of Judicial Administration, University of Birmingham. See also Young and Wilcox (2007).

[94] P. Darbyshire, 'For the New Lord Chancellor – Some Causes for Concern about Magistrates' [1997b] Criminal Law Review 861 at p. 873.    [95] Darbyshire (1997b) p. 873.

[96] H. Astor, 'The Unrepresented Defendant Revisited: A Consideration of the Role of the Clerk in Magistrates' Courts' (1986) 13 Journal of Law and Society 225.

clerk who helped two unrepresented young men to make a submission of 'no case to answer' which resulted in the case against them being dismissed. To ignore the effect of magistrates' clerks on what takes place in the courts in which they work is to obtain an incomplete picture of the working of the criminal justice system. This is not to say that all the clerks in Astor's study lived up to this ideal. She reports that some were examples of clerks who were brusque, or overbearing or simply passive, and others who used stereotypes, such as 'the hardened types', 'the barrack room lawyers', or 'the one-shotters' to decide which defendants were deserving of time and attention. However, such clerks were in the minority. It was also clear that there was a limit to the extent which even the most helpful clerks were prepared to go to help unrepresented defendants. This arose out of the fact that the allegiance of the clerks was ultimately not to the defendants, but to court procedure and legal rules. Their first concern was that the case should be properly conducted, not that the defendant should understand what was going on. This is not merely a concern with bureaucracy, but in order to preserve the legitimacy of the court. Helping the defendant is an important part of this, but it is not the only factor.

The most interesting conclusion which Astor draws, from a pluralist theoretical perspective, is that the differences she found in the way clerks operated were not differences between different courts, but between different clerks.[97] It is at this micro level that the relevance of a pluralist approach can most clearly be seen.

In recent years, the development of specialist sessions in some magistrates' courts has resulted in other actors not traditionally involved in the criminal justice process emerging to play an important role. At the end of 2009, there were over 100 magistrates' courts hosting specialist hearings for domestic violence cases. The rapid expansion of 'specialist domestic violence courts' over the last decade is part of the Government's plans to ensure the effective and efficient prosecution of domestic violence.[98] A key element of the specialist court is the presence of an *independent victim advocate* to try to ensure that the victim's interests are taken into account. Although the way that the criminal justice agencies interact with the victim's advocate varies a little from court to court, in many instances there is a close relationship between the police and the advocate and the prosecutor relies significantly on the advocate for up-to-date information about the victim's situation and attitude to the case.[99] Traditionally, the victim has played a limited role in the criminal justice process, so the development of victim advocates represents an important departure from the models of criminal justice which see no role for victims.[100] Court specialization has in some ways improved the experience of victims of domestic violence, and may have addressed some of the

[97] Astor (1986) p. 232.

[98] M. Burton, 'Judicial Monitoring of Compliance: Introducing "Problem Solving" Approaches to Domestic Violence Courts in England and Wales' (2006) 20(3) International Journal of Law, Policy and the Family 366.                                                             [99] Burton (2006).

[100] The traditional 'crime control' and 'due process' models simply ignore victims because victims' rights were not fashionable at the time they were devised. Victims can be made to fit into either model but neither model prioritizes victims' interests. See Sanders et al. (2010) ch. 1.

stereotypes non-specialist magistrates held about domestic violence, but its impact on the outcomes of cases appears to have been fairly limited. The conviction rate in some specialist courts is higher than non-specialist courts but there is still a tendency to use non-custodial penalties, including fines and conditional discharges. The main impact of the courts therefore appears to be the introduction of a victim advocate who can improve the victim's experience of the criminal justice process and perhaps in that way encourage them to continue to engage with the system and report any further incidents of violence in the future.[101]

## CONCLUSION

Although the magistrates' court has traditionally been shrouded by an ideology of triviality, it is the workhorse of the criminal justice system as far as courts are concerned and much of its business is far from trivial, least of all to the defendants and victims involved. Magistrates have significant powers to deprive defendants of their liberty pending trial and they also play an important role in deciding where defendants facing more serious charges will be tried. In exercising their discretion, they will often be dependent on the information provided to them by prosecutors and defence lawyers. Some of the research reviewed in this chapter has shown that the influence of prosecutors can be pervasive and defence lawyers do not always seem to represent their clients well, either because they share the 'crime control' goals of prosecutors or because the nature of public funding for criminal defence work is such that it is not profitable for them to protect their clients in a way that the adversarial ideal expects. As elsewhere in this book, we have sought to demonstrate the significance of actors who are not normally thought of as part of the legal system, or are given little recognition for the role that they play. Some of these actors, such as magistrates' clerks, have been performing an influential role in the work of the magistrates' courts for years; others, like victim advocates, are newly emerging onto the scene. As victim advocates come to play a role in the criminal justice process, they put traditional models of criminal justice which neglect the victim's interest under stress. They remind us of the need for a pluralist account which accommodates them.

## FURTHER READING

Cammiss, S. and Stride, C. 'Modelling Mode of Trial' (2008) 48 British Journal of Criminology 482.

Darbyshire, P., 'An Essay on the Importance and Neglect of the Magistracy' [1997a] Criminal Law Review 627.

Young, R. and Wilcox, A., 'The Merits of Legal Aid in the Magistrates' Courts Revisited' [2007] Criminal Law Review 109.

---

[101]  M. Burton, *Legal Responses to Domestic Violence* (2008) Routledge-Cavendish, Abingdon, ch. 7.

# 17

# The Crown Court

## INTRODUCTION

In popular imagination, Crown Court cases are those tried before judge and jury; however, few convictions or acquittals in the Crown Court are a product of jury trial.[1] There is a large gap between perception of how the most serious cases in the spectrum of offences are decided and the reality. Most defendants in the Crown Court end up pleading guilty. In relation to not guilty pleas, the judge plays a significant role in acquittal. Thus, the image of the Crown Court case as one which is fought out in court and where the defendant anxiously awaits the jury's verdict is just as false as the image of the civil court case litigated before a bewigged and begowned judge.

Second, we will see that while the legal rules which relate to the Crown Court might provide for serious cases to be considered seriously, the reality of most trials is rather different. Again, as before, there is a gap between the rules and the actual behaviour of lawyers, judges, court staff, and everybody else involved in individual cases.

Nevertheless, this is not to say that the jury and the judge are irrelevant to most Crown Court cases, nor that the doctrinal rules are a mere sham. The reasons why most cases do not reach the jury for their final decision, owe themselves in part to the perceptions of defendants and their lawyers about the process of criminal trial. Frequently, though not invariably, these perceptions are an accurate account of what actually happens. What happens is in part determined by the rules. Cases are either litigated before the Crown Court or settled in the shadow of Crown Court practice.

## Disclosure of evidence

In anticipation of a trial, or in order to establish whether or not to plead guilty and if so to what charge, the defendant will want to establish the strength of the prosecution case against him or her. The prosecution will also want to know what the defence case may be. In recent years, the disclosure rules have undergone significant changes

---

[1] A. Sanders, R. Young, and M. Burton, *Criminal Justice* (4th edn, 2010) Oxford University Press, Oxford, p. 554.

in response to the Government's concerns that the disclosure arrangements placed too heavy a burden on the prosecution and too little responsibility to disclose on the defence.[2] The Criminal Procedure and Investigations Act (CPIA) 1996 introduced changes in relation to the duties of disclosure imposed on both sides in criminal litigation.[3] These rules have since been amended by the Criminal Justice Act 2003.

The key provision relating to the prosecution's duty of disclosure is to be found in s. 3(1)(a) of the CPIA, which provides that the prosecutor must disclose any material which 'might reasonably be considered capable of undermining the case for the prosecution or of assisting the case for the accused'.[4] The duty of disclosure is a continuing one.[5] In Crown Court cases, the defence must respond with a statement setting out the details of its case, including any points of law and details of witnesses it intends to call or any witnesses it has consulted. Adverse inferences may be drawn if the duties of disclosure are breached, or the defence at trial departs from that previously disclosed.[6]

The amendments made by the Criminal Justice Act 2003 to the rules on disclosure were intended to address criticisms that the scheme of primary and secondary disclosure by the prosecution in the CPIA was not working as intended.[7] Critics were always sceptical about whether the amendments made by the CJA would be effective. Redmayne, for example, observed: 'Disclosure has always been a problem and very probably always will be, whatever regime is adopted'[8] it is not difficult for the prosecution agencies to hide information if they really want to. There are working cultures and not just legal rules to take into account.[9]

Sanders et al. highlight a number of problems with the disclosure regime.[10] One issue is that the CPS cannot disclose information of which they are not aware; they are reliant on police disclosure officers, who are often inadequately trained and present the information poorly.[11] The police have little incentive to do the job better because to do so might undermine their case. However, CPS caseworkers may also lack the incentive or expertise to remedy defects. The CPS Inspectorate has recently found that

---

[2] Home Office, *Disclosure: A Consultation* (1995) Cm. 2864, HMSO, London.

[3] See J. Sprack, 'The Criminal Procedure and Investigations Act 1996: (1) The Duty of Disclosure' [1997] Criminal Law Review 308.          [4] CPIA, s. 391(a) as amended by Criminal Justice Act 2003, s. 32.

[5] If prosecutors subsequently become aware of material that should, but has not been, disclosed they must disclose it (CPIA, s. 7A, as inserted by Criminal Justice Act 2003, s. 37).

[6] Prior to the CPIA 1996, there were no general duties of defence disclosure, although special rules existed for alibi evidence. A general defence duty of disclosure was first introduced by the CPIA and then expanded by s. 5 of the Criminal Justice Act 2003. Although it could be argued that the rules breach the ECHR, a successful challenge seems unlikely.

[7] J. Plotnikoff and R. Woolfson, 'A Fair Balance'? *Evaluation of the Operation of Disclosure Law* (2001) RDS Occasional Paper No. 76, Home Office, London. Plotnikoff and Woolfson found that poor police and prosecution practice in relation to disclosure was widespread. See also CPS Inspectorate, *Thematic Review of the Disclosure of Unused Material* (2000) Thematic Report 2/2000, HMCPSI, London.

[8] M. Redmayne, 'Disclosure and its Discontents' [2004] Criminal Law Review 441.

[9] H. Quirk, 'The Significance of Culture in Criminal Procedure Reform: Why the Revised Disclosure Scheme cannot Work' (2006) International Journal of Evidence and Proof 42.

[10] Sanders et al. (2010) pp. 388–93.

[11] HMCPSI, *Disclosure – Thematic Review* (2008) HMCPSI, London.

initial disclosure is inadequate in nearly half of all cases. Continuing review is satisfactory in most cases but this leads to late disclosure and delays with trials and late guilty pleas.[12]


# Cases that do not go to full trial

## Case management

Like all other disputes within 'the English legal system', Crown Court cases are 'managed'. Cases do not simply inevitably go to trial following the rules that we have described above. Rather, choices are involved. Ostensibly, these are choices made by the prosecutor or the defendant. However, in reality, as we have already seen, the defendant will often have to rely upon his or her lawyer when making these choices. Moreover, in general, these choices will probably be ones which will speed the defendant's case through the court and assist the court in dealing with its caseload. The judge now has a more active role in ensuring efficient management of cases under the Criminal Procedure Rules.[13]

Research has shown that Crown Court cases involve, on the one hand barristers and on the other hand non-qualified and lowly qualified staff from a solicitors' office, far more than they involve solicitors.[14] Despite expansion in rights of audience for solicitors in the higher courts, there has not been a large uptake of these rights. Solicitors have continued to instruct barristers to do the actual representation in court and relied upon office staff to do any preparatory work.[15] The practice of using unqualified staff to substitute for solicitors is in conflict with the notion that the Crown Court deals seriously with serious cases. While some of these staff may have enormous practical experience, notwithstanding their lack of formal qualifications, others 'simply do not understand what is going on'.[16] This situation might be ameliorated by the fact that most defendants will have a barrister to represent them. In cases where a defendant has not clearly indicated that they intend to plead guilty, there may be a case conference before the Crown Court hearing.[17] This gives a barrister an opportunity to

---

[12] HMCPSI (2008) para. 8.2.

[13] The rules are available at: <http://www.justice.gov.uk/criminal/procrules_fin/rulesmenu.htm>.

[14] M. McConville, J. Hodgson, L. Bridges, and A. Pavlovic, *Standing Accused* (1994) Clarendon Press, Oxford, pp. 240–6.

[15] The Access to Justice Act 1999 extended rights of audience to employed solicitors but, despite an upturn in the percentage of cases where CPS lawyers present Crown Court cases, the CPS continues to instruct the independent Bar to appear on its behalf (HM Crown Prosecution Service Inspectorate, *Report of the Thematic Review of the Quality of Prosecution Advocacy and Case Presentation* (2009) HMCPSI, London).

[16] McConville et al. (1994) p. 242.

[17] Zander and Henderson found that 58 per cent of defence barristers and 59 per cent of defence solicitors thought that there was no case conference in the majority of cases. However, both groups thought that a case

offer the defendant advice on the strengths and weaknesses of their case. However, barristers commonly accept more work than they can, in fact, deal with.[18] In many instances, the main purpose of the case conference is not to give formal legal advice to the defendant but, rather, to allow a barrister who is unfamiliar with the case the opportunity to familiarize themselves and give the solicitor's staff instructions about further preparation that needs to be done before the case comes to trial.[19]

Case conferences also give barristers an opportunity to prepare their clients for trial.[20] Their difficulties in doing this illustrate some of the tensions that exist in the barristers' relationships with the court on the one hand, and with their clients on the other. Barristers are officers of the court with a duty to the court. At the same time, barristers are there in court to represent their clients' best interests.[21] The problem this creates is indicated by the following exchange observed in research by McConville et al.:

Client: What do you want me to say [at trial]?
Counsel: I can't tell you what to say, only how to answer.[22]

The client wants to know what story will be most likely to lead to them being found not guilty. However, barristers are under a professional obligation not to coach their clients in lies.[23] As stories are put to them, they can indicate what will be unacceptable but they cannot make up stories for their clients.

## The barrister's relationship with the defendant

While barristers are there to represent their clients, this does not mean that they are simply there to do what their clients say. Barristers do not simply set out a legal position to their clients. Rather, the research suggests a much more active role in managing the outcome of the case. 'A central purpose of most conferences is to persuade the

---

conference was much more likely in the case of a defendant who intended to contest the case (M. Zander and P. Henderson, *The Crown Court Study* (1993) Royal Commission on Criminal Justice Research Study No. 19, HMSO, London, pp. 61–2).

[18]  Sanders et al. (2010) pp. 473–7. See also J. Flood, *Barristers' Clerks* (1983) Manchester University Press, Manchester, ch. 3.

[19]  McConville et al. (1994) pp. 247–9.

[20]  The different function that the case conference fulfils has to be analysed in the context of the likely time that it will take. Zander and Henderson reported that 26 per cent took under 30 minutes, 30 per cent took between 30 minutes and one hour, 30 per cent took between one and two hours, and 13 per cent took longer (Zander and Henderson (1993) p. 63). These percentages relate to all case conferences and not just those held with respect to not guilty pleas.

[21]  See Code of Conduct for the Bar of England and Wales (8th edn, n.d.). The Code is available from: <http://www.barstandardsboard.org.uk/standardsandguidance/codeofconduct>.

[22]  McConville et al. (1994) p. 251.

[23]  The Code of Conduct for the Bar states that: 'A practising barrister has an overriding duty to the Court to act with independence in the interests of justice: he must assist the court in the administration of justice and must not deceive or knowingly or recklessly mislead the court' (para. 302).

defendants of the likelihood of conviction and of the advantages of a guilty plea.'[24] Zander and Henderson found that in 'several' of the cases in their survey defendants reported that they had been persuaded by their lawyers to plead guilty against their wishes.[25] More usually, defendants are led to accept the value of a guilty plea by the barrister involved in their case. However, that guilty plea might be appropriate only because the solicitor has not properly prepared the case. The barrister's judgement that a defendant will be found guilty is based mainly on the papers before them, not on the story that the defendant has to tell. In McConville et al.'s research, case conferences were often dominated by 'an underlying presupposition of guilt'.[26] In many instances, it may in fact be in a defendant's interest to plead guilty but some researchers have argued that, because defence barristers are part of the same legal culture as prosecuting barristers, they owe more allegiance to keeping the system working than they do to the individual interests of their clients and that defence lawyers tend to show an 'uncritical acceptance of the prosecution case'.[27] The importance of the initial attitude of the defence barrister is reinforced by the fact that very few cases involve the barrister having to take a view of some difficult but seemingly objective point of law. Instead, their opinions are based upon the more obviously subjective assessment of the factual evidence available which in turn means assessing the reliability of the various stories from defendants, witnesses, and police.[28] Defence barristers, because they see themselves as having common cause with the court as a whole, may be predisposed to distrust their clients and find police evidence reliable.[29]

As the case progresses, so further conferences may be held.[30] The closer the case gets to full trial, the greater the pressure there is on the defendant to make quick decisions. An assumption of guilt continues to pervade most conferences, with barristers seeking to persuade defendants that they should plead guilty to all or some of the charges being brought against them. Barristers cannot force their clients to plead guilty, but in telling their clients this they can also induce them to plead guilty by emphasizing the strength of the case against them, the value of a guilty plea, the emotional dangers of a full trial, and the barrister's own weight of professional experience in advising them.[31]

---

[24] McConville et al. (1994) p. 252.    [25] Zander and Henderson (1993) p. 97.

[26] McConville et al. (1994) p. 254.

[27] M. McConville, A. Sanders, and R. Leng, *The Case for the Prosecution* (1991) Routledge, London, pp. 167 and 169.

[28] J. Morison and P. Leith, *The Barrister's World and the Nature of Law* (1992) Open University Press, Milton Keynes, pp. 116–18.

[29] Rock illustrates the common culture of the police and barristers by describing lawyers and police as part of the third circle in the Crown Court, where the first circle are judges and the second circle are court staff (P. Rock, *The Social World of an English Crown Court* (1993) Clarendon Press, Oxford, p. 191). This common culture can of course be over-emphasized.

[30] Zander and Henderson reported that more than two conferences was very rare and having just one was more common than having two (Zander and Henderson (1993) p. 62). The Criminal Procedure Rules aim to minimize delays and the number of hearings.    [31] McConville et al. (1994) pp. 257–61.

## Plea bargains

One thing that can lead to a guilty plea is a plea bargain.[32] Plea bargains take a number of different forms. They may take the form of a *sentence discount*, where a defendant agrees to plead guilty to one or more offences in expectation that he or she will receive a lesser sentence. That lesser sentence may either be a sentence of a different kind – a fine, for example, instead of a period of imprisonment – or it might be a shorter or less onerous sentence of the same kind. Plea bargains may also take the form of a *charge bargain*, where the defendant agrees to plead guilty to fewer and/or a lesser offence than the one originally charged – manslaughter, for example, instead of murder. A further form of plea bargaining, which may be described as *fact bargaining*, is where the defendant pleads guilty to the original charge but in expectation that the facts presented to the court for sentencing purposes will reflect a version of events more favourable to the defendant than might have otherwise have been the case.[33]

The sentence discount principle was first placed on a statutory footing by s. 48 of the Criminal Justice and Public Order Act 1994. This provision was subsequently replaced by the similar one in s. 144 of the Criminal Justice Act 2003. Under this provision, in determining what sentence to pass on a defendant who has pleaded guilty, the court shall take into account the stage in the proceedings at which he indicated his intention to plead guilty and the circumstances in which this indication was given. The statute does not state the amount of discount that should be given depending on the stage and circumstances of the plea; however, the Sentencing Guidelines Council has issued detailed guidance on this matter.[34] This guidance should be followed by the judiciary in most cases, although they do retain some discretion to depart from it.[35] The basic scheme is a sliding scale with a maximum one-third discount for a guilty plea at the first available opportunity, reducing to one-quarter where the trial date is set, and only one-tenth for pleas entered at the door of the court or after the trial has begun. Traditionally, one of the key circumstances relevant to plea was the strength of evidence against the defendant, such that defendants who were caught red-handed were thought to deserve no discount.[36] The guidelines do not preclude a discount for defendants who are caught red-handed, suggesting instead a sliding scale with a maximum discount of 20 per cent as opposed to one-third for guilty pleas at first reasonable opportunity. There are special rules on the reduction of sentence for some offences.[37]

---

[32] For a detailed discussion of this topic, see Sanders et al. (2010) ch. 8.

[33] A. Ashworth and M. Redmayne, *The Criminal Process* (3rd edn, 2005) Oxford University Press, Oxford, p. 274.

[34] The guidance, first issued in 2004, was revised in 2007. See Sentencing Guidelines Council, *Reduction in Sentence for a Guilty Plea: Definitive Guideline* (Revised 2007) SGC, London.

[35] Sanders et al (2010) pp. 440–1.

[36] There is no discount if the defendant has been caught 'red-handed' (*Costen* (1989) 11 Cr App R(S) 182).    [37] These include convicted murderers. See Sentencing Guidelines Council (2007).

It is possible to speculate on the impact of s. 144 and associated guidance by examining the operation of its precursor. Henham found that only a bare majority of judges in the six Crown Court centres featured in his study of 310 guilty pleas stated that they were awarding a sentence discount, and less than one-fifth stated the basis on which the discount was being given.[38] In 145 cases where the judge neither stated a discount was being given, nor that it was not, Henham asserts the likely explanation is that the judge simply did not comment on a discount that was in fact given. However, it may be that a more plausible explanation was that no discount was, in fact, given and the court is failing to deliver its side of the bargain.[39] Indeed, even when judges state they are awarding a discount for a guilty plea, Sanders et al. observe that the defendant has no way of knowing whether they really are.

Traditionally, the English courts were reluctant to acknowledge plea bargaining in its sentence discount form and set out strict rules governing its operation in *R* v *Turner*.[40] Under these rules, while barristers were permitted to consult with judges about particular cases, judges were told that they should never indicate what sentence they had in mind depending on the nature of a plea, except if they were minded to impose the same form of sentence irrespective of plea. In theory, this was supposed to make plea bargains very much less likely since a barrister would not be able to guarantee any particular sentence to the client. In practice, sentence discount plea bargains were a regular feature of court practice, despite the *Turner* rules. Baldwin and McConville's 1977 study of the Birmingham Crown Court concluded that in 18.7 per cent of their sample, defendants believed that there was a plea bargain in the full sense of the word, and that in 13.2 per cent of all cases, while there had been no explicit bargain, the defendant believed that a deal had been made on his or her behalf and therefore pleaded guilty.[41]

That judicial involvement in plea bargaining exists is unquestionable, although how frequently this involvement occurs is more difficult to assess. There was a stream of successful appeals against conviction where the *Turner* rules had been breached, indicating that judges were not always willing to implement the rules in practice.[42] Zander and Henderson's study showed that 67 per cent of all judges thought that the rules in *R* v *Turner* should be changed in order to allow barristers and judges to discuss pleas and sentence.[43] Moreover, it is important to remember that at Crown Court level, not all judges are full-time. Recorders and assistant recorders who sit in the Crown Court are appointed only on a part-time basis and will normally sit for between 20 and 50 days in a year.[44] For the rest of the time, they will normally work as barristers. In

[38]   R. Henham, 'Bargain Justice or Justice Denied? Sentence Discounts and the Criminal Process' (1999) 63 Modern Law Review 515.                                    [39]   Sanders et al. (2010)) pp. 449–50.

[40]   (1970) 54 Cr App R 352.

[41]   J. Baldwin and M. McConville, *Negotiated Justice* (1977) Martin Robertson, Oxford, p. 28.

[42]   *AG Reference No. 44 of 2000 (Peverett)* [2001] Cr App R 416.

[43]   Zander and Henderson (1993) p. 145.

[44]   'Judicial Appointments: Recorders and Assistant Recorders' Leaflet 3 (1995) Lord Chancellor's Department, London, pp. 1 and 2.

Zander and Henderson's study, 86 per cent of prosecution barristers and 88 per cent of defence barristers thought that the *Turner* rules should be amended so as to allow discussion between barristers and judges about plea and sentence.[45] It seems doubtful that part-time appointees could ever be inculcated into a culture that accepted the *Turner* rules. There is some evidence to suggest that the degree of judicial involvement in plea bargaining varies, depending upon the particular judge or the particular Crown Court centre in question.[46]

Whilst the Court of Appeal were still trying to get Crown Court judges to stick to the *Turner* rules in *R v Peverett*,[47] the rules were interpreted restrictively in *R v Nazham*,[48] where a private discussion in chambers between the judge and counsel resulted in an indication that a shorter custodial sentence would be appropriate for a guilty plea and a comment was made by the judge that the case had 'got plea written all over it and bags of credit'. The Court of Appeal in *R v Nazham* said that the indication of sentence was an irregularity but did not inhibit the defendant's freedom of choice. Finally, the Court of Appeal decided to abandon the *Turner* rules in *R v Goodyear*.[49] The Court of Appeal noted that there had been a number of significant changes since the *Turner* case had been decided and both the Runciman Commission and the Auld Review had favoured some kind of advance indication of sentence when sought by the defendant. Whilst the Court of Appeal wishes to maintain a prohibition on unsolicited sentence indication, it decided in *R v Goodyear* that the defendant should be allowed to instruct his counsel to seek an indication of sentence from the judge. Under the *Goodyear* guidelines, the judge can respond to the defendant's request to indicate the maximum sentence that would follow an immediate guilty plea, but must not go further and indicate the maximum possible level of sentence following a contested trial; the former revelation does not constitute 'improper pressure' to plead guilty, whilst the later would.[50] Judges may continue to indicate the form of sentence will remain the same regardless of plea. It should be noted that the judge should not give an advance indication of sentence if the defendant does not seek it.[51] *Goodyear* requires that the process of sentence indication be initiated by the defendant who should request in writing that his lawyer seek an indication. In practice, this probably means that defence counsel will initiate the process by advising their clients to do so. Advance indication should not be sought where there is uncertainty about acceptable pleas and/or the factual basis for plea. Flowing on from this, the judge should not be asked to indicate the sentence which he might have in mind dependent upon different possible pleas.

---

[45] Zander and Henderson (1993).    [46] Morison and Leith (1992) p. 135.

[47] [2001]1 Cr App R 416.    [48] [2004] EWCA 491.    [49] [2005] 1 WLR 2532.

[50] The Court does not, however, seem keen to reduce sentences where this aspect of the rules has been breached and the defendant has been told the sentence that will be imposed for a conviction following contest (*Clark and Ors* [2008] EWCA Crim 3221).

[51] However, judges may remind counsel, in open court and in the presence of the defendant, of the entitlement to seek an advance indication. It is said that this should be done with caution to avoid pressure, but, in practice, it may be difficult to avoid the defendant getting an impression that he is being strongly encouraged by the judge to plead guilty.

In the absence of empirical evidence on how the *Goodyear* guidelines are working in practice, it is difficult to state whether they have changed the behaviour of judges and counsel. It should be noted that the practices of the judiciary and the Bar are resistant to change and there is every possibility that, like the *Turner* rules before them, the *Goodyear* guidelines are more honoured in breach. There are already examples of the Court of Appeal criticizing multiple breaches of the *Goodyear* guidelines.[52] On the other hand, the rules themselves allow a fair amount of discretion to the courts and rest upon uncertain concepts of what consistutes acceptable and unacceptable pressure to plead guilty. Whilst it is said that indicating the maximum sentence following trial would place the defendant under unacceptable pressure to plead guilty, some judges do this in contravention of the *Goodyear* guidelines. The USA system allows defendants to be told both the sentence for plea and sentence for contesting a case and being convicted. The House of Lords has had occasion to consider whether this puts the defendant under unconscionable pressure not to contest a case and has decided that it does not.[53] The court decided that only in extreme cases, where the defendant was threatened with unlawful action, would the pressure be too much. It concluded that a promise to discount the sentence by more than half and to allow the defendant to serve it under more favourable conditions, did not constitute unlawful pressure to forego a contest.

Whilst politicians are often keen to distinguish the system of plea bargaining that operates in England and Wales from that in the USA, the courts seem more willing to acknowledge the similarities. The introduction of a more formalized process for bargaining in serious fraud cases takes the English legal system closer in the direction of the USA. The *AG Guidelines on Plea Discussions in Cases of Serious and Complex Fraud* move the charge bargaining process to the pre-charge stage, allowing prosecutors to enter negotiations with the defence to agree a plea before the prosecution has carried out extensive investigation and preparation of the case. If the defendant agrees to plead guilty as a result of these negotiations, the prosecutor can make a non-binding recommendation in relation to sentence.[54] The advantages to the system in terms of resources savings are obvious but what, if any, are the advantages to the defendant?

The advantages of plea bargaining to the defendant, victim, and the criminal justice system have been much debated. On the face of it, defendants seem to benefit from plea bargaining because, in theory, they receive a lesser sentence. They are being rewarded for not only shortening the duration of the case and avoiding the cost of a trial but because, by pleading guilty, they have supposedly shown contrition. However, the disadvantages of plea bargaining are now well documented.[55] Darbyshire observes that the discount principle may be expressed as a reward for those who plead guilty but in

---

[52] *AG Reference No. 80 of 2005* [2005] EWCA 3367.    [53] *McKinnon v US* (2008) UKHL 59.
[54] *Attorney General's Guidelines on Plea Discussions in Cases of Serious or Complex Fraud* (available at: <http://www.attorneygeneral.gov.uk>).    [55] Ashworth and Redmayne (2005) ch. 10.

reality it works as a punishment for those who plead not guilty.[56] The problems of sentence discount take on a special resonance, given the differential experience of racial groups in the criminal justice system. Afro-Caribbeans are more likely to be tried in the Crown Court, more likely to plead not guilty, and more likely to be acquitted than other racial groups. The fact that they are also more likely to receive greater sentences than other racial groups is not just due to the fact that, having elected in greater numbers to plead not guilty, they are therefore proportionately less likely to receive the advantage of a sentence discount, but it is a contributory factor.

If the defendant is genuinely guilty, then plea bargaining gives the defendant a benefit that he or she arguably does not deserve.[57] Of even greater concern is that innocent defendants may be put under pressure to plead guilty and that prosecutorial and judicial discretion to plea bargain is being used in cases where the defendant could not be proved legally guilty. The defendant does not benefit from plea bargaining where he or she would have been acquitted had the case gone to trial.[58] Nor does the victim benefit from the wrong person being convicted, or in the case where the factually guilty plead guilty, from the charge or the sentence not reflecting the true harm that they have suffered.[59] Guidance has been issued to regulate the role of prosecutors in plea bargaining. It asserts that prosecutors have an important role in protecting victims' interests and should not accept pleas that are based on misleading or untrue facts.[60] However, like all guidance, questions arise about how it is implemented in practice. There is still scope for victims' interests to be marginalized or ignored.

## A culture of crime control

The picture drawn above of the progress of the usual Crown Court case, where there is no full trial, is a long way from the theory that prosecutors must prove the guilt of defendants. While the distinction between the 'crime control' and the 'due process' models is, as we have observed in previous chapters, in general too limiting as a way of analysing the criminal process as a whole in relation to the tight, enclosed world of the Crown Court, it has much to offer. The rules of the Crown Court are constructed on the basis of the due process model but the system works on the basis of the crime control model. Defendants show a high level of appreciation of the work done in preparing their case for trial. In Zander and Henderson's study, 59 per cent thought their barristers' work was very good and 26 per cent thought their work was good. Similarly, 58 per cent thought their solicitors' work was very good, while 25 per cent thought it

---

[56] P. Darbyshire, 'The Mischief of Plea Bargaining and Sentence Rewards' [2000] Criminal Law Review 895.                                                      [57] Darbyshire (2000).

[58] Darbyshire (2000).

[59] H. Fenwick, 'Charge Bargaining and Sentence Discount: The Victim's Perspective' (1997) 5 International Review of Victimology 23.

[60] *AG Guidelines on the Acceptance of Pleas and the Prosecutor's Role in the Sentencing Exercise* (2005) Attorney General, London.

was good.[61] Notwithstanding this, the reality is that Crown Court cases are frequently prepared at some stage in the proceedings by staff who are either unqualified or who take on the case with little preparation.[62] In addition, barristers do not always work in their clients interests and may prefer their own interests,[63] or buy into the idea that their clients are guilty and should be convicted.[64] The culture of the Crown Court is one of crime control, and this is a view taken as much by most defence barristers as by those people who are associated with the prosecution.[65]

# Jury trial

'Trial begins in a state of muddle and incomplete knowledge.'[66] Notwithstanding the seemingly precise rules that govern them, criminal courts are disorderly places. Cases do not begin on time because previous cases have been held over, witnesses new to the court do not know where their case is, and defendants and defence barristers may not have met before the case.[67] It is in this atmosphere that the case is conducted.

A contested trial in the Crown Court is a trial before judge and jury, so before it can begin a jury has to be empanelled. The basic qualifications for a juror are that a person must be aged between 18 and 70, be registered as a voter, and have been ordinarily resident in England and Wales for any period of five years since they were 13 years of age.[68]

## The function of the jury

The role of juries within 'the English legal system' has been much debated over the last two centuries. The topic provokes 'comments which are frequently little short of hysterical'.[69] On the one hand, Lord Devlin, a former Lord of Appeal in Ordinary, has described it as 'the lamp that shows freedom lives'.[70] On the other hand, it has been the subject of severe criticism by police, academics, and politicians.

---

[61] Zander and Henderson (1993) p. 67.

[62] In Zander and Henderson's survey, 60 per cent of defendants reported that they first met their barrister on the day of their trial (Zander and Henderson (1993) p. 62). Even if we accept that the barristers had properly prepared their papers, it is difficult to see how this gave them the proper time to check that those papers did reflect the facts in the case.

[63] The significance of the barristers 'selfish motives' is debated. It has been argued that it is not necessarily in counsel's interest to advise guilty pleas instead of trial. See P. Tague, 'Barristers' Selfish Incentives in Counselling Clients' [2008] Criminal Law Review 3.                    [64] McConville et al. (1994).

[65] Morison and Leith (1992) pp. 114–21.        [66] Rock (1993) p. 99.

[67] Rock's study contains a description of such a case (Rock (1993) pp. 95–123).

[68] Juries Act 174, s. 1.

[69] J. Baldwin and M. McConville, Jury Trials (1979a) Clarendon Press, Oxford, p. 1.

[70] Lord Devlin, Trial by Jury (1956) Stevens, London, p. 164.

The essence of the jury trial in England and Wales, is the idea that 12 people are drawn at random and, without training, asked to assess the factual circumstances that surround a particular case. Their verdict of 'not guilty' or 'guilty', given if necessary on a majority basis of ten to two, is their view of the facts.[71] The judge takes responsibility for the law, so that if the prosecution alleges a series of factual hypotheses which, in the view of the judge, are not sufficient to constitute legal proof of the crime concerned even if they are true, the judge will direct the jury to find the defendant not guilty.[72] Although the jury can usefully be compared with lay magistrates and tribunal wing people, in that they are all non-lawyers who, nevertheless, make legally binding decisions within 'the English legal system', jurors stand out as being unique even within this group. Jurors have no qualification in terms of knowledge or skill which distinguishes them from others within England and Wales. Moreover, they are not merely untrained: since they sit as jurors for only a short time, they do not even acquire that knowledge that comes with experience.[73]

Various merits have been ascribed to the institution. It has been said that it prevents the application of unpopular laws and that it allows truth to be established against a background of community values and sentiment.[74] At the same time, it has also been said that the idea of the jury, with its emphasis on the importance of the views of the untrained amateur, 'which affirms that all grades of capacity above drivelling idiocy are alike fitted for the exalted office of sifting truth from error, may excite the derision of future times'.[75] Juries have been accused of being too quick to acquit. It has also been said that their decisions are sometimes based on irrational as well as rational considerations. Sifting these various views requires a clear view of the purpose of the jury. One cannot simply inquire into what the jury does and then decide whether or not it is performing at a satisfactory level. One must first establish what role or roles the jury *should* have.

Bankowski has argued that the role of the jury runs counter to the normal consensual processes found in the criminal court and described above. The jury, on his argument, is not there to find the truth but, rather, is there to validate truth.[76] The jury can provide an alternative to the legal construction of truth which is based upon the doctrinal rules and the lawyerly culture which we have described elsewhere in this book. This

[71] Majority verdicts were first introduced by the Criminal Justice Act 1967. The provisions for majority verdicts are now found in s. 17 of the Juries Act 1974.

[72] Judge ordered and directed acquittals outnumber jury acquittals (see J. Baldwin, 'Understanding Judge Ordered and Directed Acquittals in the Crown Court' [1997] Criminal Law Review 536) and further marginalize the significance of jury trial.

[73] Jurors normally sit for a period of about two weeks (Royal Commission on Criminal Justice, *Report* (1993) Cm. 2263, HMSO, London, p. 136). During this time, they may hear several cases but their growth in experience cannot be compared with that of a lay magistrate or a wing person on a tribunal.

[74] Baldwin and McConville (1979a) p. 2; J. Gobert, *Justice, Democracy and the Jury* (1997) Dartmouth, Aldershot.

[75] J. Frank, *The Courts on Trial* (1949) Princeton University Press, Princeton, NJ, pp. 138–9.

[76] Z. Bankowski, 'The Jury and Reality' in M. Findlay and P. Duff (eds), *The Jury under Attack* (1988) Butterworths, London, pp. 18–21.

view supports the opinion that juries have a democratic role to play, but does so at the expense of ascribing to the jury any superior ability to assess the facts in the case. The jury is there to represent community values, even sometimes when they run counter to the dictates of the law. Juries are there to decide what behaviour is permissible, and when they find behaviour permissible, to find a defendant not guilty. On this view, for lawyers to say that a particular jury's decision was 'wrong' is to miss the point of the jury. It is precisely the fact that juries may make decisions which lawyers, using legal criteria, consider to be wrong which gives the jury its place in the legal system. Gobert describes the power to return perverse verdicts as evidence that the function of the jury is not mere fact-finding, but to assess whether the defendant is morally blameworthy and whether justice, according to community standards, would be done by convicting in accordance with the law.[77] The twin difficulties with this view are, first, that it ascribes to the jury an ability to represent a single community and, second, that it leaves at risk the person who stands outside the community. A randomly selected jury might find it difficult to represent any single community and might find this task even more problematic in the context of a pluralistic multicultural society. There might be some merit in an argument opposing community values to legalistic values but it is less obvious that there is merit in opposing the values of 12 individuals drawn together in a random manner to those which come from a community of lawyers used to thinking about the application of law. A jury which refuses to convict even though a person is legally guilty might seem defensible if it refuses on the basis of a community morality of fairness but less easy to defend is the jury who adjudges the defendant's actions guilty because they live outside the self-same community morality although they and other objective observers would say that they act within the law.

Assessing the functioning of the jury is made still more difficult by the operation of s. 8 of the Contempt of Court Act 1981. This makes it a criminal offence to attempt to inquire into how decisions in actual cases were made in the jury room. The secrecy of the jury room is maintained in all but the most extreme cases of irregularities.[78] For example, the Court of Appeal has refused to investigate allegations of racial bias amongst jurors that came to light only after the defendant was convicted.[79] The Auld Review recommended that s. 8 should be amended to allow for wider inquiries by the Court of Appeal into alleged jury impropriety.[80] However, Auld LJ was not convinced of the need for academic research on the English jury to be carried out.[81] For the purposes of the Review, he preferred to rely on existing jury research, much of

---

[77] Gobert (1997).        [78] *Young* [1995] 2 WLR 430.

[79] *R v Quereshi* [2002] 1 WLR 518. This decision has been criticized (see J. Spencer, 'Did the Jury Misbehave? Don't Ask, Because We Do Not Want to Know' (2002) Cambridge Law Journal 291). See also *R v Mirza* [2004] 1 AC 1118.

[80] Sir R. Auld, *A Review of the Criminal Courts of England and Wales: Report by the Right Honourable Lord Justice Auld* (2001) The Stationery Office, London, pp. 178–9.

[81] The Royal Commission on Criminal Justice recommended that the Contempt of Court Act 1981 be amended to allow further research into the jury, but the Auld Review recommends the prohibition on jury research be maintained (pp. 164–8).

which has been carried out in other jurisdictions. Darbyshire was commissioned to provide an overview of this research.[82] Due to the limitations of comparing different legal systems, considerable caution is required when drawing insights into how juries in England and Wales may operate.

## The composition of the jury

The first problem with the jury lies in the idea that it is a randomly selected group taken from society as a whole.

The basic qualifications to be a juror have already been noted. Even these basic qualifications discriminate on grounds of age, residence, and willingness or ability to register to vote. Home Office research shows that about 8 per cent of those eligible to vote are not on the electoral register, and particular groups such as ethnic minorities are more likely not to be registered.[83] This convinced the Auld Review that the juror pool should be widened by reference to other lists.[84] As yet, this has not been done, although recent research suggests that it is not necessary to supplement the juror source list to ensure that ethnic minorities are summoned in proportion to their representation in the juror catchment area.[85]

The composition of the jury is also affected by detailed rules that either exclude or make eligible for exemption whole sections of the population. Traditionally, a number of occupational groups are excluded from jury service, including judges, lawyers, and the police. This rule makes sense given that the jury is a lay institution. However, the Auld Review took the view that no one should be ineligible for jury service simply because of his or her occupation, including police prosecutors and judges.[86] Auld LJ dismissed objections that criminal justice professionals might unduly influence other jurors, be prejudiced, or use insider knowledge of the system to make educated guesses about matters not always disclosed to the jury, such as previous convictions.[87] It is questionable whether this complacency about the impartiality of 'insiders' is justified, however; appeals against convictions by juries containing criminal justice professionals on the grounds of juror bias, or appearance of bias, have tended to be unsuccessful.

---

[82] P. Darbyshire, A. Maughan, and A. Stewart, *What Can the English Legal System Learn from Jury Research Published Up to 2001?* (2001) summarized in P. Darbyshire, with research by A. Maughan and A. Stewart, 'What Can we Learn from Published Jury Research? Findings for the Criminal Courts Review' [2001] Criminal Law Review 970.

[83] J. Airs and A. Shaw, *Jury Excusal and Deferral* (1999) Research Findings No. 102, Home Office RDS, London.

[84] In other countries, the electoral register is supplemented by other lists, like telephone directories, because young, mobile, and ethnic minority populations are underrepresented on the electoral register (see Darbyshire et al. (2001) pp. 8–10).

[85] C. Thomas with N. Bulmer, *Diversity and Fairness in the Jury System* (Ministry of Justice Research Series 2/07 (2007) MOJ, London. This research is summarized in C. Thomas, 'Exposing the Myths of Jury Service' [2008] Criminal Law Review 415.

[86] The Royal Commission on Criminal Justice could not see a reason for automatic exclusion of ministers of religion.                    [87] See Auld Review (2001) pp. 146–59.

The House of Lords has stated that a reasonable person would not suspect that a police officer juror might be biased, unless the particular juror knows a police witness in the case or there is a direct conflict between the evidence of a police witness and the defendant on a significant matter.[88] In relation to prosecutors, there is greater doubt about their ability to appear unbiased, but this does not apply where the prosecution is brought by a non-CPS authority or potentially where the juror is a junior CPS employee. Prison officers are also allowed to serve because it is thought that the only ground for suspecting they might be biased is due to encountering the defendant on remand. If this has not occurred, then no suspicion arises, and even if it has, the court does not believe that knowledge of bad character thereby acquired necessarily prejudices the defendant.[89]

In the past, individuals have been able to avoid jury service because they are excused as of right or because they can show good reason.[90] Excusal of jurors can significantly affect the composition of the jury. Evidence considered by the Auld Review showed that 38 per cent of jurors called for service are able to avoid it. It is mainly professionals and self-employed people who apply to be excused on the basis that their businesses may suffer, or parents who apply on the basis that they are unable to make alternative childcare arrangements. Auld LJ recommended a reduction in those excused as of right, a clamp-down on discretionary excusal, greater use of deferral and the introduction of fines for those who fail to turn up for service.[91] The Criminal Justice Act 2003 eliminated excusal as of right (except for serving military personnel) and the categories of ineligibility.[92] Research shows that since these reforms, there has been a reduction in the percentage of excusals, and that, contrary to earlier views, it is those of low income and the unemployed who are least likely to serve, with professionals well represented on juries,[93] except perhaps where lengthy trials are concerned.[94]

The principle of random selection of jurors is eroded by the powers of both prosecuting and defending barristers to affect the composition of the jury. The defence have the right to exclude jury members for cause by showing that there is something about them that will affect their ability to perform the job of juror.[95] However, the defence can only question potential jurors if they know something about them which suggests that they might not be suitable to act as a juror.[96] Thus, this right is of very restricted value. By contrast, the prosecution can ask jurors to 'stand by for the Crown', without giving any reason. The effect of this is that a juror so challenged returns to the jury panel from whom the individual jury is selected. The reason for the rejection of the juror will only have to be examined if there are insufficient jurors on the panel who

[88] *Abdroikov* [2007] UKHL 37.      [89] Khan (2008) 2 Cr App R 13.
[90] Juries Act 1974, ss. 8, 9; *Practice Note (Jury Service: Excusal)* [1988] 3 All ER 177.
[91] Auld Review (2001) pp. 145–6 and 149–52.      [92] Criminal Justice Act, s. 321 and Sch. 33.
[93] Thomas with Bulmer (2007).
[94] Fraud trials present particular problems in this respect. See R. Julian, 'Judicial Perspectives on the Conduct of Serious Fraud Trials' [2007] Criminal Law Review 751.
[95] Criminal Justice Act 1988, s. 118 abolished the right to peremptory challenge.
[96] *R v Chandler (No. 2)* [1964] 1 All ER 761.

the Crown does not challenge to form a jury. The prosecution has the right to vet juries to see whether disqualified persons, and in limited circumstances people of extreme political views, are on the jury panel.[97] The results of such vetting can then guide the prosecution barristers' use of their power to ask jurors to stand by for the Crown.

The asymmetry of defence and prosecution powers to affect the composition of the jury has presented particular issues in relation to ethnic minority defendants. Some studies have suggested that people from ethnic minorities are likely to be underrepresented on juries. Although recent research suggests that ethnic minority representation is not a problem in most English Crown Courts, there are some courts which have significant pockets of ethnic minority communities in their juror catchment area but due to the overall ethnic composition of the area (comprising less than 10 per cent from ethnic minority groups), random selection from the electoral register will not normally produce ethnic minority representation on juries trying ethnic minority defendants.[98] An issue then arises about whether a right of peremptory challenge, previously enjoyed by the defence, should be resurrected to enable the defence to try to influence the racial composition of the jury. Zander and Henderson's survey showed in 83 per cent of all cases, defence barristers had no concerns about the composition of juries.[99] However, where there was any concern, the greatest concern related to the racial mix of juries. Of defence barristers expressing concern about jury composition, 23 per cent expressed concern about the racial mix of the jury and this concern was expressed six times more frequently if the defendant was black than if the defendant was white.[100] Traditionally, the courts have rejected the idea that judges should interfere with jury composition to secure racial balance.[101] The Royal Commission accepted that in exceptional cases a black defendant should have a right to have at least three black jurors.[102] This recommendation was not acted upon but the Auld Review also suggested that there should be provision for ethnic minority jurors in cases where race is likely to be a relevant issue in the trial.[103] The confidence of ethnic minority defendants is at stake here. Hood et al. found that, although perceptions of racial bias amongst ethnic minority defendants appear to be less widely held than in the past, a significant proportion of ethnic minority defendants and lawyers and court staff in the Crown Court perceive bias and believed that the legitimacy of the court would be strengthened if more people from ethnic minorities were sitting in judgment.[104]

---

[97]  *Attorney-General's Guidelines on Jury Checks* (1989) 88 Cr App R 124.

[98]  Thomas with Bulmer (2007) pp. 193–6.       [99]  Zander and Henderson (1993) p. 175.

[100]  Zander and Henderson (1993) p. 176.       [101]  *R v Ford* [1989] 3 All ER 445.

[102]  Royal Commission on Criminal Justice (1993) p. 133. The proposal related only to cases where there was a 'racial dimension'.

[103]  Auld Review (2001) pp. 156–9. The Government indicated that it did not favour this recommendation (Home Office, *Justice for All* (2002) Cm. 5563, The Stationery Office, London, para. 7.29).

[104]  R. Hood, S. Shute, and F. Seemungal, *Ethnic Minorities in the Criminal Courts: Perceptions of Fairness and Equality of Treatment* (2003) Research Series Report No. 2/03, Lord Chancellor's Department, London. The main perception was bias in sentencing and therefore more ethnic minority judges were favoured. A lower proportion of defendants (3.5 per cent) said more ethnic minority jurors would increase confidence than those who said more ethnic minority judges (15 per cent) would increase confidence.

Although Thomas' research shows that racial composition of mixed juries does not influence verdicts, it does affect some individual votes, with same-race leniency being a feature where race is not an explicit issue in the case. The significant limitation of this research is that it does not examine the decision-making of all white juries, and it may be in these cases that the problems of race are most pressing.[105] Contrary to the Runciman and Auld recommendations, the bias of all white juries may be of most concern where race is not an overt issue.[106] The confidence of defendants and public confidence in the fairness of jury trial warrants further consideration to be given to the question of ethnic representation on juries.[107]

## Trial

Atypical though it is, trial in the Crown Court does take place. Once trial begins, it is the defendant who is, literally, in the dock. Although legally the prosecution must make the case for guilt, presenting witnesses, and detailing the chain of arguments that leads to the allegedly inevitable conclusion of guilty, the defence is thereby put into the position of respondent. By making the case, the prosecution determines the issues which will be argued over. The defendant could in theory remain silent, but in Zander and Henderson's survey 74 per cent of prosecution barristers and 70 per cent of defence barristers said that the defendant did in fact give evidence.[108]

Where trial takes place, argument can either be about the *factual situation* (whether there was the actus reus) or the *state of mind of the accused* (whether there was the mens rea). In Zander and Henderson's survey, in 40 per cent of all cases, the defendant admitted the facts, arguing only over the question of mens rea.[109] Depending on the particular mens rea of the offence, the trial can become a contest over whom the jury believe about the subjective beliefs of the defendant at the time of the events in dispute. Notwithstanding the legal requirement for the prosecution to prove their case, in practice the onus of proof may become that of the defence.

The jury must assess the witnesses called by each side in the light both of the initial examination of the witness and the subsequent cross-examination. Before the jury come to make their decision, the judge will sum up the evidence for them. This summing up should be a neutral recapitulation of the important points in the trial.[110]

---

[105] Thomas (2008).

[106] S. Sommers and P. Ellsworth, 'How Much Do We Really Know about Race and Juries? A Review of the Social Science Theory and Research' (2003) 78 Chicago-Kent Law Review 997.

[107] J. Roberts and M. Hough, *Public Opinion and the Jury: An International Literature Review*, Ministry of Justice Research Series 1/09 (2009) Ministry of Justice, London.

[108] Zander and Henderson (1993) p. 114.

[109] Zander and Henderson (1993) p. 121. Those defendants who had previous convictions were slightly more likely to dispute the facts than those without.

[110] This is not to say that the judge should simply repeat what was said. The judge may legitimately call the jury's attention to possible discrepancies in the evidence that they will have to consider. For the obligations of judges when summing up, see *R v Bowerman* [2000] 2 Cr App R 189 and *Admado-Taylor* [2000] Criminal

However, in Zander and Henderson's survey, between 20 and 37 per cent of lawyers questioned thought that in a particular case, the judge's summing up had been against the weight of evidence presented.[111] In theory, this summing up should be the only means by which a judge commits their view of a case to the jury. However, in Zander and Henderson's survey, in 16 per cent of cases, prosecution barristers reported that a judge had indicated his or her view of a case by tone of voice or body language, while 35 per cent of defence barristers reported the same phenomenon. This non-verbal behaviour may be difficult for appellate courts to assess, although in really excessive cases of 'huffing and puffing' or hostile intervention, the Court of Appeal has overturned convictions due to the obvious bias of the judge.[112] Any judicial bias is typically for the prosecution. Both prosecution and defence barristers reported more instances of the judge indicating approval of the prosecution case than the defence case.[113] In recent years, the power of judges to intervene in cases, to control cross-examination, and to protect vulnerable and intimidated witnesses has increased.[114] As their control over the conduct of trial has increased, so it may be argued has their possible influence over the verdict. There is pressure for judges to be more interventionist in rape trials, where the conviction rate is very low.[115]

## Decision-making by the jury

Some of the most hostile attacks on juries have been made on their ability to understand evidence. It has been suggested that, particularly in the context of complex fraud cases, randomly selected jurors do not have the intellectual ability or educational background to understand the nature of the evidence put before them.[116] Jurors themselves seem to have a high opinion of their own abilities. In Zander and Henderson's survey, 50 per cent of jurors said that the evidence was not at all difficult to understand and 41 per cent said that it was not very difficult to understand. Even when they were asked about scientific evidence, 56 per cent said that it was not that difficult to understand and 34 per cent said that it was not very difficult to understand.[117] However, this finding has to be put in the context of the fact that only 27 per cent of jurors said that they had difficulty remembering evidence where a trial lasted for more than two weeks, despite the fact that 60 per cent of jurors did not take notes

---

Law Review 618. Some have questioned whether it is really necessary for judges to comment on evidence (see N. Madge, 'Summing Up – A Judge's Perspective' [2006] Criminal Law Review 817).

[111] Zander and Henderson (1993) p. 134.    [112] See, for example, *Perren* [2009] EWCA Crim 348.

[113] Zander and Henderson (1993) p. 137.

[114] L. Ellison, *The Adversarial Process and the Vulnerable Witness* (2001) Oxford University Press, Oxford; M. Burton, R. Evans, and A. Sanders, *Are Special Measures Working? Evidence from the Criminal Justice Agencies* (2006) Home Office Online Report 01/2006, Home Office, London.

[115] For an overview of the difficulties with rape prosecutions and trials, and critical analysis of solutions, see C. McGlynn and V. Munro (eds), *Rethinking Rape Law: International and Comparative Perspectives* (2010) Routledge-Cavendish, Abingdon.

[116] M. Levi, 'The Role of the Jury in Complex Cases' in M. Findlay and P. Duff (eds), *The Jury under Attack* (1998) Butterworths, London, p. 97.    [117] Zander and Henderson (1993) p. 206.

on the evidence in a case.[118] From this, one might infer the idea that jurors do not look for a very deep understanding or recall of evidence put to them. However, even if this is so, 94 per cent of prosecution barristers and 90 per cent of defence barristers thought that jurors had no trouble understanding the evidence put before them.[119] Even in cases of complex fraud, it appears that jurors are able to understand the evidence and work cooperatively, playing to their individual strengths, to ensure that this is the case.[120]

Darbyshire et al.'s review of jury research showed that generally jurors do approach their task with seriousness, but that they find it difficult to understand judicial instructions, particularly relating to the standard of proof.[121] When juries are told that the criminal standard of proof, beyond reasonable doubt, means that they must be 'sure' that the defendant is guilty, they may fix an unrealistically high standard of 100 per cent certainty.[122] This may perhaps explain why juries have been criticized as overly inclined to acquit defendants. Assessing such criticism is difficult. Comparing jury verdicts with the views of judges, police, prosecution barristers, or even defence barristers may be doing no more than comparing an outsider's views of guilt and innocence with those of insiders who have imbibed a culture of conviction.[123] In general, Zander and Henderson's survey showed that lawyers and police were surprised by the jury's decision in only a relatively small percentage of cases.[124] However, this overall result conceals the fact that professionals in the system were more frequently surprised by acquittals than by convictions.[125] This may reflect no more than the culture of conviction noted above and should be read in the context of the fact that the police, who had greatest difficulty with jury decisions, nevertheless found the decisions explicable in the light of the evidence in 91 per cent of all cases.[126] There has been a recent flurry of mock juror research examining the decision-making of juries in sexual assault cases.[127] Despite the methodological limitations of this type of research, which tends to use limited stimuli and dubious

---

[118] Zander and Henderson (1993) pp. 209–10.    [119] Zander and Henderson (1993) p. 177.

[120] Evidence of this comes from interviews with the discharged jurors in the ill-fated Jubilee line case; a fraud trial which collapsed after 21 months (see S. Lloyd-Bostock, 'The Jubilee Line Jurors: Does their Experience Strengthen the Argument for Judge-only Trial in Long and Complex Fraud Cases?' [2007] Criminal Law Review 255.    [121] Darbyshire et al. (2001) pp. 20–7.

[122] Darbyshire et al. (2001) pp. 2–29.

[123] For a survey of various attempts to assess jury performance, including comparisons with professional views of appropriate verdicts in individual cases, see Sanders and Young (2006) pp. 535–42.

[124] The Crown Prosecution Service were surprised by the verdict in 27 per cent of cases, judges and defence barristers were surprised in 14 per cent of cases (Zander and Henderson (1993) p. 163).

[125] The police were surprised by acquittals in 47 per cent of cases, but only 10 per cent of defence barristers were surprised (Zander and Henderson (1993) p. 164).    [126] Zander and Henderson (1993) p. 165.

[127] E. Finch and V. Munro, 'Breaking Boundaries? Sexual Consent in the Jury Room' (2006) Legal Studies 303; E. Finch and V. Munro, 'The Demon Drink and the Demonised Woman: Socio-sexual Stereotypes and Responsibility Attribution in Rape Trials Involving Intoxicants' (2007) Social and Legal Studies 591; L. Ellison and V. Munro, 'Reacting to Rape' (2009b) 49(2) British Journal of Criminology 202; L. Ellison and V. Munro, 'Of "Normal Sex" and "Real Rape": Exploring the Use of Socio-sexual Scripts in (Mock) Jury Deliberation' (2009a) 18(3) Social and Legal Studies 291.

samples of mock jurors,[128] the research is important in showing the impact of stereotypes on jury decision-making. The research shows, unsurprisingly, that jurors are unable to put their personal prejudices aside at the door of the deliberation room. In general, this may not be a bad thing and we would expect these prejudices to be counterbalanced, however, where there are persistent and widespread stereotypes about such matters as the level of blame to be attributed to intoxicated complainants and the credibility of complainants who are not seriously injured, delay reporting, or appear emotionally calm rather than distressed, then it is problematic. In such circumstances, there may be a case for educating jurors to counter inappropriate stereotyping.[129]

## The further demise of jury trial

In recent years, the jury system has come under attack, for example through LJ Auld's recommendations that complex and serious cases be diverted from jury trial and that defendants should have the right to apply for trial by judge alone in the Crown Court.[130] The recommendation for defendants to waive jury trial in favour of judge alone has not been enacted but the Criminal Justice Act 2003, made provision for trial without jury in complex and lengthy fraud cases, subject to further parliamentary action.[131] The rationale of these provisions has been challenged and there may yet be considerable resistance to bringing into force the provision for fraud cases. Trial by judge alone 'runs against the grain of tradition' in England and Wales, but in Northern Ireland, judge only, so-called 'Diplock courts', operated for several decades after being introduced in the 1970s due to fears of interference with juries in terrorist cases.[132] Research on these courts found that the nature of trial is significantly altered, it becomes far more pared down and less adversarial in the absence of the jury.[133] This research needs to be weighed in the balance with research on jury decision-making when making an assessment about the value of preserving jury trial. Whilst the system of jury trial is undoubtedly imperfect, we need to have greater confidence in the alternatives before abandoning or further eroding an important injection of lay values into our criminal justice system.

---

[128] E. Finch and V. Munro, 'Lifting the Veil: The Use of Focus Groups and Trial Simulations in Legal Research' (2008) 35 Journal of Law and Society 30. Finch and Munro and Ellison and Munro were able to address some of the methodological problems in their research.

[129] L. Ellison, 'The Use and Abuse of Psychiatric Evidence in Rape Trials' (2009) 13(1) International Journal of Evidence and Proof 28; L. Ellison and V. Munro, 'Turning Mirrors in Windows? Assessing the Impact of (Mock) Juror Education in Rape Trials' (2009c) 49(3) British Journal of Criminology 363.

[130] Auld Review (2001) pp. 177–81. For an analysis of these proposals, see J. Jackson, 'Modes of Trial: Shifting the Balance towards the Professional Judge' [2002] Criminal Law Review 249.

[131] Criminal Justice Act 2003, s. 44. The latest attempt to bring this into force was defeated by the House of Lords in March 2007.

[132] The Northern Ireland Securities Act 2007 contained provisions to return to trial by jury under the 'normalization' process.

[133] J. Jackson and S. Doran, Judge without Jury (1995) Clarendon Press, Oxford.

## CONCLUSION

The Crown Court is the most inward-looking and enclosed of all the institutions that we have described in this book. Defendants are more distant from its operations and perhaps more alienated than is the case in any other court. Although discussion of the court, and its rules, typically bespeak of the due process model of legal culture, the actual practice of the court is framed in terms of crime control. The processes of crime control are evident in the operation of plea bargaining in its various forms. Historically, there has been a reluctance to acknowledge plea bargaining and the courts have insisted that it be tightly regulated. However, in practice, plea bargaining is well established and successive attempts to regulate it have been unsuccessful. The culture of the lawyers is in many ways as resistant to change as that of the police officers discussed in previous chapters.

Whilst many people define the 'English legal system' by their perceptions of jury trial, it is, in fact, a rare feature of the system. Jury trial will become even rarer as more of its business gets shifted to the magistrates' court, or allocated to judge-only trial. Whether this is a matter of regret depends upon the perspective taken about the role and function of the jury. In so far as it represents the closest approximation to the democratic ideal of involving lay participants in legal decision-making, the residual role of the jury should perhaps be prized. Jurors do not make law but they can define the limits of its application by refusing to convict. An integrated theory of law enables us to take into account the crucial role that lay persons can play, even in the enclosed world of the Crown Court.

## FURTHER READING

ELLISON, L. and MUNRO, V., 'Reacting to Rape' (2009b) 49(2) British Journal of Criminology 202.

LLOYD-BOSTOCK, S., 'The Jubilee Line Jurors: Does their Experience Strengthen the Argument for Judge-only Trial in Long and Complex Fraud Cases?' (2007) Criminal Law Review 255.

THOMAS, C. with BULMER, N., Diversity and Fairness in the Jury System Ministry of Justice Research Series 2/07 (2007) MOJ, London.

# Bibliography

*A Time for Change: Report of the Committee on the Future of the Legal Profession* (the Marre Committee) (1988) General Council of the Bar and the Council of the Law Society, London

ABE, M., 'The Internal Control of a Bureaucratic Judiciary: The Case of Japan' (1995) 23 International Journal of the Sociology of Law 303

ABEL, R., 'The Comparative Study of Dispute Institutions in Society' (1973) 8 Law and Society Review 217

ABEL, R., 'Western Courts in Non-Western Settings' in S. Burman and B. Harrell-Bond, *The Imposition of Law* (1979) Academic Press, New York

ABEL, R., 'The Contradictions of Informal Justice' in R. Abel (ed.), *The Politics of Informal Justice*, Volume 1: *The American Experience* (1982) Academic Press, New York

ABEL, R., 'Introduction' in R. Abel (ed.), *The Politics of Informal Justice*, Volume 1: *The American Experience* (1982) Academic Press, New York

ABEL, R., *The Legal Profession in England and Wales* (1988a) Basil Blackwell, Oxford

ABEL, R., 'Lawyers in the Civil Law World' in R. Abel and P. Lewis (eds), *Lawyers in Society: Volume Two* (1988b) University of California Press, Berkeley, CA

ABEL, R., 'Evaluating Evaluations: How Should Law Schools Judge Teaching?' (1990) 40 Journal of Legal Education 407

ABEL-SMITH, B. and STEVENS, R., *Lawyers and the Courts* (1967) Heinemann, London

ABEL-SMITH, B. and STEVENS, R., *In Search of Justice* (1968) Allen Lane, London

ABEL-SMITH, B., ZANDER, M., and BROOKE, R., *Legal Problems and the Citizen* (1973) Heinemann, London

ABBOTT, A., *The System of Professionals* (1988) University of Chicago Press, Chicago

ADAMS, J., 'Choice of Forum in Patent Disputes' (1995) 10 European Intellectual Property Review 497

ADDISON, N., 'The Defeatist Talk of Frightened Men' (1995) 145 New Law Journal 860

ADLER, Z., 'Rape – The Intention of Parliament and the Practice of the Courts' (1982) 45 Modern Law Review 664

ADMINISTRATIVE JUSTICE AND TRIBUNALS COUNCIL, *AJTC Annual Report 2008/9* (2009) The Stationery Office, London

*AG Guidelines on the Acceptance of Pleas and the Prosecutor's Role in the Sentencing Exercise* (2005) Attorney General, London

AIRS, J. and SHAW, A., *Jury Excusal and Deferral* (1999) Research Findings No. 102, Home Office RDS, Home Office, London

ALDRIDGE, T., 'Special Educational Needs Tribunal' (1994) 138 Solicitors' Journal 870

ALDRIDGE, T., 'Training a New Tribunal' (1995) 2(2) Tribunals 4

ALDRIDGE, T., 'Special Educational Needs Tribunal Practice' (1996) 6 Practitioners' Child Law Bulletin 21

ALLEN, T., 'Children with Special Educational Needs in a Consumer Driven Educational System' in M. Allen (ed.), *The Web Journal of Current Legal Issues 1995 Yearbook* (1995) Blackstone Press, London

AMES, J., 'Council Endorses Anti-bias Policy' (1993) 90 Law Society Gazette, 13 October

ANDREWS, N., 'Reporting Case Law: Unreported Cases, the Definition of a Ratio and the Criteria for Reporting Decisions' (1985) 5 Legal Studies 205

ANDREWS, N., 'A New Civil Procedural Code for England: Party-control "Going, Going, Gone"' (2000) 19 Civil Justice Quarterly 19

*Annual Report of the Council on Tribunals for 1996/97* (1998) The Stationery Office, London

*Annual Report of the Special Educational Needs Tribunal 2004–5* (2006) Special Educational Needs and Disability Tribunal, London

*Annual Statistical Report 1993* (1993) The Law Society, London

*Annual Statistical Report 2001* (2002) The Law Society, London

*Annual Statistical Report 2005* (2006) The Law Society, London

ARISTOTLE, *Politics* (rev. edn, 1981) Penguin Books, Harmondsworth

ARNULL, A. *The European Union and its Court of Justice* (2nd edn, 2006) Oxford University Press, Oxford

ASHWORTH, A., *The Criminal Process: An Evaluative Study* (2nd edn, 1998) Oxford University Press, Oxford

ASHWORTH, A., 'Article 6 and the Fairness of Trials' [1999] Criminal Law Review 261

ASHWORTH, A. and FIONDA, F., 'The New Code for Crown Prosecutors: Prosecution, Accountability and the Public Interest' [1994] Criminal Law Review 894

ASHWORTH, A. and REDMAYNE, M., *The Criminal Process* (3rd edn, 2005) Oxford University Press, Oxford

ASHWORTH, A., GENDERS, E., MANSFIELD, G., PEAY, J., and PLAYER, E., *Sentencing in the Crown Court* (1984) Centre for Criminological Research, Oxford

ASTOR, H., 'The Unrepresented Defendant Revisited: A Consideration of the Role of the Clerk in Magistrates' Courts' (1986) 13 Journal of Law and Society 225

ATIYAH, P., *Accidents, Compensation and the Law* (1970) Weidenfeld & Nicolson, London

ATIYAH, P., *Pragmatism and Theory in English Law* (1987) Stevens, London

AUCHMUTY, R., 'Agenda for a Feminist Legal Curriculum' (2003) 23 Legal Studies 377

AULD, SIR R., *A Review of the Criminal Courts of England and Wales: Report by the Right Honourable Lord Justice Auld* (2001) The Stationery Office, London

AUSTIN, J., *The Province of Jurisprudence Determined* (2nd edn, 1861) Burt Franklin, New York

AUSTIN, J., *Lectures on Jurisprudence* (1885) John Murray, London

AUSTIN, J., *The Province of Jurisprudence Determined* (1970) Lenox Hill Publications, New York

AYRES, A. and MURRAY, L., *Arrests for Recorded Crime (Notifiable Offences) and the Operation of Certain Police Powers under PACE: England and Wales, 2004/5* (2005) Home Office Statistical Bulletin, Home Office, London

BADAWI, Z., 'Muslim Justice in a Secular State' in M. King (ed.), *God's Law versus State Law* (1995) Grey Seal, London

BAILEY, S. and BIRCH, D., 'Recent Developments in the Law of Police Powers' [1982] Criminal Law Review 475

BAILEY, S. and GUNN, M., *Smith and Bailey on the Modern English Legal System* (2nd edn, 1991) Sweet & Maxwell, London

BAILEY, S. H., CHING, J. P. L., and TAYLOR, N. W., *Smith, Bailey and Gunn on the Modern English Legal System* (5th edn, 2007) Sweet & Maxwell, London

BALDWIN, J., 'The Social Composition of Magistrates' (1976) 16 British Journal of Criminology 171

BALDWIN, J., *Preparing the Record of Taped Interview* (1992a) Royal Commission on Criminal Justice Research Study No. 2, HMSO, London

BALDWIN, J., *The Conduct of Police Investigation* (1992b) HMSO, London

BALDWIN, J., *Video Taping Interviews with Police Suspects: A National Evaluation* (1992c) Home Office, London

BALDWIN, J., 'Police Interview Techniques: Establishing Truth or Proof?' (1993) 33 British Journal of Criminology 325

BALDWIN, J., *The Small Claims Procedure and the Consumer* (1995) Office of Fair Trading, London

BALDWIN, J., 'Understanding Judge Ordered and Directed Acquittals in the Crown Court' [1997] Criminal Law Review 586

BALDWIN, J., 'Small Claims Hearings: The "Interventionist" Role Played by District Judges' (1998) 17 Civil Justice Quarterly 20

BALDWIN, J., *Lay and Judicial Perspectives on the Expansion of the Small Claims Regime* (2002) Lord Chancellor's Department, London

BALDWIN, J. and BEDWARD, J., 'Summarising Tape Recordings of Police Interviews' [1991] Criminal Law Review 671

BALDWIN, J. and HUNT, A., 'Prosecutors Advising in Police Stations' [1998] Criminal Law Review 521

BALDWIN, J. and McCONVILLE, M., *Negotiated Justice* (1977) Martin Robertson, Oxford

BALDWIN, J. and McCONVILLE, M. *Jury Trials* (1979a) Clarendon Press, Oxford

BALDWIN, J. and McCONVILLE, M., 'Police Interrogation and the Right to See a Solicitor' [1979b] Criminal Law Review 145

BALDWIN, J. and McCONVILLE, M., *Confessions in Crown Court Trials* (1980) Royal Commission on Criminal Procedure Research Study No. 5, HMSO, London

BALDWIN, J., WIKELEY, N., and YOUNG, R., *Judging Social Security* (1992) Clarendon Press, Oxford

BANKOWSKI, Z., 'The Jury and Reality' in M. Findlay and P. Duff (eds), *The Jury under Attack* (1988) Butterworths, London

BANKOWSKI, Z. and MUNGHAM, G., *Images of Law* (1976) Routledge & Kegan Paul, London

BANKOWSKI, Z., HUTTON, N. R., and McMANUS, J. J., *Lay Justice?* (1987) T. & T. Clark, Edinburgh

BANO, S., 'In Pursuit of Religious and Legal Diversity: A Response to the Archbishop of Canterbury and the "Sharia Debate" in Britain' (2008) 10 Ecclesiastical Law Journal 282

BARNARD, D., *The Family Court in Action* (1983) Butterworths, London

BARNARD, D. and HOUGHTON, M., *The New Civil Court in Action* (1993), Butterworths, London

BARNES, B., *TS Kuhn and Social Science* (1982) Macmillan, London

BARRETT, B., 'A Plea for Conservation' (1981) 15 The Law Teacher 146

BARRINGTON BAKER, W., EEKELAAR, J., GIBSON, C., and RAIKES, S., *The Matrimonial Jurisdiction of Registrars* (1977) Centre for Socio-Legal Studies, Oxford

BAYLEY, D. H. and SHEARING, C. D., 'The Future of Policing' (1996) 30 Law and Society Review 585

BEALE, H. and DUGDALE, T., 'Contracts between Businessmen: Planning and the Use of Contractual Remedies' (1975) 2 British Journal of Law and Society 45

BECHER, T. and TROWLER, P., *Academic Tribes and Territories* (2nd edn, 2001) SRHE and the Open University Press, Buckingham

BELL, J., 'The Acceptability of Legal Arguments' in N. MacCormick and P. Birks (eds), *The Legal Mind* (1986) Clarendon Press, Oxford

BELL, J. and ENGLE, SIR G., *Cross: Statutory Interpretation* (2nd edn, 1987) Oxford University Press, Oxford

BELL, J. and ENGLE, SIR G., *Cross: Statutory Interpretation* (3rd edn, 1995) Butterworths, London

BELSEY, C., 'Re-reading the Great Tradition' in P. Widdowson (ed.), *Re-Reading English* (1982) Methuen, London

BENNION, F., *Bennion on Statute Law* (3rd edn, 1990) Longman, London

BENNION, F., *Statutory Interpretation* (2nd edn, 1992) Butterworths, London

BENNION, F., 'What Interpretation is "Possible" under Section 3(1) of the Human Rights Act 1998?' [2000] Public Law 77

BENOETVEA, J., *The Legal Reasoning of the European Court of Justice: Towards a European Jurisprudence* (1993) Clarendon Press, Oxford

BENTHAM, J., 'Truth *versus* Ashhurst' in *The Works of Jeremy Bentham* (1962) Russell and Russell, New York

BINGHAM, T., *The Rule of Law* (2010) Allen Lane, London

BIRCH, D., 'The Pace Hots Up: Confessions and Confusions under the 1984 Act' [1989] Criminal Law Review 95

BLAND, N., MILLER, J., and QUINTON, P., *Upping the PACE? An Evaluation of the Recommendations of the Stephen Lawrence Inquiry on Stops and Searches* (2000) Police Research Series Paper No. 128, Home Office, London

BLANKENBERG, E. and ROGOWSKI, R., 'German Labour Courts and the British Industrial System' (1986) 13 Journal of Law and Society 67

BLOCK, B., 'Bail Conditions: Neither Logical Nor Lawful' (1990) 154 Justice of the Peace 83

BLOM-COOPER, L. and DREWERY, G., *Final Appeal* (1972) Clarendon Press, Oxford

BOHANNAN, P., *Justice and Judgement among the Tiv* (1967) Oxford University Press for International African Institute, Oxford

BOON, A., 'From Public Service to Service Industry: The Impact of Socialization and Work on the Motivation and Values of Lawyers' (2005) 12 International Journal of the Legal Profession 229

BOON, A., DUFF, L., and SHINER, M., 'Career Paths and Choices in a Highly Differentiated Profession: The Position of Newly Qualified Solicitors' (2001) 64 Modern Law Review 563

BORGSMIDT, K., 'The Advocate General at the European Court of Justice: A Comparative Study' (1988) 13 European Law Review 106

BOTTOMLEY, A. and COLEMAN, C., *Understanding Crime Rates* (1981) Saxon House, Farnborough

BOTTOMLEY, A. K. and PEASE, K., *Crime and Punishment: Interpreting the Data* (1986) Open University Press, Milton Keynes

BOTTOMS, A. E. and McCLEAN, J. D., *Defendants in the Criminal Process* (1976) Routledge & Kegan Paul, London

BOULTON, C. (ed.), *Erskine May's Treatise on the Law, Privileges, Proceedings and Usage of Parliament* (21st edn, 1989) Butterworths, London

BOWLES, R., *Law and the Economy* (1982) Martin Robertson, Oxford

BOWLING, B. and PHILLIPS, C., *Racism, Crime and Justice* (2002) Longman, London

BOWLING, B. and PHILLIPS, C., 'Disproportionate and Discriminatory: Reviewing the Evidence on Police Stop and Search' (2007) 70(6) Modern Law Review 936

BRADGATE, R., *Commercial Law* (3rd edn, 2000) Butterworths, London

BRADLEY, A., 'Judges and the Media – The Kilmuir Rules' [1983] Public Law 383

BRADLEY, A. W. and EWING, K. D., *Constitutional and Administrative Law* (12th edn, 1997) Longman, London

BRADLEY, A. W. and EWING, K. D. *Constitutional and Administrative Law* (14th edn, 2007) Longman, London

BRADNEY, A., 'Facade: The Poplar Case' (1983) 34 Northern Ireland Legal Quarterly 1

BRADNEY, A., 'Parliamentary Sovereignty – A Question of Status' (1985a) 36 Northern Ireland Legal Quarterly 2

BRADNEY, A., 'The Changing Face of the House of Lords' [1985b] Juridical Review 178

BRADNEY, A., 'The Judicial Role of the Lord Chancellor 1946–1987: A Pellet' (1989) 16 Journal of Law and Society 360

BRADNEY, A., 'Making Cowards' [1990] Juridical Review 129

BRADNEY, A., 'Ivory Towers or Satanic Mills: Choices for University Law Schools' (1992) 17 Studies in Higher Education 5

BRADNEY, A., 'Law as a Parasitic Discipline' (1998) 25 Journal of Law and Society 71

BRADNEY, A., 'The Judicial Role of the Lord Chancellor' in P. Carmichael and B. Dickson (eds), *The House of Lords* (1999) Hart Publishing, Oxford

BRADNEY, A., 'English University Legal Education: Elite Education or Mass Education? Some Preliminary Thoughts' in P. Torremans (ed.), *Legal Convergence in the Europe of the New Millennium* (2000) Kluwers, The Hague

BRADNEY, A., *Conversations, Choices and Chances: The Liberal Law School in the Twenty-first Century* (2003a) Hart Publishing, Oxford

BRADNEY, A., 'Developing Human Rights? The Lords and Transsexual Marriages' (2003b) 33 Family Law 583

BRADNEY, A. and COWNIE, F., *Living without Law* (2000a) Ashgate, Aldershot

BRADNEY, A. and COWNIE, F., 'British University Law Schools in the Twenty-first Century' in D. Hayton (ed.), *Law's Future(s)* (2000b) Hart Publishing, Oxford

BRADNEY, A. et al., *How to Study Law* (5th edn, 2005) Sweet & Maxwell, London

BRAYNE, H., 'A Case for Getting Law Students Engaged in the Real Thing – The Challenge of the Sabre-tooth Curriculum' (2000) 34 The Law Teacher 17

BRIDGES, L., 'The Lawrence Inquiry – Incompetence, Corruption, and Institutional Racism' (1999) 26 Journal of Law and Society 298

BRIDGES, L. and CHOONGH, S., *Improving Police Station Legal Advice* (1998) Law Society, London

BRIDGES, L., CAPE, E., FENN, P., MITCHELL, A., MOORHEAD, R., and SHERR, A., *Evaluation of the Public Defender Service in England and Wales* (2007) Legal Services Commission, London

BRITISH RETAIL CONSORTIUM, *10th Annual Retail Crime Survey* (2002) BRC, London

BROMLEY, P. and LOWE, N., *Bromley's Family Law* (8th edn, 1992), Butterworths, London

BROOKE LJ (ed.), *Civil Proceedings: Volume 1* (2006) Sweet & Maxwell, London

BROWN, D., *Investigating Burglary: The Effects of PACE* (1991) Home Office Research Study No. 123, HMSO, London

BROWN, D., *PACE Ten Years On: A Review of the Research* (1997) Home Office Research Study No. 155, HMSO, London

BROWN, D., ELLIS, T., and LARCOMBE, K., *Changing the Code: Police Detention under the Revised PACE Codes of Practice* (1993) Home Office Research Study No. 129, HMSO, London

BROWNE-WILKINSON, SIR N., 'The Independence of the Judiciary in the 1980s' [1988] Public Law 4

BROWNLEE, I., 'The Statutory Charging Scheme in England and Wales: Towards a Unified Prosecution System' [2004] Criminal Law Review 896

BROWNLEE, I., 'Conditional Cautions and Fair Trial Rights in England and Wales: Form versus Substance in the Diversionary Agenda?' [2007] Criminal Law Review 129

BROWNSWORD, R., 'Teaching Contract: A Liberal Agenda' in P. Birks (ed.), *Examining the Law Syllabus: The Core* (1992) Oxford University Press, Oxford

BUCKE, T., STREET, R., and BROWN, D., *The Right of Silence: The Impact of the Criminal Justice and Public Order Act 1994* (2000) Home Office Research Study No. 199, HMSO, London

BURTON, M., 'Reviewing Crown Prosecution Service Decisions Not to Prosecute' [2001] Criminal Law Review 374

BURTON, M., 'Judicial Monitoring of Compliance: Introducing "Problem Solving" Approaches to Domestic Violence Courts in England and Wales' (2006) 20(3) International Journal of Law, Policy and the Family 366

BURTON, M., *Legal Responses to Domestic Violence* (2008) Routledge-Cavendish, Abingdon

BURTON, M., 'The Human Rights of Victims of Domestic Violence: Opuz v Turkey' (2010) 22(1) Child and Family Law Quarterly 131

BURTON, M., EVANS, R., and SANDERS, A., *Are Special Measures Working? Evidence from the Criminal Justice Agencies* (2006) Home Office Online Report 01/2006, Home Office, London

BUTLER, A., 'Declaration of Incompatibility or Interpretation Consistent with Human Rights in New Zealand' [2001] Public Law 28

BUTTON, M., *Private Policing* (2002) Willan Publishing, Cullompton

BUTTON, M. *Security Officers and Policing: Powers, Culture and Control in the Governance of Private Space* (2007) Ashgate, Aldershot

BUXTON, R., 'The Human Rights Act and Private Law' (2000) 116 Law Quarterly Review 48

BUXTON, R., 'How the Common Law Gets Made: *Hedley Byrne* and other Cautionary Tales' (2009) 125 Law Quarterly Review 60

CAIN, M., *Society and the Policeman's Role* (1973) Routledge & Kegan Paul, London

CAIN, M., 'Trends in the Sociology of Police Work' (1979) 7 International Journal of the Sociology of Law 143

CAIN, M., 'Where are the Disputes? A Study of a First Instance Civil Court in the UK' in M. Cain and K. Kulscar (eds), *Disputes and the Law* (1983) Akademia Kiado, Budapest

CAMMISS, S., '"I Will in a Moment Give You the Full History": Mode of Trial, Prosecutorial Control and Partial Accounts' [2006a] Criminal Law Review 38

CAMMISS, S., 'The Management of Domestic Violence Cases in the Mode of Trial Hearing: Prosecutorial Control and Marginalizing Victims' (2006b) 46 British Journal of Criminology, 704

CAMMISS, S. and Stride, C., 'Modelling Mode of Trial' (2008) 48 British Journal of Criminology 482

CAMPBELL, C., 'Lawyers and their Public' in D. N. MacCormick (ed.), *Lawyers in their Social Setting* (1976) W. Green, Edinburgh

CAMPBELL, C. and WILES, P., 'The Study of Law and Society in Britain' (1975–76) 10 Law and Society Review 547

CANE, P. (ed.), *Atiyah's Accidents, Compensation and the Law* (5th edn, 1993) Butterworths, London

CANE, P., *Administrative Tribunals and Adjudication* (2009) Hart Publishing, Oxford

CANTERBURY, ARCHBISHOP OF, *Civil and Religious Law in England: A Religious Perspective* (2008) <http://www.archbishopofcanterbury.org/1575>

CAPE, E., 'Incompetent Police Station Advice and the Exclusion of Evidence' [2002] Criminal Law Review 471

CAPE, E., 'The Revised PACE Codes of Practice: A Further Step Towards Inquisitorialism' [2003] Criminal Law Review 355

CARLEN, P., *Magistrates' Justice* (1976) Martin Robertson, Oxford

CARNWATH LJ, *Senior President of Tribunals First Implementation Review* (2008) available at: <http://www.tribunals.gov.uk/Tribunals/Documents/News/%5B30june%5DSPImpl ementationClean7b.pdf>

CARNWATH LJ, *Senior President of Tribunals' Annual Report: Tribunals Transformed* (2010) London, Ministry of Justice

CARRINGTON, P., 'Of Law and the River' (1984) 34 Journal of Legal Education 222

CARROLL, M., MARCHINGTON, M., EARNSHAW, J., and TAYLOR, S., 'Recruitment in Small Firms' (1999) 21 Employee Relations 230

CARSON, W., 'White-collar Crime and the Enforcement of Factory Legislation' (1970) 10 British Journal of Criminology 383

CARTER OF COLES, LORD, *Legal Aid: A Market-based Approach to Reform* (2006) Department for Constitutional Affairs, London

CASSON, D. and SCOTT, I., 'Great Britain' in S. Shetreet and J. Deschenes (eds), *Judicial Independence: The Contemporary Debate* (1985) Martinus Nijhoff, Dordrecht

CHADWICK, J., 'A Testator's Bounty to his Slayer' (1914) 30 Law Quarterly Review 211

CHAKRABORTI, N., 'Policing Muslim Communities' in Rowe, M., (ed.) *Policing beyond Macpherson* (2007) Willan, Cullompton

CHAMBERS, G. and HARWOOD, S., *Solicitors in England and Wales: Practice, Organisation and Perceptions* (1990) The Law Society, London

CHAMBERS, G. and HARWOOD-RICHARDSON, S., *Solicitors in England and Wales: Practice, Organisation and Perceptions – Second Report: The Private Practice Firm* (1991) The Law Society, London

CHAN, J., *Changing Police Culture* (1997) Cambridge University Press, Cambridge

CHEFFINS, B., 'Using Theory to Study Law: A Company Law Perspective' (1999) 58 Cambridge Law Journal 19

CHLOROS, A., 'Common Law, Civil Law and Socialist Law: Three Leading Systems of the World, Three Kinds of Legal Reasoning' in C. Varga (ed.), *Comparative Legal Cultures* (1992) Dartmouth, Aldershot

CHOO, A. and NASH, S., 'What's the Matter with Section 78?' [1999] Criminal Law Review 929

CHOONGH, S., 'Impact and Implications of the New Bill' (1996) Legal Action, 6 January

CHOONGH, S., 'Policing the Dross: A Social Disciplinary Model of Policing' (1998) 38(4) British Journal of Criminology 623

*Civil Justice Review: Personal Injuries Litigation* (1986) Lord Chancellor's Department, London

Civil Justice Review, *Report of the Review Body on Civil Justice* (1988) Cm. 394, HMSO, London

CLARK, D., *Bevan and Lidstone's The Investigation of Crime* (3rd edn, 2004) Butterworths, London

CLARK, J., 'Adversarial and Investigative Approaches to the Arbitral Resolution of Dismissal Disputes: A Comparison of South Africa and the U.K.' (1999) 28(4) Industrial Law Journal 319

CLARKE, A. et al., 'Solicitors in the Judiciary' (1999) Law Society Gazette, 13 October

CLOUTIER, A., 'The Conciliatory Function of the Superior Court' (1985) 4 Civil Justice Quarterly 342

COCKS, R., *Foundations of the Modern Bar* (1983) Sweet & Maxwell, London

COHEN LJ, 'Jurisdiction, Practice and Procedure of the Court of Appeal' (1951) 11 Cambridge Law Journal 3

COLLIER, R., 'Masculism, Law and Law Teaching' (1991) 19 International Journal of the Sociology of Law 427

COLLIER, R., '"Be Smart, Be Successful, Be Yourself…"? Representations of the Training Contract and Trainee Solicitor in Advertising by Large Law Firms' (2005) 12 International Journal of the Legal Profession 51

COLLIER, R., *Men, Law and Gender: Essays on the 'Man' in Law* (2010a) Routledge, London

COLLIER, R., 'The Restructured University: Rethinking the Gendered Law School' in R. Collier, *Men, Law and Gender: Essays on the 'Man' in Law* (2010b) Routledge, London

COMAROFF, J. and ROBERTS, S., *Rules and Processes* (1981) University of Chicago Press, Chicago

COMBAR (COMMERCIAL BAR ASSOCIATION), *Pupillage, Maternity Leave and Pro Bono Work* (2005) available at: <http://www.combar.com/index.php>

CONNOLLY, C., 'Shades of Discrimination: University Entry Data 1990–92' in S. Haselgrove (ed.), *The Student Experience* (1994) Open University Press, Milton Keynes

COOK, D., *Rich Law Poor Law* (1989) Open University Press, Milton Keynes

COOKE, LORD, 'The British Enactment of Human Rights' (1998) 3 European Human Rights Law Review 243

COOPER, C., ANSCOMBE, J., AVENELL, J., MCLEAN, F., and MORRIS, J., *A National Evaluation of Community Support Officers* (2006) Home Office Research Study No. 297, Home Office, London

COOPER, J., *Public Legal Services* (1983) Sweet & Maxwell, London

COOTE, A. and CAMPBELL, B., *Sweet Freedom* (1987) Basil Blackwell, Oxford

COOTER, R. and ULEN, T., *Law and Economics* (1988) Harper Collins, New York

COPPEN, J. 'PACE: A View from the Custody Suite', in E. Cape and R. Young (eds), *Regulating Policing* (2008) Hart, Oxford

COUSINS, M., 'Civil Legal Aid in France, Ireland, the Netherlands and the United Kingdom – A Comprehensive Survey' (1993) 12 Civil Justice Quarterly 154

COWNIE, F., 'The Reform of the Legal Profession or the End of Civilization as we Know it' in F. Patfield and R. White (eds), *The Changing Law* (1990) Leicester University Press, Leicester

COWNIE, F., 'Women in the Law School: Shoals of Fish, Starfish or Fish out of Water?' in P. Thomas (ed.), *Discriminating Lawyers* (2000) Cavendish, London

COWNIE, F., *Legal Academics: Culture and Identities* (2003) Hart Publishing, Oxford

COWNIE, F. and BRADNEY, A., 'Divided Justice, Different Voices: Inheritance and Family Provision' (2003) 23 Legal Studies 56

COWNIE, F. and COCKS, R. *'A Great and Noble Occupation': The History of the Society of Legal Scholars* (2009) Hart Publishing, Oxford

CPS INSPECTORATE, *Thematic Review of the Disclosure of Unused Material* (2000) Thematic Report 2/2000, HMCPSI, London

CRAIG, P., *Administrative Law* (3rd edn, 1994) Sweet & Maxwell, London

CRANSTON, R., 'What do Courts do? (1986) 5 Civil Justice Quarterly 123

CRANSTON, R., *How Law Works: The Machinery and Impact of Civil Justice* (2006) Oxford University Press, Oxford

CRAWFORD, L., 'Race Awareness Training and the Judges' (January/February 1994) Counsel 11

CRETNEY, A. and DAVIS, G., *Punishing Violence* (1995) Routledge, London

CRETNEY, S., MASSON, J., and BAILEY-HARRIS, R., *Principles of Family Law* (7th edn, 2002) Sweet & Maxwell, London

*Criminal Law Revision Committee: 11th Report* (1972) Cmnd 4991, HMSO, London

CROMPTON, R. and SANDERSON, K., 'Professional Women's Careers' in S. McRae, *Keeping Women In* (1990) Policy Studies Institute, London

CROSS, R., *Precedent in English Law* (3rd edn, 1977) Clarendon Press, Oxford

CROSS, R. and HARRIS, J., *Precedent in English Law* (1991) Clarendon Press, Oxford

CUNNINGHAM, J. V., *The Poems of J.V. Cunningham*, edited and with an introduction by Timothy Steele (1997) Swallow Press Ohio University Press (Athens)

DANZIG, R., 'Towards the Creation of a Complementary, Decentralised System of Criminal Justice' (1973) 26 Stanford Law Review 1

DARBYSHIRE, P., *Magistrates' Clerks* (1984) Barry Rose, Chichester

DARBYSHIRE, P., *Eddey on the English Legal System* (5th edn, 1992) Sweet & Maxwell, London

DARBYSHIRE, P., 'An Essay on the Importance and Neglect of the Magistracy' [1997a] Criminal Law Review 627

DARBYSHIRE, P., 'For the New Lord Chancellor – Some Causes for Concern about Magistrates' [1997b] Criminal Law Review 861

DARBYSHIRE, P., 'A Comment on the Powers of Magistrates' Clerks' [1999] Criminal Law Review 377

DARBYSHIRE, P., 'The Mischief of Plea Bargaining and Sentence Rewards' [2000] Criminal Law Review 895

DARBYSHIRE, P., 'Cameos from the World of District Judges' (2006) 50 Journal of Criminal Law 443

DARBYSHIRE, P., 'Where do English and Welsh Judges Come from?' (2007) 66 Cambridge Law Journal 365

DARBYSHIRE, P., MAUGHAN, A., and STEWART, A., 'What Can the English Legal System Learn from Jury Research Published Up to 2001?' (2001) at: <http:www.criminal-courts-review.org.uk>; also summarized in Darbyshire, P. with research by Maughan, A. and Stewart, A., 'What Can we Learn from Published Jury Research? Findings for the Criminal Courts Review' [2001] Criminal Law Review 970

DASHWOOD, A., 'The Advocate General in the Court of Justice of the European Communities' (1983) 2 Legal Studies 202

DAVID, R. and BRIERLEY, J., *Major Legal Systems in the World Today* (3rd edn, 1985) Stevens, London

DAVIES, M. 'Reading Cases' (1987) 50 Modern Law Review 409

DAVIES, M., 'The Ethos of Pluralism' (2005) 27 Sydney Law Review 87

DAVIS, G., *Partisans and Mediators* (1988a) Clarendon Press, Oxford

DAVIS, G., 'The Halls of Justice and Justice in Halls' in R. Dingwall and J. Eekelaar (eds), *Divorce Mediation and the Legal Process* (1988b) Clarendon Press, Oxford

DAVIS, G. and MURCH, M., *Grounds for Divorce* (1988) Clarendon Press, Oxford

DEAKIN, S. and MORRIS, G., *Labour Law* (3rd edn, 2001) Butterworths, London

DE SOUSA SANTOS, B., 'The Law of the Oppressed: The Construction and Reproduction of Legality in Pasargda' (1977) 12 Law and Society Review 5

DE SOUSA SANTOS, B., 'Law and Community: The Changing Nature of State Power in Late Capitalism' (1980) 8 International Journal of the Sociology of Law 379

DE SOUSA SANTOS, B., *Towards a New Common Sense: Law, Science and Politics in the Paradigmatic Transition* (1995) Routledge, London

DE VOIL, P., *Tax Appeals* (1969) Butterworths, London

'Define and Empower: Women Students Consider Feminist Learning' (1990) 1 Law and Critique 47

DEMPSEY, M. M., *Prosecuting Domestic Violence* (2009) Oxford University Press, Oxford

DENNING, LORD, *Misuse of Power* (1980) BBC, London

DENNIS, I., 'Silence in the Police Station: The Marginalisation of Section 34' [2002] Criminal Law Review 2

DEPARTMENT FOR CONSTITUTIONAL AFFAIRS, *Increasing Diversity in the Judiciary: Consultation Paper: CP25/04* (2004a) DCA, London

DEPARTMENT FOR CONSTITUTIONAL AFFAIRS, *Transforming Public Services: Complaints, Redress and Tribunals* (2004b) Cm. 6243, HMSO, London

DEPARTMENT FOR CONSTITUTIONAL AFFAIRS, *A Fairer Deal for Legal Aid* (2005) Cm. 6591, HMSO, London

DEPARTMENT FOR CONSTITUTIONAL AFFAIRS, *Legal Aid Reform: The Way Ahead* (2006) Cm. 6993, HMSO, London

DEPARTMENT FOR EDUCATION, *Special Educational Needs Tribunal: How to Appeal* (1994) DFE Publication Centre, London

DEPARTMENT FOR TRADE AND INDUSTRY, *Report of the Department of Trade and Industry Departmental Advisory Committee on International Commercial Arbitration* (the Mustill Report) (1985) HMSO, London

DEVLIN, Lord, *Trial by Jury* (1956) Stevens, London

DEWAR, J. with PARKER, S., *Law and the Family* (2nd edn, 1992) Butterworths, London

DHAMI, K., 'Do Bail Information Schemes Really Affect Bail Decisions' (2002) 41 Howard Journal 245

DIAMOND, A., 'The Queen's Bench Master' (1960) 76 Law Quarterly Review 504

DIAMOND, A., 'Codification of the Law of Contract' (1968) 31 Modern Law Review 361

DICEY, A. V., *Can English Law Be Taught at the Universities?* (1883) Macmillan, London

DICEY, A. V., *Introduction to the Law of the Constitution* (5th edn, 1897) Macmillan, London

DICKENS, L., JONES, M., WEEKES, B., and HART, M., *Dismissed* (1985) Basil Blackwell, Oxford

DICKSON, B., 'The Contribution of Lord Diplock to the General Law of Contract' (1989) 9 Oxford Journal of Legal Studies 441

DICKSON, B., *Introduction to French Law* (1994) Pitman Publishing, London

DICKSON, B., 'Britain's Law Lords and Human Rights' (2006) 26 Legal Studies 329

DINGWALL, R., DURKIN, T., PLEASANCE, P., FELSTINER, W., and BOWLES, R., 'Firm Handling: The Litigation Strategies of Defence Lawyers in Personal Injury Cases' (2000) 20 Legal Studies 1

DIXON, D., COLEMAN, C., and BOTTOMLEY, K., 'Consent and the Legal Regulation of Policing' (1990) 17 Journal of Law and Society 345

DIXON, D., BOTTOMLEY, A. K., COLEMAN, C., GILL, M., and WALL, D., 'Reality and Rules in the Construction and Regulation of Police Suspicion' (1989) 17 International Journal of the Sociology of Law 185

DOE, N., *The Legal Framework of the Church of England* (1996) Oxford University Press, Oxford

DOE, N., *Canon Law in the Anglican Communion* (1998) Oxford University Press, Oxford

DOHERTY, M. J. and EAST, R., 'Bail Decisions in Magistrates' Courts' (1985) 25 British Journal of Criminology 251

DOYLE, B., 'The Hidden History of English Studies' in P. Widdowson (ed.), *Re-reading English* (1982) Methuen, London

DOYLE, M. et al., *Seeking Resolutions: The Availability and Usage of Consumer-to-business Alternative Dispute Resolution in the United Kingdom* (2004) DTI, London

DRAPER, H., *Private Police* (1978) Penguin Books, Harmondsworth

DU CANN, R., *The Art of the Advocate* (rev. edn, 1993), Penguin, Harmondsworth

DUFF, E., SHINER, M., BOON, A., with WHYTE, A., *Entry into the Legal Professions: The Law Student Cohort Study: Year 6: Research Study No. 39* (2000) The Law Society, London

DURKHEIM, E., *The Division of Labour in Society* (1933) Macmillan, London

DURKHEIM, E., *The Rules of Sociological Method* (1982) Macmillan, London

DUXBURY, N., 'The Reinvention of Ideas: American Jurisprudence in the Twentieth Century' (1992) University of Nottingham Research Papers No. 3, Nottingham

DWORKIN, R., *Taking Rights Seriously* (1977) Duckworth, London

Dworkin, R., *Law's Empire* (1986) Fontana, London

Economides, K., 'Small Claims and Procedural Justice' (1980) 7 British Journal of Law and Society 111

Economides, K., 'The Country Lawyer: Iconography, Iconoclasm, and the Restoration of the Professional Image' in P. Thomas (ed.), *Tomorrow's Lawyers* (1992) Basil Blackwell, Oxford

Edwards, R., 'Judicial Deference under the Human Rights Act' (2002) 65 Modern Law Review 859

Edwards, S., *Policing Domestic Violence* (1989) Sage, London

Eekelaar, J. and Clive, E. with others, *Custody after Divorce* (1977) Oxford Centre for Socio-Legal Studies, Oxford

Ekins, R., 'Judicial Supremacy and the Rule of Law' (2003) 119 Law Quarterly Review 127

Elkins, J., 'Coping Strategies in Legal Education' (1982) 16 The Law Teacher 195

Ellison, L., *The Adversarial Process and the Vulnerable Witness* (2001) Oxford University Press, Oxford

Ellison, L., 'Responding to Victim Withdrawal in Domestic Violence Prosecutions' [2003] Criminal Law Review 760

Ellison, L., 'The Use and Abuse of Psychiatric Evidence in Rape Trials' (2009) 13(1) International Journal of Evidence and Proof 28

Ellison, L. and Munro, V., 'Of "Normal Sex" and "Real Rape": Exploring the Use of Socio-sexual Scripts in (Mock) Jury Deliberation' (2009a) 18(3) Social and Legal Studies (131) 291

Ellison, L. and Munro, V., 'Reacting to Rape' (2009b) 49(2) British Journal of Criminology 202

Ellison, L. and Munro, V., 'Turning Mirrors in Windows? Assessing the Impact of (Mock) Juror Education in Rape Trials' (2009c) 49(3) British Journal of Criminology 363

Engle Merry, S., *Getting Justice and Getting Even* (1990) University of Chicago Press, Chicago

Engle Merry, S. and Milner, N. (eds), *The Possibility of Popular Justice* (1993) University of Michigan Press, Ann Arbor, MI

Equality and Human Rights Commission, *Police and Racism: What has Been Achieved 10 Years after the Stephen Lawrence Inquiry Report?* (2009) EHRC, London

Eskridge, W. Jr, *Dynamic Statutory Interpretation* (1994) Harvard University Press, Cambridge, MA

Evans-Pritchard, E., *The Nuer* (1940) Oxford University Press, Oxford

Falk Moore, S., *Law as Process* (1978) Routledge & Kegan Paul, London

Farmer, J., *Tribunals and Government* (1974) Weidenfeld & Nicolson, London

Farrar, J. and Dugdale, A., *Introduction to Legal Method* (3rd edn, 1990) Sweet & Maxwell, London

Faulconbridge, J., Beaverstock, J., Muzio, D., and Taylor, P., 'Global Law Firms: Globalization and Organizational Spaces of Cross-border Legal Worlds' (2008) 28 Northwestern Journal of International Law and Business 455

FELDMAN, D., *Civil Liberties and Human Rights in England and Wales* (2nd edn, 2002) Oxford University Press, Oxford

FENN, P., GRAY, A., RICKMAN, N., and CARRIER, H., *The Impact of Conditional Fees on the Selection, Handling and Outcomes of Personal Injury Cases* (2002) Lord Chancellor's Department, London

FENWICK, H., 'Charge Bargaining and Sentence Discount: The Victim's Perspective' (1997) 5 International Review of Victimology 23

FIDDES, C. and LLOYD, C., 'Assessing the Impact of Bail Information Schemes' (1990) 29 Home Office Research Bulletin No. 23, Home Office, London

FINCH, E. and MUNRO. V., 'Breaking Boundaries? Sexual Consent in the Jury Room' (2006) 26(3) Legal Studies 303

FINCH, E. and MUNRO. V., 'The Demon Drink and the Demonised Woman: Socio-sexual Stereotypes and Responsibility Attribution in Rape Trials Involving Intoxicants' (2007) 16(4) Social and Legal Studies 591

FINCH, E. and MUNRO. V., 'Lifting the Veil: The Use of Focus Groups and Trial Simulations in Legal Research' (2008) 35 Journal of Law and Society 30

FINEMAN, M., 'Feminist Legal Scholarship and Women's Gendered Lives' in M. Cain and C. Harrington (eds), *Lawyers in a Postmodern World* (1994) Open University Press, Buckingham

FIONDA, J., *Public Prosecutors and Discretion: A Comparative Study* (1995) Clarendon Press, Oxford

FISHER, E., 'Community Courts: An Alternative to Conventional Criminal Adjudication' (1975) 24 American University Law Review 1253

FISS, O., 'Against Settlement' (1984) 93 Yale Law Journal 1073

FITZGERALD, M., *Final Report into Stop and Search* (1999a) at <http://www.met.police.uk>

FITZGERALD, M., *Searches in London* (1999b) Metropolitan Police Service, London

FITZPATRICK, P., 'Law, Plurality and Underdevelopment' in D. Sugarman (ed.), *Legality, Ideology and the State* (1983) Academic Press, London

FITZPATRICK, P., 'The Abstracts and Brief Chronicles of the Time: Supplementing Jurisprudence' in P. Fitzpatrick (ed.), *Dangerous Supplements* (1991) Pluto Press, London

FLOOD, J., *Barristers' Clerks* (1983) Manchester University Press, Manchester

FLOOD, J., 'Megalaw in the UK: Professionalism or Corporatism? A Preliminary Report' (1989) 64 Indiana Law Journal 569

FLOOD, J., 'The Culture of Globalization' in Y. D. Dezalay and D. Sugarman (eds), *Professional Competition and Professional Power* (1995) Routledge, London

FOSTER, J., 'The "Cooling Out" of Law Students: Facilitating Market Co-operation of Future Lawyers' in R. Gambitta, M. May, and J. Foster (eds), *Governing through Courts* (1981) Sage Publications, Beverley Hills, CA

FOSTER, N., *German Law and German Legal System* (1993) Blackstone Press, London

FOUCAULT, M., *Discipline and Punish: The Birth of Prison* (1977) Pantheon, New York

FRANCIS, A., 'Legal Executives and the Phantom of Legal Professionalism: The Rise and Rise of the Third Branch of the Legal Profession?' (2002) 9(1) International Journal of the Legal Profession 5

FRANCIS, A., 'Out of Touch and Out of Time: Lawyers, their Leaders and Collective Mobility within the Legal Profession' (2004) 24 Legal Studies 322

FRANCIS, A. and McDONALD, I., 'Part-time Law Students: The Forgotten Cohort' (2005) 39 The Law Teacher 277

FRANK, J., *The Courts on Trial* (1949) Princeton University Press, Princeton, NJ

FRANKS COMMITTEE, *Report of the Committee on Administrative Tribunals and Enquiries* (the Franks Report) (1957) Cmnd 218, HMSO, London

FRIEDMAN, L., 'Lawyers in Cross-cultural Perspective' in R. Abel and P. Lewis (eds), *Lawyers in Society: Volume Three* (1989) University of California Press, Berkeley, CA

FRUG, M., *Postmodern Legal Feminism* (1992) Routledge, London

FULTON, O., 'Elite Survivals? Entry "Standards" and Procedures for Higher Education Admissions' (1988) 13 Studies in Higher Education 15

*Further Findings: A Continuing Evaluation of the Civil Justice Reforms* (2002) <http://www.dca.gov.uk/civil/reform/ffreform.htm>

GALANTER, M., 'Why the "Haves" Come Out Ahead' (1974) 9 Law and Society Review 75

GALANTER, M., ' " . . . A Settlement Judge Not a Trial Judge": Judicial Mediation in the United States' (1985) 12 Journal of Law and Society 1

GAMBITTA, R., MAY, M., and FOSTER, J. (eds), *Governing through Courts* (1981) Sage Publications, Beverley Hills, CA

GEARY, R., 'Lord Denning and Morality' in P. Robson and P. Watchman (eds), *Justice, Lord Denning and the Constitution* (1981) Gower, Aldershot

GENN, H., 'Who Claims Compensation: Factors Associated with Claiming and Obtaining Damages' in D. Harris et al. (eds), *Compensation and Support for Illness and Injury* (1984) Clarendon Press, Oxford

GENN, H., *Hard Bargaining: Out of Court Settlement in Personal Injury Claims* (1987) Oxford University Press, Oxford

GENN, H., *The Central London County Court Pilot Mediation Scheme Evaluation Report* (1998) Lord Chancellor's Department Research Series 5/98, Lord Chancellor's Department, London

GENN, H., *Mediation in Action* (1999a) Calouste Gilbenkian Foundation, London

GENN, H., *Paths to Justice* (1999b) Hart Publishing, Oxford

GENN, H., *Court-based ADR Initiatives for Non-family Civil Disputes: The Commercial Court and the Court of Appeal* (2002) DCA Research Series 1/02, Department for Constitutional Affairs, London

GENN, H. and GENN, Y., *The Effectiveness of Representation at Tribunals* (1989) Lord Chancellor's Department, London

GEORGE, B. and BUTTON, M., 'Private Security Industry Regulation: Lessons from Abroad for the United Kingdom?' (1997) 2(3) International Journal of Risk, Security and Crime Prevention 187

GEORGE, B. and BUTTON, M., ' "Too Little Too Late"? An Assessment of Recent Proposals for the Private Security Industry in the United Kingdom' (1998) 10 Security Journal 1

GIDDENS, A., *Central Problems in Social Theory* (1979) Macmillan, London

GIFFORD, T., *Where's the Justice?* (1986) Penguin, Harmondsworth

GILCHRIST, E. and BLISSETT, J., 'Magistrates' Attitudes to Domestic Violence and Sentencing Options' (2002) 41(4) Howard Journal of Criminal Justice 348

GILCHRIST, S., 'Defendant's Rights in SFO and DTI Investigations' (1991) 135 Solicitors' Journal 1140

GILLIGAN, C., *In a Different Voice* (1982) Harvard University Press, Cambridge, MA

GLIDEWELL, SIR I., *The Review of the Crown Prosecution Service* (1998) Cm. 3960, The Stationery Office, London

GLUCKMAN, M., *The Judicial Process amongst the Barotse* (2nd edn, 1976) Manchester University Press, Manchester

GOBERT, J., *Justice, Democracy and the Jury* (1997) Dartmouth, Aldershot.

GOFF, LORD, 'The Search for Principle' (1983) 69 Proceedings of the British Academy 169

GOFF, LORD, 'Judge, Jurist and Legislator' [1987] Denning Law Journal 79

GOODE, R., *Commercial Law* (2004) Penguin, Harmondsworth

GOODHART, A., *Essays in Jurisprudence and Common Law* (1931) Cambridge University Press, Cambridge

GOODHART, A., 'Case Law – A Short Replication' (1934) 50 Law Quarterly Review 196

GOODHART, A., 'The Ratio Decidendi of a Case' (1959) 22 Modern Law Review 117

GOODRICH, P., *Reading the Law* (1986) Basil Blackwell, Oxford

GOODRICH, P., *Languages of Law* (1990) Weidenfeld & Nicolson, London

GORDON, M., 'The Conceptual Foundations of Parliamentary Sovereignty: Reconsidering Jennings and Wade' [2009] Public Law 519

GRAYCAR, R. and MORGAN, J., *The Hidden Gender of Law* (1990) The Federation Press, Leichhardt

GREER, S., 'The Right to Silence, Defence Disclosure and Confession Evidence' (1994) 21 Journal Law and Society 102

GREER, S., 'Towards a Sociological Model of the Police Informant' (1995) 46 British Journal of Sociology 509

GREER, S. and MORGAN, R. (eds), *The Right to Silence Debate* (1990) Centre for Criminal Justice, Bristol

GRIFFITH, J. A. G., *The Politics of the Judiciary* (5th edn, 1997) Fontana, London

GRIFFITH, J. A. G., 'The Brave New World of Sir John Laws' (2000) 63 Modern Law Review 159

GRIFFITH, J. A. G., 'The Common Law and the Political Constitution' (2001) 117 Law Quarterly Review 42

GUDJONSSON, G., *The Psychology of Interrogations, Confessions and Testimony* (1992) Wiley, London

GURVITCH, G., *The Sociology of Law* (1947) Routledge & Kegan Paul, London

Gus John Partnership, *Race for Justice* (2003) The Stationery Office/CPS, London

Hadfield, P., *Bar Wars: Contesting the Night in Contemporary British Cities* (2006) Oxford University Press, Oxford

Hailsham, Lord, 'The Office of Lord Chancellor and the Separation of Powers' (1989) 8 Civil Justice Quarterly 308

Hale, Dame Brenda, 'Equality and the Judiciary: Why Should We Want More Women Judges?' [2001] Public Law 489

Hale, Lady, 'Making a Difference? Why We Need a More Diverse Judiciary' (2005) 56 Northern Ireland Legal Quarterly 281

Hallsworth, S., *Street Crime* (2005) Willan, Cullompton

Halpern, D., *Entry into the Legal Professions: The Law Student Cohort Study: Years 1 and 2* (1994) The Law Society, London

Halpern, S., 'On the Politics and Pathology of Legal Education' (1982) 32 Journal of Legal Education 383

*Halsbury's Laws of England*, Volume 10 (4th edn, 1975) Butterworths, London

Harden, I. and Lewis, N., *The Noble Lie* (1988) Hutchinson, London

Harrell-Bond, B. and Smith, A., 'Dispute Treatment in an English Town' in M. Cain and K. Kulcsar (eds), *Disputes and the Law* (1983) Akademiai Kiado, Budapest

Harris, B., 'Final Appellate Courts Overruling their Own "Wrong" Precedents: The Ongoing Search for Principle' (2002) 118 Law Quarterly Review 408

Harris, D., 'Claims for Damages' in D. Harris et al. (eds), *Compensation and Support for Illness and Injury* (1984) Clarendon Press, Oxford

Harris, J., 'Legal Expenses Insurance' (1991) 135 Solicitors' Journal 668

Harris, N., *Law and Education: Regulation, Consumerism and the Education System* (1993) Sweet & Maxwell, London

Hart, H. L. A., 'Positivism and the Separation of Law and Morals' (1958) 71 Harvard Law Review 593

Hart, H. L. A., *The Concept of Law* (1961) Oxford University Press, Oxford

Hart, H. L. A., *The Concept of Law* (2nd edn, 1994) Oxford University Press, Oxford

Hartley, T. C. and Griffith, J. A. G., *Government and Law* (1975) Weidenfeld & Nicolson, London

Harvie, D., 'Equal Opportunities at the Bar' (1994) 144 New Law Journal 503

Hawkins, K., *Environment and Enforcement* (1984) Clarendon Press, Oxford

Hawkins, K., *Law as a Last Resort* (2002) Oxford University Press, Oxford

Hayek, F., *The Constitution of Liberty* (1960) Routledge & Kegan Paul, London

Hedderman, C. and Moxon, D., *Magistrates' Court or Crown Court? Mode of Trial Decisions and Sentencing* (1992) HMSO, London

Henham, R., 'Bargain Justice or Justice Denied? Sentence Discounts and the Criminal Process' (1999) 63 Modern Law Review 515

Henry, A. and Smith, D. (eds), *Transformations of Policing* (2007) Ashgate, Aldershot

HENRY, S., *Private Justice* (1983) Routledge & Kegan Paul, London

HEPPLE, B., 'The Renewal of the Liberal Law Degree' (1996) 55 Cambridge Law Journal 470

HERBERT, A., 'Mode of Trial and the Influence of Local Justice' (2004) 43 Howard Journal of Criminal Justice 65

HERBERT, P., 'Mode of Trial and Magistrates' Sentencing Powers: Will Increased Powers Inevitably Lead to a Reduction in the Committal Rate?' [2003] Criminal Law Review 314

HEUSTON, R., *Lives of the Lord Chancellors, Volume 1: 1885–1940* (1964) Clarendon Press, Oxford

HEUSTON, R., *Lives of the Lord Chancellors, Volume 2: 1940–1970* (1987) Clarendon Press, Oxford

HEWSON, B., 'A Recent Problem?' (1995) 145 New Law Journal 626

HILL, M., *Ecclesiastical Law* (3rd edn, 2007) Oxford University Press, Oxford

HM CROWN PROSECUTION SERVICE, *The Director's Guidance on Charging* (3rd edn, 2007), issued by the DPP under s. 37A of the Police and Criminal Evidence Act 1984, London, available at: <http://www.cps.gov.uk/publications/directors_guidance/dpp_guidance.html>

HM CROWN PROSECUTION SERVICE INSPECTORATE, *Report on the Evaluation of Lay Review and Lay Presentation*, Thematic Report 2/99 (1999) CPSI, London

HM CROWN PROSECUTION SERVICE INSPECTORATE, *Disclosure – Thematic Review* (2008) HMCPSI, London

HM CROWN PROSECUTION SERVICE INSPECTORATE, *Report of the Thematic Review of the Quality of Prosecution Advocacy and Case Presentation* (2009) HMCPSI, London

HM CROWN PROSECUTION SERVICE INSPECTORATE AND HM INSPECTORATE OF CONSTABULARY, *Violence at Home: The Investigation and Prosecution of Cases Involving Domestic Violence* (2004) HMCPSI, London, CPS, available at: <http://www.hmcpsi.gov.uk>

HM CROWN PROSECUTION SERVICE INSPECTORATE AND HM INSPECTORATE OF CONSTABULARY, *Joint Thematic Review of the New Charging Arrangements* (2008) HMCPSI/HMIC, London

HM CROWN PROSECUTION SERVICE INSPECTORATE, HM INSPECTORATE OF CONSTABULARY, HM INSPECTORATE OF COURT ADMINISTRATION, and HM INSPECTOR OF PRISONS, *Peart Review* (2008) HMICA, London

HM INSPECTOR OF PRISONS, *Unjust Deserts: A Thematic Review of the Chief Inspector of Prisons of the Treatment and Conditions for Unsentenced Prisoners in England and Wales* (2000) Home Office, London

HM Revenue and Customs, *Modernising, Deterrents and Safeguards: Criminal Investigation Powers – A Technical Consultation Document* (2006) HMRC, London

HOBBES, T., *Leviathan* (n.d.) Basil Blackwell, Oxford

HOBBS, D., HADFIELD, P., LISTER, S., and WINLOW, S., *Bouncers: Violence and Governance in the Night-time Economy* (2003) Oxford University Press, Oxford

HODGSON, J., 'Adding Injury to Injustice: The Suspect at the Police Station' (1994) 21(1) Journal of Law and Society 85

HOFFMAN, LORD, review of LEE, S., *Judging Judges* (1989) 105 Law Quarterly Review 140

HOGBIN, H., *Law and Order in Polynesia* (1934) Harcourt Brace, New York

HOGGETT, B., *Mental Health Law* (4th edn, 1996) Sweet & Maxwell, London

HOLDAWAY, S., *Inside the British Police* (1983) Basil Blackwell, Oxford

HOLDSWORTH, W., *A History of English Law* (3rd 1922) Methuen, London

HOLDSWORTH, SIR W., 'Case Law' (1934) 50 Law Quarterly Review 180

HOLLAND, L. and SPENCER, L., *Without Prejudice? Sex Equality at the Bar and in the Judiciary* (1992) TMS Consultants, London

HOME AFFAIRS SELECT COMMITTEE FIRST REPORT, *The Private Security Industry: Volume 1* (1995) HMSO, London

HOME OFFICE, *Disclosure: A Consultation* (1995) Cm. 2864, HMSO, London

HOME OFFICE, *Review of Police Core and Ancillary Tasks* (1995) HMSO, London

HOME OFFICE, *Determining Mode of Trial in Either-way Cases* (July 1998) Home Office Consultation Paper, Home Office, London

HOME OFFICE, *The Government's Proposals for Regulating the Private Security Industry in England and Wales* (1999) Cm. 4254, HMSO, London

HOME OFFICE, *Justice for All* (2002) Cm. 5563, The Stationery Office, London

HOME OFFICE, *Statistics on Race and the Criminal Justice System 2002: A Home Office Publication under Section 95 of the Criminal Justice Act 1991* (2003a) Home Office Research, Development and Statistics Directorate, London

HOME OFFICE, *Criminal Justice Act 2003: Bail Elsewhere than at a Police Station* (2003b) Circular 061/2003, Home Office, London

HOME OFFICE, *Crime in England and Wales 2005/06* (2006) Home Office, London

HOOD, R., SHUTE, S., and SEEMUNGAL, F., *Ethnic Minorities in the Criminal Courts: Perceptions of Fairness and Equality of Treatment* (2003) Research Series Report No. 2/03, Lord Chancellor's Department, London

HOYANO, A., HOYANO, L., DAVIS, G., and GOLDIE, S., 'A Study of the Impact of the Revised Code for Crown Prosecutors' [1997] Criminal Law Review 556

HOYLE, C., *Negotiating Domestic Violence* (1998) Oxford University Press, Oxford

HUCKLESBY, A., 'The Problem with Bail Bandits' (1992) 142 New Law Journal 558

HUCKLESBY, A., 'The Use and Abuse of Conditional Bail' (1994) 33 Howard Journal 258

HUCKLESBY, A., 'Court Culture: An Explanation of Variations in the Use of Bail in the Magistrates' Courts' (1997a) 36 Howard Journal 129

HUCKLESBY, A., 'Remand Decision Makers' [1997b] Criminal Law Review 269

HUCKLESBY, A., 'Not Necessarily a Trip to the Police Station' [2004] Criminal Law Review 803

HUCKLESBY, A. and MARSHALL, E., 'Tackling Offending on Bail' (2000) 39 Howard Journal 150

HUTCHINSON, A. and MONAHAN, P., 'Law, Politics and the Critical Legal Scholars: The Unfolding Drama of American Legal Thought' (1984) 36 Stanford Law Review 199

IHSAN, Y., 'The Challenge of Post-modern Legality and Muslim Legal Pluralism in England' (2002) 28 Journal of Ethnic and Minority Studies 343

IHSAN, Y., *Muslim Laws, Politics and Society in Modern Nation States* (2005) Ashgate, Aldershot

INDUSTRIAL TRIBUNALS, *Industrial Tribunal: England and Wales: Procedures* (1994) Industrial Tribunals, London

INGLEBY, R., 'The Solicitor as Intermediary' in R. Dingwall and J. Eekelaar (eds), *Divorce Mediation and the Legal Process* (1988) Clarendon Press, Oxford

IRVINE, LORD, 'Judges and Decision-makers: The Theory and Practice of *Wednesbury* Review' [1996] Public Law 59

ISON, T., 'Small Claims' (1972) 35 Modern Law Review 18

JACK, D. and JACK, R., 'Women Lawyers: Archetype and Alternatives' in C. Gilligan (ed.), *Mapping the Moral Domain* (1988) Harvard University Press, Cambridge, MA

JACKSON, J., 'Curtailing the Right of Silence' [1991] Criminal Law Review 404

JACKSON, J., 'The Right of Silence: Judicial Responses to Parliamentary Encroachment' (1994) 57 Modern Law Review 270

JACKSON, J., 'Modes of Trial: Shifting the Balance towards the Professional Judge' [2002] Criminal Law Review 249

JACKSON, J., 'Justice for All: Putting Victims at the Heart of Criminal Justice?' (2003) Journal of Law and Society 309

JACKSON, J. and DORAN, S., *Judge without Jury* (1995) Clarendon Press, Oxford

JACKSON, R., *The Machinery of Justice in England* (1st edn, 1940) Cambridge University Press, Cambridge

JACKSON, R., *The Machinery of Justice in England* (8th edn, 1989) Cambridge University Press, Cambridge

JACKSON, Sir R., *Review of Civil Litigation Costs: Final Report* (2010) The Stationery Office, London

JACOB, SIR J. (ed.), *Supreme Court Practice: 1995* (1994) Sweet & Maxwell, London

JACOBS, A., 'Women in Law Schools: Structural Constraint and Personal Choice in the Formation of Professional Identity' (1972) 24 Journal of Legal Education 462

JEFFERSON, T. and WALKER, M., 'Ethnic Minorities in the Criminal Justice System' [1992] Criminal Law Review 83

JOHNSON, T., *Professions and Power* (1972) Macmillan, London

JOHNSTON, H., 'Court Duty Solicitors' (1992) Legal Action, May, p. 11

JOHNSTON, L., *The Rebirth of Private Policing* (1992) Routledge, London

JONES, P., 'Remand Decisions at Magistrates' Courts' in D. Moxon (ed.), *Managing Criminal Justice* (1985) Home Office Research and Planning Unit, HMSO, London

JONES, P., TARLING, R., and VENNARD, J., 'The Effectiveness of Committal Proceedings as a Filter in the Criminal Justice System' in D. Moxon (ed.), *Managing Criminal Justice* (1985) Home Office Research and Planning Unit, HMSO, London

JONES, T. and NEWBURN, T., *Private Security and Public Policing* (1998) Clarendon Press, Oxford

JOWELL, J., 'Parliamentary Sovereignty under the New Constitutional Hypothesis' [2006] Public Law 562

*Judicial Appointments: Recorders and Assistant Recorders* Leaflet 3 (1995) Lord Chancellor's Department, London

*Judicial Appointments: Tribunal Appointments* (1995) Lord Chancellor's Department, London

*Judicial Diversity: Findings of a Consultation with Barristers, Solicitors and Judges: Final Report* (2006) Opinion Leader Research, London

*Judicial Statistics: Annual Report: 1991* (1992) Cm. 1990, Lord Chancellor's Department, London

*Judicial Statistics: 1993* (1994) Cm. 2623, Lord Chancellor's Department, London

*Judicial Statistics: 1994* (1995) Cm. 2891, Lord Chancellor's Department, London

*Judicial Statistics 2005 (Revised)* (2006) Cm. 6903, Department for Constitutional Affairs, London

JUDICIAL STUDIES BOARD, *Report 1991–1995* (1995) Judicial Studies Board, London

JULIAN, R., 'Judicial Perspectives on the Conduct of Serious Fraud Trials' [2007] Criminal Law Review 751

JUSTICE (SOCIETY), *Industrial Tribunals* (1987) Justice, London

KAGAN, R., 'The Routinization of Debt Collection: An Essay on Social Change and Conflict in the Courts' (1984) 18 Law and Society Review 323

KAIRYS, D. (ed.), *The Politics of Law* (rev. edn, 1990) Pantheon, New York

KAKALIK, J. S. and WILDHORN, S., Private *Policing in the United States: Findings and Recommendations* (1971) Rand Corporation, Santa Monica, CA

KAMALI, M. H., *Principles of Islamic Jurisprudence* (1989) Pelanduk Publications (M) Sdn Bhd, Petaling Jaya

KASSIM, S. and WRIGHTSMAN, L., *The American Jury on Trial* (1988) Hemisphere, New York

KAVANAGH, A., '*Pepper* v *Hart* and Matters of Constitutional Principle' (2005) 121 Law Quarterly Review 98

KAVANAGH, A., *Constitutional Review under the Human Rights Act* (2009) Cambridge University Press, Cambridge

KELMAN, M., 'Trashing' (1984) 36 Stanford Law Review 293

KELMAN, M., *A Guide to Critical Legal Studies* (1987) Harvard University Press, Cambridge, MA

KEMP, V. and BALMER, N., *Criminal Defence Services: User's Perspectives* (2008) Research Paper No. 21, Legal Services Research Centre, London

KENNEDY, D., 'Form and Substance in Private Law Adjudication' (1976) 89 Harvard Law Review 1685

KENNEDY, D., 'Legal Education as Training for Hierarchy' in D. Kairys (ed.), *The Politics of Law* (1990) Pantheon Books, New York

KENNEDY, T., 'The Essential Minimum: The Establishment of the Court of First Instance' (1989) 14 European Law Review 7

KIBBLE, N., 'Access to Legal Education and the Legal Professions in England' in R. Dhavan, N. Kibble, and W. Twining (eds), *Access to Legal Education and the Legal Professions* (1989) Butterworths, London

KING, M., *Bail or Custody* (1971) Cobden Trust, London

KING, M. and MAY, C., *Black Magistrates* (1985) Cobden Trust, London

KING, M., ISRAEL, M., and GOULBOURNE, S., *Ethnic Minorities and Recruitment to the Solicitors' Profession* (1990) Law Society on Behalf of the Commission for Racial Equality, London

KIRALFY, A., *The English Legal System* (1954) Sweet & Maxwell, London

KIRK, D. and WOODCOCK, A., *Serious Fraud: Investigation and Trial* (2nd edn, 1997) Butterworths, London

KLUG, F., 'The Human Rights Act 1998, *Pepper v Hart* and All That' [1999] Public Law 246

KLUG, F. and O'BRIEN, C., 'The First Two Years of the Human Rights Act' [2002] Public Law 649

KNORR-CETINA, K. and CICOUREL, A. V. (eds), *Advances in Social Theory and Methodology* (1981) Routledge & Kegan Paul, London

KRITZER, H., 'Propensity to Sue in England and the United States of America: Blaming and Claiming in Tort Cases' (1991) 18 Journal of Law and Society 400

KUHN, T., *The Structure of Scientific Revolutions* (2nd edn, 1970) University of Chicago Press, Chicago

KWAI, N., 'The Judge as Mediator: The Japanese Experience' (1991) 10 Civil Justice Quarterly 108

LANE, LORD, 'Judicial Independence and the Increasing Executive Role in Judicial Administration' in S. Shetreet and J. Deschenes (eds), *Judicial Independence: The Contemporary Debate* (1985) Martinus Nijhoff, Dordrecht

LANGAN, P., *Maxwell on the Interpretation of Statutes* (12th edn, 1969) Sweet & Maxwell, London

LARKIN, S., 'Debunking the Idea of Parliamentary Sovereignty: The Controlling Factor of Legality in the British Constitution' (2008) 28 Oxford Journal of Legal Studies 709

LARSON, M., *The Rise of Professionalism* (1977) University of California Press, Berkley

LASH, D., 'An Old Tale – The Legal Career of Sir John Glanville' (1993) Law Society Gazette, 14 July

LAW COMMISSION, *The Interpretation of Statutes* (Law Com. No. 21) (1969) HMSO, London

LAW COMMISSION, *Bail and the Human Rights Act 1998* (1999) Law Commission Consultation Paper No. 157, TSO, London

LAW COMMISSION, *Evidence of Bad Character in Criminal Proceedings* (2001) Law Commission Report No. 273

LAW SOCIETY, *Women in the Professions: A Report Compiled by the United Kingdom Inter-professional Group Working Party on Women's Issues* (1990) The Law Society, London

LAW SOCIETY, *Trends in the Solicitors' Profession: Annual Statistical Report 1994* (1994) The Law Society, London

LAW SOCIETY, *Trends in the Solicitors' Profession: Annual Statistical Report 2001* (2002) The Law Society, London

LAW SOCIETY, *Women Solicitors 2004: Research Findings* (2004) The Law Society, London

LAW SOCIETY, *Trends in the Solicitors' Profession: Annual Statistical Report 2009* (2009a) The Law Society, London

LAW SOCIETY, *Ethnicity and Earnings in Private Practice* (2009b) The Law Society, London

LAWRENCE, T., 'Judging the (Tribunal) Judges' (1995) 2(2) Tribunals 9

LAWS, SIR J., 'Is the High Court the Guardian of Fundamental Constitutional Rights?' [1993] Public Law 59

LAWS, SIR J., 'Law and Democracy' [1995] Public Law 72

LAWS, SIR J., 'Public Law and Employment Law' [1997] Public Law 455

LAWS, SIR J., 'The Limitations of Human Rights' [1998] Public Law 254

LEAVIS, F., 'The Great Tradition: George Eliot, Henry James, Joseph Conrad' (new edn, 1960) Chatto and Windus, London

LEE, G., 'An Introduction' in G. Lee, *The Changing Professions: Accountancy and Law* (1991) Aston Business School, Birmingham

LEE, R., 'From Profession to Business: The Rise and Rise of the City Law Firm' in P. Thomas (ed.), *Tomorrow's Lawyers* (1992) Basil Blackwell, Oxford

LEE, R., *Firm Views: Work of and Work in the Largest Law Firms* (1999) The Law Society, London

LEE, S., *Judging Judges* (1988) Faber and Faber, London

LEGAL SERVICES COMMISSION, *Legal Services Commission Annual Report and Accounts 2008–9* HC731 (2009) The Stationery Office, London

LEGGATT, SIR A., *Tribunals for Users: One System, One Service* (2001) Report of the Review of Tribunals by Sir Andrew Leggatt (Leggatt Review), The Stationery Office, London

LEIGHTON, P., MORTIMER, T., and WHATELY, N., *Today's Law Teachers: Lawyers or Academics?* (1995) Cavendish, London

LENG, R., *The Right to Silence in Police Interrogation: A Study of Some of the Issues Underlying the Debate* (1993) Royal Commission on Criminal Justice Research Study No. 10, HMSO, London

LENG, R., McCONVILLE, M., and SANDERS, A., 'Researching the Discretions to Charge and to Prosecute' in D. Downes (ed.), *Unravelling Criminal Justice* (1992) Macmillan, London

LEONARD, A., *Judging Inequality: The Effectiveness of the Tribunal System in Sex Discrimination and Equal Pay Cases* (1987) Cobden Trust, London

LESTER, LORD, 'The Art of the Possible – Interpreting Statutes under the Human Rights Act' (1998) 6 European Human Rights Law Review 665

LEVI, M., 'The Role of the Jury in Complex Cases' in M. Findlay and P. Duff (eds), *The Jury under Attack* (1988) Butterworths, London

LEWIS, H. and MAIR, G., *Bail and Probation Work II: The Use of London Probation/Bail Hostels for Bailees* (1988) Home Office Research and Policy Planning Unit Paper No. 46, HMSO, London

LEWIS, J. with KEEGAN, J., *Defining Legal Business: Understanding the Work of the Largest Law Firms* (1997) The Law Society, London

LIDSTONE, K., and PALMER, C., *The Investigation of Crime* (2nd edn, 1996) Butterworths, London

LIDSTONE, K. et al., *Prosecutions by Private Individuals and Non-police Agencies* (1980) Royal Commission on Criminal Procedure Research Study No. 10, HMSO, London

LIVINGSTONE, K., *Managing the 'Policing Business'* (1996) Research Paper 6, Scarman Centre for the Study of Public Order, University of Leicester

LLEWELLYN, K., *The Bramble Bush* (1960) Oceana Publications, New York

LLOYD, C., *Bail Information Schemes: Practice and Effect* (1992) Home Office Research and Policy Planning Unit Paper No. 69, Home Office, London

LLOYD-BOSTOCK, S., 'The Jubilee Line Jurors: Does their Experience Strengthen the Argument for Judge-only Trial in Long and Complex Fraud Cases?' [2007] Criminal Law Review 255

LORD CHANCELLOR'S DEPARTMENT, *Judicial Appointment* (1986) Lord Chancellor's Department, London

LORD CHANCELLOR'S DEPARTMENT, *The Work and Organisation of the Legal Profession* (1989) Cm. 570, Lord Chancellor's Department, London

LORD CHANCELLOR'S DEPARTMENT, *Legal Aid, Targeting Need: The Future of Publicly Funded Help in Solving Legal Problems and Disputes in England and Wales: A Consultation Paper* (1995) Cm. 2854, HMSO, London

LOVELL BANKS, T., 'Gender Bias in the Classroom' (1988) 38 Journal of Legal Education 135

LOWE, N. and BORRIE, G., *Borrie and Lowe's Law of Contempt* (2nd edn, 1983) Butterworths, London

LUKES, S. and SCULL, A., *Durkheim and the Law* (1983) Martin Robertson, Oxford

LUSTGARTEN, L., 'The Future of Stop and Search' [2002] Criminal Law Review 603

McAUSLAN, P., 'Administrative Law, Collective Consumption and Judicial Policy' (1983) 46 Modern Law Review 1

McBARNET, D., *Conviction* (1981) Macmillan, London

McBARNET, D., *Conviction: Law, the State and the Construction of Justice* (1983) Macmillan, London

McCABE, S., WALLINGTON, P., ALDERSON, J., GOSTIN, L., and MASON, C., *Police, Public Order and Civil Liberties* (1988) Routledge, London

McCONVILLE, M., 'Videoing Interrogations: Police Behaviour On and Off Camera' [1992] Criminal Law Review 532

McConville, M., *Corroboration and Confessions: The Impact of a Rule Requiring that No Conviction Can be Sustained on the Basis of Confession Evidence Alone* (1993) Royal Commission on Criminal Justice Research Study No. 13, HMSO, London

McConville, M. and Baldwin, J., *Courts, Prosecution and Conviction* (1981) Clarendon Press, Oxford

McConville, M. and Hodgson, J., *Custodial Legal Advice and the Right to Silence* (1993) Royal Commission on Criminal Justice Research Study No. 16, HMSO, London

McConville, M., Sanders, A., and Leng, R., *The Case for the Prosecution* (1991) Routledge, London

McConville, M., Hodgson, J., Bridges, L., and Pavlovic, A., *Standing Accused* (1994) Clarendon Press, Oxford

MacCormick, N., *Legal Rules and Legal Reasoning* (1978) Clarendon Press, Oxford

MacCormick, N., 'Why Cases have Rationes and What These Are' in L. Goldstein (ed.), *Precedent in Law* (1987) Clarendon Press, Oxford

MacCullum, G., 'Legislative Intent' (1966) 75 Yale Law Journal 754

McDonald, P., '"The Class of 81" – A Glance at the Social Class Composition of Recruits to the Legal Profession' (1982) 9 Journal of Law and Society 267

McEwen, C. and Maiman, R., 'Mediation in Small Claims Court: Achieving Compliance through Consent' (1984) 18 Law and Society Review 11

McGlynn, C., 'Soliciting Equality – The Way Forward' (1995) 145 New Law Journal 1065

McGlynn, C., *The Woman Lawyer* (1998) Butterworths, London

McGlynn, C., 'Women, Representation and the Legal Academy' (1999) 19(1) Legal Studies 68

McGlynn, C. and Munro, V., (eds), *Rethinking Rape Law: International and Comparative Perspectives* (2010) Routledge-Cavendish, Abingdon

McIvor, G. and Warner, S., *Bail Services in Scotland* (1996) Avebury, Aldershot

McKay, D., *Politics and Power in the USA* (2nd edn, 1994) Penguin, Harmondsworth

Mackay, Lord, 'Who Makes the Law' (1987) *The Times*, 3 December

Mackay, Lord, 'Presidential Address' (December 1992/January 1993) The Magistrate 196

Mackay, Lord, *The Administration of Justice* (1994) Sweet & Maxwell, London

McKenzie, I., Morgan, R., and Reiner, R., 'Helping the Police with their Enquiries' [1990] Criminal Law Review 22

McLeod, J., 'Higher Courts Curtain Raiser' (1994) 91 Law Society Gazette, 27 July

McManus, M., *From Fate to Choice: Private Bobbies, Public Beats* (1995) Avebury, Aldershot

MacMillan, J., 'Employment Tribunals: Philosophies and Practicalities' (1999) 28 Industrial Law Journal 33

MacPherson, Sir W., *The Stephen Lawrence Inquiry* (1999) Cm. 4262-I, The Stationery Office, London

Macrory, R., *Regulatory Justice: Making Sanctions Effective* (2006) Cabinet Office, London

McThenia, A. W. and Shaffer, T. L., 'For Reconciliation' (1985) 94 Yale Law Journal 1660

MADGE, N., 'Summing up – A Judge's Perspective' [2006] Criminal Law Review 817

MAGEE, I. *Review of Legal Aid Delivery and Governance* (2008) Ministry of Justice, London

MAGUIRE, M., 'Effects of the PACE: Provisions on Detention and Questioning' (1988) 28 British Journal of Criminology 19

MAGUIRE, M., 'Crime Data and Statistics' in M. Maguire, R. Morgan, and R. Reiner (eds), *The Oxford Handbook of Criminology* (4th edn, 2007) Oxford University Press, Oxford

MAGUIRE, M. and NORRIS, C., *The Conduct and Supervision of Criminal Investigations* (1992) Royal Commission on Criminal Justice Research Study No. 5, HMSO, London

MAIR, G. and LLOYD, C., 'Policy and Progress in the Development of Bail Schemes in England and Wales' in F. Paterson (ed.), *Understanding Bail in Britain* (1996) Scottish Office, Edinburgh

MAITLAND, F., 'The Making of the German Civil Code' in F. Maitland, *Collected Papers* (1911) Cambridge University Press, Cambridge

MALINOWSKI, B., *Crime and Custom in Savage Society* (1926) Routledge & Kegan Paul, London

MALLESON, K., *The New Judiciary* (1999) Ashgate, Aldershot

MALLESON, K., 'Justifying Gender Inequality on the Bench: Why Difference Won't Do' (2003) 11 Feminist Legal Studies 1

MALLESON, K., *The English Legal System* (3rd edn, 2007) Oxford University Press, Oxford

MALLESON, K. and BANDA, F., *Factors Affecting the Decision to Apply for Silk or Judicial Office* (2000) Lord Chancellor's Department, London

MANCHESTER, A., *Modern Legal History* (1980) Butterworths, London

MARKESINIS, B. and DEAKIN, S., *Tort Law* (3rd edn, 1994) Clarendon Press, Oxford

MARSH, A. and MCCARTHY, W., *Dispute Procedures in Britain* (1968) HMSO, London

MARSHALL, G., *Constitutional Theory* (1971) Clarendon Press, Oxford

MARSHALL, G., *Constitutional Conventions* (1986) Clarendon Press, Oxford

MASSON, J., BAILEY-HARRIS, R., and PROBERT, R., *Cretney's Principles of Family Law* (8th edn, 2008) Sweet & Maxwell, London

MASSON, J., NORBURY, D., and CHATTERTON, S., *Mine, Yours or Ours?* (1983) HMSO, London

MATTHEWS, R. (ed.), *The Politics of Informal Justice* (1988) Sage, London

MAWBY, R., *Policing the City* (1979) Saxon House, Farnborough

MAY, LORD JUSTICE (ed.), *Civil Proceedings: Volume 1* (2003) Sweet & Maxwell, London

MAYSON, S., FRENCH, D., and RYAN, C., *Company Law* (19th edn, 2002) Oxford University Press, Oxford

MAYSON, S., FRENCH, D., and RYAN, C., *Company Law* (26th edn, 2009) Oxford University Press, Oxford

MEGARRY, R. and WADE, W., *The Law of Real Property* (1966) Stevens, London

MELVIN, M. and DIDCOTT, P. J., *Pre-trial Bail and Custody in the Scottish Courts* (1976) Scottish Office Central Research Unit, HMSO, Edinburgh

MERRY, S. E., *Getting Justice and Getting Even* (1990) University of Chicago Press, Chicago

MERRY, S. E. and MILNER, N. (eds), *The Possibility of Popular Justice* (1993) University of Michigan Press, Ann Arbor, MI

MHLANGA, B., *Race and the CPS* (2000) The Stationery Office, London

MICHAEL, D., 'The Levels of Orientation Security Officers have Towards a Public Policing Function' (1999) 11 Security Journal 40

MIERS, D., 'Legal Theory and the Interpretation of Statutes' in W. Twining (ed.), *Legal Theory and Common Law* (1986) Basil Blackwell, Oxford

MIERS, D. and PAGE, A., *Legislation* (2nd edn, 1990) Sweet & Maxwell, London

MILLER, J., BLAND, N., and QUINTON, P., *The Impact of Stops and Searches on Crime and the Community* (2000) Police Research Series Paper 127, Home Office, London

MILLER, J., QUINTON, P., and BLAND, N., *Police Stops and Searches: Lessons from a Programme of Research, Police* (2000) Home Office Briefing Note, Home Office, London

MILLERSON, G., *The Qualifying Associations* (1964) Routledge & Kegan Paul, London

MINISTRY OF JUSTICE, *Criminal Statistics 2007* (2008a) MOJ, London

MINISTRY OF JUSTICE, *Statistics on Race and the Criminal Justice System, 2006/7* (2008b) MOJ, London

MINISTRY OF JUSTICE, *Bail and Murder: Response to Consultation*, Consultation Paper (R) 11/08 (2009a) MOJ, London

MINISTRY OF JUSTICE, *Judicial and Court Statistics 2008* (2009b) Cm. 7697, HMSO, London

MINISITRY OF JUSTICE, *Legal Aid: Funding Reforms*, Consultation Paper 18/09 (2009c) MOJ, London

MINISTRY OF JUSTICE, *Statistics on Race and the Criminal Justice System, 2007/8* (2009d) MOJ, London

MIRFIELD, P., *Silence, Confessions and Improperly Obtained Evidence: Modernising Justice: The Government's Plans for Reforming Legal Services and the Courts* (1997) Cm. 4155, The Stationery Office, London

*Modernising Justice: The Government's Plans for Reforming Legal Services and the Courts* (1998) Cm. 4155, The Stationery Office, London

MONTESQUIEU, C. DE, *The Spirit of the Laws* (1989) Cambridge University Press, Cambridge

MONTROSE, J., 'Ratio Decidendi and the House of Lords' (1957a) 20 Modern Law Review 124

MONTROSE, J., 'The *Ratio Decidendi* of a Case' (1957b) 20 Modern Law Review 587

MOORE, G., *English Canon Law* (1963) Clarendon Press, Oxford

MOORHEAD, R., 'Third Way Regulation? Community Legal Service Partnerships' (2001) 64 Modern Law Review 543

MOORHEAD, R., 'Legal Aid and the Decline of the Private Practice: Blue Murder or Toxic Job?' (2004) 11 International Journal of the Legal Profession 157

MORE, T., *Utopia* (1965) Penguin, Harmondsworth

MORGAN, P. and Henderson, P., *Remand Decisions and Offending on Bail: Evaluation of the Bail Process Project* (1988) Home Office Research Study No. 184, Home Office, London

MORGAN, R., 'Remands in Custody: Problems and Prospects' [1989] Criminal Law Review 481

MORGAN, R., 'Magistrates: The Future According to Auld' (2002) 29 Journal of Law and Society 308

MORGAN, R. and JONES, S., 'Bail or Jail?' in E. Stockdale and S. Casale (eds), *Criminal Justice under Stress* (1981) Croom Helm, London

MORGAN, R. and RUSSELL, N., *The Judiciary in the Magistrates' Courts* (2000) Home Office RDS Occasional Paper No. 66, London

MORISON, J. and LEITH, P., *The Barrister's World and the Nature of Law* (1992) Open University Press, Milton Keynes

MORISON, W., *John Austin* (1982) Edward Arnold, London

MORRIS, P. et al., *Social Needs and Legal Action* (1973) Martin Robertson, Oxford

MORTON, J., 'Liverpool 8 – Anatomy of a Law Centre' (1988) 138 New Law Journal 141

MULCAHY, L., 'Can Leopards Change their Spots? An Evaluation of the Role of Lawyers in Medical Negligence Mediation' (2001) 8 International Journal of the Legal Profession 203

MUNDAY, R., 'Tribunal Lore: Legalism and the Industrial Tribunals' (1981) 10 Industrial Law Review 146

MUNDAY, R., 'All for One and One for All: The Rise to Prominence of the Composite Judgment within the Civil Division of the Court of Appeal' (2002) 61 Cambridge Law Journal 331

MUNRO, C., *Studies in Constitutional Law* (1987) Butterworths, London

MUNRO, C., *Studies in Constitutional Law* (2nd edn, 1999) Butterworths, London

MURPHY, D., *Customers and Thieves* (1986) Gower, Aldershot

MURPHY, W. and RAWLINGS, R., 'After the Ancien Regime: The Writing of Judgments in the House of Lords 1979/80' (1981) 44 Modern Law Review 617; (1982) 45 Modern Law Review 34

MUZIO, D. and ACKROYD, S., 'Change in the Legal Profession: Professional Agency and the Legal Labour Process' in D. Muzio, S. Ackeroyd, and J. Chanlat, *Redirections in the Study of Exopert Labour: Established Professions and New Occupations* (2008) Palgrave Macmillan, London

MUZIO, D., ACKEROYD, S., and CHANLAT, J. D., *Redirections in the Study of Expert Labour: Established Professions and New Occupations* (2008) Palgrave Macmillan, London

NAFFINE, N., *Law and the Sexes* (1990) Allen & Unwin, London

National Audit Office, *Crown Prosecution Service: Effective Use of Magistrates' Court Hearings*, HC 798 Session 2005–2006, 15 February 2006

National Consumer Council, *Ordinary Justice* (1989) HMSO, London

NEVILLE BROWN, L., 'The Court of First Five Years of the Court of First Instance and Appeals to the Court of Justice: Assessment and Statistics' (1995) 32 Common Market Law Review 743

NEVILLE BROWN, L., and KENNEDY, T., *Brown & Jacobs: The Court of Justice of the European Communities* (5th edn, 2000) Sweet & Maxwell, London

NICHOLLS, SIR D., 'Keeping the Civil Law Up To Date: Flexibility and Certainty in the 1990s' [1991] Current Legal Problems 1

NICOL, A. and ROGERS, H., *Changing Contempt of Court* (1981) National Council for Civil Liberties, Campaign for Press Freedom, London

NOBLES, R. and SCHIFF, D., 'The Right to Appeal and Workable Systems of Justice' (2002) 65 Modern Law Review 676

NORRIS, C., FIELDING, N., KEMP, C., and FIELDING, J., 'Black and Blue: An Analysis of the Influence of Race on Being Stopped by the Police' (1992) 43(2) British Journal of Sociology 207

NORTON, P., *The Commons in Perspective* (1981) Martin Robertson, Oxford

NOTT, S., 'Women in Law – 2' (1989) 139 New Law Journal 785

ODA, H., *Japanese Law* (1992) Butterworths, London

O'DONOVAN, K., 'Defences for Battered Women who Kill' (1991) 18 Journal of Law and Society 219

O'DONOVAN, K. and SZYSZCZAK, E., *Equality and Sex Discrimination Law* (1988) Basil Blackwell, Oxford

OFFICE FOR CRIMINAL JUSTICE REFORM, *Criminal Statistics 2005* (2005) The Stationery Office, London

OLIVER, D., 'Politicians and the Courts' (1988) 41 Parliamentary Affairs 13

ORMEROD, D., *Smith and Hogan: Criminal Law* (12th edn, 2008) Oxford University Press, Oxford

ORMEROD, D. and ROBERTS, A., 'The Police Reform Act 2002 – Increasing Centralization, Maintaining Confidence and Contracting Out Crime Control' [2003] Criminal Law Review 141

ORMEROD, D. and TAYLOR, R., 'The Corporate Manslaughter and Corporate Homicide Act 2007' [2008] Criminal Law Review 589

OSBORN, P., *A Concise Law Dictionary* (5th edn, 1964) Sweet & Maxwell, London

OVEY, C. and WHITE, R., *Jacobs and White, The European Convention on Human Rights* (4th edn, 2006) Oxford University Press, Oxford

PACKER, H. L., *The Limits of the Criminal Sanction* (1968) Stanford University Press, Stanford, CA

PANNICK, D., *Judges* (1987) Oxford University Press, Oxford

PANNICK, D., *Advocates* (1992) Oxford University Press, Oxford

PARKER, H., SUMNER, M., and JARVIS, G., *Unmasking the Magistrates* (1989) Open University Press, Milton Keynes

PATERSON, A., *The Law Lords* (1982) Macmillan, London

PATERSON, F. (ed.), *Understanding Bail in Britain* (1996) Scottish Office, Edinburgh

PAULDEN, P., 'Corporate Fraud: Civil Disclosure in Criminal Proceedings' (1994) 57 Modern Law Review 280

PAULUS, I., *The Search for Pure Food: A Sociology of Legislation in Britain* (1974) Martin Robertson, Oxford

PEACH, SIR L., 'Independent Scrutiny of the Appointment Processes of Judges and Queen's Counsel' (1999) Lord Chancellor's Department, London

PEARL, D. and MENSKI, W., *Muslim Family Law* (3rd edn, 1998), Butterworths, London

PENN, R. and SCATTERGOOD, H., 'Ethnicity and Career Aspirations' (1992) 19 New Community 75

PERKIN, H., *The Rise of Professional Society* (1989) Routledge, London

PEYSNER, J. and BALEN, P., 'Conditional Fees' (1995) Law Society Gazette, 31 August, 13 September

PEYSNER, J. and SENEVIRATNE, M., *The Management of Civil Cases: The Courts and Post-Woolf Landscape* (2005) DCA Research Series 9/05, Department for Constitutional Affairs, London

PEYSNER, J. and SENEVIRATNE, M., 'The Management of Civil Cases: A Snapshot' (2006) 25 Civil Justice Quarterly 312

PHILLIPS, C. and BROWN, D., *Entry into the Criminal Justice System: A Survey of Police Arrests* (1998) Home Office Research Study No. 185, HMSO, London

PHILLIPS, J., 'An Alternative Method of Settling Disputes' (1992) The Lawyer, 7 January

PHILLIPS, LORD, *Equality before the law* (2008) <http://www.judiciary.gov.uk/publications_media/speeches/index.htm>

PIERPOINT, H., 'Quickening the PACE? The Use of Volunteers as Appropriate Adults in England and Wales' (2008) 18(4) Policing and Society 397

PLANT, C. (ed.), *Blackstone's Guide to the Civil Procedure Rules* (1999) Blackstone Press, London

PLEASENCE, P. and BUCK, A., BALMER, N., O'GRADY, A., GENN, H., and SMITH, M., *Causes of Action: Civil Law and Social Justice* (2004) Legal Services Commission, London

PLOTNIKOFF, J. and WOOLFSON, R., *'A Fair Balance'? Evaluation of the Operation of Disclosure Law* (2001) RDS Occasional Paper No. 76, Home Office, London

PODMORE, D., *Solicitors and the Wider Community* (1980) Heinemann, London

PODMORE, D. and SPENCER, A., 'The Law as a Sex-typed Profession' (1982) 9(1) Journal of Law and Society 21

PODMORE, D. and SPENCER, A., 'Gender in the Labour Process: The Case of Women and Men Lawyers' in D. Knights and H. Wilmott (eds), *Gender in the Labour Process* (1986) Gower, Aldershot

POVEY, D. and SMITH, K., (eds) *Police Powers and Procedures, England and Wales 2007/08*, Home Office Statistical Bulletin 7/09 (2009) Home Office, London

POWELL, N., 'Soliloquy' in *A Season of Calm Weather* (1982) Carcanet New Press, Manchester

PRINCE, S., *Court-based Mediation: A Preliminary Analysis of the Small Claims Mediation Scheme at Exeter County Court* (2004) Civil Justice Council <http://www.adr.civiljustice-council.gov.uk>

*Prison Statistics for England and Wales 2001* (2001) Cm. 5743, HMSO, London

PUNT, T. and COLE, B., *Routes into the Solicitors' Profession and the Utilisation of Professional Time* (1999) The Law Society, London

PURCELL, K. and PITCHER, J., *Great Expectations* (1996) Institute of Employment Research, University of Warwick, Warwick

QUICK, O., 'Prosecuting "Gross" Medical Negligence: Manslaughter, Discretion and the CPS' (2006) 33 Journal of Law and Society 421

QUINTON, P., BLAND, N., and MILLER, J., *Police Stops, Decision-making and Practice* (2000) Police Research Series Paper 130, Home Office, London

QUIRK, H., 'The Significance of Culture in Criminal Procedure Reform: Why the Revised Disclosure Scheme Cannot Work' (2006) 10 International Journal of Evidence and Proof 42

'Rabbinical Courts: Modern Day Solomons' (1970) 6 Columbia Journal of Law and Social Problems 49

RABINOWICZ, J. and FRIEL, J., 'The New Tribunal: First Responses' (1994) 21 British Journal of Special Education 27

RACKLEY, E., 'Representations of the (Woman) Judge Hercules, the Little Mermaid and the Vain and Naked Emperor' (2002) 22 Legal Studies 602

RACKLEY, E., 'Difference in the House of Lords' (2006) 15 Social and Legal Studies 163

RADCLIFFE, G. and CROSS, G., *The English Legal System* (3rd edn, 1954) Butterworths, London

RADCLIFFE-BROWN, A. R., *Structure and Function in Primitive Society* (1952) Cohen & West, London

RADIN, M., 'Statutory Interpretation' (1929–30) 43 Harvard Law Review 863

RAINE, J., *Local Justice: Ideals and Realities* (1989) T. & T. Clark, Edinburgh

RAMSAY, I., 'What Do Lawyers Do? Reflections on the Model for Lawyers' (1993) 21 International Journal of the Sociology of Law 355

RASMUSSEN, H., *On Law and Policy in the European Court of Justice* (1986) Martinus Nijhoff, Dordrecht

READ, G., 'The Catholic Tribunal System in the British Isles' (1991) 9 Ecclesiastical Law Journal 213

REDMAYNE, M., 'Disclosure and its Discontents' [2004] Criminal Law Review 441

*Reforming Employment Rights Disputes: Options for Reform* (1994) Cm. 2707, HMSO, London

REID, B., *A Practical Guide to Patent Law* (2nd edn, 1993) Sweet & Maxwell, London

REID, B., *A Practical Guide to Patent Law* (3rd edn, 1999) Sweet & Maxwell, London

REID, LORD, 'The Judge as Law Maker' (1972) 12 Journal of the Society of Public Teachers of Law 22

REINER, R., *The Politics of the Police* (3rd edn, 2000) Oxford University Press, Oxford

*Report of the Civil Justice Review* (1988) Cm. 394, Home Office, London

*Report of the Committee on Ministers' Powers* (1932) Cmd 4060, HMSO, London

*Report of the Home Office Working Group on the Right of Silence* (1989) HMSO, London

*Report of the Roskill Committee on Fraud Trials* (1986) HMSO, London

Revenue and Customs Prosecutions Office, *Annual Report 2005–6* (2006) RCPO, London

RICE, A., 'Solicitor Judges Face Exclusion from Senior Judicial Posts' (2007) Law Society Gazette, 16 August

ROBERTS, J. and HOUGH, M., *Public Opinion and the Jury: An International Literature Review*, Ministry of Justice Research Series 1/09 (2009) Ministry of Justice, London

ROBERTS, S., *Order and Dispute: An Introduction to Legal Anthropology* (1979) Penguin Books, Harmondsworth

ROBERTS, S., 'Three Models of Family Mediation' in R. Dingwall and J. Eekelaar (eds), *Divorce Mediation and the Legal Process* (1988) Clarendon Press, Oxford

ROBERTS, S. and PALMER, M., *Dispute Processes: ADR and the Primary Forms of Decision-making* (2005) Cambridge University Press, Cambridge

ROBSON, G., 'Judicial Situations Vacant' (1994) Law Society Gazette, 15 June

ROBSON, W., *Justice and Administrative Law* (3rd edn, 1951) Stevens, London

ROCK, P., *The Social World of an English Crown Court* (1993) Clarendon Press, Oxford

ROHL, K., 'The Judge as Mediator' (1985) 4 Civil Justice Quarterly 235

ROLFE, H. and ANDERSON, T., 'A Firm Choice: Law Firms' Preferences in the Recruitment of Trainee Solicitors' (2003) 10 International Journal of the Legal Profession 315

ROYAL COMMISSION ON ASSIZES AND QUARTER SESSIONS, *Report* (1969) Cmnd 4153, HMSO, London

ROYAL COMMISSION ON CIVIL LIABILITY AND COMPENSATION FOR PERSONAL INJURY, *Report* (the Pearson Report) (1978) Cmnd 7054, HMSO, London

ROYAL COMMISSION ON CRIMINAL JUSTICE, *Report* (1993) Cm. 2263, HMSO, London

ROYAL COMMISSION ON CRIMINAL PROCEDURE, *Report* (the Philips Report) (1981a) Cmnd 8092, HMSO, London

ROYAL COMMISSION ON CRIMINAL PROCEDURE, *The Investigation and Prosecution of Criminal Offences in England and Wales: The Law and Procedure* (1981b) Cmnd 8092-I, HMSO, London

ROYAL COMMISSION ON LEGAL SERVICES (THE BENSON COMMITTEE), *Report* (the Benson Report) (1979) Cmnd 7648, HMSO, London

ROYAL COMMISSION ON TRADE UNIONS AND EMPLOYERS ASSOCIATIONS, *Report* (the Donovan Report) (1968) Cmnd 3623, HMSO, London

RUMBLE, W., *The Thought of John Austin* (1985) Athlone Press, London

RUSSELL, C., *Academic Freedom* (1993) Routledge, London

RYAN, D., 'Conditional Fee Agreements: Strutting their Stuff Around a Circle that Cannot Be Squared?' (2006) 25 Civil Justice Quarterly 20

SACHS, A. and HOFF WILSON, J., *Sexism and the Law* (1978) Martin Robertson, Oxford

SAMUEL, G., *The Foundations of Legal Reasoning* (1994) Maklu, Antwerp

SAMUEL, G., 'Can Legal Reasoning Be Demystified?' (2009) 29 Legal Studies 181

SANDERS, A., 'Class Bias in Prosecutions' (1985a) 24 Howard Journal 176

SANDERS, A., 'Prosecution Decisions and the Attorney-General's Guidelines' [1985b] Criminal Law Review, 4

SANDERS, A., *Community Justice: Modernising the Magistracy in England and Wales* (2001) Institute for Public Policy Research, London

SANDERS, A., 'Core Values, the Magistracy, and the Auld Report' (2002) 29 Journal of Law and Society 324

SANDERS, A. and BRIDGES, L., 'Access to Legal Advice and Police Malpractice' [1990] Criminal Law Review 494

SANDERS, A. and YOUNG, R., *Criminal Justice* (3rd edn, 2006) Oxford University Press, Oxford

SANDERS, A., YOUNG, R., and BURTON, M., *Criminal Justice* (4th edn, 2010) Oxford University Press, Oxford

SANDERS, A., BRIDGES, L., MULVANEY, A., and CROZIER, G., *Advice and Assistance at Police Stations and the 24-Hour Duty Solicitor Scheme* (1989) Lord Chancellor's Department, London

SANDERSON, P. and SOMMERLAD, H., 'Professionalism, Discrimination, Difference and Choice in Women's Experience in Law Jobs' in P. Thomas (ed.), *Discriminating Lawyers* (2000) Cavendish Publishing, London

SARTRE, J., *Existentialism and Humanism* (1973) Eyre Methuen, London

SAYERS, M. and WEBB, A., 'Franks Revisited: A Model of the Ideal Tribunal' (1990) 9 Civil Justice Quarterly 36

SCARMAN, LORD, *The Brixton Disorders* (1981) Cmnd 8427, HMSO, London

SCHWARTZ, R. and MILLER, J., 'Legal Evolution and Social Control' (1964–5) 70 American Journal of Sociology 159

SCRUTTON, T., 'The Work of the Commercial Courts' (1921) 1 Cambridge Law Journal 6

SEAGO, P., WALKER, C., and WALL, D., 'The Development of the Professional Magistracy in England and Wales' [2000] Criminal Law Review 361

SEDLEY, J., 'Human Rights: A Twenty-first Century Agenda' [1995] Public Law 386

SEDLEY LJ, *Freedom, Law and Justice* (1999) Sweet & Maxwell, London

SEDLEY, S., 'The Common Law and the Political Constitution: A Reply' (2001) 117 Law Quarterly Review 68

SENTENCING GUIDELINES COUNCIL, *Reduction in Sentence for a Guilty Plea: Definitive Guideline* (Revised 2007) SGC, London

SHAH, S. and POOLE, T. 'The Impact of the Human Rights Act on the House of Lords' [2009] Public Law 361

SHAPLAND, J. and SCORSBY, A., *Starting Practice: Work and Training at the Junior Bar* (1995) Institute for the Study of the Legal Profession, Faculty of Law, University of Sheffield, Sheffield

SHAPLAND, J. and VAGG, J., *Policing by the Public* (1988) Routledge, London

SHARPE, S. D., 'Article 6 and the Disclosure of Evidence in Criminal Trials' [1999] Criminal Law Review 273

SHEARING, C. D. and STENNING, P. C., 'Modern Private Security: Its Growth and Implications' in M. Tonry and N. Morris (eds), *Crime and Justice*, Volume 3 (1981) University of Chicago Press, Chicago

SHEARING, C. D. and STENNING, P. C., 'Private Security: Implications for Social Control' (1983) 30 Social Problems 500

SHEARING, C. D., FARNELL, M. F., and STENNING, P. C., *Contract Security in Ontario* (1980) Centre of Criminology, University of Toronto, Toronto

SHEARING, C. D., STENNING, P. C., and ADDARIO, S. M., 'Corporate Perceptions of Private Security' (1985) 9 Canadian Police College Journal 367

Shepherd, E., *Investigative Interviewing: The Conversation Management Approach* (2007) Oxford University Press, Oxford

SHERR, A. and WEBB, J., 'Law Students, the External Market and Socialization: Do We Make Them Turn to the City?' (1989) 16 Journal of Law and Society 225

SHINER, M., *Entry into the Legal Professions: The Law Student Cohort Study: Year 5* (1999) The Law Society, London

SHINER, M., *The National Implementation of the Recording of Police Stops* (2006) Home Office, London

SHURY, J., SPEED, M., VIVIAN, D., KUECHEL, A., and NICHOLAS, S., *Crime against Retail and Manufacturing Premises: Findings from the 2002 Commercial Victimisation Survey* (2005) Home Office Online Report 37/05, Home Office, London

SIME, S. 'What Price Justice?' (2010) Counsel, March, 12

SIMON, F. and WEATHERITT, M., *The Use of Bail and Custody by London Magistrates' Courts before and after the Criminal Justice Act 1967* (1974) Home Office Research Unit Report No. 20, HMSO, London

SIMPSON, A., 'The *Ratio Decidendi* of a Case' (1957) 20 Modern Law Review 413

SIMPSON, A., 'The *Ratio Decidendi* of a Case' (1958) 21 Modern Law Review 155

SKINNS, L., '"Let's Get It Over With": Early Findings on Factors Affecting Detainees' Access to Custodial Legal Advice' (2009a) 19(1) Policing and Society 58

SKINNS, L., '"I'm a Detainee; Get Me Out of Here"' (2009b) 49(3) British Journal of Criminology 399

SKOGAN, W., *The Police and Public in England and Wales – A British Crime Survey Report* (1990) Home Office Research Study No. 117, Home Office, London

SKRYME, SIR T., *The Changing Image of the Magistracy* (2nd edn, 1983) Macmillan, London

SMITH, A. T. H., 'The Human Rights Act 1998 (1) The Human Rights Act and the Criminal Lawyer: The Constitutional Context' [1999] Criminal Law Review 25

SMITH, D. J., *Police and People in London*: Volume 3: *A Survey of Police Officers* (1983a) Policy Studies Institute, London

SMITH, D. J. and GRAY, J., *Police and People in London*: Volume 4: *The Police in Action* (1983b) Policy Studies Institute, London

SMITH, I., WOOD, J., and THOMAS, G., *Industrial Law* (5th edn, 1993) Butterworths, London

SMITH, J. C., *The Law of Contract* (1989) Sweet & Maxwell, London

SMITH, SIR J. C., *Smith and Hogan's Criminal Law* (10th edn, 2002) Butterworths, London

SMITH, P., 'Reducing Legal Aid Eligibility Criteria: The Impact for Immigration Law Practitioners and their Clients' (1993) 12 Civil Justice Quarterly 167

SMITH, P. F. and BAILEY, S. H., *The Modern English Legal System* (1984) Sweet & Maxwell, London

SOFTLEY, P., *Police Interrogation* (1980) Royal Commission on Criminal Procedure Research Study No. 4, HMSO, London

SOMMERLAD, H., 'Women in a Changing Profession: The Myth of Feminisation' in J. Shapland and R. Le Grys (eds), *The Changing Shape of the Legal Profession* (1994a) Institute for the Study of the Legal Profession, University of Sheffield, Sheffield

SOMMERLAD, H., 'The Myth of Feminisation: Women and Cultural Change in the Legal Profession' (1994b) 1 International Journal of the Legal Profession 31

SOMMERLAD, H., '"I've Lost the Plot": An Everyday Story of the "Political" Legal Aid Lawyer' (2001) 28 Journal of Law and Society 335

SOMMERLAD, H., 'Women Solicitors in a Fractured Profession: Intersections of Gender and Professionalism in England and Wales' (2002) 29 International Journal of the Legal Profession 213

SOMMERLAD, H., and SANDERSON, P., *Gender, Choice and Commitment: Women Solicitors in England and Wales and the Struggle for Equal Status* (1998) Ashgate, Aldershot

SOMMERS, S. and ELLSWORTH, P., 'How Much Do We Really Know about Race and Juries? A Review of the Social Science Theory and Research' (2003) 78 Chicago-Kent Law Review, 997

SOOTHILL, K., WALBY, S., and BAIGGULEY, P., 'Judges, the Media and Rape' (1990) 17 Journal of Law and Society 211

SOUTH, N., 'The Corruption of Private Justice: The Case of the Private Security Sector' in M. Clarke (ed.), *Corruption: Causes, Consequences and Control* (1983) Pinter, London

SOUTH, N., 'Private Security, the Division of Policing Labour and the Commercial Compromise of the State' in S. Spitzer and A. T. Scull (eds), *Research in Law, Deviance and Social Control*, Volume 6 (1984) JAI Press, Greenwich, CT

SOUTHGATE, P. and CRISP, D., *Public Satisfaction with Police Services* (1993) Home Office Research and Planning Unit Paper No. 73, Home Office, London

SPENCER, A. and PODMORE, D., 'Women Lawyers – Marginal Members of a Male-dominated Profession' in A. Spencer and D. Podmore (eds), *In a Man's World* (1987) Tavistock Publications, London

SPENCER, J., 'Did the Jury Misbehave? Don't Ask, Because We Do Not Want to Know' (2002) Cambridge Law Journal 291

SPENCER, J. R., *Jackson's Machinery of Justice in England* (8th edn, 1989) Cambridge University Press, Cambridge

SPRACK, J., 'The Criminal Procedure and Investigations Act 1996: (1) The Duty of Disclosure' [1997] Criminal Law Review 308

STALLWORTHY, M., 'Local Government Lawyers: The 1980s and Beyond' in P. Thomas (ed.), *Tomorrow's Lawyers* (1992) Basil Blackwell, Oxford

STALLYBRASS, W., 'Law in the Universities' [1948] Journal of the Society of Public Teachers of Law 157

STANKO, E., 'Missing the Mark? Police Battering' in J. Hanmer, J. Radford, and E. Stanko (eds), *Women, Policing and Male Violence: International Perspectives* (1989) Routledge, London

STANLEY, C., 'Training for the Hierarchy? Reflections on the British Experience of Legal Education' (1988) 22 The Law Teacher 78

STANLEY, C., 'Legal Fictions: Discourse and Archaeology. Notes on the Construction of a Jurisprudence Course' (1991) 25 The Law Teacher 241

STARMER, K., 'Two Years of the Human Rights Act' (2003) 1 European Human Rights Law Review 14

STEER, D., *Uncovering Crime: The Police Role* (1980) Royal Commission on Criminal Procedure Research Study No. 7, HMSO, London

STEVENS, P. and WILLIS, C. F., *Race, Crime and Arrests* (1979) Home Office Research Study No. 58, Home Office, London

STEVENS, R., *Law and Politics* (1979) Weidenfeld & Nicolson, London

STEVENS, R., *The Independence of the Judiciary* (1993) Oxford University Press, Oxford

STEVENS, R., *The English Judge: Their Role in the Changing Constitution* (2002) Hart Publishing, Oxford

STEYN, LORD, 'The Weakest and Least Dangerous Department of Government' [1997] Public Law 84

STEYN, LORD, 'Incorporation and Devolution – A Few Reflections on the Changing Scene' (1998) 2 European Human Rights Law Review 153

STEYN, [Lord] J., '*Pepper* v *Hart*: A Re-examination' (2001) 21 Oxford Journal of Legal Studies 59

STEYN, LORD, 'Democracy through Law' (2002) 6 European Human Rights Law Review 723

STEYN, LORD, '2000–2005: Laying the Foundations of Human Rights Law in the United Kingdom' (2005) 4 European Human Rights Law Review 349

STEYN, LORD, 'Democracy, the Rule of Law and the Role of Judges' (2006) 3 European Human Rights Law Review 243

STONE, C., *Bail Information for the Crown Prosecution Service* (1988) Vera Institute of Justice, London

STONE, J., 'The *Ratio* of the *Ratio Decidendi*' (1959) 22 Modern Law Review 597

STONE, R., *Entry, Search and Seizure* (4th edn, 2005) Oxford University Press, Oxford

STONE, V. and PETTIGREW, N., *The Views of the Public on Stops and Searches* (2000) Police Research Series Paper 129, Home Office, London

STYCHIN, C. and MULCAHY, L., *Legal Method* (3rd edn, 2003) Sweet & Maxwell, London

SUGARMAN, D., 'Legal Theory, the Common Law Mind and the Making of the Textbook Tradition' in W. Twining (ed.), *Legal Theory and Common Law* (1986) Basil Blackwell, Oxford

Supreme Court Act 1981, *Current Law Annotated Statutes* (1981) Sweet & Maxwell, London

SWANN, J., 'Comment' (2002) Law Society Gazette, 30 August

SWIFT, J., *Gulliver's Travels* (1975) JM Dent, London

TAGUE, P., 'Barristers' Selfish Incentives in Counselling Clients' [2008] Criminal Law Review 3

TAMANAHA, B., *A General Jurisprudence of Law and Society* (2001) Oxford University Press, Oxford

TAPPER, C., *Cross and Tapper on Evidence* (8th edn, 1995) Butterworths, London

TAYLOR, C., (2006) *Criminal Investigation and Pre-trial Disclosure in the United Kingdom: How Detectives Put Together a Case* (2006) Edwin Mellen Press, Lampeter

TAYLOR, J., 'Law School Stress and the Deformation Professionelle' (1975–6) 27 Journal of Legal Education 251

TAYOR, R., WASIK, M., and LENG, R., *Blackstone's Guide to the Criminal Justice Act 2003* (2003) Oxford University Press, Oxford

TEMKIN, J., *Rape and the Legal Process* (1987) Sweet & Maxwell, London

TEUBNER, G., *Law as an Autopoetic System* (1993) Basil Blackwell, Oxford

THOMAS, C., 'Exposing the Myths of Jury Service' [2008] Criminal Law Review 415

THOMAS, C. with BULMER, N., *Diversity and Fairness in the Jury System* Ministry of Justice Research Series 2/07 (2007) MOJ, London

THOMPSON, A., 'Critical Legal Education in Britain' in P. Fitzpatrick and A. Hunt (eds), *Critical Legal Studies* (1987) Basil Blackwell, London

THOMPSON, P. (ed.), *The County Court Practice: 1995* (1995) Butterworths, London

TMS CONSULTANTS, *Without Prejudice? Sex Equality at the Bar and in the Judiciary* (1992) TMS Management Consultants, Bournemouth

TOMBS, J. and MOODY, S., 'Alternatives to Prosecution: The Public Interest Redefined' [1993] Criminal Law Review 357

TOMBS, S. and WHYTE, S., *A Crisis of Enforcement: The Decriminalisation of Death and Injury at Work* (2008) Centre for Crime and Justice Studies Briefing No. 6, King's College London, London

TREMLETT, N., *The 1992 Survey of Industrial Tribunal Applications* (1994) Employment Department, London

TWINING, W., 'Pericles and the Plumber' (1967) 83 Law Quarterly Review 396

TWINING, W., *Karl Llewellyn and the Realist Movement* (1973) Weidenfeld & Nicolson, London

TWINING, W., *Blackstone's Tower* (1994) Sweet & Maxwell, London

TWINING, W., 'A Post-Westphalian Conception of Law' (2003) 37 Law and Society Review 199

UNGER, R., *The Critical Legal Studies Movement* (1986) Harvard University Press, Cambridge, MA

USHER, J., *European Court Practice* (1983) Sweet & Maxwell, London

VENNARD, J., *Contested Trials in Magistrates' Courts: The Case for the Prosecution* (1980) Royal Commission on Criminal Procedure Research Study No. 6, HMSO, London

VENNARD, J., 'The Outcome of Contested Trials' in D. Moxon (ed.), *Managing Criminal Justice* (1985) HMSO, London

VERKAILC, R., 'Be the Judge' (1996) Law Society Gazette, 31 January

VESTERDORF, B., 'The Community Court System Ten Years from Now and Beyond: Challenges and Possibilities' (2003) 28 European Law Review 303

VIGNAENDRA, S., *Social Class and Entry into the Solicitors' Profession: Research Study 41* (2001) The Law Society, London

VILE, M., *Constitutionalism and the Separation of Powers* (1967) Clarendon Press, Oxford

VINCENT-JONES, P., 'Private Property and Public Order: The Hippy Convoy' (1986) 13 Journal of Law and Society 343

VINCENT-JONES, P., 'Contract Litigation in England and Wales 1975–1991' (1993) 12 Civil Justice Quarterly 370

WADDINGTON, P., 'Police (Canteen) Sub-culture: An Appreciation' (1999) 39 British Journal of Criminology 286

WADDINGTON, P., STENSON K., and DON, D., 'In Proportion: Race, and Police Stop and Search' (2004) 44 British Journal of Criminology 889

WADE, W., *Towards Administrative Justice* (1963) University of Michigan Press, Ann Arbor, MI

WADE, W. and FORSYTH, C., *Administrative Law* (10th edn, 2009) Oxford University Press, Oxford

WAKEFIELD, A., *Selling Security* (2003) Willan, Cullompton

WALKER, R. and WALKER, M., *The English Legal System* (1965) Sweet & Maxwell, London

WALSH, D. and BULL, R., 'Interviewing Suspects of Fraud' (2009) 37 Journal of Psychiatry and Law 1

WALSH, D. and MILNE, R., 'Giving P.E.A.C.E. a Chance: A Study of DWP's Investigators' Perceptions of their Interviewing Practices' (2007) 85 Public Administration 525

WALSH, D. and MILNE, R., 'Keeping the Peace? A Study of Investigative Practice in the Public Sector' (2008) 13 Legal and Criminological Psychology 39

WARD, R., *Walker and Walker's English Legal System* (8th edn, 1998) Butterworths, London

WARD, R. and AKHTAR, A., *Walker and Walker's English Legal System* (10th edn, 2008) Oxford University Press, Oxford

WARNOCK, BARONESS, *Universities: Knowing our Minds* (1989) Chatto and Windus, London

WASIK, M., *Emmins on Sentencing* (1998) Blackstone Press, London

WASIK, M., 'Legislating in the Shadow of the Human Rights Act: The Criminal Justice and Police Act 2001' [2001] Criminal Law Review 931

WEAIT, M., 'The Letter of the Law?' (1989) 29 British Journal of Criminology 57

WEBLEY, L. and DUFF, L., 'Women Solicitors as a Barometer for Problems within the Legal Profession – Time to Put Values before Profits?' (2007) 34 Journal of Law and Society 374

WELLS, C., 'Battered Woman Syndrome and Defences to Homicide: Where now?' (1994) 14 Legal Studies 266

WHELAN, C., 'The Role of Research in Civil Justice Reform: Small Claims in the County Court' (1987) 6 Civil Justice Quarterly 237

WHITE, R., 'Legal Expenses Insurance' (1984) 3 Civil Justice Quarterly 245

WHITE, R., *The Administration of Justice* (1st edn, 1985) Blackwells, Oxford

WHITE, R., *The Administration of Justice* (2nd edn, 1991) Blackwells, Oxford

WHITE, R., *The English Legal System in Action: The Administration of Justice* (3rd edn, 1999) Oxford University Press, Oxford

WHITE, R., 'Investigators and Prosecutors or, Desperately Seeking Scotland: Reformulation of the "Philips Principle"' (2006) 69 Modern Law Review 143

WHITE, R. and ATKINSON, R., 'Personal Injury Litigation, Conditional Fees and After-the-event Insurance' (2000) 19 Civil Justice Quarterly 118

WIKELEY, N. 'So What Exactly *is* the Upper Tribunal?' [2010] The Reporter, Society of Legal Scholars

WILLIAMS, G. (ed.), *Salmond on Jurisprudence* (11th edn, 1957) Sweet & Maxwell, London

WILLIAMS, G., *Learning the Law* (11th edn, 1982) Stevens, London

WILLIAMS, G., 'The Lords and Impossible Attempts, or Quis Custodiet Ipsos Custodes?' (1986) 45 Cambridge Law Journal 33

WILLIAMS, T. and GORIELY, T., *Recruitment and Retention of Solicitors in Small Firms: Research Study 44* (2003) The Law Society, London

WILLIAMS, T. and MOSTON, S., 'The Extent of Silence in Police Interviews' in S. Greer and R. Morgan (eds), *The Right to Silence Debate* (1990) Centre for Criminal Justice, Bristol

WILLIS, C., *The Use, Effectiveness and Impact of Police Stop and Search Powers* (1983) Home Office Research and Policy Planning Unit Paper No. 15, Home Office, London

WITTGENSTEIN, L., *Philosophical Investigations* (1963) Basil Blackwell, Oxford

WOOLF LJ, *Prison Disturbances April 1990: Report of an Inquiry by Lord Justice Woolf (Parts 1 and 2) and His Honour Judge Stephen Tumin (Part 2)* Cm. 1456 (1991) HMSO, London

WOOLF, LORD, *Access to Justice: Interim Report to the Lord Chancellor on the Civil Justice System in England and Wales* (1995a) Lord Chancellor's Department, London

WOOLF, LORD, 'Droit Public – English Style' [1995b] Public Law 57

WOOLF, LORD, *Access to Justice: Final Report to the Lord Chancellor on the Civil Justice System in England and Wales* (the Woolf Report) (1996) Lord Chancellor's Department, London

WOOLF, LORD, 'Judicial Review – The Tensions between the Executive and the Judiciary' (1998) 114 Law Quarterly Review 579

WOOLFSON, R., PLOTKINOFF, J., and WILSON, D., *Solicitors in the Employed Sector* (1994) The Law Society, London

WRIGHT, LORD, 'The Common Law in its Old Home' in Lord Wright, *Legal Essays and Addresses* (1939) Cambridge University Press, Cambridge

WYATT, D. and DASHWOOD, A., *Wyatt and Dashwood's European Community Law* (3rd edn, 1993) Sweet & Maxwell, London

YOUNG, R. and WILCOX, A., 'The Merits of Legal Aid in the Magistrates' Courts Revisited' [2007] Criminal Law Review 109

YOUNG, R., MOLONEY, T., and SANDERS, A., *In the Interests of Justice?* (1992) Institute of Judicial Administration, University of Birmingham, Birmingham

ZANDER, M., *Lawyers and the Public Interest* (1968) Weidenfeld & Nicolson, London

ZANDER, M., *Legal Services for the Community* (1978) Temple Smith, London

ZANDER, M., 'The Investigation of Crime: A Study of Cases Tried at the Old Bailey' [1979] Criminal Law Review 203

ZANDER, M., 'The Final Woolf Report: Forwards or backwards for the New Lord Chancellor?' (1997) 16 Civil Justice Quarterly 208

ZANDER, M., 'Advance Disclosure' (2002) 146 Solicitors' Journal 824

ZANDER, M. and HENDERSON, P., *The Crown Court Study* (1993) Royal Commission on Criminal Justice Research Study No. 19, HMSO, London

ZUCKERMAN, A., 'Lord Woolf's Access to Justice: Plus ça change...' (1996) 59 Modern Law Review 773

ZYL SMIT, J. VAN, 'The New Purposive Interpretation of Statutes: HRA Section 3 after *Ghaidan v Godin-Moendoza*' (2007) 70 Modern Law Review 294

# Index